Teacher Edition
Volume 2

HARCOURT
Math
NORTH CAROLINA EDITION

Harcourt

Orlando   Austin   Chicago   New York   Toronto   London   San Diego

Visit *The Learning Site!*
www.harcourtschool.com

Requests for permission to make copies of any part of the work should be addressed to School Permissions and Copyrights, Harcourt, Inc., 6277 Sea Harbor Drive, Orlando, Florida 32887-6777. Fax: 407-345-2418.

HARCOURT and the Harcourt Logo are trademarks of Harcourt, Inc., registered in the United States of America and/or other jurisdictions.

Grateful acknowledgment is made to Flint Public Library, 1026 East Kearsley, MI, 48502-1994 for permission to reprint from "Cobbler, Cobbler" in *Ring a Ring o' Roses: Finger Plays for Pre-School Children,* Tenth Edition. Text copyright © 1996 by Flint Public Library.

Printed in the United States of America

ISBN 0-15-336624-9

3 4 5 6 7 8 9 10 030 10 09 08 07 06 05 04

Teacher's Edition Contents

Volume 1

Pupil Edition

UNIT 1 Understand Numbers and Operations Chapters 1–3

UNIT 2 Addition, Subtraction, Money, and Time Chapters 4–7

UNIT 3 Multiplication Concepts and Facts Chapters 8–11

Volume 2

Pupil Edition

UNIT 4 Division Concepts and Facts Chapters 12–14

UNIT 5 Data and Measurement Chapters 15–18

UNIT 6 Geometry Chapters 19–22

Volume 3

Authors

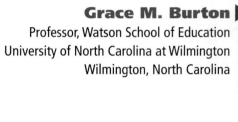

Senior Author

Evan M. Maletsky
Professor of Mathematics
Montclair State University
Upper Montclair, New Jersey

Angela Giglio Andrews
Math Teacher, Scott School
Naperville District #203
Naperville, Illinois

Jennie M. Bennett
Houston Independent School District
Houston, Texas

Grace M. Burton
Professor, Watson School of Education
University of North Carolina at Wilmington
Wilmington, North Carolina

Lynda A. Luckie
K-12 Mathematics Coordinator
Gwinnett County Public Schools
Lawrenceville, Georgia

Joyce C. McLeod
Visiting Professor
Rollins College
Winter Park, Florida

Tom Roby
Associate Professor of Mathematics
California State University
Hayward, California

Vicki Newman
Classroom Teacher
McGaugh Elementary School
Los Alamitos Unified School District
Seal Beach, California

Janet K. Scheer
Executive Director
Create A Vision
Foster City, California

Mathematics
Advisors

The development of **HARCOURT MATH** was guided by prominent, accomplished mathematicians from across the United States. Their guidance helped ensure accurate mathematics and appropriate conceptual development.

Richard Askey
Professor of Mathematics
University of Wisconsin
Madison, Wisconsin
Grades 5–6

Tom Roby
Associate Professor of Mathematics
California State University
Hayward, California
Grade 4

David Singer
Professor of Mathematics
Case Western Reserve University
Cleveland, Ohio
Grade 3

Contributions to the Professional Handbook

Roger Howe
Professor of Mathematics
Yale University
New Haven, Connecticut

David Wright
Professor of Mathematics
Brigham Young University
Provo, Utah

Liping Ma
Mathematics Researcher and Educator
Palo Alto, California

Tom Roby
Associate Professor of Mathematics
Hayward, California

Marilee Sprenger
Educational Consultant
Two Rivers Professional Development Center
Edwards, Illinois

Program Consultants and Specialists

Janet S. Abbott
Mathematics Consultant
California

Elsie Babcock
Director, Mathematics and Science Center
Mathematics Consultant
Wayne Regional Educational Service Agency
Wayne, Michigan

William J. Driscoll
Professor of Mathematics
Department of Mathematical Sciences
Central Connecticut State University
New Britain, Connecticut

Lois Harrison-Jones
Education and Management Consultant
Dallas, Texas

Rebecca Valbuena
Language Development Specialist
Stanton Elementary School
Glendora, California

The Bag Ladies
Karen Simmons
Cindy Guinn
Palm Beach County, Florida
bagladiesonline.com

Reviewers and Field-Test Teachers

Britta Abinger
Teacher
Corkery School
Chicago, Illinois

Lynne D. Allen
Teacher
Wakefield Elementary
Raleigh, North Carolina

Ann Allison
Teacher
Woodward Elementary
Lock Haven, Pennsylvania

Elizabeth Arcement
DEEP Math Teacher/LINCS
    Coordinator
Iberia Parish Educational Center
New Iberia, Louisiana

Audrey A. Arellano-Davie
Assistant Principal
Side Creek Elementary
Aurora, Colorado

Angela M. Ascencio
Teacher
Bunche Elementary
Flint, Michigan

Sister Mary Berryman
Teacher
St. Peter Celestine School
Cherry Hill, New Jersey

Linda Bierkortte
Teacher
Parkmoor Urban Academy
Columbus, Ohio

Hazel Bills
Teacher
Corkery School
Chicago, Illinois

David A. Bond
Gifted and Talented Resource
    Teacher
Bollman Bridge Elementary
Ellicott City, Maryland

Henry Boyd
Teacher
Graham Elementary
Shelby, North Carolina

Kris Buechner
Teacher
Rowena Kyle Elementary School
Portage, Indiana

Wanda Bullock
Teacher
B.O. Barnes Elementary
Wilson, North Carolina

Stephanie Cahoon
Teacher
C. Wayne Collier Elementary
Hope Mills, North Carolina

Desiree A. Charles
Cayman Department of
    Education
Georgetown, Grand Cayman

Gail L. Clark
Teacher
Southhampton School #2
Delran, New Jersey

LaJuan Conley
Teacher
Burton Geo-World
Durham, North Carolina

Elizabeth Culpepper
Teacher
Princeton Elementary
Orlando, Florida

Carolyn A. Day
Director of Programs:
    Math/Science
Dayton Public Schools
Dayton, Ohio

Paul G. Dillenberger
Classroom 2000 Coordinator
Education Service Center
Minneapolis, Minnesota

Gail R. Englert
Teacher
Norfolk Public Schools/Sewells
    Point
Norfolk, Virginia

Judy Fisher
Teacher
James L. Dennis Elementary
Oklahoma City, Oklahoma

Kelly L. Fleming
Teacher
Windy Hill Elementary
Owings, Maryland

Mia Freeman
Teacher
Westchase Elementary School
Tampa, Florida

Ellen Galdieri
Teacher
Dowell Elementary
Huntingtown, Maryland

Susan Gaspich
Teacher
Chelsea Heights Elementary
Atlantic City, New Jersey

Kathryn George
Teacher
East Park Elementary
Danville, Illlinois

Lou Gerbi
Teacher
Westinghouse Elementary
Wilmerding, Pennsylvania

Elizabeth Q. Gilbert
Teacher
Roosevelt Elementary
West Palm Beach, Florida

James Giordano
Teacher
W.B. Powell Elementary
Washington, D.C.

Susan Googins
Teacher
Philip Schuyler Elementary
Albany, New York

Becky Hamilton
Teacher
Scull Elementary
North Huntingdon, Pennsylvania

Cheryl Harkins
Teacher
Bashaw Elementary
Bradenton, Florida

Elizabeth Harris
Teacher
Springfield Elementary
Providence, Rhode Island

Diane Hastings
Teacher
Thoreau Park
Parma, Ohio

Earl Heddle
Teacher
Richland Elementary
Gibsonia, Pennsylvania

Sarah Hillyer
Teacher
Craddock Elementary
Aurora, Ohio

Russell Hinson
Math Facilitator
Nathaniel Alexander
Charlotte, North Carolina

Tim Horton
Teacher
Quarryville Elementary
Quarryville, Pennsylvania

Heather Hunt
Teacher
Horizon Elementary
Hanover Park, Illinois

Travis Ivory
Teacher
Lyle Creek Elementary School
Conover, North Carolina

Michelle Jaronik
Coordinator, Gifted Math
Lincoln Center
Waukegan, Illinois

Catheline Jones
Teacher
Gateway Elementary
St. Louis, Missouri

Carolyn Rebecca Kniceley
Teacher
Breckinridge Elementary
    School
Fincastle, Virginia

Kim Lawrence
Teacher
Elmont Elementary
Ashland, Virginia

Jacqueline Leccia
Teacher
Timber Trace Elementary School
Palm Beach Gardens, Florida

Inell Lemon
Math Coordinator
Jensen Scholastic Academy
Chicago, Illinois

Carol C. Livingston
Teacher
Martin Luther King, Jr.
    Elementary
Woodbridge, Virginia

Arlene D. Loughlin
Teacher
Lake St. George
Palm Harbor, Florida

Ruth Loveland
Curriculum Director
Boundary County School
    District #101
Bonners Ferry, Idaho

Sarah Meadows
Title I Instructional Liaison
Topeka Public
Topeka, Kansas

Ruth Harbin Miles
Math Coordinator
Unified School District 233
Olathe, Kansas

Faye H. Miller
Teacher
Roosevelt Elementary
Plover, Wisconsin

Elaine Millie
Teacher
Bryant Elementary
Sioux City, Iowa

Susan Milstein
Teacher
Dag Hammerskjold School
Brooklyn, New York

Kathleen Mineau
Teacher
Public School # 19
Albany, New York

Ethel T. Munro
Teacher
Windom Elementary
Orchard Park, New York

Amy Musten
Teacher
Francisco Elementary School
Westfield, North Carolina

Patti Ogle
Teacher
Glen Arden Elementary School
Arden, North Carolina

Maritza Perez
Teacher
Huff Elementary
Elgin, Illinois

Jill E. Perkins
Teacher
Edwardsburg Primary
Cassopolis, Michigan

Kayanna Pitchford
Teacher
Alger B. Wilkins Elementary
Fayetteville, North Carolina

Paulette Prentice
Teacher
Anne Sullivan
Minneapolis, Minnesota

Suzanne Regali
Teacher
C.W. Holmes School
Derry, New Hampshire

Augustus Reid
Teacher
Greensboro, North Carolina

Pauline E. Robinson
Teacher
Star Hill Elementary
Dover, Delaware

Shana M. Runge
Teacher
Marion Intermediate School
Shelby, North Carolina

Telkia Rutherford
Mathematics Support Manager
Department of Instruction
Chicago, Illinois

Janae Shackelford
Teacher
Roosevelt Elementary
West Palm Beach, Florida

Therese Shields
Teacher
Parkside Elementary
Camden, New Jersey

Bonnie Short
Teacher
Snow Rogers Elementary
Gardendale, Alabama

Patti Smith
Teacher
Jefferson Elementary School
Ft. Riley, Kansas

Ivy Soffin
Teacher
Sunrise Park Elementary
Boca Raton, Florida

Ann H. Spencer
Teacher
Liberty Elementary
Shelbyville, Tennessee

Valerie J. Spindler
Teacher
L.V. Denti Elementary
Ava, New York

Ionia U. Stemple
Teacher
Norwood
Stonewood, West Virginia

Cathy L. Summa
Principal
Fountain City Elementary
Knoxville, Tennessee

Sylvia Teahan
Teacher
New Albany Elementary
Cinnaminson, New Jersey

Mary Thomas
Math Coordinator
Jersey Shore Area Junior High
Jersey Shore, Pennsylvania

Peter Tuttle
Teacher
Noble Elementary
Cleveland Heights, Ohio

Michelle Vancheri
Teacher
School #11
Paterson, New Jersey

Shelli Van Waes
K-1 Looping Teacher
Lyle Creek Elementary School
Conover, North Carolina

Suzanne Voos
Teacher
Roselawn-Condon Elementary
Cincinnati, Ohio

Beverly A. White
Teacher
Cecil Elementary
Cecil, Pennsylvania

Karen D. White
Teacher
Gardendale Elementary
Gardendale, Alabama

Lorraine White
Teacher
North Mami Elementary
North Miami, Florida

HARCOURT

Math

NORTH CAROLINA EDITION

Harcourt

Orlando   Austin   Chicago   New York   Toronto   London   San Diego

Visit *The Learning Site!*
www.harcourtschool.com

ISBN 0-15-336607-9

2 3 4 5 6 7 8 9 10 032 10 09 08 07 06 05 04

Senior Author

Evan M. Maletsky
Professor of Mathematics
Montclair State University
Upper Montclair, New Jersey

Mathematics Advisor

David Singer
Professor of Mathematics
Case Western Reserve University
Cleveland, Ohio

Authors

Angela Giglio Andrews
Math Teacher, Scott School
Naperville District #203
Naperville, Illinois

Jennie M. Bennett
Houston Independent School District
Houston, Texas

Grace M. Burton
Professor, Watson School of Education
University of North Carolina
 at Wilmington
Wilmington, North Carolina

Lynda A. Luckie
K–12 Mathematics Coordinator
Gwinnett County Public Schools
Lawrenceville, Georgia

Joyce C. McLeod
Visiting Professor
Rollins College
Winter Park, Florida

Vicki Newman
Classroom Teacher
McGaugh Elementary School
Los Alamitos Unified School District
Seal Beach, California

Tom Roby
Associate Professor of Mathematics
California State University
Hayward, California

Janet K. Scheer
Executive Director
Create A Vision
Foster City, California

Program Consultants and Specialist

Janet S. Abbott
Mathematics Consultant
California

Lois Harrison-Jones
*Education and
 Management Consultant*
Dallas, Texas

Elsie Babcock
*Director, Mathematics and
 Science Center
Mathematics Consultant*
Wayne Regional
 Educational Service
 Agency
Wayne, Michigan

William J. Driscoll
Professor of Mathematics
Department of
 Mathematical Sciences
Central Connecticut State
 University
New Britain, Connecticut

Rebecca Valbuena
*Language Development
 Specialist*
Stanton Elementary School
Glendora, California

UNIT 1
CHAPTERS 1-3

Understand Numbers and Operations

Technology Link

Harcourt Mega Math
Chapter 1: pp. 2, 8; Chapter 2: pp. 22, 25
Chapter 3: p. 43
The Harcourt Learning Site:
www.harcourtschool.com
Multimedia Math Glossary:
www.harcourtschool.com/mathglossary

UNIT 2
CHAPTERS 4-7

Addition, Subtraction, Money, and Time

Technology Link

Harcourt Mega Math
Chapter 4: pp. 70, 77; Chapter 5: p. 91
Chapter 6: pp. 111, 119; Chapter 7: pp. 134, 139
The Harcourt Learning Site: www.harcourtschool.com
Multimedia Math Glossary:
www.harcourtschool.com/mathglossary

UNIT 3 Multiplication Concepts and Facts

Technology Link

Harcourt Mega Math
Chapter 8: pp. 158, 162; Chapter 9: p. 182
Chapter 10: p. 200; Chapter 11: pp. 213, 216
The Harcourt Learning Site:
www.harcourtschool.com
Multimedia Math Glossary:
www.harcourtschool.com/mathglossary

ix

UNIT 4

CHAPTERS 12-14

Division Concepts and Facts

Technology Link

Harcourt Mega Math
Chapter 12: pp. 242, 247; Chapter 13: p. 261
Chapter 14: pp. 274, 281
The Harcourt Learning Site:
www.harcourtschool.com
Multimedia Math Glossary:
www.harcourtschool.com/mathglossary

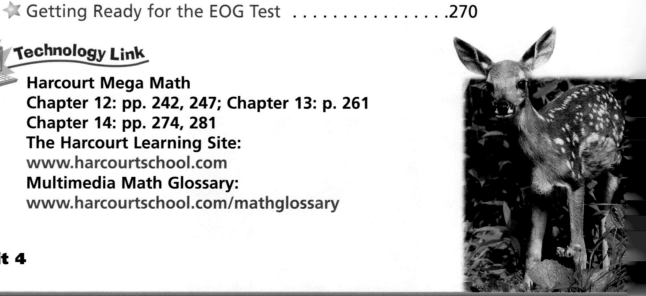

UNIT 5
CHAPTERS 15-18

Data and Measurement

Technology Link

Harcourt Mega Math
Chapter 15: pp. 311, 315; Chapter 16: pp. 325, 330
Chapter 17: p. 348; Chapter 18: p. 359
The Harcourt Learning Site:
www.harcourtschool.com
Multimedia Math Glossary:
www.harcourtschool.com/mathglossary

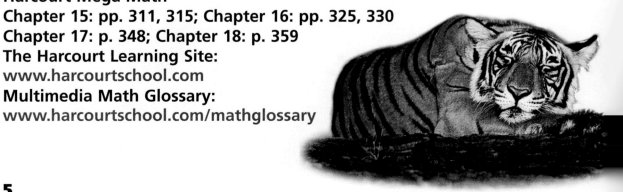

UNIT 6 Geometry

Technology Link

Harcourt Mega Math
Chapter 19: p. 396; Chapter 20: pp. 408, 414
Chapter 21: p. 424; Chapter 22: p. 452
The Harcourt Learning Site:
www.harcourtschool.com
Multimedia Math Glossary:
www.harcourtschool.com/mathglossary

UNIT 7 Patterns and Probability

Technology Link

Harcourt Mega Math
Chapter 23: p. 476
Chapter 24: pp. 489, 493
The Harcourt Learning Site:
www.harcourtschool.com
Multimedia Math Glossary:
www.harcourtschool.com/mathglossary

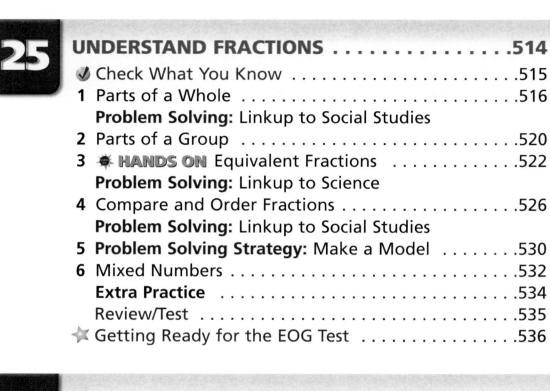

Technology Link

Harcourt Mega Math
Chapter 25: p. 527; Chapter 26: p. 547
Chapter 27: pp. 560, 562; Chapter 28: p. 580
The Harcourt Learning Site:
www.harcourtschool.com
Multimedia Math Glossary: www.harcourtschool.com/mathglossary

UNIT 9
CHAPTERS 29-30

Multiply and Divide by 1-Digit Numbers

Technology Link

Harcourt Mega Math
Chapter 29: p. 603
Chapter 30: p. 619
The Harcourt Learning Site:
www.harcourtschool.com
Multimedia Math Glossary:
www.harcourtschool.com/mathglossary

Teaching Notes

Additional Ideas:

Good Questions to Ask:

Additional Resources:

Notes for Next Time:

Unit at a Glance

PROFESSIONAL DEVELOPMENT

EXCERPTS FROM THE RESEARCH

" . . . open number sentences provide children symbolic representations that they can relate to their informal counting and modeling strategies. Teaching children to write a variety of open sentences to represent different word problems may be a way to build on children's intuitive concepts of addition and subtraction." (Carpenter, Moser, and Bebout, 1988)

Assessment Options

Assessing Prior Knowledge

Determine whether students have the required prerequisite concepts and skills.

Check What You Know, PE pp. 237, 257, 273

Test Preparation

Provide review and practice for chapter and standardized tests.

Getting Ready for the EOG Test, PE pp. 239, 241, 245, 249, 254–255, 259, 261, 263, 265, 270–271, 277, 279, 283, 285, 290–291

Study Guide and Review, PE pp. 294–295

Formal Assessment

Assess students' mastery of chapter concepts and skills.

Chapter Review/Test PE pp. 253, 269, 289

Pretest and Posttest Options

    Chapter Test, Form A

        pp. AG77–78, 81–82, 85–86

    Chapter Test, Form B

        pp. AG79–80, 83–84, 87–88

Unit 4 Test • Chapters 12–14

    Form A, pp. AG89–92

    Form B, pp. AG93–96

Daily Assessment

Obtain daily feedback on students' understanding of concepts.

Quick Review, See the first page of each PE lesson.

Getting Ready for the EOG Test

    See the last page of each PE skill lesson.

Number of the Day

    See the first page of each TE lesson.

Problem of the Day

    See the first page of each TE lesson.

Lesson Quiz

    See the *Assess* section of each TE lesson.

Performance Assessment

Assess students' understanding of concepts applied to real-world situations.

Performance Assessment (Tasks A–B), PE p. 296; pp. PA30–31

Student Self-Assessment

Have students evaluate their own work.

How Did I Do?, p. AGxvii

A Guide to My Math Portfolio, p. AGxix

Math Journal

    See *Write* in the *Assess* section of each TE lesson and TE pages 242B, 264B, 278B, 280B.

 Harcourt Assessment System

Make and grade chapter tests electronically.

This software includes:

- **multiple-choice items**
- **free-response items**
- **customizable tests**
- **the means to build your own tests from available items**
- **customizable student and class reports**

 Portfolio

Portfolio opportunities appear throughout the Pupil and Teacher's Editions.

Suggested work samples:

Problem Solving Project, TE pp. 236, 256, 272

Write About It, PE pp. 239, 261, 279

Chapter Review/Test, PE pp. 253, 269, 289

KEY   AG Assessment Guide   TE Teacher's Edition   PA Performance Assessment   PE Pupil Edition

LEARNING GOAL	TAUGHT IN LESSONS	CAT/ TERRA NOVA	CTBS/ TERRA NOVA	ITBS FORM A	MAT 8	STANFORD 10	NORTH CAROLINA STANDARDS
12A To model the meaning of division	12.1						1.03
12B To relate division to subtraction	12.2						1.03
12C To write division facts by using multiplication facts and fact families	12.3, 12.4	•		•		•	1.03 5.03 5.04
12D To solve problems by using an appropriate strategy such as *write a number sentence*	12.5	•	•	•	•	•	1.06
13A To write division facts with divisors of 2, 5, 3, and 4, and to understand the special properties of 0 and 1 in division	13.1, 13.2, 13.3	•	•	•	•	•	1.03
13B To write expressions and complete number sentences by using addition, subtraction, multiplication, or division	13.4	•	•	•	•	•	maintains (2) Goal 5
13C To solve problems by using an appropriate skill such as *choose the operation*	13.5	•	•	•	•	•	1.06
14A To write division facts with divisors of 6, 7, 8, 9, and 10	14.1, 14.2, 14.3	•	•	•	•	•	1.03
14B To write the unit or total cost of multiple items	14.4	•	•	•	•	•	1.03
14C To solve problems by using an appropriate strategy such as *work backward*	14.5		•			•	1.06

Technology Links

 ## Harcourt Mega Math
CD-ROM Series

The learning activities in this exciting, new, comprehensive math software series complement, enrich, and enhance the Pupil Edition lessons.

Harcourt Mega Math Correlation		
Lesson	**Activity/Level**	**Skill**
12.1	Country Countdown, Counting Critters/Levels X & Y	Meaning of Division
12.3 & 12.4	Ice Station Exploration, Arctic Algebra, Level E	Relate Multiplication and Division
13.1	Country Countdown, Counting Critters/Level AA	Divide by 2 and 5
13.2	The Number Games, Up, Up, and Array/Level E	Divide by 3 and 4
14.1	The Number Games, Up, Up, and Array/Level F	Divide by 6, 7, and 8
14.2	The Number Games, Up, Up, and Array/Level G	Divide by 9 and 10
14.3	Ice Station Exploration, Arctic Algebra, Level F	Practice Division Facts

The Harcourt Learning Site

www.harcourtschool.com

 GO ON-LINE

Visit THE LEARNING SITE at **www.harcourtschool.com** for a variety of activities and resources that can be used to explore, reinforce, practice, and extend the learning of the chapter.

- Multimedia Math Glossary
- Activities and instructional resources
- E-Lab activities
- Show Me math models

Intervention CD-ROMs

 These CD-ROMs help you

- assess prerequisite concepts and skills for each chapter and assess problem-solving at point of use.
- diagnose to determine whether intervention is necessary or if enrichment is appropriate for a concept or skill.
- diagnose to determine whether intervention is necessary for a specific problem-solving strategy or skill.
- prescribe intervention for concepts, skills, and problem-solving strategies and skills.
- provide enrichment for students who mastered the prerequisite concepts and skills.

For the Student

The following technology can be used with students that need more instruction with skills or problem solving, and with students that will benefit from reinforcement, practice, and extension of skills from this chapter.

 ## Intervention CD-ROMs

- Support and enrichment for prerequisite skills
- Support for problem solving

 ## Harcourt Mega Math CD-ROMs

- Reinforcement, practice, and extension

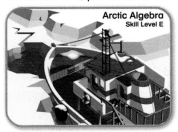

Arctic Algebra
Skill Level E

Up, Up, and Array
Skill Level F

 ## The Harcourt Learning Site
www.harcourtschool.com

- Multimedia Math Glossary
- E-Lab activities
- Show Me math models
- Games and activities

For the Teacher

 ## Intervention CD-ROMs

- Diagnose and prescribe intervention for prerequisite skills.
- Provide enrichment for prerequisite skills.
- Diagnose and prescribe intervention for problem-solving strategies and skills.

 ## Harcourt Mega Math CD-ROMs

- Customize additional practice for each student in your class.
- The leveled activities increase in difficulty as students progress.

 ## The Harcourt Learning Site
www.harcourtschool.com

- Find activities and other resources.

 ## Harcourt Assessment System

This software includes:

- Online test taking and automatic scoring
- A bank of items from which to build tests
- Immediate feedback on students' performance
- Correlation of items to textbook and state standards
- Comprehensive program management and class reporting
- Prescriptive reports

 ## ePlanner

This on-line resource allows you to:

- Customize planning and pacing.
- Select resources for daily instruction.
- Reorder content to meet your state, district, or local needs.

For the Parent

 ## The Harcourt Learning Site
www.harcourtschool.com

Encourage parents to visit the Math section of the Harcourt Learning Site to help them reinforce mathematics vocabulary, concepts, and skills with their children.

- Multimedia Math Glossary
- E-Lab interactive learning experiences
- Show Me math models
- Family Involvement tips and activities

Cross-Curricular Connections

Use these topics to help integrate mathematics into your daily planning.
See the pages indicated to find out more about each topic.

Science

- **Tadpoles,** PE p. 245
- **Goldfish,** TE p. 250B
- **Pelicans,** PE/TE p. 256
- **Pine trees,** PE p. 265
- **Weights on the moon,** TE p. 274B

Writing

- **Division word problems,** TE p. 242B
- **Write expressions,** TE p. 264B
- **Word problems,** TE p. 278B
- **Explain methods,** TE p. 280B

Social Studies

- **Whitewater rapids,** PE/TE, p. 236
- **Egyptian math game,** TE p. 240B
- **History of zero,** TE p. 262B
- **History of pizza,** PE/TE p. 272
- **Bagel baking,** PE p. 277

Language Arts/Reading

- **Analyze information,** TE p. 250B
- **Use context,** TE p. 266B
- **Label problems,** TE p. 274B
- **Choose important information,** PE/TE p. 277
- **Sequence,** TE p. 286B

Literature

- *The Doorbell Rang* by Pat Hutchins (Greenwillow Books, 1986), TE p. 236G
- *One Hundred Hungry Ants* by Elinor J. Pinczes (Houghton Mifflin Company, 1993), TE p. 236G

Reaching All Learners

Differentiated Instruction

PURPOSE To demonstrate an understanding of division as repeated subtraction.

USING THE ACTIVITY WHEEL Have each student choose one activity to complete independently. *Use after Lesson 12.2.*

*The Activity Wheel provides each student with a choice, according to learning style, for practicing an important skill.

Check students' work.

ACTIVITY WHEEL*

Model with counters 12 ÷ 3 = 4 as repeated subtraction. Explain your model.

Think of a real-world situation that models repeated subtraction, like pairing up socks from the dryer. Draw a picture of the situation and explain how it shows division as repeated subtraction.

Design a poster that shows the meaning of division as repeated subtraction. Use real-world objects that are naturally divided into equal groups such as pens (separated by color), marbles, and socks.

Literature Connections

These books provide students with additional ways to explore division.

The Doorbell Rang by Pat Hutchins (Greenwillow Books, 1986) tells the story of more and more friends who arrive to share a plate of cookies and illustrates the process of division.

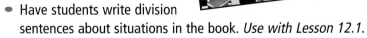

- Have students write division sentences about situations in the book. *Use with Lesson 12.1.*

One Hundred Hungry Ants by Elinor J. Pinczes (Houghton Mifflin Company, 1993). One hundred hungry ants head toward a picnic, but stop to change their line formation, showing different divisions of 100.

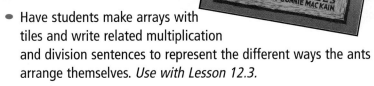

- Have students make arrays with tiles and write related multiplication and division sentences to represent the different ways the ants arrange themselves. *Use with Lesson 12.3.*

PRACTICE GAME

Fact Family

PURPOSE To practice multiplication and division fact families

MATERIALS *For each group* game cards, p. TR74; scissors

ABOUT THE GAME

- Groups of four cut out the cards, mix them up, and pass out ten to each player.

- Players take turns taking one card from the player to their right.

- The object is to complete sets of four facts that make up a fact family. Players place each completed fact family face up.

- After all cards have been matched, the player with the greatest number of fact families wins the game. *Use with Lesson 12.4.*

VISUAL LOGICAL/ MATHEMATICAL

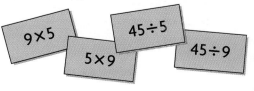

CHAPTER 12

Understand Division

NCTM Standards 2000

1. Number and Operations *Lessons 12.1, 12.2, 12.3, 12.4, 12.5*	6. Problem Solving *Lessons 12.1, 12.2, 12.3, 12.4, 12.5*
2. Algebra *Lessons 12.2, 12.3, 12.4, 12.5*	7. Reasoning and Proof *Lessons 12.1, 12.2, 12.3, 12.4, 12.5*
3. Geometry	8. Communication *Lessons 12.2, 12.3, 12.4, 12.5*
4. Measurement	9. Connections *Lessons 12.1, 12.2, 12.3, 12.4*
5. Data Analysis and Probability	10. Representation *Lessons 12.1, 12.3, 12.4, 12.5*

Chapter Planner

Getting Ready for Chapter 12 • Assessing Prior Knowledge and INTERVENTION (See PE and TE page 237.)

LESSON	NORTH CAROLINA STANDARDS	PACING	VOCABULARY*	MATERIALS	RESOURCES AND TECHNOLOGY
12.1 Hands On: The Meaning of Division pp. 238–239 Objective To model the meaning of *division*	1.03a	1 Day (For Lessons 12.1 and 12.2)	**divide**	*For each group* counters	Reteach, Practice, Problem Solving, Challenge 12.1 ▢ Transparency 12.1 ⊙ **Intervention,** *Skills 26–29* (CD or Book) ⊙ **Harcourt Mega Math Country Countdown,** *Counting Critters*
12.2 Subtraction and Division pp. 240–241 Objective To relate division to subtracting equal groups	1.03c				Reteach, Practice, Problem Solving, Challenge 12.2 ▢ Transparency 12.2 ⊙ **Intervention,** *Skills 26–29* (CD or Book)
12.3 Algebra: Multiplication and Division pp. 242–245 Objective To relate division to multiplication and to use a variable for an unknown number	1.03c *also* 5.03 5.04	1 Day	**dividend** **divisor** **quotient** **inverse operations** **variable**		Reteach, Practice, Problem Solving, Challenge 12.3 ▢ Transparency 12.3 ▣ **Math Jingles® CD 3–4** ⊙ **Intervention,** *Skills 26–29* (CD or Book) ⊙ **Harcourt Mega Math Ice Station Exploration,** *Arctic Algebra*
12.4 Algebra: Fact Families pp. 246–249 Objective To use multiplication and division fact families	1.03c *also* 5.04	2 Days	**fact family** factor product	*For each student or each pair* square pieces of paper, scissors	Reteach, Practice, Problem Solving, Challenge 12.4 ▢ Transparency 12.4 ▣ **Math Jingles® CD 3–4** ⊙ **Intervention,** *Skills 26–29* (CD or Book) ⊙ **Harcourt Mega Math Ice Station Exploration,** *Arctic Algebra*
12.5 Problem Solving Strategy: Write a Number Sentence pp. 250–251 Objective To solve problems using the strategy *write a number sentence*	1.06	1 Day			Reteach, Practice, Reading Strategy, Challenge 12.5 ⊙ **Intervention • Problem Solving,** *Strategy/Skill 12* (CD or Book) ▢ Transparency 12.5 ▢ Scaffolded Instruction Transparency 12 ▢ Reading Transparency 12

Ending Chapter 12 • Extra Practice, p. 252 • Chapter 12 Review/Test, p. 253 • Getting Ready for the EOG Test, pp. 254–255

****Boldfaced** terms are the key mathematical terms for the chapter. Other terms are review vocabulary.

Vocabulary Power

Review Vocabulary

To be ready for Chapter 12, students should know the following vocabulary term:

- **group** (p. 237)—a collection of items that share the same attributes

Develop Key Chapter Vocabulary

The **boldfaced** words are the key vocabulary terms in the chapter.

- **divide** (p. 238)—to separate into equal groups
- **dividend** (p. 242)—the number that is being divided in a division problem
- **divisor** (p. 242)—the number that divides the dividend
- **quotient** (p. 242)—the number, not including the remainder, that is the result of dividing
- **inverse operations** (p. 242)—mathematical actions that undo each other, or that are opposites
- **variable** (p. 243)—a symbol or letter, used in mathematics, that represents a number or many numbers
- **fact family** (p. 246)—a set of related number sentences

Vocabulary Cards

Have students use the Vocabulary Cards on *Teacher's Resource Book* pages TR153–154 for the key terms in the chapter. The cards can be added to a file of mathematics terms.

Multimedia Math Glossary

For vocabulary support, visit
GO ON-LINE www.harcourtschool.com/mathglossary

Math Journal

Have students define the key vocabulary terms: *divide, dividend, divisor, quotient, inverse operations, variable,* and *fact family.* Have students use their own words and give an example of each.

MATH Word Work

Objective To reinforce vocabulary concepts
Use after Lesson 12.4.

Materials *For each student* counters, sheet of paper

Have students fold a sheet of paper in half 2 times so that the paper has 4 sections. Have students write the multiplication and division fact family for 4, 6, and 24. There should be one number sentence at the bottom of each section. Direct students to use counters to model each of the number sentences and sketch the models. Have students label each part of the division sentences using the vocabulary terms *dividend, divisor,* and *quotient.*

Discuss the different models used to display each fact. Explain how the model for a multiplication sentence might look the same as a model for a division sentence.

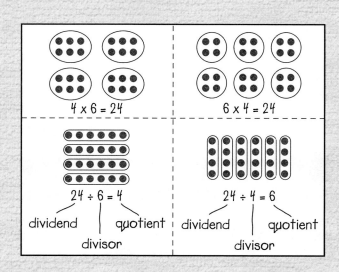

Mathematics Across the Grades

LOOKING BACK • Prerequisite Skills

To be ready for Chapter 12, students should have the following understandings and skills:

- **Multiplication Facts Through 10**—review basic multiplication facts through 10

- **Make Equal Groups**—determine the number of groups and the number in each group

Check What You Know

Use page 237 to determine students' knowledge of prerequisite concepts and skills.

Intervention

Help students prepare for the chapter by using the intervention resources described on TE page 237.

LOOKING AT CHAPTER 12 • Essential Skills

Students will

- model the meaning of *division*.

- relate division to subtracting equal groups.

- **relate division to multiplication.**

- use multiplication and division fact families.

- use the problem solving strategy *write a number sentence.*

Example

Complete the number sentence:

$$30 \div 6 = \blacksquare$$

Model	Solution
$6 \times 5 = 30$	$30 \div 6 = 5$

LOOKING AHEAD • Applications

Students will apply what they learn in Chapter 12 to the following new concepts:

- Write Division Facts with Divisors of 1–5 (Chapter 13)

- Write Division Facts with Divisors of 6–10 (Chapter 14)

- Find the Cost (Chapter 14)

- Divide with Remainders (Chapter 30)

Differentiated Instruction

PROFESSIONAL DEVELOPMENT

FROM RESEARCH TO PRACTICE

 Meeting the Needs of All Learners

Extra Support	Activities for All	Enrichment
Alternative Teaching Strategy TE Lessons 12.1, 12.2, 12.3, 12.4, 12.5 **ESOL/ESL** TE Lessons 12.1, 12.2, 12.3, 12.4, 12.5 **Special Needs** TE Lessons 12.3, 12.5	**Cross-Curricular Connections** **Career:** TE Lesson 12.4 **Reading:** TE Lesson 12.5 **Science:** TE Lesson 12.5 **Social Studies:** Chapter Opener, TE Lesson 12.2 **Vocabulary:** TE p. 236I, PE/TE p. 237 **Writing:** TE Lesson 12.3	**Advanced Learners** TE Lesson 12.4 **Early Finishers** TE Lesson 12.1

Combination and Multi-age Classrooms

Grade 2	Grade 3	Grade 4
Skills Trace Across the Grades		
Relate addition and multiplication; explore division by making equal groups.	**Model division with equal groups and arrays; relate subtraction and division; relate multiplication and division; write fact families.**	Relate multiplication and division; practice multiplication and division facts to 12.
Instructional Strategies		
Students on this level may require more time to build conceptual understanding. **Assignments** **Grade 3 Pupil Edition** • Have students use counters with Lessons 12.1, 12.2, and 12.3. • Have students work in pairs on Lessons 12.4 and 12.5. **Grade 2 Pupil Edition**—pages 529–536	Students on this level should be able to complete all the lessons in the Pupil Edition and all the activities in the Teacher's Edition with minimal adjustments. **Assignment** **Grade 3 Pupil Edition**—pages 236–253	Students on this level will probably require less time to build conceptual understanding. **Assignments** **Grade 3 Pupil Edition** • Compact Lessons 12.1 and 12.2. **Grade 4 Pupil Edition**—pages 162–201

Understand Division

Introducing the Chapter

To *divide* means "to separate into equal groups," or "to make equal numbers of groups." Have students look at the bar graph. Ask: If a group of people in a small raft switched to canoes, how many canoes would they need? 2 canoes

Using Data

To begin study of the chapter, have students

• Write a number sentence to show how many groups of canoe paddlers would fit into a big raft.
$2 + 2 + 2 = 6$

• Begin with the number of persons that a big raft can hold and subtract 3 from it as many times as you can. Then tell how many groups of 3 there are.
$6 - 3 = 3$; $3 - 3 = 0$; There are 2 groups of 3 in 6.

• How many people can ride in each small raft? 4 people Write a multiplication sentence to show how many small rafts would be needed for 24 people to go rafting. $6 \times 4 = 24$; 6 small rafts

Problem Solving Project

Purpose To practice finding equal groups

Grouping pairs

Materials catalogs of outdoor equipment

Background Rapids and rivers are rated Class I through Class VI. These ratings depend on the volume of water, geography of the rapids, and any downstream dangers. The following classifications are used: Class I-II Mild/Easy; Class III-IV Very Major Rapids; Class V-VI Very Difficult.

UNDERSTAND • PLAN • SOLVE • CHECK

Have students

• Plan an outdoor trip for 5–10 people.

• Make a table listing equipment and food needed for the trip.

• Write number sentences showing how many of each item each person will receive. Check students' work.

 Graphing Investigations
Begin Week 12.

≡FAST FACT • SOCIAL STUDIES
North Carolina has more than 150 white-water rapids. In the sport of white-water rafting, people use paddles to move boats along rivers through shallow, fast-moving water called rapids.

PROBLEM SOLVING The graph shows different kinds of white-water boats and the number of people each can hold. If 24 friends want to go white-water rafting together, how many big rafts will they need? Explain.

4; $24 \div 6 = 4$

WHITE-WATER RIVER BOATS

236

WHY LEARN MATH? Tour guides use division to find the number of rafts needed for the number of people going white-water rafting. Ask: **If 36 people are going white-water rafting, how many big rafts will be needed?** 6 big rafts Ask: **What are some times when you use division?** Possible answer: when dividing snacks to share with friends; when dividing into teams to play a game

Family Involvement Activities

These activities provide:

• Letter to the Family

• Math Vocabulary

• Family Game

• Practice (Homework)

Family Involvement Activities, p. FA45

CHECK WHAT YOU KNOW

Use this page to help you review and remember
important skills needed for Chapter 12.

✔ MULTIPLICATION FACTS THROUGH 10

Find the product.

1. $6 \times 7 = $ ■ 42
2. $3 \times 8 = $ ■ 24
3. ■ $= 8 \times 9$ 72
4. $9 \times 0 = $ ■ 0

5. $5 \times 7 = $ ■ 35
6. ■ $= 10 \times 4$ 40
7. $4 \times 4 = $ ■ 16
8. $2 \times 4 = $ ■ 8

9. ■ $= 9 \times 9$ 81
10. ■ $= 6 \times 8$ 48
11. $8 \times 7 = $ ■ 56
12. $4 \times 3 = $ ■ 12

✔ MAKE EQUAL GROUPS

Complete.

13.
■ groups
■ in each group 4; 2

14. 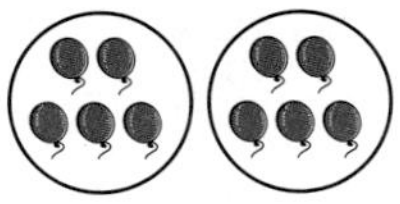
■ groups
■ in each group 2; 5

15. 
■ groups
■ in each group 3; 2

16. 
■ groups
■ in each group 4; 1

17.
■ groups
■ in each group 4; 3

18. 
■ groups
■ in each group 4; 4

✔ VOCABULARY POWER

REVIEW	PREVIEW
group [grōop] *noun*	divide — quotient
Group means "a number of persons or things that are collected." Suppose you have 20 marbles. How many groups of 5 marbles do you have? **4 groups**	dividend — inverse operations
	divisor — variable
	fact family

GO ON-LINE www.harcourtschool.com/mathglossary

Chapter 12 **237**

Assessing Prior Knowledge

Use the **Check What You Know** page to determine whether your students have mastered the prerequisite skills critical for this chapter.

Intervention

- **Diagnose and Prescribe**
Evaluate your students' performance on this page to determine whether intervention is necessary or if enrichment is appropriate. Options that provide instruction, practice, and a check are listed in the chart.

✔ CHECK WHAT YOU KNOW RESOURCES

Intervention Copying Masters or CD-ROMs

Enrichment Copying Masters

VOCABULARY POWER

For activities and information about the vocabulary in this chapter, see page 236I.

Were students successful with ✔ CHECK WHAT YOU KNOW?

IF . . . NO THEN . . . INTERVENE — **INTERVENTION OPTIONS** — **IF . . . YES THEN . . . ENRICH**

Skill/Items	Missed more than	Intervene with
Multiplication Facts Through 10, 1–12	3	• *Intervention*, Skills 26, 27, 28
Make Equal Groups, 13–18	2	• *Intervention*, Skill 29

Skill/Items	Missed fewer than	Enrich with
Multiplication Facts Through 10, 1–12	4	• *Intervention*, Enrichment p. IN351
Make Equal Groups, 13–18	3	• *Intervention*, Enrichment p. IN352

Lesson Planning

PROFESSIONAL DEVELOPMENT

Objective To model the meaning of division

Materials *For each group* counters

NCTM Standards
1. Number and Operations
6. Problem Solving
7. Reasoning and Proof
9. Connections
10. Representation

Math Background
These ideas will help students understand the meaning of division.

- Division can help you find how many items are in each group and how many equal groups there are.

- Division can be modeled with counters.

- Division and multiplication are opposite, or inverse, operations.

Vocabulary
divide to share a number of items to find how many equal groups can be made or how many items will be in each group

Warm-Up Resources

Build Number Sense
3
2
1

Number of the Day
Transparency **12.1**

The number of the day is the number of days in the month of February in a non-leap year. 28

Review Basic Facts
8
+3

Daily Facts Practice

Have students practice addition and subtraction facts by completing Set F of *Teacher's Resource Book*, p. TR91.

Solve a Problem
Transparency **12.1**

Problem of the Day

Rudy is saving $6 a week to buy a computer game that costs $24. Al is saving $4 a week to buy the same game. Who will be able to buy the game sooner? Rudy How much sooner? 2 weeks

Solution Problem of the Day tab, p. PD12

Intervention and Extension Resources

Alternative Teaching Strategy

MATERIALS *For each group* tape or string

Organize a student role-play activity to help students **understand the meaning of division.** Form groups of students that are divisible by 2, 3, 4, 5, or 6. Have each group use the tape or string to divide their group into smaller, equal groups. To begin, ask one group to demonstrate the first example in the lesson. Continue with the exercises in Try It. Check students' work.

KINESTHETIC

BODILY/KINESTHETIC

ESOL/ESL

Have students **practice the concept of division** by writing a story about a number such as 10, 12, or 15. Have them include information about who is sharing, how many groups they will need to make, and how many will be in each group. Encourage students to draw pictures to illustrate their stories and share them with the class. Check students' work.

AUDITORY

INTRAPERSONAL/INTROSPECTIVE

Multistep and Strategy Problems

The following multistep or strategy problem is provided in Lesson 12.1:

Page	Item
239	6

Early Finishers

Have students find models in the classroom to **reinforce the concept of division.** Ask students to work in pairs to find items they can divide into equal groups and then write a word problem for each item. Have students exchange their problems with other students and solve. Check students' work.

KINESTHETIC

BODILY/KINESTHETIC

Technology Link

Intervention, *Skills 26–29*

Harcourt Mega Math Country Countdown, *Counting Critters,* Levels X and Y

GO The Harcourt Learning Site www.harcourtschool.com

Lesson 12.1 Organizer

Objective To model the meaning of division

Vocabulary divide

Materials *For each group* counters

1 INTRODUCE

QUICK REVIEW provides review of prerequisite skills.

WHY LEARN THIS? You can use division if you want to share something equally with friends. *Share the lesson objective with students.*

2 TEACH

Guided Instruction

- *Refer students to Activities 1 and 2.*

  How can counters or other objects help you divide? Possible answer: You can see how many items are in each group or how many groups there are.

  What would you do differently if you were to divide 14 counters into 7 equal groups? You would begin by placing 1 counter in each of 7 groups until all 14 counters are used, making 7 groups of 2.

MODIFYING INSTRUCTION You may wish to show Steps 2 and 3 in either activity by drawing the counters and having students draw a picture to show the counters in equal groups.

3 PRACTICE

Guided Practice

Do Try It Exercises a–b with your students. Identify students who are having difficulty and choose appropriate lesson resources to provide assistance.

REASONING How are Activity 1 and Activity 2 alike? How are they different? Possible answer: Both show dividing 14 counters into equal groups; in Activity 1, counters are placed into 2 groups of 7; in Activity 2, 14 counters are placed in 7 groups of 2.

LESSON

1

The Meaning of Division

VOCABULARY
divide

MATERIALS
counters

▶ **Explore**

When you multiply, you put equal groups together. When you **divide**, you separate into equal groups.

Activity 1 Divide 14 counters into 2 equal groups. How many counters are in each group?

STEP 1
Use 14 counters.

STEP 2
Show 2 groups. Place a counter in each group

STEP 3
Continue until all counters are used.

So, there are 7 counters in each of 2 groups.

Activity 2 Divide 14 counters into groups of 2. How many groups of 2 counters can you make?

STEP 1
Use 14 counters.

STEP 2
Make groups of 2.

STEP 3
Continue making groups of 2 until all counters are used.

So, there are 7 groups of 2 counters.

Try It

Use counters to make equal groups. Draw a picture to show how you divided.

a. Divide 15 counters into 5 equal groups. How many are in each group?
   3 counters

b. Divide 15 counters into groups of 5. How many groups of 5 counters can you make?
   3 groups

We are putting 15 counters in 5 equal groups. How many should be in each group?
3 counters

238

MATH IDEA You can divide to find how many items are in each group or how many equal groups there are.

Four friends share 20 marbles equally. How many marbles will each person get?

Put one marble in each group until all marbles are used.

Each person will get 5 marbles.

Each person wants 4 marbles. How many people can share 20 marbles?

Make equal groups of 4 marbles until all marbles are used.

Five people can share 20 marbles.

Practice and Problem Solving

6. Possible answers: 2 groups of 9, 9 groups of 2, 3 groups of 6, 6 groups of 3, 18 groups of 1, 1 group of 18.

Copy and complete the table. Use counters to help.

	COUNTERS	NUMBER OF EQUAL GROUPS	NUMBER IN EACH GROUP
1.	15	5	▦ 3
2.	21	▦ 7	3
3.	24	3	▦ 8
4.	28	▦ 4	7

For 5–8, use counters and draw a picture. Check students' drawings.

5. Five friends share 30 stickers equally. How many will each person get? **6 stickers**

6. Elijah has 18 books that he wants to put into equal groups. List three different ways that he could do this. **See above.**

7. **REASONING** Three friends share some grapes equally. If each gets 9 grapes, how many grapes are there altogether? **27 grapes**

8. ✎ **Write About It** Explain how to divide 32 counters into 4 equal groups. **Start with 32 counters. Put counters in each of 4 groups until all counters are used. There are 8 counters in each group.**

Getting Ready for the EOG Test

9. Gina, Mike, Sharon, and Nita are sharing 16 cookies equally. How many cookies will each person get? **A**

   A 4   **B** 6   **C** 8   **D** 16

Chapter 12 **239**

North Carolina Standards 1.03 Develop fluency with multiplication from 1 × 1 to 12 × 12 and division of two-digit by one-digit numbers using: a) Strategies for multiplying and dividing numbers.

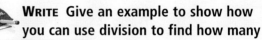
Independent Practice

Note that Exercise 6 is a **multistep or strategy problem.** Assign Exercises 1–8.

Point out that sharing equally means each person will have the same amount.

4 ASSESS

Summarize the lesson by having students:

DISCUSS What does it mean to divide something equally? to separate it into equal groups

WRITE Give an example to show how you can use division to find how many items are in a group. Possible answer: Divide 6 counters into 3 equal groups to find 2 in each group.

LESSON QUIZ

For 1–2, use counters.

Transparency **12.1**

1. Ten books are divided into 2 equal groups. How many books are in each group? 5 books

2. Fourteen snacks are divided so that each boy gets 2 snacks. How many boys get 2 snacks? 7 boys

---

Challenge 12.1

Paintbrush Division

The jars in each row need to be filled with the same number of paintbrushes. Draw the paintbrushes in each jar and complete the number sentence. Check students' drawings.

1.
Total number of paintbrushes: 12
Paintbrushes in each jar: 4
12 ÷ 3 = 4

2.
Total number of paintbrushes: 8
Paintbrushes in each jar: 2
8 ÷ 4 = 2

3.
Total number of paintbrushes: 12
Paintbrushes in each jar: 6
12 ÷ 2 = 6

4.
Total number of paintbrushes: 15
Paintbrushes in each jar: 3
15 ÷ 5 = 3

5.
Total number of paintbrushes: 18
Paintbrushes in each jar: 6
18 ÷ 3 = 6

6.
Total number of paintbrushes: 20
Paintbrushes in each jar: 5
20 ÷ 4 = 5

Complete the chart.

Number of Paintbrushes	Number of Jars	Number of Paintbrushes in Each Jar
24	4	6
21	3	7
30	5	6

CW62 Challenge

Problem Solving 12.1

Meaning of Division

Understand ➡ Plan ➡ Solve ➡ Check

Write the correct answer.

1. Three friends want to share 18 star stickers equally. How many stars will each person get? Draw a picture to help.
6 stars

2. Tyra is at her friend's house. She has to be home at 4:00 P.M. The clock below shows the time right now. How many minutes is it until Tyra needs to be home?
40 minutes

3. Mike has $7.45 in his pocket. Make a list of bills and coins that he could have.
Possible answer: a $5 bill, 2 $1 bills, 1 quarter, and 2 dimes

4. Four friends want to share 12 cookies equally. How many cookies will each person get? Draw a picture to help.
3 cookies

Choose the letter of the correct answer.

5. Find the difference.
1,780 − 907
A 887   **C** 877
B 883   **(D)** 873

6. There are 32 counters. How many equal groups of 8 can be made?
F 40   **(H)** 4
G 24   **J** 3

7. Which number of friends could not share 8 marbles equally?
A 2   **C** 4
(B) 3   **D** 8

8. What is the product of 5 and 9?
F 4   **(H)** 45
G 14   **J** 54

9. **Write About It** Describe the strategy you used to find the correct answer for Problem 7.
Possible answer: I drew three circles and tried to divide 8 marbles equally among the three circles.

PS62 Problem Solving

Subtraction and Division

Lesson Planning

PROFESSIONAL DEVELOPMENT

Objective To relate division to subtracting equal groups

NCTM Standards
1. **Number and Operations**
2. **Algebra**
6. **Problem Solving**
7. **Reasoning and Proof**
8. **Communication**
9. **Connections**

Math Background
These ideas will help students understand the meaning of division and relate division to subtraction.

- Repeated subtraction may be used to solve a division problem.

- When using repeated subtraction, start with the total and subtract equal groups until you reach 0. Count the number of times you subtracted to find the quotient.

- When using repeated subtraction to find a quotient, you are skip-counting backward.

- Division may be written in two forms: with a division house or as a division sentence.

Warm-Up Resources

Number of the Day

Transparency 12.2

Choose an even number from 10–20. How many different equal groups of 2 can you make?
Answers will vary.

Daily Facts Practice

Have students practice addition and subtraction facts by completing Set G of *Teacher's Resource Book*, p. TR91.

Transparency 12.2

Problem of the Day

Krista has 8 dimes and 20 pennies. She divides them equally among 3 friends and herself. How many dimes does each get? 2 dimes How many pennies does each get? 5 pennies How much money does each person have? 25¢

Solution Problem of the Day tab, p. PD12

Intervention and Extension Resources

Alternative Teaching Strategy

MATERIALS *For each student* number line, p. TR5

ESOL/ESL

Help students **make the connection between repeated subtraction and division**. Tell students to skip-count backward along the number line from the first number in the division sentence until they reach zero. For example, to solve $20 \div 4 = $ ■, show skip-counting backward by 4 from 20 to 0.

Have students practice with the following exercises:

$21 \div 3 = $ ■ 7

$24 \div 8 = $ ■ 3

$15 \div 3 = $ ■ 5

KINESTHETIC

MUSICAL/RHYTHMIC

Multistep and Strategy Problems

The following multistep or strategy problem is provided in Lesson 12.2:

Page	Item
241	18

Technology • *Calculator*

MATERIALS *For each group* calculator

Students can use a calculator to **make the connection between repeated subtraction and division**. Start with the problem $20 \div 4 = $ ■. Have students input the following keystrokes on a calculator and record their findings as shown here.

$$20 - 4 = \blacksquare \ 16$$
$$= \blacksquare \ 12$$
$$= \blacksquare \ 8$$
$$= \blacksquare \ 4$$
$$\underline{= \blacksquare \ 0}$$
$$5 \text{ times}$$

Have students count the number of times they need to press the $=$ key before they reach 0. Ask students: Each time you press the key with the equal sign, what are you actually doing? subtracting 4

Have students practice with exercises from the lesson.

VISUAL

VISUAL/SPATIAL

Social Studies Connection

Have students **apply repeated subtraction** to the Egyptian game Mancala. Mancala was created about 3,000 years ago. The game is played with 48 stones equally divided into 12 bins, 6 on each side of the game board. Each player has a bin, called a mancala, to store captured stones. Have students draw a diagram of the game board. Have them use repeated subtraction to find how many stones are placed in each bin to begin the game.

$48 \div 12 = \underline{\ ?\ }$ 4 stones

VISUAL

VISUAL/SPATIAL

Technology Link

Intervention, *Skills 26–29*

Lesson 12.2 Organizer

Objective To relate division to subtracting equal groups

1 INTRODUCE

QUICK REVIEW provides review of prerequisite skills.

WHY LEARN THIS? Knowing how to subtract equal groups can help you share game pieces or treats with your friends. *Share the lesson objective with students.*

2 TEACH

Guided Instruction

- *Direct students' attention to the Learn section.*
  Why do you count back or continue to subtract until you reach zero? to separate all the pieces equally
  How can you model the repeated subtraction steps using counters? Start with 12 counters and subtract groups of 4 until no counters remain.

- *Ask students to look at the Write and Read statements and apply their knowledge.*
  What are the two ways you can write thirty-five divided by seven equals five?
  $35 \div 7 = 5$; $7\overline{)35}^{\,5}$

- *Have students read the Math Idea.*
  How is division like repeated subtraction?
  Possible answer: Both separate the objects into equal groups.

LESSON 2 Subtraction and Division

Quick Review
How many are there in all?

1. 2 groups of 3 6
2. 4 groups of 4 16
3. 5 groups of 2 10
4. 3 groups of 9 27
5. 1 group of 8 8

▶ **Learn**

GET IN THE GAME Ana has 12 game pieces for a game. Each player gets 4 pieces. How many people can play?

$$12 \div 4 = \blacksquare$$

number of pieces | number for each player | number of players

One Way Use a number line. Start at 12. Count back by 4s until you reach 0. Count the number of times you subtract 4.

You subtract 4 three times.

So, 3 people can play.

Another Way Start with 12. Take away groups of 4 until you reach 0. Count the number of times you subtract 4.

$$\begin{array}{ccc} 12 & 8 & 4 \\ -\ 4 & -\ 4 & -\ 4 \\ \hline 8 & 4 & 0 \end{array}$$

Number of times you subtract 4: **1** **2** **3**

Since you subtract 4 from 12 three times, there are 3 groups of 4 in 12.

Write: $12 \div 4 = 3$ or $4\overline{)12}^{\,3}$
Read: Twelve divided by four equals three.

MATH IDEA You can count back on a number line or use repeated subtraction to find how many groups when you know how many in all and how many in each group.

- **Discuss** how to count back to find $15 \div 5$.
  Count backward by 5s three times to zero, so $15 \div 5 = 3$.

240

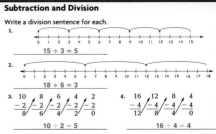

Reteach 12.2

Subtraction and Division

Division is like repeated subtraction.
How many groups of 2 are there in 8?
Start at 8 on the number line.
Count back 2 spaces at a time until you reach 0.

$$\begin{array}{cccc} 8 & 6 & 4 & 2 \\ -2 & -2 & -2 & -2 \\ \hline 6 & 4 & 2 & 0 \end{array}$$

You can subtract 2 from 8 four times because there are 4 groups of 2 in 8.
So, $8 \div 2 = 4$.

Find the quotient. You may use the number line to help.

1. $12 \div 2 = \underline{\ 6\ }$

2. $12 \div 6 = \underline{\ 2\ }$

3. $12 \div 3 = \underline{\ 4\ }$

4. $12 \div 4 = \underline{\ 3\ }$

5. $10 \div 2 = \underline{\ 5\ }$

6. $10 \div 5 = \underline{\ 2\ }$

7. $9 \div 3 = \underline{\ 3\ }$

8. $8 \div 4 = \underline{\ 2\ }$

Reteach RW63

Practice 12.2

Subtraction and Division

Write a division sentence for each.

1. $15 \div 3 = 5$

2. $18 \div 6 = 3$

3. $\begin{array}{ccccc} 10 & 8 & 6 & 4 & 2 \\ -2 & -2 & -2 & -2 & -2 \\ \hline 8 & 6 & 4 & 2 & 0 \end{array}$
   $10 \div 2 = 5$

4. $\begin{array}{cccc} 16 & 12 & 8 & 4 \\ -4 & -4 & -4 & -4 \\ \hline 12 & 8 & 4 & 0 \end{array}$
   $16 \div 4 = 4$

Use a number line or subtraction to solve. Possible solutions shown.

5. $12 \div 3 = \underline{\ 4\ }$

6. $20 \div 4 = \underline{\ 5\ }$

7. $30 \div 5 = \underline{\ 6\ }$
   $\begin{array}{cccccc} 30 & 25 & 20 & 15 & 10 & 5 \\ -5 & -5 & -5 & -5 & -5 & -5 \\ \hline 25 & 20 & 15 & 10 & 5 & 0 \end{array}$

8. $6 \div 2 = \underline{\ 3\ }$
   $\begin{array}{ccc} 6 & 4 & 2 \\ -2 & -2 & -2 \\ \hline 4 & 2 & 0 \end{array}$

Mixed Review

9. $\begin{array}{r} 271 \\ +409 \\ \hline 680 \end{array}$

10. $\begin{array}{r} 9,006 \\ -7,847 \\ \hline 1,159 \end{array}$

11. $\begin{array}{r} 7 \\ \times 6 \\ \hline 42 \end{array}$

12. $\begin{array}{r} 4 \\ \times 9 \\ \hline 36 \end{array}$

13. $7 \times 7 = \underline{\ 49\ }$ 14. $8 \times 3 = \underline{\ 24\ }$ 15. $8 \times 6 = \underline{\ 48\ }$

Practice PW63

Check

1. **Explain** how to use repeated subtraction to prove that $18 \div 6 = 3$. **Possible answer: $18 - 6 = 12$, $12 - 6 = 6$, $6 - 6 = 0$. You can subtract 6 from 18 three times to get to zero, so 18 divided by 6 equals 3.**

Write the division sentence for each.

2.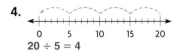
0 1 2 3 4 5 6 7 8 9 10 11 12
$12 \div 3 = 4$

3.
$$\begin{array}{cccc} 8 & 6 & 4 & 2 \\ -2 & -2 & -2 & -2 \\ \hline 6 & 4 & 2 & 0 \end{array}$$
$8 \div 2 = 4$

Practice and Problem Solving

Extra Practice, page 252, Set A

Write a division sentence for each.

4.
0   5   10   15   20
$20 \div 5 = 4$

5.
$$\begin{array}{ccc} 24 & 16 & 8 \\ -8 & -8 & -8 \\ \hline 16 & 8 & 0 \end{array}$$
$24 \div 8 = 3$

Use a number line or subtraction to solve.

6. $15 \div 3 = \blacksquare$ **5**
7. $21 \div 7 = \blacksquare$ **3**
8. $30 \div 5 = \blacksquare$ **6**
9. $36 \div 6 = \blacksquare$ **6**
10. $2\overline{)10}$ **5**
11. $8\overline{)16}$ **2**
12. $7\overline{)35}$ **5**
13. $5\overline{)25}$ **5**

✸**ALGEBRA** **Complete. Write $+$, $-$, $\times$, or $\div$ for each ●.**

14. $20 - 5 = 5 \, \bullet \, 3$ **×**
15. $24 \div 6 = 18 \, \bullet \, 14$ **−**
16. $32 \, \bullet \, 8 = 4 \times 10$ **+**
17. $8 \, \bullet \, 2 = 2 + 2$ **÷**

18. Scott buys 22 baseball cards. He keeps 10 cards and divides the rest equally between 2 friends. How many cards will each friend get? **6 cards**

19. **REASONING** Nora says that $8 \div 4 = 0$ because $8 - 4 = 4$ and $4 - 4 = 0$. Is Nora correct? Explain. **No; Nora subtracted 4 from 8 two times, so $8 \div 4 = 2$.**

20. Explain how to use repeated subtraction to find $100 \div 10$. **Possible answer: Subtract 10 from 100 ten times. So, $100 \div 10 = 10$.**

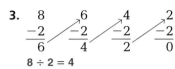

Getting Ready for the EOG Test

21. Some students earned 15 quarters for raking leaves. Each student received 3 quarters. Which number sentence could be used to find how many students received quarters? **D**

0 1 2 3 4 5 6 7 8 9 10 11 12 13 14 15

A $15 - 3 = \blacksquare$
B $3 + 15 = \blacksquare$
C $15 - 3 - 3 = \blacksquare$
D $15 \div 3 = \blacksquare$

Chapter 12 **241**

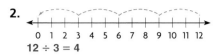

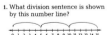 **North Carolina Standards 1.03** Develop fluency with multiplication from 1×1 to 12×12 and division up to two-digit by one-digit numbers using: c) Relationships between operations.

---

3 PRACTICE

Guided Practice

Do Check Exercises 1–3 with your students. Identify students who are having difficulty and choose appropriate lesson resources to provide assistance.

Independent Practice

Note that Exercise 18 is a **multistep or strategy problem.** Assign Exercises 4–20.

4 ASSESS

Summarize the lesson by having students:

DISCUSS What are two ways to find $25 \div 5 = \blacksquare$? Possible answer: Use repeated subtraction or skip-count backward; 5.

WRITE How can you use subtraction to find $12 \div 3 = \blacksquare$? Possible answer: by subtracting 3 until you reach 0 and counting the number of times you subtracted; 4

LESSON QUIZ

Use a number line or subtraction to solve.

Transparency **12.2**

1. $12 \div 3 = \blacksquare$ 4;
   $12 - 3 = 9$,
   $9 - 3 = 6$,
   $6 - 3 = 3$,
   $3 - 3 = 0$

2. $14 \div 7 = \blacksquare$ 2;
   $14 - 7 = 7$,
   $7 - 7 = 0$

3. $27 \div 9 = \blacksquare$ 3;
   $27 - 9 = 18$,
   $18 - 9 = 9$,
   $9 - 9 = 0$

4. $12 \div 4 = \blacksquare$ 3;
   $12 - 4 = 8$,
   $8 - 4 = 4$,
   $4 - 4 = 0$

Challenge 12.2

Animal Division

Separate the animals into groups. Draw a circle around each group. Then complete the number sentence. Check students' work.

1. 4 cats in each group

$8 \div 4 = \underline{2}$

2. 3 dogs in each group
$9 \div 3 = \underline{3}$

3. 3 birds in each group

$12 \div 3 = \underline{4}$

4. 5 turtles in each group
$10 \div 5 = \underline{2}$

5. 5 mice in each group

$15 \div 5 = \underline{3}$

6. 3 fish in each group
$18 \div 3 = \underline{6}$

Complete the chart.

Number of Animals	Number in Each Group	Number of Equal Groups
18 puppies	3	6
20 kittens	4	5
24 gerbils	6	4
30 guinea pigs	5	6

Challenge CW63

Problem Solving 12.2

Subtraction and Division

Understand ▸ Plan ▸ Solve ▸ Check

Write the correct answer.

1. What division sentence is shown by this number line?
0 1 2 3 4 5 6 7 8 9 10 11 12 13 14 15
$15 \div 5 = 3$

2. Draw a picture to show 6 counters divided into 2 equal groups.

3. Mary cut 8 flowers from her garden. She gave 2 flowers to each teacher. How many teachers received flowers?
4 teachers

4. Felix's team scored 3 runs each inning for 9 innings. How many runs did they score?
27 runs

Choose the letter of the correct answer.

5. Which division sentence is shown by this repeated subtraction?
$$\begin{array}{cccc} 12 & 9 & 6 & 3 \\ -3 & -3 & -3 & -3 \\ \hline 9 & 6 & 3 & 0 \end{array}$$
A $12 \div 6 = 2$ C $12 \div 3 = 4$
B $12 \div 1 = 12$ D $12 \div 2 = 6$

6. Cecily and Ashley shared 12 cookies equally. How many did each girl have?
F 12
G 6
H 4
J 2

7. What is 7 times 8?
A 49
B 54
C 56
D 64

8. Tom had $4.68. He spent $1.93. How much does he have left?
F $3.75   H $2.35
G $2.75   J $1.35

9. **Write About It** Explain how Problem 3 can be solved with repeated subtraction.
Possible answer: You can start with 8 and keep subtracting groups of 2 until you get to 0. It takes 4 subtractions to get to 0.

Problem Solving PS63

241

Lesson Planning

PROFESSIONAL DEVELOPMENT

Objective To relate division to multiplication and to use a variable for an unknown number

NCTM Standards
1. **Number and Operations**
2. **Algebra**
6. **Problem Solving**
7. **Reasoning and Proof**
8. **Communication**
9. **Connections**
10. **Representation**

Math Background
These ideas will help students relate division to multiplication.

- To find a quotient, use an array and count the number in each equal row.

- Use a related multiplication fact to find a quotient.

- Multiplication and division are inverse operations. If $a \times b = c$, then $c \div a = b$.

Vocabulary
dividend the number that is to be divided in a division problem

divisor the number that divides the dividend

quotient the answer in a division problem

inverse operations operations that are opposite, such as multiplication and division

variable a symbol or letter that stands for an unknown number

Warm-Up Resources

Number of the Day

Transparency **12.3**

What number times 3 equals 18? Double that number to find the number of the day. 12

Daily Facts Practice

Have students practice subtraction facts by completing Set A of *Teacher's Resource Book*, p. TR92.

Transparency **12.3**

Problem of the Day

Replace each ■ with a digit from 1 to 9. Use each digit only once. Make each number sentence true. Possible answers:

1. $36 \div ■ = ■$ 4, 9
2. $■ \times ■ = 30$ 6, 5
3. $11 - ■ = ■$ 8, 3
4. $■ + ■ + ■ = 10$ 1, 2, 7

Solution Problem of the Day tab, p. PD12

Intervention and Extension Resources

Alternative Teaching Strategy

Help students **connect an array to a division sentence**. For a given array, have students do the following:

ESOL/ESL

1. Copy each array and circle the rows.

2. To describe the array, write a multiplication sentence in the form:

number of rows	×	number in each row	=	total number
↓		↓		↓
factor 1	×	factor 2	=	product

3. Use the multiplication sentence to write a division sentence:

product	÷	factor 1	=	factor 2

Have students use exercises from the lesson to practice this strategy. Check students' work.

See also page 244.

VISUAL

LOGICAL/MATHEMATICAL

Multistep and Strategy Problems

The following multistep or strategy problems are provided in Lesson 12.3:

Page	Item
244	33
245	35

Special Needs

MATERIALS *For each group* counters, play money, cubes, color tiles

Have students **model multiplication and division sentences**. Let pairs of students choose items to use for modeling multiplication and division sentences. Read aloud the following number sentences one at a time: $4 \times 2 = 8$, $8 \div 4 = 2$; $3 \times 3 = 9$, $9 \div 3 = 3$; $14 \div 7 = 2$, $7 \times 2 = 14$.

Ask one student to model the sentence you read and the other one to check the model. Then reverse the roles. Check students' work.

KINESTHETIC

BODILY/KINESTHETIC

Writing in Mathematics

Have students **write and solve a division word problem** that involves sharing equally among friends. Have them represent their problems by writing a number sentence with a variable to describe the unknown number. Next, encourage students to exchange problems and number sentences with classmates and solve. Then have students compare their solutions. Check students' work.

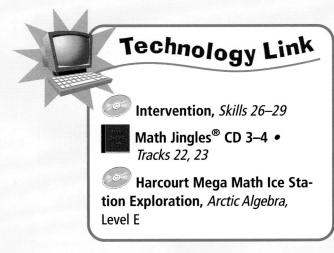

Technology Link

Intervention, *Skills 26–29*

Math Jingles® CD 3–4 • *Tracks 22, 23*

Harcourt Mega Math Ice Station Exploration, *Arctic Algebra, Level E*

Lesson 12.3 Organizer

Objective To relate division to multiplication and to use a variable for an unknown number

Vocabulary dividend, divisor, quotient, inverse operations, variable

① INTRODUCE

QUICK REVIEW provides review of prerequisite skills.

WHY LEARN THIS? You can use division to find how many items are in each group or how many groups there are. *Share the lesson objective with students.*

② TEACH

Guided Instruction

- *Direct students' attention to the Learn section.* **The dividend stands for the total number of stamps. What does the divisor stand for? the quotient?** the number of rows; the number in each row

  REASONING The product in the multiplication sentence becomes what part in the division sentence? the dividend

  What division sentence relates to the multiplication sentence, 5 × 8 = 40? Possible answers: 40 ÷ 8 = 5 or 40 ÷ 5 = 8

  REASONING Explain why multiplication and division are called opposite, or inverse, operations. Possible answer: The operations are opposite because multiplication puts together equal groups while division separates equal groups.

---

③ Algebra: Multiplication and Division

▶ Learn

STICK WITH STAMPS Use what you know about arrays and multiplication to understand division.

Mark is putting stamps into his stamp album. Each page holds 18 stamps in 3 equal rows. How many stamps are in each row?

$$18 \div 3 = \blacksquare$$
↑ number of stamps ↑ number of rows ↑ number in each row

VOCABULARY
dividend divisor
quotient
inverse operations
variable

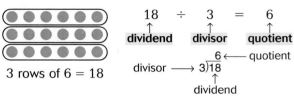

Show an array with 18 in 3 equal rows. Find how many are in each row.

Since 3 × 6 = 18, then 18 ÷ 3 = 6.

$$18 \div 3 = 6$$
↑ dividend ↑ divisor ↑ quotient

3 rows of 6 = 18

$$\text{divisor} \longrightarrow 3\overline{)18} \quad \begin{array}{l} 6 \longleftarrow \text{quotient} \end{array}$$
↑ dividend

So, there are 6 stamps in each row.

MATH IDEA Multiplication and division are opposite or **inverse operations**.

Technology Link
More Practice:
Harcourt Mega Math
Ice Station Exploration,
Arctic Algebra, Level E

Examples

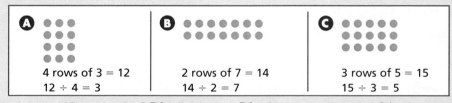

Ⓐ
4 rows of 3 = 12
12 ÷ 4 = 3

Ⓑ
2 rows of 7 = 14
14 ÷ 2 = 7

Ⓒ
3 rows of 5 = 15
15 ÷ 3 = 5

242

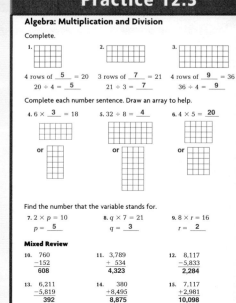

Use Variables

A **variable** is something that stands for an unknown number.
A box, , can be a variable.

$16 \div 2 = $

Think: $2 \times $ $ = 16$
$2 \times 8 = 16$

So, $16 \div 2 = 8$.

A letter can also be a variable.

$24 \div 4 = a$

Think: $4 \times a = 24$
$4 \times 6 = 24$

So, $24 \div 4 = 6$.

2 rows of $= 16$

4 rows of $a = 24$

Examples

A $12 \div 2 = b$	**B** $15 \div 5 = c$
Think: $2 \times b = 12$	Think: $5 \times c = 15$
$2 \times 6 = 12$, so, $b = 6$.	$5 \times 3 = 15$, so, $c = 3$.
So, $12 \div 2 = 6$.	So, $15 \div 5 = 3$.

 MATH IDEA You can use a variable to stand for an unknown number.

 Check

Possible answer: The number of rows and columns can show $3 \times 7 = 21$ or $21 \div 3 = 7$.

1. **Explain** how to use this array to multiply and divide.

Copy and complete.

2. 3 rows of $= 24$ 8
$24 \div 3 = $ 8

3. 2 rows of $= 18$ 9
$18 \div 2 = $ 9

4. 3 rows of $= 18$ 6
$18 \div 3 = $ 6

Find the number that the variable stands for.

5. $12 \div 3 = r$
$r = \underline{?}$ 4

6. $16 \div 4 = s$
$s = \underline{?}$ 4

7. $20 \div 4 = t$
$t = \underline{?}$ 5

LESSON CONTINUES ▶

 North Carolina Standards 1.03 Develop fluency with multiplication from 1×1 to 12×12 and division up to two-digit by one-digit numbers using: c) Relationships between operations. *also* 5.03, 5.04

Challenge 12.3

Missing Numbers

Complete each table.

1.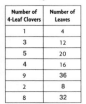

Number of Students	Number of Hands
1	2
4	8
6	12
2	4
9	18
7	14
5	10

2.

Number of Tricycles	Number of Wheels
1	3
3	9
7	21
6	18
9	27
4	12
8	24

3.

Number of 4-Leaf Clovers	Number of Leaves
1	4
3	12
5	20
4	16
9	36
2	8
8	32

4.

Number of Ants	Number of Legs
1	6
2	12
5	30
3	18
4	24
7	42
8	48

Problem Solving 12.3

Algebra: Multiplication and Division

Understand ▶ Plan ▶ Solve ▶ Check

Write the correct answer.

1. Use the array to find the quotient.

$5\overline{)25}$

5

2. There are 4 third-grade classes and 12 math games. Write an expression to show how the classes can each get the same number of games.

$12 \div 4$

3. There are 18 tiles in 3 equal rows. How many tiles are there in each row?

6 tiles

4. Ana is decorating 8 frames. She uses 8 buttons for each frame. How many buttons does she need?

64 buttons

Choose the letter of the correct answer.

5. In which division sentence is 8 the divisor?

A $8 \div 2 = 4$
B $40 \div 8 = 5$
C $8 \div 4 = 2$
D $48 \div 6 = 8$

6. Which addition sentence is related to this subtraction sentence?

$9 - 6 = 3$

F $8 + 1 = 9$
G $6 + 3 = 9$
H $5 + 4 = 9$
J $2 + 7 = 9$

7. A school bus has 9 rows of seats with 4 seats in each row. Which shows how to find the number of seats on the bus?

A $9 + 4$
B $9 - 4$
C $13 \div 4$
D 9×4

8. Mr. Lee has 259 books at home and 447 books in his office. Which is the best way to estimate the total number of books he has?

F $300 + 500$
G $300 + 400$
H $200 + 300$
J $200 + 400$

9. **Write About It** Explain the 3 parts in the division sentence, $10 \div 5 = 2$.

Possible answer: The dividend, 10, is the number being divided by the divisor, 5. The quotient, 2, is the answer.

• Direct students' attention to the top of page 243.
How does the array of 16 relate to the division sentence shown? Possible answer: It shows 16 divided into 2 rows.
What are two different ways the quotient can be represented before the division is completed? by a box or a variable

• Direct students' attention to Examples A and B. **How is the quotient represented before the division is completed?** by a letter

MODIFYING INSTRUCTION Have students recall the different ways their textbooks have represented an unknown number. List missing factors by using $\underline{\quad ? \quad}$, , or letters. Point out that no matter what variable is used, the idea is the same and is something that students have already practiced.

③ PRACTICE

Guided Practice

Do Check Exercises 1–7 with your students. Identify students who are having difficulty and choose appropriate lesson resources to provide assistance.

Independent Practice

Note that Exercises 33 and 35 are **multistep or strategy problems.** Assign Exercises 8–35.

For Exercises 8–10, tell students that they do not need to copy the arrays.

ALGEBRAIC THINKING For Exercises 27–29, tell students that an unknown can be used for either factor. Wherever a variable appears, use the inverse, or opposite, operation to find its value.

Vocabulary Power Discuss with students how to use an *array* to find $4 \times \blacksquare = 28$ and $28 \div 4 = \blacksquare$. Have students draw an array to show their answers. Check students' drawings. Drawings should show 4 rows of 7 = 28 and 28 ÷ 4 = 7.

 **Practice and Problem Solving** Extra Practice, page 252, Set B

Copy and complete.

8.

3 rows of $\blacksquare$ = 21 **7**
21 ÷ 3 = $\blacksquare$ **7**

9.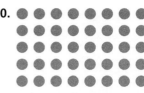

5 rows of $\blacksquare$ = 30 **6**
30 ÷ 5 = $\blacksquare$ **6**

10.

5 rows of $\blacksquare$ = 40 **8**
40 ÷ 5 = $\blacksquare$ **8**

Complete each number sentence. Draw an array to help.

11. $3 \times \blacksquare = 18$ **6** $18 \div 3 = \blacksquare$ **6**
12. $5 \times \blacksquare = 25$ **5** $25 \div 5 = \blacksquare$ **5**
13. $6 \times \blacksquare = 24$ **4** $24 \div 6 = \blacksquare$ **4**
14. $3 \times \blacksquare = 24$ **8** $24 \div 3 = \blacksquare$ **8**

Find the number that the variable stands for.

15. $12 \div 2 = a$
$a = \underline{?}$ **6**

16. $15 \div 3 = b$
$b = \underline{?}$ **5**

17. $18 \div 6 = c$
$c = \underline{?}$ **3**

18. $14 \div 7 = p$
$p = \underline{?}$ **2**

19. $25 \div 5 = q$
$q = \underline{?}$ **5**

20. $24 \div 8 = r$
$r = \underline{?}$ **3**

21. $5 \times a = 20$
$a = \underline{?}$ **4**

22. $6 \times b = 18$
$b = \underline{?}$ **3**

23. $3 \times c = 21$
$c = \underline{?}$ **7**

24. $p \times 4 = 16$
$p = \underline{?}$ **4**

25. $q \times 5 = 10$
$q = \underline{?}$ **2**

26. $r \times 7 = 14$
$r = \underline{?}$ **2**

ALGEBRA Complete.

27. $4 \times 2 = 24 \div a$
$a = \underline{?}$ **3**

28. $b \times 3 = 30 \div 5$
$b = \underline{?}$ **2**

29. $4 \times 1 = c \div 4$
$c = \underline{?}$ **16**

30. Tory arranged 28 stamps so that 7 were in each row. How many rows did she make? **4 rows**

31. **? What's the Question?** Christy puts 36 pennies into 4 equal piles. The answer is 9 pennies. How many pennies are in each pile?

32. **Vocabulary Power** One definition of *array* is "a number of objects arranged in rows and columns." Tell the number of rows and columns shown in the array in Exercise 10. **5 rows, 8 columns**

33. **REASONING** Mark bakes 14 muffins. He eats 2 muffins and divides the rest equally among 6 friends. What division sentence shows how many muffins each friend gets? **12 ÷ 6 = 2; each friend gets 2 muffins.**

244

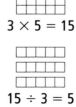

34. ≡**FAST FACT** • **SCIENCE** Frogs lay many eggs which hatch into tadpoles. In about 12 to 16 weeks, the tadpoles become frogs. About how many months does it take for a tadpole to become a frog? **3 to 4 months**

35. Colin has 24 toy cars. He puts an equal number of cars into each of 3 boxes. How many cars will be in 2 of the boxes? **16 cars**

4. Possible answer: Mr. Burns wants to put 3 shells in each box. How many boxes will he need to display 12 shells? 12 ÷ 3 = 4 boxes

Getting Ready for the EOG Test

36. There are 28 days in February and 7 days in one week. How many weeks are in February? **C**

February						
Sun	Mon	Tue	Wed	Thu	Fri	Sat
	1	2	3	4	5	6	7
8	9	10	11	12	13	14
15	16	17	18	19	20	21
22	23	24	25	26	27	28

A 2 **B** 3 **C** 4 **D** 5

37. Aaron is putting 32 sports cards in an album. Each page holds 4 cards. Which of the following can be used to find how many pages Aaron will use? **D**

A $4 \times \blacksquare = 16$
B $4 + \blacksquare = 32$
C $36 - \blacksquare = 32$
D $4 \times \blacksquare = 32$

Problem Solving — Thinker's Corner

THE HOBBY STORE

VISUAL THINKING Mr. Burns wrote number sentences to help him remember how to place the shells in the display cases at the Hobby Store.

For 1–3, draw a picture to show how the shells will be displayed. Check students' drawings. Possible answers: 1. 5 rows or groups of 8   2. 4 rows or groups of 7   3. 4 rows or groups of 9

1. $5 \times 8 = 40$
   $40 \div 5 = 8$

2. $4 \times 7 = 28$
   $28 \div 4 = 7$

3. $4 \times 9 = 36$
   $36 \div 4 = 9$

4. Write a problem using division to find how many equal groups. Write a number sentence to solve.
See above.

5. Mr. Burns has 16 new shells. He wants to put them into 8 equal groups. Write a problem using division to find how many shells are in each group. Write a number sentence to solve.
See below.

5. Possible answer: Mr. Burns has 8 boxes and 16 shells. How many shells can he place in each box if he wants to divide them equally? 16 ÷ 8 = 2 shells

Chapter 12 **245**

MULTISTEP OR STRATEGY PROBLEM To solve Exercise 35, students can divide the number of toy cars by 3 and then multiply the quotient by 2 to find the number of cars in 2 boxes.

Problem Solving — Thinker's Corner

• *Have students complete Problems 1–5.*
Suppose Mr. Burns wants to display 24 cups. Write number sentences and describe different ways he can display the cups. Possible answer: $6 \times 4 = 24$, $24 \div 6 = 4$, 6 shelves with 4 cups on each; $2 \times 12 = 24$, $24 \div 2 = 12$, 2 shelves with 12 cups on each.

4 ASSESS

Summarize the lesson by having students:

DISCUSS How are the dividend and the product alike? Each tells the total number.

WRITE Explain how you would divide 10 into 5 equal groups using arrays. Then write a division sentence using a variable, label each part of the sentence, and solve. Show an array with 10 in 5 equal rows of 2; 10 (dividend) ÷ 5 (divisor) = n (quotient); $n = 2$

LESSON QUIZ
Complete each number sentence. Draw an array to help.

Transparency **12.3**

1. $8 \times \blacksquare = 24$ 3 $24 \div 8 = \blacksquare$ 3

2. $2 \times \blacksquare = 14$ 7 $14 \div 2 = \blacksquare$ 7

3. $4 \times \blacksquare = 28$ 7 $28 \div 4 = \blacksquare$ 7

4. $3 \times \blacksquare = 12$ 4 $12 \div 3 = \blacksquare$ 4

Algebra: Fact Families

Lesson Planning

PROFESSIONAL DEVELOPMENT

Objective To use multiplication and division fact families

Materials *For each student or each pair* square pieces of paper, scissors

NCTM Standards
1. Number and Operations
2. Algebra
6. Problem Solving
7. Reasoning and Proof
8. Communication
9. Connections
10. Representation

Math Background
These ideas will help students use fact families to find a quotient or missing divisor.

• A fact family is a set of related multiplication and division number sentences.

• Think of the quotient or missing divisor as one of the missing factors in the related multiplication sentence.

• To use a multiplication table and related multiplication fact to find a quotient or missing divisor, find the given divisor or quotient in the top row, look down to find the dividend, and then look to the left to find the missing number.

Vocabulary
fact family a set of related multiplication and division number sentences

Warm-Up Resources

Build Number Sense
3 2 1

Number of the Day

Transparency
12.4

The number of the day is your age in years. Write a multiplication sentence using the number as a factor and a division sentence using the number as the quotient. Answers will vary.

Review Basic Facts
8 +3

Daily Facts Practice

Have students practice subtraction facts by completing Set B of *Teacher's Resource Book*, p. TR92.

Transparency
12.4

Solve a Problem

Problem of the Day

Find the two numbers whose product is 6 and quotient is 6. What is the sum and difference of the two numbers? 6, 1; 7, 5

Solution Problem of the Day tab, p. PD12

Intervention and Extension Resources

Alternative Teaching Strategy

MATERIALS *For each pair* 8 index cards

ESOL/ESL

Have students work in pairs to **review vocabulary words**. Write each word below on an index card.

divide	divisor
factor	quotient
product	inverse operations
dividend	multiply

Divide the cards in half so each student has 4 cards. Have each student write the definition of the word on the back of the card.

Then have students quiz their partner by holding up one card at a time with the word showing. If the partner is having trouble defining a word, the student can give the partner clues.

See also p. 248.

VISUAL, AUDITORY

VERBAL/LINGUISTIC

Multistep and Strategy Problems

The following multistep or strategy problems are provided in Lesson 12.4:

Page	Item
248	49
249	51

Career Connection

MATERIALS *For each group* research materials

Have students **research how they might use multiplication and division in a future career**. Suggest that students identify a career they find interesting and then research how that career uses multiplication and division. For example, a baker might have to multiply to double a recipe or divide to pack items in containers. Have them use research materials or interview people they know. Encourage students to share their findings with the class.

VISUAL, AUDITORY

VERBAL/LINGUISTIC

Advanced Learners

Challenge students to **write a division sentence** that has the same quotient as the division sentence given below. Students may want to use a multiplication table to help them.

1. $24 \div 3 = 8$
Possible answers: $16 \div 2 = 8, 40 \div 5 = 8$

2. $18 \div 2 = 9$
Possible answers: $27 \div 3 = 9, 36 \div 4 = 9$

VISUAL

LOGICAL/MATHEMATICAL

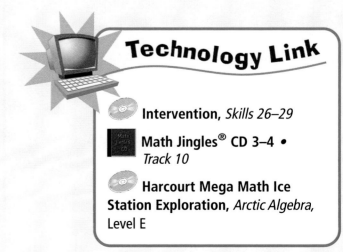

Technology Link

Intervention, *Skills 26–29*

Math Jingles® CD 3–4 • *Track 10*

Harcourt Mega Math Ice Station Exploration, *Arctic Algebra,* Level E

Lesson 12.4 Organizer

Objective To use multiplication and division fact families

Vocabulary fact family *Review* factor, product

Materials *For each student or each pair* square pieces of paper, scissors

---

1 INTRODUCE

QUICK REVIEW provides review of prerequisite skills.

WHY LEARN THIS? You can use related multiplication sentences to help you solve division problems. *Share the lesson objective with students.*

---

2 TEACH

Guided Instruction

- *Have students refer to the information about fact families.*
  Does a fact family always include inverse operations? Explain. Possible answer: Yes; fact families show facts that are related by using opposite, or inverse operations.

- *Have students read the Activity.*
  Why is it helpful to use cards shaped like triangles? Since fact families use 3 numbers, 1 number is put on each corner of the triangle.

Algebra: Fact Families

Learn

FUN FACTS A set of related multiplication and division number sentences is called a **fact family**.

Fact Family for 3, 5, and 15

factor		factor		product		dividend	divisor		quotient
3	×	5	=	15		15	÷ 5	=	3
5	×	3	=	15		15	÷ 3	=	5

Activity

Materials: square pieces of paper, scissors

Use this triangle fact card to think of the fact family for 3, 5, and 15.

Make a set of triangle fact cards. Use them to write fact families.

Product
15
Factor 3   5 Factor

A Fold each paper in half three times. Open up the paper and cut along the folds to make triangle cards.

Fold
Fold   Fold

B Make triangle fact cards for each of these products: 12, 15, 18, 20, 24, 25, and 30.

C Write fact families for at least 3 triangle fact cards.

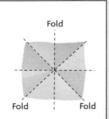

- **REASONING** How many triangle fact cards can you make for the product 12? Explain.
  Possible answer: 3; you can write a fact family for 1, 12, and 12, for 2, 6, and 12, and for 3, 4, and 12.

246

Quick Review
1. $3 \times \blacksquare = 18$ 6
2. $\blacksquare \times 6 = 18$ 3
3. $18 \div 6 = \blacksquare$ 3
4. $5 \times \blacksquare = 25$ 5
5. $25 \div 5 = \blacksquare$ 5

VOCABULARY
fact family

Reteach 12.4

Algebra: Fact Families

Use multiplication and division to tell about the cookies in opposite ways.

Use multiplication to put same-size groups together.	$3 \times 4 = 12$ or $4 \times 3 = 12$
Use division to separate the total into same-size groups.	$12 \div 3 = 4$ or $12 \div 4 = 3$

The four number sentences are called a **fact family**. Each of the four sentences uses the same numbers.

Complete each fact family.

1. $4 \times 2 = 8$
$2 \times 4 = 8$
$8 \div 2 = 4$
$8 \div 4 = 2$

2. $3 \times 2 = 6$
$2 \times 3 = 6$
$6 \div 3 = 2$
$6 \div 2 = 3$

3. $3 \times 5 = 15$
$5 \times 3 = 15$
$15 \div 3 = 5$
$15 \div 5 = 3$

4. $6 \times 3 = 18$
$3 \times 6 = 18$
$18 \div 6 = 3$
$18 \div 3 = 6$

5. $6 \times 4 = 24$
$4 \times 6 = 24$
$24 \div 6 = 4$
$24 \div 4 = 6$

6. $7 \times 3 = 21$
$3 \times 7 = 21$
$21 \div 7 = 3$
$21 \div 3 = 7$

Reteach RW65

Practice 12.4

Algebra: Fact Families

Write the fact family.

1. 4, 9, 36
$4 \times 9 = 36,$
$9 \times 4 = 36,$
$36 \div 9 = 4,$
$36 \div 4 = 9$

2. 8, 3, 24
$8 \times 3 = 24,$
$3 \times 8 = 24,$
$24 \div 3 = 8,$
$24 \div 8 = 3$

3. 6, 4, 24
$6 \times 4 = 24,$
$4 \times 6 = 24,$
$24 \div 4 = 6,$
$24 \div 6 = 4$

4. 6, 6, 36
$6 \times 6 = 36,$
$36 \div 6 = 6$

5. 7, 7, 49
$7 \times 7 = 49,$
$49 \div 7 = 7$

6. 5, 5, 25
$5 \times 5 = 25,$
$25 \div 5 = 5$

Find the quotient or product.

7. $5 \times 7 = \underline{35}$ 8. $7 \times 5 = \underline{35}$ 9. $35 \div 7 = \underline{5}$ 10. $35 \div 5 = \underline{7}$

Write the other three sentences in the fact family.

11. $6 \times 3 = 18$
$3 \times 6 = 18,$
$18 \div 3 = 6,$
$18 \div 6 = 3$

12. $4 \times 5 = 20$
$5 \times 4 = 20,$
$20 \div 4 = 5,$
$20 \div 5 = 4$

13. $2 \times 7 = 14$
$7 \times 2 = 14,$
$14 \div 7 = 2,$
$14 \div 2 = 7$

Mixed Review

Write +, −, ×, or ÷ in each ◯.

14. $36 \oplus 4 = 9$
15. $18 \ominus 12 = 6$
16. $2 \otimes 8 = 16$
17. $72 \oplus 9 = 8$
18. $14 \ominus 4 = 10$
19. $9 \otimes 6 = 54$

Practice PW65

---

246 Chapter 12

Using a Multiplication Table

 MATH IDEA Use related multiplication facts to find quotients or missing divisors in division sentences.

Examples

A Find the quotient.

$12 \div 3 = \blacksquare$

Think: $3 \times \blacksquare = 12$

Find the row for the factor 3. Look across to find the product 12. Look up to find the missing factor, 4.

$3 \times 4 = 12$

So, $12 \div 3 = 4$.

B Find the missing divisor.

$30 \div \blacksquare = 5$

Think: $\blacksquare \times 5 = 30$

Find the factor 5 in the top row. Look down to find the product 30. Look left to find the missing factor, 6.

$6 \times 5 = 30$

So, $30 \div 6 = 5$.

Remember

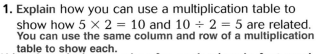

$$3 \quad \times \quad 4 \quad = \quad 12$$
$$\uparrow \qquad \uparrow \qquad \uparrow$$
$$\text{factor} \quad \text{factor} \quad \text{product}$$

×	0	1	2	3	4	5	6
0	0	0	0	0	0	0	0
1	0	1	2	3	4	5	6
2	0	2	4	6	8	10	12
3	0	3	6	9	12	15	18
4	0	4	8	12	16	20	24
5	0	5	10	15	20	25	30
6	0	6	12	18	24	30	36

- **REASONING** How can you use multiplication to check $20 \div 5 = 4$? **Possible answer: multiply the divisor, 5, by the quotient, 4, to find the dividend, 20.**

 Technology Link

More Practice: Harcourt Mega Math Ice Station Exploration, *Arctic Algebra*, Level E

Check

1. Explain how you can use a multiplication table to show how $5 \times 2 = 10$ and $10 \div 2 = 5$ are related. **You can use the same column and row of a multiplication table to show each.**

Write the missing number for each triangle fact card.

2.
15 / 3 / 5

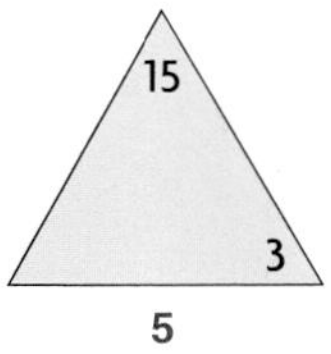

3.
24 / 4 / 6

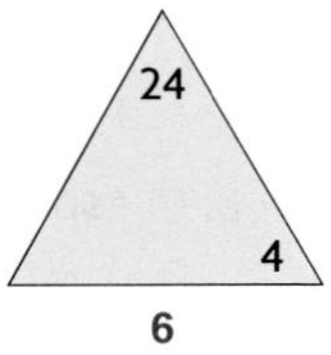

4.
30 / 6 / 5

5.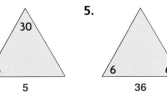
6 / 6 / 36

Write the fact family.

6. 3, 6, 18   7. 4, 4, 16   8. 4, 5, 20   9. 3, 7, 21

6. $3 \times 6 = 18$, $6 \times 3 = 18$, $18 \div 3 = 6$, $18 \div 6 = 3$.
Answers for 7–9 should follow the same style.

LESSON CONTINUES ▶

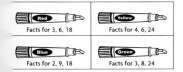

- *Direct students' attention to Example A.*
How do you know what multiplication sentence to think of to find the quotient? Possible answer: Write the fact family so the divisor becomes a factor and the dividend becomes the product.
How can you use the table to find the quotient without using a multiplication sentence? Find the row for the given divisor, 3. Look across to find the dividend, 12. Look up to find the missing quotient, 4.

- *Have students refer to Example B.*
How can you use the table to find the missing divisor without using a multiplication sentence? Find the quotient, 5, in the top row. Look down to find the dividend, 30. Look left to find the missing divisor, 6.

3 PRACTICE

Guided Practice

Do Check Exercises 1–9 with your students. Identify students who are having difficulty and choose appropriate lesson resources to provide assistance.

Chapter 12 **247**

 North Carolina Standards 1.03 Develop fluency with multiplication from 1×1 to 12×12 and ...sion up to two-digit by one-digit numbers using: c) Relationships between operations. *also 5.04*

Challenge 12.4

Fact Family Patterns

1. Fill in the missing numbers in the first three rows of the Fact Table to complete each number sentence.

Fact Table

Blue $18 \div 2 = \underline{9}$	Red $3 \times 6 = \underline{18}$	Green $24 \div 8 = \underline{3}$	Yellow $6 \times 4 = \underline{24}$
Red $6 \times \underline{3} = 18$	Green $24 \div 3 = \underline{8}$	Yellow $4 \times \underline{6} = 24$	Blue $9 \times \underline{2} = 18$
Green $3 \times \underline{8} = 24$	Yellow $24 \div \underline{4} = 6$	Blue $2 \times \underline{9} = 18$	Red $18 \div 6 = \underline{3}$
Yellow $\underline{24} \div 6 = 4$	Blue $18 \div 9 = 2$	Red $\underline{18} \div 3 = 6$	Green $8 \times 3 = 24$

2. Use the colors shown below to color all the facts in the Fact Table above that belong to each fact family. **Check students' work.**

Red — Facts for 3, 6, 18

Yellow — Facts for 4, 6, 24

Blue — Facts for 2, 9, 18

Green — Facts for 3, 8, 24

3. Notice the color pattern in the Fact Table, and notice that each fact family is missing a fact. Write the missing fact from each fact family in the bottom row of the Fact Table. Arrange the facts so that the color pattern continues.

Challenge **CW65**

Problem Solving 12.4

Algebra: Fact Families   Understand ▶ Plan ▶ Solve ▶ Check

Write the correct answer.

1. What number sentence is missing from this fact family?

$27 \div 3 = 9$
$27 \div 9 = 3$
$9 \times 3 = 27$

$3 \times 9 = 27$

2. Solve. Then write a multiplication sentence to check your work.

$7)\overline{35}$

$5; 5 \times 7 = 35$

3. Mrs. Cruz asked Ron why there are only two number sentences in the fact family for 4, 4, and 16. What is the reason?

Both factors are the same.

4. Aunt Jill has 32 silver dollars. She wants to divide them evenly among her 8 nieces. How many should each niece get?

4 silver dollars

Choose the letter of the correct answer.

5. Which number sentence does **not** belong in the fact family for 7, 9, and 63?

A $7 \times 9 = 63$
B $63 \div 9 = 7$
C $63 \div 7 = 9$
(D) $7 + 9 = 16$

6. Devon has 3 notebooks with 9 sheets of paper in each notebook. Which number sentence shows how many sheets of paper he has in all?

F $3 + 9 = 12$
G $9 \div 3 = 3$
(H) $3 \times 9 = 27$
J $9 - 3 = 6$

7. **Write About It** Could a multiplication table help you solve Problem 2? Why or why not?

Possible answer: Yes, it could help. Since division is the opposite of multiplication you can use a multiplication table to find a quotient.

Problem Solving **PS65**

247

Independent Practice

Note that Exercises 49 and 51 are **multistep or strategy problems**. Assign Exercises 10–52.

MULTISTEP OR STRATEGY PROBLEM To solve Exercise 49, students can subtract 2 from 20 and then divide the difference by 3 to find the number of bookmarks in each gift box.

 Practice and Problem Solving Extra Practice, page 252, Set C

Write the missing number for each triangle fact card.

10. 24 / 3 / 8   **11.** 8 / 2 / 4   **12.** 12 / 6 / 2   **13.** 5 / 5 / 25

Write the fact family.

14. 5, 6, 30   **15.** 2, 8, 16   **16.** 4, 7, 28   **17.** 5, 5, 25
$6 \times 5 = 30, 5 \times 6 = 30, 30 \div 6 = 5, 30 \div 5 = 6$ **Answers for 15–17 should follow the same style.**

Find the quotient or product.

18. $3 \times 6 =$ ▧ **18**   **19.** $6 \times 3 =$ ▧ **18**   **20.** $18 \div 3 =$ ▧ **6**   **21.** $18 \div 6 =$ ▧ **3**

22. $4 \times 9 =$ ▧ **36**   **23.** $9 \times 4 =$ ▧ **36**   **24.** $36 \div 4 =$ ▧ **9**   **25.** $36 \div 9 =$ ▧ **4**

26. $8 \times 5 =$ ▧ **40**   **27.** $5 \times 8 =$ ▧ **40**   **28.** $40 \div 8 =$ ▧ **5**   **29.** $40 \div 5 =$ ▧ **8**

Write the other three sentences in the fact family.

30. $3 \times 7 = 21$ $7 \times 3 = 21,$ **31.** $1 \times 5 = 5$ $5 \times 1 = 5,$ **32.** $4 \times 3 = 12$ $3 \times 4 = 12,$
    $21 \div 3 = 7, 21 \div 7 = 3$ $5 \div 5 = 1, 5 \div 1 = 5$ $12 \div 4 = 3, 12 \div 3 = 4$

33. $5 \times 3 = 15$ $3 \times 5 = 15,$ **34.** $6 \times 4 = 24$ $4 \times 6 = 24,$ **35.** $9 \times 2 = 18$ $2 \times 9 = 18,$
    $15 \div 5 = 3, 15 \div 3 = 5$ $24 \div 6 = 4, 24 \div 4 = 6$ $18 \div 9 = 2, 18 \div 2 = 9$

Find the quotient or the missing divisor.

36. $8 \div 4 =$ ▧ **2**   **37.** $16 \div 2 =$ ▧ **8**   **38.** $7 = 21 \div$ ▧ **3**   **39.** $2 = 12 \div$ ▧ **6**

40. $24 \div 8 =$ ▧ **3**   **41.** $10 \div$ ▧ $= 2$ **5**   **42.** $30 \div$ ▧ $= 6$ **5**   **43.** $28 \div 4 =$ ▧ **7**

⭐ALGEBRA Complete.

44. ▧ $\div 5 = 6 + 3$ **45**   **45.** $6 \times$ ▧ $= 54 \div 9$ **1**   **46.** $42 - 6 =$ ▧ $\times 9$ **4**

47. What do you notice about the fact family for 6, 6, and 36? **There are only 2 number sentences.**

48. REASONING How are $20 \div 5 = 4$ and $20 \div 4 = 5$ alike? How are they different? **members of same fact family; the divisor and quotient switched places.**

49. Geri made 20 bookmarks. She kept 2 and then put an equal number in each of 3 gift boxes. How many bookmarks are in each box? **6 bookmarks**

50. REASONING Kendra says, "There are 3 teaspoons in 1 tablespoon, so there are 15 teaspoons in 5 tablespoons." Do you agree or disagree? Explain. **Agree; $3 \times 5 = 15$, so Kendra's statement is true.**

248

Alternative Teaching Strategy | Scaffolded Instruction

PURPOSE Students make multiplication and division fact families.

MATERIALS *For each student* several pieces of paper

Have students fold sheets of paper into fourths and label the sections *a, b, c,* and *d,* respectively.

Write one multiplication number sentence such as: $3 \times 5 = 15$.

Have students copy the number sentence into section *a* on their papers. Then ask students to write another multiplication sentence in section *b* using the same three numbers: 3, 5, and 15.

Finally, have students fill in sections *c* and *d* with division number sentences that use the same three numbers.

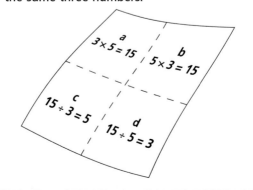

Tell students they have just made a fact family for 3, 5, and 15. Discuss with them the meaning of a fact family.

Repeat this exercise several times. Each time start with either a multiplication number sentence or a division number sentence.

Ask students:

- How many number sentences are usually in a fact family? 4
- Give an example of a fact family that does not have four number sentences. Possible answer: $5 \times 5 = 25, 25 \div 5 = 5$

51. Mr. Tapia has a water bowl and a food bowl for each cat and dog in his pet store. He has 5 dogs and 4 cats. How many bowls does he have? **18 bowls**

52. **What's the Error?** John says that since $4 + 4 = 8$, then $8 \div 4 = 4$. Describe his error and give the correct quotient. **8 ÷ 4 does not equal 4. There are 2 fours in 8, so 8 ÷ 4 = 2.**

Getting Ready for the EOG Test

53. Four friends want to share 36 marbles equally. Which of the following can they use to help them find $36 \div 4$? **A**

A $4 \times 9 = 36$ **C** $12 \times 3 = 36$

B $3 \times 12 = 36$ **D** $1 \times 36 = 36$

54. Which number completes each of the sentences in this fact family? **C**

$5 \times \blacksquare = 45$ $45 \div 5 = \blacksquare$

$\blacksquare \times 5 = 45$ $45 \div \blacksquare = 5$

A 7
B 8
C 9
D 10

Problem Solving   Thinker's Corner

OPERATIONS AND PARENTHESES Parentheses help you know which part of the problem to do first. Look at Examples A and B. The problems use the same numbers, but the parentheses are in different places.

Examples

A	**B**
$(3 + 6) \div 3 = a$ First add. $3 + 6 = 9$	$3 + (6 \div 3) = b$ First divide. $6 \div 3 = 2$
$9 \div 3 = a$ Then divide. $9 \div 3 = 3$	$3 + 2 = b$ Then add. $3 + 2 = 5$
$3 = a$	$5 = b$

Solve each number sentence.

1. $(3 \times 4) - 3 = a$
$3 \times (4 - 3) = b$ **9; 3**

2. $(6 + 9) \div 3 = a$
$6 + (9 \div 3) = b$ **5; 9**

3. $(5 \times 4) - 3 = a$
$5 \times (4 - 3) = b$ **17; 5**

Chapter 12   **249**

Problem Solving   Thinker's Corner

- *Use this page to show students that parentheses can make a difference in an answer.*

- *Write the following on the chalkboard:*

  $2 \times 2 + 4 = a$ $2 \times 2 + 4 = b$

  What are two ways to use parentheses to solve this problem?

  $(2 \times 2) + 4 = a$ $2 \times (2 + 4) = b$
  $4 + 4 = a$ $2 \times 6 = b$
  $8 = a$ $12 = b$

- *Where should you place the parentheses to make this sentence true?*

  $2 + (8 \div 4) = 4$

  REASONING Is the value of *a* the same as the value of *b* in these number sentences? Explain.

  $2 \times (6 \div 3) = a$ $(2 \times 6) \div 3 = b$
  yes; $2 \times 2 = 4$ and $12 \div 3 = 4$

---

4   ASSESS

Summarize the lesson by having students:

DISCUSS Without dividing, tell which quotient will be greater, $63 \div 7$ or $63 \div 9$. Explain. $63 \div 7$; If the same number is being divided into fewer groups, there will be more in each of the groups.

WRITE How are multiplication and division related? Possible answer: They are opposite, or inverse, operations. When multiplying, you put equal groups of objects together; when dividing, you separate objects into equal groups.

LESSON QUIZ   Transparency **12.4**

Write the fact family.

1. 2, 7, 14
$2 \times 7 = 14$, $7 \times 2 = 14$, $14 \div 2 = 7$, $14 \div 7 = 2$

2. 6, 9, 54
$6 \times 9 = 54$, $9 \times 6 = 54$, $54 \div 9 = 6$, $54 \div 6 = 9$

3. 4, 8, 32
$4 \times 8 = 32$, $8 \times 4 = 32$, $32 \div 4 = 8$, $32 \div 8 = 4$

4. 4, 5, 20
$4 \times 5 = 20$, $5 \times 4 = 20$, $20 \div 5 = 4$, $20 \div 4 = 5$

Lesson Planning

PROFESSIONAL DEVELOPMENT

Objective To solve problems using the strategy *write a number sentence*

Lesson Resources Reading Transparency 12; Intervention • Problem Solving, Strategy/Skill 12

NCTM Standards
1. **Number and Operations**
2. **Algebra**
6. **Problem Solving**
7. **Reasoning and Proof**
8. **Communication**
10. **Representation**

Math Background
These ideas will help students use the strategy *write a number sentence* to solve problems.

● Read the problem and determine what you are asked to find and what information you will use in the number sentence.

● Identify what each number in the number sentence represents in the problem.

● Use an equal sign in each number sentence.

Warm-Up Resources

Number of the Day

Transparency **12.5**

The number of the day is the number of minutes in a half hour. Divide this number by 5. Find the quotient. $30 \div 5 = 6$

Daily Facts Practice

Have students practice subtraction facts by completing Set C of *Teacher's Resource Book*, p. TR92.

Solve a Problem

Transparency **12.5**

Problem of the Day

Alicia is twice as old as Jon. Tina is twice as old as Alicia. Tina is 12 years old. What is the difference between Tina's age and Jon's? 9 years

Solution Problem of the Day tab, p. PD12

Intervention and Extension Resources

Alternative Teaching Strategy

Have students work in groups to **practice solving problems using the strategy** *write a number sentence*. Have them solve the problem in the lesson by following these steps:

- Answer the question: What operation do you need to use to solve the problem? How do you know? Division; you need to find how many groups and you're given the total number and the number in each group.
- Begin a number sentence by writing the operation you chose, an equal sign, and blank boxes where the numbers belong. $\square \div \square = \square$
- Discuss what should go in each box.
- Fill in the numbers and solve. Check students' work.

AUDITORY, VISUAL

INTERPERSONAL/SOCIAL

Special Needs

ESOL/ESL

MATERIALS *For each student* index cards

Help students **write number sentences** by providing them with the following reminders for choosing the correct operation:

Add—put together
Subtract—separate; compare
Multiply—put equal groups together
Divide—separate into equal groups; share equally among groups

Encourage students to place a reminder for each operation on a card and use these cards as they complete exercises from the lesson. Check students' work.

VISUAL

VERBAL/LINGUISTIC

Reading Strategy

Analyze Information When you write a number sentence to solve a problem, you need to analyze the meanings of the numbers in the problem and think about how the numbers are related.

Have students identify the operation symbol they would use to solve each problem. Then have them solve.

1. There are 7 cards in each pile. If there are 3 piles, how many cards are there? $\times$; $7 \times 3 = 21$ cards

2. There are 6 boxes of pens. In all, there are 60 pens. How many pens are in each box? $\div$; $60 \div 6 = 10$ pens

3. There are 5 sticks of gum in a pack. How many packs do you need to have 40 sticks of gum? $\div$; $40 \div 5 = 8$ packs of gum

Transparency
12 Reading Transparency 12

Science Connection

Have students use the information below to **write a number sentence** to solve the problem.

Goldfish are originally from China and Eastern Europe. Goldfish like shallow and cool freshwater ponds and creeks. Some goldfish live for 25 to 30 years.

Goldfish living in bowls as pets need their water changed and their bowls cleaned about 2 times a week. About how many times does a goldfish bowl need to be cleaned in 4 weeks? $2 \times 4 = 8$, or about 8 times

AUDITORY

LOGICAL/MATHEMATICAL

Multistep and Strategy Problems

The following multistep or strategy problems are provided in Lesson 12.5:

Page	Item
251	1–8

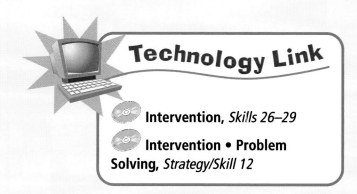

Technology Link

Intervention, *Skills 26–29*

Intervention • Problem Solving, *Strategy/Skill 12*

Lesson 12.5 Organizer

Objective To solve problems using the strategy *write a number sentence*

Lesson Resources Reading Transparency 12; Intervention • Problem Solving, Strategy/Skill 12

1 INTRODUCE

QUICK REVIEW provides review of prerequisite skills.

WHY LEARN THIS? You can use the strategy *write a number sentence* to solve everyday problems. *Share the lesson objective with students.*

2 TEACH

Guided Instruction

• *Have students read the Problem and the Understand step.*
Restate the problem in your own words.
Possible answer: If Megan has 36 cards and puts 9 on each page, how many pages will she need?
Is there any additional information you need to solve the problem? Explain. No; you know the total number of trading cards and how many cards go on each page.

MODIFYING INSTRUCTION Students may find a solution by modeling with counters or drawing a diagram.

• *Direct students' attention to the number sentence in the Solve section.*
How do you know what operation to use to solve the problem? You need to divide the cards into equal groups of 9 to find how many pages are needed.
Could you have used a different operation to solve the problem? Explain. Possible answer: Yes; you could use multiplication and solve for the missing factor.

LESSON 5

Problem Solving Strategy
Write a Number Sentence

Quick Review

1. $8 \times 4 = \blacksquare$ 32
2. $30 = 6 \times \blacksquare$ 5
3. $10 \times 5 = \blacksquare$ 50
4. $18 = \blacksquare \times 6$ 3
5. $27 = 9 \times \blacksquare$ 3

PROBLEM Megan puts 36 animal trading cards in her binder. She puts 9 cards on each page. How many pages will Megan need for her cards?

UNDERSTAND
• What are you asked to find?
How many pages Megan needs for her cards.
• What information will you use?
36 cards; 9 cards on each page.
• Is there information you will not use? If so, what? **No**

PLAN
• What strategy can you use?
Write a number sentence to find the number of pages Megan will need.

SOLVE
• How can you use the strategy to solve the problem?
Write a number sentence and solve.

$$36 \div 9 = 4$$

number of trading cards | number on each page | number of pages

So, Megan needs 4 pages for her cards.

CHECK
• How can you decide if your answer is correct? **Think of multiplication to check. 4 groups of 9 is 36 or $4 \times 9 = 36$.**
• What other strategy could you use?
You could separate 36 objects into 4 groups of 9.

250

Reteach 12.5

Problem Solving Strategy

Write a Number Sentence

You can write a number sentence to help you solve a problem.

Example: There are 18 students in Josh's class. They are working in groups of 3. How many groups are there in all?

$$18 \div 3 = 6$$

number of students | number in each group | number of groups

Remember

Multiply
• when you are joining groups of equal size.
• when you know the size of the groups and the number of same-size groups.

Divide
• when you are separating a total into groups of equal size.
• when you know the total.
• when you know either the number of same-size groups or the number in each group.

Write a number sentence to solve. Then write the answer.

1. Mary rode her bicycle 4 miles every day for 5 days. How many miles did she ride in all?

$5 \times 4 = 20$

20 mi

2. Twelve campers want to canoe. Each canoe holds 3 people. How many canoes are needed?

$12 \div 3 = 4$

4 canoes

3. Jeff earns $3 an hour for raking leaves. How many hours does he need to work to earn $15?

$15 \div 3 = 5$

5 hr

4. Jackie made a cartoon book that is 8 pages long. There are 4 cartoons on each page. How many cartoons are in the book?

$8 \times 4 = 32$

32 cartoons

RW66 Reteach

Practice 12.5

Problem Solving Strategy

Write a Number Sentence

Write a number sentence to solve.

1. Mrs. Scott bought 3 packages of hot dogs. Each package has 8 hot dogs. How many hot dogs did she buy in all?

$3 \times 8 = 24$ hot dogs

2. A class of 27 students is working in groups of 3 on an art project. How many groups are there?

$27 \div 3 = 9$ groups

3. Melissa took 24 photographs. She put 4 photographs on each page of her album. How many pages did she use?

$24 \div 4 = 6$ pages

4. Tim planted 5 rows of corn. There are 6 corn plants in each row. How many corn plants are there in all?

$5 \times 6 = 30$ corn plants

Mixed Review

5. $\begin{array}{r} \$2.42 \\ +\$5.65 \\ \hline \$8.07 \end{array}$

6. $\begin{array}{r} \$4.91 \\ -\$0.76 \\ \hline \$4.15 \end{array}$

7. $\begin{array}{r} \$8.56 \\ -\$3.28 \\ \hline \$5.28 \end{array}$

8. $\begin{array}{r} \$7.99 \\ +\$1.99 \\ \hline \$9.98 \end{array}$

9. $\begin{array}{r} 8 \\ \times 5 \\ \hline 40 \end{array}$

10. $\begin{array}{r} 5 \\ \times 8 \\ \hline 40 \end{array}$

11. $\begin{array}{r} 9 \\ \times 9 \\ \hline 81 \end{array}$

12. $\begin{array}{r} 6 \\ \times 8 \\ \hline 48 \end{array}$

13. $3 \times 7 = \underline{21}$ 14. $6 \times 9 = \underline{54}$ 15. $10 \times 4 = \underline{40}$ 16. $4 \times 7 = \underline{28}$

Write $+$, $-$, $\times$, or $\div$ in each $\bigcirc$.

17. $84 \ominus 25 = 59$ 18. $6 \otimes 8 = 48$ 19. $32 \oplus 73 = 105$

20. $54 \oplus 9 = 63$ 21. $7 \otimes 6 = 42$ 22. $9 \otimes 5 = 45$

PW66 Practice

---

250   Chapter 12

Strategies

Draw a Diagram or Picture
Make a Model or Act It Out
Make an Organized List
Find a Pattern
Make a Table or Graph
Predict and Test
Work Backward
Solve a Simpler Problem
▶ **Write a Number Sentence**
Use Logical Reasoning

Problem Solving

Write a number sentence to solve.

1. **What if** Megan buys 27 trading cards to add to her collection? How many pages will she need for the new cards?
   27 ÷ 9 = 3; 3 pages

2. Rosita has 28 cards. She wants to keep 4 cards and divide the rest equally among 4 friends. How many cards will each friend get?
   24 ÷ 4 = 6; 6 cards

Jorge has 45 trading cards in his collection. His binder holds 10 pages. Each page holds 9 trading cards.

3. How many pages will Jorge use for the cards he has? **A**

   A 5
   B 10
   C 45
   D 90

4. Which number sentence shows how to find how many trading cards fit in Jorge's binder? **G**

   F 45 + 10 = 55   H 10 + 9 = 19
   G 9 × 10 = 90   J 45 ÷ 9 = 5

Mixed Strategy Practice

USE DATA For 5–8, use the graph.

5. Sebastian collects coins. How many coins in all are in Sebastian's coin collection? **50 coins**

6. Tim has 4 times as many quarters in his collection as Sebastian has. How many quarters are in Tim's collection? **20 quarters**

7. Sebastian added some half dollars to his collection. There are 5 more pennies than half dollars in his collection. How many half dollars did Sebastian add to his collection? **10 half dollars**

SEBASTIAN'S COIN COLLECTION

pennies	
nickels	
dimes	
quarters	

Key: Each 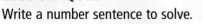 = 5 coins.

8. ✏ Write a problem using the data in the pictograph.
   Check students' problems.

Chapter 12 251

North Carolina Standards 1.06 Develop flexibility in solving problems by selecting strategies and ...g mental computation, estimation, calculators or computers, and paper and pencil.

---

3 PRACTICE

Guided Practice

Do Problem Solving Practice Exercises 1–4 with your students. Identify students who are having difficulty and choose appropriate lesson resources to provide assistance. Note that Exercises 1–4 are **multistep or strategy problems.**

Independent Practice

Note that Exercises 5–8 are **multistep or strategy problems.** Assign Exercises 5–8.

SCAFFOLDED INSTRUCTION Use the prompts on Transparency 12 to guide instruction for the multistep or strategy problem in Exercise 7.

Transparency **12**

4 ASSESS

Summarize the lesson by having students:

DISCUSS How can you check your solution to a problem? Possible answers: use an inverse operation; model the problem

 **WRITE** List the number sentences in the fact family for 3, 6, and 18. Write a word problem in which one of these number sentences is a solution. Provide the solution. 3 × 6 =18; 6 × 3 = 18; 18 ÷ 6 = 3; 18 ÷ 3 = 6. Possible answer: Sharon divided 18 apples among 3 friends. How many apples did each friend receive? 18 ÷ 3 = 6 apples

LESSON QUIZ

Write a number sentence to solve.

Transparency **12.5**

1. Find the number of days in 8 weeks. 8 × 7 = 56; 56 days

2. There are 35 books stacked in 7 equal stacks. How many books are in each stack? 35 ÷ 7 = 5; 5 books

3. There are 42 pencils shared equally among 6 children. How many pencils does each child get? 42 ÷ 6 = 7; 7 pencils

4. Each pack of gum has 5 pieces. How many pieces of gum are in 3 packs? 3 × 5 =15; 15 pieces

---

Challenge 12.5

Number Sentences

Complete the division and multiplication sentences that solve each problem.

Problem	Division Sentence	Multiplication Sentence
1. There are 12 kittens. There are 3 kittens in each basket. How many baskets are there in all?	12 ÷ 3 = __4__	__4__ × 3 = 12
2. There are 15 chairs. There are 5 equal rows of chairs. How many chairs are there in each row?	15 ÷ 5 = __3__	5 × __3__ = 15

Write a division sentence that can be used to solve each problem. Then write a related multiplication sentence.

Problem	Division Sentence	Multiplication Sentence
3. There are 21 children. There are 3 equal groups. How many are there in each group?	21 ÷ 3 = 7	3 × 7 = 21
4. There are 15 postcards. There is 1 postcard on a page. How many pages have postcards?	15 ÷ 1 = 15	1 × 15 = 15
5. There are 20 mice. There are 4 cages, with the same number of mice in each cage. How many mice are in each cage?	20 ÷ 4 = 5	4 × 5 = 20
6. There are 24 wheels. How many cars are there?	24 ÷ 4 = 6	6 × 4 = 24
7. There are 16 eyes. How many people are there?	16 ÷ 2 = 8	8 × 2 = 16

W66 Challenge

Reading Strategy 12.5

Use Context Clues

Understand ▸ Plan ▸ Solve ▸ Check

VOCABULARY context clues

To understand a word problem, look for **context clues,** or important words or phrases. If a problem asks "How many in all?" add or multiply to find a total. If the problem is about equal groups, you can multiply. If the problem asks "How many are left?" you subtract. If it asks "How many in each group?" you will usually divide.

Read the following problem.

▸ Brandon and his 3 friends caught 12 fish. Each person will get the same number of fish. How many fish will each person get?

1. Which question is this problem asking: *How many in all?*, *How many are left?*, or *How many in each group?* What operation will you use?
   How many in each group?; division

2. What information will you use to solve the problem?
   There are 12 fish and 4 people.

3. Solve the problem.
   12 ÷ 4 = 3; 3 fish

4. Describe the strategy you used.
   Possible answer: I found clues about the number in each group, so I divided to get the answer.

Look for clues and solve.

5. Ed, Nina, and Frank each filled 2 boxes with decorations after the party. How many boxes did they fill in all?
   3 × 2 = 6; 6 boxes

6. Maria, Joe, and Gwen carried 27 trays back to the cafeteria. They each took the same number of trays. How many trays did each student take?
   27 ÷ 3 = 9; 9 trays

PS66 Reading Strategy

251

CHAPTER 12 Extra Practice

Purpose To provide extra practice for the skills presented in this chapter

The blue page references in each set of exercises refer to the lesson pages where each skill is taught.

Internet Resources

Visit **THE LEARNING SITE** at **www.harcourtschool.com** for a listing of practice activities.

Extra Practice

Set A (pp. 240–241)

Write a division sentence for each.

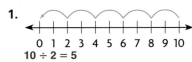

1.
```
<——∩—∩—∩—∩—∩——>
|—|—|—|—|—|—|—|—|—|—|
0 1 2 3 4 5 6 7 8 9 10
```
10 ÷ 2 = 5

2.
$$\begin{array}{r} 36 \\ -\ 9 \\ \hline 27 \end{array} \quad \begin{array}{r} 27 \\ -\ 9 \\ \hline 18 \end{array} \quad \begin{array}{r} 18 \\ -\ 9 \\ \hline 9 \end{array} \quad \begin{array}{r} 9 \\ -\ 9 \\ \hline 0 \end{array} \quad 36 \div 9 = 4$$

Use a number line or subtraction to solve.

3. $15 \div 5 = \blacksquare$ **3**
4. $18 \div 3 = \blacksquare$ **6**
5. $12 \div 4 = \blacksquare$ **3**
6. $16 \div 4 = \blacksquare$ **4**

7. $7\overline{)14}$ **2**
8. $5\overline{)20}$ **4**
9. $3\overline{)24}$ **8**
10. $8\overline{)40}$ **5**

Set B (pp. 242–245)

Complete each number sentence. Draw an array to help.

1. $4 \times \blacksquare = 8$ **2** $8 \div 4 = \blacksquare$ **2**
2. $6 \times \blacksquare = 30$ **5** $30 \div 6 = \blacksquare$ **5**
3. $8 \times \blacksquare = 32$ **4** $32 \div 8 = \blacksquare$ **4**
4. $4 \times \blacksquare = 12$ **3** $12 \div 4 = \blacksquare$ **3**

5. What division sentence could you write for an array that shows $5 \times 8 = 40$?
Possible answer: 40 ÷ 5 = 8

6. How can you use $5 + 5 + 5 + 5 = 20$ to help you find $20 \div 5$? **5 + 5 + 5 + 5 = 20 shows four 5's. There are four 5's in 20, so 20 ÷ 5 = 4.**

Find the number that the variable stands for.

7. $2 \times a = 12$
   $a = \underline{\ ?\ }$ **6**

8. $b \times 4 = 36$
   $b = \underline{\ ?\ }$ **9**

9. $20 \div 4 = c$
   $c = \underline{\ ?\ }$ **5**

Set C (pp. 246–249)

1. 2 × 3 = 6, 3 × 2 = 6, 6 ÷ 2 = 3, 6 ÷ 3 = 2.

Write the fact family. **Answers for 2–8 should follow the same style.**

1. 2, 3, 6
2. 3, 7, 21
3. 3, 9, 27
4. 3, 6, 18
5. 4, 6, 24
6. 4, 8, 32
7. 5, 5, 25
8. 3, 8, 24

Find the quotient or the missing divisor.

9. $6 \div \blacksquare = 3$ **2**
10. $18 \div 6 = \blacksquare$ **3**
11. $\blacksquare = 12 \div 3$ **4**
12. $20 \div \blacksquare = 4$ **5**

13. $30 \div 6 = \blacksquare$ **5**
14. $3 = 15 \div \blacksquare$ **5**
15. $9 \div \blacksquare = 3$ **3**
16. $16 \div 4 = \blacksquare$ **4**

17. Jerome made 30 cookies. He ate 3 and divided the rest equally among 3 friends. How many cookies did each friend get? **9 cookies**

252

Review/Test

✓ CHECK VOCABULARY AND CONCEPTS

Choose the best term from the box.

> variable
> divide
> divisor
> quotient
> inverse operations

1. Multiplication and division are opposite operations, or ___?___ . (p. 242) **inverse operations**

2. In $18 \div 6 = 3$, the number 3 is called the ___?___ . (p. 242) **quotient**

3. When you separate into equal groups, you ___?___ . (p. 238) **divide**

4. A letter that is used to stand for an unknown number is called a ___?___ . (p. 243) **variable**

Use a number line or subtraction to solve. (pp. 240–241)

5. $10 \div 5 = \blacksquare$ **2**   6. $27 \div 9 = \blacksquare$ **3**   7. $4\overline{)20}$ **5**   8. $8\overline{)32}$ **4**

✓ CHECK SKILLS

Complete each number sentence.
Draw an array to help. (pp. 242–245)

9. $2 \times \blacksquare = 6$ **3** $6 \div 2 = \blacksquare$ **3**   10. $3 \times \blacksquare = 15$ **5** $15 \div 3 = \blacksquare$ **5**

11. $4 \times \blacksquare = 4$ **1** $4 \div 4 = \blacksquare$ **1**   12. $5 \times \blacksquare = 30$ **6** $30 \div 5 = \blacksquare$ **6**

Find the number that the variable stands for. (pp. 242–245)

13. $14 \div 2 = a$
$a = $ ___?___ **7**

14. $b \times 5 = 20$
$b = $ ___?___ **4**

15. $18 \div 9 = c$
$c = $ ___?___ **2**

Write the fact family. (pp. 246–249)

16. 4, 5, 20
17. 2, 7, 14
18. 4, 9, 36

16. $4 \times 5 = 20$, $5 \times 4 = 20$, $20 \div 4 = 5$, $20 \div 5 = 4$. Answers for 17–18 should follow the same style.

✓ CHECK PROBLEM SOLVING

Write a number sentence to solve. (pp. 250–251)

19. Ms. Kraft has 20 pencils to divide equally among 5 groups of students. How many pencils does each group get? $20 \div 5 = 4$; 4 pencils

20. Fernando has 24 rocks in his collection. If a box holds 6 rocks, how many boxes will Fernando need for his collection? $24 \div 6 = 4$; 4 boxes

Chapter 12   **253**

Review/Test

Purpose To check understanding of concepts, skills, and problem solving presented in Chapter 12

Using the Page

The Chapter 12 Review/Test can be used as a **review** or a **test**.

- Items 1–8 check understanding of concepts and new vocabulary.
- Items 9–18 check skill proficiency.
- Items 19–20 check students' abilities to choose and apply problem solving strategies to real-life division problems.

Suggest that students place the completed Chapter 12 Review/Test in their portfolios.

Using the Assessment Guide

- Multiple-choice format of Chapter 12 Posttest— See *Assessment Guide*, pp. AG77–78.
- Free-response format of Chapter 12 Posttest— See *Assessment Guide*, pp. AG79–80.

Using Student Self-Assessment

The How Did I Do? survey helps students assess what they have learned and how they learned it. This survey is available as a copying master in *Assessment Guide*, p. AGxvii.

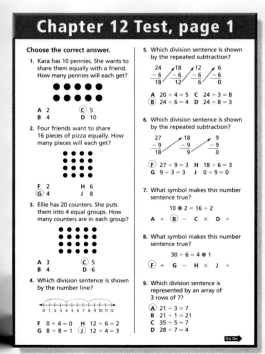

CHAPTER 12

Getting Ready for the EOG Test

Chapters 1–12

Using the Pages

These pages may be used to help students get ready for the North Carolina EOG Test. The test items are written in the same style and arranged in the same format as those on the EOG Test.

The pages are cumulative. They cover the standards from the North Carolina Mathematics Standard Course of Study that have been taught up to this point in the text or in a previous grade. Each Getting Ready for the EOG Test also reviews the North Carolina mathematics strands shown below.

- Number and Operations
- Measurement
- Geometry
- Data Analysis and Probability
- Algebra

These pages can be assigned at the end of the chapter as classwork or as a homework assignment. You may want to have students use individual recording sheets presented in a multiple-choice (standardized) format. A Test Answer Sheet is available as a black-line master in the *Assessment Guide* (p. AGlii).

You may wish to have students describe how they solved each problem and share their solutions.

Getting Ready for the ⭐EOG Test

⭐ **NUMBER AND OPERATIONS**

1. Scott had 20 juice boxes. He gave 4 juice boxes to each friend. How many friends received juice boxes? **C**

- **A** 8
- **B** 2
- **C** 5
- **D** 4

2. Jon bought 9 packs of trading cards. There were 8 cards in each pack. How many cards did Jon buy? **C**

- **A** 17
- **B** 64
- **C** 72
- **D** 81

3. Which subtraction fact belongs to the same fact family as these addition facts? **D**

$$3 + 8 = 11 \qquad 8 + 3 = 11$$

- **A** $11 - 2 = 9$
- **B** $11 - 4 = 7$
- **C** $11 - 6 = 5$
- **D** $11 - 8 = 3$

4. **Explain It** Which pair of numbers has a difference of *about* 500? Explain how you know. See page 255.

- **a.** 647 and 374
- **b.** 659 and 188

⭐ **MEASUREMENT AND GEOMETRY**

5. Holly signed up for flute lessons on April 7. Her first lesson was 2 weeks later. On which date was her first lesson? **D**

April						
Sun	Mon	Tue	Wed	Thu	Fri	Sat
				1	2	3
4	5	6	7	8	9	10
11	12	13	14	15	16	17
18	19	20	21	22	23	24
25	26	27	28	29	30	

- **A** April 7
- **B** April 9
- **C** April 16
- **D** April 21

6. Where is Erica at 11:10? **A**

ERICA'S CAMP SCHEDULE	
Time	Activity
7:30	Breakfast
8:45	Nature hike
10:00	Horseshoes
10:45	Swim lessons
12:00	Lunch
1:00	Bugs and plants

- **A** Swim lessons
- **B** Lunch
- **C** Nature hike
- **D** Horseshoes

7. **Explain It** Brad has two $1 bills, 6 quarters, 4 dimes, and 5 nickels. How much money does he have in all? Tell how you found your answer. See page 255.

254

⭐ ALGEBRAIC THINKING

8. Pam read 8 pages of a book on Monday, 16 pages on Tuesday, and 24 pages on Wednesday. If this pattern continues, how many pages will Pam read on Friday? **D**

A 8
B 32
C 34
D 40

9. What rule could be used to make this table? **C**

Starfish	1	2	3	4
Arms	5	10	15	20

A Multiply by 6.
B Add 4.
C Multiply by 5.
D Divide by 4.

> **TIP** **Understand the problem.** See item 10. Use the rule with an odd number and an even number. See if the product is always an even number. Remember to think about the first number in the pattern.

10. Explain It Julie wants to make a pattern that uses only even numbers. She uses the rule *multiply by 10.* Will Julie's rule form a pattern of even numbers? Explain why or why not. **See below.**

⭐ DATA ANALYSIS AND PROBABILITY

11. Tim's class took a survey and made this bar graph. Which activity received the most votes? **D**

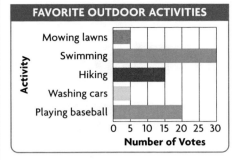

FAVORITE OUTDOOR ACTIVITIES

Activity: Mowing lawns, Swimming, Hiking, Washing cars, Playing baseball

Number of Votes: 0 5 10 15 20 25 30

A Playing baseball
B Hiking
C Washing cars
D Swimming

12. Explain It Geri's class took a survey to find out their favorite ice cream flavors. They made the bar graph below to show the results. How many students answered the survey? Explain how you found your answer. **See below.**

FAVORITE ICE CREAM

Flavor: Vanilla, Chocolate, Butter pecan, Strawberry

Number of Students: 0 3 6 9 12 15 18 21

Chapters 1–12

Item Analysis

You may wish to use the item analysis to determine which North Carolina standards need additional review.

Item	North Carolina Standard	Lesson
1	1.03	12.1
2	1.03	10.2
3	1.02	1.1
4	1.06	5.1
5	2.01	7.5
6	2.01	7.4
7	Goal 2	6.1
8	5.02	9.3
9	5.02	11.2
10	5.02	11.1
11	(2) 4.01	Grade 2
12	(2) 4.01	Grade 2

SCORING RUBRIC
Explain It

2 Demonstrates a complete understanding of the problem and chooses an appropriate strategy to determine the solution

1 Demonstrates a partial understanding of the problem and chooses a strategy that does not lead to a complete and accurate solution

0 Demonstrates little understanding of the problem and shows little evidence of using any strategy to determine a solution

Explain It • Written Response

4. b; possible answer: round and subtract to estimate the differences:
a. $600 - 400 = 200$; b. $700 - 200 = 500$

7. $4.15; added $2.00 + $1.50 + $0.40 + $0.25

10. Possible answer: yes, all the numbers in the pattern will be even because the product of any number and 10 is an even number.

12. 48 students; possible answer: I added the total number of students who voted for each flavor: $6 + 21 + 9 + 12 = 48$.

NCTM Standards 2000

1. Number and Operations
Lessons 13.1, 13.2, 13.3, 13.4, 13.5
2. Algebra
Lesson 13.4
3. Geometry
4. Measurement
5. Data Analysis and Probability

6. Problem Solving
Lessons 13.4, 13.5
7. Reasoning and Proof
Lessons 13.1, 13.2, 13.3
8. Communication
Lessons 13.1, 13.2, 13.3, 13.4, 13.5
9. Connections
10. Representation

Chapter Planner

Getting Ready for Chapter 13 • Assessing Prior Knowledge and INTERVENTION (See PE and TE page 257.)

LESSON	NORTH CAROLINA STANDARDS	PACING	VOCABULARY*	MATERIALS	RESOURCES AND TECHNOLOGY
13.1 Divide by 2 and 5 pp. 258–259 **Objective** To divide by 2 and 5	1.03a	1 Day	*Review* dividend divisor quotient		Reteach, Practice, Problem Solving, Challenge 13.1 Worksheets Transparency 13.1 **Intervention,** *Skill 21* (CD or Book) **Harcourt Mega Math Country Countdown,** *Counting Critters* **Math Jingles® CD 3–4**
13.2 Divide by 3 and 4 pp. 260–261 **Objective** To divide by 3 and 4	1.03a	1 Day			Reteach, Practice, Problem Solving, Challenge 13.2 Worksheets Transparency 13.2 **Intervention,** *Skill 25* (CD or Book) **Harcourt Mega Math The Number Games,** *Up, Up and Array* Scaffolded Instruction Transparency 13 **Math Jingles® CD 3–4**
13.3 Divide with 1 and 0 pp. 262–263 **Objective** To divide with 1 and 0	1.03a	1 Day			Reteach, Practice, Problem Solving, Challenge 13.3 Worksheets Transparency 13.3 **Intervention,** *Skill 24* (CD or Book) **Math Jingles® CD 3–4**
13.4 Algebra: Expressions and Equations pp. 264–265 **Objective** To write expressions and equations that represent situations	maintains (2) Goal 5	1 Day	**equation** *Review* expression		Reteach, Practice, Problem Solving, Challenge 13.4 Worksheets Transparency 13.4 **Intervention,** *Skill 28* (CD or Book)
13.5 Problem Solving Skill: Choose the Operation pp. 266–267 **Objective** To use the problem solving skill *choose the operation* to solve problems	1.06	1 Day		🖩	Reteach, Practice, Reading Strategy, Challenge 13.5 Worksheets Transparency 13.5 Reading Transparency 13 **Intervention • Problem Solving,** *Strategy/Skill 13* (CD or Book)

Ending Chapter 13 • Extra Practice, p. 268 • Chapter 13 Review/Test, p. 269 • Getting Ready for the EOG Test, pp. 270–271

****Boldfaced** terms are the key mathematical terms for the chapter. Other terms are review vocabulary.

Vocabulary Power

Review Vocabulary

To be ready for Chapter 13, students should know the following vocabulary terms:

- **divide** (p. 257)—a mathematical operation in which a group is separated into equal groups. When you divide, you find the number of equal groups that can be made or how many are in each equal group.

- **dividend** (p. 258)—the number that is being divided in a division problem

- **divisor** (p. 258)—the number that divides the dividend

- **quotient** (p. 258)—the number, not including the remainder, that is the result of dividing

- **expression** (p. 264)—part of a number sentence that combines numbers and operation signs, but does not include an equal sign.

Develop Key Chapter Vocabulary

The **boldfaced** word is the key vocabulary term in the chapter.

- **equation** (p. 264)—a mathematical sentence that states the equality between two quantities

Vocabulary Cards

Have students use the Vocabulary Card on *Teacher's Resource Book* pages TR155–156 for the key term in the chapter. The card can be added to a file of mathematics terms.

Multimedia Math Glossary

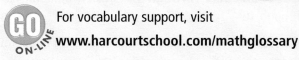

For vocabulary support, visit
www.harcourtschool.com/mathglossary

Math Journal

Have students define the key vocabulary term: *equation*. Have students use their own words and give an example.

M A T H Word Work

Objective To reinforce vocabulary concepts
Use after Lesson 13.4

Materials *For each pair* 12 index cards

Students can review expressions and equations by deciding which expressions name the same amount. Have each student write 2 different expressions for the quantities 8, 12, and 15. Each expression should be written on an index card. Encourage students to use addition, subtraction, multiplication, and division in their expressions.

Have pairs shuffle the cards and turn them face-down on the table. Partners can play a memory game in which they must find pairs of expressions with the same value. You may wish to have partners record each of the equations they form during the activity.

	15 – 3		
		4 × 3	

Mathematics Across the Grades

LOOKING BACK • Prerequisite Skills

To be ready for Chapter 13, students should have the following understandings and skills:

- **Multiplication Facts Through 10**—review of multiplication facts through 10

- **Model Division**—review modeling division with equal rows of counters

Check What You Know

Use page 257 to determine students' knowledge of prerequisite concepts and skills.

Intervention

Help students prepare for the chapter by using the intervention resources described on TE page 257.

LOOKING AT CHAPTER 13 • Essential Skills

Students will

- divide by 2, 3, 4, and 5.

- divide using 1 and 0.

- **write expressions and equations that represent situations.**

- use the problem solving skill *choose the operation* to solve problems.

Example

Raymond had 25 apples. He divided the apples equally among 5 friends. Write an expression to show how many apples Raymond gave each friend.

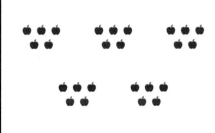

Answer:

$25 \div 5$

LOOKING AHEAD • Applications

Students will apply what they learn in Chapter 13 to the following new concepts:

- Divide by 6, 7, 8, 9, and 10 (Chapter 14)

- Find the Cost (Chapter 14)

- Divide with Remainders (Chapter 30)

- Divide 2-Digit Numbers (Chapter 30)

Differentiated Instruction

FROM RESEARCH TO PRACTICE

 Meeting the Needs of All Learners

Extra Support	Activities for All	Enrichment
Alternative Teaching Strategy TE Lessons 13.1, 13.2, 13.3, 13.4, 13.5 **ESOL/ESL** TE Lessons 13.1, 13.2, 13.3, 13.4, 13.5 **Special Needs** TE Lesson 13.2	**Cross-Curricular Connections** **Reading:** TE Lesson 13.5 **Science:** Chapter Opener **Social Studies:** TE Lesson 13.3 **Vocabulary:** TE p. 256B, PE/TE, p. 257 **Writing:** TE Lesson 13.4	**Advanced Learners** TE Lesson 13.1 **Early Finishers** TE Lessons 13.2, 13.3, 13.4, 13.5

Combination and Multi-age Classrooms

Grade 2	Grade 3	Grade 4
Skills Trace Across the Grades		
Relate addition and multiplication; explore division by making equal groups.	**Divide by 2, 3, 4, and 5; divide with 1 and 0; write expressions and equations using division.**	Relate multiplication and division; practice multiplication and division facts to 12.
Instructional Strategies		
Students on this level may require more time to build conceptual understanding. **Assignments** **Grade 3 Pupil Edition** • Have students work in pairs on Lessons 13.1, 13.2, 13.3, and 13.4. Skip Lesson 13.5. **Grade 2 Pupil Edition**—pages 529–535	Students on this level should be able to complete all the lessons in the Pupil Edition and all the activities in the Teacher's Edition with minimal adjustments. **Assignment** **Grade 3 Pupil Edition**—pages 256–269	Students on this level will probably require less time to build conceptual understanding. **Assignments** **Grade 3 Pupil Edition** • Compact Lessons 13.1, 13.2, and 13.3. **Grade 4 Pupil Edition**—pages 162–201

Division Facts Through 5

Introducing the Chapter

Placing items into equal groups is called *division*. It is the opposite of multiplication. Have students skip-count the number of fish for Pelican 1. Ask: Is skip-counting like multiplication or division? multiplication

Using Data

To begin the study of the chapter, ask students

• How many equal groups of fish are in the pictograph for Pelican 2? There are 8 equal groups of 2.

• What two multiplication sentences show how to find the total number of fish for Pelican 3? $4 \times 2 = 8$ and $2 \times 4 = 8$

• How many fish would Pelican 1 have if each picture represented 3 fish caught? Pelican 1 would have 18 fish.

Problem Solving Project

Purpose To express equal groups of objects with number sentences

Grouping Small groups

Background The brown pelican is the official state bird of Louisiana.

UNDERSTAND • PLAN • SOLVE • CHECK
Have students

• Locate objects in the classroom that have been divided into groups: books on shelves, paintbrushes in cups, and so on.

• Write 2 number sentences with markers to describe each group.

• Tape the number sentences to the groups of objects. Have one student from each group explain the number sentence.

Have students write an explanation of their number sentences for their portfolios.

Graphing Investigations
Begin Week 13.

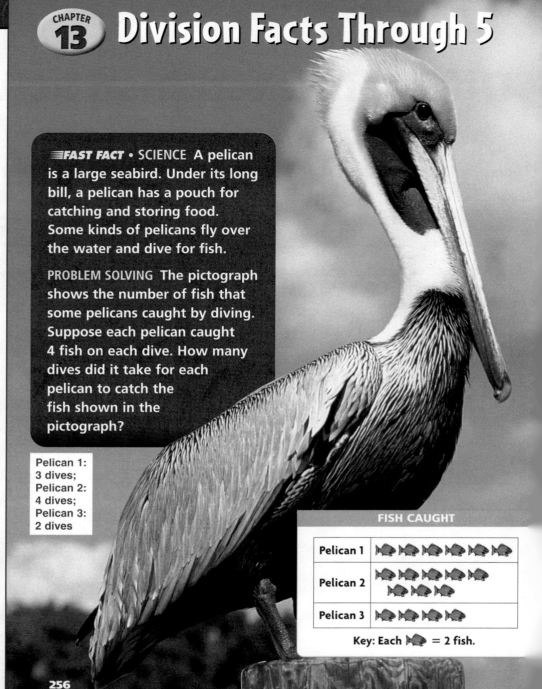

Division Facts Through 5

≡FAST FACT • SCIENCE A pelican is a large seabird. Under its long bill, a pelican has a pouch for catching and storing food. Some kinds of pelicans fly over the water and dive for fish.

PROBLEM SOLVING The pictograph shows the number of fish that some pelicans caught by diving. Suppose each pelican caught 4 fish on each dive. How many dives did it take for each pelican to catch the fish shown in the pictograph?

Pelican 1: 3 dives;
Pelican 2: 4 dives;
Pelican 3: 2 dives

FISH CAUGHT

Pelican 1	🐟🐟🐟🐟🐟🐟
Pelican 2	🐟🐟🐟🐟🐟🐟🐟🐟
Pelican 3	🐟🐟🐟🐟

Key: Each 🐟 = 2 fish.

256

WHY LEARN MATH? Nature magazine writers sometimes express animal behavior in terms of mathematical relationships. Suppose 2 pelicans eat a total of 10 fish per day. If they each eat the same number of fish, how many does each pelican eat? 5 fish each How many fish would 20 pelicans eat each day? 100 fish

Family Involvement Activities

These activities provide:

• Letter to the Family
• Math Vocabulary
• Family Game
• Practice (Homework)

Family Involvement Activities, p. FA49

Use this page to help you review and remember
important skills needed for Chapter 13.

✓ MULTIPLICATION FACTS THROUGH 5

Find each product.

1. $6 \times 3 =$ ■ **18**   **2.** $3 \times 5 =$ ■ **15**   **3.** ■ $= 9 \times 2$ **18**   **4.** $7 \times 4 =$ ■ **28**

5. ■ $= 1 \times 7$ **7**   **6.** ■ $= 3 \times 1$ **3**   **7.** $5 \times 8 =$ ■ **40**   **8.** $3 \times 9 =$ ■ **27**

9. $1 \times 1 =$ ■ **1**   **10.** $6 \times 5 =$ ■ **30**   **11.** $4 \times 6 =$ ■ **24**   **12.** ■ $= 2 \times 8$ **16**

✓ MODEL DIVISION

Copy and complete.

13.  ● ● ● ● ● ●
● ● ● ● ● ●
● ● ● ● ● ●

14. ● ● ● ● ● ● ●
● ● ● ● ● ● ●

15. ● ● ● ● ●
● ● ● ● ●
● ● ● ● ●
● ● ● ● ●

3 rows of ■ $= 18$ 2 rows of ■ $= 14$ 4 rows of ■ $= 20$

$18 \div 3 =$ ■ **6, 6** $14 \div 2 =$ ■ **7, 7** $20 \div 4 =$ ■ **5, 5**

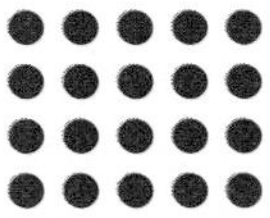

16. $3 \times 7 = 21; 7 \times 3 = 21; 21 \div 3 = 7; 21 \div 7 = 3$

✓ FACT FAMILIES

17. $2 \times 4 = 8; 4 \times 2 = 8; 8 \div 2 = 4; 8 \div 4 = 2$

18. $3 \times 5 = 15; 5 \times 3 = 15; 15 \div 3 = 5; 15 \div 5 = 3$

19. $4 \times 4 = 16; 16 \div 4 = 4$

Write the fact family.
See above.

16. 3, 7, 21   **17.** 2, 4, 8   **18.** 5, 3, 15   **19.** 4, 4, 16

✓ VOCABULARY POWER

REVIEW

divide [di•vīd'] *verb*

When you *multiply*, you use
multiplication. When you *divide*, what
operation do you use? Use *multiply*
and *divide* in a sentence.
division; Check students' work.

PREVIEW

equation

 GO ON-LINE   www.harcourtschool.com/mathglossary

Assessing Prior Knowledge

Use the **Check What You Know** page to determine
whether your students have mastered the prerequisite skills critical for this chapter.

Intervention

- **Diagnose and Prescribe**
  Evaluate your students' performance on this page
  to determine whether intervention is necessary or
  if enrichment is appropriate. Options that provide
  instruction, practice, and a check are listed in the
  chart below.

✓ CHECK WHAT YOU KNOW RESOURCES

Intervention Copying Masters or CD-ROMs

Enrichment Copying Masters

VOCABULARY POWER

For activities and information about the vocabulary in this chapter, see page 256B.

Were students successful with ✓ **CHECK WHAT YOU KNOW?**

IF . . . **NO** THEN . . . INTERVENE   **INTERVENTION OPTIONS**   IF . . . **YES** THEN . . . ENRICH

Skill/Items	Missed more than	Intervene with
Multiplication Facts Through 5, 1–12	3	• *Intervention,* Skill 21
Model Division, 13–15	1	• *Intervention,* Skill 30
Fact Families, 16–19	1	• *Intervention,* Skill 31

Skill/Items	Missed fewer than	Enrich with
Multiplication Facts Through 5, 1–12	4	• *Intervention,* Enrichment p. IN354
Model Division, 13–15	2	• *Intervention,* Enrichment p. IN353
Fact Families, 16–19	2	• *Intervention,* Enrichment p. IN354

Lesson Planning

PROFESSIONAL DEVELOPMENT

Objective To divide by 2 and 5

NCTM Standards
1. Number and Operations
7. Reasoning and Proof
8. Communication

Math Background

These ideas will help students divide by 2 and 5.

- To find a quotient when you have 2 as the divisor, solve for the missing factor of a multiplication sentence with 2 as a factor and a product equal to the dividend.

- To find a quotient when you have 5 as the divisor, solve for the missing factor of a multiplication sentence with 5 as a factor and a product equal to the dividend.

- When using repeated subtraction to find a quotient, you are skip-counting backward.

- Use multiplication to check division facts. The divisor multiplied by the quotient equals the dividend.

Warm-Up Resources

Number of the Day

Transparency **13.1**

October has 1 more day than September does. Find the total number of days in September and October. 61 days

Daily Facts Practice

Have students practice addition and subtraction facts by completing Set D of *Teacher's Resource Book*, p. TR92.

Transparency **13.1**

Problem of the Day

Find the number that does not belong in each group.
1. 12, 16, 10, 5, 8 5
2. 45, 18, 20, 15, 50 18
3. 24, 35, 56, 63, 42 24
4. 32, 40, 24, 48, 23 23
5. 38, 24, 15, 12, 28 15

Solution Problem of the Day tab, p. PD13.

Intervention and Extension Resources

Alternative Teaching Strategy

MATERIALS *For each pair* 10 index cards

Help students **find related multiplication and division sentences**. Have one student write two related multiplication sentences, such as $2 \times 5 = 10$, $5 \times 2 = 10$, on the front of one of the index cards. Have the partner write the related division sentences, such as $10 \div 2 = 5$, $10 \div 5 = 2$, on the back of the card. After five turns, have students reverse roles. Check students' work.

VISUAL

VISUAL/SPATIAL, INTERPERSONAL/SOCIAL

Multistep and Strategy Problems

The following multistep or strategy problem is provided in Lesson 13.1:

Page	Item
259	26

ESOL/ESL

MATERIALS *For each pair* 2 number cubes numbered 0–5 and 4–9

ESOL/ESL

Help students **practice dividing by 2 and 5**. Have a student roll the cubes and use the digits to form numbers that can be divided by 2 or 5. The two digits may be added, subtracted, or multiplied, such as $7 + 1$ or 6×5, to arrive at a dividend. Have the other student state a division sentence using the numbers formed by the partner. Students reverse roles and repeat several times. Check students' work.

KINESTHETIC

BODILY/KINESTHETIC, VERBAL/LINGUISTIC

Advanced Learners

MATERIALS *For each student* multiplication table

Challenge students to **find all the numbers on the multiplication table that can be divided by both 2 and 5**.

Have students:

- highlight the rows and columns of 2 and 5.
- circle all the numbers that can be divided by both 2 and 5, and use multiplication to check their answers. 10, 20, 30, 40, 50, 60, 70, 80, 90, 100

Ask: What do you notice about the numbers on your list? Possible answers: All the numbers end in zero; you can divide every number by 10.

VISUAL

VISUAL/SPATIAL, LOGICAL/MATHEMATICAL

Technology Link

Intervention, *Skill 21*

Harcourt Mega Math
Country Countdown, *Counting Critters,* Level AA

Math Jingles® CD 3–4 • *Track 7*

GO The Harcourt Learning Site
www.harcourtschool.com

Lesson 13.1 Organizer

Objective To divide by 2 and 5

Vocabulary *Review* dividend, divisor, quotient

1 INTRODUCE

Quick Review provides review of prerequisite skills.

Why Learn This? You can find how many hats are on each shelf. *Share the lesson objective with students.*

2 TEACH

Guided Instruction

Modifying Instruction Use counters to model the division word problems.

- *Check students' understanding of using multiplication to solve division problems.*
  How can you use a multiplication fact to solve 8 ÷ 2 = 4? I know 2 × 4 = 8, so 8 ÷ 2 = 4.
  Why can you use a multiplication sentence to solve a division problem? Possible answer: Multiplication and division are inverse operations.

- *Direct students' attention to the Math Idea.*
  What multiplication number sentence could you use to help you solve 14 ÷ 2 = ■?
  Possible answer: 2 × ■ = 14
  Reasoning You are given two division problems to solve: 10 ÷ 2 = ■ and 10 ÷ 5 = ■. **What do you know about the multiplication facts that you can use to solve the division problems?** They are in the same fact family.

3 PRACTICE

Guided Practice

Do Check Exercises 1–3 with your students. Identify students who are having difficulty and choose appropriate lesson resources to provide assistance.

Divide by 2 and 5

Quick Review
1. $2 \times ■ = 10$ 5
2. $4 \times ■ = 8$ 2
3. $5 \times ■ = 20$ 4
4. $■ \times 5 = 35$ 7
5. $■ \times 2 = 18$ 9

▶ Learn

CRAFTY MATH Mrs. Jackson knit 12 hats. She put an equal number of hats on each of 2 shelves in the craft shop. How many hats are on each shelf?

$12 \div 2 = ■$

Use a related multiplication fact to find the quotient.

Think: $2 \times ■ = 12$

$2 \times 6 = 12$

$12 \div 2 = 6$, or $2\overline{)12}^{\,6}$

So, there are 6 hats on each shelf.

What if Mrs. Jackson knits 15 hats and puts an equal number of hats on each of 5 shelves? How many hats are on each shelf?

$15 \div 5 = ■$

Use the multiplication table to find the quotient.

Think: $5 \times ■ = 15$ $5 \times 3 = 15$

$15 \div 5 = 3$, or $5\overline{)15}^{\,3}$

So, there are 3 hats on each shelf.

 MATH IDEA You can find missing factors in related multiplication facts to help you divide.

- How can you use $3 \times 2 = 6$ to help you find $6 \div 2$? **There are 3 groups of 2 in 6, so 6 ÷ 2 = 3.**

▶ Check

1. **Explain** how you can use multiplication to check $20 \div 5 = 4$. **Possible answer: Check that the divisor multiplied by the quotient equals the dividend; 5 × 4 = 20**

258

Remember

$$16 \div 2 = 8$$
$$\underset{\text{dividend}}{\uparrow} \quad \underset{\text{divisor}}{\uparrow} \quad \underset{\text{quotient}}{\uparrow}$$

×	0	1	2	3	4	5
0	0	0	0	0	0	0
1	0	1	2	3	4	5
2	0	2	4	6	8	10
3	0	3	6	9	12	15
4	0	4	8	12	16	20
5	0	5	10	15	20	25
6	0	6	12	18	24	30

Reteach 13.1

Divide by 2 and 5

You can use the multiplication facts you know to find quotients.

Here are two examples.

Example A

$$16 \div 2 = ?$$
$$\underset{\text{dividend}}{\uparrow} \quad \underset{\text{divisor}}{\uparrow} \quad \underset{\text{quotient}}{\uparrow}$$

Think: $2 \times \underline{?} = 16$

$2 \times \mathbf{8} = 16$

So, $16 \div 2 = 8$ or $2\overline{)16}^{\,8}$

Example B

$$30 \div 5 = ?$$
$$\underset{\text{dividend}}{\uparrow} \quad \underset{\text{divisor}}{\uparrow} \quad \underset{\text{quotient}}{\uparrow}$$

Think: $5 \times \underline{?} = 30$

$5 \times \mathbf{6} = 30$

So, $30 \div 5 = 6$ or $5\overline{)30}^{\,6}$

Find each quotient.

1. $18 \div 2 = \underline{9}$ 2. $35 \div 5 = \underline{7}$ 3. $10 \div 2 = \underline{5}$

Think: $2 \times \underline{9} = 18$ Think: $5 \times \underline{7} = 35$ Think: $2 \times \underline{5} = 10$

4. $50 \div 5 = \underline{10}$ 5. $14 \div 2 = \underline{7}$ 6. $6 \div 2 = \underline{3}$

Think: $5 \times \underline{10} = 50$ Think: $2 \times \underline{7} = 14$ Think: $2 \times \underline{3} = 6$

7. $40 \div 5 = \underline{8}$ 8. $2 \div 2 = \underline{1}$ 9. $20 \div 5 = \underline{4}$

10. $20 \div 2 = \underline{10}$ 11. $25 \div 5 = \underline{5}$ 12. $45 \div 5 = \underline{9}$

13. $8 \div 2 = \underline{4}$ 14. $12 \div 2 = \underline{6}$ 15. $5 \div 5 = \underline{1}$

16. $5\overline{)20}^{\,4}$ 17. $2\overline{)18}^{\,9}$ 18. $5\overline{)30}^{\,6}$ 19. $5\overline{)50}^{\,10}$

20. $2\overline{)10}^{\,5}$ 21. $2\overline{)12}^{\,6}$ 22. $5\overline{)35}^{\,7}$ 23. $5\overline{)40}^{\,8}$

Reteach RW67

Practice 13.1

Divide by 2 and 5

Find each missing factor or quotient.

1. $2 \times \underline{4} = 8$ 2. $30 \div 5 = \underline{6}$ 3. $16 \div 2 = \underline{8}$

4. $45 \div 5 = \underline{9}$ 5. $5 \times \underline{5} = 25$ 6. $8 \div 2 = \underline{4}$

7. $5 \times \underline{3} = 15$ 8. $2 \times \underline{10} = 20$ 9. $2 \times \underline{6} = 12$

Find each quotient.

10. $18 \div 2 = \underline{9}$ 11. $35 \div 5 = \underline{7}$ 12. $40 \div 5 = \underline{8}$

13. $4 \div 2 = \underline{2}$ 14. $10 \div 2 = \underline{5}$ 15. $5 \div 5 = \underline{1}$

16. $5\overline{)30}^{\,6}$ 17. $2\overline{)14}^{\,7}$ 18. $5\overline{)20}^{\,4}$ 19. $5\overline{)5}^{\,1}$

20. $2\overline{)12}^{\,6}$ 21. $2\overline{)8}^{\,4}$ 22. $5\overline{)15}^{\,3}$ 23. $5\overline{)40}^{\,8}$

Complete.

24. $20 \div 2 = \underline{4} + 6$ 25. $15 \div 5 = \underline{3} \times 1$ 26. $40 \div 5 = \underline{4} \times 2$

Mixed Review

Solve.

27. $9 \times 3 \times \underline{3} = 81$ 28. $\underline{1} \times 6 \times 2 = 12$ 29. $9 \times \underline{7} = 63$

Add 1,000 to each.

30. 32,605   31. 20,001   32. 518   33. 6

   $\underline{33,605}$ $\underline{21,001}$ $\underline{1,518}$ $\underline{1,006}$

Write A.M. or P.M.

34. ten minutes after midnight 35. time to go to bed 36. ten minutes before noon 37. ten minutes before midnight

   $\underline{\text{A.M.}}$ $\underline{\text{P.M.}}$ $\underline{\text{A.M.}}$ $\underline{\text{P.M.}}$

Practice PW67

Copy and complete each table.

2.

÷	2	4	6	8
2	▦	▦	▦	▦
	1	2	3	4

3.

÷	10	15	20	25
5	▦	▦	▦	▦
	2	3	4	5

▶ **Practice and Problem Solving**   (Extra Practice, page 268, Set A)

Copy and complete each table.

4.

÷	10	12	14	16
2	▦	▦	▦	▦
	5	6	7	8

5.

÷	30	35	40	45
5	▦	▦	▦	▦
	6	7	8	9

Find each missing factor and quotient.

6. $2 \times ▦ = 4$ **2** $4 \div 2 = ▦$ **2**

7. $5 \times ▦ = 20$ **4** $20 \div 5 = ▦$ **4**

8. $5 \times ▦ = 35$ **7** $35 \div 5 = ▦$ **7**

9. $2 \times ▦ = 16$ **8** $16 \div 2 = ▦$ **8**

Find each quotient.

10. $6 \div 2 = ▦$ **3**

11. $10 \div 2 = ▦$ **5**

12. $▦ = 10 \div 5$ **2**

13. $5 \div 5 = ▦$ **1**

14. $25 \div 5 = ▦$ **5**

15. $▦ = 14 \div 2$ **7**

16. $40 \div 5 = ▦$ **8**

17. $20 \div 2 = ▦$ **10**

18. $2\overline{)2}$ **1**

19. $5\overline{)15}$ **3**

20. $5\overline{)35}$ **7**

21. $2\overline{)16}$ **8**

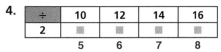 **ALGEBRA** Complete.

27. Philip used the wrong multiplication fact. He should have used $2 \times 4 = 8$ to find $8 \div 2 = 4$.

22. $10 \div 2 = ▦ \times 1$ **5**

23. $40 \div 5 = 4 \times ▦$ **2**

24. $▦ \div 2 = 3 + 4$ **14**

25. **REASONING** What do you notice about the numbers that can be evenly divided by 2? **Possible answers:** They end in 0, 2, 4, 6, or 8; They are even numbers.

26. Mrs. Jackson sells hats for $5. She has $15. How many more hats must she sell to have $35 in all? **4 hats**

27. ❓ **What's the Error?** Philip used the multiplication fact $2 \times 8 = 16$ to find $8 \div 2 = ▦$. Describe his error. What is the correct quotient? **See above.**

▶ **Getting Ready for the EOG Test**

28. Erin makes 12 cards. She puts an equal number of cards in each of 2 boxes. How many cards are in each box? **A**

A 6   **B** 7   **C** 8   **D** 12

★ **North Carolina Standards 1.03** Develop fluency with multiplication from 1×1 to 12×12 and division to two-digit by one-digit numbers using: a) Strategies for multiplying and dividing numbers.

Challenge 13.1

Favorite Numbers

Karen, Tyler, and Daniela are friends who have made posters of their favorite numbers. Think about each of their favorite numbers and then answer the questions below.

1. Which friends have favorite numbers that can all be divided by 2?

   Karen and Tyler

2. Which friends have favorite numbers that can all be divided by 5?

   Daniela and Tyler

3. Which friend has favorite numbers that can all be divided by both 2 and 5?

   Tyler

4. What else do Karen's favorite numbers have in common?

   Possible answer: They are all even numbers.

5. What else do Daniela's favorite numbers have in common?

   Possible answer: The ones digits are either 0 or 5.

Challenge **CW67**

Problem Solving 13.1

Divide by 2 and 5

Understand ▸ Plan ▸ Solve ▸ Check

Write the correct answer.

1. Some crayons are divided equally among 6 students. Each student gets 8 crayons. How many crayons are there in all?

   48 crayons

2. A music class began at 9:40 A.M. The class spent 25 minutes singing and 10 minutes listening to music. What time did the class end?

   10:15 A.M.

3. There are 15 students in art class. There are 5 students sitting at each table. How many tables are there?

   3 tables

4. Miranda has 12 mittens in her winter clothes box. How many pairs of mittens does she have?

   6 pairs

Choose the letter of the correct answer.

5. A store sells 2 balloons for $3. How much would it cost to buy 4 balloons?

   A $12
   B $9
   Ⓒ $6
   D $4

6. If you divide 30 by a number, the quotient is 6. What is the number you divide by?

   F 4
   Ⓖ 5
   H 14
   J 24

7. Phil wants to trade in his 40 nickels for quarters. How many quarters can he get?

   A 35 quarters
   B 10 quarters
   C 9 quarters
   Ⓓ 8 quarters

8. Rosita practiced the piano 2 hours every day for a week. How many hours did she practice in all?

   F 2
   G 10
   Ⓗ 14
   J 20

9. **Write About It** Tell how you solved Problem 5.

   Possible answer: Since I multiplied the number of balloons by 2, I also multiplied the price by 2. $3 \times 2 = $6

Problem Solving **PS67**

▧▧▧ **COMMON ERROR ALERT** ▧▧▧

For the problem $12 \div 2 = ▦$, students may think the related multiplication fact is $12 \times 2 = ▦$.

$$12 \div 2 = ▦$$
$$12 \times 2 = 24$$

Remind students that the dividend is the same as the product. The quotient is the same as the missing factor.

Independent Practice

Note that Exercise 26 is a **multistep or strategy problem.** Assign Exercises 4–27.

ALGEBRAIC THINKING For Exercises 22–24, encourage students to start by simplifying the side of the equation without the unknown number.

4 ASSESS

Summarize the lesson by having students:

DISCUSS What are 4 methods you can use to solve division problems? Possible answer: skip-counting, using counters, using a related multiplication fact, using repeated subtraction

WRITE Think of a division word problem. Write the problem and solve it. **Explain your solution strategy.** Possible answer: How would you divide 45 pencils equally among 5 friends? Each friend would get 9 pencils; I knew the multiplication fact $5 \times 9 = 45$, so $45 \div 5 = 9$.

LESSON QUIZ   Transparency **13.1**

Find each missing factor and quotient.

1. $5 \times ▦ = 25$ **5** $25 \div 5 = ▦$ **5**

2. $2 \times ▦ = 14$ **7** $14 \div 2 = ▦$ **7**

3. $2 \times ▦ = 20$ **10** $20 \div 2 = ▦$ **10**

4. $5 \times ▦ = 40$ **8** $40 \div 5 = ▦$ **8**

Lesson Planning

PROFESSIONAL DEVELOPMENT

Objective To divide by 3 and 4

NCTM Standards

1. Number and Operations
7. Reasoning and Proof
8. Communication

Math Background

These ideas will help students divide by 3 and 4.

- To find a quotient when you have 3 as a divisor, solve for the missing factor of a multiplication sentence with 3 as a factor and a product equal to the dividend.

- To find a quotient when you have 4 as a divisor, solve for the missing factor of a multiplication sentence with 4 as a factor and a product equal to the dividend.

Warm-Up Resources

Number of the Day

Transparency **13.2**

The number of the day completes both of these number sentences: $2 \times \blacksquare = 10$, $10 \div 2 = \blacksquare$ 5

Daily Facts Practice

Have students practice subtraction facts by completing Set E of *Teacher's Resource Book*, p. TR92.

Solve a Problem

Transparency **13.2**

Problem of the Day

All of the even numbers less than 9 are factors of me. Who am I? Possible answer: the number 24

Solution Problem of the Day tab, p. PD13.

Intervention and Extension Resources

Alternative Teaching Strategy

MATERIALS counters, paper plates

ESOL/ESL

Help students **find quotients**. Tell students that the paper plates represent the divisor and the counters represent the dividend. Have students divide 18 counters among 3 plates so that 6 counters are in each group. Using the plates and counters, ask students to find the quotients for the following:

$36 \div 4 = $ ■ 9 $24 \div 3 = $ ■ 8

$30 \div 3 = $ ■ 10 $20 \div 4 = $ ■ 5

$18 \div 3 = $ ■ 6 $28 \div 4 = $ ■ 7

KINESTHETIC

BODILY/KINESTHETIC, LOGICAL/MATHEMATICAL

Multistep and Strategy Problems

The following multistep or strategy problems are provided in Lesson 13.2:

Page	Item
261	33–34

Special Needs

MATERIALS *For each student* 20 index cards, crayons

Help students **reinforce division and multiplication fact families**. Have them write a multiplication fact for threes or fours on the front of an index card and the related division fact on the reverse side. Then have them circle factors, divisors, and quotients in red, and products and dividends in blue. Check students' work.

VISUAL

VISUAL/SPATIAL, VERBAL/LINGUISTIC

Early Finishers

MATERIALS *For each group* 10 ones blocks, 12 counters, 20 paper clips

Help students **review the division facts** they have learned. Ask students if they can divide the items evenly by 2, 3, 4, and/or 5. Have them write the multiplication facts they used to find the quotients and then write the quotients. Check students' work.

KINESTHETIC

BODILY/KINESTHETIC, VERBAL/LINGUISTIC

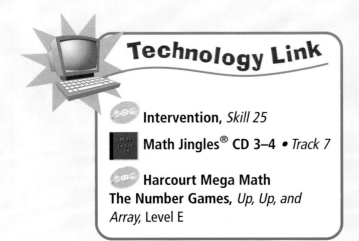

Technology Link

Intervention, *Skill 25*

Math Jingles® CD 3–4 • *Track 7*

Harcourt Mega Math
The Number Games, *Up, Up, and Array,* Level E

Lesson 13.2 Organizer

Objective To divide by 3 and 4

2 Divide by 3 and 4

Quick Review

1. ■ × 3 = 18 6
2. 4 × ■ = 12 3
3. ■ × 4 = 16 4
4. 4 × ■ = 32 8
5. 3 × ■ = 21 7

1 INTRODUCE

QUICK REVIEW provides review of prerequisite skills.

WHY LEARN THIS? If you know the number of people in a group and how many people a vehicle can hold, you can determine how many vehicles are needed. *Share the lesson objective with students.*

2 TEACH

Guided Instruction

• *Discuss the Paddle Power problem.*
What is the meaning of each number in the division sentence 24 ÷ 3 = 8? 24 is the number of people in the group; 3 is the number of people one canoe can hold; 8 is the number of canoes needed.

• *Check students' understanding of the What If problem.*
Tell what each number in the division sentence 24 ÷ 4 = 6 means. 24 is the number of people in the group; 4 is the number of people one rowboat can hold; 6 is the number of rowboats needed.

MODIFYING INSTRUCTION Use counters to model the division problems in both examples.

• *Ask students to think about using a multiplication table to solve the division problems.*
How do you use a multiplication table differently to solve 24 ÷ 3 = ■ than to solve 24 ÷ 4 = ■? For 24 ÷ 3, start by finding row 3 in the table. For 24 ÷ 4, start by finding row 4 in the table.

3 PRACTICE

Guided Practice

Do Check Exercises 1–5 with your students. Identify students who are having difficulty and choose appropriate lesson resources to provide assistance.

▶ Learn

PADDLE POWER The Traveler Scouts want to rent canoes. There are 24 people in the group. A canoe can hold 3 people. How many canoes should the group rent?

24 ÷ 3 = ■

Use the multiplication table to find a related multiplication fact.

Think: 3 × ■ = 24
3 × 8 = 24   24 ÷ 3 = 8, or 3)24 (8)

So, the group should rent 8 canoes.

What if the group wants to rent rowboats instead? If each rowboat holds 4 people, how many rowboats should they rent?

24 ÷ 4 = ■

Think: 4 × ■ = 24
4 × 6 = 24   24 ÷ 4 = 6, or 4)24 (6)

So, the group should rent 6 rowboats.

• **REASONING** How can you use 21 ÷ 3 = 7 to find 24 ÷ 3? **There are 7 groups of 3 in 21. There is one more group of 3 in 24. So, 24 ÷ 3 = 8.**

×	0	1	2	3	4	5	6	7	8	9
0	0	0	0	0	0	0	0	0	0	0
1	0	1	2	3	4	5	6	7	8	9
2	0	2	4	6	8	10	12	14	16	18
3	0	3	6	9	12	15	18	21	24	27
4	0	4	8	12	16	20	24	28	32	36
5	0	5	10	15	20	25	30	35	40	45

▶ Check

1. Explain how you can use multiplication to find 12 ÷ 4.
4 × 3 = 12, so 12 ÷ 4 = 3.

Write the multiplication fact you can use to find the quotient. Then write the quotient.

2. 12 ÷ 3 = ■
3 × 4 = 12; 4

3. 8 ÷ 4 = ■
4 × 2 = 8; 2

4. 15 ÷ 3 = ■
3 × 5 = 15; 5

5. 28 ÷ 4 = ■
4 × 7 = 28; 7

260

Reteach 13.2

Divide by 3 and 4

You can use the multiplication facts you know to find quotients.

Here are two examples.

Example A	**Example B**
15 ÷ 3 = ?	28 ÷ 4 = ?
↑ ↑ ↑	↑ ↑ ↑
dividend divisor quotient	dividend divisor quotient
Think: 3 × ? = 15	Think: 4 × ? = 28
3 × 5 = 15	4 × 7 = 28
So, 15 ÷ 3 = 5 or 3)15 (5)	So, 28 ÷ 4 = 7 or 4)28 (7)

Find each quotient.

1. 18 ÷ 3 = **6**   2. 32 ÷ 4 = **8**   3. 12 ÷ 4 = **3**
Think: 3 × **6** = 18   Think: 4 × **8** = 32   Think: 4 × **3** = 12

4. 40 ÷ 4 = **10**   5. 16 ÷ 4 = **4**   6. 6 ÷ 3 = **2**
Think: 4 × **10** = 40   Think: 4 × **4** = 16   Think: 3 × **2** = 6

7. 21 ÷ 3 = **7**   8. 20 ÷ 4 = **5**   9. 24 ÷ 3 = **8**

10. 24 ÷ 4 = **6**   11. 27 ÷ 3 = **9**   12. 30 ÷ 3 = **10**

13. 8 ÷ 4 = **2**   14. 12 ÷ 3 = **4**   15. 3 ÷ 3 = **1**

16. 3)21 (7)   17. 4)32 (8)   18. 3)9 (3)   19. 4)20 (5)

20. 4)28 (7)   21. 3)27 (9)   22. 4)36 (9)   23. 4)4 (1)

RW68 Reteach

Practice 13.2

Divide by 3 and 4

Write the multiplication fact you can use to find the quotient. Then write the quotient.

1. 36 ÷ 4   2. 21 ÷ 3   3. 28 ÷ 4
   9 × 4 = 36;   7 × 3 = 21;   7 × 4 = 28;
   9   7   7

Find each quotient.

4. 18 ÷ 3 = **6**   5. 32 ÷ 4 = **8**   6. 30 ÷ 3 = **10**

7. 8 ÷ 2 = **4**   8. 12 ÷ 3 = **4**   9. 12 ÷ 4 = **3**

10. 3)15 (5)   11. 4)28 (7)   12. 3)27 (9)   13. 4)16 (4)

14. 4)32 (8)   15. 3)9 (3)   16. 4)8 (2)   17. 3)30 (10)

Complete.

18. 12 ÷ 4 = **1** × 3   19. 24 ÷ 4 = **2** × 3   20. 27 ÷ 3 = **3** × 3

Mixed Review

Solve.

21. 8   22. 7   23. 6   24. 5   25. 4
   ×9   ×8   ×7   ×6   ×5
   72   **56**   **42**   **30**   **20**

26. 9   27. 8   28. 7   29. 6   30. 5
   ×9   ×8   ×7   ×6   ×5
   81   **64**   **49**   **36**   **25**

31. $13.87   32. $45.16   33. $63.27   34. $49.95
   + $25.62   + $82.37   + $37.92   + $77.85
   $39.49   **$127.53**   **$101.19**   **$127.80**

PW68 Practice

Practice and Problem Solving Extra Practice, page 268, Set B

Write the multiplication fact you can use to find
the quotient. Then write the quotient.

Technology Link
More Practice:
Harcourt Mega Math
The Number Games,
Up, Up, and Array,
Level E

6. $27 \div 3 = \blacksquare$
$3 \times 9 = 27; 9$

7. $\blacksquare = 4 \div 4$
$4 \times 1 = 4; 1$

8. $30 \div 3 = \blacksquare$
$3 \times 10 = 30; 10$

9. $16 \div 4 = \blacksquare$
$4 \times 4 = 16; 4$

10. $18 \div 3 = \blacksquare$
$3 \times 6 = 18; 6$

11. $\blacksquare = 20 \div 4$
$4 \times 5 = 20; 5$

Copy and complete each table.

12.

÷	9	12	15	18
3	■	■	■	■
	3	4	5	6

13.

÷	16	20	24	28
4	■	■	■	■
	4	5	6	7

Find each quotient.

14. $12 \div 4 = \blacksquare$ 3

15. $\blacksquare = 6 \div 3$ 2

16. $\blacksquare = 14 \div 2$ 7

17. $12 \div 2 = \blacksquare$ 6

18. $15 \div 3 = \blacksquare$ 5

19. $25 \div 5 = \blacksquare$ 5

20. $24 \div 4 = \blacksquare$ 6

21. $\blacksquare = 40 \div 4$ 10

22. $\blacksquare = 18 \div 2$ 9

23. $32 \div 4 = \blacksquare$ 8

24. $\blacksquare = 9 \div 3$ 3

25. $30 \div 5 = \blacksquare$ 6

26. $3\overline{)3}$ 1

27. $3\overline{)18}$ 6

28. $4\overline{)36}$ 9

29. $5\overline{)20}$ 4

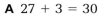 **ALGEBRA** Complete.

30. $20 \div 4 = 8 - \blacksquare$ 3

31. $24 \div 3 = \blacksquare \times 2$ 4

32. $36 \div \blacksquare = 18 \div 2$ 4

33. Yusef collected 38 pinecones. He
kept 11 pinecones for himself and
divided the rest equally among
3 friends. How many pinecones
did each friend get?
9 pinecones

34. The scouts saw squirrels and
birds. If there were 4 animals and
12 legs, how many squirrels and
birds were there? Draw a picture
to show your answer. 2 squirrels and
2 birds; check students' drawings.

35. **REASONING** Two numbers have a
product of 16 and a quotient of
4. What are they? 8 and 2

36. 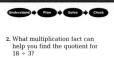 Write About It Explain how to
solve $32 \div 4$ in 2 different ways.
Possible answers: $4 \times 8 = 32$; draw an
array with 4 rows of 8 to find $32 \div 4 = 8$.

Getting Ready for the EOG Test

37. John has 27 books divided equally among
3 shelves. Which number sentence could
you use to find the number of books on
each shelf? D

A $27 + 3 = 30$

C $3 \times 3 = 9$

B $27 - 3 = 24$

D $27 \div 3 = 9$

Chapter 13 **261**

North Carolina Standards 1.03 Develop fluency with multiplication from 1×1 to 12×12 and division
to two-digit by one-digit numbers using: a) Strategies for multiplying and dividing numbers.

Independent Practice

Note that Exercises 33–34 are **multistep or
strategy problems.** Assign Exercises 6–36.

SCAFFOLDED INSTRUCTION Use the
prompts on Transparency 13 to guide
instruction for the multistep or strategy
problem in Exercise 33.

Transparency **13**

 4 ASSESS

Summarize the lesson by having students:

**DISCUSS How do you know what multiplication
fact will help you find a quotient?** One of the
factors is the divisor. The product should equal the
dividend. The missing factor is equal to the quotient.

 **WRITE What are four methods you can
use to solve division problems?** Possible
answers: model groups with counters, use repeated
subtraction, use a related multiplication fact, use a
multiplication table

LESSON QUIZ

Write the multiplication fact you can
use to find the quotient. Then write
the quotient.

Transparency **13.2**

1. $18 \div 3 = \blacksquare$ $3 \times 6 = 18; 6$

2. $12 \div 4 = \blacksquare$ $4 \times 3 = 12; 3$

3. $28 \div 4 = \blacksquare$ $4 \times 7 = 28; 7$

4. $27 \div 3 = \blacksquare$ $3 \times 9 = 27; 9$

Challenge 13.2

The Same and Different

Divide. In each row, circle the problem that is different
from the other problems in that row. Explain how the
remaining problems are alike.
Answers may vary. Possible answers are given.

1. $24 \div 3 =$ __8__   **2.** $40 \div 4 =$ __10__   **3.** $15 \div 3 =$ __5__

quotients are even numbers

4. $36 \div 4 =$ __9__   **5.** $32 \div 4 =$ __8__   **6.** $18 \div 3 =$ __6__

quotients are even numbers

7. $20 \div 4 =$ __5__   **8.** $21 \div 3 =$ __7__   **9.** $12 \div 3 =$ __4__

quotients are odd numbers

10. $16 \div 4 =$ __4__   **11.** $9 \div 3 =$ __3__   **12.** $6 \div 3 =$ __2__

quotient is same as divisor

13. $30 \div 3 =$ __10__   **14.** $8 \div 4 =$ __2__   **15.** $20 \div 4 =$ __5__

quotients are divisible by 5

16. Write two division problems that are alike in some
way and one division problem that is different in
some way. Have a classmate solve your problems
and tell which two problems are alike and why.

___ ÷ ___ = ___   ___ ÷ ___ = ___   ___ ÷ ___ = ___

Check students' work.

W68 **Challenge**

Problem Solving 13.2

Divide by 3 and 4   Understand → Plan → Solve → Check

Write the correct answer.

1. Mario's rock collection has
7 rows of rocks. Each row has
5 rocks. How many rocks are in
Mario's collection?

35 rocks

2. What multiplication fact can
help you find the quotient for
$18 \div 3$?

$3 \times 6 = 18$

3. What dividend is missing from
the table? What quotient?

÷	4	8	12	16	20	■
4	1	■	3	4	5	6

24; 2

4. Homer has $24 to buy sheets of
music. Each sheet of music costs
$3. How many sheets of music
can he buy?

8

Choose the letter of the correct answer.

5. Which clock shows 2 hours
after 7:15?

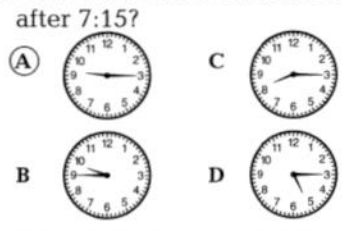

Ⓐ   C

B   D

6. Summer is the favorite season
of 12 students. Fall is the
favorite of 8 students. How
many more students prefer
summer than fall?

F 2   H 6
Ⓖ 4   J 8

7. Anna is filling 4 pages of a report
with 24 pictures. If she puts the
same number of pictures on each
page, how many pictures will
there be on each page?

A 24   C 8
B 20   Ⓓ 6

8. What multiplication fact can
you use to help you find the
quotient for $24 \div 3$?

Ⓕ $3 \times 8 = 24$
G $6 \times 4 = 24$
H $9 \times 6 = 54$
J $5 \times 4 = 20$

9. **Write About It** How can repeated subtraction help
you solve Problem 4?

Possible answer: I can subtract 3 from 24 until I reach 0. I reach
0 after 8 subtractions.

PS68 **Problem Solving**

261

Lesson Planning

PROFESSIONAL DEVELOPMENT

Objective To divide with 1 and 0

NCTM Standards
1. Number and Operations
7. Reasoning and Proof
8. Communication

Math Background
These rules will help students divide with 1 and 0.

- Any number divided by 1 equals that number. Guide students to understand that 9 ÷ 1 means "How many groups of 1 are in 9?"

- Any number (except 0) divided by itself equals 1. Think: How many groups of 9 are in 9?

- Zero divided by any number (except 0) equals 0. Think: How many sets of 9 are in zero?

- You cannot divide by 0. It is impossible to divide a group into 0 sets.

Warm-Up Resources

Number of the Day

Transparency **13.3**

The number of the day is the number of hours in one day. A work shift lasts 8 hours. Find the number of shifts in one full day. 3 shifts

Daily Facts Practice

Have students practice multiplication facts by completing Set F of *Teacher's Resource Book,* p. TR92.

Transparency **13.3**

Problem of the Day

Jannelle has 50 pennies. How many pennies will she put in a group if she wants to exchange them for nickels? for dimes? for quarters? 5 pennies; 10 pennies; 25 pennies

Solution Problem of the Day tab, p. PD13.

Intervention and Extension Resources

Alternative Teaching Strategy

MATERIALS *For each student* 5 counters

ESOL/ESL

Help students **model division with 1 and 0**. Read the following problem. Have students use counters to model the problem and answer the questions.

- Tim's garden has 5 tomato plants, divided among 5 rows. How many plants are in each row? 1 plant
- Write a division sentence to explain your answer. $5 \div 5 = 1$
- What happens when the dividend and divisor are the same? The quotient is 1.
- Suppose all the tomato plants were removed. How many tomato plants are in the garden? 0 plants
- Now divide the 0 plants in the garden into 5 rows. How many plants are in each row? 0 plants. Write a division sentence to explain your answer. $0 \div 5 = 0$

KINESTHETIC

BODILY/KINESTHETIC, LOGICAL/MATHEMATICAL

Multistep and Strategy Problems

The following multistep or strategy problem is provided in Lesson 13.3:

Page	Item
263	43

Social Studies Connection

MATERIALS *For each group* encyclopedia or reference book

Help students **understand 0**. Many scholars believe that the ancient Hindus first developed the number zero, possibly as far back as the third century A.D. The Hindu symbol for zero was a heavy dot, called *sunya*, which meant *void* or *empty*. Have students research other ways zero has been used or is being used and share their research with the class. Possible answer: Zero is represented with the symbol 0, or omicron, a letter in the Greek alphabet.

VISUAL

VISUAL/SPATIAL

Early Finishers

Help students **reinforce division with 1 and 0**. Have students complete the following table by writing and solving the division facts through 9. The first 3 examples are shown.

$1 \div 1 = \blacksquare\ 1$ $1 \div 1 = \blacksquare\ 1$ $0 \div 1 = \blacksquare\ 0$

$2 \div 2 = \blacksquare\ 1$ $2 \div 1 = \blacksquare\ 2$ $0 \div 2 = \blacksquare\ 0$

$3 \div 3 = \blacksquare\ 1$ $3 \div 1 = \blacksquare\ 3$ $0 \div 3 = \blacksquare\ 0$

Check students' work.

VISUAL

VISUAL/SPATIAL, LOGICAL/MATHEMATICAL

Technology Link

Intervention, *Skill 24*

Math Jingles® CD 3–4 • *Track 7*

Lesson 13.3 Organizer

Objective To divide with 1 and 0

1 INTRODUCE

QUICK REVIEW provides review of prerequisite skills.

WHY LEARN THIS? When you understand the rules for dividing with 1 and 0, you don't have to memorize division facts for them. *Share the lesson objective with students.*

2 TEACH

Guided Instruction

- *Introduce Rules A and B.*
  What is another situation that could be used to describe the division sentence 3 ÷ 1 = 3?
  Possible answer:

  $$3 \quad ÷ \quad 1 \quad = \quad 3$$
  ↑ ↑ ↑
  number of | number of | number of people
  people | boats | in each boat

  Write another situation that could describe the division sentence 3 ÷ 3 = 1.
  Possible answer:

  $$3 \quad ÷ \quad 3 \quad = \quad 1$$
  ↑ ↑ ↑
  number of | number of | number of people
  people | cars | in each car

- *Discuss Rule C.*
  How can you use multiplication to check 0 ÷ 3 = 0? Show that the divisor, 3, multiplied by the quotient, 0, equals the dividend, 0.

- *Check students' understanding of Rule D.*
  Compare dividing by 1 in Rule A to dividing by 0 in Rule D. You divide by 1 because there is 1 stall; if there are no stalls, you can't divide.

262 Chapter 13

LESSON 3 Divide with 1 and 0

Quick Review
1. $8 \times \blacksquare = 8$ 1
2. $3 \times 0 = \blacksquare$ 0
3. $\blacksquare \times 1 = 4$ 4
4. $0 \times 10 = \blacksquare$ 0
5. $1 \times \blacksquare = 7$ 7

▶ **Learn**

MOO . . . VE OVER Here are some rules for dividing with 1 and 0.

RULE A

Any number divided by 1 equals that number.

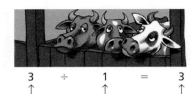

$$3 \quad ÷ \quad 1 \quad = \quad 3$$
↑ ↑ ↑
number of | number of | number in
cows | stalls | each stall

If there is only 1 stall, then all of the cows must be in that stall.

RULE B

Any number (except 0) divided by itself equals 1.

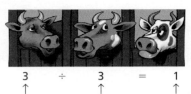

$$3 \quad ÷ \quad 3 \quad = \quad 1$$
↑ ↑ ↑
number of | number of | number in
cows | stalls | each stall

If there are the same number of cows and stalls, then one cow goes in each stall.

RULE C

Zero divided by any number (except 0) equals 0.

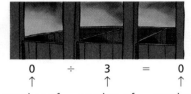

$$0 \quad ÷ \quad 3 \quad = \quad 0$$
↑ ↑ ↑
number of | number of | number in
cows | stalls | each stall

If there are no cows, then no matter how many stalls you have, there won't be any cows in the stalls.

RULE D

You cannot divide by 0.

If there are no stalls, then you aren't separating cows into equal groups. So, using division doesn't make sense.

- **REASONING** How can you use multiplication to show that $3 ÷ 0 = \blacksquare$ doesn't make sense? **Possible answer: There is no number that can be multiplied by 0 to get 3, so dividing by 0 doesn't make sense.**

262

Reteach 13.3

Divide with 1 and 0

$6 ÷ 6 = ?$ Divide 6 counters into 6 groups.	$6 ÷ 1 = ?$ Divide 6 counters into 1 group.	$0 ÷ 6 = ?$ Divide 0 counters into groups of 6.
●●●●●●	●●●●●●	
There is 1 in each group. $6 ÷ 6 = 1$	There are 6 in each group. $6 ÷ 1 = 6$	There are 0 groups. $0 ÷ 6 = 0$
Any number divided by itself is 1.	Any number divided by 1 is that number.	Zero divided by any number is 0.

Find each quotient.

1. $8 ÷ 8 =$ ⊿1
2. $4 ÷ 1 =$ ④
3. $0 ÷ 5 =$ ☐0
4. $7 ÷ 1 =$ ⑦
5. $3 ÷ 3 =$ ⊿1
6. $9 ÷ 9 =$ ⊿1
7. $0 ÷ 3 =$ ☐0
8. $1 ÷ 1 =$ ⊿1
9. $0 ÷ 7 =$ ☐0
10. $8 ÷ 1 =$ ⑧
11. $2 ÷ 2 =$ ⊿1
12. $4 ÷ 4 =$ ⊿1
13. $7 ÷ 7 =$ ⊿1
14. $5 ÷ 1 =$ ⑤
15. $0 ÷ 2 =$ ☐0

Look at Exercises 1–15 again. If a number is divided by itself, put a triangle around the quotient. If a number is divided by 1, put a circle around the quotient. If the dividend is 0, put a box around the quotient.

Find each missing factor.

16. $1 \times \underline{8} = 8$
17. $7 \times \underline{0} = 0$
18. $1 \times \underline{5} = 5$
19. $\underline{0} \times 8 = 0$
20. $4 \times \underline{1} = 4$
21. $\underline{3} \times 1 = 3$
22. $\underline{1} \times 3 = 3$
23. $\underline{0} \times 3 = 0$
24. $6 \times \underline{1} = 6$

Reteach RW69

Practice 13.3

Divide with 1 and 0

Find each quotient.

1. $7 ÷ 7 = \underline{1}$
2. $0 ÷ 5 = \underline{0}$
3. $4 ÷ 1 = \underline{4}$
4. $8 ÷ 1 = \underline{8}$
5. $6 ÷ 6 = \underline{1}$
6. $0 ÷ 3 = \underline{0}$
7. $2 ÷ 2 = \underline{1}$
8. $0 ÷ 8 = \underline{0}$
9. $2 ÷ 1 = \underline{2}$
10. $0 ÷ 4 = \underline{0}$
11. $3 ÷ 1 = \underline{3}$
12. $5 ÷ 5 = \underline{1}$
13. $4 ÷ 4 = \underline{1}$
14. $9 ÷ 1 = \underline{9}$
15. $0 ÷ 2 = \underline{0}$
16. $7 ÷ 1 = \underline{7}$
17. $9 ÷ 9 = \underline{1}$
18. $6 ÷ 1 = \underline{6}$
19. $0 ÷ 1 = \underline{0}$
20. $0 ÷ 9 = \underline{0}$
21. $3 ÷ 3 = \underline{1}$

Compare. Write <, >, or = for each ◯.

22. $7 ÷ 7$ ⊙< $7 ÷ 1$
23. $9 ÷ 9$ ⊙= $10 - 9$
24. $5 ÷ 1$ ⊙< $5 + 1$
25. $0 ÷ 6$ ⊙< $6 + 0$
26. $2 + 4$ ⊙> $0 ÷ 6$
27. $3 ÷ 1$ ⊙= 3×1

Mixed Review

Solve.

28. $\begin{array}{r} 475 \\ -352 \\ \hline 123 \end{array}$
29. $\begin{array}{r} 450 \\ +640 \\ \hline 1,090 \end{array}$
30. $\begin{array}{r} 7,991 \\ -4,328 \\ \hline 3,663 \end{array}$
31. $\begin{array}{r} 665 \\ +392 \\ \hline 1,057 \end{array}$
32. $\begin{array}{r} \$3.67 \\ +\$2.33 \\ \hline \$6.00 \end{array}$
33. $\begin{array}{r} \$4.27 \\ +\$3.59 \\ \hline \$7.86 \end{array}$
34. $\begin{array}{r} \$28.95 \\ -\$17.60 \\ \hline \$11.35 \end{array}$
35. $\begin{array}{r} \$13.40 \\ -\$11.72 \\ \hline \$1.68 \end{array}$

Find each missing number.

36. $6 ÷ \underline{3} = 2$
37. $8 ÷ \underline{2} = 4$
38. $\underline{4} ÷ 4 = 1$
39. $\underline{21} ÷ 7 = 3$

Practice PW69

Check

1. **Explain** how you can use multiplication to check $0 \div 9 = 0$. **Possible answer: Check that the divisor multiplied by the quotient equals the dividend; $9 \times 0 = 0$**

Find each quotient.

2. $3 \div 3 = $ ■ **1**   3. ■ $= 5 \div 1$ **5**   4. $0 \div 2 = $ ■ **0**   5. ■ $= 6 \div 6$ **1**

6. $7 \div 1 = $ ■ **7**   7. $0 \div 6 = $ ■ **0**   8. ■ $= 4 \div 4$ **1**   9. $10 \div 1 = $ ■ **10**

Practice and Problem Solving
Extra Practice, page 268, Set C

Find each quotient.

10. $2 \div 1 = $ ■ **2**   11. $8 \div 8 = $ ■ **1**   12. ■ $= 6 \div 3$ **2**   13. $1 \div 1 = $ ■ **1**

14. $20 \div 5 = $ ■ **4**   15. ■ $= 0 \div 4$ **0**   16. ■ $= 5 \div 5$ **1**   17. $10 \div 2 = $ ■ **5**

18. $3 \div 1 = $ ■ **3**   19. $21 \div 3 = $ ■ **7**   20. $32 \div 4 = $ ■ **8**   21. ■ $= 0 \div 7$ **0**

22. ■ $= 0 \div 8$ **0**   23. $18 \div 2 = $ ■ **9**   24. ■ $= 9 \div 1$ **9**   25. $24 \div 4 = $ ■ **6**

26. Divide 2 by 2. **1**   27. Divide 4 by 1. **4**   28. Divide 0 by 3. **0**   29. Divide 14 by 2. **7**

30. $5\overline{)35}$ **7**   31. $9\overline{)9}$ **1**   32. $2\overline{)16}$ **8**   33. $5\overline{)0}$ **0**   34. $2\overline{)14}$ **7**

35. $3\overline{)18}$ **6**   36. $1\overline{)8}$ **8**   37. $4\overline{)36}$ **9**   38. $7\overline{)7}$ **1**   39. $1\overline{)0}$ **0**

ALGEBRA Compare. Write $<$, $>$, or $=$ for each ●.

40. $4 \div 1$ ● $4 \div 4$ **>**   41. $0 \div 9$ ● $9 \div 1$ **<**   42. $6 + 4$ ● $5 \div 1$ **>**

43. A farmer has 6 bales of hay. He feeds 2 bales to his cows. He divides the rest equally among 4 stalls. How many bales are in each stall? **1 bale of hay**

44. **REASONING** Chelsea says, "Ask me to divide any number by 1, and I'll give you the quotient." What is her strategy? **Any number divided by 1 is that number.**

45. Use what you know about 0 and 1 to find each quotient.
   a. $398 \div 398 = $ ■ **1**   b. $971 \div 1 = $ ■ **971**   c. $0 \div 426 = $ ■ **0**

Getting Ready for the EOG Test

46. Which division sentence shows the number of ears of corn on each plate? **D**

   A $5 \div 5 = 1$ **C** $10 \div 1 = 10$
   B $0 \div 10 = 0$ **D** $10 \div 2 = 5$

*North Carolina Standards 1.03 Develop fluency with multiplication from 1×1 to 12×12 and division to two-digit by one-digit numbers using: a) Strategies for multiplying and dividing numbers.

Challenge 13.3

Writing Equations

In each table below, the numbers in the ☐ column are dividends. The numbers in the △ column are quotients. Find the divisor that works for each table. Then, write the equation below the table, and complete the table. The first equation has been written for you.

1.
☐	△
4	2
8	4
0	0
6	3
10	5
20	10
14	7

Equation:
$☐ \div 2 = △$

2.
☐	△
15	3
35	7
10	2
25	5
5	1
0	0
45	9

Equation:
$☐ \div 5 = △$

3.
☐	△
20	5
16	4
4	1
12	3
8	2
36	9
0	0

Equation:
$☐ \div 4 = △$

4.
☐	△
12	2
24	4
6	1
30	5
42	7
0	0
18	3

Equation:
$☐ \div 6 = △$

5.
☐	△
12	4
27	9
6	2
3	1
0	0
18	6
9	3

Equation:
$☐ \div 3 = △$

6.
☐	△
4	4
8	8
7	7
5	5
0	0
3	3
2	2

Equation:
$☐ \div 1 = △$

Challenge **CW69**

Problem Solving 13.3

Divide with 1 and 0

Understand → Plan → Solve → Check

Write the correct answer.

1. What happens when you divide a number by 1?

   The quotient is that number.

2. What is zero divided by eight?

   0

3. If 4 math groups share 4 sets of flashcards equally, how many sets will each group get?

   1 set

4. Mr. Olson needs 16 batteries. There are 4 batteries in each pack. How many packs should he buy?

   4 packs of batteries

Choose the letter of the correct answer.

5. What is the quotient when a number is divided by itself?

   A 2   **C** zero
   B that number   **D** 1

6. Which number is thirteen thousand, nine hundred seventeen in standard form?

   F 3,917   **H** 13,917
   G 3,970   **J** 30,917

7. Bob had $3.50. He loaned his brother $1.65. How much does Bob have left?

   A $1.80
   B $1.85
   C $1.95
   D $2.25

8. Namie had $6. She earned $1 and spent $2.25 on a snack. How much does she have now?

   F $4.75
   G $5.75
   H $7.25
   J $9.25

9. **Write About It** How did you choose the operation you used to solve Problem 3?

   Possible answer: I divided because I needed to find how many sets each group should get.

Problem Solving **PS69**

COMMON ERROR ALERT

Students may try to divide by zero. Remind students that they can't have zero divisions, so 0 can never be a divisor.

$$8 \div 0 =$$

3 PRACTICE

Guided Practice

Do Check Exercises 1–9 with your students. Identify students who are having difficulty and choose appropriate lesson resources to provide assistance.

Independent Practice

Note that Exercise 43 is a **multistep or strategy problem.** Assign Exercises 10–45.

4 ASSESS

Summarize the lesson by having students:

Discuss How does knowing the rules for dividing with 1 and 0 help you learn division facts more easily? If you learn the rules for 1 and 0, you have fewer division facts to memorize.

Write What is the missing dividend for ■ $\div 8 = 0$? How do you know? 0; The quotient multiplied by the divisor equals the dividend. Since the quotient is 0, the dividend must be 0. **What examples can you give in which the quotient is 1?** Possible answers: $8 \div 8 = 1$, $6 \div 6 = 1$

LESSON QUIZ
Find each quotient.

Transparency
13.3

1. $6 \div 6 = $ ■ **1**   2. $6 \div 1 = $ ■ **6**

3. $0 \div 6 = $ ■ **0**   4. $0 \div 4 = $ ■ **0**

5. $9 \div 1 = $ ■ **9**   6. $7 \div 7 = $ ■ **1**

Lesson Planning

PROFESSIONAL DEVELOPMENT

Objective To write expressions and equations that represent situations

NCTM Standards

1. Number and Operations
2. Algebra
6. Problem Solving
8. Communication

Math Background

These ideas will help students understand how to write expressions and equations.

- An expression is part of a number sentence. It contains only numbers and symbols. It does not have an equal sign.

- You can use operation symbols (+ , −, ×, ÷) and numbers to write an expression that describes a problem.

- An equation contains numbers, symbols, and an equal sign. It shows that two amounts are equal.

Vocabulary

equation a number sentence that uses an equal sign to show that two amounts are equal.

Warm-Up Resources

Build Number Sense 3 2 1

Number of the Day

Transparency 13.4

If you divide this number by 3, the quotient is 8. What is the quotient if the number is divided by 4?
6

Review Basic Facts 8 +3

Daily Facts Practice

Have students practice multiplication facts by completing Set G of *Teacher's Resource Book*, p. TR92.

Solve a Problem

Transparency 13.4

Problem of the Day

Joey wants to plant 4 rows of beans with 5 bean seeds in each row. He also plans to plant 3 pepper seeds in each of the 4 rows. How many seeds will he need in all? 32 seeds

Solution Problem of the Day tab, p. PD13.

Intervention and Extension Resources

Alternative Teaching Strategy

MATERIALS *For each student* 22 small squares of paper

Help students **model equations**. On six of the squares, have students write the symbols $+$, $-$, $\times$, $\div$, $=$, and $\neq$. On the remaining squares, have them write the following numbers: 21, 3, 4, 5, 16, 35, 36, 20, 7, 18, 10, 12, 6, 24, 30, 15. Then have students combine the squares to form equations. Check students' work.

KINESTHETIC, VISUAL

BODILY/KINESTHETIC, VISUAL/SPATIAL

Multistep and Strategy Problems

The following multistep or strategy problem is provided in Lesson 13.4:

Page	Item
265	9

Writing in Mathematics

Have students **write expressions using each of the four operation symbols.** Have them exchange their expressions with a partner, who will write the equations and solve. Check students' work.

Early Finishers

Help students **reinforce the concept of writing expressions.** Have students list the number of a particular object they have at home, such as games, CDs, or books. Then ask them to write expressions about the objects, similar to the following examples.

I had 20 CDs. I received 3 more for my birthday. $20 + 3$

I had 20 CDs. I gave 4 to my friend. $20 - 4$ Check students' work.

VISUAL

VERBAL/LINGUISTIC

Technology Link

Intervention, *Skill 28*

Lesson 13.4 Organizer

Objective To write expressions and equations that represent situations

Vocabulary equation *Review* expression

Algebra: Expressions and Equations

1 INTRODUCE

QUICK REVIEW provides review of prerequisite skills.

WHY LEARN THIS? You can write an expression or an equation to help solve a word problem. *Share the lesson objective with students.*

2 TEACH

Guided Instruction

- *Direct students' attention to the Remember box and the definition of equation.*
  REASONING What is the difference between an expression and an equation? An expression is only part of a number sentence. An equation is a number sentence that has an equal sign; an expression does not.
  Write an equation for each of the expressions. $3 + 4 = 7$, $25 - 12 = 13$, $4 \times 2 = 8$, $12 \div 6 = 2$

- *Discuss the Happy Campers problem.*
  How do you know when to use a division symbol? Possible answer: when you see words or phrases in the problem such as *divided, 3 equal groups, how many in each group*
  What equation includes the expression $21 \div 3$? $21 \div 3 = 7$

- *Check students' understanding of the relay race problem.*
  Give an example of a multiplication number sentence using the symbol $\neq$. Possible answer: $6 \times 7 \neq 40$.

3 PRACTICE

Guided Practice

Do Check Exercises 1–6 with your students. Identify students who are having difficulty and choose appropriate lesson resources to provide assistance.

▶ Learn

HAPPY CAMPERS The 21 campers were divided into 3 equal groups. How many campers are in each group?

Write an expression to show how many campers are in each group.

21 campers	divided into	3 groups
↓	↓	↓
21	÷	3

You can use the expression to write an equation. An **equation** is a number sentence. It uses an equal sign to show that two amounts are equal. Use the equation to solve the problem.

21 campers	divided into	3 groups	is equal to	7 campers in each group.
↓	↓	↓	↓	↓
21	÷	3	=	7

So, there are 7 campers in each group.

Mr. Gonzales is lining up 4 rows of 5 campers for relay races. There are 20 campers lined up.

$$4 \; \bullet \; 5 = 20$$

Which symbol will complete the equation?

Try $+$ $4 + 5 \neq 20$
Try $-$ $4 - 5 \neq 20$
Try $\div$ $4 \div 5 \neq 20$
Try $\times$ $4 \times 5 = 20$

So, the correct symbol is $\times$.

▶ Check

1. **Write** an expression to describe the relay race problem above. **Possible answer:** $5 + 5 + 5 + 5$

264

Reteach 13.4

Algebra: Expressions and Equations

An expression is part of an equation. You can use the operation symbols ($+, -, \times, \div$) in expressions to show how to solve problems.

To choose an operation symbol for an expression, think about how the action is taking place.

Multiply	**Add**
• Combine equal groups.	• Combine groups.
Six friends each ate 4 crackers. How many crackers did the friends eat altogether?	The friends ate 3 crackers the first hour. They ate 7 crackers the second hour. How many crackers did they eat in all?
the expression: 6×4	the expression: $3 + 7$
Divide	**Subtract**
• Share equally. • Make equal groups.	• Take away. • Compare. • Separate.
Three friends shared 15 crackers equally. How many crackers did each friend get?	Bill ate 3 fewer crackers than Jane. Jane ate 5 crackers. How many crackers did Bill eat?
the expression: $15 \div 3$	the expression: $5 - 3$

Write an expression to describe each problem.

1. Five friends each made 8 greeting cards. How many greeting cards did the friends make altogether?
5×8

2. Mel made 9 greeting cards. He sent 6 of them. How many greeting cards does he have left?
$9 - 6$

Write an equation to solve.

3. Erin made 4 greeting cards. Louise made 5 greeting cards. How many greeting cards did they make altogether?
$4 + 5 = 9$ cards

4. Sarah bought 30 stamps for her greeting cards. The stamps came in 5 equal rows. How many stamps were in each row?
$30 \div 5 = 6$ stamps

RW70 **Reteach**

Practice 13.4

Algebra: Expressions and Equations

Write an expression to describe each problem.

1. Kim has 18 craft sticks. His mother gives him 3 more. How many craft sticks does he have now?
$18 + 3$

2. Four students share 36 tacks. How many tacks does each student get?
$36 \div 4$

3. Beth has an album with 9 pages. She can fit 8 photos on each page. How many photos can be in the album?
9×8

4. Tim stacked 20 blocks. He then took away 8 of them. How many blocks remained in the stack?
$20 - 8$

Write an equation to solve.

5. Vinnie is 5 years younger than Carly. Vinnie is 15 years old. How old is Carly?
$15 + 5 = 20$ years old

6. Mindy has $1.00. She spends $0.85 on lunch. How much money does she have left?
$\$1.00 - \$0.85 = \$0.15$

7. Pauline has 35 baseball cards. She buys 5 more cards. How many cards does she have altogether?
$35 + 5 = 40$ cards

8. Matthew is 2 times as old as Greg. Greg is 6 years old. How old is Matthew?
$2 \times 6 = 12$ years old

Mixed Review

Add, subtract, multiply, or divide.

9. $\begin{array}{r} 6 \\ \times 3 \\ \hline 18 \end{array}$

10. $\begin{array}{r} 45 \\ +68 \\ \hline 113 \end{array}$

11. $\begin{array}{r} 101 \\ -73 \\ \hline 28 \end{array}$

12. $5\overline{)45}^{\,9}$

Write the missing number in each problem.

13. $\begin{array}{r} 3,672 \\ +348 \\ \hline 4,020 \end{array}$

14. $\begin{array}{r} 888 \\ -565 \\ \hline 323 \end{array}$

15. $\begin{array}{r} 4 \\ \times 9 \\ \hline 36 \end{array}$

16. $9\overline{)36}^{\,4}$

PW70 **Practice**

Write an expression to describe each problem.

2. Nine campers each ate 7 carrot sticks. How many carrot sticks did the campers eat in all? 9×7

3. Jo had 9 carrot sticks. She ate 7 of them. How many carrot sticks does she have left? $9 - 7$

Write +, −, ×, or ÷ to complete the equation.

4. $9 = 18 \underset{-}{\bullet} 9$

5. $6 \times 6 = 4 \underset{\times}{\bullet} 9$

6. $72 \underset{\div}{\bullet} 8 = 3 \times 3$

▶ Practice and Problem Solving   Extra Practice, page 268, Set D

Write an expression to describe each problem.

7. On the nature hike, Beth picked up two pinecones. There were 48 seeds in one and 55 seeds in the other. How many seeds were in the two pinecones in all?
$48 + 55$

8.  **FAST FACT • SCIENCE** About 65 species of pine trees grow in North America. Thirty-six of them grow in the United States. How many do not grow in the United States?
$65 - 36$

Write an equation to solve.

9. Matt and 7 other campers made bird feeders from pinecones and peanut butter. They shared 40 pinecones equally. How many pinecones did each camper use?
$40 \div 8 = 5$; 5 pinecones

10. Vocabulary Power A *symbol* can be used to show something easily and quickly. A stop sign is a symbol that tells drivers to stop. Name other symbols that you see every day. **Possible answers: traffic lights, rest room signs, traffic signs; math symbols such as operation signs, comparison symbols, dollar and cent symbols**

Write +, −, ×, or ÷ to complete the equation.

11. $13 \underset{-}{\bullet} 7 = 2 \times 3$

12. $12 + 5 = 9 \underset{+}{\bullet} 8$

13. $6 \times 4 = 8 \underset{\times}{\bullet} 3$

14. ✎ **Write a problem** for each expression.

a. $35 \div 5$ **b.** 7×3 **c.** $15 - 3$
Check students' problems.

Getting Ready for the EOG Test

15. Jenny and her sister went to the store and bought the crayons shown in the picture. Which number sentence shows how many crayons are in each box? **C**

A $2 \times 5 = 10$ **C** $15 \div 3 = 5$
B $15 - 5 = 10$ **D** $15 \div 5 = 3$

North Carolina Standards maintains (2) Goal 5 The learner will recognize and represent patterns simple mathematical relationships.

Challenge 13.4

Write a Problem

Write an expression that describes each picture. Then write a word problem to go with the picture and the expression.
Answers may vary. Possible answers are given.

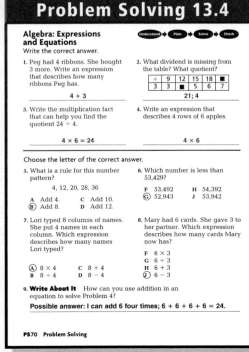

1.
Expression: $8 \div 2$

The Problem
A pet store has 8 kittens. It keeps an equal number of kittens in each of two cages. How many kittens are in each cage?

2.
Expression: $6 + 5$

The Problem
Six birds are sitting in a tree. Five more birds join them. How many birds are in the tree now?

3.
Expression: $9 - 3$

The Problem
The boy had 9 balloons. Three of the balloons blew away. How many balloons does he have now?

4.
Expression: 5×8

The Problem
The grocery store displays apples in 5 equal rows of 8 apples. How many apples are in the display?

W70   Challenge

Problem Solving 13.4

Algebra: Expressions and Equations

Understand ➡ Plan ➡ Solve ➡ Check

Write the correct answer.

1. Peg had 4 ribbons. She bought 3 more. Write an expression that describes how many ribbons Peg has.
$4 + 3$

2. What dividend is missing from the table? What quotient?

÷	9	12	15	18	■
3	3	■	5	6	7

$21; 4$

3. Write the multiplication fact that can help you find the quotient $24 \div 4$.
$4 \times 6 = 24$

4. Write an expression that describes 4 rows of 6 apples.
4×6

Choose the letter of the correct answer.

5. What is a rule for this number pattern?
4, 12, 20, 28, 36
A Add 4.   C Add 10.
Ⓑ Add 8.   D Add 12.

6. Which number is less than 53,429?
F 53,492   H 54,392
Ⓖ 52,943   J 53,942

7. Lori typed 8 columns of names. She put 4 names in each column. Which expression describes how many names Lori typed?
Ⓐ 8×4 C $8 + 4$
B $8 \div 4$ D $8 - 4$

8. Mary had 6 cards. She gave 3 to her partner. Which expression describes how many cards Mary now has?
F 6×3
G $6 \div 3$
H $6 + 3$
Ⓙ $6 - 3$

9. **Write About It** How can you use addition in an equation to solve Problem 4?
Possible answer: I can add 6 four times; 6 + 6 + 6 + 6 = 24.

PS70   Problem Solving

Independent Practice

Note that Exercise 9 is a **multistep or strategy problem**. Assign Exercises 7–14.

Vocabulary Power Have students make a list of all of the math symbols they know and what they stand for. Suggest students choose a symbol and find its history and/or give examples of how it is used. Have students report their findings to the class. Check students' work.

ALGEBRAIC THINKING For Exercises 7–8, remind students that they just need to write an expression, not an equation, to describe each problem, and no solution is required.

4 ASSESS

Summarize the lesson by having students:

DISCUSS Give an example of an expression using each of the operation symbols. Possible answers: $2 + 3$, $16 - 12$, 4×9, $25 \div 5$

WRITE Write a word problem for the situation described by the expression $10 - 4$. Check students' work.

LESSON QUIZ
Write an equation to describe each problem.

Transparency **13.4**

1. Shauna picked 10 apples, 6 pears, and 8 oranges. How many pieces of fruit did she pick altogether? $10 + 6 + 8 = 24$

2. Yogurt cups come in packages of 4. How many packages do you need for a class of 28 students? $28 \div 4 = 7$

3. Chris planted 4 rows of 7 tiger lilies each. How many tiger lilies did he plant? $4 \times 7 = 28$

Lesson Planning

PROFESSIONAL DEVELOPMENT

Objective To use the problem solving skill *choose the operation* to solve problems

Lesson Resources Reading Transparency 13; Intervention • Problem Solving, Strategy/Skill 13

NCTM Standards
1. Number and Operations
6. Problem Solving
8. Communication

Math Background

These ideas will help students use the problem solving skill *choose the operation*.

- Use addition to join groups of different sizes; use subtraction to take away or compare amounts.

- Use multiplication to join equal groups; use division to separate into equal groups or to find the number in each group.

- Use operation symbols ($+$, $-$, $\times$, $\div$), numbers, and an equal sign ($=$) to write a number sentence or equation.

Warm-Up Resources

Number of the Day

Transparency
13.5

The number of the day is 4. Write expressions using each of the four operations with this number.
Possible answers: 4×2, $12 \div 4$, $4 + 12$, $14 - 4$

Daily Facts Practice

Have students practice multiplication facts by completing Set A of *Teacher's Resource Book*, p. TR93.

Solve a Problem

Transparency
13.5

Problem of the Day

Billy's mother cut each of 2 pizzas into 6 pieces. Billy and 3 of his friends shared the pieces equally. How many pieces did each of them get? 3 pieces

Solution Problem of the Day tab, p. PD13.

Intervention and Extension Resources

Alternative Teaching Strategy

Have students **practice choosing operations**. The following questions are only parts of word problems. Read each question and have students choose the operation that would help answer the question.

- How many are in each group? divide
- How many are there in all? add or multiply
- How much more does Carol have than Stephen? subtract
- How many apples are in the 3 baskets? add or multiply
- How many equal groups are there? divide

AUDITORY

VERBAL/LINGUISTIC

Reading Strategy

Use Context Context includes words or phrases that help you understand the meaning of the word. Have students copy Exercises 1 and 2 on PE page 267. Then have them

- circle important numbers and their labels.
- highlight words or phrases that help them decide what operation to use.
- use all this information to write number sentences.
- solve. Check students' work.

 13 **Reading Transparency 13**

Multistep and Strategy Problems

The following multistep and strategy problems are provided in Lesson 13.5:

Page	Item
267	1–4, 7–8

ESOL/ESL

MATERIALS *For each pair* 4 index cards

Help students **review the four operations**. Using the chart on PE page 266 as a guide, have pairs of students copy 4 word problems you have displayed on the front of the index cards. Ask students to underline the words that help them decide which operation to use. On the reverse side, have students draw the operation symbol and write the name of the operation. Students may take turns quizzing each other by reading the problem, paying close attention to the underlined words, and having their partner identify the operation.

While working on exercises, have students use these cards to help them choose the correct operation. Check students' work.

AUDITORY

VERBAL/LINGUISTIC, INTERPERSONAL/SOCIAL

Early Finishers

Help students **select operation symbols to make number sentences true**.

Have students copy the following number sentences and make them true by changing the operation symbols.

$25 + 5 = 5 \div$

$9 \div 4 = 36 \times$

$10 \div 5 = 15 +$

$18 \div 6 = 12 -$

Have students write their own false number sentences, exchange with a partner, and change the operation symbols to make the number sentences true. Check students' work.

VISUAL

VISUAL/SPATIAL, VERBAL/LINGUISTIC

Technology Link

Intervention • Problem Solving, *Strategy/Skill 13*

Lesson 13.5 Organizer

Objective To use the problem solving skill *choose the operation* to solve problems

Lesson Resources Reading Transparency 13; Intervention • Problem Solving, Strategy/Skill 13

1 INTRODUCE

QUICK REVIEW provides review of prerequisite skills.

WHY LEARN THIS? You'll be able to solve real-world problems when you know which operation to use. *Share the lesson objective with students.*

2 TEACH

Guided Instruction

- *Have students read the Nature Walk problem.*
  What information is not needed to solve the problem? The campers saw 6 chipmunks, 4 deer, and 8 butterflies.
  How do you know that you are joining equal groups? Since there are 3 turtles on each of 4 rocks, you put together 4 groups of 3 to find the total number of turtles.
  How can you check your answer? by adding 4 groups of 3; $3 + 3 + 3 + 3 = 12$

- *Direct students' attention to the chart.*
  How can you use the chart? Possible answer: It can help you decide what operation to use when solving a problem.
  When would you use division to solve a problem? Give an example. Possible answer: to find the number in each group; there are 6 turtles with the same number on each of 3 rocks, so, there are 2 turtles on each rock.

LESSON 5 Problem Solving Skill
Choose the Operation

UNDERSTAND ▶ PLAN ▶ SOLVE ▶ CHECK

NATURE WALK On a hike, the campers saw 6 chipmunks, 4 deer, and 8 butterflies. They also saw 3 turtles on each of 4 large rocks. How many turtles did they see in all?

This chart can help you decide when to use each operation.

ADD	• Join groups of different sizes.
SUBTRACT	• Take away. • Compare amounts.
MULTIPLY	• Join equal groups.
DIVIDE	• Separate into equal groups. • Find the number in each group.

 MATH IDEA Before you solve a problem, decide what operation to use. Write an equation to solve the problem.

Since you are joining equal groups, multiply.

$$4 \quad \times \quad 3 \quad = \quad 12$$

number of rocks	number of turtles on each rock	total number of turtles

So, they saw 12 turtles in all.

- **REASONING** When would you use division to solve a problem? **Possible answer: Use division to separate into equal groups.**
- Write an equation to find how many animals they saw in all. $6 + 4 + 8 + 12 = 30$

266

Reteach 13.5

Problem Solving Skill

Choose the Operation

The table below shows examples of problems in which you add, subtract, multiply, or divide.

There are 18 children and 6 adults at the park. How many people are at the park?	**Add** - You are joining groups of different size. $18 + 6 = 24$ 24 people
There are 10 boys and 8 girls at the park. How many more boys are there than girls?	**Subtract** - You are comparing two different amounts. $10 - 8 = 2$ 2 more boys
There are 3 sets of swings. Each swing set has 4 swings. How many swings are there in all?	**Multiply** - You are joining groups of equal size. $3 \times 4 = 12$ 12 swings
The 18 students in a class divide into teams of 6 to play a game. How many teams of students are there?	**Divide** - You are separating a total into groups of equal size. $18 \div 6 = 3$ 3 teams

Choose the operation you need to use. Write *add, subtract, multiply,* or *divide*. Then solve.

1. Mrs. Shaw buys 6 packages of muffins. There are 4 muffins in each package. How many muffins does she buy?

   multiply;
   _____
   24 muffins

2. Louisa bakes 12 small cookies and 9 large cookies. How many cookies does she bake in all?

   add;
   _____
   21 cookies

3. Mr. Mason uses 20 apples to make pies. He uses 5 apples in each pie. How many pies does he make?

   divide;
   _____
   4 pies

4. A large pizza costs $9.00, and a small pizza costs $5.25. How much more does the large pizza cost than the small one?

   subtract;
   _____
   $3.75

Reteach RW71

Practice 13.5

Problem Solving Skill

Choose the Operation

Choose the operation. Write an equation. Then solve.

1. There are 9 mice in each cage. There are 3 cages. How many mice are there in all?

   $9 \times 3 = 27;$
   _____
   27 mice

2. Izzy and Tom are cats. Izzy weighs 9 pounds and Tom weighs 12 pounds. How much more does Tom weigh than Izzy?

   $12 - 9 = 3;$
   _____
   3 pounds

3. Mrs. Ellis buys 9 cans of cat food. She already has 8 cans of cat food at home. How many cans does she have now?

   $9 + 8 = 17;$
   _____
   17 cans

4. Mr. Davis has 24 goldfish. He puts 8 fish in each fish bowl. How many fish bowls does he use?

   $24 \div 8 = 3;$
   _____
   3 bowls

Mixed Review

5. $0 \div 3 =$ __0__

6. $18 \div 2 =$ __9__

7. $42 + 39 + 72 =$ __153__

8. $742 - 329 =$ __413__

9. Divide 30 by 3. __10__

10. Divide 36 by 4. __9__

11. $\begin{array}{r} 4,422 \\ - 3,795 \\ \hline 627 \end{array}$

12. $\begin{array}{r} 6,219 \\ - 1,706 \\ \hline 4,513 \end{array}$

13. $\begin{array}{r} 3,290 \\ + 2,416 \\ \hline 5,706 \end{array}$

14. $\begin{array}{r} 5,554 \\ - 4,787 \\ \hline 767 \end{array}$

Find each missing factor, divisor, or quotient.

15. __6__ $\times 4 = 24$

16. $49 \div$ __7__ $= 7$

17. $35 \div 5 =$ __7__

18. $8 \times$ __8__ $= 64$

Practice PW71

Problem Solving

Choose the operation. Write an equation. Then solve.

1. David collected 8 acorns and 16 wildflowers. He put the same number of wildflowers in each of 8 vases. How many wildflowers were in each vase? $16 \div 8 = 2$; **2 wildflowers**

2. The camp counselor put 4 pears, 5 apples, and 7 bananas in a basket. If 3 pieces of fruit were eaten, how many pieces of fruit were left? $4 + 5 + 7 = 16$; $16 - 3 = 13$; **13 pieces of fruit**

3. Beth has a scrapbook. Each page can hold 8 small postcards or 6 large postcards. How many small postcards fit on 4 pages? $4 \times 8 = 32$; **32 postcards**

4. Shawn took 8 photos of birds, 9 photos of wildflowers, and 15 photos of campers. How many photos did he take? $8 + 9 + 15 = 32$; **32 photos**

Thirty students went on a camp cookout. Six students sat at each picnic table. How many tables did they fill?

5. Which number sentence can you use to solve the problem? **C**

   A $30 + 6 = $ ▪   C $30 \div 6 = $ ▪
   B $30 - 6 = $ ▪   D $30 \times 6 = $ ▪

6. What is the answer to the question? **G**

   F 24 students
   G 5 tables
   H 5 students
   J 1 table

Mixed Applications

USE DATA For 7–9, use the graph.

7. Gina took 5 packs of soda to the cookout. Were there enough bottles of soda for 28 people? Explain. **Yes; There were 30 bottles of soda.**

8. Khar bought 3 packs of water. He gave 4 bottles to friends. How many bottles of water did he have left? **20 bottles**

9. ❓ **What's the Question?** The answer is 30 bottles of juice.
   Possible question: How many bottles of juice are in 3 packs?

NUMBER OF BOTTLES IN A PACK	
Soda	🍾🍾🍾
Juice	🍾🍾🍾🍾🍾
Water	🍾🍾🍾🍾

Key: Each 🍾 = 2 bottles.

North Carolina Standards 1.06 Develop flexibility in solving problems by selecting strategies and ing mental computation, estimation, calculators or computers, and paper and pencil.

Challenge 13.5

Solving Problems at the Aquarium

Aquarium	Admission	Sea Lion Show
🐟	$6 adults $4 children under 12 $45 Family membership— free admission for one year	10:30, 12:00, 1:30, 3:00

1. Mr. and Mrs. Young and their 6-year-old triplets go to the aquarium. How much do they pay?
   $24.00 (or $45 for 1 yr. membership)

2. The sea lion show lasts 45 minutes. How much time is there between shows?
   45 min

3. The theater where the sea lions perform can seat 600 people. There are 475 people sitting in the theater for the 12:00 show. How many more people can be seated before the theater is full?
   125 more people

4. Mr. Ruiz buys a family membership. He goes to the aquarium with his 4-year-old son 6 times during the year. How much money does he save?
   $15.00

5. A class of 24 students visits the aquarium. They divide into 4 groups. How many students are in each group?
   6 students

6. John buys a book about sharks for $4.95 and a shell for $1.35. How much money does he spend?
   $6.30

7. Meg counts 12 starfish and 9 hermit crabs in a display. How many more starfish are there than hermit crabs?
   3 more starfish

8. Jesse learned that a seahorse egg hatches in 50 to 60 days. About how many weeks is this?
   about 8 weeks

Challenge CW71

Reading Strategy 13.5

Follow Directions   Understand ➤ Plan ➤ Solve ➤ Check

The first thing to do when you start your homework is to read the directions. Reading and following directions will help you to solve problems correctly.

Here are examples of direction lines you have seen in your math book. After each direction is a problem. Write what task, operation, or process you are asked to do. Then solve the problem. **Possible answers are given.**

1. Write the value of the underlined digit.   1**5**6
   Look at the underlined digit and then write its value; **50**

2. Find the sum. $8 + 5$
   Add the numbers and write the answer; **13**

3. Find the difference. $8 - 5$
   Subtract the numbers and write the answer; **3**

4. Write >, <, or = for the ●.   8 ● 5
   Compare the numbers.Then write the correct symbol to make the expression true; **>**

5. Write in order from greatest to least.   21, 37, 18, 14
   Put the numbers in order. Start with the greatest number; **37, 21, 18, 14**

6. Write + or − to make the number sentence true.   9 ● 7 = 2
   Decide if addition or subtraction would make the number sentence true. Then write + or − where the ● is; **−**

7. Write the product. 8×5
   Multiply the numbers and write the answer; **40**

Reading Strategy PS71

---

3 **PRACTICE**

Guided Practice

Do Problem Solving Practice Exercises 1–6 with your students. Identify students who are having difficulty and choose appropriate lesson resources to provide assistance. Note that Exercises 1–4 are **multistep or strategy problems.**

Independent Practice

Note that Exercises 7 and 8 are **multistep or strategy problems.** Assign Exercises 7–9.

4 **ASSESS**

Summarize the lesson by having students:

DISCUSS Why is it important to decide what operation to use before solving a problem? You need to know what operation to use before you can write an equation and solve.

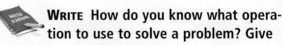

WRITE How do you know what operation to use to solve a problem? Give an example. Possible answer: The operation depends on the problem and the information given; answers will vary.

LESSON QUIZ

Choose the operation. Write an equation. Then solve.

Transparency **13.5**

1. Richard planted 3 rows of onions with 4 plants in each row. How many plants were there in all? $3 \times 4 = 12$; **12 plants**

2. Carrie bought a package of 8 pens. Her sister, Lily, bought a box of 20 pens. How many more pens does Lily have than Carrie? $20 - 8 = 12$; **12 more pens**

3. David picked 16 oranges and 8 apricots. He put the same number of oranges in each of 8 bags. How many oranges were in each bag? $16 \div 8 = 2$; **2 oranges**

CHAPTER 13 Extra Practice

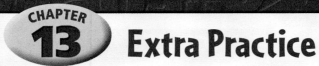

Purpose To provide extra practice for the skills presented in this chapter

The blue page references in each set of exercises refer to the lesson pages where each skill is taught.

Internet Resources

Visit **THE LEARNING SITE** at **www.harcourtschool.com** for a listing of practice activities.

Extra Practice

Set A (pp. 258–259)

Find each missing factor and quotient.

1. $2 \times \blacksquare = 10$ 5 $10 \div 2 = \blacksquare$ 5
2. $5 \times \blacksquare = 30$ 6 $30 \div 5 = \blacksquare$ 6

Find each quotient.

3. $15 \div 5 = \blacksquare$ 3
4. $\blacksquare = 16 \div 2$ 8
5. $\blacksquare = 45 \div 5$ 9
6. $10 \div 5 = \blacksquare$ 2
7. $2\overline{)2}$ 1
8. $5\overline{)20}$ 4
9. $2\overline{)18}$ 9
10. $5\overline{)25}$ 5
11. $2\overline{)12}$ 6
12. Divide 20 by 2. 10
13. Divide 35 by 5. 7
14. Divide 6 by 2. 3

Set B (pp. 260–261)

Write the multiplication fact you can use to find the quotient. Then write the quotient.

1. $18 \div 3 = \blacksquare$
   $3 \times 6 = 18$; 6
2. $32 \div 4 = \blacksquare$
   $4 \times 8 = 32$; 8
3. $9 \div 3 = \blacksquare$
   $3 \times 3 = 9$; 3

Find each quotient.

4. $28 \div 4 = \blacksquare$ 7
5. $12 \div 3 = \blacksquare$ 4
6. $\blacksquare = 27 \div 3$ 9
7. $\blacksquare = 8 \div 4$ 2
8. $4\overline{)16}$ 4
9. $3\overline{)15}$ 5
10. $4\overline{)24}$ 6
11. $3\overline{)21}$ 7
12. $4\overline{)12}$ 3
13. Divide 30 by 3. 10
14. Divide 20 by 4. 5
15. Divide 36 by 4. 9

Set C (pp. 262–263)

Find each quotient.

1. $0 \div 4 = \blacksquare$ 0
2. $\blacksquare = 3 \div 3$ 1
3. $\blacksquare = 8 \div 1$ 8
4. $10 \div 10 = \blacksquare$ 1
5. $7\overline{)7}$ 1
6. $8\overline{)0}$ 0
7. $1\overline{)4}$ 4
8. $3\overline{)0}$ 0
9. $9\overline{)9}$ 1

Set D (pp. 264–265)

Write an expression to describe each problem.

1. Four friends share 28 stickers equally. How many stickers does each friend get? $28 \div 4$
2. Melinda had $15. She buys slippers for $8. How much money does she have now?
   $15 - $8

Write +, −, ×, or ÷ to complete the equation.

3. $6 \times 3 = 12 \blacksquare 6$ +
4. $5 \times 7 = 38 \blacksquare 3$ −
5. $24 \div 3 = 4 \blacksquare 2$ ×

268

Review/Test

✓ CHECK VOCABULARY

Choose the best term from the box.

equation
divided
multiplied
zero

1. You cannot divide by _?_. (p. 262) **zero**

2. Any number (except 0) _?_ by itself equals 1. (p. 262) **divided**

3. A number sentence like $12 \div 2 = 6$ or $3 \times 5 = 15$ is called an _?_. (p. 264) **equation**

✓ CHECK SKILLS

Find each quotient. (pp. 258–263)

4. $16 \div 4 = \blacksquare$ **4**   5. $\blacksquare = 21 \div 3$ **7**   6. $6 \div 1 = \blacksquare$ **6**   7. $\blacksquare = 25 \div 5$ **5**

8. $8 \div 2 = \blacksquare$ **4**   9. $0 \div 5 = \blacksquare$ **0**   10. $\blacksquare = 9 \div 3$ **3**   11. $\blacksquare = 8 \div 1$ **8**

12. $4\overline{)32}$ **8**   13. $1\overline{)10}$ **10**   14. $2\overline{)18}$ **9**   15. $3\overline{)0}$ **0**   16. $5\overline{)15}$ **3**

17. $2\overline{)14}$ **7**   18. $3\overline{)15}$ **5**   19. $5\overline{)0}$ **0**   20. $4\overline{)24}$ **6**   21. $5\overline{)40}$ **8**

Write an expression to describe each problem. (pp. 264–265)

22. Lila made 18 muffins. She put 3 muffins in each bag. How many bags did Lila fill? **18 ÷ 3**

23. Kyle had 32 shells. He gave 8 to his friend. How many shells does Kyle have now? **32 − 8**

✓ CHECK PROBLEM SOLVING

Choose the operation. Write an equation. Then solve. (pp. 266–267)

24. Chiang has 24 trading cards. She puts the cards into piles of 6. How many piles does she make? **24 ÷ 6 = 4; 4 piles**

25. Casey has 5 packs of stickers. Each pack has 8 stickers. How many stickers does he have? **5 × 8 = 40; 40 stickers**

Chapter 13 269

Review/Test

Purpose To check understanding of concepts, skills, and problem solving presented in Chapter 13

Using the Page

The Chapter 13 Review/Test can be used as a **review** or a **test**.

- Items 1–3 check understanding of concepts and new vocabulary.
- Items 4–23 check skill proficiency.
- Items 24–25 check students' abilities to choose and apply problem solving strategies to real-life division problems.

 Suggest that students place the completed Chapter 13 Review/Test in their portfolios.

Using the Assessment Guide

- Multiple-choice format of Chapter 13 Posttest— See *Assessment Guide*, pp. AG81–82.
- Free-response format of Chapter 13 Posttest— See *Assessment Guide*, pp. AG83–84.

Using Student Self-Assessment

The How Did I Do? survey helps students assess what they have learned and how they learned it. This survey is available as a copying master in *Assessment Guide*, p. AGxvii.

Chapter 13 Test, page 1

Choose the correct answer.

1. What number completes both number sentences?

   $5 \times \blacksquare = 30$ $30 \div 5 = \blacksquare$

   A 7   C 5
   B 6   D 4

2. $2\overline{)14}$

   F 16   H 7
   G 12   J 6

3. $2\overline{)18}$

   A 8   C 14
   B 9   D 16

4. Amber has 40 stickers. She divides the stickers equally among her 5 friends. How many stickers does each friend get?

   F 10   H 6
   G 8   J 5

5. Eric has 25 pennies. He spends 5 of them to buy a pencil and divides the rest equally among his 4 sisters. How many pennies does each sister get?

   A 20   C 5
   B 16   D 1

6. Two numbers have a product of 16 and a quotient of 1. What are the numbers?

   F 8 and 2   H 4 and 4
   G 6 and 3   J 3 and 3

7. Which number completes the number sentence?

   $27 \div \blacksquare = 18 \div 2$

   A 3   C 8
   B 6   D 9

8. $24 \div 3 = \blacksquare$

   F 27   H 8
   G 21   J 7

9. Which multiplication fact can be used to find $32 \div 4$?

   A $2 \times 16 = 32$
   B $4 \times 8 = 32$
   C $4 \times 9 = 36$
   D $4 \times 10 = 40$

10. $0 \div 4 = \blacksquare$

    F 0   H 2
    G 1   J 4

11. What symbol makes this number sentence true?

    $0 \div 9 \bullet 8 \div 8$

    A <   B >   C =

   Go On

Chapter 13 Test, page 2

12. $8 \div 1 = \blacksquare$

    F 0   H 8
    G 1   J 9

13. Tyler has 3 bags of carrots. There are 10 carrots in each bag. Which expression shows the number of carrots Tyler has in all?

    A $10 \div 3$ C $10 + 10 + 3$
    B $10 - 3$ D 10×3

14. Dennis had 28 packages of raisins. He gave 4 packages to each of his friends. Which expression shows the number of friends that received raisins?

    F $28 \div 4$ H $28 + 28$
    G $28 - 4$ J $4 + 4$

15. A pet store has 8 puppies. Each puppy gets 2 treats each day. Which expression shows the number of treats that are needed each day?

    A $8 \div 2$ C $8 \div 2$
    B 8×2 D $2 + 2 + 2$

16. Sean saw 3 ducks flying overhead and 6 ducks swimming in the pond. Which expression shows the number of ducks he saw in all?

    F 6×3
    G $6 \div 3$
    H $6 - 3$
    J $6 + 3$

17. Miss Jana received 20 flowers from her students. Each student brought 2 flowers. Which number sentence shows how to find the number of students who brought flowers?

    A $20 \div 2 = 10$
    B $20 - 2 = 18$
    C $20 + 2 = 22$
    D $20 + 20 = 40$

18. Each box contains 6 candy bars. Which number sentence shows how to find the number of bars in 3 boxes?

    F $6 \div 3 = 2$
    G $6 - 3 = 3$
    H $3 + 6 = 9$
    J $3 \times 6 = 18$

19. Mrs. Walls received 5 pieces of mail on Monday and 10 on Tuesday. Which number sentence shows how to find the number of pieces she received in all?

    A $10 \div 5 = 2$
    B $10 - 5 = 5$
    C $10 + 5 = 15$
    D $10 \times 5 = 50$

20. Jon has 18 games. Barry has 6 games. Which number sentence shows how to find how many more games Jon has than Barry?

    F $6 + 6 + 6 = 18$
    G $18 + 6 = 3$
    H $6 + 18 = 24$
    J $18 - 6 = 12$

   Stop

CHAPTER 13

Getting Ready for the EOG Test

Chapters 1–13

Using the Pages

These pages may be used to help students get ready for the North Carolina EOG Test. The test items are written in the same style and arranged in the same format as those on the EOG Test.

The pages are cumulative. They cover the standards from the North Carolina Mathematics Standard Course of Study that have been taught up to this point in the text or in a previous grade. Each Getting Ready for the EOG Test also reviews the North Carolina mathematics strands shown below.

• Number and Operations

• Measurement

• Geometry

• Data Analysis and Probability

• Algebra

These pages can be assigned at the end of the chapter as classwork or as a homework assignment. You may want to have students use individual recording sheets presented in a multiple-choice (standardized) format. A Test Answer Sheet is available as a black-line master in the *Assessment Guide* (p. AGlii).

You may wish to have students describe how they solved each problem and share their solutions.

Getting Ready for the EOG Test

⭐ **NUMBER AND OPERATIONS**

1. Joe wrote these multiplication facts.

$4 \times 6 = 24 \qquad 6 \times 4 = 24$

Which division fact belongs to the same fact family as these multiplication facts? **D**

A $24 \div 2 = 12$
B $24 \div 3 = 8$
C $24 \div 8 = 3$
D $24 \div 6 = 4$

2. Which division fact does the picture show? **B**

3 rows of 7 = 21

A $24 \div 3 = 8$ C $12 \div 3 = 4$
B $21 \div 3 = 7$ D $12 \div 6 = 2$

3. Ella bakes 18 muffins. She puts 3 muffins in each bag. How many bags does Ella use? **B**

A 9   C 4
B 6   D 3

4. Explain It Todd said that both of these multiplication facts should be completed with the same number. Do you agree? Tell why or why not.

$8 \times \blacksquare = 8 \qquad 5 \times \blacksquare = 5$
See page 271.

270

⭐ **DATA ANALYSIS AND PROBABILITY**

5. The pictograph shows the goals scored. What information does the key tell you? **D**

GOALS SCORED	
Dave	⚽⚽⚽
Gina	⚽⚽
Kyle	⚽⚽⚽⚽
Melanie	⚽⚽⚽⚽⚽⚽
Zack	⚽⚽⚽

Key: Each ⚽ = 3 goals.

A how many goals Gina scored
B how many players are on a soccer team
C the total number of goals scored by the team
D what each ball stands for

6. Look at the pictograph above. Which players scored an equal number of goals? **B**

A Gina and Kyle
B Dave and Zack
C Kyle and Melanie
D Dave and Gina

7. Explain It Tell how you can use the pictograph above to order the players from *least* to *greatest* number of goals scored. Then order the players. **See page 271.**

⭐ ALGEBRA

8. Which numbers complete this table? **C**

×	4	5			
5	20	25	30	35	40

A 4, 5, 6
B 5, 6, 7
C 6, 7, 8
D 7, 8, 9

> **TIP** **Get the information you need.** See item 9. Determine how the numbers are alike. The answer describes these common characteristics.

9. How would you describe this group of numbers? **A**

1, 3, 5, 9

A odd numbers less than 10
B odd numbers greater than 1
C odd numbers less than 6
D odd numbers greater than 8

10. Explain It Katie practiced the piano for 15 minutes on Monday, 30 minutes on Tuesday, and 45 minutes on Wednesday. If this pattern continues, how long will she practice the piano on Friday? Explain how you found your answer. **See below.**

⭐ MEASUREMENT AND GEOMETRY

11. Which figure shows a line of symmetry? **A**

A. 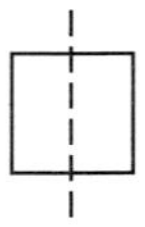   C.

B. 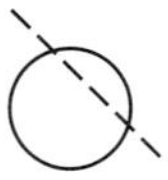   D.

12. Diane has 3 feet of wire. How many inches of wire does she have? **D**

A 12 inches
B 18 inches
C 24 inches
D 36 inches

13. Tim had $4.75. He bought markers and construction paper for $2.89. How much money did he have left? **D**

A $7.64
B $2.86
C $2.14
D $1.86

14. Explain It Jean traced the top of this solid figure on a sheet of paper. What figure appeared on her paper? Explain how you found your answer.
See below.

Chapters 1–13

Item Analysis

You may wish to use the item analysis to determine which North Carolina standards need additional review.

Item	North Carolina Standard	Lesson
1	1.03	12.4
2	1.03	13.2
3	1.03	13.2
4	1.04	11.4
5	(2) 4.01	Grade 2
6	(2) 4.01	Grade 2
7	(2) 4.01	Grade 2
8	5.01	8.2
9	5.01	2.1
10	5.01	2.5
11	(2) 3.03	Grade 2
12	(2) 2.01	Grade 2
13	Goal 2	6.4
14	(2) 3.02	Grade 2

SCORING RUBRIC
Explain It

2 Demonstrates a complete understanding of the problem and chooses an appropriate strategy to determine the solution

1 Demonstrates a partial understanding of the problem and chooses a strategy that does not lead to a complete and accurate solution

0 Demonstrates little understanding of the problem and shows little evidence of using any strategy to determine a solution

Explain It • Written Response

4. Possible answer: yes; according to the Identity Property, any number multiplied by 1 equals that number.

7. Possible answer: compare the number of soccer balls shown beside each player's name. The players in order are Gina, Dave, Zack, Kyle, and Melanie.

10. 1 hour 15 minutes; Possible answer: the pattern is to add 15 minutes to the previous time.

14. A circle; possible answer: the top and bottom of a cylinder are circles.

Division Facts Through 10

NCTM Standards 2000

1. Number and Operations *Lessons 14.1, 14.2, 14.3, 14.4, 14.5*	6. Problem Solving *Lessons 14.1, 14.2, 14.3, 14.4, 14.5*
2. Algebra *Lessons 14.1, 14.2, 14.3, 14.4*	7. Reasoning and Proof *Lessons 14.1, 14.2, 14.3, 14.4, 14.5*
3. Geometry	8. Communication *Lessons 14.1, 14.2, 14.3, 14.4, 14.5*
4. Measurement	9. Connections *Lessons 14.1, 14.2, 14.3, 14.4*
5. Data Analysis and Probability	10. Representation *Lessons 14.1, 14.2, 14.3, 14.4, 14.5*

Chapter Planner

Getting Ready for Chapter 14 • Assessing Prior Knowledge and INTERVENTION (See PE and TE page 273.)

LESSON	NORTH CAROLINA STANDARDS	PACING	VOCABULARY*	MATERIALS	RESOURCES AND TECHNOLOGY
14.1 Divide by 6, 7, and 8 pp. 274–277 **Objective** To divide by 6, 7, and 8	1.03a	2 Days			Reteach, Practice, Problem Solving, Challenge 14.1 Transparency 14.1 **Intervention**, *Skills 22, 32–34, 62* (CD or Book) **Harcourt Mega Math The Number Games,** *Up, Up, and Array*
14.2 Divide by 9 and 10 pp. 278–279 **Objective** To divide by 9 and 10	1.03a	1 Day			Reteach, Practice, Problem Solving, Challenge 14.2 Scaffolded Instruction Transparency 14 Transparency 14.2 **Intervention**, *Skills 22, 32–34, 62* (CD or Book) **Harcourt Mega Math The Number Games,** *Up, Up, and Array*
14.3 Practice Division Facts pp. 280–283 **Objective** To practice division facts through 10 by using various strategies	1.03a	1 Day			Reteach, Practice, Problem Solving, Challenge 14.3 Transparency 14.3 **Intervention**, *Skills 22, 32–34, 62* (CD or Book) **Harcourt Mega Math Ice Station Exploration,** *Arctic Algebra* **Math Jingles® CD 3–4**
14.4 Algebra: Find the Cost pp. 284–285 **Objective** To use multiplication and division to find the cost of multiple items or the cost of one item	1.03a	1 Day			Reteach, Practice, Problem Solving, Challenge 14.4 Transparency 14.4 **Intervention**, *Skills 22, 32–34, 62* (CD or Book) **Math Jingles® CD 3–4**
14.5 Problem Solving Strategy: Work Backward pp. 286–287 **Objective** To use the problem solving strategy *work backward* to solve problems	1.06	1 Day		🖩	Reteach, Practice, Reading Strategy, Challenge 14.5 Transparency 14.5 Reading Transparency 14 **Intervention • Problem Solving,** *Strategy/Skill 14* (CD or Book)

Ending Chapter 14 • **Extra Practice,** p. 288 • **Chapter 14 Review/Test,** p. 289 • **Getting Ready for the EOG Test,** pp. 290–291

Ending Unit 4 • **It's in the Bag,** p. 292; **Challenge,** p. 293; **Study Guide and Review,** pp. 294–295; **Performance Assessment,** p. 296; **Technology Linkup,** p. 297; **Problem Solving in North Carolina,** pp. 298–299

Vocabulary Power

MATH Word Work

Objective To reinforce vocabulary concepts
Use after Lesson 14.1.

Materials *For each pair* color tiles

Have students work in pairs. One partner uses color tiles to model a division fact. The other partner draws the model of that division fact and writes the number sentence. Have this partner label the *dividend, divisor,* and *quotient* in the number sentence. Students trade roles and repeat the activity.

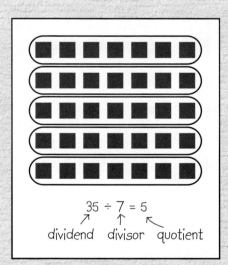

CHAPTER 14 · Division Facts Through 10

Mathematics Across the Grades

LOOKING BACK • Prerequisite Skills

To be ready for Chapter 14, students should have the following understandings and skills:

- **Vocabulary**—*quotient, dividend,* and *divisor*

- **Commutative Property of Multiplication**—use the Commutative Property of Multiplication to find products

- **Division Facts Through 5**—divide by 1, 2, 3, 4, and 5

- **Missing Factors**—find the missing factor in a multiplication sentence

Check What You Know

Use page 273 to determine students' knowledge of prerequisite concepts and skills.

Intervention

Help students prepare for the chapter by using the intervention resources described on TE page 273.

LOOKING AT CHAPTER 14 • Essential Skills

Students will

- **divide by 6, 7, and 8.**

- divide by 9 and 10.

- practice division facts through 10 by using various strategies.

- use multiplication and division to find the cost of multiple items or the cost of one item.

- use the problem solving strategy *work backward* to solve problems.

Example

Find the quotient.

$$8\overline{)32}$$

Strategy	Answer
Use the related multiplication fact. Think: $8 \times \blacksquare = 32$ $8 \times 4 = 32$	$8\overline{)32}^{\,4}$ So, the quotient of $32 \div 8$ is 4.

LOOKING AHEAD • Applications

Students will apply what they learn in Chapter 14 to the following new concepts:

- Change Units (Chapter 17)

- Divide with Remainders (Chapter 30)

- Divide by 1-Digit Numbers (Chapter 30)

- Divide by 2-Digit Numbers (Grade 4)

Differentiated Instruction

FROM RESEARCH TO PRACTICE

Meeting the Needs of All Learners

Extra Support	Activities for All	Enrichment
Alternative Teaching Strategy TE Lessons 14.1, 14.2, 14.3, 14.4, 14.5 **ESOL/ESL** TE Lessons 14.1, 14.2, 14.3, 14.4, 14.5	**Cross-Curricular Connections** **Reading:** TE Lesson 14.5 **Science:** TE Lesson 14.1 **Social Studies:** Chapter Opener **Vocabulary:** TE p. 272B, PE/TE p. 273, TE Lesson 14.1 **Writing:** TE Lessons 14.2, 14.3	**Advanced Learners** TE Lessons 14.3, 14.4 **Early Finishers** TE Lessons 14.2, 14.4, 14.5

Combination and Multi-age Classrooms

Grade 2	Grade 3	Grade 4
Skills Trace Across the Grades		
Relate addition and multiplication; use arrays; explore equal sizes of groups and equal numbers of groups.	**Divide by 6, 7, 8, 9, and 10; practice division facts through 10; write the unit or total cost of multiple items.**	Relate multiplication and division; multiply facts through 12; write expressions with multiplication and division; multiply with tens and 1- and 2-digit numbers.
Instructional Strategies		
Students on this level may require more time to build conceptual understanding. **Assignments** **Grade 3 Pupil Edition** • Have students work in pairs on Lessons 14.1 and 14.2. • Skip Lesson 14.4. **Grade 2 Pupil Edition**—pages 529–536	Students on this level should be able to complete all the lessons in the Pupil Edition and all the activities in the Teacher's Edition with minimal adjustments. **Assignment** **Grade 3 Pupil Edition**—pages 272–289	Students on this level will probably require less time to build conceptual understanding. **Assignments** **Grade 3 Pupil Edition** • Compact Lessons 14.1 and 14.2. **Grade 4 Pupil Edition**—pages 162–201

Division Facts Through 10

Introducing the Chapter

Remind students that division involves separating equal groups. Have students focus on the picture and ask them to write a number sentence to describe how many slices of pizza each person can have if 4 people share a pizza with 8 slices. 8 ÷ 4 = 2 slices

Using Data

To begin the study of this chapter, have students

- Find which restaurant has the fewest pieces of pepperoni per slice and which has the most, if each pizza has 8 slices. Mario's Pizza has the fewest and Broadway Pizza has the most.

- Determine how many pieces of pepperoni are on each slice of a pizza at Lorenzo's Pizza if it is divided into 6 slices. 8 pieces of pepperoni

- Determine how many pieces of pepperoni each person will get if 5 students equally divide a pizza from Mamma Mia's. 8 pieces of pepperoni

Problem Solving Project

Purpose To use division facts through 10 to solve a problem

Grouping small groups

Materials construction paper and scissors

Background One of the largest pizzas ever made had a diameter of 122 feet. A pizza that large can feed over 11,000 people.

UNDERSTAND • PLAN • SOLVE • CHECK

Have students

- Make pizzas and pepperoni slices out of construction paper.

- Cut the pizzas so that each person in the group has 2 equal slices of pizza with the same number of pepperoni pieces on each slice.

- Write a division sentence to represent the problem and the solution. Check students' work.

Graphing Investigations
Begin Week 14.

Division Facts Through 10

≡**FAST FACT** • SOCIAL STUDIES The first pizzeria in the United States was opened in 1905 in New York City. America's favorite pizza topping is pepperoni.

PROBLEM SOLVING Suppose each pizza in the table is cut into 8 slices and the pieces of pepperoni are divided equally among the 8 slices. How many pieces of pepperoni are on 1 slice of pizza from each restaurant?

PEPPERONI PIZZA	
Restaurant	Pieces of Pepperoni
Mario's Pizza	32
Broadway Pizza	56
Mamma Mia's	40
Lorenzo's Pizza	48

Mario's Pizza, 4; Broadway Pizza, 7; Mamma Mia's, 5; Lorenzo's Pizza, 6

272

WHY LEARN MATH? Restaurateurs use division when making decisions about ordering food. Ask: If the restaurant has 35 pounds of carrots and it uses 7 pounds of carrots per day in salads, how many days' worth of carrots does the restaurant have? 5 days

Family Involvement Activities

These activities provide:

- Letter to the Family
- Math Vocabulary
- Family Game
- Practice (Homework)

Family Involvement Activities, p. FA53

HARCOURT MATH	Name
GRADE 3	Date
Chapter 14	
WHAT WE ARE LEARNING	**Dear Family,**
Division Facts Through 10	Your child is learning to divide by 6, 7, 8, 9, and 10.
	Your child has learned to understand division in these ways:
VOCABULARY	• As repeated subtraction
Here are the vocabulary words we continue to use in class:	• As arrays showing a group as smaller equal groups
	• As the inverse of multiplication
Factor One of the numbers in a multiplication problem	• As part of a table of division facts
Factor × Factor = Product	Use the example here and the activity that follows to help your child find the cost of one item. Encourage your child to do this activity with you and other members of your family.
Quotient The answer in a division problem	
Dividend ÷ Divisor = Quotient	To help guide your child's thinking, ask questions such as these:
Fact family A set of numbers that form related multiplication and division number sentences	Six tickets cost $42. Find the cost of 1 ticket.	If $42 is the total cost for 6 tickets, what operation can you use to find the cost of 1 ticket?
The numbers 3, 5, and 15 form a fact family.	42 ÷ 6 = ▢	What multiplication fact can you use to find 42 ÷ 6?
3 × 5 = 15, 5 × 3 = 15, 15 ÷ 3 = 5, and 15 ÷ 5 = 3.	Think: 6 × 7 = 42 So, the cost of 1 ticket is $7.	
Inverse operations Opposite operations such as addition and subtraction or multiplication and division	Knowing division facts through 10 will help your child divide greater numbers later in the year. Being able to find the total cost and the cost of one item are useful shopping skills.	
	Sincerely,	

Family Involvement Activities FA53

CHECK WHAT YOU KNOW

Use this page to help you review and remember
important skills needed for Chapter 14.

✓ COMMUTATIVE PROPERTY OF MULTIPLICATION

Use the Commutative Property of Multiplication to help you
find each product.

1. $7 \times 8 = \blacksquare$ 56 $8 \times 7 = \blacksquare$ 56   2. $6 \times 8 = \blacksquare$ 48 $8 \times 6 = \blacksquare$ 48

3. $7 \times 9 = \blacksquare$ 63 $9 \times 7 = \blacksquare$ 63   4. $6 \times 10 = \blacksquare$ 60 $10 \times 6 = \blacksquare$ 60

✓ DIVISION FACTS THROUGH 5

Find each quotient.

5. $35 \div 5 = \blacksquare$ 7   6. $8 \div 2 = \blacksquare$ 4   7. $20 \div 4 = \blacksquare$ 5   8. $0 \div 5 = \blacksquare$ 0

9. $\blacksquare = 18 \div 3$ 6   10. $12 \div 4 = \blacksquare$ 3   11. $\blacksquare = 9 \div 1$ 9   12. $16 \div 2 = \blacksquare$ 8

✓ MISSING FACTORS

Find the missing factor.

13. $3 \times \blacksquare = 27$ 9   14. $25 = \blacksquare \times 5$ 5   15. $\blacksquare \times 6 = 12$ 2   16. $45 = 9 \times \blacksquare$ 5

17. $6 \times \blacksquare = 48$ 8   18. $\blacksquare \times 8 = 32$ 4   19. $35 = 5 \times \blacksquare$ 7   20. $20 = \blacksquare \times 4$ 5

REVIEW

quotient [kwoʹshənt] *noun*

The word *quotient* comes from the Latin root *quot*, which
means "how many." Write a word problem that could be
solved by finding a quotient. Use the words *how many* in
your problem. **Possible answer: Bob divided 24 marbles equally among
4 friends. How many marbles did each friend get?**

 www.harcourtschool.com/mathglossary

Were students successful with ✓ **CHECK WHAT YOU KNOW?**

IF . . . **NO** THEN . . . INTERVENE   **INTERVENTION OPTIONS**   IF . . . **YES** THEN . . . ENRICH

Skill/Items	Missed more than	Intervene with
Commutative Property of Multiplication, 1–4	1	• *Intervention*, Skill 22
Division Facts Through 5, 5–12	2	• *Intervention*, Skills 32, 33, 34
Missing Factors, 13–20	2	• *Intervention*, Skill 62

Skill/Items	Missed fewer than	Enrich with
Commutative Property of Multiplication, 1–4	2	• *Intervention*, Enrichment p. IN355
Division Facts Through 5, 5–12	3	• *Intervention*, Enrichment p. IN356
Missing Factors, 13–20	3	• *Intervention*, Enrichment p. IN356

Divide by 6, 7, and 8

Lesson Planning

PROFESSIONAL DEVELOPMENT

Objective To divide by 6, 7, and 8

NCTM Standards
1. Number and Operations
2. Algebra
6. Problem Solving
7. Reasoning and Proof
8. Communication
9. Connections
10. Representation

Math Background
Use these ideas to help students divide by 6, 7, and 8.

- Use a related multiplication fact. The missing factor is equal to the quotient.
- To find a quotient, use counters to model equal groups.
- To find a quotient, model the problem with an array.

Warm-Up Resources

Build Number Sense

Number of the Day

Transparency **14.1**

The number of the day is one more than two times the number of feet in a yard. Write two division sentences with quotients equal to this number.
Possible answers: $14 \div 2 = 7$, $21 \div 3 = 7$

Review Basic Facts

Daily Facts Practice

Have students practice addition facts by completing Set B of *Teacher's Resource Book*, p. TR93.

Solve a Problem

Transparency **14.1**

Problem of the Day

Mrs. Martin baked some cupcakes. She put 8 chocolate chips and 4 nuts on each. If she used 48 chocolate chips, how many nuts did she use? 24 nuts

Solution Problem of the Day tab, p. PD14

Intervention and Extension Resources

Alternative Teaching Strategy

MATERIALS multiplication table, p. TR19

Have students **use a multiplication table to find quotients.**

Provide the steps for finding $24 \div 6 = \blacksquare$.

- Run your finger along the top row and stop on the divisor, 6.
- Move your finger down the column until you reach the dividend, 24.
- Move your finger left along that row to the number in the first column. This missing factor, 4, is the quotient.

Have students practice this method with exercises from the lesson. Check students' work.

See also page 276.

VISUAL, KINESTHETIC

VISUAL/SPATIAL

Multistep and Strategy Problems

The following multistep or strategy problems are provided in Lesson 14.1:

Page	Item
277	53–54, Linkup 1

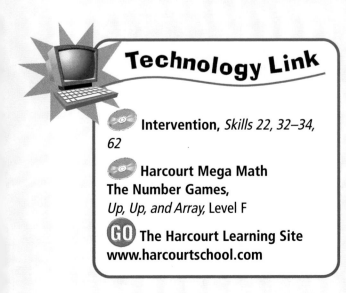

Technology Link

Intervention, *Skills 22, 32–34, 62*

**Harcourt Mega Math
The Number Games,**
Up, Up, and Array, Level F

GO **The Harcourt Learning Site**
www.harcourtschool.com

Vocabulary Strategy

To help students **solve division problems**, have them rewrite the problem with a label next to each fact. Labels may include: *dividend, divisor,* or *not needed* (if the fact is not needed to solve the problem). For example:

ESOL/ESL

Mrs. Taylor baked 6 batches (divisor) of muffins. She has a total of 48 muffins (dividend). She also baked 2 cakes (not needed). How many muffins were in each batch? 8 muffins

VISUAL

VISUAL/SPATIAL

Science Connection

Have students **divide by 6** to find weights on the moon.

Tell students that their weight is a measure of the force of gravity between them and Earth. The moon's gravity is about one-sixth of Earth's gravity. If you know what something weighs on Earth, you can divide by 6 to find about how much it would weigh on the moon. For example, a 60-pound child would weigh about 10 pounds on the moon.

Have students find about how much each of the following would weigh on the moon.

1. a 36-pound dog about 6 pounds
2. a 12-pound telescope about 2 pounds
3. a 6-pound camera about 1 pound
4. an 18-pound spacesuit about 3 pounds

VISUAL

LOGICAL/MATHEMATICAL

Lesson 14.1 Organizer

Objective To divide by 6, 7, and 8

1 INTRODUCE

QUICK REVIEW provides review of prerequisite skills.

WHY LEARN THIS? You can put items into equal groups. *Share the lesson objective with students.*

2 TEACH

Guided Instruction

- *Discuss the Learn section.*
  When can you use division to solve a problem? when you want to find out how many equal groups there are or how many in each group

- *Check students' understanding of Example A.*
  How do you know what multiplication fact to use to find the quotient? The divisor, 7, should be one of the factors, and the dividend, 63, should be the product.

- *Check students' understanding of Example B.*
  How do you know what multiplication fact to use to find the quotient? The divisor, 8, should be one of the factors, and the dividend, 56, should be the product.

- *Direct students' attention to the Math Idea.*
  How are multiplication and division sentences related? The sentences are in the same fact family.

274 Chapter 14

LESSON

1 Divide by 6, 7, and 8

▶ Learn

IT'S IN THE BAG The Bagel Stop sells bagels in bags of 6. Ramona has 24 fresh bagels to put in bags. How many bags does she need?

$24 \div 6 = $ ■

Use a related multiplication fact to find the quotient.

Think: $6 \times $ ■ $ = 24$
$6 \times 4 = 24$

$24 \div 6 = 4$, or $6\overline{)24}$ with 4 above

So, Ramona needs 4 bags.

Examples

A $63 \div 7 = $ ■
Think: $7 \times $ ■ $ = 63$
$7 \times 9 = 63$

$63 \div 7 = 9$, or $7\overline{)63}$ with 9 above

B $56 \div 8 = $ ■
Think: $8 \times $ ■ $ = 56$
$8 \times 7 = 56$

$56 \div 8 = 7$, or $8\overline{)56}$ with 7 above

MATH IDEA Think of related multiplication facts to help you divide.

- What multiplication fact can you use to find $42 \div 7$? What is the quotient?
  $7 \times 6 = 42$; 6

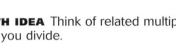

Technology Link
More Practice:
Harcourt Mega Math
The Number Games,
Up Up and Array,
Level F.

274

Reteach 14.1

Divide by 6, 7, and 8

You can use the multiplication facts you know to find quotients.

Here are three examples.

Example A	Example B	Example C
$24 \div 6 = $?	$28 \div 7 = $?	$48 \div 8 = $?
↑ ↑ ↑	↑ ↑ ↑	↑ ↑ ↑
dividend divisor quotient	dividend divisor quotient	dividend divisor quotient
Think: $6 \times $? $ = 24$	Think: $7 \times $? $ = 28$	Think: $8 \times $? $ = 48$
$6 \times 4 = 24$	$7 \times 4 = 28$	$8 \times 6 = 48$
So, $24 \div 6 = 4$ or $6\overline{)24}$.	So, $28 \div 7 = 4$ or $7\overline{)28}$.	So, $48 \div 8 = 6$ or $8\overline{)48}$.

Complete.

1. $18 \div 6 = $ __3__
   Think: $6 \times $ __3__ $ = 18$

2. $32 \div 8 = $ __4__
   Think: $8 \times $ __4__ $ = 32$

3. $14 \div 7 = $ __2__
   Think: $7 \times $ __2__ $ = 14$

4. $72 \div 8 = $ __9__
   Think: $8 \times $ __9__ $ = 72$

5. $42 \div 6 = $ __7__
   Think: $6 \times $ __7__ $ = 42$

6. $49 \div 7 = $ __7__
   Think: $7 \times $ __7__ $ = 49$

7. $6 \div 6 = $ __1__

8. $21 \div 7 = $ __3__

9. $24 \div 8 = $ __3__

10. $40 \div 8 = $ __5__

11. $36 \div 6 = $ __6__

12. $56 \div 7 = $ __8__

13. $64 \div 8 = $ __8__

14. $12 \div 6 = $ __2__

15. $30 \div 6 = $ __5__

16. $6\overline{)54}$ 9

17. $7\overline{)63}$ 9

18. $7\overline{)42}$ 6

19. $6\overline{)48}$ 8

20. $8\overline{)56}$ 7

21. $8\overline{)16}$ 2

22. $7\overline{)0}$ 0

23. $6\overline{)54}$ 9

RW72 Reteach

Practice 14.1

Divide by 6, 7, and 8

Find the missing factor and quotient.

1. $6 \times $ __5__ $ = 30$ $30 \div 6 = $ __5__

2. $8 \times $ __7__ $ = 56$ $56 \div 8 = $ __7__

3. $7 \times $ __9__ $ = 63$ $63 \div 7 = $ __9__

Find the quotient.

4. $18 \div 6 = $ __3__

5. $32 \div 8 = $ __4__

6. $40 \div 8 = $ __5__

7. $49 \div 7 = $ __7__

8. $12 \div 6 = $ __2__

9. $35 \div 7 = $ __5__

10. $7\overline{)14}$ 2

11. $7\overline{)28}$ 4

12. $6\overline{)24}$ 4

13. $7\overline{)56}$ 8

14. $7\overline{)63}$ 9

15. $6\overline{)30}$ 5

16. $6\overline{)54}$ 9

17. $8\overline{)24}$ 3

Complete.

18. $36 \div 6 = $ __2__ $ \times 3$

19. $56 \div 7 = $ __5__ $ + 3$

20. $8 \div 8 = $ __4__ $ - 3$

Mixed Review

Write the numbers in order from greatest to least.

21. 19
    43
    38
    __43, 38, 19__

22. 2,013
    2,130
    3,120
    __3,120; 2,130;__
    __2,013__

23. 315
    272
    156
    __315, 272,__
    __156__

24. 30,500
    30,099
    30,122
    __30,500; 30,122;__
    __30,099__

Add.

25. 14
    22
    + 69
    __105__

26. 74
    28
    + 32
    __134__

27. 411
    260
    + 591
    __1,262__

28. 7,000
    3,000
    + 1,000
    __11,000__

29. 6,100
    5,100
    + 3,000
    __14,200__

PW72 Practice

Equal Groups

Remember, you can also use equal groups and arrays to help you find a quotient.

Here are two different ways to find $28 \div 7$.

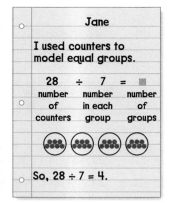

Jane
I used counters to model equal groups. $28 \div 7 = \blacksquare$ number number number of   in each   of counters group groups So, $28 \div 7 = 4$.

Kevin
I modeled the problem with an array. $28 \div 7 = \blacksquare$ number number number in   in each of array row rows So, $28 \div 7 = 4$.

- **REASONING** You have used equal groups and arrays to help you find products. Why can you also use them to help you find quotients? **Possible answer: Multiplication and division are related. Separate a given number of equal groups or equal rows to divide.**

▶ Check

1. **Explain** how you would use a related multiplication fact to find $18 \div 6$. **Possible answer: $6 \times 3 = 18$. So, $18 \div 6 = 3$.**

Find the missing factor and quotient.

2. $8 \times \blacksquare = 16$ **2** $16 \div 8 = \blacksquare$ **2**   3. $7 \times \blacksquare = 35$ **5** $35 \div 7 = \blacksquare$ **5**

4. $6 \times \blacksquare = 36$ **6** $36 \div 6 = \blacksquare$ **6**   5. $6 \times \blacksquare = 30$ **5** $30 \div 6 = \blacksquare$ **5**

Copy and complete each table.

6.
÷	14	21	28	35
7	▦ 2	▦ 3	▦ 4	▦ 5

7.
÷	6	12	18	24
6	▦ 1	▦ 2	▦ 3	▦ 4

Find the quotient.

8. $21 \div 7 = \blacksquare$ **3** 9. $42 \div 6 = \blacksquare$ **7** 10. $\blacksquare = 56 \div 7$ **8** 11. $32 \div 8 = \blacksquare$ **4**

12. $8)\overline{40}$ **5**   13. $7)\overline{42}$ **6**   14. $8)\overline{24}$ **3**   15. $6)\overline{24}$ **4**

LESSON CONTINUES ▶

Chapter 14 **275**

- *Compare Jane's and Kevin's ways to solve $28 \div 7$.* **How are these two methods alike?** Both methods form equal groups.

3 PRACTICE

Guided Practice

Do Check Exercises 1–15 with your students. Identify the students who are having difficulty and choose appropriate lesson resources to provide assistance.

North Carolina Standards 1.03 Develop fluency with multiplication from 1×1 to 12×12 and division of two-digit by one-digit numbers using: a) Strategies for multiplying and dividing numbers.

Challenge 14.1

Fun with Facts

Follow the arrows to solve each problem. Write the answer inside the empty box. You may use a multiplication table to help you multiply and divide.

1. $36 \rightarrow \div 6 \rightarrow \times 4 \rightarrow \div 8 \rightarrow$ **3**
2. $48 \rightarrow \div 8 \rightarrow +15 \rightarrow \div 7 \rightarrow$ **3**
3. $63 \rightarrow \div 7 \rightarrow \times 2 \rightarrow \div 6 \rightarrow$ **3**
4. $56 \rightarrow \div 7 \rightarrow -2 \rightarrow \div 6 \rightarrow$ **1**
5. $35 \rightarrow \div 7 \rightarrow +27 \rightarrow \div 8 \rightarrow$ **4**
6. $16 \rightarrow \div 8 \rightarrow \times 6 \rightarrow -4 \rightarrow$ **8**
7. $8 \rightarrow \times 3 \rightarrow \div 6 \rightarrow +4 \rightarrow$ **8**

Write an operation and a number in the empty box.

8. $72 \rightarrow \div 8 \rightarrow \div 3 \rightarrow$ **×7 or + 18** $\rightarrow 21$
9. $24 \rightarrow \div 6 \rightarrow \times 9 \rightarrow$ **÷6 or − 30** $\rightarrow 6$
10. $8 \rightarrow \times 8 \rightarrow -8 \rightarrow$ **÷7 or − 48** $\rightarrow 8$

Make up your own problems. Use at least one multiplication or division step in each. **Check students' work. Answers will vary.**

1. $\square \rightarrow \square \rightarrow \square \rightarrow \square$
2. $\square \rightarrow \square \rightarrow \square \rightarrow \square$

N72 Challenge

Problem Solving 14.1

Divide by 6, 7, and 8

Write the correct answer.

Understand ▶ Plan ▶ Solve ▶ Check

1. Tonya has 16 pictures of her new kitten. She put an equal number in each of two rows. How many pictures did she put in each row?

8 pictures

2. Which quotient is greater, $49 \div 7$ or $24 \div 3$?

24 ÷ 3

3. Jason bought 35 postcards. He mailed 8 postcards on Monday and 7 postcards on Tuesday. How many does he still have?

20 postcards

4. Kendra looked at the clock. It was 5:20 P.M. She was 30 minutes late for an appointment. What time was her appointment?

4:50 P.M.

Choose the letter of the correct answer.

5. Which is equivalent to $0.95?
  A 3 quarters, 2 dimes, 1 nickel
  B 3 quarters, 1 dime, 1 nickel
  Ⓒ 2 quarters, 4 dimes, 1 nickel
  D 1 quarter, 7 dimes, 1 nickel

6. Gina put 72 pennies into 8 equal stacks. How many did she put in each stack?
  F 7   H 64
  Ⓖ 9   J 80

7. Victor made 2 cookies for each of 5 friends. He put 8 chocolate chips in each cookie. How many chocolate chips did he use?
  Ⓐ 80   C 16
  B 40   D 15

8. There are 54 people in Gary's choir. They stand in 6 rows. Each row has the same number of people. How many people are in each row?
  F 8   H 13
  Ⓖ 9   J 49

9. **Write About It** Explain how you found your answer to Problem 2.

Possible answer: First, I found each quotient; $49 \div 7 = 7$

and $24 \div 3 = 8$. Then I compared the quotients. $7 < 8$ or $8 > 7$.

PS72 Problem Solving

COMMON ERROR ALERT

Since students are using a multiplication fact to help them divide, they may give the product (or dividend) as the quotient.

$8 \times 4 = 32; 32 \div 8 = 32$

Remind students to check their answer by using multiplication. The product of the quotient and divisor should equal the dividend.

Independent Practice

Note that Exercises 53–54 and Linkup 1 are **multistep or strategy problems**. Assign Exercises 16–54 and Linkup 1.

ALGEBRAIC THINKING For Exercises 16–21, remind students that the unknown factor in the multiplication sentence is the same as the unknown quotient in the division sentence.

MULTISTEP OR STRATEGY PROBLEM To solve Exercise 53, students can divide $48 \div 6 = 8$ to find the total number of bagels in one bag and then multiply $8 \times 2 = 16$ to find the total number of bagels in 2 bags. Guide students to conclude that the division must be completed before the multiplication.

Find the missing factor and quotient.

16. $7 \times \blacksquare = 14$ 2 $14 \div 7 = \blacksquare$ 2
17. $6 \times \blacksquare = 60$ 10 $60 \div 6 = \blacksquare$ 10
18. $6 \times \blacksquare = 48$ 8 $48 \div 6 = \blacksquare$ 8
19. $8 \times \blacksquare = 72$ 9 $72 \div 8 = \blacksquare$ 9
20. $7 \times \blacksquare = 42$ 6 $42 \div 7 = \blacksquare$ 6
21. $8 \times \blacksquare = 40$ 5 $40 \div 8 = \blacksquare$ 5

Copy and complete each table.

22.

÷	42	63	56	49
7	■ 6	■ 9	■ 8	■ 7

23.

÷	56	40	48	32
8	■ 7	■ 5	■ 6	■ 4

Find the quotient.

24. $36 \div 6 = \blacksquare$ 6
25. $80 \div 8 = \blacksquare$ 10
26. $\blacksquare = 0 \div 7$ 0
27. $8 \div 1 = \blacksquare$ 8
28. $\blacksquare = 15 \div 3$ 5
29. $\blacksquare = 18 \div 6$ 3
30. $45 \div 5 = \blacksquare$ 9
31. $24 \div 8 = \blacksquare$ 3

32. $8\overline{)64}$ 8
33. $2\overline{)14}$ 7
34. $7\overline{)28}$ 4
35. $6\overline{)0}$ 0

36. $5\overline{)10}$ 2
37. $7\overline{)7}$ 1
38. $8\overline{)0}$ 0
39. $3\overline{)30}$ 10

40. Divide 42 by 6. 7
41. Divide 8 by 8. 1
42. Divide 35 by 5. 7

Write a division sentence for each.

43.

$30 \div 5 = 6$ or $30 \div 6 = 5$

44.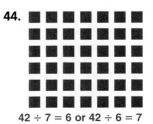

$42 \div 7 = 6$ or $42 \div 6 = 7$

ALGEBRA Complete.

45. $3 + \blacksquare = 49 \div 7$ 4
46. $8 \times 5 = \blacksquare \times 10$ 4
47. $\blacksquare - 4 = 24 \div 6$ 8
48. $\blacksquare \times 4 = 8 \times 3$ 6
49. $6 \div 6 = 0 + \blacksquare$ 1
50. $5 + 3 = 16 \div \blacksquare$ 2

51. **REASONING** Is the quotient $24 \div 6$ greater than or less than the quotient $24 \div 4$? How do you know? Possible answer: less than; since the same number is divided into more groups, there are fewer in each group.

52. **? What's the Question?** Hikara bought 35 fruit chews. Fruit chews come in packs of 5. The answer is 7 packs. How many packs of fruit chews did Hikara buy?

276

Alternative Teaching Strategy   Scaffolded Instruction

PURPOSE Students use a table to find a quotient.

Have students make a table with 12 columns and 2 rows. 6 is the divisor. Dividends of 0 through 60 are listed in the first row. The quotients are placed in the second row. Have students use the table to find $24 \div 6 = \blacksquare$.

÷	0	6	12	18	24	30	36	42	48	54	60
6	0	1	2	3	4	5	6	7	8	9	10

Have students:

• Find the dividend, 24, in the top row.

• Highlight that column. Tell students that the quotient is the number below the dividend. 4

÷	0	6	12	18	24	30	36	42	48	54	60
6	0	1	2	3	4	5	6	7	8	9	10

Have students make a table with 7 as the divisor and find $42 \div 7 = \blacksquare$. 6

PROFESSIONAL DEVELOPMENT

Have students make a table with 8 as the divisor and find $32 \div 8 = \blacksquare$. 4

Have them use their tables to solve additional division problems that require dividing by 6, 7, or 8. Check students' work.

53. **≡FAST FACT** • **SOCIAL STUDIES**
The bagel is the only bread product that is boiled before it is baked. A baker made 48 bagels and placed an equal number in each of 6 bags. How many bagels are in 2 bags? **16 bagels**

54. Asha had 24 pictures of her friends. She put 8 pictures on each page in a photo album. Her album has 20 pages. How many album pages do not have pictures? **17 pages**

Getting Ready for the EOG Test

55. Mr. Luis has 72 chairs. He puts the chairs in rows of 8 for the school play. How many rows does Mr. Luis make? **D**

A 6   **B** 7   **C** 8   **D** 9

56. Jared wants to solve the problem 54 ÷ 6. Which of the following can he use to help him? **A**

A $6 \times 9 = 54$

B $6 \times 8 = 48$

C $7 \times 6 = 42$

D $5 \times 9 = 45$

Problem Solving LiNKUP . . . to Reading

STRATEGY • CHOOSE IMPORTANT INFORMATION

Some word problems have more information than you need. Before you solve a problem, find the facts you need to solve the problem.

Mrs. Taylor baked 8 batches of muffins. She had a total of 48 muffins. She also baked 2 cakes. How many muffins were in each batch?

Facts You Need: baked 8 batches of muffins, total of 48 muffins

Fact You Don't Need: baked 2 cakes

$$48 \div 8 = 6$$

So, there were 6 muffins in each batch.

Write the important facts. Solve the problem.

1. Bonnie made 4 batches of cookies and 3 pies in the morning. She made 3 batches of cookies in the afternoon. She made 63 cookies in all. How many cookies were in each batch? **4 + 3 = 7 batches, 63 cookies; 9 cookies**

Chapter 14   277

Problem Solving LiNKUP . . . to Reading

• Direct students' attention to the Link Up.
REASONING How do you know that "baked 2 cakes" is a fact you don't need? Possible answer: The question asks about muffins, not cakes.

What multiplication fact can you use to find the quotient? $6 \times 8 = 48$

4 ASSESS

Summarize the lesson by having students:

DISCUSS How do multiplication facts help you solve division problems? Possible answer: The dividend is the product. One factor is the divisor. The other factor is the quotient.

WRITE Compare solving the division problem 48 ÷ 6 by using counters to modeling the problem with an array. Using counters: make equal groups of counters and count the number of groups. Using an array: form equal rows of tiles, and then count the number of rows.

Transparency **14.1**

LESSON QUIZ
Find the missing factor and quotient.

1. $6 \times \blacksquare = 30$ 5 $30 \div 6 = \blacksquare$ 5

2. $8 \times \blacksquare = 56$ 7 $56 \div 8 = \blacksquare$ 7

3. $8 \times \blacksquare = 32$ 4 $32 \div 8 = \blacksquare$ 4

4. $7 \times \blacksquare = 63$ 9 $63 \div 7 = \blacksquare$ 9

Lesson Planning

PROFESSIONAL DEVELOPMENT

Objective To divide by 9 and 10

NCTM Standards
1. **Number and Operations**
2. **Algebra**
6. **Problem Solving**
7. **Reasoning and Proof**
8. **Communication**
9. **Connections**
10. **Representation**

Math Background
These ideas may help students divide by 9 and 10.

- To divide by 9, think of a related multiplication fact with a factor of 9.

- To divide by 10, think of a related multiplication fact with a factor of 10.

- The missing factor in a related multiplication sentence is equal to the quotient.

Warm-Up Resources

Number of the Day

Transparency **14.2**

The number of the day multiplied by 3 is 30. What is this number? 10

Daily Facts Practice

Have students practice multiplication facts by completing Set C of *Teacher's Resource Book*, p. TR93.

Solve a Problem

Transparency **14.2**

Problem of the Day

If you divide this number by 2, the quotient is 8. What is the quotient if the number is divided by 4? 4

Solution Problem of the Day tab, p. PD14

Intervention and Extension Resources

Alternative Teaching Strategy

MATERIALS paper plates, counters

ESOL/ESL

Have students **model division by 9 and 10** by using counters, then comparing.

- Have students use plates and counters to model and solve the following problem:
  There are 30 counters. If 10 counters are placed on each plate, how many plates do you need? 3 plates with 10 counters on each plate; $30 \div 10 = 3$
- Have them use the same groups of counters again. Ask: What do you need to do to these plates and counters to model $27 \div 9$? Take away one counter from each plate. $27 \div 9 = 3$

KINESTHETIC, VISUAL

BODILY/KINESTHETIC

Multistep and Strategy Problems

The following multistep or strategy problems are provided in Lesson 14.2:

Page	Item
279	35–36

Writing in Mathematics

Ask students to **write and solve a word problem that involves dividing by 9 or 10.** Have them write and solve a word problem about a collection they have or would like to have. Have students exchange their word problems and solve each other's problems. Check students' work.

Early Finishers

MATERIALS *For each pair* 30 index cards

Have pairs of students **match related facts**. Ask students to write 15 pairs of related 9's and 10's facts such as $18 \div 9 = 2$ and $9 \times 2 = 18$ on separate cards. Have them place the 30 cards face down in rows. Students take turns picking two cards to find a match. Check students' work.

VISUAL

VISUAL/SPATIAL; BODILY/KINESTHETIC

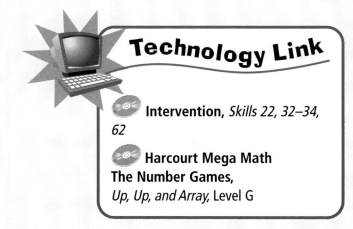

Technology Link

Intervention, *Skills 22, 32–34, 62*

Harcourt Mega Math
The Number Games,
Up, Up, and Array, Level G

Lesson 14.2 Organizer

Objective To divide by 9 and 10

1 INTRODUCE

QUICK REVIEW provides review of prerequisite skills.

WHY LEARN THIS? You can divide to find the number of boxes you need to hold pins or other collectibles. *Share the lesson objective with students.*

2 TEACH

Guided Instruction

- *Discuss Example A.*
  How else could you solve the problem? Possible answers: make an array; use repeated subtraction.

- *Refer to Example B.*
  When dividing by 10, how can you find the quotient just by looking at the dividend? The quotient is equal to the first digit of the dividend; 60 is the same as 6 tens.

- *Point out the bar graph.*
  REASONING Katie wants to use the fewest boxes possible for her animal pins. Should she put them in boxes that hold 9 or 10 pins? 10 pins

3 PRACTICE

Guided Practice

Do Check Exercises 1–3 with your students. Identify students who are having difficulty and choose appropriate lesson resources to provide assistance.

Divide by 9 and 10

Quick Review
1. $9 \times 3 = \blacksquare$ 27
2. $9 \times 5 = \blacksquare$ 45
3. $10 \times 4 = \blacksquare$ 40
4. $8 \times 10 = \blacksquare$ 80
5. $9 \times 10 = \blacksquare$ 90

▶ **Learn**

PLENTY OF PINS Katie collects different kinds of pins. She has boxes that hold 9 or 10 pins. Help Katie organize her collection.

Examples

A Katie puts her 45 state flag pins in boxes that hold 9 pins each. How many boxes does she need?

$45 \div 9 = \blacksquare$

Think: $9 \times \blacksquare = 45$
$9 \times 5 = 45$

$45 \div 9 = 5$, or $9\overline{)45}^{5}$

So, Katie needs 5 boxes for her state flag pins.

B Katie puts her 60 flower pins in boxes that hold 10 pins each. How many boxes does she need?

$60 \div 10 = \blacksquare$

Think: $10 \times \blacksquare = 60$
$10 \times 6 = 60$

$60 \div 10 = 6$, or $10\overline{)60}^{6}$

So, Katie needs 6 boxes for her flower pins.

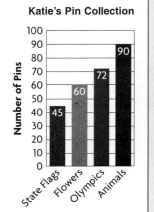

Katie's Pin Collection

Bar graph — Number of Pins vs. Type of Pin: State Flags 45, Flowers 60, Olympics 72, Animals 90.

▶ **Check**

1. **Explain** how to use a related multiplication fact to find $36 \div 9$. What is the quotient?
   Possible answer: $9 \times 4 = 36$; So, $36 \div 9 = 4$.

Copy and complete each table.

2.

$\div$	9	18	27	36
9	1	2	3	4

3.

$\div$	20	30	40	50
10	2	3	4	5

278

Reteach 14.2

Divide by 9 and 10

You can use the multiplication facts you know to find quotients.

Here are two examples.

Example A

$72 \div 9 = \underline{\ ?\ }$

↑ dividend ↑ divisor ↑ quotient

Think: $9 \times \underline{\ ?\ } = 72$
$9 \times 8 = 72$

So, $72 \div 9 = 8$ or $9\overline{)72}^{8}$.

Example B

$30 \div 10 = \underline{\ ?\ }$

↑ dividend ↑ divisor ↑ quotient

Think: $10 \times \underline{\ ?\ } = 30$
$10 \times 3 = 30$

So, $30 \div 10 = 3$ or $10\overline{)30}^{3}$.

Complete.

1. $18 \div 9 = \underline{2}$
   Think: $9 \times \underline{2} = 18$

2. $20 \div 10 = \underline{2}$
   Think: $10 \times \underline{2} = 20$

3. $36 \div 9 = \underline{4}$
   Think: $9 \times \underline{4} = 36$

4. $50 \div 10 = \underline{5}$
   Think: $10 \times \underline{5} = 50$

5. $45 \div 9 = \underline{5}$
   Think: $9 \times \underline{5} = 45$

6. $80 \div 10 = \underline{8}$
   Think: $10 \times \underline{8} = 80$

7. $90 \div 10 = \underline{9}$

8. $10 \div 10 = \underline{1}$

9. $54 \div 9 = \underline{6}$

10. $27 \div 9 = \underline{3}$

11. $63 \div 9 = \underline{7}$

12. $70 \div 10 = \underline{7}$

13. $40 \div 10 = \underline{4}$

14. $81 \div 9 = \underline{9}$

15. $60 \div 10 = \underline{6}$

16. $9\overline{)36}^{4}$

17. $10\overline{)80}^{8}$

18. $9\overline{)9}^{1}$

19. $9\overline{)72}^{8}$

20. $10\overline{)60}^{6}$

21. $9\overline{)63}^{7}$

22. $10\overline{)100}^{10}$

23. $9\overline{)90}^{10}$

Reteach RW73

Practice 14.2

Divide by 9 and 10

Complete each table.

1.

$\div$	18	27	36	45
9	2	3	4	5

2.

$\div$	30	40	50	60
10	3	4	5	6

Find the quotient.

3. $72 \div 9 = \underline{8}$

4. $63 \div 9 = \underline{7}$

5. $40 \div 8 = \underline{5}$

6. $60 \div 10 = \underline{6}$

7. $9 \div 1 = \underline{9}$

8. $81 \div 9 = \underline{9}$

9. $10\overline{)10}^{1}$

10. $9\overline{)27}^{3}$

11. $9\overline{)54}^{6}$

12. $10\overline{)70}^{7}$

13. $9\overline{)63}^{7}$

14. $9\overline{)90}^{10}$

15. $10\overline{)90}^{9}$

16. $10\overline{)100}^{10}$

Complete.

17. $54 \div 9 = \underline{2} \times 3$

18. $80 \div 10 = \underline{15} - 7$

19. $36 \div 9 = \underline{1} + 3$

Write $+$, $-$, $\times$, or $\div$ for each ◯.

20. $36 \ (+) \ 4 = 9$

21. $18 \ (-) \ 6 = 12$

22. $9 \ (\times) \ 3 = 27$

23. $16 \ (+) \ 8 = 24$

Mixed Review

Solve.

24. Divide 45 by 5.
    $\underline{9}$

25. Divide 24 by 6.
    $\underline{4}$

26. Divide 48 by 8.
    $\underline{6}$

Write the time.

27. 18 minutes after noon
    $\underline{12:18 \text{ P.M.}}$

28. 18 minutes before noon
    $\underline{11:42 \text{ A.M.}}$

29. 20 minutes before 1:15 P.M.
    $\underline{12:55 \text{ P.M.}}$

Practice PW73

Copy and complete each table.

4.

÷	54	72	63	81
9	■ 6	■ 8	■ 7	■ 9

5.

÷	70	90	80	100
10	■ 7	■ 9	■ 8	■ 10

Find the quotient.

37. Possible answer: In division you take apart one number to find how many smaller numbers are in it.

6. $45 \div 9 = $ ■ 5   **7.** ■ $= 10 \div 10$ 1   **8.** ■ $= 0 \div 9$ 0   **9.** $60 \div 10 = $ ■ 6

10. $9 \div 1 = $ ■ 9   **11.** $12 \div 6 = $ ■ 2   **12.** $18 \div 3 = $ ■ 6   **13.** ■ $= 36 \div 9$ 4

14. ■ $= 50 \div 10$ 5   **15.** $14 \div 2 = $ ■ 7   **16.** ■ $= 12 \div 4$ 3   **17.** $40 \div 5 = $ ■ 8

18. $6\overline{)0}$ ⁰   **19.** $6\overline{)42}$ ⁷   **20.** $9\overline{)90}$ ¹⁰   **21.** $9\overline{)63}$ ⁷

22. $8\overline{)64}$ ⁸   **23.** $5\overline{)25}$ ⁵   **24.** $7\overline{)28}$ ⁴   **25.** $3\overline{)24}$ ⁸

26. Divide 72 by 8. 9   **27.** Divide 42 by 7. 6   **28.** Divide 70 by 10. 7

ALGEBRA Write +, −, ×, or ÷ for each ●.

29. $10 ● 10 = 2 − 1$ ÷   **30.** $8 \times 3 = 20 ● 4$ +   **31.** $12 ● 7 = 50 \div 10$ −

32. $3 \times 6 = 2 ● 9$ ×   **33.** $81 ● 9 = 3 \times 3$ ÷   **34.** $6 \times 7 = 35 ● 7$ +

35. REASONING Ken has 89 patches in his collection. He puts 8 patches on his vest and puts the rest in boxes of 9 patches each. How many boxes does Ken need?
9 boxes

36. REASONING Boxes for 9 pins cost $4 each. Boxes for 10 pins cost $5 each. Janine has 90 pins. If she wants to spend the least amount of money, what type of boxes should she buy? **boxes for storing 9 pins**

37. Vocabulary Power The words *division, dividend,* and *divisor* come from a Latin word that means "to take apart." How is division like taking something apart? **See above.**

38. ✎ **Write About It** Make a table showing the 9's division facts. Describe any patterns you see in your table. **Possible answer: The tens digit of the dividend is 1 less than the quotient, and the sum of the digits is 9.**

Getting Ready for the EOG Test

39. Sandi is buying adult tickets for the train. She gives the clerk $70. How many tickets can Sandi buy? **B**

A 5   **B** 7   **C** 9   **D** 10

TRAIN TICKETS	
Type of Ticket	**Price**
Adult	$10
Child	$5
Senior	$9

Chapter 14 **279**

North Carolina Standards **1.03** Develop fluency with multiplication from 1 × 1 to 12 × 12 and division o two-digit by one-digit numbers using: a) Strategies for multiplying and dividing numbers.

Challenge 14.2

Divide by 9 and 10

Divide. Connect the dots in order from least to greatest quotient.

$9\overline{)81}$ 9
$9\overline{)90}$ 10
$9\overline{)72}$ 8
$9\overline{)63}$ 7
$9\overline{)54}$ 6
$9\overline{)36}$ 4
$10\overline{)10}$ 1
$10\overline{)50}$ 5
$10\overline{)30}$ 3
$9\overline{)18}$ 2

n grid paper, design your own connect-the-dots picture ng the division facts you know. Have a friend solve.

Challenge CW73

Problem Solving 14.2

Divide by 9 and 10

Understand ▸ Plan ▸ Solve ▸ Check

Write the correct answer.

1. Ted plans to practice the piano ten minutes every day for one week. How many minutes will he practice the piano?

70 minutes

2. Lee has 100 stamps to put in his stamp book. He wants to make 10 equal rows of stamps. How many stamps will he put in each row?

10 stamps

3. Omar visits his grandparents twice a week. How many times has he visited them in the last 8 weeks?

16 times

4. Katie has 16 more problems to solve than Leslie. Leslie has 8 more problems to solve than Meg. Meg has 5 problems to solve. How many problems does Katie have?

29 problems

Choose the letter of the correct answer.

5. Mrs. Lopez was born in 1928. What was her age in 2000?

A 82   C 73
B 78   **D** 72

6. Which amount is greater than $5.03?

F $4.99   H $5.02
G $5.00   **J** $5.20

7. Wendy has 81 treats to give to nine dogs at the animal shelter. If she gives each dog the same number of treats, how many will each dog get?

A 90   **C** 9
B 72   D 8

8. Tameo has 12 cards. Barb has 8 more cards than Tameo and 10 times as many cards as Lori. How many cards does Lori have?

F 2   H 14
G 4   J 20

9. **Write About It** Explain how you found your answer to Problem 8.

Possible answer: I added 12 + 8 to find out how many cards Barb had. Then I divided 20 by 10 to get 2.

Problem Solving PS73

Independent Practice

Note that Exercises 35–36 are **multistep or strategy problems.** Assign Exercises 4–38.

SCAFFOLDED INSTRUCTION Use the prompts on Transparency 14 to guide instruction for the multistep or strategy problem in Exercise 35.

Transparency **14**

Vocabulary Power Discuss with students the meaning of *division, dividend,* and *divisor.* Have students write a division sentence and draw a picture to show what it means. Then have students label the *dividend* and *divisor.* Check students' work.

4 ASSESS

Summarize the lesson by having students:

DISCUSS What is $0 \div 9$? $0 \div 10$? **Explain.**
0; 0; zero divided by any number is equal to zero. It is not possible to divide sets that contain nothing.

WRITE What if you do not know the answer to $27 \div 9 = $ ■? List several ways you can find the answer.
Possible answers:
1. Make an array with 9 tiles in each row until you use 27 tiles. Count the number of rows.
2. Put 27 counters one-by-one in 9 groups; count the number in each group.
3. Use a related multiplication fact.
4. Use repeated subtraction.

LESSON QUIZ
Find the quotient.

Transparency **14.2**

1. $60 \div 10 = $ ■ 6   **2.** $27 \div 9 = $ ■ 3

3. $81 \div 9 = $ ■ 9   **4.** $70 \div 10 = $ ■ 7

Practice Division Facts

Lesson Planning

Professional Development

Objective To practice division facts through 10 by using various strategies

NCTM Standards

1. Number and Operations
2. Algebra
6. Problem Solving
7. Reasoning and Proof
8. Communication
9. Connections
10. Representation

Math Background

These ideas will help students remember division facts and various ways of finding quotients.

- Use counters or arrays to make equal groups.
- Use repeated subtraction.
- Relate division to multiplication by using fact families or a multiplication table.

Warm-Up Resources

Number of the Day

Transparency 14.3

The number of the day is the number of seconds in one minute. Divide this number by 10. 6

Daily Facts Practice

Have students practice multiplication facts by completing Set D of *Teacher's Resource Book*, p. TR93.

Solve a Problem

Transparency 14.3

Problem of the Day

Two sisters and two brothers need to share $36 equally. How much money will each person get? $9

Solution Problem of the Day tab, p. PD14

Intervention and Extension Resources

Alternative Teaching Strategy

MATERIALS index cards

Have groups of students **practice division facts**.

Have students use the multiplication table on PE page 281 to make flash cards to practice division facts through 10. The front of each card should have a division expression such as 24 ÷ 8. The quotient, 3, should be placed on the back.

Partners can use these cards to quiz each other.

See also page 282.

AUDITORY, VISUAL

VISUAL/SPATIAL; VERBAL/LINGUISTIC

Multistep and Strategy Problems

The following multistep or strategy problems are provided in Lesson 14.3:

Page	Item
283	53–54

Writing in Mathematics

Have students **write about solving division problems**.

Have students choose a method from the lesson that they prefer to use and explain why. Have them provide an example with their explanation. Check students' work.

Advanced Learners

MATERIALS self-stick notes

Challenge students to **practice division facts** by playing "Find the Dividends!"

Write various dividends, such as 4, 16, 24, 27, 35, 48, 50, and 63, on large self-stick notes and post them.

Display number sentences with missing dividends. Ask students to place the correct dividend in each number sentence. For example:

16 ■ ÷ 2 = 8   35 ■ ÷ 5 = 7

63 ■ ÷ 7 = 9   4 ■ ÷ 1 = 4

48 ■ ÷ 6 = 8   24 ■ ÷ 4 = 6

27 ■ ÷ 9 = 3   50 ■ ÷ 10 = 5

VISUAL

VISUAL/SPATIAL

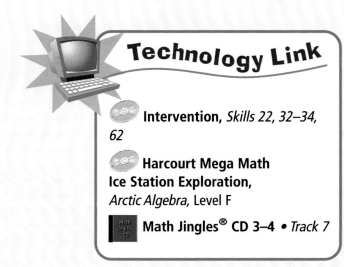

Technology Link

Intervention, *Skills 22, 32–34, 62*

Harcourt Mega Math
Ice Station Exploration,
Arctic Algebra, Level F

Math Jingles® CD 3–4 • *Track 7*

Lesson 14.3 Organizer

Objective To practice division facts through 10 by using various strategies

1 INTRODUCE

QUICK REVIEW provides review of prerequisite skills.

WHY LEARN THIS? You'll be able to choose from a variety of ways to find a quotient. *Share the lesson objective with students.*

2 TEACH

Guided Instruction

- *Compare solutions A and D.*
  How is using counters like using an array?
  Both involve forming equal groups or rows and counting them.

- *Direct students' attention to solution B.*
  How do you know when to stop subtracting?
  when you get a difference equal to zero

- *Check students' understanding of solution C.*
  How many facts usually make a fact family?
  4 facts
  REASONING When you multiply, is the product usually greater than or less than the two factors? Give an example. Possible answer: greater than; $6 \times 4 = 24$.
  When you divide, is the quotient usually greater than or less than the dividend? Give an example. Possible answer: less than; $12 \div 6 = 2$.

---

3 Practice Division Facts

Quick Review
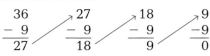
1. $7 \times \blacksquare = 56$ 8
2. $\blacksquare \times 3 = 27$ 9
3. $6 \times \blacksquare = 30$ 5
4. $\blacksquare \times 4 = 16$ 4
5. $5 \times \blacksquare = 40$ 8

▶ Learn

BOXED CARS Bobby has 36 toy cars that he wants to put in display boxes. Each display box holds 9 cars. How many display boxes will Bobby need?

$36 \div 9 = \blacksquare$

There are many ways to find the quotient.

A. Use counters.

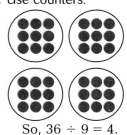

So, $36 \div 9 = 4.$

B. Use repeated subtraction.

$$\begin{array}{cccc} 36 & 27 & 18 & 9 \\ -\ 9 & -\ 9 & -\ 9 & -9 \\ \hline 27 & 18 & 9 & 0 \end{array}$$

Number of times you subtract 9:   1   2   3   4

So, $36 \div 9 = 4.$

C. Use fact families.

Fact Family for 4, 9, and 36

factor	factor	product		dividend	divisor	quotient
4	× 9	= 36		36	÷ 9	= 4
9	× 4	= 36		36	÷ 4	= 9

So, $36 \div 9 = 4.$

D. Use an array.

Make an array with 36 tiles.
Count the rows of 9 tiles each.
There are 4 rows of 9 tiles.

Since $4 \times 9 = 36$, then $36 \div 9 = 4.$

Reteach 14.3

Practice Division Facts

One way to recall a division fact is to think of a related multiplication fact.

Find $18 \div 3$.

Think: How many groups of 3 are in 18?
Or, what number multiplied times 3 equals 18?

$? \times 3 = 18$

$6 \times 3 = 18$, so $18 \div 3 = 6.$

Complete.

1. __6__ × 4 = 24, so 24 ÷ 4 = __6__
2. __3__ × 10 = 30, so 30 ÷ 10 = __3__
3. __7__ × 5 = 35, so 35 ÷ 5 = __7__
4. __6__ × 6 = 36, so 36 ÷ 6 = __6__
5. __10__ × 8 = 80, so 80 ÷ 8 = __10__
6. __3__ × 7 = 21, so 21 ÷ 7 = __3__

Find the quotient. Think about multiplication facts that have 5 as a factor.

7. 25 ÷ 5 = __5__
8. 40 ÷ 5 = __8__
9. 15 ÷ 5 = __3__
10. 10 ÷ 5 = __2__
11. 45 ÷ 5 = __9__
12. 20 ÷ 5 = __4__
13. 35 ÷ 5 = __7__
14. 5 ÷ 5 = __1__
15. 30 ÷ 5 = __6__

Find the quotient. Think about multiplication facts that have 9 as a factor.

16. 63 ÷ 9 = __7__
17. 72 ÷ 9 = __8__
18. 18 ÷ 9 = __2__
19. 45 ÷ 9 = __5__
20. 27 ÷ 9 = __3__
21. 54 ÷ 9 = __6__
22. 9 ÷ 9 = __1__
23. 36 ÷ 9 = __4__
24. 81 ÷ 9 = __9__

RW74 Reteach

Practice 14.3

Practice Division Facts

Write a division sentence for each. Possible answers are given.

1. $8 \div 2 = 4$
2. $21 \div 3 = 7$
3. $\begin{array}{cc} 20 & 10 \\ -10 & -10 \\ \hline 10 & 0 \end{array}$ $20 \div 10 = 2$

Find the missing factor and quotient.

4. 7 × __7__ = 49   49 ÷ 7 = __7__
5. 6 × __9__ = 54   54 ÷ 6 = __9__

Find the quotient.

6. 36 ÷ 6 = __6__
7. 24 ÷ 8 = __3__
8. 42 ÷ 7 = __6__
9. 56 ÷ 8 = __7__
10. 63 ÷ 7 = __9__
11. 14 ÷ 2 = __7__
12. 8)‾64 → 8
13. 10)‾10 → 1
14. 5)‾35 → 7
15. 9)‾27 → 3
16. 7)‾70 → 10
17. 5)‾30 → 6
18. 4)‾36 → 9
19. 7)‾49 → 7

Compare. Write <, >, or = for each ◯.

20. 36 − 6 ⊙ 8 × 3   21. 18 ÷ 9 ⊙ 0 + 3   22. 64 ÷ 8 ⊙ 2 × 4

Mixed Review

Write a multiplication sentence for each. Possible answers are given.

23.   24.   25.   26.

$3 \times 3 = 9$ $4 \times 2 = 8$ $5 \times 4 = 20$ $6 \times 3 = 18$

PW74 Practice

Find Missing Factors

E. Use a multiplication table.

Think: $\blacksquare \times 9 = 36$

- Find the given factor 9 in the top row.

- Look down the column to find the product, 36.

- Look left across the row to find the missing factor, 4.

$4 \times 9 = 36 \quad 36 \div 9 = 4$

So, Bobby needs 4 display boxes.

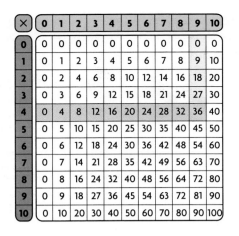

×	0	1	2	3	4	5	6	7	8	9	10
0	0	0	0	0	0	0	0	0	0	0	0
1	0	1	2	3	4	5	6	7	8	9	10
2	0	2	4	6	8	10	12	14	16	18	20
3	0	3	6	9	12	15	18	21	24	27	30
4	0	4	8	12	16	20	24	28	32	36	40
5	0	5	10	15	20	25	30	35	40	45	50
6	0	6	12	18	24	30	36	42	48	54	60
7	0	7	14	21	28	35	42	49	56	63	70
8	0	8	16	24	32	40	48	56	64	72	80
9	0	9	18	27	36	45	54	63	72	81	90
10	0	10	20	30	40	50	60	70	80	90	100

 MATH IDEA Use equal groups, repeated subtraction, fact families, arrays, and multiplication tables to help you find quotients.

Technology Link
More Practice:
Harcourt Mega Math
Ice Station Exploration,
Arctic Algebra, Level F

▶ Check

1. Explain how to find $56 \div 8$ in two different ways.
Possible answer: Model 56 in 8 equal groups of 7; Think:
$8 \times 7 = 56$. So, $56 \div 8 = 7$.

Write a division sentence for each. Possible answers are given.

2.
$18 \div 6 = 3$

3.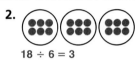
$24 \div 4 = 6$

4.
$\begin{array}{r} 21 \\ -7 \\ \hline 14 \end{array} \quad \begin{array}{r} 14 \\ -7 \\ \hline 7 \end{array} \quad \begin{array}{r} 7 \\ -7 \\ \hline 0 \end{array}$
$21 \div 7 = 3$

Find the missing factor and quotient.

5. $3 \times \blacksquare = 15$ **5** $15 \div 3 = \blacksquare$ **5**

6. $8 \times \blacksquare = 32$ **4** $32 \div 8 = \blacksquare$ **4**

7. $4 \times \blacksquare = 40$ **10** $40 \div 4 = \blacksquare$ **10**

8. $7 \times \blacksquare = 56$ **8** $56 \div 7 = \blacksquare$ **8**

Find the quotient.

9. $10 \div 2 = \blacksquare$ **5**   **10.** $18 \div 9 = \blacksquare$ **2**   **11.** $\blacksquare = 49 \div 7$ **7**   **12.** $80 \div 10 = \blacksquare$ **8**

13. $6\overline{)0}$ **0**   **14.** $9\overline{)9}$ **1**   **15.** $8\overline{)40}$ **5**   **16.** $5\overline{)20}$ **4**

LESSON CONTINUES ▶

- *Check students' understanding of solution E.*
How is using a multiplication table like using a related multiplication fact to find a quotient? You use the divisor as a factor, the dividend as the product, and the second factor for the quotient.

③ PRACTICE

Guided Practice

Do Check Exercises 1–16 with your students. Identify students who are having difficulty and choose appropriate lesson resources to provide assistance.

North Carolina Standards 1.03 Develop fluency with multiplication from 1×1 to 12×12 and division to two-digit by one-digit numbers using: a) Strategies for multiplying and dividing numbers.

Challenge 14.3

The Quotient Game

Play with a partner.

Materials:
2 game tokens
2 sets of number cards with the numbers 1–10

How to Play:
Place the game tokens on **Start**. Shuffle the number cards and turn them face down.

Take turns drawing a number card. Move forward to the closest space with a quotient that matches the number on the card. The first player to reach **Finish** wins!

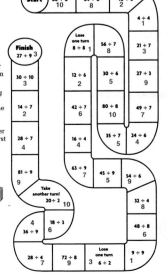

CW74 Challenge

Problem Solving 14.3

Practice Division Facts

Understand ▸ Plan ▸ Solve ▸ Check

Write the correct answer.

1. What dividend is missing from the table? What quotient?

÷	42	49	56	■	70
7	6	7	■	9	10

_63; 8_

2. What are the two division sentences in the fact family for 7, 3, and 21?

$21 \div 3 = 7$ and $21 \div 7 = 3$

3. There are 9 people at a table. Each person has a salad fork, a dinner fork, and a dessert fork. How many forks are on the table?

27 forks

4. Jacob took $45 to the school office to buy tickets to the tournament. He bought 9 tickets. How much did each ticket cost?

_$5_

Choose the letter of the correct answer.

5. What is the value of the 3 in 43,207?

A   30,000   C   300
Ⓑ   3,000   D   30

6. What is the total value of 5 quarters and 5 nickels?

Ⓕ $1.50   H $1.56
G $1.55   J $1.75

7. At the flower shop, Mitch is putting 3 roses into each vase. If there are 27 roses in all, how many vases can Mitch fill?

A   24   Ⓒ   9
B   14   D   8

8. Mr. Adams is displaying some students' drawings. If he has 24 drawings in 3 equal rows, how many are in each row?

F   5   H   7
G   6   Ⓙ   8

9. Write About It How can repeated subtraction help you solve Problem 7?

Possible answer: I can subtract 3 from 27 until I reach 0.

I reach 0 after 9 subtractions.

PS74 Problem Solving

Independent Practice

Note that Exercises 53 and 54 are **multistep or strategy problems.** Assign Exercises 17–54.

Emphasize the importance of memorizing the division facts.

ALGEBRAIC THINKING For Exercises 45–50, tell students to complete the multiplication or division on each side of the ● and then to compare and write >, <, or =.

MULTISTEP OR STRATEGY PROBLEM To solve Exercise 53, students can multiply $9 \times 7 = 63$ to find the number of stickers on 1 sheet, and add $63 + 63 = 126$ to find the number of stickers on 2 sheets. Students then multiply $2 \times 7 = 14$ to find the number of stickers in 2 rows, and subtract $126 - 14 = 112$ to find the number of stickers left. Guide students to conclude that the multiplication must be completed before the addition and subtraction.

Extra Practice, page 288, Set C

Practice and Problem Solving

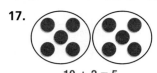

Write a division sentence for each. **Possible answers are given.**

17.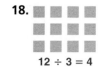
$10 \div 2 = 5$

18.
$12 \div 3 = 4$

19.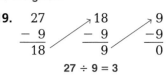
$27 \div 9 = 3$

Find the missing factor and quotient.

20. $10 \times \blacksquare = 90$ **9** $90 \div 10 = \blacksquare$ **9** 21. $7 \times \blacksquare = 35$ **5** $35 \div 7 = \blacksquare$ **5**

22. $4 \times \blacksquare = 16$ **4** $16 \div 4 = \blacksquare$ **4** 23. $9 \times \blacksquare = 63$ **7** $63 \div 9 = \blacksquare$ **7**

Find the quotient.

24. $10 \div 1 = \blacksquare$ **10** 25. $\blacksquare = 35 \div 5$ **7** 26. $50 \div 10 = \blacksquare$ **5** 27. $\blacksquare = 16 \div 2$ **8**

28. $\blacksquare = 81 \div 9$ **9** 29. $\blacksquare = 20 \div 10$ **2** 30. $60 \div 6 = \blacksquare$ **10** 31. $24 \div 3 = \blacksquare$ **8**

32. $9\overline{)54}$ **6** 33. $7\overline{)28}$ **4** 34. $8\overline{)72}$ **9** 35. $10\overline{)100}$ **10**

36. $8\overline{)24}$ **3** 37. $2\overline{)0}$ **0** 38. $4\overline{)4}$ **1** 39. $3\overline{)21}$ **7**

40. Divide 63 by 7. **9** 41. Divide 30 by 5. **6** 42. Divide 0 by 9. **0**

Choose the letter of the division sentence that matches each.

   a. $42 \div 6 = 7$ b. $32 \div 8 = 4$ c. $56 \div 7 = 8$ d. $24 \div 8 = 3$

43. **c**

44. **b**

Compare. Write <, >, or = for each ●.

45. $9 \times 6 ● 9 \times 5$ **>** 46. $24 \div 6 ● 16 \div 4$ **=** 47. $4 + 4 ● 72 \div 8$ **<**

48. $8 \times 5 ● 10 \times 4$ **=** 49. $23 - 18 ● 45 \div 5$ **<** 50. $3 \times 3 ● 70 \div 10$ **>**

51. **REASONING** Roberta has some boxes that hold 8 cars in each. Could the full boxes hold 20 cars in all? Explain. **Possible answer: No; 20 does not divide evenly by 8.**

52. ✏ **Write a problem** about Jonah buying several toy cars that cost $3 each. Use division in your problem. **Check students' problems.**

282

Scaffolded Instruction

Alternative Teaching Strategy

PURPOSE Students practice division strategies.

Divide the class into 5 groups of students. Assign each group one of the five strategies shown in the lesson: A (use counters), B (use repeated subtraction), C (use fact families), D (use an array), or E (use a multiplication table to find missing factors).

Have each group:

• Solve the problem $63 \div 7 = \blacksquare$ by using its assigned strategy. **9**

• Make a display or visual of the strategy to share with the rest of the class.

$63 \div 7 = 9$

• Present its solution to the class and explain why the group thinks this strategy is a good way to solve the problem. Check students' work.

• Have each group choose a different strategy from the one previously assigned to solve $48 \div 6 = \blacksquare$. **8**

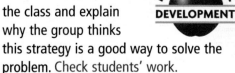

PROFESSIONAL DEVELOPMENT

53. Chi has 2 sheets of stickers. Each sheet has 9 rows of 7 stickers. If Chi uses 2 rows of stickers, how many stickers will Chi have left?
112 stickers

54. Carla put 24 toy animals in 4 boxes. Each box has the same number of animals. How many animals are in 3 boxes? **18 animals**

Getting Ready for the EOG Test

55. Erica has 28 slices of meat. She puts 4 slices of meat on each sandwich. How many sandwiches can Erica make? **D**

A 4   **B** 5   **C** 6   **D** 7

56. James has 63 marbles. He puts an equal number into each of 9 bags. How many marbles are in each bag? **C**

A 9   **B** 8   **C** 7   **D** 6

Problem Solving Thinker's Corner

MAKE A PREDICTION Using what you know about multiplication and division, make a prediction to complete each statement. Choose from the terms below.

greater than   less than   equal to

1. The quotient will be __?__ the dividend in the division problems below. **less than**

2. The product will be __?__ each factor in the multiplication problems below. **greater than**

Check your predictions by completing the number sentences below. Use each number in the box only once. **Possible answers:**

48	6	4
30	63	8
9	5	36

3. ▪ ÷ 6 = ▪
48 ÷ 6 = 8

4. 9 × ▪ = ▪
9 × 4 = 36

5. ▪ ÷ 7 = ▪
63 ÷ 7 = 9

6. ▪ × ▪ = ▪
5 × 6 = 30

Chapter 14   **283**

Reading Strategy

K-W-L CHART Before having students read the Thinker's Corner, have them look at the problems and the chart. Ask them to predict what the Thinker's Corner will be about. Then have students make a three-column chart headed *What I Know, What I Want to Know,* and *What I Learned.* Ask them to fill in the first two columns. Have them fill in the third column as they read through the statements.

K-W-L Chart

What I Know	What I Want to Know	What I Learned

Problem Solving Thinker's Corner

- *Have students read the first statement.* **In a division problem, which number is the quotient and which is the dividend?** The quotient is the answer. The dividend is the number being divided.

- *Have students read the second statement.* **In a multiplication problem, what is a product and a factor?** The product is the answer; the factors are the numbers that are multiplied.

4 ASSESS

Summarize the lesson by having students:

DISCUSS How can you use multiplication to find 24 ÷ 6? Possible answer: Think of the fact family and the related multiplication sentence; $6 \times 4 = 24$, so $24 \div 6 = 4$.

WRITE Describe how you would find 42 ÷ 7 by using one of the strategies in the lesson. Possible answer: Make an array with 7 in each row to find the quotient, 6.

LESSON QUIZ
Find the quotient.

Transparency **14.3**

1. 12 ÷ 3 = ▪ 4

2. 45 ÷ 5 = ▪ 9

3. 24 ÷ 8 = ▪ 3

4. 10 ÷ 1 = ▪ 10

5. 14 ÷ 2 = ▪ 7

6. 54 ÷ 9 = ▪ 6

Lesson Planning

PROFESSIONAL DEVELOPMENT

Objective To use multiplication and division to find the cost of multiple items or the cost of one item

NCTM Standards

1. **Number and Operations**
2. **Algebra**
6. **Problem Solving**
7. **Reasoning and Proof**
8. **Communication**
9. **Connections**
10. **Representation**

Math Background

These ideas will help students find the cost of multiple items or of one item.

● Write a number sentence to help find the cost.

● Multiply the number of items by the cost of one item to find the total cost of multiple items.

● Divide the total amount spent by the number of items to find the cost of one item.

Warm-Up Resources

Number of the Day

Transparency **14.4**

The number of the day is 8.

● Write three multiplication sentences with a product of 8. Possible answers: $8 \times 1 = 8$, $2 \times 4 = 8$, $4 \times 2 = 8$

● Write three division sentences with a quotient of 8. Possible answers: $16 \div 2 = 8$, $24 \div 3 = 8$, $32 \div 4 = 8$

Daily Facts Practice

Have students practice multiplication facts by completing Set E of *Teacher's Resource Book*, p. TR93.

Transparency **14.4**

Problem of the Day

Ben, Carl, and Evan are each less than 15 years old. Last year, Evan was 10 years older than Ben. Next year, Evan will be 3 times as old as Carl. How old are the children now? Ben and Carl: 4 years, Evan: 14 years

Solution Problem of the Day tab, p. PD14

Intervention and Extension Resources

Alternative Teaching Strategy

MATERIALS *For each group* play money, p. TR53

ESOL/ESL

Have students use play money to **find the cost**. Provide each group with a set of one-dollar bills, or have each group make a set. Have students model the problems in the Learn section on page 284.

Then instruct each group to use the one-dollar bills to model and solve the exercises on page 285. Have students separate or combine groups of dollars to find the cost. Check students' work.

KINESTHETIC

BODILY/KINESTHETIC

Multistep and Strategy Problems

The following multistep or strategy problem is provided in Lesson 14.4:

Page	Item
285	27

Early Finishers

MATERIALS catalogs or newspapers

Have students **compare costs**. Have them choose similar items from different advertisements and find the best buy. Check students' work.

VISUAL

VISUAL/SPATIAL

Advanced Learners

Challenge students to **use tables to find missing costs**. Challenge students to use patterns and reasoning to find numbers of items as well as missing costs in the following tables.

Notebooks:	1	2	▓	4	▓	3; 5
Cost:	$2	▓	$6	▓	$10	$4; $8

Bracelets:	1	2	3	▓	5	4
Cost:	▓	$8	▓	$16	▓	$4; $12; $20

Flowers:	1	2	▓	10	12	5
Cost:	$3	▓	$15	▓	▓	$6; $30; $36

VISUAL

LOGICAL/MATHEMATICAL

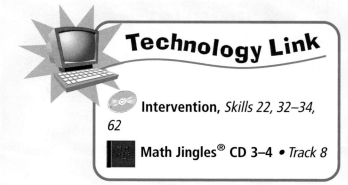

Technology Link

Intervention, *Skills 22, 32–34, 62*

Math Jingles® CD 3–4 • *Track 8*

Lesson 14.4 Organizer

Objective To use multiplication and division to find the cost of multiple items or the cost of one item

Algebra: Find the Cost

① INTRODUCE

QUICK REVIEW provides review of prerequisite skills.

WHY LEARN THIS? You can find the total cost to see if you have enough money to buy several items, or you can find the cost of one item to help you find the best buy. *Share the lesson objective with students.*

② TEACH

Guided Instruction

• *Have students look at the first number sentence in Learn.*
  How do you know the cost of one pizza? Look at the sign.

• *Check students' understanding of the number sentence in the second problem.*
  Why are there dollar signs ($) in front of the dividend and the quotient? These are both costs: the dividend, $12, is the total cost of a box of 6 tacos; and the quotient, $2, is the cost of one taco.
  How can you check your answer? by multiplying $6 \times \$2 = \$12$

• *Discuss the Math Idea.*
  How can you decide whether to divide or multiply to find a cost? Possible answer: Multiply to find the cost of multiple items. Divide to find the cost of one item.

MODIFYING INSTRUCTION You may wish to have students make a table listing the costs of 1 pizza, 2 pizzas, 3 pizzas, and so on.

③ PRACTICE

Guided Practice

Do Check Exercises 1–3 with your students. Identify students who are having difficulty and choose appropriate lesson resources to provide assistance.

▶ Learn

WHAT'S FOR LUNCH? Mrs. Hugo buys 3 pizzas for her family. How much does Mrs. Hugo spend?

To find the total amount spent, multiply the number of pizzas by the cost of one pizza.

3	×	$9	=	$27
↑		↑		↑
number of pizzas		cost of one		total spent

So, Mrs. Hugo spends $27 for 3 pizzas.

Nicolas buys a box of 6 tacos. How much does each taco cost?

To find the cost of one taco, divide the total amount spent by the number of tacos bought.

$12	÷	6	=	$2
↑		↑		↑
total spent		number of tacos		cost of one

So, each taco costs $2.

MATH IDEA Multiply to find the cost of multiple items. Divide to find the cost of one item.

▶ Check

1. Possible answer: 4 cookies cost $4; $4 \div 4 = 1$; so, one cookie costs $1.

1. **Explain** how you can find the cost of one cookie. See above.

For 2–3, write a number sentence. Then solve.

2. Alan bought 4 salads. Each salad cost $3. How much did Alan spend? $4 \times \$3 = \$12$; Alan spent $12.

3. Kim spent $12 on bags of cookies. How many cookies did she buy? $\$12 \div \$4 = 3$ bags; $3 \times 4 = 12$ cookies

The Lunch Box

Pizza	$9
Box of 6 Tacos	$12
Salad	$3
Bag of 4 Cookies	$4

284

Reteach 14.4

Algebra: Find the Cost

You can multiply to find the cost of multiple items.

Example A

Alex bought 5 sandwiches. Each sandwich cost $3. How much did Alex spend?	5 × $3 = $15
	number of sandwiches / cost of one / total spent

Alex spent a total of $15 on sandwiches.

You can divide to find the cost of one item.

Example B

Silva paid $24 for 8 sandwiches. How much does one sandwich cost?	$24 ÷ 8 = $3
	total spent / number of sandwiches / cost of one

One sandwich costs $3.

For 1–9, one notebook costs $3 and one highlighter costs $2. Find the cost of each number of items.

1. 2 highlighters   2. 3 notebooks   3. 4 highlighters
   $2 \times \$2 = \$4$ $3 \times \$3 = \$9$ $4 \times \$2 = \$8$

4. 9 notebooks   5. 7 highlighters   6. 6 notebooks
   $9 \times \$3 = \$27$ $7 \times \$2 = \$14$ $6 \times \$3 = \$18$

7. 5 highlighters   8. 8 notebooks   9. 5 notebooks
   $10 $24 $15

For 10–18, find the cost of one of each item.

10. 8 hats cost $72   11. 6 stamps cost $12   12. 4 T-shirts cost $40
    $72 ÷ 8 = $9 $12 ÷ 6 = $2 $40 ÷ 4 = $10

13. 5 toy trucks cost $25   14. 3 books cost $27   15. 9 CD's cost $81
    $25 ÷ 5 = $5 $27 ÷ 3 = $9 $81 ÷ 9 = $9

16. 3 pies cost $30   17. 7 belts cost $49   18. 10 watches cost $80
    $10 $7 $8

Reteach RW75

Practice 14.4

Algebra: Find the Cost

Complete the table. Use the price list at the right.

Lunch To Go	
Tuna salad	$5
Soft drink	$1
Hot dog	$2
Hamburger	$4

1.
Hot dogs	2	4	6	8	10
Cost	$4	$8	$12	$16	$20

For 2–10, use the price list at the right to find the cost of each number of items.

2. 5 soft drinks   3. 8 hamburgers   4. 9 tuna salads
   $5 $32 $45

5. 7 tuna salads   6. 5 hot dogs   7. 6 hamburgers
   $35 $10 $24

8. 9 hot dogs   9. 3 soft drinks   10. 5 tuna salads
   $18 $3 $25

Find the cost of one of each item.

11. 6 pens cost $18.   12. 4 CDs cost $36.   13. 9 salads cost $36.
    $3 $9 $4

14. 8 mice cost $40.   15. 7 gerbils cost $56.   16. 9 hamsters cost $45.
    $5 $8 $5

17. 3 cages cost $30.   18. 8 balls cost $48.   19. 5 games cost $35.
    $10 $6 $7

Mixed Review

Continue each pattern.

20. 3, 10, 13, 20, 23, 30, __33__, __40__   21. 9, 7, 10, 8, 11, 9, __12__, __10__

Add.

22. 1,382
     7,344
   + 2,196
   ———
    10,922

23. 1,152
      634
    + 776
   ———
    2,562

24. 4,848
     7,474
   + 4,994
   ———
    17,316

25. 618
     554
   + 920
   ———
    2,092

Practice PW75

For 4–5, write a number sentence. Then solve.

4. Sherry bought 4 hot dogs. Each hot dog cost $4. How much did Sherry spend? **4 × $4 = $16; Sherry spent $16.**

5. Mr. Hess spends $18 for an order of 6 sandwiches. How much does each sandwich cost? **$18 ÷ 6 = $3; Each sandwich costs $3.**

USE DATA For 6–16, use the price list at the right to find the cost of each number of items.

6. 4 videos $36   **7.** 6 CDs $42   **8.** 8 CDs $56

9. 7 books $28   **10.** 2 CDs $14   **11.** 5 videos $45

12. 3 books $12   **13.** 9 CDs $63   **14.** 5 books $20

15. 2 videos and 6 books $42

16. 4 books and 5 CDs $51

PRICE LIST	
Books	$4 each
CDs	$7 each
Videos	$9 each

Find the cost of one of each item.

17. 9 markers cost $27. **$3**   **18.** 6 notepads cost $18. **$3**   **19.** 3 stamps cost $15. **$5**

20. 5 baseballs cost $30. **$6**   **21.** 8 pencils cost $8. **$1**   **22.** 4 games cost $32. **$8**

23. 7 toy cars cost $28. **$4**   **24.** 10 pens cost $20. **$2**   **25.** 2 T-shirts cost $12. **$6**

26. REASONING Ako has $20. She wants to buy rubber stamps that cost $6 each. How many rubber stamps can she buy? Explain. **3 rubber stamps; 3 stamps cost $18. 4 stamps cost $4 more than she has.**

27. Heidi buys 3 puzzle books for $24. She gives the clerk $30. How much does each book cost? How much change does she get? **$8 for each book; $6 change**

Getting Ready for the EOG Test

28. Tom bought one cap. How much did he spend? Which number sentence can you use to solve the problem? **B**

A 3 × $4 = $12   **C** $4 + $4 = $8

B $16 ÷ 4 = $4   **D** $16 − $4 = $12

Save-A-Bunch Sale!

5 shirts for	$40
4 caps for	$16
3 T-shirts for	$18
2 ties for	$10

✏ **North Carolina Standards 1.03** Develop fluency with multiplication from 1 × 1 to 12 × 12 and division to two-digit by one-digit numbers using: a) Strategies for multiplying and dividing numbers.

Independent Practice

Note that Exercise 27 is a **multistep or strategy problem.** Assign Exercises 4–27.

ALGEBRAIC THINKING Encourage students to write number sentences to help them solve Exercises 6–25.

4 ASSESS

Summarize the lesson by having students:

DISCUSS You and two friends go out to lunch. Each of you orders the same item. What information do you need to know to find the total cost? Explain. The cost of one item. Multiply this cost by 3 to find the total cost.

WRITE Make a price list that includes the cost of multiple items. Write a problem in which you need to find the cost of one item. Check students' work.

LESSON QUIZ
Find the cost of each number of items.

Transparency **14.4**

1. 5 cereal boxes at $3 each $15

2. 6 shirts at $9 each $54

Find the cost of one of each item.

3. 4 stuffed bears cost $24. $6 each

4. 3 greeting cards cost $6. $2 each

Challenge 14.4

What's the Cost?

Complete the table and solve each problem.

1. Mr. Brown pays $3 for 1 bag of dog food. How much will he pay for 4 bags of food?

Bags	1	2	3	4	5
Cost	$3	$6	$9	$12	$15

$12

2. In Jill's class, 5 students paid a total of $25 for a field trip. If each student pays an equal amount, how much will 3 students pay?

Students	1	2	3	4	5
Cost	$5	$10	$15	$20	$25

$15

3. During the summer, Liza earns $6 every 2 days walking her neighbor's pets. How much does she earn in 5 days?

Days	1	2	3	4	5
Earns	$3	$6	$9	$12	$15

$15

4. It costs $16 for every 4 times the Moran family goes swimming at the pool. If the cost of each visit remains the same, how much will it cost for the Morans to go to the pool 10 times?

Times	1	2	3	4	5
Cost	$4	$8	$12	$16	$20

Times	6	7	8	9	10
Cost	$24	$28	$32	$36	$40

$40

5. A student can buy 9 lunch tokens for $18. If the cost of each token remains the same, how much will a student pay for 3 lunch tokens? How much will 10 lunch tokens cost?

Tokens	1	2	3	4	5
Cost	$2	$4	$6	$8	$10

Tokens	6	7	8	9	10
Cost	$12	$14	$16	$18	$20

$6; $20

Challenge CW75

Problem Solving 14.4

Algebra: Find the Cost   Understand → Plan → Solve → Check

Write the correct answer.

1. Beth bought 9 bracelets to give as gifts. Each bracelet cost $6. How much did Beth spend?

$54

2. Tammy reads 14 hours each week. She reads the same number of hours each day. How many hours does she read each day?

2 hours

3. Jared runs 2 miles at each track practice. He has practice 3 days a week. How many miles will he run in 4 weeks?

24 miles

4. Lin paid $28 for 4 movie tickets. What is the cost of one ticket?

$7

Choose the letter of the correct answer.

5. Jerome spent $36 for 9 packs of baseball cards. Each pack costs the same amount. How much does one pack cost?

A $27   **C** $4.50
B $5   **Ⓓ** $4

6. Kimberly has $15. She wants to buy socks that cost $3 a pair. How many pairs of socks can she buy?

F 4   **H** 6
Ⓖ 5   **J** 10

7. Nancy buys 3 books for $24. She gives the clerk $30. How much change does she get?

A $2   **Ⓒ** $6
B $4   **D** $8

8. Tony has $20. He spends $5 on lunch and $6 on dinner. How much money does he have left?

F $31   **H** $14
G $15   **Ⓙ** $9

9. Write About It Explain how you found your answer to Problem 8.

Possible answer: First I added $5 + $6 = $11 to find the amount Tony spent. Then I subtracted $20 − $11 = $9 to find the amount that Tony had left.

Problem Solving PS75

Problem Solving Strategy
Work Backward

Lesson Planning

Objective To use the problem solving strategy *work backward* to solve problems

Lesson Resources Reading Transparency 14; Intervention • Problem Solving, Strategy/Skill 14

NCTM Standards
1. Number and Operations
6. Problem Solving
7. Reasoning and Proof
8. Communication
10. Representation

Math Background
These ideas will help students understand how to use the strategy *work backward* to solve problems.

- Start with the total and reverse the steps in the problem to find the answer.

- Decide what operations you need to use to work backward through the problem.

- Remember addition and subtraction are inverse, or opposite, operations as are multiplication and division.

- Write number sentences to show each step of the process.

Warm-Up Resources

 Number of the Day Transparency **14.5**

Take the number of centimeters in a meter and divide by 10 to find the number of the day. 10

 Daily Facts Practice

Have students practice addition and subtraction facts by completing Set F of *Teacher's Resource Book*, p. TR93.

 Transparency **14.5**

Problem of the Day

Rachel has 40 trading cards. She wants to share them equally among herself and 4 friends. How many cards does each friend get? 8 cards

Solution Problem of the Day tab, p. PD14

Intervention and Extension Resources

Alternative Teaching Strategy

MATERIALS counters, paper plates

Have students **use counters to solve problems**.

Have students model the problem on page 286 by using their counters to represent popovers and paper plates to represent batches. Have them solve Exercise 1 on page 287 using the same method. Check students' work.

KINESTHETIC

BODILY/KINESTHETIC

Reading Strategy

Sequence Understanding the sequence of events is important to solving problems. Reinforce that to *work backward*, students start with a concluding fact or action. Then they use that fact to "rebuild" the problem from the end to the beginning.

Demonstrate how to make a fact time line for the Problem.

3 × number in each batch + 4 extra popovers = 31 popovers

Have students start with 31 popovers.

31 popovers − 4 extra popovers ÷ 3 batches
   total   →   →

Have students use the *work backward* strategy to solve problems from the lesson. Check students' work.

14 **Reading Transparency 14**

Multistep and Strategy Problems

The following multistep or strategy problems are provided in Lesson 14.5:

Page	Item
287	1–7

ESOL/ESL

MATERIALS play money, pp. TR51–53

ESOL/ESL

Have students **model problems using play money and the *work backward* strategy**.

Present the following problem:

You spent $5.45 on a T-shirt and $4.05 on equipment. You have $2.50 left. How much money did you begin with? $12

- Have students work backward by thinking about turning back time. Have students pose as a T-shirt and equipment salesperson and return the money. Students add it to the amount left to find what they started with.
- Have students solve the money problems in the lesson by using play money and working backward. Have them act out the situation first and then record their solutions. Check students' work.

VISUAL, KINESTHETIC

BODILY/KINESTHETIC

Early Finishers

Have students **work backward to find missing addends**. Have students complete the following:

1. ■ + 41 + 33 = 108 34

2. ■ + 67 + 88 = 245 90

3. ■ + 76 + 89 = 276 111

4. ■ + 46 + 27 = 123 50

Have them write a similar problem for a classmate to solve. Check students' work.

VISUAL

VISUAL/SPATIAL

Technology Link

Intervention • Problem Solving, *Strategy/Skill 14*

Lesson 14.5 Organizer

Objective To use the problem solving strategy *work backward* to solve problems

Lesson Resources Reading Transparency 14; Intervention • Problem Solving, Strategy/Skill 14

1 INTRODUCE

QUICK REVIEW provides review of prerequisite skills.

WHY LEARN THIS? You can use the *work backward* strategy to solve problems with more than one step. *Share the lesson objective with students.*

2 TEACH

Guided Instruction

MODIFYING INSTRUCTION Have students try to solve the problem first. Then they can compare their strategies with those of other students and then with the solution in the book.

- *Read the Problem.*
  What is meant by "3 batches"? This means he filled and baked popovers in the tin 3 times.

- *Discuss the Plan section.*
  To work backward, what information will you start with? He made 31 popovers in all.
  What other strategies could you use to solve the problem? Possible answers: predict and test, draw a picture, use logical reasoning, make a model

- *Check students' understanding of the Solve section.*
  Why do you subtract and then divide? You take away the extras before separating the popovers into equal groups.

- *Have students apply their knowledge.*
  REASONING Suppose Mike made these popovers by tripling his popover recipe. About how many popovers would 1 recipe yield? Explain. Tripling his popover recipe yielded 31 popovers as given in the problem. 31 is close to 30, so one recipe would yield about $30 \div 3 = 10$ popovers.

286 Chapter 14

Problem Solving Strategy
Work Backward

Quick Review
1. $18 \div 3 = \blacksquare$ 6
2. $12 \div 4 = \blacksquare$ 3
3. $24 \div 6 = \blacksquare$ 4
4. $20 \div 2 = \blacksquare$ 10
5. $10 \div 5 = \blacksquare$ 2

PROBLEM Mike baked 3 batches of popovers. The extra batter made 4 more popovers. He made 31 popovers in all. How many popovers does the tin hold?

UNDERSTAND

- What are you asked to find?
  how many popovers the popover tin holds
- What information will you use? **31 popovers in all; 3 batches using the popover tin and 4 extra popovers**

PLAN

- What strategy can you use to solve the problem?

  You can *work backward* to find how many popovers the tin holds.

SOLVE

- How can you use the strategy to solve the problem?

  Begin with the total number of popovers. Subtract the number of extra popovers from the total.

$$31 \quad - \quad 4 \quad = \quad 27$$

| total popovers | extra popovers | popovers in 3 batches |

Divide to find the number of popovers in each batch.

$$27 \quad \div \quad 3 \quad = \quad 9$$

| popovers in 3 batches | number of batches | number in each batch |

So, Mike's tin holds 9 popovers.

CHECK

- Look back. Does your answer make sense?
  Yes; 3 batches of 9 popovers equal 27 popovers. Add 4 extra popovers to get 31 popovers.

286

Reteach 14.5

Problem Solving Strategy

Work Backward

Tiko spent 4 days building a 98 cm bridge out of craft sticks. He built 24 cm of the bridge on Tuesday, 29 cm of the bridge on Wednesday, and 27 cm on Thursday. How much of the bridge did Tiko build on Monday?

UNDERSTAND

1. What are you asked to do? **to find how much of the bridge Tiko built on Monday**

2. What information will you use? **the bridge's length; 24 cm on Tuesday, 29 cm on Wednesday, and 27 cm on Thursday**

PLAN

3. What strategy can you use to solve the problem?
   work backward

SOLVE

4. How can you work backward to solve the problem?
   Add the lengths built on Tuesday, Wednesday, and Thursday; subtract the total from the total length of the bridge.

5. How much of the bridge did he build on Monday? **18 cm**

CHECK

6. Look back. Does your answer make sense? **Yes; 18 cm + 24 cm + 29 cm + 27 cm = 98 cm**

RW76 Reteach

Practice 14.5

Problem Solving Strategy

Work Backward

Work backward to solve.

1. Mr. Ruiz sells mailboxes. He sold 5 mailboxes and then made 12 more. Now he has 15 mailboxes. How many did he begin with?

   8 mailboxes

2. Paul has 23 outfielders and 19 pitchers in his baseball card collection. If he has a total of 95 cards, how many are not outfielders or pitchers?

   53 cards

3. Josh has 17 quarters and 28 dimes in his bank. There are 102 coins in the bank. How many are not quarters or dimes?

   57 coins

4. Tim sells picture frames. He sold 14 and then made 8 more. Now he has 23 frames. How many did he begin with?

   29 frames

Mixed Review

Solve.

5. 274	6. $1.92	7. $2.52	8. 381
36	$3.34	$1.12	77
+183	+$0.57	+$0.67	+342
493	$5.83	$4.31	800

Continue each pattern.

9. 2, 9, 16, 23, **30**, **37**   10. 36, 31, 26, 21, **16**, **11**

11. 11, 14, 17, 20, **23**, **26**   12. 64, 58, 52, 46, **40**, **34**

Multiply.

13. $9 \times 10 =$ **90**   14. $7 \times 4 =$ **28**   15. $8 \times 8 =$ **64**

16. $4 \times 3 =$ **12**   17. $5 \times 9 =$ **45**   18. $7 \times 5 =$ **35**

19. $6 \times 7 =$ **42**   20. $9 \times 7 =$ **63**

PW76 Practice

▶ Problem Solving Practice

Work backward to solve.

1. What if Mike used a different tin to bake 4 batches of popovers? Then he used the extra batter to make 3 more popovers. He made 27 popovers in all. How many popovers does this tin hold? **6 popovers**

2. Mr. Jones spent $30 at the sports shop. He bought a mitt for $10 and 4 balls. How much did each ball cost? **$5 for each ball**

Strategies

Draw a Diagram or Picture
Make a Model or Act It Out
Make an Organized List
Find a Pattern
Make a Table or Graph
Predict and Test
▶ **Work Backward**
Solve a Simpler Problem
Write a Number Sentence
Use Logical Reasoning

Mr. Lo bought 2 books that cost the same amount. He gave the cashier $20 and received $6 in change. How much money did each book cost?

3. Which number sentence shows how to find the total cost of the 2 books? **C**

A $20 + $6 = $26
B $2 \times $6 = $12
C $20 - $6 = $14
D $20 \div 2 = $10

4. How much money did each book cost? **G**

F $6
G $7
H $10
J $14

7. 3 quarters; 2 quarters, 2 dimes, 1 nickel; 2 quarters, 2 dimes, 5 pennies; 2 quarters, 1 dime, 2 nickels, 5 pennies

Mixed Strategy Practice

USE DATA For 5–7, use the price list.

5. Zach pays for an apple pie and a bag of cookies with a $10 bill. He gets his change in quarters and dimes. There are 13 coins in all. How many of each coin does Zach get? **8 quarters and 5 dimes**

6. **What's the Error?** Lara says a lemon tart and 2 boxes of muffins cost $11.65. Describe Lara's error and give the correct cost of the items. **Lara found the cost of a lemon tart and only 1 box of muffins; $15.10**

Bake Sale Price List
- Bag of 3 Cookies $0.75
- Box of 6 Muffins $3.45
- Apple Pie $6.75
- Lemon Tart $8.20

7. Tim has 3 quarters, 2 dimes, 2 nickels, and 5 pennies. List all the ways he can pay for a bag of cookies. **See above.**

Chapter 14 **287**

⟡ **North Carolina Standards 1.06** Develop flexibility in solving problems by selecting strategies and using mental computation, estimation, calculators or computers, and paper and pencil.

---

3 PRACTICE

Guided Practice

Do Problem Solving Practice Exercises 1–4 with your students. Identify students who are having difficulty and choose appropriate lesson resources to provide assistance. Note that Exercises 1–4 are **multistep or strategy problems.**

Independent Practice

Note that Exercises 5–7 are **multistep or strategy problems.** Assign Exercises 5–7.

4 ASSESS

Summarize the lesson by having students:

DISCUSS How do you know when the *work backward* strategy might be a good one to use? Possible answer: if you're given a concluding fact or if you have to go backward in time to find the answer

WRITE Describe a problem you can work backward to solve. Exchange with a partner and solve. Check students' work.

LESSON QUIZ
Work backward to solve.

Transparency
14.5

1. A sales clerk sold 12 shirts on Wednesday and 6 shirts on Thursday. On Friday morning, the clerk stocked the shelves with 20 more shirts, so there were 42 shirts on display. How many shirts were on display when the store opened on Wednesday? 40 shirts

2. Carol's mom spent $10 on ice cream. She bought a sundae for $4 and 3 small ice cream cones. How much did each cone cost? $2

Challenge 14.5

What Number Am I?

Read each number riddle. Use the clues to identify each number.

1. If you add 7 to me and then divide the result by me, the answer is 8. What number am I?

1

2. Multiply me by 5, and you get a number that is 5 more than 20. What number am I?

5

3. Divide me by 3, or multiply me by 6. The answer will be the same. What number am I?

0

4. When you multiply me by myself, you get me again! What number am I?

1 or 0

5. Divide 12 by 3, and you get me. Divide 12 by me, and you get 3. What number am I?

4

6. If you multiply any number by me, the sum of the digits in the product equals me. What number am I?

9

7. If you divide 30 by me, the answer is 3 doubled. What number am I?

5

8. If you divide any number by me, your answer will be that number again! What number am I?

1

9. Write your own number riddle. After solving it yourself, ask a classmate to try it.

Answers will vary.

CW76 Challenge

Reading Strategy 14.5

Sequence Information   Understand ▶ Plan ▶ Solve ▶ Check

When several events happen in a story, it is important to understand the order of the events, or the **sequence**. Sequence is also important in math problems because sometimes you will work from beginning to end, and other times you will work backward to solve problems.

VOCABULARY
sequence

Read the following problem.

▶ Mrs. Hechter is knitting an afghan. Today the afghan is 74 inches long. During the week of January 7, she knitted 12 inches. By January 14 Mrs. Hechter had knitted 16 inches more. She is now working on the border. How long was the afghan before January 7?

List the sequence of events in the order they happened.

Week of January 7 – She knitted 12 inches.
Week of January 14 – She knitted 16 inches more.
Now the afghan is 74 inches long.

1. Solve the problem.

Start with 74. Subtract amounts knitted each week. 74 − 16 = 58;

58 − 12 = 46; the afghan was 46 in. long before January 7.

2. Describe the problem solving strategy you used. **Possible answer:**

I worked backward from 74 in. by subtracting the amount

knitted each week to find the length before January 7.

Sequence the events in order. Solve.

3. Emma bought a package of stamps. She gave her brother 6 stamps. She used 17 stamps to send cards. She has 27 stamps left. How many stamps were in the package she bought?

Possible answer: gave brother 6; used 17; has 27 left;

6 + 17 + 27 = 50; there were 50 in package

PS76 Reading Strategy

287

CHAPTER 14 Extra Practice

Purpose To provide extra practice for the skills presented in this chapter

The blue page references in each set of exercises refer to the lesson pages where each skill is taught.

Internet Resources

Visit **THE LEARNING SITE** at **www.harcourtschool.com** for a listing of practice activities.

Extra Practice

Set A (pp. 274–277)

Find the missing factor and quotient.

1. $8 \times \blacksquare = 32$ 4 $\quad 32 \div 8 = \blacksquare$ 4 **2.** $7 \times \blacksquare = 35$ 5 $\quad 35 \div 7 = \blacksquare$ 5

Find the quotient.

3. $42 \div 6 = \blacksquare$ 7 **4.** $\blacksquare = 24 \div 4$ 6 **5.** $64 \div 8 = \blacksquare$ 8 **6.** $\blacksquare = 21 \div 7$ 3

7. $7\overline{)49}$ 7 **8.** $2\overline{)2}$ 1 **9.** $6\overline{)36}$ 6 **10.** $5\overline{)40}$ 8 **11.** $8\overline{)48}$ 6

12. Divide 63 by 7. 9 **13.** Divide 80 by 8. 10 **14.** Divide 15 by 3. 5

Set B (pp. 278–279)

Find the quotient.

1. $\blacksquare = 36 \div 9$ 4 **2.** $20 \div 10 = \blacksquare$ 2 **3.** $\blacksquare = 20 \div 5$ 4 **4.** $54 \div 6 = \blacksquare$ 9

5. $3\overline{)12}$ 4 **6.** $10\overline{)70}$ 7 **7.** $9\overline{)72}$ 8 **8.** $4\overline{)16}$ 4 **9.** $9\overline{)27}$ 3

10. Divide 56 by 8. 7 **11.** Divide 60 by 6. 10 **12.** Divide 100 by 10. 10

Set C (pp. 280–283)

Find the quotient.

1. $6 \div 6 = \blacksquare$ 1 **2.** $\blacksquare = 7 \div 1$ 7 **3.** $\blacksquare = 0 \div 5$ 0 **4.** $28 \div 7 = \blacksquare$ 4

5. $9\overline{)81}$ 9 **6.** $3\overline{)18}$ 6 **7.** $6\overline{)24}$ 4 **8.** $2\overline{)20}$ 10 **9.** $7\overline{)0}$ 0

10. Divide 32 by 4. 8 **11.** Divide 40 by 10. 4 **12.** Divide 16 by 8. 2

Set D (pp. 284–285)

USE DATA For 1–4, use the price list at the right to find the cost of each number of items.

PRICE LIST	
Mugs	$4
Aprons	$8

1. 3 aprons $24 **2.** 5 mugs $20 **3.** 6 aprons $48 **4.** 8 mugs $32

Find the cost of one of each item.

5. 2 pizzas cost $14. $7 **6.** 4 tapes cost $32. $8 **7.** 5 books cost $25. $5

8. 6 pens cost $12. $2 **9.** 7 balls cost $21. $3 **10.** 3 shirts cost $27. $9

288

Review/Test

✓ CHECK CONCEPTS

Write a division sentence for each. (pp. 280–283) **Possible answers are given.**

1.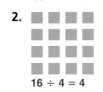

   12 ÷ 3 = 4

2.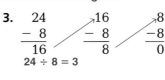

   16 ÷ 4 = 4

3.
$$24 \quad \nearrow16 \quad \nearrow8$$
$$-\;8 \quad -\;8 \quad -\;8$$
$$\overline{16} \quad \overline{8} \quad \overline{0}$$

   24 ÷ 8 = 3

✓ CHECK SKILLS

Find the missing factor and quotient. (pp. 274–277)

4. 8 × ■ = 40 **5**   40 ÷ 8 = ■ **5**

5. 6 × ■ = 42 **7**   42 ÷ 6 = ■ **7**

6. 7 × ■ = 56 **8**   56 ÷ 7 = ■ **8**

7. 8 × ■ = 32 **4**   32 ÷ 8 = ■ **4**

Find the quotient. (pp. 274–283)

8. 14 ÷ 7 = ■ **2**   9. ■ = 30 ÷ 5 **6**   10. 40 ÷ 4 = ■ **10**   11. ■ = 63 ÷ 9 **7**

12. 8)24 **3**   13. 10)90 **9**   14. 2)14 **7**   15. 9)18 **2**   16. 3)27 **9**

For 17–20, use the price list at the right to find the
cost of each number of items. (pp. 284–285)

17. 4 balloons
    $12

18. 7 noisemakers
    $14

19. 3 noisemakers
    $6

20. 9 balloons
    $27

PARTY SUPPLIES PRICE LIST	
Balloons	$3 each
Noisemakers	$2 each

Find the cost of one of each item. (pp. 284–285)

21. 5 notebooks cost $10.
    $2

22. 6 markers cost $18.
    $3

23. 5 caps cost $35.
    $7

✓ CHECK PROBLEM SOLVING

Work backward to solve. (pp. 286–287)

24. Nikki used a tin to make 3
    batches of popovers. Then she
    made 2 extra popovers. She
    made 26 popovers in all. How
    many popovers does the tin hold?
    8 popovers

25. Roger earned $35. He made $15
    from a paper route. He also
    walked 4 dogs after school. How
    much did Roger charge to walk
    each dog? **$5**

Chapter 14 **289**

Review/Test

Purpose To check understanding of concepts,
skills, and problem solving presented in Chapter 14

Using the Page

The Chapter 14 Review/Test can be used as a
review or a **test**.

- Items 1–3 check understanding of new concepts.
- Items 4–23 check skill proficiency.
- Items 24–25 check students' abilities to choose
  and apply problem solving strategies to real-life
  division problems.

Portfolio — Suggest that students place the completed Chapter 14 Review/Test in their
portfolios.

Using the Assessment Guide

- Multiple-choice format of Chapter 14 Posttest—
  See *Assessment Guide*, pp. AG85–86.
- Free-response format of Chapter 14 Posttest—
  See *Assessment Guide*, pp. AG87–88.

Using Student Self-Assessment

The How Did I Do? survey helps students assess
what they have learned and how they learned it.
This survey is available as a copying master in
Assessment Guide, p. AGxvii.

Chapter 14 Test, page 1

Choose the correct answer.

1. 40 ÷ 8 = ■
   - A 4
   - Ⓑ 5
   - C 6
   - D 7

2. 6)54
   - F 7
   - G 8
   - Ⓗ 9
   - J 10

3. ■ = 14 ÷ 7
   - A 98
   - B 21
   - C 7
   - Ⓓ 2

4. What number completes the number sentence?
   32 ÷ ■ = 8 − 5
   - F 4
   - G 6
   - Ⓗ 8
   - J 9

5. Morgan worked 16 hours in 3 days. He worked 4 hours 1 day and the same number of hours on each of the other 2 days. How many hours did he work on each of the other days?
   - A 2
   - B 3
   - Ⓒ 6
   - D 7

6. 9)36
   - F 2
   - G 3
   - Ⓗ 4
   - J 5

7. 81 ÷ 9 = ■
   - A 7
   - B 8
   - Ⓒ 9
   - D 10

8. 10)50
   - F 4
   - Ⓖ 5
   - H 6
   - J 7

9. Compare. What symbol makes this number sentence true?
   9 ● 9 = 5 − 4
   - A +
   - B −
   - C ×
   - Ⓓ ÷

10. Paul bought 60 pencils. There were 10 pencils in each box. How many boxes did he buy?
    - F 70
    - G 50
    - H 16
    - Ⓙ 6

Go On ▶

Chapter 14 Test, page 2

11. Compare. What symbol makes this true?
    2 × 3 ● 72 ÷ 9
    - Ⓐ <
    - B >
    - C =

12. Find the missing factor and quotient.
    7 × ■ = 21   21 ÷ 7 = ■
    - Ⓕ 3
    - G 7
    - H 14
    - J 28

13. Divide 0 by 10.
    - Ⓐ 0
    - B 1
    - C 7
    - D 8

14. Each watermelon costs $2. How much will 10 watermelons cost?
    - F $5
    - G $10
    - H $15
    - Ⓙ $20

15. Greta bought 8 yards of ribbon. She gave the clerk $40 and got $8 in change. How much did one yard of ribbon cost?
    - A $3
    - Ⓑ $4
    - C $13
    - D $24

16. Each ticket costs $5. How much will 6 tickets cost?
    - F $42
    - Ⓖ $30
    - H $18
    - J $11

17. Eight notebooks cost $24. How much does 1 notebook cost?
    - Ⓐ $3
    - B $4
    - C $8
    - D $16

18. Mrs. Wilson spends $15 for 5 sandwiches. How much does each sandwich cost?
    - Ⓕ $3
    - G $5
    - H $6
    - J $7

19. Bob threw 6 of the fish he caught back in the water. He divided the rest equally among 4 people. Each person got 4 fish. How many fish did Bob catch?
    - A 12
    - B 13
    - Ⓒ 22
    - D 27

20. Angie was thinking of a number. She added 5 to the number. She divided that sum by 2 and got 10. What was her number?
    - F 0
    - G 10
    - Ⓗ 15
    - J 25

Stop ■

Division Facts Through 10 **289**

CHAPTER 14

Getting Ready for the EOG Test
Chapters 1–14

Using the Pages

These pages may be used to help students get ready for the North Carolina EOG Test. The test items are written in the same style and arranged in the same format as those on the EOG Test.

The pages are cumulative. They cover the standards from the North Carolina Mathematics Standard Course of Study that have been taught up to this point in the text or in a previous grade. Each Getting Ready for the EOG Test also reviews the North Carolina mathematics strands shown below.

- Number and Operations
- Measurement
- Geometry
- Data Analysis and Probability
- Algebra

These pages can be assigned at the end of the chapter as classwork or as a homework assignment. You may want to have students use individual recording sheets presented in a multiple-choice (standardized) format. A Test Answer Sheet is available as a blackline master in the *Assessment Guide* (p. AGlii).

You may wish to have students describe how they solved each problem and share their solutions.

Getting Ready for the EOG Test

⭐ NUMBER AND OPERATIONS

1. Which of the multiplication facts belongs to the same fact family as these division facts? **B**

    $56 \div 8 = 7$ $56 \div 7 = 8$

    A $8 \times 8 = 64$
    B $7 \times 8 = 56$
    C $7 \times 7 = 49$
    D $5 \times 6 = 30$

2. Ramona baked 36 muffins. She put 9 muffins in each bag. How many bags did Ramona use? **D**

    A 24   **C** 9
    B 18   **D** 4

3. Which of the following number sentences does the drawing show? **C**

    A $10 \div 2 = 5$
    B $80 \div 10 = 8$
    C $40 \div 5 = 8$
    D $50 \div 5 = 10$

4. **Explain It** Barb scored 211 points in a video game. Kelsey scored 58 fewer points than Barb. *About* how many points did Kelsey score? Tell how you found your answer. **See page 291.**

⭐ MEASUREMENT AND GEOMETRY

5. How many lines of symmetry does the figure have? **B**

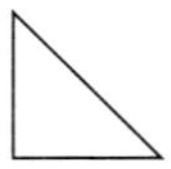

    A 0   **B** 1   **C** 2   **D** 3

6. Which pair of figures appears to be congruent? **D**

    A

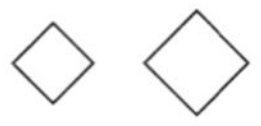

    B

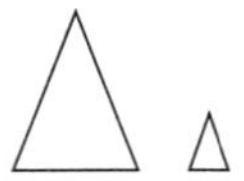

    C

    D

    TIP **Eliminate choices.** See item 7. The answer is a 5-sided figure. So, you can eliminate any choice that does not have 5 sides.

7. Helen drew a polygon with 5 equal sides. Which shape did she draw? **A**

    A pentagon   **C** triangle
    B square   **D** circle

8. **Explain It** Tony traced the faces of a solid figure. He counted 6 squares. What solid figure did Tony trace? Explain how you found your answer. **See page 291.**

290

⭐ ALGEBRA

9. What is the next number in this pattern? **C**

90, 81, 72, 63, ■

A 64   **C** 54
B 59   **D** 51

10. Which group contains only numbers that are multiples of 6? **C**
A 3, 6, 20
B 15, 30, 45
C 12, 18, 30
D 16, 33, 36

11. Kevin bought 6 pies at the farmers' market.

Pies	1	2	3	4	5	6
Cost	$6	$12	$18	$24	$30	■

How much did Kevin spend on the 6 pies? **A**

A $36   **C** $32
B $35   **D** $6

12. Explain It Lee made this division table. Find a rule for his pattern. What is the missing number? Explain how you found your answer. **See below.**

LEE'S DIVISION TABLE	
56	8
49	7
42	6
35	5
28	■

⭐ DATA ANALYSIS AND PROBABILITY

13. What is the probability of pulling a green tile? **B**

A impossible   **C** certain
B unlikely   **D** likely

14. Jada made a pictograph to show the sales at her snow cone stand. How many **more** snow cones did Jada sell on Monday than on Wednesday? **C**

SNOW CONE SALES

Sat	🍦🍦🍦🍦🍦🍦🍦🍦
Sun	🍦🍦🍦🍦🍦🍦🍦
Mon	🍦🍦🍦🍦🍦🍦
Tue	🍦🍦🍦
Wed	🍦🍦

Key: Each 🍦 = 5 snow cones.

A 5   **C** 20
B 10   **D** 30

15. Explain It After looking at the pictograph above, Jada said that people bought more snow cones on Saturday and Sunday than on weekdays. Do you agree with her? Explain why or why not. **See below.**

Chapters 1–14

Item Analysis

You may wish to use the item analysis to determine which North Carolina standards need additional review.

Item	North Carolina Standard	Lesson
1	1.03	12.4
2	1.03	14.2
3	1.03	13.1
4	1.06	5.1
5	(2) 3.03	Grade 2
6	(2) 3.03	Grade 2
7	(2) 3.01	Grade 2
8	(2) 3.01	Grade 2
9	5.01	2.5
10	5.01	10.1
11	5.02	10.1
12	5.01	14.1
13	(2) 4.02	Grade 2
14	(2) 4.01	Grade 2
15	(2) 4.01	Grade 2

SCORING RUBRIC
Explain It

2 Demonstrates a complete understanding of the problem and chooses an appropriate strategy to determine the solution

1 Demonstrates a partial understanding of the problem and chooses a strategy that does not lead to a complete and accurate solution

0 Demonstrates little understanding of the problem and shows little evidence of using any strategy to determine a solution

Explain It • Written Response

4. About 140 points; possible answer: round 211 to 200 and 58 to 60, then subtract: 200 − 60 = 140.

8. Possible answer: Tony traced a cube; all 6 faces of a cube are squares.

12. 4; Possible rule: divide the numbers in the first column by 7; 56 ÷ 7 = 8 and 49 ÷ 7 = 7; so divide the numbers in the first column by 7 to get the numbers in the second column.

15. Yes; possible answer: there are 15 snow cone symbols for Saturday and Sunday and only 11 symbols for the weekdays.

IT'S IN THE BAG

It's in the Bag
Candy Bar Division

Purpose To make a candy bar wrapper booklet to practice division facts

Materials *For each student* construction paper, silver foil, ruler, 2 sheets of $8\frac{1}{2}$ inch × 11 inch unlined paper, pencil, scissors, glue or tape, candy wrapper pattern, pp. TR186–187

Using the Page

Preparing the Materials

- Gather all of the materials needed for the class.

Making the Project

- Students may wish to use the pattern on pp. TR186–187. Cut 2 thin strips of silver foil that equal the length of the construction paper. When preparing the wrapper, attach the 2 strips of silver foil to the side edges of the construction paper so that when the construction paper wrapper is folded around the bar, the foil appears to cover the bar inside. Have students tape the 2 sheets of unlined paper together and then fold the paper accordion style so that the space between each fold measures about 1 to 2 inches. Using 2 or more sheets of paper and taping them together enables students to write more problems in their booklet. Encourage students to write problems on both sides of the papers.

Extending the Project

- Challenge students to write division story problems in their booklets. Encourage students to think of the different ways division can be modeled, such as by separating into equal groups and finding the number in each group or by finding the number of equal groups in a set. Students can draw diagrams to show how to solve each story problem.

Candy Bar Division

PROJECT Make a "candy bar" booklet for practicing division facts.

Materials

- Silver foil
- Construction paper
- Wrapper pattern
- Ruler
- 2 sheets of $8\frac{1}{2}'' \times 11''$ unlined paper
- Pencil
- Scissors
- Glue or tape

Directions

1. Using the construction paper and the pattern make and decorate a large "candy bar" wrapper. Glue a piece of silver foil inside each end of the wrapper to look like a real candy bar. Name the candy bar.

2. Measure the width of the wrapper. *(Picture A)* Draw a line slightly shorter than that width on unlined paper. Fold the paper accordion style (back and forth) so that the folded paper will fit into the wrapper.

3. Cut the folded paper about 1 inch longer than the length of the candy bar wrapper. Repeat with the second sheet of paper and glue or tape the two folded sheets together. *(Picture B)*

4. Write a different division problem on each space of the folded paper. *(Picture C)*

5. Fold up the paper and then solve the problems in the candy bar booklet.

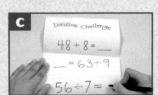

292 Unit 4 • It's in the Bag

Challenge

Divide by 11 and 12

Mr. Samson gathered 132 eggs. He wants to put them into egg cartons that hold 12 eggs each. How many egg cartons does Mr. Samson need?

$$132 \div 12 = \blacksquare$$

number of eggs   number in each carton   number of cartons

×	0	1	2	3	4	5	6	7	8	9	10	11	12
0	0	0	0	0	0	0	0	0	0	0	0	0	0
1	0	1	2	3	4	5	6	7	8	9	10	11	12
2	0	2	4	6	8	10	12	14	16	18	20	22	24
3	0	3	6	9	12	15	18	21	24	27	30	33	36
4	0	4	8	12	16	20	24	28	32	36	40	44	48
5	0	5	10	15	20	25	30	35	40	45	50	55	60
6	0	6	12	18	24	30	36	42	48	54	60	66	72
7	0	7	14	21	28	35	42	49	56	63	70	77	84
8	0	8	16	24	32	40	48	56	64	72	80	88	96
9	0	9	18	27	36	45	54	63	72	81	90	99	108
10	0	10	20	30	40	50	60	70	80	90	100	110	120
11	0	11	22	33	44	55	66	77	88	99	110	121	132
12	0	12	24	36	48	60	72	84	96	108	120	132	144

Use a multiplication table to find the quotient.

Think: $12 \times \blacksquare = 132$

Find the factor 12 in the top row. Look down the column to find the product, 132. Look left along the row to find the missing factor, 11.

$12 \times 11 = 132$

$132 \div 12 = 11$

So, Mr. Samson needs 11 egg cartons.

Talk About It

• Explain how to use repeated subtraction to find
  $48 \div 12$. **$48 - 12 = 36$, $36 - 12 = 24$, $24 - 12 = 12$, $12 - 12 = 0$. Subtract 12 from 48 four times. So, $48 \div 12 = 4$.**
• What patterns do you notice in the column for 11 on the multiplication table? **Possible answer: the ones digits start at 0 and increase by 1 up to 9. Then the ones digits start at 0 again.**

Try It

Use the multiplication table to solve.

1. $99 \div 11 = \blacksquare$ 9   2. $\blacksquare = 108 \div 12$ 9   3. $110 \div 11 = \blacksquare$ 10   4. $\blacksquare = 84 \div 12$ 7

5. $72 \div 12 = \blacksquare$ 6   6. $66 \div 11 = \blacksquare$ 6   7. $\blacksquare = 144 \div 12$ 12   8. $0 \div 11 = \blacksquare$ 0

9. $12\overline{)120}$ 10   10. $11\overline{)121}$ 11   11. $11\overline{)77}$ 7   12. $12\overline{)36}$ 3

Challenge

Divide by 11 and 12

Objective To extend the concepts and skills of Chapters 12–14

Using the Page

• *Direct students' attention to the multiplication table.*
  Explain how you could use a multiplication table to find $96 \div 12$. Find the factor 12 in the top row. Look down the column to find the product 96. Look left to find the missing quotient, 8.
  Name other ways to find $96 \div 12$. repeated subtraction, equal groups, a related multiplication fact, or an array
  Explain how you could use an array to find $77 \div 11$. Possible answer: divide 77 into 11 equal rows and count how many are in each row; $77 \div 11 = 7$

Try It Before assigning the Try It exercises, remind students that there are many ways to solve these division sentences.

Intervention and Extension Resources

Special Needs

Help students **understand division by drawing pictures.** Have students draw an array of $60 \div 12$. Have them use an object other than a square to draw the array, such as hearts, flowers, or baseballs. When students have finished, have them write a division sentence to go with their picture. Have them repeat this for other exercises. Check students' work.

VISUAL

VISUAL/SPATIAL

UNIT 4

Study Guide and Review

Purpose To help students review concepts and skills presented in Chapters 12–14

Using the Pages

☑ Assessment Checkpoint

The Study Guide and Review includes content from Chapters 12–14.

Chapter 12

12.1 Hands On: The Meaning of Division

12.2 Subtraction and Division

12.3 Algebra: Multiplication and Division

12.4 Algebra: Fact Families

12.5 Problem Solving Strategy: *Write a Number Sentence*

Chapter 13

13.1 Divide by 2 and 5

13.2 Divide by 3 and 4

13.3 Divide with 1 and 0

13.4 Algebra: Expressions and Equations

13.5 Problem Solving Skill: *Choose the Operation*

Chapter 14

14.1 Divide by 6, 7, and 8

14.2 Divide by 9 and 10

14.3 Practice Division Facts

14.4 Algebra: Find the Cost

14.5 Problem Solving Strategy: *Work Backward*

The blue page numbers in parentheses provided with each group of exercises indicate the pages on which the concept or skill was presented.

Study Guide and Review

VOCABULARY

Choose the best term from the box.

> one
> fact family
> quotient
> zero

1. A set of related multiplication and division sentences is a __?__ . (p. 246) **fact family**

2. Any number divided by __?__ is that number. (p. 262) **one**

STUDY AND SOLVE

Chapter 12

Use repeated subtraction to divide.

$28 \div 7 = \blacksquare$

$$\begin{array}{ccccccc} 28 & & 21 & & 14 & & 7 \\ -7 & \nearrow & -7 & \nearrow & -7 & \nearrow & -7 \\ \hline 21 & & 14 & & 7 & & 0 \end{array}$$

You subtracted 7 from 28 four times.
So, $28 \div 7 = 4$.

Write the division sentence shown by the repeated subtraction. (pp. 240–241)

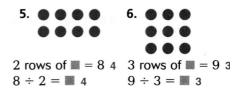

3.
$$\begin{array}{ccccc} 15 & & 10 & & 5 \\ -5 & \nearrow & -5 & \nearrow & -5 \\ \hline 10 & & 5 & & 0 \end{array}$$
$15 \div 5 = 3$

4.
$$\begin{array}{ccccc} 32 & & 24 & & 16 & & 8 \\ -8 & \nearrow & -8 & \nearrow & -8 & \nearrow & -8 \\ \hline 24 & & 16 & & 8 & & 0 \end{array}$$
$32 \div 8 = 4$

Use arrays to divide.

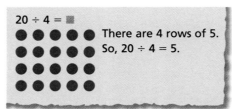

$20 \div 4 = \blacksquare$

There are 4 rows of 5.
So, $20 \div 4 = 5$.

Use the array to find the quotient. (pp. 242–245)

5. ● ● ● ● ●
● ● ● ● ●

6. ● ● ●
● ● ●
● ● ●

2 rows of ■ = 8 4
$8 \div 2 = \blacksquare$ 4

3 rows of ■ = 9 3
$9 \div 3 = \blacksquare$ 3

Write fact families.

This is the fact family for 3, 4, and 12.
$3 \times 4 = 12 \quad 12 \div 4 = 3$
$4 \times 3 = 12 \quad 12 \div 3 = 4$

Write the fact family for each set of numbers. (pp. 246–249) Check students' number sentences.

7. 3, 9, 27   8. 6, 7, 42

9. 5, 8, 40   10. 4, 9, 36

Chapter 13

Use related multiplication facts to find quotients.

45 ÷ 5 = ▨
Think: 5 × ▨ = 45
    5 × 9 = 45
So, 45 ÷ 5 = 9, or 5)45.

Find each quotient. (pp. 258–263)

11. 18 ÷ 3 = ▨ **6**   **12.** 30 ÷ 5 = ▨ **6**

13. 20 ÷ 4 = ▨ **5**   **14.** 16 ÷ 2 = ▨ **8**

15. 40 ÷ 5 = ▨ **8**   **16.** 24 ÷ 4 = ▨ **6**

17. 4)32 **8**   **18.** 3)9 **3**   **19.** 2)10 **5**

Chapter 14

Multiply to find the cost of multiple items.

Pens cost $4 each. Find the cost of 7 pens.
7 × $4 = $28
So, 7 pens cost $28.

Divide to find the cost of one item.

8 erasers cost $16.
$16 ÷ 8 = $2
So, each eraser costs $2.

Beach balls cost $3 each. Find the cost of each number of items. (pp. 284–285)

20. 6 beach balls **$18**

21. 2 beach balls **$6**

22. 5 beach balls **$15**

Find the cost of one of each item. (pp. 284–285)

23. 9 tennis balls cost $18. **$2**

24. 7 baskets cost $42. **$6**

25. 10 notepads cost $10. **$1**

PROBLEM SOLVING PRACTICE

Solve. (pp. 250–251, 266–267, 286–287)

26. Marcie bought 5 packs of juice. There are 3 juice boxes in each pack. How many juice boxes did Marcie buy? Write a number sentence and solve.
5 × 3 = 15; 15 juice boxes

27. Noah spent 15 minutes eating lunch and then played kickball for 25 minutes. Now it is 12:45 P.M. At what time did Noah start eating lunch? **12:05 P.M.**

28. Janet had $7.35 and spent $2.50 on a snack. How much money does Janet have left? **$4.85**

✔ Assessment Checkpoint

Portfolio Suggestions The portfolio represents the growth, talents, achievements, and reflections of the mathematics learner. Students might spend a short time selecting work samples for their portfolios and completing A Guide to My Math Portfolio from *Assessment Guide*, page AGxix.

You may want to have students respond to the following questions:

• **What new understanding of math have I developed in the past several weeks?**

• **What growth in understanding or skills can I see in my work?**

• **What can I do to improve my understanding of math ideas?**

• **What would I like to learn more about?**

For information on how to organize, share, and evaluate portfolios, see *Assessment Guide*, page AGxviii.

Use the item analysis in the **Intervention** chart to diagnose students' errors. You may wish to reinforce content or remediate misunderstandings by using the text pages or lesson resources.

Unit Test

• Multiple-choice format of Unit 4 Posttest—See *Assessment Guide*, pp. AG89–92.

• Free-Response format of Unit 4 Posttest—See *Assessment Guide*, pp. AG93–96.

Study Guide and Review Intervention • How to Help Options

Items	Text Pages	Reteach and Practice Resources
3–4	240–241	Worksheets for Lesson 12.2
5–6	242–245	Worksheets for Lesson 12.3
7–10	246–249	Worksheets for Lesson 12.4
11–19	258–263	Worksheets for Lessons 13.1, 13.2, 13.3
20–25	284–285	Worksheets for Lesson 14.4
26–28	250–251, 266–267, 286–287	Worksheets for Lessons 12.5, 13.5, 14.5

Performance Assessment

Purpose To provide performance assessment tasks for Chapters 12–14

Using the Page

- *Have students work individually or in pairs as an alternative to formal assessment.*

- *Use the performance indicators and work samples below to evaluate Tasks A–B.*

See *Performance Assessment* for

- a complete scoring rubric, p. PAx, for this unit.
- additional student work samples for this unit.
- copying masters for this unit.

 You may suggest that students place completed Performance Assessment tasks in their portfolios.

Performance Indicators

Task A

A student with a Level 3 paper

✓ Makes and draws an array.

✓ Writes multiplication and division sentences for model.

✓ Explains relationship between multiplication and division in model.

Task B

A student with a Level 3 paper

✓ Divides to find the cost of one item.

✓ Writes a division sentence.

✓ Adds money amounts.

PERFORMANCE ASSESSMENT

TASK A • DAISY GARDEN

Materials: counters

Blair has 30 daisy plants. She wants to plant them in her garden so that each row has the same number of plants.

a. Use counters to make a model. Show one way Blair could place the plants in her garden. Draw a picture of your model. **Possible models are 5 × 6, 6 × 5, 3 × 10, 10 × 3, 2 × 15, or 15 × 2.**

b. Write the multiplication and division sentences that belong to the fact family for the model you drew. **Possible answer: 6 × 5 = 30, 5 × 6 = 30, 30 ÷ 5 = 6, 30 ÷ 6 = 5**

c. How does the model you drew show that multiplication and division are related? **Possible answer: The model shows that 6 groups of 5 equal 30 and that 30 divided into 6 rows has 5 in each row.**

TASK B • AT THE BALL PARK

Kade and Lydia are going to a baseball game. There are special bargains at the ball park if you buy more than one of the same item. Kade and Lydia will buy items with friends who want the same thing. Each friend will get one item and will pay an equal part.

Kade has $3 and Lydia has $4.
See additional answers on p. 297.

a. What is one item Kade could buy? **Possible answers: poster, cap, mug**

b. Lydia wants to buy a different item. Which item could she buy? Write a division sentence to show how much Lydia's item will cost. **Possible answer: T-shirt; $12 ÷ 3 = $4**

c. If Kade and Lydia combine their money, can they pay for one baseball to share? Explain. **Yes; One baseball costs $5, so they would have $2 left.**

Specials
4 baseballs for $ 20
3 posters for $ 6
6 caps for $ 18
3 T-shirts for $12
8 mugs for $ 8

Work Samples for Task A and Task B

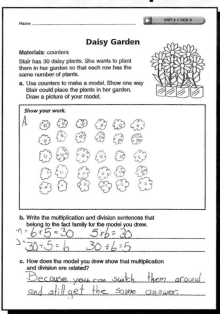

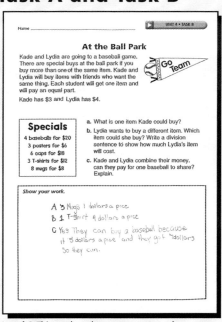

Level 3 The student shows good understanding of the task. The multiplication and division sentences are correct, although the explanation in part c is nonstandard.

Level 3 This student demonstrates a good understanding of the task. Answers are complete and accurate. All questions are addressed.

Technology Linkup

Calculator • Find the Unit Cost

Joanne sees a sign that says, "Kites—4 for $15!"
How much would Joanne pay for 1 kite?

The unit cost will tell you. The **unit cost** is the cost of
one item when several items are sold for a single price.

Find the unit cost. Use a calculator.

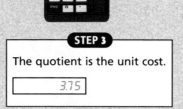

STEP 1	STEP 2	STEP 3
Enter the total cost. 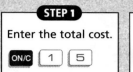	Divide by the number of items. 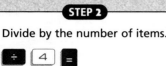	The quotient is the unit cost. 3.75

So, Joanne would pay $3.75 for 1 kite.

Practice and Problem Solving

Use a calculator to find each unit cost.

1. 4 for $18
   $4.50
2. 2 for $7
   $3.50
3. 8 for $18
   $2.25
4. 2 for $24
   $12
5. 5 for $35
   $7
6. 6 for $39
   $6.50
7. 3 for $27
   $9
8. 4 for $27
   $6.75
9. 4 for $11
   $2.75

Use a calculator to solve.

10. A hobby shop sells 6 puzzles for $12.
    How much will 2 puzzles cost?
    Explain. **$4; Possible explanation: since
    6 puzzles cost $12, 1 puzzle costs $2;
    $2 × 2 = $4.**

11. **STRETCH YOUR THINKING** Ricardo
    bought 5 toy cars for $8.45. How
    much did each toy car cost? **$1.69**

GO ON-LINE

Multimedia Math Glossary www.harcourtschool.com/mathglossary
Vocabulary Power Look up *dividend*, *divisor*, and *quotient* in the
Multimedia Math Glossary. Write a riddle that someone could use to
help remember these terms. **Check students' work.**

Additional Answers, p. 296
Task B
a. $20 ÷ 4 = $5 (baseball); $6 ÷ 3 = $2 (poster); $18 ÷ 6 = $3 (cap); $12 ÷ 3 =
$4 (T-shirt); $8 ÷ 8 = $1 (mug)
Kade could buy 1 poster for $2. Other possibilities are a cap for $3, or a mug for $1.
b. If Kade buys a poster, then Lydia could buy a cap. The division sentence showing
the cost of the cap is $18 ÷ 6 = $3. The other possibility is that she could buy a mug,
$8 ÷ 8 = $1.
If Kade buys a cap, then Lydia could buy a poster, $6 ÷ 3 = $2, or a mug, $8 ÷ 8 = $1.
If Kade buys a mug, then Lydia could buy a cap, $18 ÷ 6 = $3, or a poster, $6 ÷ 3 = $2.
Lydia could buy a T-shirt regardless of what Kade buys.
c. If Kade and Lydia combine their money, $3 + $4 = $7, they will have enough to buy
a baseball. They both cannot buy something different and share the cost of buying the
baseball.
Kade could pay $1 and Lydia $4 and Kade could buy something else.
Kade could pay $2 and Lydia $3 and each could buy a mug.

Technology Linkup

Objective To use a calculator to find the unit cost

Optional Technology Tools TI–108, Casio SL–450, or
another calculator

Using the Page

Students will learn that when items are sold as a
group, they can calculate the *unit cost* to find the
price for one of the items.

Using the Calculator

Students may use a TI–108, Casio SL–450, or
another calculator to find unit cost.

- *Have students use their calculators to do
  Steps 1–3.*
  **How will you write the quotient so that it
  is an amount of money?** Using a dollar sign
  with the quotient shows that it is an amount of
  money.

- *Direct students' attention to Exercise 1.*
  **Which number should you enter into the cal-
  culator for the dividend? Explain.** 18, because
  that is the total cost; I will divide 18 by 4 to find
  the unit cost for each of the 4 items.
  What is the quotient? 4.5

Reasoning **Why doesn't this quotient look
like an amount of money?** It doesn't have two
digits to the right of the decimal point or a dollar
sign.
What is the unit cost? $4.50

Remind students that when they are writing
amounts of money in dollars and cents, there are
two numbers to the right of the decimal point.
They need to use a zero as a place holder to the
right of the 5.

Practice and Problem Solving

You can extend the lesson by having students write
their own unit cost problems and exchange with a
partner to solve.

Multimedia Math Glossary

Dividend, divisor, quotient, and all other vocabulary words in this unit can be found in the
Harcourt Multimedia Math Glossary.
www.harcourtschool.com/mathglossary

Problem Solving
in North Carolina

Purpose To provide additional practice for concepts and skills in Chapters 12–14

Using the Page

AT THE NORTH CAROLINA ZOOLOGICAL PARK

- *Direct students to the table of data.*
  How many inches taller is an Arctic fox than a horned puffin? Explain. 22 in.; height of Arctic fox: 3 ft; 3 ft = 36 in.; 36 − 14 = 22.
  Reasoning Suppose an Arctic fox weighing 15 pounds is placed on one side of a balance scale. About how many peregrine falcons can be placed on the right side so that the scale balances? Explain. Possible answer: about 8–15 peregrine falcons; You can place as many as fifteen 1-lb falcons on the scale. You can place as few as seven 2-lb falcons and one 1-lb falcon.
  7 × 2 = 14; 14 + 1 = 15

- *Direct students to Exercise 3.*
  Suppose a female horned puffin laid her eggs on March 4. On about what date should these eggs hatch? April 15

Extension Have students decide how they could design the rows of seats in a tram. Tell students how many seats to include, using numbers such as 18, 24, 36, or 48. Then have students draw different arrays for the same total number of seats. Have students write a division sentence for each array to find the number of seats in each row. Check students' work.

▲ The Rocky Coast exhibit looks like the Pacific coast from Alaska to California. It has cliffs and trees.

AT THE NORTH CAROLINA ZOOLOGICAL PARK

Asheboro

The North Carolina Zoological Park in Asheboro is the country's largest walk-through zoo. The animals and plants in its exhibits are seen in settings that are like natural habitats.

USE DATA For 1 and 4, use the table.

1. At the Rocky Coast exhibit, you can see seals, sea lions, horned puffins, peregrine falcons, and Arctic foxes. A group of horned puffins weighs a total of about 8 pounds. How many horned puffins are in the group? **8 horned puffins**

2. A tram carries visitors around the park. Each row of seats can hold 4 people. There are 32 people on the tram. How many rows are filled? **8 rows**

3. It takes about 40 days for a horned puffin to hatch. About how many weeks is that? **about 6 weeks**

ANIMALS IN THE ROCKY COAST EXHIBIT		
Animal	**Height**	**Weight**
Horned puffin (seabird)	14 inches	about 1 pound
Peregrine falcon	15–20 inches	1–2 pounds
Arctic fox	3 feet	7–15 pounds

4. **STRETCH YOUR THINKING** Three Arctic foxes weigh about the same amount. What is the least they could weigh in all? What is the most they could weigh in all?
   21 pounds; 45 pounds

298 Unit 4 • Problem Solving in North Carolina

HELPING ENDANGERED SPECIES

Scientists at the North Carolina Zoological Park work in the United States and in other countries to help save endangered species like the red wolf and the African elephant.

Solve.

1. An African elephant can replace its worn molar teeth up to six times in its lifetime. If an African elephant lives about 60 years, about how long will a set of molars last? **about 10 years**

2. An African elephant can hold about 16 cups of water in its trunk. How many gallons of water is this? **1 gallon**

▲ African elephants are the largest land animals. A male elephant can weigh up to 13,000 pounds.

3. **REASONING** Red wolves live in packs of 2 to 8 members. Gray wolves live in larger packs, with up to 20 members. Scientists found an area with about 14 wolves. They think there are 2 packs living in the area. Are these red wolves or gray wolves? Explain. **See Number 3.**

The red wolf is the smallest member of the North American wolf family. In 2002 there were fewer than 100 red wolves living in the wild. ▶

4. In one week, a red wolf ate about 35 pounds of food. If the wolf ate about the same amount each day, how many pounds of food did it eat each day? **about 5 pounds**

3. red wolves; Possible answer: There may be 7 wolves in each of the 2 packs. The red wolf lives in smaller packs than the gray wolf.

Using the Page

HELPING ENDANGERED SPECIES

- *After students have completed Exercise 1, ask:* **Reasoning** How old is an African elephant who now has his third set of molars? **Explain.** Between 20 and 30 years old; since each set of molars lasts about 10 years, the elephant should be older than 2 × 10 or 20 years. The third set of molars could last until he is about 30 years old.

- *Direct students to Exercise 4.* **Suppose a gray wolf eats about 28 pounds of food a week. Make a table to show the total number of pounds of food the wolf eats day 1 through day 7.**

Day	1	2	3	4	5	6	7
Food	4	8	12	16	20	24	28

Algebraic Thinking If *n* represents the number of days, what expression represents the number of pounds of food eaten by the gray wolf? $4n$

Extension Have students research the average litter size of other endangered animals. Have them use the data to write their own problem. Then have each student exchange problems with a classmate, and solve. Check students' work.

Teaching Notes

Additional Ideas:

Good Questions to Ask:

Additional Resources:

Notes for Next Time:

UNIT 5

Data and Measurement

Unit at a Glance

EXCERPTS FROM THE RESEARCH

"Graphing helps a child see that mathematical knowledge is an integral part of daily life and can be applied to many situations. . . . Graphing gives the child an opportunity to compare, count, add, subtract, sequence, and classify data." (Choate and Okey, 1981)

UNIT 5
Data and Measurement

Assessment Options

Assessing Prior Knowledge

Determine whether students have the required prerequisite concepts and skills.

Check What You Know, PE pp. 301, 321, 337, 357

Test Preparation

Provide review and practice for chapter and standardized tests.

Getting Ready for the EOG Test, PE pp. 303, 305, 307, 313, 315, 318–319, 325, 327, 329, 331, 334–335, 341, 343, 345, 347, 349, 354–355, 361, 365, 367, 369, 372–373

Study Guide and Review, PE pp. 376–377

Formal Assessment

Assess students' mastery of chapter concepts and skills.

Chapter Review/Test, PE pp. 317, 333, 353, 371

Pretest and Posttest Options

   Chapter Test, Form A

      pp. AG97–98, 101–102, 105–106, 109–110

   Chapter Test, Form B

      pp. AG99–100, 103–104, 107–108, 111–112

   Unit 5 Test • Chapters 15–18

      Form A, pp. AG113–116

      Form B, pp. AG117–120

Daily Assessment

Obtain daily feedback on students' understanding of concepts.

Quick Review, See the first page of each PE lesson.

Getting Ready for the EOG Test

   See the last page of each PE skill lesson.

Number of the Day

   See the first page of each TE lesson.

Problem of the Day

   See the first page of each TE lesson.

Lesson Quiz

   See the *Assess* section of each TE lesson.

Performance Assessment

Assess students' understanding of concepts applied to real-world situations.

Performance Assessment (Tasks A–B), PE p. 378; pp. PA39–40

Student Self-Assessment

Have students evaluate their own work.

How Did I Do?, p. AGxvii

A Guide to My Math Portfolio, p. AGxix

Math Journal

   See *Write* in the *Assess* section of each TE lesson and TE pages 308B, 310B, 326B, 348B, 350B, 364B.

 Harcourt Assessment System

Make and grade chapter tests electronically.

This software includes:
- multiple-choice items
- free-response items
- customizable tests
- the means to build your own tests from available items
- customizable student and class reports

 Portfolio

Portfolio opportunities appear throughout the Pupil and Teacher's Editions.

Suggested work samples:

Problem Solving Project, TE pp. 300, 336

Write About It, PE pp. 305, 312, 313, 315, 331, 343, 351, 360, 367

Chapter Review/Test, PE pp. 317, 333, 353, 371

KEY   **AG** Assessment Guide   **TE** Teacher's Edition   **PA** Performance Assessment   **PE** Pupil Edition

Correlation to STANDARDIZED TESTS

LEARNING GOAL	TAUGHT IN LESSONS	CAT/ TERRA NOVA	CTBS/ TERRA NOVA	ITBS FORM A	MAT 8	STANFORD 10	NORTH CAROLINA STANDARDS
15A To collect, record, and classify data	15.1, 15.2, 15.3	•	•		•		4.01
15B To solve problems by using an appropriate strategy such as *make a table*	15.4	•	•		•	•	4.01
15C To read and interpret data from a survey and in a line plot; to find the range, mode, and median of the data	15.5, 15.6	•	•	•	•	•	4.01
16A To solve problems by using an appropriate strategy such as *make a graph*	16.1	•	•				4.01
16B To read, interpret, and draw bar graphs	16.2, 16.3	•	•	•	•	•	4.01
16C To locate points on a grid	16.4	•	•			•	3.02
16D To read and interpret line graphs	16.5	•	•	•	•	•	4.01
17A To estimate and measure length, distance, capacity, and weight using appropriate customary units	17.1, 17.2, 17.3, 17.4	•	•	•	•	•	maintains (2) 2.01 2.01 2.02
17B To use a variety of methods to convert units within the customary system of measurement	17.5	•	•		•		2.01
17C To solve problems by using an appropriate skill such as *estimate or measure*	17.6			•			2.02
18A To estimate and measure length by using metric units	18.1	•	•		•	•	2.02
18B To solve problems by using an appropriate strategy such as *make a table*	18.2	•	•		•	•	2.01
18C To estimate and measure capacity and mass using metric units	18.3, 18.4	•			•	•	2.02
18D To estimate and measure temperature by using metric and customary units	18.5	•	•	•		•	2.02

Technology Links

 ## Harcourt Mega Math CD-ROM Series

The learning activities in this exciting, new comprehensive math software series complement, enrich, and enhance the Pupil Edition lessons.

Harcourt Mega Math Correlation		
Lesson	**Activity/Level**	**Skill**
15.5 & 15.6	The Number Games, ArachnaGraph, Levels E and F	Line Plots; Mean and Median
16.2 & 16.3	The Number Games, ArachnaGraph, Levels B and C	Bar Graphs; Make Bar Graphs
16.4 & 16.5	The Number Games, ArachnaGraph, Levels G and I	Ordered Pairs; Line Graphs
17.1 & 17.2	Ice Station Exploration, Linear Lab, Levels A, B, C, D, and E	Customary Length; Inch, Foot, Yard, and Mile
17.4	Country Countdown, Harrison's Comparisons, Level G	Weight (Nonstandard Units)
17.5	The Number Games, Tiny's Think Tank, Level M	Ways to Change Units
18.1	Ice Station Exploration, Linear Lab, Levels H and I	Metric – Length

The Harcourt Learning Site

www.harcourtschool.com

Visit **THE LEARNING SITE** at **www.harcourtschool.com** for a variety of activities and resources that can be used to explore, reinforce, practice, and extend the learning of the chapter.

- Multimedia Math Glossary
- Activities and instructional resources
- E-Lab Activities
- Show Me math models

Intervention CD-ROMs

These CD-ROMs help you

- assess prerequisite concepts and skills for each chapter and assess problem-solving at point of use.
- diagnose to determine whether intervention is necessary or if enrichment is appropriate for a concept or skill.
- diagnose to determine whether intervention is necessary for a specific problem-solving strategy or skill.
- prescribe intervention for concepts, skills, and problem-solving strategies and skills.
- provide enrichment for students who mastered the prerequisite concepts and skills.

For the Student

The following technology can be used with students that need more instruction with skills or problem solving, and with students that will benefit from reinforcement, practice, and extension of skills from this chapter.

 Intervention CD-ROMs
- Support and enrichment for prerequisite skills
- Support for problem solving

 Harcourt Mega Math CD-ROMs
- Reinforcement, practice, and extension

ArachnaGraph
Skill Level E

Linear Lab
Skill Level D

 The Harcourt Learning Site
www.harcourtschool.com
- Multimedia Math Glossary
- E-Lab activities
- Show Me math models
- Games and activities

For the Teacher

 Intervention CD-ROMs
- Diagnose and prescribe intervention for prerequisite skills.
- Provide enrichment for prerequisite skills.
- Diagnose and prescribe intervention for problem-solving strategies and skills.

 Harcourt Mega Math CD-ROMs
- Customize additional practice for each student in your class.
- The leveled activities increase in difficulty as students progress.

 The Harcourt Learning Site
www.harcourtschool.com
- Find activities and other resources.

 Harcourt Assessment System

This software includes:
- Online test taking and automatic scoring
- A bank of items from which to build tests
- Immediate feedback on students' performance
- Correlation of items to textbook and state standards
- Comprehensive program management and class reporting
- Prescriptive reports

 ePlanner

This on-line resource allows you to:
- Customize planning and pacing.
- Select resources for daily instruction.
- Reorder content to meet your state, district, or local needs.

For the Parent

 The Harcourt Learning Site
www.harcourtschool.com

Encourage parents to visit the Math section of the Harcourt Learning Site to help them reinforce mathematics vocabulary, concepts, and skills with their children.
- Multimedia Math Glossary
- E-Lab interactive learning experiences
- Show Me math models
- Family Involvement tips and activities

Cross-Curricular Connections

Use these topics to help integrate mathematics into your daily planning.
See the pages indicated to find out more about each topic.

Science

- **Dinosaurs,** PE/TE p. 300
- **Giant pandas,** PE/TE p. 320
- **Saturn V rocket,** PE/TE p. 336
- **Animal fact cards,** TE p. 342B
- **Temperature,** PE/TE p. 356

Literature

- *Lemonade for Sale* by Stuart J. Murphy (HarperCollins, 1998), TE p. 300G
- *Math Counts: Capacity* by Henry Pluckrose (Children's Press, 1995), TE p. 300G

Art

- **Types of music,** TE p. 302B
- **Grid designs,** TE p. 328B

Writing

- **Write and answer questions,** TE p. 304B
- **Write a paragraph about tables,** TE p. 308B
- **Write a summary about line plots,** TE p. 310B
- **Explain how to make a bar graph,** TE p. 326B
- **Write a word problem,** TE p. 348B
- **Explain when to estimate or measure,** TE p. 350B
- **Describe a solution,** TE p. 364B

Language Arts/Reading

- **Use graphic aids,** PE/TE p. 313; TE pp. 308B, 322B, 350B
- **Make visual aids for vocabulary,** TE p. 324B
- **Compare pictographs, bar graphs, and line graphs,** TE p. 330B
- **Discuss estimation,** TE p. 338B
- **Review usage of** *estimate*, TE p. 350B
- **Choose important information,** TE p. 362B
- **Acrostic poems,** TE p. 366B

Reaching All Learners

Differentiated Instruction

PURPOSE To collect, organize, and interpret data.

USING THE ACTIVITY WHEEL Have each student choose one activity to complete independently. *Use after Lesson 15.2.*

*The Activity Wheel provides each student with a choice, according to learning style, for practicing an important skill.

Check students' work.

ACTIVITY WHEEL*

Write step-by-step directions for collecting and organizing data into a table. Include sample questions that could be asked in a survey.

Cut out a table from a magazine or newspaper. Tape it to a larger piece of paper. Briefly explain to the class the information it contains.

Write survey questions that help you obtain information about something you're interested in. Decide on a subject. Then write 2 lists of questions: 1 set that is inappropriate and 1 set that is appropriate.

Literature Connections

These books provide ways to explore data and measurement.

Lemonade for Sale by Stuart J. Murphy (HarperCollins, 1998) is a lively book in which four kids open a lemonade stand and make a bar graph to track their sales.

- Have students make bar graphs to chart how many pieces of mail their family receives each day for a week. *Use with Lesson 16.3.*

Math Counts: Capacity by Henry Pluckrose (Children's Press, 1995). The realistic photographs in this book illustrate both metric and customary measures.

- Have students guess which containers pictured on pages 8–9 would hold the least or most water. *Use with Lessons 17.3 and 18.3.*

PRACTICE GAME
Ready, Set, Measure!

PURPOSE To choose the correct metric unit of measure

MATERIALS *For each pair* blank number cube, p. TR65, labeled cm, cm, m, m, dm, dm; gameboard, p. TR77; 2 colored pencils

ABOUT THE GAME

- Each player chooses a different-colored pencil.

- Players take turns tossing the cube, finding one item on the list that would be measured using that unit, and writing the unit next to that item.

- Answers are checked with the answer key. The player with more correct units wins the game. *Use with Lesson 18.1.*

VISUAL; LOGICAL/MATHEMATICAL

How would ou measure each item?
Use centimeter (cm), decimeter (dm), or meter (m)

☐ 1. Measure length of swimming pool.
☐ 2. Measure length of referee's whistle.
☐ 3. Measure length of track or running race.
☐ 4. Measure length of tennis racket.
☐ 5. Measure length of baseball diamond.
☐ 6. Measure length of bicycle tire.
☐ 7. Measure length of arrows for archery.
☐ 8. Measure size of table tennis balls.
☐ 9. Measure length of soccer field.
☐ 10. Measure width of wheels on roller skates.
☐ 11. Measure height of basketball goal.
☐ 12. Measure length of paper clip.

Collect and Record Data

NCTM Standards 2000

1. Number and Operations *Lessons 15.1–15.6*	6. Problem Solving *Lessons 15.1–15.6*
2. Algebra *Lesson 15.3*	7. Reasoning and Proof *Lessons 15.1, 15.2, 15.3, 15.4, 15.6*
3. Geometry	8. Communication *Lessons 15.1–15.6*
4. Measurement	
5. Data Analysis and Probability *Lessons 15.1–15.6*	9. Connections *Lessons 15.1–15.6*
	10. Representation *Lessons 15.1–15.6*

Chapter Planner

Getting Ready for Chapter 15 • Assessing Prior Knowledge and INTERVENTION (See PE and TE page 301.)

LESSON	NORTH CAROLINA STANDARDS	PACING	VOCABULARY*	MATERIALS	RESOURCES AND TECHNOLOGY
15.1 Hands On: Collect Data pp. 302–303 **Objective** To collect and organize data into a table	4.01	1 Day (For Lessons 15.1 and 15.2)	**data** **tally table** **frequency table**	*For each student* pencils, paper	Reteach, Practice, Problem Solving, Challenge 15.1 Transparency 15.1 **Intervention**, *Skills 9, 64* (CD or Book)
15.2 Use Data from a Survey pp. 304–305 **Objective** To interpret survey results	4.01		**survey** **results**		Reteach, Practice, Problem Solving, Challenge 15.2 Transparency 15.2 **Intervention**, *Skills 9, 64* (CD or Book)
15.3 Classify Data pp. 306–307 **Objective** To use a table to group data in more than one way	4.01	1 Day	**classify**		Reteach, Practice, Problem Solving, Challenge 15.3 Transparency 15.3 **Intervention**, *Skills 9, 64* (CD or Book)
15.4 Problem Solving Strategy: Make a Table pp. 308–309 **Objective** To use the problem solving strategy *make a table*	4.01	1 Day		▦	Reteach, Practice, Reading Strategy, Challenge 15.4 Transparency 15.4 Scaffolded Instruction Transparency 15 Reading Transparency 15 **Intervention • Problem Solving,** *Strategy/Skill 15* (CD or Book)
15.5 Line Plots pp. 310–313 **Objective** To read and interpret data in line plots	4.01	1 Day	**line plot** **mode** **range** **circle graph**	*For each student* unlabeled number line	Reteach, Practice, Problem Solving, Challenge 15.5 Transparency 15.5 **Intervention**, *Skills 9, 64* (CD or Book) **Harcourt Mega Math The Number Games,** *ArachnaGraph* **Math Jingles® CD 3–4**
15.6 Hands On: Mean and Median pp. 314–315 **Objective** To find the mean and median of a set of data	4.01	1 Day	**mean** **median**	*For each student* connecting cubes	Reteach, Practice, Problem Solving, Challenge 15.6 Transparency 15.6 **Intervention**, *Skills 9, 64* (CD or Book) **Harcourt Mega Math The Number Games,** *ArachnaGraph*

Ending Chapter 15 • Extra Practice, p. 316 • Chapter 15 Review/Test, p. 317 • Getting Ready for the EOG Test, pp. 318–319

****Boldfaced** terms are the key mathematical terms for the chapter.

Vocabulary Power

Review Vocabulary

To be ready for Chapter 15, students should know the following vocabulary term:

- **table** (p. 301)—an arrangement of data in columns and rows

Develop Key Chapter Vocabulary

The **boldfaced** words are the key vocabulary terms in the chapter.

- **data** (p. 302)—information gathered by survey, observation, or measurement
- **tally table** (p. 302)—a table that uses tally marks to record data
- **frequency table** (p. 302)—a table that uses numbers to record data
- **survey** (p. 304)—method of gathering information or data
- **results** (p. 304)—the answers from a survey
- **classify** (p. 306)—to group information according to specific traits, such as size, color, shape
- **line plot** (p. 310)—a diagram that uses X's above a number line to show the frequency of each value
- **mode** (p. 310)—the number or item occurring most often in a set of data
- **range** (p. 310)—the difference between the least and the greatest numbers in a set of data
- **circle graph** (p. 313)—display of data as parts of a whole circle
- **mean** (p. 314)—the average of a set of data
- **median** (p. 314)—the middle number in an ordered set of data

Vocabulary Cards

Have students use the Vocabulary Cards on *Teacher's Resource Book* pages TR155–158 for the key terms in the chapter. The cards can be added to a file of mathematics terms.

Multimedia Math Glossary

 For vocabulary support, visit **www.harcourtschool.com/mathglossary**

Math Journal

Have students define the key vocabulary terms: *data, tally table, frequency table, survey, results, classify, line plot, mode, range, circle graph, mean,* and *median*. Have students use their own words and give an example of each.

M A T H Word Work

Objective To reinforce vocabulary concepts
Use after Lesson 15.6.

Materials *For each group* 1 large sheet of drawing paper, connecting cubes

Separate the class into an odd number of small groups. Conduct a survey. Ask groups to find the total number of pets all members of the group have. Ask a volunteer to record the results as each group responds. Then have students work together to show the results in frequency tables, line plots, or bar graphs. Have each group use connecting cubes to find the median of the data. Ask each group to present their median displays and tell the median they found. Discuss with the class which displays were most effective in showing the results of the survey.

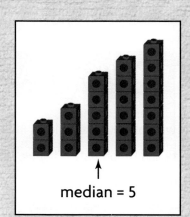

median = 5

Mathematics Across the Grades

LOOKING BACK • Prerequisite Skills

To be ready for Chapter 15, students should have the following understandings and skills:

- **Column Addition**—single-digit addition of four addends

- **Read a Table**—interpret information in a table

Check What You Know

Use page 301 to determine students' knowledge of prerequisite concepts and skills.

Intervention

Help students prepare for the chapter by using the intervention resources described on TE page 301.

LOOKING AT CHAPTER 15 • Essential Skills

Students will

- collect and organize data into a table.

- **interpret survey results.**

- use a table to classify data in more than one way.

- read and interpret data in line plots.

- find the mean and median of a set of data.

- use the problem solving strategy *make a table*.

Example

What was the favorite color for both boys and girls?

FAVORITE COLORS		
	Red	**Blue**
Boys	4	6
Girls	3	4

Solution

Add the column for each color to find 7 votes for red and 10 votes for blue. 10 > 7, so blue is the more popular color.

LOOKING AHEAD • Applications

Students will apply what they learn in Chapter 15 to the following new concepts:

- Analyze and Graph Data (Chapter 16)

- Probability (Chapter 24)

- Make a Table to Show Metric Units (Chapter 18)

- Make Stem-and-Leaf Plots (Grade 4)

Differentiated Instruction

Meeting the Needs of All Learners

Extra Support	Activities for All	Enrichment
Alternative Teaching Strategy TE Lessons 15.1, 15.2, 15.3, 15.4, 15.5, 15.6 **ESOL/ESL** TE Lessons 15.1, 15.2, 15.3, 15.4, 15.5, 15.6 **Special Needs** TE Lesson 15.1	**Cross-Curricular Connections** **Music:** TE Lesson 15.1 **Reading:** TE Lesson 15.4 **Science:** Chapter Opener **Vocabulary:** TE p. 300I, PE/TE p. 301, TE Lesson 15.2 **Writing:** TE Lessons 15.4, 15.5	**Advanced Learners** TE Lessons 15.2, 15.4, 15.5, 15.6 **Early Finishers** TE Lesson 15.3

Combination and Multi-age Classrooms

Grade 2	Grade 3	Grade 4
Skills Trace Across the Grades		
Gather information to make a tally table; compare data in tally tables; make and interpret data in concrete and pictographs; find the range, median, and mode.	**Collect, record, and classify data; find the range, mode, and median of the data.**	Organize, summarize, and interpret data by using cumulative frequency tables, line plots, stem-and-leaf plots, mean, median, and mode.
Instructional Strategies		
Students on this level may require more time to build conceptual understanding. **Assignments** **Grade 3 Pupil Edition** • Have students work in small groups on Lessons 15.1, 15.2, and 15.3. • Have students skip Lessons 15.5 and 15.6. **Grade 2 Pupil Edition**—pages 49–62 and 275–288	Students on this level should be able to complete all the lessons in the Pupil Edition and all the activities in the Teacher's Edition with minimal adjustments. **Assignment** **Grade 3 Pupil Edition**—pages 300–317	Students on this level will probably require less time to build conceptual understanding. **Assignments** **Grade 3 Pupil Edition** • Compact Lessons 15.1, 15.2, and 15.3. **Grade 4 Pupil Edition**—pages 112–131

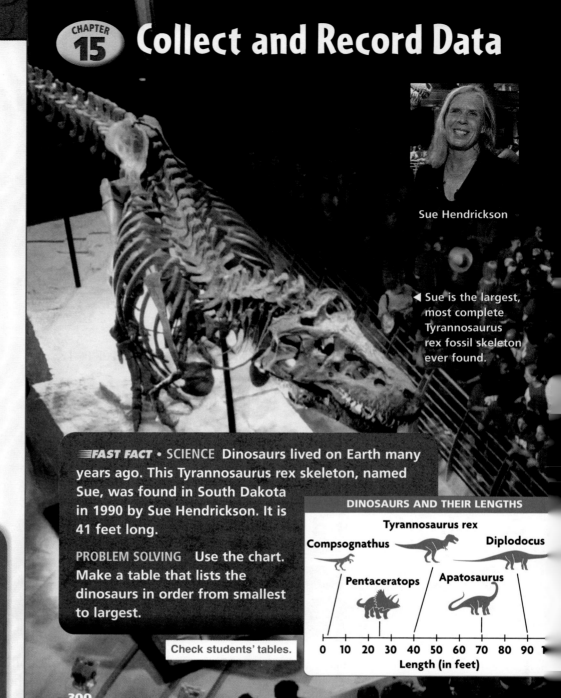

Sue Hendrickson

◀ Sue is the largest, most complete Tyrannosaurus rex fossil skeleton ever found.

Collect and Record Data

Introducing the Chapter

Explain that collecting and recording data can help students organize and understand information. Ask students to think of times when collecting data can be useful.

Using Data

To begin the study of this chapter, have students

• Order the lengths of dinosaurs from longest to shortest. Check students' work.

• Determine the difference in size between the largest dinosaur and the smallest dinosaur listed in the graph. about 85 feet

• Explain what kinds of data have been organized in this graph. dinosaurs and their lengths

Problem Solving Project

Purpose To collect and record data

Grouping small groups

Background Dinosaurs are the largest animals ever to have lived on land. The largest dinosaurs weighed as much as 85 tons. These creatures would have been 10 times as heavy as a full-grown elephant. The only animals that grow to this size today are a few kinds of whales.

UNDERSTAND • PLAN • SOLVE • CHECK

Have students

• Take a survey of the number of times students have visited a dinosaur exhibit in a museum.

• Make a tally table of the results.

• Organize and record the data in a frequency table.

Portfolio

Suggest that students place the tables and data in their portfolios.

DATA

Graphing Investigations
Begin Week 15.

≡**FAST FACT** • SCIENCE Dinosaurs lived on Earth many years ago. This Tyrannosaurus rex skeleton, named Sue, was found in South Dakota in 1990 by Sue Hendrickson. It is 41 feet long.

PROBLEM SOLVING   Use the chart. Make a table that lists the dinosaurs in order from smallest to largest.

Check students' tables.

DINOSAURS AND THEIR LENGTHS

Tyrannosaurus rex

Compsognathus   Diplodocus

Pentaceratops   Apatosaurus

| 0 | 10 | 20 | 30 | 40 | 50 | 60 | 70 | 80 | 90 | |

Length (in feet)

300

WHY LEARN MATH? Archaeologists are people who study the life and culture of ancient civilizations. To do this, they dig up objects from the past such as pieces of pottery and animal bones. It is important that they collect and organize their data very carefully. Ask: How might archaeologists organize the data they find? tally table, frequency table Ask students why it's important that the data be collected and organized carefully. Possible answer: so important facts of the past are accurate

Family Involvement Activities

These activities provide:

• Letter to the Family

• Math Vocabulary

• Family Game

• Practice (Homework)

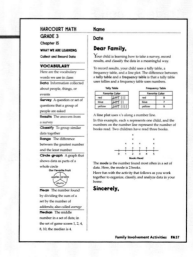

Family Involvement Activities, p. FA57

CHECK WHAT YOU KNOW

Use this page to help you review and remember important skills needed for Chapter 15.

✓ COLUMN ADDITION

Find the sum.

1.	2.	3.	4.	5.
8	9	8	5	9
3	3	6	4	5
4	1	4	7	9
+7	+6	+2	+3	+3
22	19	20	19	26

✓ READ A TABLE

For 6–9, use the information in this table.

6. What is the title of the table?
Our Favorite Weather

7. How many students like snowy weather best? 8 students

8. What kind of weather had the fewest votes? cloudy weather

9. How many students were asked?
22 students

OUR FAVORITE WEATHER

Type	Students
☀ Sunny	7
💧 Rainy	4
❄ Snowy	8
☁ Cloudy	3

VOCABULARY POWER

REVIEW

table [tā'bəl] *noun*

Table comes from the French word for *tablet,* which means "a slab of metal, stone, or wood used for writing." In mathematics, the meaning of *table* is "an arrangement of data in rows and columns." What is another meaning of *table*? Possible answer: a piece of furniture with a flat surface and legs, often found in a kitchen, and at which meals are eaten

PREVIEW

data	line plot
tally table	mode
frequency table	range
survey	circle graph
results	mean
classify	median

 www.harcourtschool.com/mathglossary

Chapter 15 **301**

Assessing Prior Knowledge

Use the **Check What You Know** page to determine whether your students have mastered the prerequisite skills critical for this chapter.

Intervention

- **Diagnose and Prescribe**
Evaluate your students' performance on this page to determine whether intervention is necessary or if enrichment is appropriate. Options that provide instruction, practice, and a check are listed in the chart below.

✓ CHECK WHAT YOU KNOW RESOURCES

Intervention Copying Masters or CD-ROMs

Enrichment Copying Masters

VOCABULARY POWER

For activities and information about the vocabulary in this chapter, see page 300I.

Were students successful with ✓ **CHECK WHAT YOU KNOW?**

IF ... NO THEN ... INTERVENE — **INTERVENTION OPTIONS** — **IF ... YES** THEN ... ENRICH

Skill/Items	Missed more than	Intervene with
Column Addition 1–5	1	• *Intervention,* Skill 9
Read a Table, 6–9	1	• *Intervention,* Skill 64

Skill/Items	Missed fewer than	Enrich with
Column Addition 1–5	2	• *Intervention,* Enrichment p. IN30
Read a Table, 6–9	2	• *Intervention,* Enrichment p. IN30

Collect Data

Lesson Planning

Objective To collect and organize data into a table

Materials *For each student* pencils, paper

NCTM Standards
1. Number and Operations
5. Data Analysis and Probability
6. Problem Solving
7. Reasoning and Proof
8. Communication
9. Connections
10. Representation

Math Background
These ideas will help students collect and organize data.

- Data can be organized in tally tables and frequency tables.

- A survey is a form of data collection.

- Skip-counting by fives and adding ungrouped tallies is a quick way to count responses from a tally table.

- Making a tally table is a logical first step before making a frequency table.

Vocabulary
data information collected about people or things

tally table a table that uses tally marks to record data

frequency table a table that uses numbers to record data

Warm-Up Resources

Number of the Day

Transparency **15.1**

The number of the day is 20. During what calendar year will you have your twentieth birthday? Answers will vary.

Daily Facts Practice

Have students practice multiplication facts by completing Set G of *Teacher's Resource Book*, p. TR93.

Transparency **15.1**

Problem of the Day

The survey of Kathy's class of 32 students showed that 6 students have birthdays in the shortest month of the year. In each of the months with only 30 days, there were 3 students who have birthdays. In each of the other months, the same number of students have birthdays. Tell the number of students who have birthdays in each month of the year. January, 2; February, 6; March, 2; April, 3; May, 2; June, 3; July, 2; August, 2; September, 3; October, 2; November, 3; December, 2

Solution Problem of the Day tab, p. PD15

Intervention and Extension Resources

Alternative Teaching Strategy

Help students **collect and organize data** by displaying a table with no data. Ask students to identify its parts. title, column, row, label As students correctly name the parts, write the names of the parts in the proper places. Then review how and where tally marks would be recorded.

ESOL/ESL

VISUAL

VISUAL/SPATIAL

Special Needs

Help students **practice collecting data**. Have pairs of students go on a data hunt around the classroom. Discuss types of data that can be collected and recorded, such as the number of library books, chairs, or windows. Give them time to collect the data in a tally table and share their results with the class. Check students' work.

KINESTHETIC/VISUAL

INTERPERSONAL/SOCIAL

Multistep and Strategy Problems

The following multistep or strategy problem is provided in Lesson 15.1:

Page	Item
303	4

Music Connection

Have students work in groups to **make a tally table** showing the preferences of their classmates for one of the following: types of music, musical groups, singers, favorite instruments, or current songs. When they are finished with their tallies, challenge students to **make a frequency table** with the same data. Check students' work.

VISUAL

VISUAL/SPATIAL

Technology Link

GO The Harcourt Learning Site
www.harcourtschool.com

Intervention, *Skills 9, 64*

Lesson 15.1 Organizer

Objective To collect and organize data into a table

Vocabulary data, tally table, frequency table

Materials *For each student* pencils, paper

---

1 INTRODUCE

QUICK REVIEW provides review of prerequisite skills.

WHY LEARN THIS? You can use a frequency table to find out which sport or products people prefer. *Share the lesson objective with students.*

2 TEACH

Guided Instruction

- *Have students read the Explore section.*
  Give some examples of data. Possible answer: number of people who wear different shoe sizes; number of people who prefer dogs, cats, or fish as pets

- *Ask students to look at the tables.*
  What does the second column of the tally table show? one tally mark for each person who named each kind of dinosaur as a favorite
  Why might it be a good idea to make a tally table before making a frequency table?
  Possible answer: First you can record the data one by one. Then you can find the sum for each category.
  REASONING How is the frequency table the same as the tally table? How is it different?
  Both tables show the same data about favorite dinosaurs; the frequency table uses numbers instead of tally marks.

3 PRACTICE

Guided Practice

Discuss the Try It activity with your students. Identify students who are having difficulty and choose appropriate lesson resources to provide assistance.

LESSON 1

Collect Data

▶ Explore

Information collected about people or things is called **data**.

The students in Kelly's class voted for their favorite dinosaurs and made tables to show the results.

A **tally table** uses tally marks to record data.

A **frequency table** uses numbers to record data.

FAVORITE DINOSAUR

Name	Tally
Apatosaurus	||||̄	
Brachiosaurus	||||̄ ||
Tyrannosaurus	||||̄ ||||̄ ||
Stegosaurus	|||

FAVORITE DINOSAUR

Name	Number
Apatosaurus	6
Brachiosaurus	7
Tyrannosaurus	12
Stegosaurus	3

Collect data about your classmates' favorite dinosaurs. Organize the data in a tally table.

Activity 1

STEP 1
Write the title and headings. List four answer choices.

STEP 2
Ask classmates *What's your favorite dinosaur?* Make a tally mark for each answer.

Favorite Dinosaur	
Name	Tally

• Why is a tally table good for recording data?
Possible answer: It's an easy way to keep track of people's answers.

Try It

Decide on a question to ask your classmates.

a. Write four answer choices in a tally table.

b. Ask your classmates the question. Complete the tally table.

302

Reteach 15.1

Collect Data

Information about people or things is called **data**. Data can be collected and organized in different ways.

Tally Table

A **tally table** uses tally marks to record data. Each tally shows the kind of pants one person is wearing.

Kinds of Pants

Pants	Tally
Dark	///
Striped	||||̄ /
Light	//

Frequency Table

A **frequency table** uses numbers to record data. This table shows the number of tallies used in the tally table.

Kinds of Pants

Pants	Number
Dark	3
Striped	6
Light	2

Remember, tally marks are grouped by fives.

Complete the tally table and the frequency table for the picture below.

1.
Kinds of Shirts

Shirt	Tally
Stripes	||||̄ ||||̄
Polka-dots	||||̄ ||
Flowers	////
Logos	///
Plain	/

2.
Kinds of Shirts

Shirt	Number
Stripes	10
Polka-dots	7
Flowers	4
Logos	3
Plain	1

Reteach RW77

Practice 15.1

Collect Data

1. Make a tally table of four kinds of pets. Ask some of your classmates which pet they like best. Make a tally mark beside the name of the pet each one chooses.

2. Use the data from your tally table to make a frequency table.

3. Which type of pet did the most classmates choose? the fewest?

   Answers will vary.

4. Compare your tables with those of your classmates. Did everyone get the same results?

   Answers will vary.

Tables will vary.

FAVORITE PETS

Name	Tally

FAVORITE PETS

Name	Number

Mixed Review

Write <, >, or = for each ○.

5. 6 ÷ 1 ⊘ 6 ÷ 6   6. 10 × 4 ⊘ 5 × 9

7. 12 + 12 ⊘ 10 + 13   8. 354 ⊘ 370 − 30

9. 236 + 3 ⊜ 239   10. 54 ÷ 9 ⊘ 70 ÷ 10

11. 3 × 3 ⊘ 10 × 1   12. 0 ÷ 6 ⊜ 0 ÷ 7

Solve.

13. 500	14. 104	15. 78	16. 518	17. 729
− 238	− 57	+ 46	+ 203	+ 819
262	47	124	721	1,548

Practice PW77

▶ Connect

Use the data you organized in the tally table on page 302 to make a frequency table.

Activity 2

STEP 1
Write the title and headings. List the four answer choices.

STEP 2
Count the number of tally marks in each row. Write each number in the frequency table.

Favorite Dinosaur	
Name	Number

- Why is a frequency table a good way to show data?
  Possible answer: It is easier to read numbers than count tallies.

▶ Practice and Problem Solving

1. Make a tally table about three after-school activities. Ask your classmates which activity they like best. For each answer, make a tally mark beside the activity.
Check students' tables.

2. Use the data from your tally table to make a frequency table. Which activity was chosen by the greatest number of classmates? the least number?
Check students' tables and answers.

3. Which table is better for reading results? Which table is better for collecting data?
a frequency table; a tally table

4. How many more students chose oranges and apples than chose bananas? **1 student**

5. ✎ **Write a problem** using the information in the Favorite Fruit tally table. **Check students' problems.**

FAVORITE FRUIT	
Name	**Tally**
Grapes	||||| ||||| ||||
Oranges	||||
Apples	|||||
Bananas	||||| |||

Getting Ready for the ✏EOG Test

6. Lily made this table to show her classmates' favorite kind of music. What kind of music had the same number of votes as rock? **C**

FAVORITE KINDS OF MUSIC	
Kind	**Tally**
rock	||||| |||
hip hop	|||||
country	||||| ||||
jazz	||||| |||

A hip hop   **C** jazz
B country   **D** classical

Chapter 15 303

North Carolina Standards 4.01 Collect, organize, analyze, and display data (including circle graphs and tables) to solve problems.

Independent Practice

Note that Exercise 4 is a **multistep or strategy problem**. Assign Practice Exercises 1–5.

4 ASSESS

Summarize the lesson by having students:

Discuss What do the tally marks in a tally table show? Possible answer: They show how many in each category.

✎ **Write** Give two reasons why people might use tables to record data.

Possible answer: Tables help organize data so it can be studied and so that it is easier to read.

LESSON QUIZ

For 1–2, use the tally table.

Transparency **15.1**

FAVORITE SANDWICH	
Type	**Tally**
Tuna	||||
Cheese	|||||
Peanut Butter	||||
Turkey	|||

1. Make a frequency table of the data in the tally table. Check students' work.

2. How many voted for their favorite sandwich? 16

303

Use Data from a Survey

Lesson Planning

PROFESSIONAL DEVELOPMENT

Objective To interpret survey results

NCTM Standards
1. Number and Operations
5. Data Analysis and Probability
6. Problem Solving
7. Reasoning and Proof
8. Communication
9. Connections
10. Representation

Math Background
These ideas will help students interpret survey results.

- Surveys involve asking one or more questions, recording results, and interpreting results.

- Surveys can tell about preferences and behaviors; results from surveys can be useful in decision making.

- Surveys are useful when people can readily interpret the collected data.

Vocabulary
survey a method of gathering information or data

results answers from a survey

Warm-Up Resources

Number of the Day

Transparency 15.2

The number of the day is 72. Write all the numbers you could skip-count by from 0 to reach 72. 2, 3, 4, 6, 8, 9, 12, 18, 24, 36

Daily Facts Practice

Have students practice multiplication facts by completing Set A of *Teacher's Resource Book*, p. TR94.

Solve a Problem

Transparency 15.2

Problem of the Day

Rashana asked her 28 classmates which flavor of yogurt they like best—lemon, vanilla, or strawberry. The number of tallies she recorded for lemon was 2 more than the number for strawberry but 3 less than the number for vanilla. How many students said they like vanilla best? 12 students

Solution Problem of the Day tab, p. PD15

Intervention and Extension Resources

Alternative Teaching Strategy

Conduct a classroom survey to help students understand data.

ESOL/ESL

- Ask students whether they prefer to go to one of three locations such as the zoo, the science museum, or the planetarium for a field trip.
- Invite students to form groups according to how they responded. Explain that the three groups represent survey results.
- Construct a tally table to record the results of this survey.
- Have students record the actual results by placing a tally mark in the correct category to represent themselves.

Check students' work.

KINESTHETIC

BODILY/KINESTHETIC

Multistep and Strategy Problems

The following multistep or strategy problem is provided in Lesson 15.2:

Page	Item
305	15

Vocabulary Strategy

Help students **extend their knowledge of data** by answering the following questions using the terms *survey* and *results*.

- Which comes first, the survey or the results? survey
- Which term means "a method of gathering information or data"? survey
- Which term can be shown by means of tally marks? results
- Complete these analogies: *problem* is to *test* as a *question* is to a _____. survey *Answers* are to *solutions* as *responses* are to _____. results

Invite students to add other questions, analogies, or riddles to this list. Check students' work.

AUDITORY

VERBAL/LINGUISTIC

Advanced Learners

Challenge students to **understand data** by having them write a paragraph about how to conduct a survey about favorite after-school activities and show the results in either a tally table or a frequency table. Remind them to tell the steps in order and to use transitional words such as *first, next, then,* and *last.* Check students' work.

VISUAL

VERBAL/LINGUISTIC

Technology Link

Intervention, *Skills 9, 64*

Lesson 15.2 Organizer

Objective To interpret survey results
Vocabulary survey, results

1 INTRODUCE

QUICK REVIEW provides review of prerequisite skills.

WHY LEARN THIS? You can interpret the results of a survey in the news. *Share the lesson objective with students.*

2 TEACH

Guided Instruction

- *Discuss the Learn section.*
  What are the results of Jillian and Ted's survey? Possible answers: the responses shown by the tally marks in the table; their classmates' answers

- *Point out the table labeled Favorite Snack.*
  What other type of table could be used to show these results? a frequency table
  REASONING How might the data in Jillian and Ted's survey be used? Possible answer: If a class trip or party is planned, it could help them decide on the snacks to serve.
  ALGEBRAIC THINKING Displaying data in a tally table or frequency table helps students develop representational-thinking skills. Ask students to explain which method of organizing data they prefer.

3 PRACTICE

Guided Practice

Do Check Exercises 1–4 with your students. Identify students who are having difficulty and choose appropriate lesson resources to provide assistance.

LESSON 2 Use Data from a Survey

Quick Review

1. $17 + 21 + 12$ 50
2. $13 + 9 + 6$ 28
3. $24 + 5 + 7$ 36
4. $8 + 14 + 7$ 29
5. $19 + 13 + 21 + 5$ 58

▶ **Learn**

SURVEY SAYS . . . A **survey** is a method of gathering information or data. The answers from a survey are called the **results** of the survey.

Jillian and Ted took a survey to find their classmates' favorite snacks. The tally table shows the choices and votes of their classmates.

What are the favorite snacks of their classmates?

Since cookies got the greatest number of votes, 12, cookies are the favorite snack.

VOCABULARY
survey
results

▶ **Check**

1. **Explain** how you can find the number of students who answered Jillian and Ted's survey. **You can count all the tally marks.**
2. **List** the snacks at the right in order from the most votes to the fewest votes. **cookies, apples, granola bars, popcorn, pretzels**

FAVORITE SNACK	
Snack	**Tally**
Popcorn	IIII
Cookies	ℍℍ ℍℍ II
Granola bars	ℍℍ
Apples	ℍℍ II
Pretzels	II

For 3–4, use the tally table below.

DO YOU HAVE AN OLDER BROTHER OR SISTER?	
Answer	**Tally**
Yes	ℍℍ ℍℍ II
No	ℍℍ ℍℍ ℍℍ II

3. How many people were surveyed? **29 people**

4. Write a statement that describes the survey results. **Possible answer: Most of the people surveyed did not have an older brother or sister.**

304

Reteach 15.2

Use Data from a Survey

This is a survey question.

What is your favorite flavor of ice cream?
  Chocolate
  Vanilla
  Strawberry

Chocolate
Vanilla
Strawberry

The survey question about ice cream was asked of 14 people. Their answers are the results of the survey.

Look at the tally table at the right. The results of the survey are recorded using tally marks. It's an easy way to see what flavor of ice cream people like best.

OUR FAVORITE ICE-CREAM FLAVORS	
Flavor	**Tally**
Chocolate	ℍℍ ///
Vanilla	////
Strawberry	//

For 1, use the survey results in the tally table below.

1. List the drinks in order from the most to the least chosen.
   Rooting Root Beer; Paradise Punch; Kooky-Kola; Strawberry Surprise

OUR FAVORITE DRINKS	
Drink	**Tally**
Kooky-Kola	///
Strawberry Surprise	//
Rooting Root Beer	ℍℍ ///
Paradise Punch	ℍℍ

For 2–3, use the frequency table.

2. How many people were surveyed?
   59 people

3. How many more people answered yes than no?
   5 more people

DO YOU OWN A PET?	
Answer	**Number**
Yes	32
No	27

RW78 Reteach

Practice 15.2

Use Data from a Survey

For 1–4, use the tally table.

1. List the games in order from the most to the least chosen.
   jump rope, tether ball, follow-the-leader, four-square

OUR FAVORITE GAMES	
Game	**Tally**
Follow-the-Leader	ℍℍ //
Jump Rope	ℍℍ ℍℍ ℍℍ /
Tether Ball	ℍℍ ℍℍ /
Four-Square	////

2. How many people answered the survey?
   38 people

3. How many more people like jump rope than four-square?
   12 people

4. How many fewer people like follow-the-leader than jump rope?
   9 people

Mixed Review

5. $\begin{array}{r} 106 \\ + 894 \\ \hline 1,000 \end{array}$
6. $\begin{array}{r} 1,219 \\ + 6,537 \\ \hline 7,756 \end{array}$
7. $\begin{array}{r} 9,213 \\ - 3,219 \\ \hline 5,994 \end{array}$
8. $\begin{array}{r} 4,266 \\ - 875 \\ \hline 3,391 \end{array}$

9. $\begin{array}{r} 8 \\ \times 4 \\ \hline 32 \end{array}$
10. $\begin{array}{r} 1 \\ \times 9 \\ \hline 9 \end{array}$
11. $\begin{array}{r} 12 \\ \times 0 \\ \hline 0 \end{array}$
12. $\begin{array}{r} 4 \\ \times 6 \\ \hline 24 \end{array}$
13. $\begin{array}{r} 7 \\ \times 7 \\ \hline 49 \end{array}$

14. Find the sum of 804 and 159. __963__

15. Which number is greater: 6,232 or 6,323? __6,323__

16. Round 2,975 to the nearest thousand. __3,000__

PW78 Practice

For 5–8, use the tally table.

5. List the subjects in order from the most votes to the fewest votes.
   reading, math, science, art, social studies
6. How many students answered the survey? **50 students**

7. How many more students chose math than chose social studies?
   7 students
8. How many fewer students chose art than chose reading? **8 students**

FAVORITE SCHOOL SUBJECT	
Subject	Tally
Math	卌 卌 Ⅲ
Science	卌 ⅢⅠ
Reading	卌 卌 卌
Social Studies	卌 Ⅰ
Art	卌 Ⅱ

For 9–12, use the frequency table.

9. How many more students chose basketball than chose baseball?
   9 students
10. Which sport did the greatest number of students choose?
    swimming
11. How many students answered this survey? **109 students**

FAVORITE SPORT	
Sport	Number
Basketball	26
Football	15
Baseball	17
Hockey	21
Swimming	30

12. What if 5 more students chose basketball? How would that change the results of the survey? **Possible answer: Basketball would have the most votes.**

14. **Write About It** Think of a survey question. Write four possible answers. Survey your classmates. Make a tally table and a frequency table to record your classmates' choices. Explain the results.
    Check students' work.

13. ⚡ **What's the Error?** Lily wrote the following number sentence: $24 \times 0 = 24$. What's her error? **See below.**

15. Jamie has 48 stickers. They are arranged on 6 sheets so that each sheet has the same number of stickers. How many stickers do 3 sheets contain? **24 stickers**

13. **Possible answer: She forgot that any number multiplied by 0 equals 0.**

Getting Ready for the EOG Test

16. How many more students chose cat than chose bird? **c**

    A 2   **C** 5
    B 3   **D** 11

FAVORITE PET	
Pet	Number
dog	10
cat	8
bird	3
hamster	5

Chapter 15   **305**

North Carolina Standards 4.01 Collect, organize, analyze, and display data (including circle ~phs and tables) to solve problems.

Independent Practice

Note that Exercise 15 is a **multistep or strategy problem.** Assign Exercises 5–15.

For Exercise 5, suggest that students count the groups of fives first by skip-counting and then add the remaining tally marks.

For Exercise 10, suggest that students order the sports from greatest to least.

4 ASSESS

Summarize the lesson by having students:

Discuss How could you find out which computer game is the most popular among the third graders in your school? Possible answer: write questions for a survey; ask third graders to answer the questions; make a tally table of the results; count the tally marks

 Write Name some benefits of taking a survey about books. Possible answer: You can learn what people like and dislike. You can collect information that may help the school make a decision about what books might be ordered for the school library.

LESSON QUIZ

Use the "Favorite School Subject" tally table on page 305.

Transparency **15.2**

1. How many more students like reading than like science? 6

2. What if 7 more students had voted for art. How would that change the results of the survey? Explain. It would increase the total number of students whose favorite subject is art. It would not change which subject is most popular; $7 + 7 = 14$, $15 > 14$

Challenge 15.2

You Decide

You work at a grocery store.

You must decide what brand of crackers to order.

A survey is conducted to help you.

Think about the price of the crackers and the number of votes when you decide.

CRACKERS		
Brand of Crackers	Number of Votes	Price per Bag
Wavy	23	30¢
Light 'n' Salty	13	36¢
Crispy Crunchies	45	27¢
Toasties	22	20¢
Frickles	61	23¢
Ring-a-Ling	48	18¢
Goodies	27	25¢

Examine the table. Pick three brands to order.
Explain your decision.

Possible answers: I would stock Frickles, Crispy Crunchies, and

Goodies because they are priced in the middle and had

a large number of votes. I think the names are fun.

Problem Solving 15.2

Use Data from a Survey   Understand ▸ Plan ▸ Solve ▸ Check

For 1–4, use the table.

1. How many people answered the survey?

   _____ 45 people _____

The Garden Club's Favorite Vegetables	
Vegetable	Tallies
peas	卌 卌
corn	卌 Ⅱ
potatoes	卌 卌 卌
zucchini	卌 Ⅲ
broccoli	卌

2. Which vegetable did the most people like best?

   _____ potatoes _____

3. How many more people prefer peas than prefer corn?

   _____ 3 more people _____

Choose the letter of the correct answer.

4. Which vegetable is preferred by 3 times as many people as those who prefer broccoli?

   A peas   **C** corn
   B potatoes   **D** tomatoes

5. A group of 7 students were asked to prepare a 35-minute presentation. If each one speaks for the same length of time, how long will each one speak?

   F 5 minutes   **H** 7 minutes
   G 6 minutes   **J** 8 minutes

6. Brendon saved $307. Ellen saved $573. About how much more did Ellen save than Brendon?

   A about $500
   B about $400
   C about $300
   D about $200

7. On Saturday, the Webers made $88 at their yard sale. On Sunday, they made $37. Which is the best way to estimate the total amount they made?

   F $80 + $30   **H** $90 + $30
   G $80 + $40   **J** $90 + $40

8. **Write About It** How did you find the answer to Problem 5?

   Possible answer: I divided the number of minutes, 35, by the

   number of students, 7, to get 5 minutes.

Lesson Planning

PROFESSIONAL DEVELOPMENT

Objective To use a table to group data in more than one way

NCTM Standards

1. Number and Operations
2. Algebra
5. Data Analysis and Probability
6. Problem Solving
7. Reasoning and Proof
8. Communication
9. Connections
10. Representation

Math Background

These ideas will help students use a table to group data in more than one way.

- When there is more than one category of data, information may be located by reading across and down a table.

- Once data are classified, then statements can easily be made about the results.

Vocabulary

classify to place data in groups

Warm-Up Resources

Number of the Day

Transparency 15.3

The number of the day is 45. Write three number sentences using three different operations with the number. Possible answer: $9 \times 5 = 45$, $45 - 3 = 42$, $45 + 6 = 51$

Daily Facts Practice

Have students practice multiplication facts by completing Set B of *Teacher's Resource Book*, p. TR94.

Transparency 15.3

Problem of the Day

Thirty students answered a survey about 3 favorite recess games. Two more liked kickball than tag, and two more liked tag than hide and seek. What numbers appeared for each recess game on the frequency table? 12 for kickball, 10 for tag, 8 for hide and seek

Solution Problem of the Day tab, p. PD15

Intervention and Extension Resources

Alternative Teaching Strategy

Have students **model classifying data** by forming one large group.

- Ask students to think of two ways they could classify themselves into smaller groups. Possible answers: boys and girls; color of eyes; color of hair
- Have students separate into smaller groups and make a tally table of data that shows each classification.
- Then challenge students to make a frequency table with the same data. Check students' work.

VISUAL

BODILY/KINESTHETIC

Multistep and Strategy Problems

The following multistep or strategy problem is provided in Lesson 15.3:

Page	Item
307	9

ESOL/ESL

ESOL/ESL

Help students **reinforce the vocabulary used in the lesson**. Have students work in pairs to construct word crosses that use the terms *tally*, *classify*, and *data* such as the following:

		D				
T	A	L	L	Y		
		T				
C	L	A	S	S	I	F	Y

Students should provide clues for their word crosses and then exchange them with another pair of students to solve. Check students' work.

VISUAL

VISUAL/SPATIAL

Early Finishers

MATERIALS box of different-sized objects, such as buttons

Challenge students to **classify a collection of objects** that can be sorted in two ways. Ask them to find two ways in which to sort the objects. Possible answers: color, shape, number of holes Then have students make a frequency table to show the data. Check students' work.

KINESTHETIC

VISUAL/SPATIAL

Technology Link

Intervention, *Skills 9, 64*

Lesson 15.3 Organizer

Objective To use a table to group data in more than one way

Vocabulary classify

---

1 INTRODUCE

QUICK REVIEW provides review of prerequisite skills.

WHY LEARN THIS? You can classify data in ways that let you show preferences, such as color and size. *Share the lesson objective with students.*

---

2 TEACH

Guided Instruction

• *Discuss the Learn section.*

The table groups two kinds of information. What are they? size and color

How many different kinds of blue marbles are there? 3 different kinds: small, medium, and large

REASONING For each color of marble, there are three different sizes. How many different kinds of marbles are there? How do you know? 9 different kinds; You can add 3 kinds of blue to 3 kinds of red and 3 kinds of multi-colored, or you can count the number of groupings in the table.

What steps could you use to add all the marbles in the bag? Possible answer: Add the numbers in each column in the table to get 3 sums; then add those 3 sums.

---

3 PRACTICE

Guided Practice

Do Check Exercises 1–6 with your students. Identify students who are having difficulty and choose appropriate lesson resources to provide assistance.

Classify Data

Quick Review

1. $6 + 2 + 3$ 2. $5 + 7 + 6$
   11   18
3. $9 + 1 + 4$ 4. $3 + 8 + 5$
   14   16
5. $13 + 4 + 8$
   25

VOCABULARY
classify

▶ Learn

MARBLES IN MOTION You can group, or **classify**, data in many different ways, such as by size, color, or shape.

Ms. Vernon gave each pair of students in her class a bag of marbles. She asked students to think about ways that they could group the marbles.

Luis and Joey made a table to show what they did.

Bag of Marbles

	Small	Medium	Large
Blue	2	2	5
Red	3	1	5
Multicolor	3	3	2

• **How did Luis and Joey classify their data?** by color: blue, red, multicolored and by size: small, medium, and large

▶ Check

1. Explain 3 things that the groupings in the table helped you know about the marbles.
   See above.
2. How many small blue marbles are there?
   2 small blue marbles
3. How many large red marbles are there?
   5 large red marbles
4. How many multicolored marbles are there?
   8 multicolored marbles
5. How many medium-size marbles are there?
   6 medium-size marbles
6. How many more large marbles than small marbles are there?
   4 more large marbles

306

1. Possible answers: There are more large blue and red marbles than multi-colored ones. The fewest small marbles are blue. There is only 1 medium-size red marble.

For 7–10, use the table.

COLOR OF SHIRTS IN OUR CLASS				
	Green	Blue	Red	Yellow
Girls	1	6	2	5
Boys	3	4	4	0

7. How many girls are wearing red shirts? **2 girls**

8. How many students are wearing blue shirts? **10 students**

9. How many more students' shirts are red than are green?
2 more

10. How many students are in the class? **25 students**

For 11–13, use the table.

PICTURES IN THE ART SHOW				
	Chalk	Crayon	Paint	Pencil
People	3	5	8	1
Animals	4	5	4	3
Plants	6	2	9	5

11. How many pictures are in the art show in all? **55 pictures**

12. What is the subject of the greatest number of pictures in the art show: people, animals, or plants?
plants

13. There are 12 possible categories of pictures in the art show. Which one was represented the least?
people drawn with pencil

14. **REASONING** Look at the figures below. Make a table to classify, or group, them. Explain how you grouped the figures.

[figures: circles and triangles in two rows]

Check students' tables.
Possible answer: I grouped the figures by shape and by color.

15. ▤**FAST FACT** • **SOCIAL STUDIES**
The first machine to make marbles was invented in about 1905 in Akron, Ohio. How many years ago was this?
Possible answer: 99 years ago (in 2004)

16. There are 11 girls and 8 boys in a music club. Of the girls, 6 are dancers and the rest are singers. Of the boys, 3 are dancers and the rest are singers. Make a table to classify, or group, the students. **Check students' tables.**

Getting Ready for the EOG Test

17. Kylie sorted some figures as shown. How did Kylie sort them? **A**

KYLIE'S FIGURES		
Color	Square	Triangle
red	2	1
yellow	1	2
blue	2	1

A by color and shape
B by shape and size
C by size and color
D by size and shape

Chapter 15 **307**

* **North Carolina Standards 4.01** Collect, organize, analyze, and display data (including circle
graphs and tables) to solve problems.

Challenge 15.3

You Group

The first table shows one way to group the shapes below. Find another way to group the shapes. Then make a table to show the other way.

NUMBER OF LINES			
	One Line	Two Lines	Four Lines
Circles	7	6	7
Triangles	3	6	5

Possible answers are shown.

DIRECTION OF LINES			
	Horizontal Lines	Vertical Lines	Diagonal Lines	All Three Lines
Circles	6	6	6	2
Triangles	4	5	3	2

Challenge CW79

Problem Solving 15.3

Classify Data

Understand ➔ Plan ➔ Solve ➔ Check

For 1–6, use the table.

Class Magazine			
Item	1 Page	2 Pages	3 Pages
True Stories	2	8	5
Make-Believe Stories	3	10	4
Poems	12	2	0

1. How many poems are in the magazine?
14 poems

2. How many true stories are more than one page long?
13

3. How many items are in the magazine altogether?
46 items

4. Which item can be found most often in the magazine?
make-believe stories

Choose the letter of the correct answer.

5. How many more 2-page items are in the magazine than 3-page items?
A 3
B 6
C 11
D 12

6. How many fewer poems than true stories are in the magazine?
F 1
G 3
H 6
J 10

7. Matthew took $10 to the movies. He spent $8.35. How much does he have left?
A $0.65
B $1.55
C $1.65
D $2.55

8. Nora had $7.55. Her mother gave her another $5.25. How much does she have now?
F $12.80
G $12.75
H $11.80
J $2.30

9. **Write About It** How did you solve Problem 2?
Possible answer: I used the table to find out how many
2-page and 3-page true stories there were. 8 + 5 = 13

Problem Solving PS79

Students may fail to identify a value because they are not reading both across and down the table. Display a table, and circle or highlight how you would read down one column and across a row to find a single number that describes two criteria, such as *red* and *large*.

BAG OF MARBLES

	Small	Medium	Large
Blue	2	2	5
Red	3	1	5
Multicolor	3	3	2

Independent Practice

Note that Exercise 9 is a **multistep or strategy problem**. Assign Exercises 7–16.

Remind students who are having difficulty with Exercise 12 to add the number of pictures made of people, then add the number of pictures of animals, then add the number of pictures of plants, and then compare the numbers.

4 ASSESS

Summarize the lesson by having students:

DISCUSS What are some ways you can classify data? Possible answers: by size and color; by shape and color; by size and shape

WRITE Make a frequency table from the data below and use it to answer the following questions: How many boys in all chose either fishing or camping? 22 How many more girls like hiking than camping? 5

FAVORITE OUTDOOR ACTIVITY		
	Boys	Girls
Fishing	卌 II	卌 卌 IIII
Hiking	卌 卌 I	卌 卌 III
Camping	卌 卌 卌	卌 III

LESSON QUIZ

Use the "Pictures in the Art Show" table on page 307.

Transparency
15.3

1. How many different kinds of pictures does this table classify? 12 kinds

2. What was the least popular subject? animals

307

Lesson Planning

PROFESSIONAL DEVELOPMENT

Objective To use the problem solving strategy *make a table*

Lesson Resources Reading Transparency 15; Intervention • Problem Solving, Strategy/Skill 15

NCTM Standards
1. **Number and Operations**
5. **Data Analysis and Probability**
6. **Problem Solving**
7. **Reasoning and Proof**
8. **Communication**
9. **Connections**
10. **Representation**

Math Background
These ideas will help students use the problem solving strategy *make a table*.

- Tables organize data, making results such as *most often* and *least often* easier to determine.

- Making a table is a step-by-step process that begins with an analysis of a word problem.

- Making a table is a way of interpreting and solving a word problem.

Warm-Up Resources

Number of the Day

Transparency **15.4**

The number of the day is the number that represents the day of the month. Use that number and at least two different operations to write four number sentences. Answers will vary.

Daily Facts Practice

Have students practice addition facts by completing Set C of *Teacher's Resource Book*, p. TR94.

Transparency **15.4**

Problem of the Day

Show this data in a table. In Ali's class, 3 girls have long, straight, blond hair, and 1 has short, straight, blond hair. The only redhead has long, straight hair. No girls have long, curly hair. The only girls with short, curly hair are 3 whose hair is brown. Of the 3 other brown-haired girls, 2 have long hair, and one has short hair. Find the type of hair that is most common. long, straight, blond and short, curly, brown

Solution Problem of the Day tab, p. PD15

Intervention and Extension Resources

Alternative Teaching Strategy

Help students **review the steps in the process of using the strategy *make a table* to solve a problem**. Display the following steps:

- Read the problem.
- Determine what you are being asked to find.
- Make a table with a title and labels for the columns.
- Put the data you want to organize in the columns.
- Solve the problem.

Have students copy the steps on strips of paper, turn the strips over, mix them up, turn them back over, and put the steps in the correct order. Check students' work.

VISUAL

VISUAL/SPATIAL

Reading Strategy

Use Graphic Aids Remind students that sometimes the best way to solve a problem is to organize the information in a table. A table can help them see the information more clearly. Help students make a table to solve the following problem:

Nick and Elena each roll a number cube with the numbers 1–6. They record the differences between the two numbers. They get the following data: 0, 5, 1, 1, 2, 4, 0, 3, 2, 4, 3, 0, 2, 1, 2. What difference did they get most often? 2

You may want to remind students of the steps required to make a table. Check students' work.

 15 **Reading Transparency 15**

Multistep and Strategy Problems

The following multistep or strategy problems are provided in Lesson 15.4:

Page	Item
309	2, 5–9

Writing in Mathematics

Help **reinforce students' understanding of the strategy *make a table*** by having them write a paragraph. The first sentence can tell what a table is. The second sentence can tell when or why a person might decide to make a table. The third sentence can conclude with how tables help people solve problems. Check students' work.

VISUAL

VERBAL/LINGUISTIC

Advanced Learners

After students solve Exercise 3 on page 309, challenge them to **make a table** that would show all the possible combinations that would yield the differences from rolling the two number cubes, numbered 1–6.

Difference of:	Roll:
5	(6,1) (1,6)
4	(6,2) (2,6) (5,1) (1,5)
3	(6,3) (3,6) (5,2) (2,5) (4,1) (1,4)
2	(6,4) (4,6) (5,3) (3,5) (4,2) (2,4) (3,1) (1,3)
1	(6,5) (5,6) (5,4) (4,5) (4,3) (3,4) (3,2) (2,3) (2,1) (1,2)
0	(6,6) (5,5) (4,4) (3,3) (2,2) (1,1)

VISUAL

VISUAL/SPATIAL

Technology Link

Intervention • Problem Solving, *Strategy/Skill 15*

Lesson 15.4 Organizer

Objective To use the problem solving strategy *make a table*

Lesson Resources Reading Transparency 15; Intervention • Problem Solving, Strategy/Skill 15

1 INTRODUCE

QUICK REVIEW provides review of prerequisite skills.

WHY LEARN THIS? Making a table helps you organize information which can help you make decisions. *Share the lesson objective with students.*

2 TEACH

Guided Instruction

• *Discuss the Problem.*
What do the results of the spins mean? Each result is the sum of the two numbers that were spun.
REASONING Why is it hard to tell which sum occurred most often just by reading the problem? The sums are not in any particular order.

• *Direct students' attention to the table titled Spinner Sum.*
What are the parts of this table? It has a title and two columns. The columns have labels. The sums are recorded in one column, and tally marks showing the number of spins are recorded in the second column.

What can you learn from the table besides the answer to the Problem? Possible answer: what the next most frequent and least frequent sums were

---

Problem Solving Strategy
Make a Table

Quick Review
1. 6 + 4 10   2. 3 + 5 8
3. 8 + 7 15   4. 9 + 6 15
5. 6 + 7 13

PROBLEM   Leo and Sally used the two spinners shown at the right. They spun the pointers and recorded the sum of the two numbers. They spun 20 times. Their results were 2, 4, 6, 5, 4, 5, 4, 4, 2, 4, 4, 3, 4, 5, 6, 4, 6, 4, 3, and 4. Which sum occurred most often?

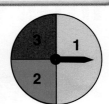

3 + 1 = 4

UNDERSTAND
• What are you asked to find?
the sum that occurred most often
• What information will you use?
the sums that are the results of their experiment

PLAN
• What strategy can you use to solve the problem?
You can *make a table* to organize the data.

SOLVE
• What should you put in the table?
Leo and Sally recorded the sums of the two numbers. So, label one column *Sums*. In this column, list all the sums that are possible. Label another column *Number of Spins*. Use a tally mark to record each spin.

So, the sum 4 occurred most often.

SPINNER SUM	
Sums	**Number of Spins**
2			
3			
4									
5				
6				

CHECK
• What other strategy could you use to solve the problem? **make an organized list**

308

Reteach 15.4

Problem Solving Strategy

Make a Table

Sam and Matilda are using the two spinners at the right. They will spin each pointer 20 times to find the sum they spin the most often and the least often. After spinning each of the two pointers, they will add the two numbers they spun. They will need to record the sums. What would be the best way to organize and record which sums were spun?

SPINNER EXPERIMENT	
Sum	**Number of Spins**
2						
3				
4				
5					
6				

Step 1 Make a table. List all of the different possible sums.

Step 2 Spin the pointers 20 times each. Record one tally mark for each sum.

Make a table to solve. **Answers will vary. Check students' tables.**

1. Joe and Maria are using the two spinners shown below. They will spin the pointers on the spinners and then record the results. They will spin the pointers 50 times. Show how they can organize the data in a table.

2. Heather is using the two spinners shown below. One spinner has two sections: a light section and a dark section. The other spinner has two sections: A and B. Heather will spin the pointer and record the results 50 times. Show how she can organize the data in a table.

RW80 Reteach

Practice 15.4

Problem Solving Strategy

Make a Table

Solve. **Check students' tables.**

1. Karen and José are using the spinner and coin shown below. They spin the spinner and flip the coin. Then they record the results. They repeat this 15 times. Show how they could organize the data in a table.

COIN-SPINNER EXPERIMENT	
Coin-Spin	Tally
Heads-1	
Tails-1	
Heads-2	
Tails-2	
Heads-3	
Tails-3	

2. Phillip is using the two coins shown below. He will toss both coins 25 times and record the results after each pair of tosses. Show how he could organize the data in a table.

TWO COINS EXPERIMENT	
Coins	Tally
Heads-Heads	
Heads-Tails	
Tails-Tails	

Mixed Review

Round to the nearest 100 and 1,000.

3. 1,355 _1,400; 1,000_
4. 5,667 _5,700; 6,000_
5. 7,572 _7,600; 8,000_
6. 4,140 _4,100; 4,000_
7. 9,454 _9,500; 9,000_
8. 6,905 _6,900; 7,000_

Divide.

9. 15 ÷ 3 = _5_
10. 49 ÷ 7 = _7_
11. 63 ÷ 9 = _7_
12. 8 ÷ 8 = _1_
13. 30 ÷ 5 = _6_
14. 48 ÷ 6 = _8_

PW80 Practice

Solve.

1. **What if** Leo and Sally spin the pointers 25 times and record the sums in a table? How many tallies should there be?
   25 tallies

2. Marta and Dan rolled two number cubes 15 times and recorded the sums. Their results were 9, 9, 5, 6, 9, 3, 7, 7, 3, 5, 12, 12, 10, 8, and 5. Make a table and find the sum rolled most often. **Check students' tables; 9 and 5 were both rolled 3 times.**

Strategies

Draw a Diagram or Picture
Make a Model or Act It Out
Make an Organized List
Find a Pattern
▶ **Make a Table or Graph**
Predict and Test
Work Backward
Solve a Simpler Problem
Write a Number Sentence
Use Logical Reasoning

Problem Solving

Roll two number cubes, numbered 1–6, twenty times to find out what difference you will roll most often.

3. What are all the differences you will list in your table? **C**
   A 0, 2, 4, 6
   B 0, 1, 2, 3, 4, 5, 6
   C 0, 1, 2, 3, 4, 5
   D 1, 2, 3, 4, 5, 6

4. What should the total number of tallies be in your table for this experiment? **H**
   F 10   H 20
   G 15   J 25

Mixed Strategy Practice

5. **REASONING** Louise is older than Jim and Marsha. Marsha is younger than Jim. Al is the youngest of the group. What is the order of the group from youngest to oldest? **Al, Marsha, Jim, Louise**

6. The clock shows the time when the game ended. If the game lasted 2 hours and 15 minutes, when did it start?
   11:55 A.M.

7. In the library, there are 3 shelves with 9 new books on each shelf. How many new books are on the shelves? **27 books**

8. Lonnie has 48 dinosaur models. He puts them into 8 bags so that there are the same number in each bag. How many models do 2 bags contain? **12 models**

9. **? What's the Question?** Sylvia spent $7 at the movies. She still had $8 when she got home. The answer is $15. **How much did Sylvia have to begin with?**

Chapter 15 **309**

▶ **North Carolina Standards 4.01** Collect, organize, analyze, and display data (including circle graphs and tables) to solve problems.

Challenge 15.4

Spinning

Use a paper clip and a pencil.
Put your pencil in the paper clip to hold the paper clip in the center point of the circle. Spin the paper clip on each spinner.
In the table, record the sum of the two numbers you spin. Repeat this 50 times. **Tallies will vary. Possible answers are given.**

1. Which sum happened the most?

   The sum of 8 happened

   the most.

2. Which sum happened the least?

   The sum of 5 happened

   the least.

SPINNER SUMS	
Sum	Tally
5	
6	
7	
8	
9	

3. Which two sums do you think should happen more times?

   Possible answer: 7 and 8, since the sections for 2, 3, and 5 are

   larger than the other sections on the spinners.

Reading Strategy 15.4

Use Graphic Aids   Understand ▶ Plan ▶ Solve ▶ Check

Sometimes the best way to solve a word problem is to organize the information in a table. A table can help you see the information more clearly.

Read the following problem.

▶ Anita used the spinner at the right. In the first trial, Anita spun yellow 12 times and green 13 times. In the second trial, she spun yellow 9 times and green 16 times. In the third trial, she spun yellow 14 times and green 11 times. Which color did she spin more often?

1. Use the information in the problem to complete the table.

	Yellow	Green
Trial 1	12	13
Trial 2	9	16
Trial 3	14	11
Total	35	40

2. Solve the problem. **Anita spun green more often.**

3. Describe the strategy you used to solve the problem.
   Possible answer: I recorded the spins for each color in the
   table, added the numbers, and compared the totals.

Make a table to solve each problem. **Check students' tables.**

4. Nick has two number cubes. Each cube has the numbers 1, 1, 2, 2, 3, and 3. He rolls the two cubes and finds the sum. What sums can he roll?
   2, 3, 4, 5, 6

5. Keesha tossed a coin 30 times. She tossed heads twice as many times as tails. How many times did she toss heads?
   20 times

---

3 PRACTICE

Guided Practice

Do Problem Solving Practice Exercises 1–4 with your students. Identify students who are having difficulty and choose appropriate lesson resources to provide assistance. Note that Exercise 2 is a **multistep or strategy problem.**

For Exercise 3, remind students that finding differences means subtracting lesser numbers from greater numbers.

Independent Practice

Note that Exercises 5–9 are **multistep or strategy problems.** Assign Exercises 5–9.

SCAFFOLDED INSTRUCTION Use the prompts on Transparency 15 to guide instruction for the multistep or strategy problem in Exercise 8.

Transparency
15

4 ASSESS

Summarize the lesson by having students:

DISCUSS Why is *make a table* a good problem solving strategy? A table helps you organize information so that you can find the answer.

WRITE Why is analyzing the problem an important step in problem solving? You can't choose a strategy until you understand the problem.

LESSON QUIZ

Solve.

Transparency
15.4

1. Marta and Dan roll two number cubes 12 times and record the sums 7, 5, 9, 7, 8, 4, 8, 7, 12, 3, 6, and 7. Make a table and find the sum rolled most often. Check students' work; 7 was the sum rolled most often.

2. Leo and Sally use two spinners and record 10 differences: 2, 3, 5, 5, 2, 4, 3, 5, 4, 4. Show how they could make a table to find the differences landed on most often. Check students' work; 4 and 5 were the differences landed on most often.

309

Lesson Planning

PROFESSIONAL DEVELOPMENT

Objective To read and interpret data in line plots

Materials *For each student* unlabeled number line, p. TR16

NCTM Standards
1. **Number and Operations**
5. **Data Analysis and Probability**
6. **Problem Solving**
8. **Communication**
9. **Connections**
10. **Representation**

Math Background
These ideas will help students read and interpret line plots.

- Line plots are useful for displaying the frequency of data.
- You can identify the range of data and the mode, at a glance, on a line plot. In a given set of data, there may be more than one mode.
- Line plots are one of many options for displaying data in a clear, organized, and easy-to-read format.

Vocabulary
line plot a diagram that shows the frequency of data

mode the number or item that occurs most often in a set of data

range the difference between the greatest number and the least number in a set of data

circle graph a graph in the shape of a circle that shows data as a whole made up of different parts

Warm-Up Resources

Number of the Day

Transparency **15.5**

Determine the number of months you have been in school so far this year. If you had that number of pennies, nickels, and dimes, what would be the value of your coins? Answers will vary.

Daily Facts Practice

Have students practice multiplication facts by completing Set D of *Teacher's Resource Book*, p. TR94.

Transparency **15.5**

Problem of the Day

Three students made 3 graphs. The boy who made the horizontal bar graph was not Jeff. Amy did not make the vertical bar graph. Paul did not make the pictograph. Which of the 3 graphs did each student make? Paul: horizontal bar graph; Jeff: vertical bar graph; Amy: pictograph

Solution Problem of the Day tab, p. PD15

Intervention and Extension Resources

Alternative Teaching Strategy

To **help students identify the range**, have them follow these steps for the line plots shown in the lesson: **ESOL/ESL**

- Look at the number line.
- Identify the greatest number and the least number.
- Subtract the least number from the greatest number.
  Check students' work.

See also page 312.

VISUAL

VISUAL/SPATIAL

Writing in Mathematics

 Have students **summarize what they have learned about line plots**. Have students use the following terms in their explanation: *graphic aid, number line, data, range,* and *mode.*

Possible answer: A line plot is a <u>graphic aid</u> that shows the frequency of <u>data</u>. A line plot consists of a <u>number line</u> that is labeled with the greatest and least numbers in a set of data. If you subtract the least number from the greatest number, you get the <u>range</u>. Above the number line are *x*'s showing how frequently each number or item occurs in the set. The <u>mode</u> is the number that occurs most often.

Multistep and Strategy Problems

The following multistep or strategy problems are provided in Lesson 15.5:

Page	Item
311	3
312	6

Advanced Learners

Challenge students to **make a line plot**. Have them work in groups to choose a topic and collect data that can be represented in a line plot. After they have completed their line plots, have them identify the range and the mode and display the line plots in the classroom. Check students' work.

VISUAL

INTERPERSONAL/SOCIAL

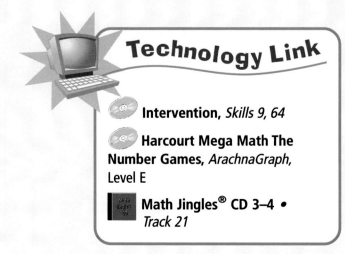

Technology Link

Intervention, *Skills 9, 64*

Harcourt Mega Math The Number Games, *ArachnaGraph,* Level E

Math Jingles® CD 3–4 • *Track 21*

Lesson 15.5 Organizer

Objective To read and interpret data in line plots

Vocabulary line plot, mode, range, circle graph

Materials *For each student* unlabeled number line, p. TR16

---

1 INTRODUCE

QUICK REVIEW provides practice of mental math skills.

WHY LEARN THIS? You can use line plots to summarize information. *Share the lesson objective with students.*

---

2 TEACH

Guided Instruction

• *Direct students' attention to the line plot.*
How is a line plot like a number line? The numbers increase as you move to the right.
Explain how you can use the numbers that the line plot begins and ends with to find the range. Subtract the beginning, or least, number from the ending, or greatest, number.
How do you show each tally mark on the chart in the line plot? Put one *x* in the line plot for each tally mark in the chart. Place it above the number it represents.

• *Have students read the definition of* mode.
What if there were two fewer students who measured 53 inches? What would the mode be? Explain. 52 inches; it would be the height that would occur most often.

LESSON 5 Line Plots

Quick Review
1. 27 − 12 15
2. 36 − 18 18
3. 98 − 35 63
4. 74 − 47 27
5. 56 − 39 17

► Learn

LOTS OF PLOTS All 24 third-grade students were measured to find their heights in inches.

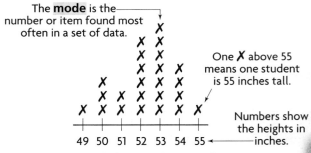

HEIGHTS OF THIRD GRADERS	
Height in Inches	**Number of Students**
49	|
50	|||
51	||
52	⦀|
53	⦀||
54	||||
55	|

VOCABULARY
line plot
mode
range
circle graph

You can make a **line plot** to record each piece of data on a number line.

The **mode** is the number or item found most often in a set of data.

One **X** above 55 means one student is 55 inches tall.

Numbers show the heights in inches.

```
                    X
                  X X
                  X X
                  X X X
            X     X X X
            X X X X X X
        X X X X X X X X
        ┼─┼─┼─┼─┼─┼─┼─┼
       49 50 51 52 53 54 55
```
Heights of Third Graders in Inches

The **range** is the difference between the greatest number and the least number.

greatest number — least number = range
55 − 49 = 6

• What are the range and mode for this data? **6 in.; 53 in.**
• How many students are 50 inches tall? **3 students**

310

Reteach 15.5

Line Plots

Ms. Ryan is teaching a cartooning class for students ages 8 to 12. She made a **line plot** to show the number of students of each age in the class. How many students are 10 years old?

```
        X
        X
        X X
      X X X X X
      X X X X X
      ┼─┼─┼─┼─┼
      8  9 10 11 12
   Ages of Students in Class
```

Step 1 Locate 10 on the line plot.

Step 2 Count the number of **X**'s above the number 10.

There are 4 students who are 10 years old.

For 1–4, use the line plot above.

1. There are __3__ students who are 11 years old.

2. The same number of students are __8__ and __12__ years old.

3. The **range** is the difference between the greatest and least numbers in a set of data. The range in ages of students in the class is __4 years__.

4. The **mode** is the number that occurs most often in a set of data. The number on the line plot with the most **X**'s is 9. So, the **mode** for this set of data is __9 years old__.

5. After the first morning of cartooning class, the students counted the number of cartoon pages they had completed. Use the data in the table to complete the line plot.

CARTOON PAGES COMPLETED					
Number of Pages	2	3	4	5	6
Number of Students	2	4	7	2	1

```
        X
        X
        X
      X X
      X X
    X X X X
    X X X X X
    ┼─┼─┼─┼─┼
    2 3 4 5 6
 Cartoon Pages Completed
```

Reteach RW81

Practice 15.5

Line Plots

For 1–3, use the line plot at the right.

1. The **X**'s on this line plot represent the number of students. What do the numbers on the line plot represent?
   the number of children in a family

2. What is the range of numbers used in this line plot?
   6 children

3. What is the mode, or number that occurs most often, for this set of data?
   2 children

```
        X
        X
        X
        X
      X X
      X X
      X X X X
      X X X X   X
      ┼─┼─┼─┼─┼─┼─┼
      1 2 3 4 5 6 7
 Number of Children in Family
```

4. Use the data in the table to complete the line plot.

Slices of Pizza Eaten	
Number of Slices	**Number of Students**
0	||
1	⦀|
2	⦀
3	|||
4	|
5	||

```
        X
      X X
      X X
      X X X
    X X X X   X
    X X X X X X
    ┼─┼─┼─┼─┼─┼
    0 1 2 3 4 5
  Slices of Pizza Eaten
```

Mixed Review

Find each product or quotient.

5. 10 × 7 = __70__   6. 7 × 9 = __63__   7. 6 × 1 = __6__   8. 8 × 2 = __16__

9. 8 ÷ 4 = __2__   10. 36 ÷ 6 = __6__   11. 0 ÷ 22 = __0__   12. 45 ÷ 9 = __5__

Practice PW81

Make a Line Plot

Debbie took a survey in her third-grade class to find out how many peanut butter and jelly sandwiches the students ate last week.

She put the survey data in a tally table.

PEANUT BUTTER AND JELLY SANDWICHES

Number of Sandwiches	Tallies
0		
1						
2				
3							
4					
5			

Activity

Materials: number line

Make a line plot of the data in the table.

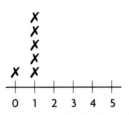

STEP 1

Write a title for the line plot. Label the numbers from 0 to 5.

```
+--+--+--+--+--+
0  1  2  3  4  5
```
Peanut Butter and Jelly Sandwiches Eaten Last Week

STEP 2

Draw **X**'s above the number line to show how many students ate each number of sandwiches.

```
            X
            X
            X
            X
      X  X
+--+--+--+--+--+
0  1  2  3  4  5
```
Peanut Butter and Jelly Sandwiches Eaten Last Week

• How are the tally table and the line plot alike? How are they different? **Alike: They both represent the same data. Different: The tally table uses tallies; the line plot uses Xs and a number line.**

Technology Link

More Practice: Harcourt Mega Math The Number Games, *Arachna-Graph,* Level E

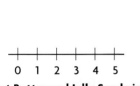 **Check**

1. **Explain** how to find the mode for the data above.
Possible answer: Find the number that has the most Xs. 3 is the mode.

For 2–3, use your line plot.

2. How many students ate exactly 3 peanut butter and jelly sandwiches last week? **6 students**

3. How many more students ate 1 or 2 sandwiches than ate 4 or 5 sandwiches? **2 more students**

LESSON CONTINUES

Chapter 15 **311**

• *Refer to Steps 1 and 2.*

Why do you label the number line with the numbers 0 to 5? to match the data in the tally table

REASONING How do you know when your line plot is complete? when the number of tally marks equals the number of *x*'s

3 PRACTICE

Guided Practice

Do Check Exercises 1–3 with your students. Identify the students who are having difficulty and choose appropriate lesson resources to provide assistance. Note that Exercise 3 is a **multistep or strategy problem.**

North Carolina Standards 4.01 Collect, organize, analyze, and display data (including circle graphs and tables) to solve problems.

Challenge 15.5

What's in a Name?

Jennifer is comparing the number of letters in her classmates' first names. She printed each student's name on a piece of paper. She then began to count and record the number of letters in each name.

1. Complete Jennifer's line plot by recording the number of letters in the first names of the students in her class.

Jennifer	Zachary	Lee	Elizabeth	Dimitri
Ted	Juan	Trudi	Malcolm	Chiang
Carl	Paul	Courtney	Kevin	Alan

```
      X
      X        X
   X  X     X  X
   X  X  X  X  X  X  X
  +--+--+--+--+--+--+--+
  3  4  5  6  7  8  9
Number of Letters in First Name
```

For 2–5, use the completed line plot.

2. How many students have 7 letters in their first name?
3 students

3. What is the mode for the number of letters for a first name in Jennifer's class?
4 letters

4. What is the range in this data?
6 letters

5. Would the data be different if you made a line plot for the number of letters in the first names of students in your class? Make a list of names and show the data in a line plot.
Yes; Check students' work.

```
+--+--+--+--+--+--+--+--+--+
2  3  4  5  6  7  8  9 10 11
Number of Letters in First Name
```

Challenge **CW81**

Problem Solving 15.5

Line Plots

Understand ▸ Plan ▸ Solve ▸ Check

Write the correct answer.

1. Each *x* on the line plot stands for one student. How many students watched 4 movies?

___1 student___

2. What is the mode of the data in the line plot?

___1 movie___

3. How many students are included in the line plot?

___22 students___

4. What is the range for the data in the line plot?

___7 movies___

```
      X
      X     X
   X  X     X
   X  X  X     X
   X  X  X  X  X     X
   X  X  X  X  X  X     X
  +--+--+--+--+--+--+--+--+
  0  1  2  3  4  5  6  7
      Number of Movies
```

Choose the letter of the correct answer.

5. In the line plot above, how many students saw *fewer than* 3 movies?
A 17   C 10
B 12   D 5

6. In the line plot above, which number of students watched 2 movies?
F 0   **H 2**
G 1   J 3

7. Harry is 7 years old. Lucy is 4 years younger than Harry. Susan is 6 years older than Lucy. Which is true?
A Harry is older than Susan.
B Lucy is older than Harry.
C Lucy is older than Susan.
D Susan is older than Harry.

8. Find the sum.
```
  35
  42
+49
```
F 116   H 127
G 126   J 136

9. **Write About It** Describe how you solved Problem 7.

Possible answer: I made a list of the names and wrote down their ages as I worked through the problem. I compared this list with the answer choices.

Problem Solving **PS81**

COMMON ERROR ALERT

When two sets of data such as the number of students and the number of sandwiches are both expressed in numbers, students may confuse the two categories. Remind them that the first set of numbers on the left are placed on the number line and show the range. The x's on the line plot represent each tally mark and show the frequency.

Independent Practice

Note that Exercise 6 is a **multistep or strategy problem.** Assign Exercises 4–13.

MULTISTEP OR STRATEGY PROBLEM To solve Exercise 6, students can add the number of x's above the numbers *2, 3,* and *4,* and add the number of x's above the numbers *6, 7, 8, 9,* and *10.* Next, they should compare these sums.

To help students make the line plot in Exercise 12, you may wish to have them use an unlabeled number line from pp. TR 5, 6, or 16.

Vocabulary Power Explain that the root of the word *mode* is *med.* Its original meaning was related to measuring. Another math word from the same root is *median.*

For 4–6, use the line plot at the right.

4. The **X**'s on the line plot stand for the band members. What do the numbers stand for? **the number of hours practiced**
5. What is the greatest number of hours any student practiced? What is the least number? What is the range for this set of data? **greatest: 10; least: 2; range: 8**
6. Did more band members practice for *less than* 5 hours or for *more than* 5 hours? Explain. **See above.**

6. less than; 2 + 3 + 7 = 12 and 5 + 2 + 1 + 1 = 9; 12 > 9

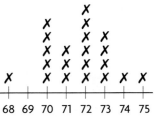

Hours Band Members Practiced

7. **Vocabulary Power** To remember the meaning of *mode,* think of the word *most.* In this set of numbers, what is the mode? 9, 2, 8, 9, 7, 3, 9, 5, 6, 9 **9**

For 8–11, use the line plot below.

Mrs. Brown's class recorded the high temperature each day for 3 weeks.

8. What high temperature occurred most often in the 3 weeks? On how many days? **72 degrees; 6 days**
9. On how many days was the high temperature below 70 degrees? **1 day**
10. What was the range of high temperatures? **7 degrees**
11. Predict what you think the high temperature will be the fourth week. Explain. **Possible answers: 70°–73°; The most X's are from 70° to 73° on the line plot.**
12. Take a survey to find out how many pets each student in your class has. Show the results in a tally table and a line plot. **Check students' tally tables and line plots.**

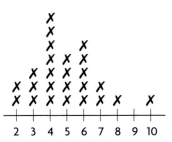

High Temperatures Each Day (in Degrees)

13. ✎ **Write About It** Explain how you decided which numbers to use in your line plot in Problem 12. **Students should explain how they found the range of the data from their survey.**

312

Alternative Teaching Strategy | Scaffolded Instruction

PURPOSE Students model the data on a line plot to understand a plot, range, and mode.

MATERIALS chalk or washable marker

Step 1

Ask students which number comes closest to the number of hours they have exercised in the last week: 1, 2, 3, or 4. Have students form groups according to the number of hours each has chosen.

Step 2

Bring students to a large, empty space. Along one side of that space, draw a large number line with the numbers 1–4.

Step 3

Have each group place itself on the number line according to the number of hours exercised. Then have each group form a straight row, beginning at that number and extending away.

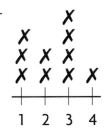

Step 4

Explain that students have formed a line plot. Also explain that the line you drew is a number line, from which the range can be found by subtracting 1 from 4. Ask students to determine the range of their data. 3

Step 5

Have students identify the longest of the four rows. Count the number of students and explain that the number that occurs most often is the mode. Answers will vary.

PROFESSIONAL DEVELOPMENT

14. Todd made a line plot to show the number of hours he slept each night during two weeks. What is the *mode* for this set of data? **C**

A 8
B 9
C 10
D 11

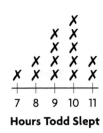

```
              X
          X   X
          X   X
      X   X   X   X
  X   X   X   X   X
  +---+---+---+---+---+
  7   8   9  10  11
```
Hours Todd Slept

15. What is the *range* of this data? **B**

A 7   B 4   C 3   D 2

Problem Solving — LiNKUP ...to Reading

STRATEGY • USE GRAPHIC AIDS Graphic aids organize information so that it can be compared and analyzed. When you use a graphic aid, you "read" a picture rather than just words.

Brandi took a survey to find her classmates' favorite pets. She made a line plot and a circle graph of the data.

A **circle graph** shows data as parts of a whole circle.

1. How many classmates did Brandi survey?
   16 classmates
2. What is the mode of the data? **dogs**

3. Which pet received half of the votes? **dogs**

4. Which two pets received the same number of votes? **birds and fish**

5. 🖊 **Write About It** Tell whether you think the circle graph or the line plot is easier to read. Explain the reason for your choice.
   Answers will vary.

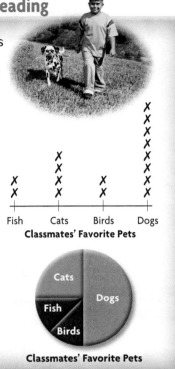

```
                              X
                              X
                              X
                              X
              X               X
              X               X
  X           X       X       X
  X           X       X       X
  +-------+-------+-------+-------+
 Fish    Cats   Birds   Dogs
```
Classmates' Favorite Pets

Classmates' Favorite Pets

Reading Strategy

K-W-L CHART Before having students read the Linkup, have them look at the line plot and circle graph. Ask them to predict what the Linkup will be about. Then have students make a three-column chart headed *What I Know, What I Want to Know,* and *What I Learned.* Ask them to fill in the first two columns. Have them fill in the third column as they study the diagrams.

K-W-L Chart

What I Know	What I Want to Know	What I Learned

Problem Solving LiNKUP ...to Reading

• *Have students read about using graphic aids.*
  What are the two kinds of graphic aids shown? a line plot and a circle graph
  What is the same and what is different about these graphic aids? Both show the same data and have the same titles. The line plot uses *x*'s to show each student's vote. The circle graph uses parts of a circle to show the number of students' votes.
  REASONING How could this data be shown using another graphic aid? Possible answer: pictograph; bar graph

---

4 ASSESS

Summarize the lesson by having students:

DISCUSS How is the range found on a line plot? Look at the number line. Subtract the first, or least, number from the last, or greatest, number to find the range.

📓 **WRITE How is the mode shown on a line plot?** The number with the most *x*'s is the mode.

LESSON QUIZ
For 1–2, use the line plot titled *Hours Band Members Practiced* on page 312.

Transparency **15.5**

1. What is the mode? 4 hours

2. If one student had practiced 12 hours, what would the range be? 10 hours

Lesson Planning

Objective To find the mean and median of a set of data

Materials *For each student* connecting cubes

NCTM Standards
1. **Number and Operations**
5. **Data Analysis and Probability**
6. **Problem Solving**
7. **Reasoning and Proof**
8. **Communication**
9. **Connections**
10. **Representation**

Math Background
These ideas will help students understand how to find the mean and the median.

- The mean is an average.
- You can find the mean by dividing the sum of a set of numbers by the number of addends.
- The median is the middle number when all the numbers in a set of data are placed in order.

Vocabulary
mean the average of a set of data
median the middle number in an ordered set of data

Warm-Up Resources

Number of the Day

Transparency **15.6**

Record the number of boys in your class and the number of girls. Subtract the lesser number from the greater number. What is the difference? Check students' answers.

Daily Facts Practice

Have students practice multiplication facts by completing Set E of *Teacher's Resource Book*, p. TR94.

Transparency **15.6**

Problem of the Day

Graham saved for 5 weeks to buy a train set that cost $29.56. About how much did he set aside each week? He saved about $6.00 per week.

Solution Problem of the Day tab, p. PD15

Intervention and Extension Resources

Alternative Teaching Strategy

MATERIALS *For each group* 30 counters per 5 students

To help students **practice finding mean and median,** have one student in each group pass out the counters randomly. Each student should have a different number. Then have students line up each group of counters in order and identify the middle number. Remind them that the middle number of any group of data is called the median.

Next, ask students to find how many counters each student would get if they were divided evenly. Allow groups to experiment until they discover that each would get 6. So the average number of counters per student is 6. The average number is the mean.

KINESTHETIC

LOGICAL/MATHEMATICAL, BODILY/KINESTHETIC

Multistep and Strategy Problems

The following multistep or strategy problem is provided in Lesson 15.6:

Page	Item
315	8

ESOL/ESL

Help students **build understanding of the word** *median.* Display these numbers: 3, 6, 4, 8, and 5. Ask a volunteer to order the numbers from least to greatest. Then have the student circle the middle number and say the word *median.* Explain that on a highway, the median is a strip of land that separates the lanes going in opposite directions. This may help students remember that the median is the middle.

VISUAL/AUDITORY

VERBAL/LINGUISTIC

Advanced Learners

Give students the following puzzle to solve. Explain that there is more than one way to solve it, but certain numbers in the data set will be the same no matter how it is solved.

The mode of a set of data is 3. There are 9 numbers in the set. The range of the set is 7. The median is 8. What are the numbers in the set? Possible answer: 3, 3, 3, 4, 8, 8, 9, 9, 10; The numbers that must be the same in all solutions are 3 and 10 as the first and last numbers, and 8 as the fifth number in the set. All other numbers can vary as long as there are more 3s than any other number.

LOGICAL/MATHEMATICAL

INTERPERSONAL

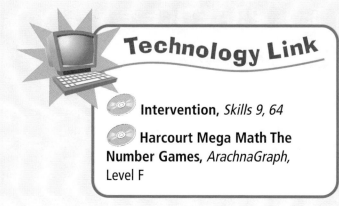

Technology Link

Intervention, *Skills 9, 64*

Harcourt Mega Math The Number Games, *ArachnaGraph,* Level F

Lesson 15.6 Organizer

Objective To find the mean and median of a set of data

Vocabulary mean, median

Materials *For each student* connecting cubes

Mean and Median

HANDS ON

---

1 INTRODUCE

QUICK REVIEW provides review of mental math skills.

WHY LEARN THIS? Collecting and understanding data of the world around you can help you appreciate it in new and different ways. *Share the lesson objective with students.*

---

2 TEACH

Guided Instruction

- *Direct students' attention to Activity 1, One Way.*
  How are the stacks of connecting cubes in Step 1 like the tally sheet that Cari made? There are 3 cubes for the 3 robins Cari saw on Monday; 8 cubes for the 8 robins she saw on Tuesday, and so on.
  How can you check the mean in Another Way? You can multiply the mean by the number of addends. The product should equal the sum of the addends. $4 \times 5 = 20$

- *Direct students' attention to Activity 2.*
  Why is it important to arrange the stacks of cubes in order from least to greatest? The number in the middle would not be the median if the stacks were not ordered.
  REASONING Is it possible for the mean and the median to be the same number? Give an example. Yes; in the set of numbers 9, 10, and 11, the median and the mean are 10.

---

3 PRACTICE

Guided Practice

Do Try It Exercises a and b with your students. Identify students who are having difficulty and choose appropriate lesson resources to provide assistance.

▶ Explore

BIRD COUNT Cari recorded in a tally table the number of robins she saw on her way to school. Find the mean and median of this data.

The **mean** is the average of a set of data. The **median** is the middle number in an ordered set of data.

Robins I Saw	
Monday	|||
Tuesday	||||
Wednesday		
Thursday	||||
Friday	||

Activity 1 Find the mean.
One Way Use connecting cubes.

STEP 1
Model the number of robins counted each day.

STEP 2
Rearrange the cubes so each stack has the same number of cubes.
The mean is the number of cubes in each stack. So, the mean is 4 robins.

Another Way Use addition and division.

STEP 1
Add the numbers for each day.
$3 + 8 + 1 + 6 + 2 = 20$

STEP 2
Divide the sum by the number of addends.
$20 \div 5 = 4$ So, the mean is 4 robins.

Activity 2 Find the median.

STEP 1
Model the number of robins counted each day. Arrange the stacks in order from least to greatest.

STEP 2
Count the number of cubes in the middle stack. So, the median is 3 robins.

median

Try It

Find the mean and median.

a. 4, 9, 8 **7; 8**   b. 5, 7, 6, 3, 9 **6; 6**

314

▶ Connect

If a set of data uses numbers, you can find the median of the data without using connecting cubes.

In the spring, Travis and his friends saw 7 robins' nests with eggs and used a picture to show their data. What is the median?

Record the number of eggs that are in each nest. List the data in order from least to greatest. Then find the middle number.

3, 3, 3, 4, 4, 5, 6

So, the median of the set of data is 4 eggs.

- What are the mode and the range of this set of data?
  mode: 3 eggs; range: 3 eggs
- What is the mean of this set of data? Use connecting cubes to help. **mean: 4 eggs**

Technology Link
More Practice:
Harcourt Mega Math
The Number Games,
Arachna-Graph,
Level F

▶ Practice and Problem Solving

Find the mean and the median.

1. 7, 2, 6 **mean: 5; median: 6**

2. 5, 8, 5 **mean: 6; median: 5**

3. 5, 8, 9, 6, 7 **mean: 7; median: 7**

4. 1, 5, 3, 2, 4 **mean: 3; median: 3**

5. 1, 4, 0, 3, 1, 2, 3 **mean: 2; median: 2**

6. 2, 6, 5, 3, 1, 7, 4 **mean: 4; median: 4**

7. **REASONING** Teri says using connecting cubes to find the mean of a set of data is like dividing. Do you agree or disagree? Explain.
   Possible answer: agree; rearranging the cubes into equal stacks is like separating a set into equal groups.

8. ✎ **Write About It** Choose your favorite fruit. Record in a tally table the number of times you eat the fruit each day for one week. Then find the range, mode, and median of the data. **Check students' work.**

◀ Getting Ready for the EOG Test ▶

9. Teri used stickers to show how many hours she babysat each week. What is the mode of the data? **B**

   A 4   **C** 16

   B 10   **D** 20

HOURS TERI BABYSAT	
Week 1	
Week 2	
Week 3	
Week 4	
Key: Each ⏰ = 2 hours.	

Chapter 15   **315**

North Carolina Standards 4.01 Collect, organize, analyze, and display data (including circle graphs and tables) to solve problems.

COMMON ERROR ALERT

When finding the mean, students may not divide the sum by the correct number of addends.

$$6 + 8 + 3 + 7 = 24$$
$$24 \div 6 = 4$$

Suggest that students either circle each addend or draw an X through each as they count it.

Independent Practice

Note that Exercise 8 is a **multistep or strategy problem.** Assign Exercises 1–8.

4 ASSESS

Summarize the lesson by having students:

DISCUSS What are two ways to find the mean? Using models for the data, you can combine the smaller unequal groups into one group, and then divide the group evenly. You can divide the sum of a set of numbers by the number of addends.

WRITE Describe how to find the mean and median of 6, 8, 7, 4, and 10.
Mean: Find $6 + 8 + 7 + 4 + 10 = 35$. Find $35 \div 5 = 7$. The mean is 7. Median: order the numbers. $4 < 6 < 7 < 8 < 10$. The number in the middle, or the median, is 7.

LESSON QUIZ

Find the mean and the median.

Transparency **15.6**

1. 9, 4, 7, 2, 3 median, 4; mean, 5

2. 6, 7, 5 median, 6; mean, 6

3. 4, 5, 5, 9, 9, 3, 7 median, 5; mean, 6

Challenge 15.6

Mean and Median Pathway

Find the mean and median for each of the following sets of numbers. Then, find and color the sets of numbers whose mean and median are equal. Find a path from Start to Finish.

START

7, 4, 1
4; 4

8, 1, 3, 9, 4
5; 4

9, 1, 5, 6, 9
6; 6

4, 1, 4
3; 4

8, 5, 5, 2
9, 5, 8
6; 5

3, 8, 4, 1,
8, 7, 4
5; 4

2, 4, 8, 3, 5,
6, 7
5; 5

9, 2, 1
4; 2

3, 9, 6
6; 6

2, 2, 6, 7, 3
4; 3

8, 6, 3, 9, 9
7; 8

1, 1, 9, 8,
2, 7, 7
5; 7

6, 4, 7, 1
6, 3, 8
5; 6

4, 2, 8, 6, 5
5; 5

2, 1, 7, 5, 5
4; 5

6, 6, 1, 9
9, 8, 3
6; 6

FINISH

CW82 Challenge

Problem Solving 15.6

Mean and Median

Understand → Plan → Solve → Check

For 1–5, use the table.

1. What is the mode for this data?
   6 books

Books Read During the Summer	
Child	Number of Books
Beth	5
Tim	6
Toya	4
Marc	6
Shawn	9

2. What is the mean for this data?
   6 books

3. What is the median for this data?
   6 books

4. How many children read more than 5 books?
   3 children

Choose the letter of the correct answer.

5. What is the range for the data in the table above?
   A 4 books **C** 6 books
   Ⓑ 5 books **D** 9 books

6. To find the mean of 9, 7, 3, and 5, by what number would you divide?
   F 9 Ⓗ 4
   G 5 **J** 1

7. What is the best description of the median of a set of data?
   A the number that occurs most often
   B the difference between the greatest and least numbers
   Ⓒ the middle number in an ordered set
   D the number that occurs least often

8. Every afternoon Beth reads from 3:20 P.M. to 4:30 P.M. How long does Beth read?
   F 50 minutes
   Ⓖ 1 hour 10 minutes
   H 1 hour 30 minutes
   J 1 hour 50 minutes

9. **Write About It** Explain how you solved Problem 2.
   Possible answer: I added the number of books each child read and divided the sum by the number of children.

PS 82 Problem Solving

315

CHAPTER 15 Extra Practice

Purpose To provide extra practice for the skills presented in this chapter

The blue page references in each set of exercises refer to the lesson pages where each skill is taught.

Internet Resources

Visit **The Learning Site** at **www.harcourtschool.com** for a listing of practice activities.

Extra Practice

Set A (pp. 304–305)

For 1–3, use the tally table.

FAVORITE HOBBY	
Hobby	**Tally**
Collecting stamps	IIII
Collecting sports cards	JHT JHT
Collecting coins	II
Reading	JHT III

1. How many people answered the survey? **24 people**

2. What is the most popular hobby? **collecting sports cards**

3. How many fewer people chose collecting coins than chose reading? **6 fewer people**

For 4–6, use the frequency table.

4. How many people answered the survey? **27 people**

5. Did more people choose peas or carrots? **Neither; the same number of people chose peas and carrots.**

6. How many more people chose corn than chose beans? **9 more people**

FAVORITE VEGETABLE	
Type	**Number**
Carrots	6
Peas	6
Beans	3
Corn	12

Set B (pp. 306–307)

For 1–3, use the table.

FAVORITE BREAKFAST FOOD				
	Bacon and Eggs	**French Toast**	**Cereal**	**Muffins**
Boys	9	6	4	1
Girls	4	8	5	3

1. How many girls were surveyed? **20 girls**

2. How many boys liked French toast the best? **6 boys**

3. How many students chose bacon and eggs? **13 students**

Set C (pp. 310–313)

For 1–2, use the line plot.

1. What are the range and the mode of the data? Explain. **range is 5; 6 − 1 = 5; mode is 4; the number with the most x's is 4.**

2. How many students were surveyed? **1 + 3 + 4 + 3 + 1 = 12 students**

Number of Chores Students Did Last Week

316

Review/Test

✓ CHECK VOCABULARY

Choose the best term from the box.

| data |
| survey |
| tally table |
| frequency table |
| median |
| mode |

1. A method of gathering information is a __?__ . (p. 304)
   survey
2. Information collected about people or things is called __?__ . (p. 302) **data**
3. A table that uses numbers to record data is a __?__ .
   (p. 302) **frequency table**
4. The number or item found most often in a set of data is the __?__ . (p. 310) **mode**

✓ CHECK SKILLS

For 5–6, use the tally table. (pp. 304–305)

5. List the instruments in order from the most votes to the fewest votes.
   drums, guitar, piano, flute
6. How many people answered the survey? **55 people**

FAVORITE MUSICAL INSTRUMENT

Musical Instrument	Tally
Guitar	﷼﷼﷼
Flute	﷼||||
Drums	﷼﷼﷼|||
Piano	﷼﷼|||

For 7–8, use the frequency table.
(pp. 306–307)

7. How many students have brown eyes?
   15 students
8. How many girls were surveyed?
   13 girls

EYE COLOR OF STUDENTS

	Blue	Brown	Green
Girls	4	8	1
Boys	5	7	2

✓ CHECK PROBLEM SOLVING

Solve. (pp. 308–309)

9. There are 12 fourth graders and 13 fifth graders in the Science Club. Five of the fourth graders and 9 of the fifth graders are girls. Make a table to group the students in the Science Club.
   Check students' tables.

10. Sancho rolled two number cubes 10 times and recorded the sums. His results were 7, 6, 11, 2, 8, 9, 6, 8, 11, and 8. Make a table and find the sum rolled most often.
    Check students' tables; 8 was rolled most often.

Review/Test

Purpose To check understanding of concepts, skills, and problem solving presented in Chapter 15

Using the Page

The Chapter 15 Review/Test can be used as a **review** or a **test**.

- Items 1–4 check understanding of concepts and new vocabulary.
- Items 5–8 check skill proficiency.
- Items 9–10 check students' abilities to choose and apply problem solving strategies to real-life problems.

 Portfolio

Suggest that students place the completed Chapter 15 Review/Test in their portfolios.

Using the Assessment Guide

- Multiple-choice format of Chapter 15 Posttest—See *Assessment Guide*, pp. AG97–98.
- Free-response format of Chapter 15 Posttest—See *Assessment Guide*, pp. AG99–100.

Using Student Self-Assessment

The How Did I Do? survey helps students assess what they have learned and how they learned it. This survey is available as a copying master in *Assessment Guide*, p. AGxvii.

Chapter 15 Test, page 1

Choose the correct answer.

For 1–3, use the tally table.

FAVORITE FOOD

Name	Tally
Hamburger	||||
Taco	﷼
Chicken	|||
Grilled Cheese	﷼	

1. How many students answered this survey?
   Ⓐ 18   C 20
   B 19   D 21

2. How many more students chose taco than chose chicken?
   F 1   H 3
   Ⓖ 2   J 5

3. How many students in all chose hamburger and grilled cheese?
   Ⓐ 10   C 8
   B 9   D 7

For 4–7, use the frequency table.

FAVORITE CAR COLOR

Color	Number
White	30
Blue	18
Black	23
Red	17

4. How many people were surveyed?
   F 78   H 98
   Ⓖ 88   J 100

5. How many more people chose white than red?
   A 23   C 12
   Ⓑ 13   D 7

6. Which group of colors is in order from **greatest** to **least** votes?
   F white, black, red, blue
   G white, red, blue, black
   H white, blue, red, black
   Ⓙ white, black, blue, red

7. How many fewer people chose blue than chose black?
   A 12   Ⓒ 5
   B 6   D 2

For 8–10, use the following information.

Jordan is doing an experiment with a cube numbered 1 through 6. He will roll the cube 30 times and record the number in a tally table.

8. How many tallies should there be on Jordan's table?
   F 6   Ⓗ 30
   G 24   J 36

9. What will Jordan be able to find out from his table?
   Ⓐ the number rolled most often
   B the difference between the numbers
   C the color rolled most often
   D the sum of the numbers from 1 through 6

Go On ▶

Chapter 15 Test, page 2

10. Which number should Jordan NOT list on his tally table?
    F 2   Ⓗ 6
    G 5   Ⓙ 7

For 11–12, use the two spinners.

Sally is doing an experiment. She will use the two spinners 25 times and record the sum of the two numbers.

11. How many tallies should there be on Sally's table?
    A 5   B 10   C 20   Ⓓ 25

12. What sums should Sally list on her tally table?
    F 1, 2, 3, 4   Ⓗ 3, 4, 5, 6
    G 2, 3, 4, 6   J 2, 4, 6, 9

For 13–16, use the line plot.

```
              X
          X   X
      X   X   X
      X   X   X   X   X   X
      +---+---+---+---+---+---+
      2   3   4   5   6   7   8
      Number of Family Members
```

13. What is the mode for this set of data?
    Ⓐ 7   C 3
    B 4   D 2

14. What is the range for this set of data?
    F 4   Ⓗ 6
    G 5   J 7

15. How many families have 3 or fewer members?
    A 3   C 10
    Ⓑ 7   D 14

16. What is the **greatest** number of family members in this set of data?
    F 5   H 7
    G 6   Ⓙ 8

For 17–18, find the median.

17. 8, 12, 5, 9, 11
    A 8   C 11
    Ⓑ 9   D 12

18. 5, 9, 2, 1, 7, 6, 8
    F 2   H 5
    G 4   Ⓙ 6

For 19–20, find the mean.

19. 8, 1, 9
    A 1   Ⓒ 6
    B 3   D 18

20. 1, 9, 3, 7, 5
    Ⓕ 1   H 9
    G 5   J 25

Stop ■

CHAPTER 15

Getting Ready for the EOG Test

Chapters 1–15

Using the Pages

These pages may be used to help students get ready for the North Carolina EOG Test. The test items are written in the same style and arranged in the same format as those on the EOG Test.

The pages are cumulative. They cover the standards from the North Carolina Mathematics Standard Course of Study that have been taught up to this point in the text or in a previous grade. Each Getting Ready for the EOG Test also reviews the North Carolina mathematics strands shown below.

- Number and Operations
- Measurement
- Geometry
- Data Analysis and Probability
- Algebra

These pages can be assigned at the end of the chapter as classwork or as a homework assignment. You may want to have students use individual recording sheets presented in a multiple-choice (standardized) format. A Test Answer Sheet is available as a blackline master in the *Assessment Guide* (p. AGlii).

You may wish to have students describe how they solved each problem and share their solutions.

Getting Ready for the ⭐EOG Test

⭐ NUMBER AND OPERATIONS

1. Crystal has 6 packages of stickers. Each package has 8 stickers. How many stickers does she have? **C**

A 42		**C** 48	
B 46		**D** 54	

2. The table shows three players' scores in a computer game.

COMPUTER GAME SCORES	
Player	**Score**
Mark	4,591
Shelby	4,287
Trisha	4,538

How would you list the scores from *least* to *greatest*? **B**

A 4,591; 4,538; 4,287
B 4,287; 4,538; 4,591
C 4,538; 4,591; 4,287
D 4,287; 4,591; 4,538

3. Explain It This jar has 50 jellybeans in it. Which jar below has about 200 jellybeans in it? Explain your thinking. **See page 319.**

A   **B**

⭐ MEASUREMENT AND GEOMETRY

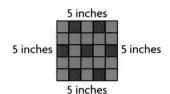

TIP **Understand the problem.** See item 4. The length around Venus' design is measured in inches. Each side of a square on the design shows 1 inch.

4. Venus made a tile design that is 5 inches long and 5 inches wide. What is the length around her design? **C**

```
        5 inches
5 inches [grid] 5 inches
        5 inches
```

A 10 inches
B 15 inches
C 20 inches
D 25 inches

5. Explain It Arthur made this schedule for his class field day. *About* how many hours will Arthur's class spend playing softball? Explain how you estimated the elapsed time.

FIELD DAY SCHEDULE	
Activity	**Time**
Relay Races	9:00 A.M. to 10:15 A.M.
Scavenger Hunt	10:30 A.M. to 11:45 A.M.
Lunch	Noon to 12:45 P.M.
Softball Game	12:50 P.M. to 4:00 P.M.
Team Awards	4:10 P.M. to 4:45 P.M.

See page 319.

⭐ ALGEBRA

6. Davis grouped these numbers together.

11, 13, 15, 17

What rule did Davis use to form this group? **D**

A even numbers less than 20

B odd numbers less than 20

C numbers greater than 10 but less than 16

D odd numbers greater than 10 but less than 18

7. Tanya has to read a book. On Monday she read 22 pages. On Tuesday, she read 26 pages. On Wednesday, she read 30 pages. If this pattern continues, how many pages will Tanya read on Friday? **C**

A 32

B 34

C 38

D 40

8. Explain It A package of 4 books costs $32. Write a number sentence to show the cost of 1 book. Explain how you decided what number sentence to write. **See below.**

⭐ DATA ANALYSIS AND PROBABILITY

9. Carla surveyed her classmates to find their favorite breakfast foods. The tally table below shows the results of Carla's survey.

FAVORITE BREAKFAST FOODS	
Type of Food	**Tally**
Cereal	ЖЖ ЖЖ III
Eggs	ЖЖ II
Oatmeal	III
Pancakes	ЖЖ ЖЖ I

Which types of food each received at least 10 votes? **C**

A pancakes and eggs

B eggs and oatmeal

C cereal and pancakes

D cereal and eggs

10. Which color is the pointer of the spinner *more likely* to land on? **B**

A red   **C** blue

B green   **D** yellow

11. Explain It Look at the line plot. Tell how to find the number of students who read 5 or more books. **See below.**

```
                    X
                    X
                    X
              X  X  X
              X  X  X
              X  X  X
           X  X  X  X
        X  X  X  X  X  X
        +--+--+--+--+--+
        2  3  4  5  6  7
```

Books Students Read

Chapters 1–15

Item Analysis

You may wish to use the item analysis to determine which North Carolina standards need additional review.

Item	North Carolina Standard	Lesson
1	1.03	10.1
2	1.01	3.3
3	1.06	3.1
4	(2) 2.01	Grade 2
5	(2) 2.02	Grade 2
6	(2) 5.01	Grade 2
7	5.02	9.3
8	5.03	13.2
9	4.01	15.2
10	(2) 4.02	Grade 2
11	4.01	15.5

SCORING RUBRIC
Explain It

2 Demonstrates a complete understanding of the problem and chooses an appropriate strategy to determine the solution

1 Demonstrates a partial understanding of the problem and chooses a strategy that does not lead to a complete and accurate solution

0 Demonstrates little understanding of the problem and shows little evidence of using any strategy to determine a solution

Explain It • Written Response

3. Jar A; Possible answer: Jar B has about twice as many jellybeans as the jar shown with 50 jellybeans. So, Jar B has about 100 jellybeans. Jar A has about twice as many jellybeans as Jar B. So Jar A has about 200 jellybeans.

5. about 3 hours; Possible answer: 12:50 P.M. is close to 1:00 P.M. The elapsed time from 1:00 P.M. to 4:00 P.M. is 3 hours.

8. Possible answer: 32 ÷ 4 = 8; each book cost $8. Since I know the cost of 4 books, I need to divide that cost by the number of books to find the cost of 1 book.

11. Possible answer: To find the number of students who read 5 or more books, add the number of X's above the numbers 5, 6, and 7. 8 + 5 + 1 = 14.

CHAPTER 16

Analyze and Graph Data

NCTM Standards 2000

1. Number and Operations
Lessons 16.1, 16.2, 16.3, 16.5
2. Algebra
Lessons 16.2, 16.4
3. Geometry
4. Measurement
5. Data Analysis and Probability
Lessons 16.1, 16.2, 16.3, 16.4, 16.5

6. Problem Solving
Lessons 16.1, 16.2, 16.3, 16.4, 16.5
7. Reasoning and Proof
Lessons 16.1, 16.2, 16.4
8. Communication
Lessons 16.1, 16.2, 16.3, 16.4, 16.5
9. Connections
Lessons 16.2, 16.4, 16.5
10. Representation
Lessons 16.1, 16.2, 16.3, 16.4, 16.5

Chapter Planner

Getting Ready for Chapter 16 • Assessing Prior Knowledge and INTERVENTION (See PE and TE page 321.)

LESSON	NORTH CAROLINA STANDARDS	PACING	VOCABULARY*	MATERIALS	RESOURCES AND TECHNOLOGY
16.1 **Problem Solving Strategy: Make a Graph** pp. 322–323 **Objective** To use the problem solving strategy *make a graph* to solve problems	4.01	1 Day	graph pictograph		Reteach, Practice, Reading Strategy, Challenge 16.1 Worksheets ▢ Transparency 16.1 ▢ Reading Transparency 16 ⊙ **Intervention • Problem Solving,** *Strategy/Skill 16* (CD or Book)
16.2 **Bar Graphs** pp. 324–325 **Objective** To read and interpret data in bar graphs	4.01	1 Day (For Lessons 16.2 and 16.3)	**bar graph** **scale** **horizontal bar graph** **vertical bar graph**		Reteach, Practice, Problem Solving, Challenge 16.2 Worksheets ▢ Transparency 16.2 ⊙ **Intervention,** *Skill 61* (CD or Book) ⊙ **Harcourt Mega Math The Number Games,** *ArachnaGraph*
16.3 **Hands On: Make Bar Graphs** pp. 326–327 **Objective** To make bar graphs	4.01			*For each student* bar graph pattern, crayons	Reteach, Practice, Problem Solving, Challenge 16.3 Worksheets ▢ Transparency 16.3 ⊙ **Intervention,** *Skills 65, 66* (CD or Book) ⊙ **Harcourt Mega Math The Number Games,** *ArachnaGraph*
16.4 **Algebra: Ordered Pairs** pp. 328–329 **Objective** To locate points on a coordinate grid by using ordered pairs	3.02a *also* 3.02b	1 Day	**grid** **ordered pair**		Reteach, Practice, Problem Solving, Challenge 16.4 Worksheets ▢ Transparency 16.4 ⊙ **Intervention,** *Skill 61* (CD or Book) ⊙ **Harcourt Mega Math The Number Games,** *ArachnaGraph*
16.5 **Line Graphs** pp. 330–331 **Objective** To read and interpret data in line graphs	4.01	1 Day	**line graph** **trends**		Reteach, Practice, Problem Solving, Challenge 16.5 Worksheets ▢ Transparency 16.5 ▢ Scaffolded Instruction Transparency 16 ⊙ **Intervention,** *Skills 61, 65, 66* (CD or Book) ⊙ **Harcourt Mega Math The Number Games,** *ArachnaGraph*

Ending Chapter 16 • **Extra Practice,** p. 332 • **Chapter 16 Review/Test,** p. 333 • **Getting Ready for the EOG Test,** pp. 334–335

*Boldfaced terms are the key mathematical terms for the chapter. Other terms are review vocabulary.

Vocabulary Power

Review Vocabulary

To be ready for Chapter 16, students should know the following vocabulary term:

- **graph** (p. 321)—a diagram in the form of bars, lines, or symbols that represents a collection of data

Develop Key Chapter Vocabulary

The **boldfaced** words are the key vocabulary terms in the chapter.

- **bar graph** (p. 324)—a graph that uses bars to show data

- **scale** (p. 324)—the numbers on a bar graph that help you read the number each bar shows

- **horizontal bar graph** (p. 324)—a bar graph in which the bars go across from left to right

- **vertical bar graph** (p. 324)—a bar graph in which the bars go from the bottom to the top

- **grid** (p. 328)—evenly spaced horizontal and vertical lines on a map

- **ordered pair** (p. 328)—a pair of numbers that names a point on a grid. The first number tells the horizontal position and the second number tells the vertical position.

- **line graph** (p. 330)—a graph that uses a line to show how data change over time

- **trends** (p. 330)—on a graph, areas where the data increase, decrease, or stay the same over time

Vocabulary Cards

Have students use the Vocabulary Cards on *Teacher's Resource Book* pages TR157–160 for the key terms in the chapter. The cards can be added to a file of mathematics terms.

Multimedia Math Glossary

 For vocabulary support, visit
www.harcourtschool.com/mathglossary

Math Journal

Have students define the key vocabulary terms: *bar graph, scale, horizontal bar graph, vertical bar graph, grid, ordered pair, line graph,* and *trends.* Have students use their own words and give an example of each.

MATH Word Work

Objective To reinforce vocabulary concepts
Use after Lesson 16.4.

Materials *For each pair* coordinate grids, p. TR62; paper, pencil

Have students design coordinate grid puzzles for a partner to solve. Have one student draw a picture on the coordinate grid. Then have that student write directions, using ordered pairs. The partner then uses these directions to draw the picture. Have students share with the class the pictures they drew. If time permits, have students reverse roles.

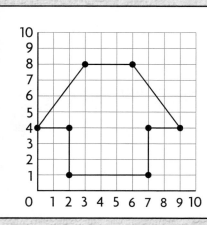

Start at (2,1).
Draw a line to (2,4),
then to (0,4),
then to (3,8),
then to (6,8),
then to (9,4),
then to (7,4),
then to (7,1),
and back to (2,1).

Analyze and Graph Data

Mathematics Across the Grades

LOOKING BACK • Prerequisite Skills

To be ready for Chapter 16, students should have the following understandings and skills:

- **Use a Tally Table**—interpret information in a tally table
- **Skip-Count**—skip-count by 2, 3, 4, and 5
- **Use Symbols**—use symbols to find missing numbers

Check What You Know

Use page 321 to determine students' knowledge of prerequisite concepts and skills.

Intervention

Help students prepare for the chapter by using the intervention resources described on TE page 321.

LOOKING AT CHAPTER 16 • Essential Skills

Students will

- use the problem solving strategy *make a graph*.
- read and interpret data in bar and line graphs.
- make bar graphs.
- locate points on a coordinate grid by using ordered pairs.

Example

Kevin made this bar graph of his classmates' favorite winter sports.

How many students in all voted?	How many more students voted for skiing than for snowboarding?
4 + 10 + 5 + 7 = 26 26 students	10 − 7 = 3 3 more students

LOOKING AHEAD • Applications

Students will apply what they learn in Chapter 16 to the following new concepts:

- Probability (Chapter 24)
- Make Line and Circle Graphs (Grade 4)
- Analyze and Graph Data in Double-Bar Graphs (Grade 4)
- Analyze and Graph Data in Circle Graphs (Grade 4)

Differentiated Instruction

Meeting the Needs of All Learners

Extra Support	Activities for All	Enrichment
Alternative Teaching Strategy TE Lessons 16.1, 16.2, 16.3, 16.4, 16.5 **ESOL/ESL** TE Lessons 16.1, 16.2, 16.3, 16.4, 16.5 **Special Needs** TE Lesson 16.1	**Cross-Curricular Connections** **Fine Arts:** TE Lesson 16.4 **Reading:** TE Lesson 16.1 **Science:** Chapter Opener **Vocabulary:** TE p. 320B, PE/TE p. 321, TE Lessons 16.2, 16.5 **Writing:** TE Lesson 16.3	**Advanced Learners** TE Lessons 16.2 16.5 **Early Finishers** TE Lessons 16.1, 16.3

Combination and Multi-age Classrooms

Grade 2	Grade 3	Grade 4
Skills Trace Across the Grades		
Make and interpret data in concrete graphs and pictographs; find the range, median, and mode; locate points on a grid and interpret data in a line graph.	**Read, interpret, and draw bar graphs; read and interpret data in a line plot and locate points on a grid; read and interpret line graphs.**	Interpret, analyze, and display data in bar graphs and line graphs; make line graphs and circle graphs; choose an appropriate graph; locate and draw points on a coordinate grid.
Instructional Strategies		
Students on this level may require more time to build conceptual understanding. **Assignments** **Grade 3 Pupil Edition** • Have students work in pairs on Lessons 16.1, 16.3, and 16.4. • Have students skip Lesson 16.1. **Grade 2 Pupil Edition**—pages 49–62, 275–288	Students on this level should be able to complete all the lessons in the Pupil Edition and all the activities in the Teacher's Edition with minimal adjustments. **Assignment** **Grade 3 Pupil Edition**—pages 320–333	Students on this level will probably require less time to build conceptual understanding. **Assignments** **Grade 3 Pupil Edition** • Compact Lessons 16.2 and 16.3. **Grade 4 Pupil Edition**—pages 134–151

Analyze and Graph Data

Introducing the Chapter

Explain to students that a graph presents data in a way that is easy for others to understand. Have students look at the pictograph and determine which animal populations at the Smithsonian National Zoological Park are even numbers. giant panda, Asian elephant, leopard gecko, and green tree python

Using Data

To begin the study of this chapter, have students

- Determine how many gorillas are at the Smithsonian National Zoological Park. 9 gorillas

- Find out how many more leopard geckos than brown pelicans there are at the Smithsonian National Zoological Park. 3 more

Problem Solving Project

Purpose To record data by using a pictograph

Background Some of the animals at the Smithsonian National Zoological Park are endangered. The giant panda, Asian elephant, and gorilla are threatened with extinction. The Smithsonian National Zoological Park is helping to save these endangered species.

UNDERSTAND • PLAN • SOLVE • CHECK

Have students:

- Make a pictograph using the data below to show about how many of these endangered animals were alive in the wild in the year 2000.

Each Picture = 1,000 Animals.

Giant panda	1,000
Asian elephant	35,000
Gorilla	500

- Make each picture represent 1,000 animals.
- Include a key. Check students' work.

Graphing Investigations
Begin Week 16.

≡FAST FACT • SCIENCE
There are about 1,000 giant pandas in the world today. Giant pandas can be 5 feet tall and can weigh more than 300 pounds!

PROBLEM SOLVING Look at the pictograph and make a bar graph of the data.

Check students' bar graphs.

SMITHSONIAN NATIONAL ZOOLOGICAL PARK	
Giant panda	🐾
Asian elephant	🐾 🐾
Gorilla	🐾 🐾 🐾 🐾 🐾
Leopard gecko	🐾 🐾 🐾 🐾 🐾
Green tree python	🐾 🐾 🐾 🐾 🐾 🐾 🐾 🐾 🐾 🐾 🐾
Brown pelican	🐾 🐾 🐾 🐾

Key: Each 🐾 = 2 animals.

Giant panda eating bamboo

320

WHY LEARN MATH? A zoologist is a scientist who studies animals. Zoologists collect data on animals by observing their behavior. They use graphs to help them organize and analyze the data. For example, a zoologist may collect data on how much an animal eats each day. Ask: What other kinds of data might a zoologist collect? Possible answers: how much time an animal spends sleeping, how much an animal grows

Family Involvement Activities

These activities provide:

- Letter to the Family
- Math Vocabulary
- Family Game
- Practice (Homework)

Family Involvement Activities, p. FA61

HARCOURT MATH
GRADE 3
Chapter 16
WHAT WE ARE LEARNING
Analyze and Graph Data

VOCABULARY
Here are the vocabulary words we use in class:
Bar graph A graph that uses bars to show data
Scale The numbers that tell what each bar shows
Horizontal bar graph A bar graph in which the bars go from left to right
Vertical bar graph A bar graph in which the bars go up from bottom to top
Grid The horizontal and vertical lines on a map
Ordered pair Two numbers, such as (2,3), that name a point on a grid
Line graph A graph that uses a line to show how data changes over time
Trends Areas on a graph where the data increase, decrease, or stay the same over time

Name
Date
Dear Family,
Your child is learning to analyze and graph data. This is what we are learning:
To make a pictograph:
- Choose a title.
- Write labels.
- Choose a key. Decide the value of one picture.
- Decide how many pictures to use to represent the data.
To make a bar graph:
- Write a title.
- Write labels along one side and numbers (the scale) along the other side.
- Complete by drawing the bars. Make their lengths show the number for each bar. For a value midway between two numbers, end the bar there.
To locate points on a grid:
- Read the ordered pair to locate the point. An ordered pair (3,1) names a point on a grid. The first number tells how many spaces to move to the right. The second number tells how many spaces to move up.
- Start at 0 on the grid. Move to the right the first number of spaces. Move up the second number of spaces.
Your child is also learning to read line graphs. Use the activity that follows.
Sincerely,

Family Involvement Activities FA61

CHECK WHAT YOU KNOW

Use this page to help you review and remember important skills needed for Chapter 16.

✓ USE A TALLY TABLE

For 1–3, use the tally table.

HOW DO YOU GET TO SCHOOL?	
Car	⊪⊪ |||||
Walk	⊪⊪ ⊪⊪ ⊪⊪
Bus	⊪⊪ ⊪⊪ ||
Bike	⊪⊪ ⊪⊪	

1. How many children ride in a car to school?
   9 children
2. How many children ride their bikes?
   11 children
3. How many children answered the question?
   47 children

✓ SKIP-COUNT

Find the missing numbers in the pattern.

4. 2, 4, 6, 8, 10, ■, ■, ■
   12, 14, 16
5. 4, 8, 12, 16, 20, ■, ■, ■
   24, 28, 32
6. 45, 40, 35, 30, ■, ■, ■
   25, 20, 15
7. 3, 6, 9, 12, 15, ■, ■, ■
   18, 21, 24

✓ USE SYMBOLS

Use the value of the symbol to find the missing number.

8. If $\Delta = 2$, then
   $\Delta + \Delta + \Delta = ■$.
   6

9. If $\square = 3$, then
   $\square + \square + \square + \square = ■$.
   12

10. If ❀ = 4, then
    ❀ + ❀ + ❀ + ❀ + ❀ + ❀ = ■.
    24

11. If ♥ = 5, then
    ♥ + ♥ + ♥ + ♥ + ♥ + ♥ + ♥ = ■.
    35

VOCABULARY POWER ✓

REVIEW

graph [graf] *noun*

Graph comes from the Greek word *graphein*, which means "to write." In a pictograph, what are you writing or drawing to show the data?
Possible answer: the pictures or symbols

PREVIEW

bar graph	grid
scale	ordered pair
horizontal bar graph	line graph
vertical bar graph	trends

GO ON-LINE www.harcourtschool.com/mathglossary

Assessing Prior Knowledge

Use the **Check What You Know** page to determine whether your students have mastered the prerequisite skills critical for this chapter.

Intervention

- **Diagnose and Prescribe**
  Evaluate your students' performance on this page to determine whether intervention is necessary or if enrichment is appropriate. Options that provide instruction, practice, and a check are listed in the chart below.

✓ CHECK WHAT YOU KNOW RESOURCES

Intervention Copying Masters or CD-ROMs

Enrichment Copying Masters

VOCABULARY POWER

For activities and information about the vocabulary in this chapter, see page 320B.

Were students successful with ✓ **CHECK WHAT YOU KNOW?**

IF ... NO THEN ... INTERVENE — **INTERVENTION OPTIONS** — **IF ... YES** THEN ... ENRICH

Skill/Items	Missed more than	Intervene with
Use a Tally Table, 1–3	1	• *Intervention*, Skill 65
Skip-Count, 4–7	1	• *Intervention*, Skill 61
Use Symbols, 8–11	1	• *Intervention*, Skill 66

Skill/Items	Missed fewer than	Enrich with
Use a Tally Table, 1–3	2	• *Intervention*, Enrichment p. IN360
Skip-Count, 4–7	2	• *Intervention*, Enrichment p. IN359
Use Symbols, 8–11	2	• *Intervention*, Enrichment p. IN360

Lesson Planning

PROFESSIONAL DEVELOPMENT

Objective To use the problem solving strategy *make a graph* to solve problems

Lesson Resources Reading Transparency 16; Intervention • Problem Solving, Strategy/Skill 16

NCTM Standards
1. Number and Operations
5. Data Analysis and Probability
6. Problem Solving
7. Reasoning and Proof
8. Communication
10. Representation

Math Background
These ideas will help students use the problem solving strategy *make a graph*.

- Pictographs organize and display data by using a title, labels, a key, and picture symbols.

- In pictographs, pictures represent values. The pictures may represent one unit or multiple units.

- The picture symbol in a pictograph should be relevant to the subject of the graph.

Warm-Up Resources

Number of the Day

Transparency **16.1**

The number of the day is 40. Name all the numbers you can use to skip-count from 0 to end at 40.
2, 4, 5, 8, 10, 20

Daily Facts Practice

Have students practice multiplication facts by completing Set F of *Teacher's Resource Book*, p. TR94.

Solve a Problem

Transparency **16.1**

Problem of the Day

The third graders at Lincoln School are trying to collect 100 soup cans for a food drive. Each time they collect 4 cans of soup they make a tally mark. There are 6 tally marks for Mrs. Blake's class, 4 tally marks for Mr. Wu's class, and 5 tally marks for Ms. Carr's class. How many more soup cans do students need to collect? 40 cans

Solution Problem of the Day tab, p. PD16

Intervention and Extension Resources

Alternative Teaching Strategy

To help students **make the connection between a frequency table and a pictograph**, display this data.

Phones in Homes

Number of Phones	Number of Families
1	20
2	25
3	10
4 or more	5

Have students explain how to make a pictograph from this data. Have them determine what title, labels, key, and symbol they will use. Make the pictograph following students' directions.

VISUAL

INTERPERSONAL/SOCIAL

Reading Strategy

Use Graphic Aids Sometimes the information needed to solve a problem may be provided in a graphic aid. Show students this data: In third grade, 20 students have one pet; 12 have two pets; 10 have three pets; and 8 have more than three pets.

Have students make a pictograph using the data. Have them use the graph to find the most common and least common number of pets in the third grade. 1 pet; more than 3 pets

16 **Reading Transparency 16**

Multistep and Strategy Problems

The following multistep or strategy problems are provided in Lesson 16.1:

Page	Item
323	1–10

Special Needs

Have students work in pairs to **practice determining what key they would use for a pictograph** for each set of data: 5, 20, 25; 6, 12, 15; 14, 18, 8; 16, 24, 32, 34. Once students decide on a key, have them represent each number pictorially and then check that representation by multiplying. Check students' work.

VISUAL

VISUAL/SPATIAL

Early Finishers

Have pairs of students **make a pictograph** that reflects classroom or school data. For example, they might show how many hours last week students spent on each subject, such as reading, math, physical education, social studies, and science; or how many students selected certain stories as their favorites. Invite students to display their completed pictographs in the classroom. Check students' work.

VISUAL

BODILY/KINESTHETIC

Technology Link

Intervention • Problem Solving, *Strategy/Skill 16*

GO The Harcourt Learning Site
www.harcourtschool.com

Lesson 16.1 Organizer

Objective To use the problem solving strategy *make a graph* to solve problems

Lesson Resources Reading Transparency 16; Intervention • Problem Solving, Strategy/Skill 16

---

1 INTRODUCE

QUICK REVIEW provides practice of prerequisite skills.

WHY LEARN THIS? You'll be able to understand pictographs you see in books, magazines, and newspapers. *Share the lesson objective with students.*

---

2 TEACH

Guided Instruction

MODIFYING INSTRUCTION You may want to simplify the problem by using less data.

- *Review the definition of a pictograph—a graph that shows data by using pictures.*
  What does every pictograph need so that users can understand what the pictures mean? a key telling what each picture stands for

- *Review the meaning of half symbols taught in Lesson 10.3.*
  If Rafael had sold 17 boxes of cards, how many pictures would be shown? $8\frac{1}{2}$ pictures

- *Call students' attention to the key.*
  REASONING Why was a key of 2 chosen, rather than 4 or 5? Possible answer: All the numbers that show boxes sold are even, except 7, which doesn't divide evenly by 4 or 5.
  With a key of 2, how do you show 1 box? Use one-half of a picture.

Problem Solving Strategy
Make a Graph

PROBLEM The soccer team sold boxes of greeting cards to raise money. Rafael sold 14 boxes, Joselyn sold 7, Phil sold 24, Ken sold 12, and Felicia sold 10. What is one way the sales could be shown in a graph?

Quick Review
1. $4 + 4 + 4 = $ ■ 12
2. $3 + 3 + 3 + 3 = $ ■ 12
3. $2 + 2 + 2 + 2 = $ ■ 8
4. $5 + 5 + 5 = $ ■ 15
5. $2 + 2 + 2 = $ ■ 6

UNDERSTAND

- What are you asked to do?
  find one way to show the data in a graph

PLAN

- What strategy can you use to solve the problem?
  You can make a pictograph.

SOLVE

- How can you show the data in a pictograph?

  a. Choose a **title** that tells about the graph.

  b. Write a **label** for each row.

  c. Look at the numbers. Choose a **key** to tell how many each picture stands for.

  d. Decide how many **pictures** should be placed next to each person's name.

BOXES OF GREETING CARDS SOLD

Rafael	✉✉✉✉✉✉✉
Joselyn	✉✉✉⸰
Phil	✉✉✉✉✉✉✉✉✉✉✉
Ken	✉✉✉✉✉✉
Felicia	✉✉✉✉✉

Key: Each ✉ = 2 boxes.

CHECK

- How can you know if the total number of pictures in your graph is correct? Possible answer: Multiply the number of whole symbols by 2, and then add the value of a half symbol.
- Why was a key of 2 used? Possible answer: 10, 12, 14, and 24 are multiples of 2.

322

Reteach 16.1

Problem Solving Strategy

Make a Graph

A pictograph uses pictures to show information. Use the data from this frequency table to make a pictograph.

FAVORITE PETS	
Kind of Pet	Number of Students
Dog	16
Cat	10

- Title the pictograph *Favorite Pets.*
- Label column 1 *Kind of Pet.*
- Label column 2 *Number of Students.*
- List the kinds of pets in the first column.
- Make a key that shows that each picture equals 2 students.
- Draw pictures to show the number of students for each row.

FAVORITE PETS	
Kind of Pet	Number of Students
Dog	●●●●●●●●
Cat	●●●●●

Key: Each ● = __2__ students.

Find *Dog* on the frequency table. Locate the number next to the name. The key says each symbol equals 2 students. Since 16 ÷ 2 = 8, draw 8 pictures.
To complete the pictograph, follow the same steps for *Cat*.

Make a pictograph that shows the data from the frequency table below. The key should show that each picture stands for 5 students. **Check students' pictographs.**

FAVORITE DR. SEUSS® STORY	
Story	Number of Votes
Green Eggs and Ham	25
Hop on Pop	15
The Foot Book	20

FAVORITE DR. SEUSS® STORY	
Story	Number of Votes
Green Eggs and Ham	▢▢▢▢▢
Hop on Pop	▢▢▢
The Foot Book	▢▢▢▢

Key: Each ▢ = 5 students.

Reteach RW83

Practice 16.1

Problem Solving Strategy

Make a Graph

Choose one of the ideas shown at the right for making a pictograph.

Take a survey to collect the data. Then make a pictograph in the space below. Decide on a symbol and key for the graph. Include a title and labels. **Check students' surveys and graphs.**

Pictograph—Menu of Ideas
- Favorite Team Sport
- Favorite Pizza Topping
- Favorite TV Show

Key: Each _____ = _____.

1. Tell how you chose a symbol, or picture, for your pictograph.
   Answers will vary.

2. Explain how you chose a key for your pictograph.
   Answers will vary.

Mixed Review

Write the value of the underlined digit.

3. 2,235 __2,000__   4. 21,507 __500__   5. 16,110 __10,000__

Practice PW83

1. What if Derek sold 30 boxes of cards, Andy sold 25 boxes, and Kay sold 15 boxes? Make a pictograph to show the information. **Check students' graphs.**
2. Barry sold 11 boxes of cards. Using a key of 2, explain how you would show his sales in a pictograph. **Use 5 symbols to show 10 boxes and one-half of a symbol to show the 11th box.**

Torrie and Jeremy made pictographs using the data in the table.

3. Torrie used a key of 3. How many symbols should she draw to show the votes for soccer? **D**

   A 2   **C** 5
   B 3   **D** 6

4. What key did Jeremy use if he drew $7\frac{1}{2}$ symbols to show the votes for football? **G**

   F key of 1   **H** key of 3
   G key of 2   **J** key of 4

FAVORITE SPORTS	
Sport	Number of Votes
Soccer	18
Softball	12
Basketball	21
Football	15

Strategies

Draw a Diagram or Picture
Make a Model or Act It Out
Make an Organized List
Find a Pattern
▶ Make a Table or Graph
Predict and Test
Work Backward
Solve a Simpler Problem
Write a Number Sentence
Use Logical Reasoning

Problem Solving

Mixed Strategy Practice

5. It was 12:05 P.M. when Liza and Nick began eating lunch. Nick finished in 15 minutes. Liza finished 8 minutes later than Nick. At what time did Liza finish lunch? **12:28 P.M.**

6. ≣**FAST FACT** • SCIENCE Panda cubs are born weighing about one-fourth of a pound. There are 16 ounces in one pound. About how many ounces does a newborn panda weigh? Think: $16 \div 4 = ?$ **about 4 ounces**

7. Lloyd spent $3.59, $4.50, and $9.75 for games. He gave the clerk $20.00. How much change should he receive? **$2.16**

8. **REASONING** If December 1 is on a Wednesday, on which day of the week is December 15? **Wednesday**

9. Sydney's team scored 89 points, 96 points, 98 points, and 107 points. How many points did the team score in all? **390 points**

10. **What's the Question?** Marty bought 2 packs of trading cards. He gave the clerk $10. His change was $4. The answer is $3. How much did each pack of cards cost?

✳ **North Carolina Standards 4.01** Collect, organize, analyze, and display data (including circle graphs and tables) to solve problems.

---

3 PRACTICE

Guided Practice

Do Problem Solving Practice Exercises 1–4 with your students. Identify students who are having difficulty and choose appropriate lesson resources to provide assistance. Note that Exercises 1–4 are **multistep or strategy problems.**

For Exercise 3, ask how Torrie decided on a key of 3. Lead students to understand that they can skip-count by 3 each time to find the number of votes.

Independent Practice

Note that Exercises 5–10 are **multistep or strategy problems.** Assign Exercises 5–10.

4 ASSESS

Summarize the lesson by having students:

DISCUSS What are the parts of a pictograph? title, labels that identify the information, key, and pictures

WRITE How are a tally table, frequency table, and pictograph alike? How are they different? Possible answer: They all have a title and labels that identify the information; a tally table uses tally marks; a frequency table uses numbers; and a pictograph uses pictures and a key.

LESSON QUIZ   Transparency **16.1**

Jorge and Sue made pictographs using this data.

FAVORITE BREAKFAST	
Item	Number of Students
Eggs	5
Toaster pop-ups	15
Cereal	20

1. Jorge used a key of 5. How many symbols should he draw to show the votes for cereal? 4 symbols

2. What key did Sue use if she drew $2\frac{1}{2}$ symbols to show the votes for eggs? key of 2

Challenge 16.1

Parts of a Picture

The pictograph shows the number of students in seven third-grade classes.

Third-Grade Classes	
Mr. Jones	○○○○○○○
Mrs. Smith	○○○○○○◖
Mr. Flores	○○○○○○○
Mr. Brown	○○○○○○○○○◖◗
Ms. Tanaka	○○○○○○
Mrs. Hanson	○○○○○○○○◗
Mrs. Wright	○○○○○○○◖

Key: Each ○ = 4 students.

1. Each ○ equals how many students?

   4 students

2. Each ◖ equals how many students? Explain.

   2 students; it is only half of a symbol. Half of 4 is 2.

3. Each ◗ equals how many students? Explain.

   1 student; it is only one fourth of a symbol.

   One fourth of 4 is 1.

4. List the number of students each teacher has in order from most students to fewest students.

   Mr. Brown, 38; Mrs. Hanson, 33; Mr. Jones, 32; Mrs. Wright, 30;

   Mr. Flores, 28; Mrs. Smith, 26; Ms. Tanaka, 24

   Challenge **CW83**

Reading Strategy 16.1

Summarize   Understand ▶ Plan ▶ Solve ▶ Check

To **summarize** is to say something in a shorter way. Sometimes using a graph to display information is a good way to summarize.   **VOCABULARY** summarize

Read the following problem.

Grades 1–3 collected money for new computer software. Grade 1 collected three $5 bills and twenty-five $1 bills. Grade 2 collected two $10 bills, six $5 bills, and ten $1 bills. Grade 3 collected four $10 bills and thirty $1 bills. Which grade collected the most money?

1. Complete the pictograph to summarize the data in the problem.

Collection for Computer Software	
Grade 1	○○○○
Grade 2	○○○○○○
Grade 3	○○○○○○○
Key: Each ○ = $10.	

2. Solve the problem.

   Grade 3; there are more pictures for Grade 3 than for

   Grade 1 or Grade 2.

3. Describe the strategy you used.

   Possible answer: I found the total amount that each grade

   collected. Then, I summarized the information in a pictograph.

Make a pictograph to summarize. Solve.

4. Kim sold 8 red boxes and 4 blue boxes of paper. Dan sold 7 red boxes and 7 blue boxes of paper. Deanna sold 11 red boxes and 5 blue boxes of paper. Who sold the most boxes of paper?

   Deanna

Number of Boxes Sold	
Kim	□□□□□□
Dan	□□□□□□□
Deanna	□□□□□□□□
Key: Each □ = 2 Boxes.	

Reading Strategy **PS83**

Lesson Planning

PROFESSIONAL DEVELOPMENT

Objective To read and interpret data in bar graphs

NCTM Standards
1. Number and Operations
2. Algebra
5. Data Analysis and Probability
6. Problem Solving
7. Reasoning and Proof
8. Communication
9. Connections
10. Representation

Math Background

These ideas will help students read and interpret data in bar graphs.

- Bar graphs can represent the same data using a horizontal or vertical format.

- A bar graph consists of a title, bars, labels, and a scale; the scale is often represented in increments of 2, 5, 10, or 25.

- Different scales can be used to present the same information in a bar graph.

Vocabulary

bar graph a graph that uses bars to show data

scale the numbers on a bar graph that help you read the number each bar shows

horizontal bar graph a graph with bars going across from left to right

vertical bar graph a graph with bars going up from the bottom

Warm-Up Resources

Number of the Day

Transparency **16.2**

I am the number that was selected for the key on a pictograph to show the data: 16, 36, 28, 12. What number am I? Possible answer: 4

Daily Facts Practice

Have students practice addition and subtraction facts by completing Set G of *Teacher's Resource Book*, p. TR94.

Transparency **16.2**

Problem of the Day

The numbers in Alicia's table are 16, 26, 32, 12, and 22, and those in Ian's table are 20, 8, 36, 24, and 40. What number could they both use for the key of their pictographs? 2 Is there another number that Ian could use? 4

Solution Problem of the Day tab, p. PD16

Intervention and Extension Resources

Alternative Teaching Strategy

Take a quick classroom survey and **make a bar graph**.

- Ask: Which do you like best—spaghetti, pizza, chicken nuggets, or tacos? Have students raise their hands, and tally the data.
- Construct a bar graph to show the data. Follow students' directions for what to title the graph, how to label it, what scale to use, and how to draw the bars.
- Invite a pair of volunteers to make the horizontal or vertical equivalent of the graph you constructed. Check students' work.

VISUAL

VISUAL/SPATIAL

Multistep and Strategy Problems

The following multistep or strategy problem is provided in Lesson 16.2:

Page	Item
325	8

Vocabulary Strategy

Have students **make a visual aid for the terms** ***bar graph, horizontal bar graph, vertical bar graph*, and *scale*.** Have them draw a horizontal bar graph and a vertical bar graph. Have them label the graphs with the terms and identify what the scale is on each graph. Check students' work.

ESOL/ESL

Advanced Learners

Challenge students to **compare bar graphs and pictographs**. Have students work in pairs to discuss how making a bar graph is the same as or different from making a pictograph. Encourage students to share the ideas they list. Possible answer: they both have a title that tells what the graph is about; a bar graph has a scale and a pictograph has a key.

AUDITORY, VISUAL

INTERPERSONAL/SOCIAL

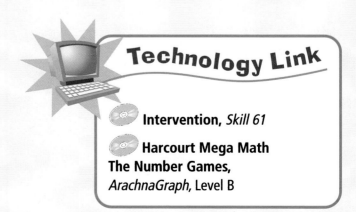

Technology Link

- **Intervention,** *Skill 61*
- **Harcourt Mega Math** **The Number Games,** *ArachnaGraph*, Level B

Lesson 16.2 Organizer

Objective To read and interpret data in bar graphs

Vocabulary bar graph, scale, horizontal bar graph, vertical bar graph

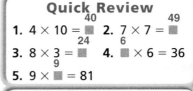

---

1 INTRODUCE

QUICK REVIEW provides practice of mental math skills.

WHY LEARN THIS? You can understand bar graphs that you see in reference books and newspapers. *Share the lesson objective with students.*

---

2 TEACH

Guided Instruction

• *Discuss the Learn section.*

What do the bars show on these graphs? the number of hours per day each animal sleeps

How do you use the bars to find out how long each animal sleeps? Possible answer: look at where the bar ends; check the scale to find the number of hours.

ALGEBRAIC THINKING Why is it better to use 4 for the scale on these bar graphs than a greater number? Possible answer: If you used a greater number for the scale, it might not be as easy to tell the exact number of hours.

• *Direct students' attention to Examples A and B.*

REASONING The two bar graphs use different scales to show the same data. Are there any advantages to either scale? Explain. Possible answer: yes; both are clear and easy to read. The graph with the scale of 25 can show more miles per hour in the same amount of space. The graph with the scale of 10 is easy to read because the bars either line up with labels or fall halfway between.

---

2 Bar Graphs

Quick Review
1. $4 \times 10 =$ ■ 40
2. $7 \times 7 =$ ■ 49
3. $8 \times 3 =$ ■ 24
4. ■ $\times 6 = 36$ 6
5. $9 \times$ ■ $= 81$ 9

▶ **Learn**

SLEEPY ANIMALS A **bar graph** uses bars to show data. A **scale** of numbers helps you read the number each bar shows.

These bar graphs show the same data.

VOCABULARY
bar graph   scale
horizontal bar graph
vertical bar graph

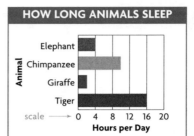

In a **horizontal bar graph**, the bars go across from left to right.

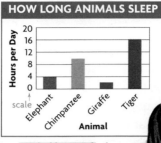

In a **vertical bar graph**, the bars go up from the bottom.

• What scale is used in the bar graphs? Why is this a good scale? **scale of 4; some of the numbers can be divided by 4.**
• How do you read the bar for the chimpanzee, which ends halfway between two lines? **A bar that ends halfway between 8 and 12 stands for 10 hours.**

Examples

Ⓐ HOW FAST LAND ANIMALS RUN

Cheetah, Lion, Hyena, Rabbit
0 10 20 30 40 50 60 70 80
Miles per Hour

Ⓑ HOW FAST LAND ANIMALS RUN

Cheetah, Lion, Hyena, Rabbit
0 25 50 75 100
Miles per Hour

• How are these graphs alike? How are they different? **Alike: Both are horizontal bar graphs. Different: Example A has a scale of 10 and Example B has a scale of 25.**

324

Reteach 16.2

Bar Graphs

A **bar graph** uses bars to show data. In a **vertical** bar graph, the bars go up from the bottom. In a **horizontal** bar graph, the bars go across from left to right.

COINS IN A JAR

COINS IN A JAR

Reading a Vertical Bar Graph
• The title is on top.
• Each bar stands for something.
• Run your finger to the top of a bar.
• Read the number to the left of the top of the bar to see how many.
• The numbers of the **scale** on the left show how many items.

Reading a Horizontal Bar Graph
• The title is on top.
• Each bar stands for something.
• Run your finger to the far right of a bar.
• Read the number below the end of the bar to see how many.
• The numbers of the **scale** on the bottom show how many items.

For 1–4, use the bar graphs above.
1. Find the number of nickels in the jar. _____ 8 nickels
2. Which coin is there the most of? the fewest of? How can you tell?
   Pennies: the bar is either the highest or the longest; dimes:
   the bar is either the lowest or the shortest.
3. Find the number of pennies in the jar. _____ 12 pennies
4. How many more pennies are there than quarters? 6 more pennies

RW84 Reteach

Practice 16.2

Bar Graphs

For 1–4, use the bar graph.
1. What type of bar graph is this?
   horizontal bar graph
2. How many students named lions as their favorite stuffed animal? frogs? dogs?
   10 students; 4 students;
   6 students

FAVORITE STUFFED ANIMALS
Seals, Dogs, Lions, Frogs, Giraffes, Teddy Bears
0 2 4 6 8 10 12
Number of Votes

3. Which stuffed animal is the favorite of the most students? of the fewest students?
   lions; giraffes
4. How many students in all voted for their favorite stuffed animal?
   31 students

Mixed Review
Find the missing factor.
5. $20 = 10 \times$ _2_
6. _9_ $\times 3 = 27$
7. $8 \times$ _4_ $= 32$
8. _5_ $\times 5 = 25$
9. $6 \times$ _4_ $= 24$
10. $1 \times$ _11_ $= 11$
11. $7 \times$ _8_ $= 56$
12. $24 = 8 \times$ _3_
13. _0_ $\times 6 = 0$

Solve.
14. $12 \div 2 =$ _6_
15. $7 \div 1 =$ _7_
16. $8 \div 2 =$ _4_
17. $9 \div 3 =$ _3_
18. $10 \div 5 =$ _2_
19. $6 \div 3 =$ _2_
20. $9 \div 9 =$ _81_
21. $6 \times 9 =$ _54_
22. $4 \times 7 =$ _28_
23. $6,890$ $+8,054$ $14,944$
24. $3,211$ $+7,618$ $10,829$
25. $5,765$ $+5,765$ $11,530$
26. $9,298$ $+5,431$ $14,729$

PW84 Practice

Technology Link

More Practice:
Harcourt Mega Math
The Number Games,
ArachnaGraph, Level B

1. Explain how you would use the graph in Example A to tell how fast a rabbit runs.

For 2–3, use the bar graphs in Examples A and B.

2. How fast can a lion run?
50 miles per hour

3. How fast can a cheetah run?
70 miles per hour

► **Practice and Problem Solving** — Extra Practice, page 332, Set A

For 4–6, use the Length of Sea Animals bar graph.

4. Is this a vertical or horizontal bar graph?
vertical bar graph

5. How long is a giant squid?
55 feet

6. How much longer is a gray whale than a bottlenose dolphin? 40 feet

For 7–8, use the Favorite Wild Animals bar graph.

7. Which animal received the most votes?
lion

8. Were there more votes in all for crocodile and lion, or for giraffe and elephant? Explain. giraffe and elephant: 2 + 15 = 17 and 6 + 12 = 18; 18 > 17

9. **Vocabulary Power** The word *scale* has more than one meaning. What meaning is found in your math book? What is another meaning for *scale*?
Possible answers: A scale helps you read the number each bar on a bar graph shows. A scale is part of the protective covering on a fish and on some reptiles.

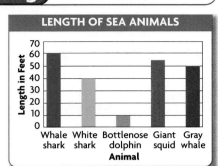
LENGTH OF SEA ANIMALS
Length in Feet — Whale shark, White shark, Bottlenose dolphin, Giant squid, Gray whale — Animal

FAVORITE WILD ANIMALS
Wild Animal — Giraffe, Crocodile, Elephant, Lion — Number of Votes

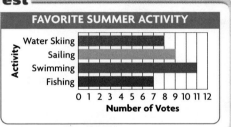

Getting Ready for the EOG Test

10. Avery's class voted for their favorite summer activity. How many more votes did swimming get than water skiing? C

FAVORITE SUMMER ACTIVITY
Activity — Water Skiing, Sailing, Swimming, Fishing — Number of Votes

A 1   C 3

B 2   D 4

Chapter 16   **325**

* **North Carolina Standards 4.01** Collect, organize, analyze, and display data (including circle phs and tables) to solve problems.

Challenge 16.2

What Is Left?

Starting with 2, put a diagonal line from upper left to lower right through every second number.

Starting with 3, put a diagonal line from lower left to upper right through every third number.

Starting with 5, put a vertical line through every fifth number.

Starting with 7, put a horizontal line through every seventh number.

[grid of numbers 1–100]

1. Circle any numbers not marked. What numbers are circled?
1, 11, 13, 17, 19, 23, 29, 31, 37, 41, 43, 47, 53, 59, 61, 67, 71, 73, 79, 83, 89, 97

2. Which numbers have all four types of lines drawn through them?
none of them

W84 Challenge

Problem Solving 16.2

Bar Graphs — Understand ► Plan ► Solve ► Check

OUR FAVORITE ICE CREAM FLAVORS
Flavor — strawberry, vanilla, chocolate, cherry vanilla, chocolate chip — Number of Students

For 1–5, use the graph.

1. What flavor do the most students like best? the fewest students?
chocolate; cherry vanilla

2. How many more students voted for chocolate than cherry vanilla?
7 more students

3. How many students said that vanilla is their favorite flavor?
9 students

4. How many students said that either vanilla or strawberry is their favorite flavor?
17 students

Choose the letter of the correct answer.

5. How many students answered the survey on favorite ice cream flavors?
A 48   C 38
(B) 40   D 30

6. There are 24 children sitting at 6 tables. If the same number sit at each table, how many are seated at 1 table?
F 18   H 6
G 12   (J) 4

7. **Write About It** If the bar graph were vertical instead of horizontal, where would its scale be? Where would 0 be?
Possible answer: The scale would be on the left side; 0 would be at the bottom.

PS84 Problem Solving

---

3 PRACTICE

Guided Practice

Do Check Exercises 1–3 with your students. Identify students who are having difficulty and choose appropriate lesson resources to provide assistance.

Independent Practice

Note that Exercise 8 is a **multistep or strategy problem**. Assign Exercises 4–9.

For Exercise 5, point out that the bar is midway between two numbers on the scale.

Vocabulary Power Suggest that students think of a *scale* on a bar graph as a tool to help them measure the bars on the graph.

4 ASSESS

Summarize the lesson by having students:

Discuss How are the horizontal and vertical bar graphs in the Learn section alike and different? They show the same data, but the bars go in different directions.

Write Why does a bar graph use a scale? Possible answer: a scale helps you determine what number each bar shows.

LESSON QUIZ

Transparency 16.2

For 1–2, use the graphs in Examples A and B on page 324.

1. What is the difference in miles per hour between the fastest and slowest animals shown? 35 miles per hour

2. How much faster can a lion run than a rabbit? 15 miles per hour

325

Lesson Planning

Objective To make bar graphs

Materials *For each student* bar graph pattern, p. TR61; crayons

NCTM Standards
1. Number and Operations
5. Data Analysis and Probability
6. Problem Solving
8. Communication
10. Representation

Math Background
These ideas will help students make bar graphs.

- A bar graph is a way of organizing and displaying data.

- Making a bar graph is a step-by-step process: students should decide whether the graph will be horizontal or vertical, title and label the graph, and determine its scale before completing the graph.

- The scale on a bar graph always begins with zero; however, different scales can be used to represent the same information.

Warm-Up Resources

Number of the Day

Transparency **16.3**

Write four number sentences that use 36 as a dividend or product. Possible answer: $6 \times 6 = 36$; $9 \times 4 = 36$; $36 \div 6 = 6$; $36 \div 4 = 9$

Daily Facts Practice

Have students practice division facts by completing Set A of *Teacher's Resource Book*, p. TR95.

Transparency **16.3**

Problem of the Day

Nathan marked the scale on his bar graph by skip-counting by sixes. If he drew a bar graph to show 28 flowers, between what two numbers should he end the bar? 24 and 30

Solution Problem of the Day tab, p. PD16

Intervention and Extension Resources

Alternative Teaching Strategy

Have students **practice completing a bar graph**. Give each student a tally table showing data about the class, such as students' favorite colors, and provide them with a partially completed bar graph. For example, the graph might show the scale and the bar for the color red, but be lacking a title, bars for other colors, and labels. Ask students to work in small groups to complete the graph. Repeat with partially completed bar graphs displaying other data. Check students' work.

ESOL/ESL

VISUAL

VISUAL/SPATIAL

Multistep and Strategy Problems

The following multistep or strategy problem is provided in Lesson 16.3:

Page	Item
327	5

Writing in Mathematics

Have students **describe the process of making a bar graph**. Encourage them to explain the step-by-step process including writing a title and labels, making a scale, and drawing and shading the bars. Remind students to use order words such as *first, second, next, then*, and *last*. Check students' work.

Early Finishers

MATERIALS *For each pair* magazines

Have pairs of early finishers **find examples of bar graphs** in children's magazines and other classroom materials. Invite them to identify the parts of each graph and to summarize the data displayed by sharing the graphs with other pairs or with the class. Check students' work.

VISUAL

VERBAL/LINGUISTIC

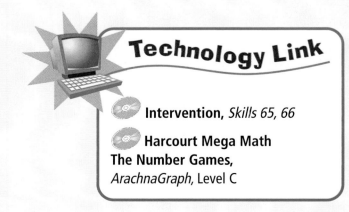

Technology Link

Intervention, *Skills 65, 66*

Harcourt Mega Math
The Number Games,
ArachnaGraph, Level C

Lesson 16.3 Organizer

Objective To make bar graphs

Materials *For each student* bar graph pattern, p. TR61; crayons

---

1 INTRODUCE

QUICK REVIEW provides practice of mental math skills.

WHY LEARN THIS? You'll be able to show data you collect in a way that will make it clear to others. *Share the lesson objective with students.*

2 TEACH

Guided Instruction

- *Direct students' attention to the Explore section.*
  How do you select a title and labels for the bar graph? Decide what the graph is about and what the bars show.
  How is making a scale on a bar graph like making a key for a pictograph? Possible answer: You start by looking for patterns in the data.
  Which bar on your graph will be the longest? goats **the shortest?** turtles

Suggest that students leave enough space in their bar graphs for the tortoises and deer they will be asked to add in Try It.

3 PRACTICE

Guided Practice

Do Try It Exercises a–b with your students. Identify students who are having difficulty and choose appropriate lesson resources to provide assistance.

LESSON 3 — Make Bar Graphs
HANDS ON

MATERIALS
bar graph pattern, crayons

▶ Explore

You can make a bar graph to show the number of each type of animal at the Oglebay Zoo in West Virginia. Use the data in the table to make a horizontal bar graph.

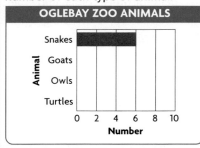

Oglebay Zoo — Wheeling — WEST VIRGINIA

OGLEBAY ZOO	
Animal	**Number**
Snakes	6
Goats	10
Owls	4
Turtles	3

Activity

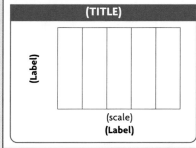

STEP 1
Write a title and labels. Decide on the best scale to use, and write the numbers.

(TITLE)
(Label)
(scale)
(Label)

STEP 2
Complete the bar graph. Make the length of each bar equal to the number of each type of animal.

OGLEBAY ZOO ANIMALS
Animal: Snakes, Goats, Owls, Turtles
Number: 0 2 4 6 8 10

- Name the parts of a bar graph.
  title, labels, scale, bars
- Explain where you would draw the bar for turtles.
  I would draw the bar to end halfway between 2 and 4 on the scale.

Try It

Use your bar graph.
Check students' bar graphs.
a. There are 5 tortoises at the Oglebay Zoo. Make a bar for the tortoises.
b. There are 6 deer at the Oglebay Zoo. Make a bar for the deer.

326

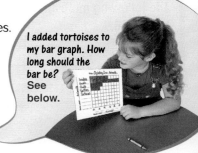

I added tortoises to my bar graph. How long should the bar be? See below.

The bar should end halfway between 4 and 6.

Reteach 16.3

Make Bar Graphs

Make a horizontal bar graph of the data in the frequency table.

- Use the same title.
- Label rows with the names of the meals.
- Use a scale of 2. Write the numbers along the bottom of the graph
- Write *Number of Votes* under the scale. Write *Meal* beside the names of the meals.
- For each meal, make a bar as long as the number of votes.

OUR FAVORITE MEAL	
Meal	**Number of Votes**
Breakfast	6
Snack	4
Lunch	10
Dinner	2

OUR FAVORITE MEAL
MEAL: Breakfast, Snack, Lunch, Dinner
0 2 4 6 8 10 12
Number of Votes

For 1–3, use the completed bar graph.
1. For which meal is the bar the longest? lunch
2. For which meal is the bar the shortest? dinner
3. If the number of votes for *Snack* had been 5, where would the bar end?
   halfway between 4 and 6.

Reteach RW85

Practice 16.3

Make Bar Graphs

Make a horizontal bar graph of the data in the table at the right. Use a scale of 2. Remember to write a title and labels for the graph. Check students' graphs.

FAVORITE DRINKS	
Drink	**Number of Votes**
Water	4
Punch	2
Milk	5
Juice	8
Soda	12

Favorite Drinks
Drink: Water, Punch, Milk, Juice, Soda
0 2 4 6 8 10 12
Number of Votes

For 1–2, use your bar graph.
1. What does the graph show? <u>favorite drinks</u>
2. How many bars end halfway between two lines?
   1 bar: the bar for milk

Mixed Review
Write $<$, $>$, or $=$ in each $\bigcirc$.

3. $32 \div 8 \bigcirc 1 \times 4$ 4. $6 + 6 \bigcirc 20$ 5. $5 \times 2 \bigcirc 10 - 1$
6. $7 \times 7 \bigcirc 9 \times 6$ 7. $18 \div 2 \bigcirc 3 + 11$ 8. $72 - 30 \bigcirc 9 \times 3$

Practice PW85

You can make a bar graph of data you collect from a survey. Check students' graphs. For bulleted questions, answers will vary.

- Take a survey in your classroom. Decide on a question. Give your classmates four possible choices. Record the choices in a table. Make a bar graph of the data in the table.

- How many classmates answered your survey?

- What scale did you use?

- What is the title of your graph?

- What did you find from your survey?

Title: Survey

Data Label:

Scale Label: _____

▶ **Practice and Problem Solving**

1. Copy and complete the Wildlife Center bar graph. Use the data in the table at the right.
   Check students' graphs.

2. Why is 2 a good scale to use?
   Possible answer: Two of the numbers are multiples of 2.

WILDLIFE CENTER	
Animal	**Number**
Monkeys	3
Zebras	8
Polar bears	2

WILDLIFE CENTER

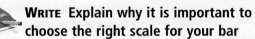

For 3–5, use the Favorite Pets table.

3. Make a bar graph. Why is 5 a good scale to use? **Check students' graphs. All the numbers are multiples of 5.**

4. For which pet is the bar the longest? **dogs**

5. Are there more birds and cats, or more dogs and fish? Explain. **There are more birds and cats; 30 + 40 = 70 and 50 + 15 = 65; 70 > 65**

FAVORITE PETS	
Animal	**Number**
Birds	30
Fish	15
Dogs	50
Cats	40

Getting Ready for the EOG Test

6. Reba's class voted for their favorite type of book. How many *more* students voted for fables than for nonfiction? **B**

   A 2   **B** 4   **C** 16   **D** 18

FAVORITE BOOKS	
Type	**Number**
Nonfiction	6
Fables	10
Legends	8

Chapter 16 **327**

North Carolina Standards 4.01 Collect, organize, analyze, and display data (including circle graphs and tables) to solve problems.

Independent Practice

Note that Exercise 5 is a **multistep or strategy problem.** Assign Exercises 1–5.

4 ASSESS

Summarize the lesson by having students:

Discuss What are the parts of a bar graph? title, labels, scale, and bars that show data

Write Explain why it is important to choose the right scale for your bar graph. Possible answer: You want the bar graph to be easy to read. If your scale is too small, your graph will take up too much space; if it is too large, you may not be able to determine what number a bar represents.

LESSON QUIZ

For 1–2, use the table.

Transparency

FAVORITE ZOO ANIMALS	
Animal	**Number**
Monkeys	20
Zebras	10
Lions	25
Elephants	5

1. Make a bar graph with a scale of 5. Check students' work.

2. Which animal has the longest bar? lions the shortest bar? elephants

---

Challenge 16.3

Pay Up

Mr. Santos rewards his students for doing their homework. Each time they do a homework assignment, he gives them a smiling face sticker. When students have collected 8 smiling face stickers, they receive a pencil.

Complete the chart for each student.

Name	Stickers	Number of Pencils	Stickers Left Over
Sylvia	☺☺☺☺☺☺☺	0	7
Joshua	☺☺☺☺☺☺☺☺☺☺☺☺☺☺☺	1	7
Hidori	☺☺☺☺☺☺☺☺☺☺☺☺☺☺☺☺☺☺☺☺☺☺	2	6
Brandon	☺☺☺☺☺☺☺☺☺☺☺☺☺☺☺☺☺☺☺☺☺	2	0
Jessica	☺☺☺☺☺☺☺☺☺☺☺☺	1	4
Martha	☺☺☺☺☺☺☺☺☺☺☺☺☺☺☺☺☺☺☺☺☺☺☺☺☺☺☺☺	3	4
Tiffany	☺☺☺☺☺☺☺☺☺☺	1	2
George	☺☺☺	0	3
Tony	☺☺☺☺☺☺☺☺☺☺☺☺☺☺☺☺☺	2	7
Justin	☺☺☺☺☺☺☺☺☺☺☺☺☺☺	1	6
Paola	☺☺☺☺☺☺☺☺☺☺☺☺☺☺☺☺☺☺☺☺☺☺☺☺☺☺☺☺☺☺☺☺☺	4	1

1. Who received the most pencils? the fewest pencils?
   Paola; George and Sylvia

2. If they all decided to share, are there enough pencils? Explain.
   Everyone could have 1 pencil. There would be 6 left over.

Challenge **CW85**

Problem Solving 16.3

Make Bar Graphs Understand ▶ Plan ▶ Solve ▶ Check

Write the correct answer.

1. Complete the bar graph using the information in the table.
   Check students' graphs.

2. How many people voted in all?
   18

3. How many people voted for either cats or dogs?
   15

4. How many more people voted for dogs than birds?
   6

OUR FAVORITE PETS	
Pet	**Votes**
Cats	6
Dogs	9
Birds	3

OUR FAVORITE PETS

Choose the letter of the correct answer.

5. Which group of numbers is in order from greatest to least?

   A 542; 432; 299; 651
   ⓑ 551; 542; 432; 299
   C 432; 599; 542; 551
   D 499; 432; 542; 651

6. Which number is between 154 and 187?

   F 146
   ⓖ 167
   H 189
   J 314

7. The key in a pictograph shows that each picture stands for 8 books. How many books do 6 pictures stand for?

   A 56 books   C 14 books
   ⓑ 48 books   D 2 books

8. Mrs. Carter paid for her groceries with a $20 bill. Her change was $3.53. How much did the groceries cost?

   ⓕ $16.47   H $17.47
   G $16.57   J $17.57

9. **Write About It** How are vertical bar graphs and horizonal bar graphs alike?
   Possible answer: They can both show the same information.
   They both have a scale, a title, and labels.

Problem Solving **PS85**

327

Algebra: Ordered Pairs

Lesson Planning

PROFESSIONAL DEVELOPMENT

Objective To locate points on a coordinate grid by using ordered pairs

NCTM Standards

2. Algebra
5. Data Analysis and Probability
6. Problem Solving
7. Reasoning and Proof
8. Communication
9. Connections
10. Representation

Math Background

Consider the following when introducing locating points on a grid.

- The first number in the ordered pair always indicates how many spaces to move horizontally. The second number indicates how many spaces to move vertically.

- An ordered pair identifies an exact location on a grid. No other ordered pair can name that location.

- If *a* and *b* are different numbers, then the ordered pairs *(a,b)* and *(b,a)* have different locations.

Vocabulary

grid horizontal and vertical lines forming squares used as a reference for locating points

ordered pair a pair of numbers used to locate a point on a grid

Warm-Up Resources

Build Number Sense

Number of the Day

Transparency 16.4

The range on a line plot is 9. Write three number sentences that might show how the range was determined. Possible answers: $21 - 12 = 9$; $10 - 1 = 9$; $55 - 46 = 9$

Review Basic Facts
8 +3

Daily Facts Practice

Have students practice division facts by completing Set B of *Teacher's Resource Book*, p. TR95.

Solve a Problem

Transparency 16.4

Problem of the Day

A bar graph showed that Barb read twice as many library books as Lisa. Mike read 25 more books than Lisa, but 15 fewer than Barb. How many books did each read? Lisa read 40 books, Mike read 65 books, and Barb read 80 books.

Solution Problem of the Day tab, p. PD16

Intervention and Extension Resources

Alternative Teaching Strategy

MATERIALS chalk

Help students **model ordered pairs** through movement.

- In a stretch of blacktop or concrete that can be marked and washed off, use chalk to draw a large grid.
- Have students label the horizontal and vertical scales.
- Review the term *grid* and label some points on it. Have students identify the ordered pair for each point. Check students' work.
- Then call out ordered pairs and, one by one, have students use the coordinates to find each point. Explain that they will use the following process to find a point: place themselves at zero, hop right to find the first number, and then jump "up" to the second number.

KINESTHETIC

BODILY/KINESTHETIC

Multistep and Strategy Problems

The following multistep or strategy problem is provided in Lesson 16.4:

Page	Item
329	20

ESOL/ESL

MATERIALS *For each group* poster board, masking tape, 2 sets of index cards numbered 1–8

ESOL/ESL

Have groups of three or four students **reinforce locating points on a grid** by playing a game. Use four large sheets of poster board, taped together, to make one 8-by-8 labeled grid. Place the grid on the floor. Have students take turns drawing 2 cards and reading the numbers as an ordered pair. Have 2 students stand along the axes at each of the numbers drawn. Have them walk up and across to meet at the point represented by the ordered pair.

KINESTHETIC

BODILY/KINESTHETIC

Fine Arts Connection

MATERIALS *For each student* grid paper, p. TR62

Have students **practice locating points on a grid**. Ask students to make a dot-to-dot design on a grid and write directions for other students to follow to duplicate the design. If students need help getting started making a design, have them locate and connect the following ordered pairs, in order, on a grid: (4,0), (5,1), (6,2), (7,3), (7,4), (6,5), (5,5), (4,4), (3,5), (2,5), (1,4), (1,3), (2,2), (3,1), (4,0). Ask students to describe the design. heart shape

VISUAL

VERBAL/LINGUISTIC

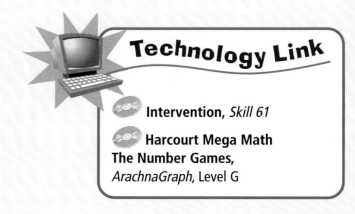

Technology Link

Intervention, *Skill 61*

Harcourt Mega Math
The Number Games,
ArachnaGraph, Level G

328B

Lesson 16.4 Organizer

Objective To locate points on a coordinate grid by using ordered pairs

Vocabulary grid, ordered pair

1 INTRODUCE

QUICK REVIEW provides practice of mental math skills.

WHY LEARN THIS? You can locate places by using a map. *Share the lesson objective with students.*

2 TEACH

Guided Instruction

- *Discuss the Learn section.*
  What is the "order" of an ordered pair? The first number is how many to the right and the second number is how many up.
  REASONING Why do you need to know a pair of numbers, instead of just one number, to find a point on a grid? Possible answer: The point is where the horizontal and vertical lines meet or cross, so you have to identify the two numbers that represent the movement to the right of zero and the movement up from there.
  ALGEBRAIC THINKING What four ordered pairs describe the square created by this grid? (0,0), (7,0), (7,7), (0,7)

- *Direct students' attention to the N, S, E, and W labels on the grid.*
  What directions do these letters stand for? north, south, east, and west
  REASONING If Jack wants to see the zebras after the elephants, in which direction should he go? south

---

4 Algebra: Ordered Pairs

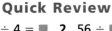
Quick Review
1. $28 \div 4 = \blacksquare$ 2. $56 \div \blacksquare = 7$
    7   8
3. $35 \div 5 = \blacksquare$ 4. $45 \div 5 = \blacksquare$
    7   9
5. $30 \div 3 = \blacksquare$ 10

▷ **Learn**

GET TO THE POINT Jack is using a map to help him find different animal areas at the zoo. He wants to see the elephants first. How can this map help Jack find the elephants?

The horizontal and vertical lines on the map make a **grid**.

VOCABULARY
grid
ordered pair

Start at 0. Move 2 spaces to the right. Then move 3 spaces up. The elephants are located at (2,3).

(2,3)

The first number tells how many spaces to move to the right.

The second number tells how many spaces to move up.

☀ **MATH IDEA** An **ordered pair** of numbers within parentheses, like (2,3), names a point on a grid.

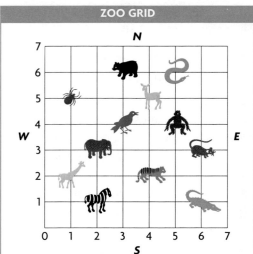
ZOO GRID

Example

Which animal is found at (5,4) on the grid?

Start at 0.
Move 5 spaces to the right.
Then move 4 spaces up.

So, the monkey is found at (5,4).

- Suppose a butterfly is at (6,5). Tell how you locate that point on the grid. **Start at 0. Move 6 spaces to the right. Then move 5 spaces up.**

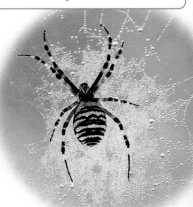
Wasp spider ▲

328

Reteach 16.4

Algebra: Ordered Pairs

The horizontal and vertical lines in the square form a **grid**. An **ordered pair** of numbers such as (2,3) helps you find points on a grid. The numbers tell you how many spaces to move to the right of zero and how many spaces to move up.

Locate the point (2,3) on the grid.

- Start at zero and move two spaces to the right.
- From that point, move up three spaces.

Look at each ordered pair. Name the sports equipment you find at the point named by the ordered pair.

1. (3,1) ___baseball___
2. (1,2) ___baseball bat___
3. (4,4) ___basketball___
4. (5,6) ___tennis racket___
5. (6,2) ___football___
6. (2,3) ___hockey stick___
7. (7,5) ___soccer ball___
8. (1,6) ___volleyball___
9. (5,1) ___baseball glove___
10. (2,5) ___sneakers___

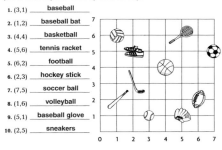

RW86 Reteach

Practice 16.4

Algebra: Ordered Pairs

For 1–4, use the grid at the right. Write the letter of the point named by the ordered pair.

1. (4,5) ___R___   2. (1,6) ___E___
3. (6,2) ___W___   4. (2,2) ___C___

For 5–10, locate each ordered pair. Draw a point. Label it with the type of fruit.

5. (1,1) apple   6. (5,5) orange
7. (2,4) banana   8. (3,2) grape
9. (4,3) kiwi   10. (6,1) peach

Mixed Review

Find the missing factor.

11. $3 \times$ __7__ $= 21$ 12. $4 \times$ __4__ $= 16$ 13. __6__ $\times 4 = 24$
14. $7 \times$ __8__ $= 56$ 15. __6__ $\times 9 = 54$ 16. $5 \times$ __10__ $= 50$

Solve.

17. $\begin{array}{r} 767 \\ -234 \\ \hline 533 \end{array}$ 18. $\begin{array}{r} 9,870 \\ -5,925 \\ \hline 3,945 \end{array}$ 19. $\begin{array}{r} 611 \\ +382 \\ \hline 993 \end{array}$ 20. $\begin{array}{r} 2,195 \\ +8,214 \\ \hline 10,409 \end{array}$

21. $0 \times 8 =$ __0__   22. $3 \times 5 =$ __15__   23. $48 \div 8 =$ __6__   24. $81 \div 9 =$ __9__
25. $2 \times 10 =$ __20__   26. $9 \times 8 =$ __72__   27. $36 \div 4 =$ __9__   28. $42 \div 7 =$ __6__
29. $4 \times 3 =$ __12__   30. $5 \times 6 =$ __30__   31. $12 \div 1 =$ __12__   32. $0 \div 7 =$ __0__

PW86 Practice

1. Explain how you would locate (11,12) on a grid. **Start at 0. Move 11 spaces to the right. Then move 12 spaces up.**
2. Does (4,3) show the same point on a grid as (3,4)? Explain. **No; (4,3) is 4 spaces to the right and 3 spaces up. (3,4) is 3 spaces to the right and 4 spaces up.**

For 3–5, use the zoo grid on page 328.
Write the ordered pair for each animal.

3. tiger (4,2)   4. bear (3,6)   5. giraffe (1,2)

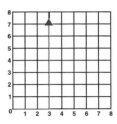

▲ Emerald tree boa

Practice and Problem Solving
Extra Practice, page 332, Set B

For 6–11 and 18, use the zoo grid on page 328.
Write the ordered pair for each animal.

6. bird (3,4)   7. snake (5,6)   8. zebra (2,1)

9. mouse (6,3)   10. deer (4,5)   11. alligator (6,1)

For 12–17, copy the grid. Locate each ordered pair.
Draw a point. Label it with the letter. **See answers on grid.**

12. (6,3) A   13. (1,3) B   14. (4,4) C
15. (2,6) D   16. (7,1) E   17. (3,2) F

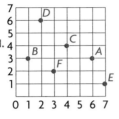

18. **REASONING** Rachel saw the zebra at (2,1) on the zoo grid. Mary saw the elephant at (2,3). What ordered pair names the point between the zebra and the elephant? **(2,2)**

19. **? What's the Error?** Jerry said, "To find the point (2,3), start at 0, move 2 spaces up and 3 spaces to the right." What error did Jerry make? **He found the point (3,2), not the point (2,3). He should have moved 2 spaces to the right and 3 spaces up to find the point (2,3).**

20. Walt has 45 pennies. Arthur has 11 nickels. Which boy has more money? How much more does he have? **Arthur; 10¢ more**

Getting Ready for the EOG Test

21. Tyra made a map of the playground at the park. Which ordered pair names the point on the grid for the slide? **C**

   A (3,1)   B (2,3)   C (1,3)   D (2,2)

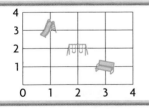

Chapter 16 **329**

North Carolina Standards 3.02 Use a rectangular coordinate system to solve problems. a) Graph and identify points with whole number and/or letter coordinates. *also* 3.02b

---

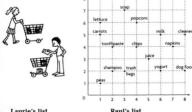

PRACTICE

Guided Practice

Do Check Exercises 1–5 with your students. Identify students who are having difficulty and choose appropriate lesson resources to provide assistance.

/// **COMMON ERROR ALERT** \\\

Watch for students who do not accurately locate a point on a grid. Ask them to "translate" ordered pairs aloud and then find the point. Display a grid large enough so that students can start at (0,0) and can move their hand right along it and then reach up the appropriate number of spaces.

Independent Practice

Note that Exercise 20 is a **multistep or strategy problem.** Assign Exercises 6–20.

ASSESS

Summarize the lesson by having students:

DISCUSS How could you use the grid on page 328 to explain to a friend at (0,0) how to get to the bear? **Move to the right three spaces, and then move up six spaces.**

WRITE What are four ordered pairs you can connect to make a square? Draw your solution on a grid. **Possible answer: (1,1), (4,1), (4,4), (1,4); Check students' work.**

LESSON QUIZ

Copy the grid below. Locate each ordered pair. Draw a point. Label it with the letter. **See answers on grid.**

Transparency **16.4**

1. (3,2) J
2. (7,3) K
3. (0,1) L
4. (2,6) M

329

Line Graphs

Lesson Planning

PROFESSIONAL DEVELOPMENT

Objective To read and interpret data in line graphs

NCTM Standards

1. Number and Operations
5. Data Analysis and Probability
6. Problem Solving
8. Communication
9. Connections
10. Representation

Math Background

Consider the following when introducing how to read and interpret data in line graphs.

- Line graphs are similar to bar graphs in that they have a title, scale, and labels.
- Line graphs differ from bar graphs because they show how data change over time.
- On a line graph, the vertical scale and the vertical and horizontal grid lines are used to plot points. These points are then connected by a line.

Vocabulary

line graph a graph that uses a line to show how data change over time
trends on a graph, areas where the data increase, decrease, or stay the same over time

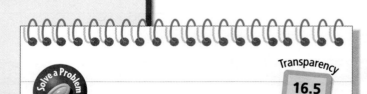

Warm-Up Resources

Build Number Sense

Number of the Day

Transparency 16.5

I come after the fifth number and before the seventh number when you skip-count by fives on a hundred chart. What number am I? 30

Review Basic Facts

Daily Facts Practice

Have students practice division facts by completing Set C of *Teacher's Resource Book*, p. TR95.

Solve a Problem

Transparency 16.5

Problem of the Day

The streets and avenues on a map are one block apart. Stan's house is at 4th Avenue and 6th Street (4,6). His grandmother's house is at 7th Avenue and 2nd Street (7,2). How many blocks is it from his house to his grandmother's house? 7 blocks

Solution Problem of the Day tab, p. PD16

Intervention and Extension Resources

Alternative Teaching Strategy

Have students **practice reading a line graph**. Display the data shown in the graph on page 330 in a table. Explain that you are going to show this data in a line graph. Draw a 7-by-7 grid, and label the horizontal scale *Month* and *January, February, March, April,* and *May.*

- Have students give the graph a title.
- Ask students where you will put the temperatures in degrees and what scale you might use. Follow their instructions and label the temperatures on the vertical scale.
- Demonstrate how to place a point on the grid for each number in the table.
- Connect the points to make the line and ask students to tell what the graph shows about the temperature in Des Moines. The normal temperature in Des Moines, Iowa, increases from month to month from January to May.

VISUAL

VERBAL/LINGUISTIC

Multistep and Strategy Problems

The following multistep or strategy problems are provided in Lesson 16.5:

Page	Item
331	12–13

Vocabulary Strategy

ESOL/ESL

Have students **compare pictographs, bar graphs, and line graphs**. Have students make a book about graphs, with one page for each of the three types of graphs studied in the chapter. On each page students may include the following:

- a definition of the type of graph
- an illustration of each graph with the parts labeled
- examples of kinds of data each graph might show
  Check students' work.

Advanced Learners

Challenge students to **analyze line graphs**. Have students work in pairs to discuss the following:

- Does a line graph have a scale? yes
- Does a line graph show a range? yes
- Does a line graph show the mode? yes
- Do you think you can make predictions based on the data in a line graph? Explain, using an example of a line graph from the lesson. Possible answer: Yes; you can predict that the temperature in Des Moines will increase from May to June.

AUDITORY

VERBAL/LINGUISTIC

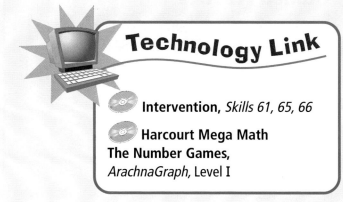

Technology Link

Intervention, *Skills 61, 65, 66*

Harcourt Mega Math
The Number Games,
ArachnaGraph, Level I

Lesson 16.5 Organizer

Objective To read and interpret data in line graphs

Vocabulary line graph, trends

1 INTRODUCE

QUICK REVIEW provides practice of mental math skills.

WHY LEARN THIS? You can understand line graphs in books and newspapers. *Share the lesson objective with students.*

2 TEACH

Guided Instruction

- *Discuss the Learn section.*
  What time period is shown in this line graph? January through May
  How many temperatures does this graph show for each month? one "normal" temperature
  How can you find the month when the normal temperature is 50 degrees? Find 50 degrees on the vertical scale on the left. Move right to find the point that is at 50. Follow the line down to find the month.
  What is the month? April
  What range of temperatures is shown from January to May? 40 degrees Fahrenheit
  REASONING If the line graph showed normal temperatures from January through December, what trend might you notice from September to December? Possible answer: The temperature decreases each month.

3 PRACTICE

Guided Practice

Do Check Exercises 1–3 with your students. Identify students who are having difficulty and choose appropriate lesson resources to provide assistance.

---

5 Line Graphs

Quick Review

1. $5 \times \blacksquare = 0$ 2. $\blacksquare \times 9 = 63$
   0   7
3. $30 = \blacksquare \times 6$ 4. $9 \times 4 = \blacksquare$
   5   36
5. $7 \times \blacksquare = 7$
   1

▶ **Learn**

LINE UP A **line graph** uses a line to show how data change over time. What was the normal, or average, temperature in Des Moines, Iowa, in March?

A line graph is like a grid.

a. From 0, find the vertical line for March. Move up to the point.

b. Follow the horizontal line left to the scale.

c. The point for March is at 40 degrees.

So, the normal temperature in Des Moines in March is 40 degrees.

In a line graph, you can see **trends**, or areas where data increase, decrease, or stay the same over time.

- Describe a trend you see in the line graph.
  Possible answer: The temperature increases each month.

VOCABULARY
line graph
trends

NORMAL TEMPERATURE IN DES MOINES, IOWA

▶ **Check**

1. **Explain** how the line graph would look if the normal temperature in Des Moines was getting colder each month.
   Possible answer: The line would start to go down.

For 2–3, use the line graph above.

2. What is the normal temperature in January? **20 degrees**

3. In what month is the normal temperature 60 degrees? **May**

Technology Link

More Practice:
Harcourt Mega Math
The Number Games,
ArachnaGraph, Level I

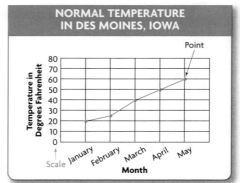

Reteach 16.5

Line Graphs

Mr. King made this line graph to show the number of bicycles he sold each month for the first seven months of the year. This **line graph** shows how bike sales change over time.

BICYCLES SOLD

How many bicycles were sold in April?

Step 1 Find the line labeled April. Put your finger on the line. Follow that line up to the point (•).

Step 2 Move your finger along the line to the left to locate the number of bicycles sold in April.

Mr. King sold 30 bicycles during April.

For 1–4, use the graph above.

1. Mr. King sold the greatest number of bicycles during
   __May__ and __June__.

2. During March, Mr. King sold __20__ bicycles.

3. During February, Mr. King sold __15__ bicycles.

4. Mr. King sold __30__ more bicycles in June than in January.

Reteach RW87

Practice 16.5

Line Graphs

For 1–5, use the line graph at the right.

1. Joyce made this line graph to show the number of pages she read each day in a mystery book. On what day did Joyce read the most pages? the fewest?

   __Sunday; Monday__

2. How many pages did Joyce read on Thursday?

   __15 pages__

3. On which two days did Joyce read the same number of pages?

   __Tuesday and Wednesday__

PAGES JOYCE READ

4. How many more pages did Joyce read on Friday than on Monday?

   __20 more pages__

5. Describe a trend you see in the line graph.

   Possible answer: Joyce read more pages on the weekend than during the week.

Mixed Review

Solve.

6. $3\overline{)18}$ 7. $5\overline{)25}$ 8. $6\overline{)24}$ 9. $7\overline{)63}$
   6   5   4   9

10. $10\overline{)10}$ 11. $8\overline{)24}$ 12. $10\overline{)20}$ 13. $2\overline{)14}$
    1   3   2   7

14.   1,234   15.   3,179   16.   2,051   17.   8,233
     +5,673   +3,298   −1,009   −4,649
      6,907   6,477   1,042   3,584

Practice PW87

For 4–7, use the Alaska line graph.

4. What is the normal temperature in December? **15 degrees**

5. In what month is the normal temperature 50 degrees? **September**

6. How many degrees higher is the normal temperature in August than in November? **35 degrees higher**

7. Describe a trend you see in the line graph. **Possible answer: Each month the temperature decreases.**

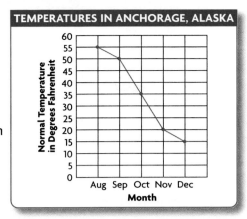

TEMPERATURES IN ANCHORAGE, ALASKA

For 8–10, use the Pencils line graph.

8. In what month were the most pencils sold? the fewest? **September; December**

9. In which months were more than 400 pencils sold? **September, October**

10. In which two months were the same number of pencils sold? How many pencils? **August, November; 400 pencils**

11. ✏️ **Write About It** Why do you think more pencils are sold in September? **Possible answer: The school year begins in September.**

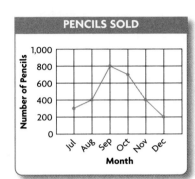

PENCILS SOLD

12. Sachio decorated 17 cookies and Linda decorated 12 cookies. They gave 20 cookies to their neighbors. How many cookies are left? **9 cookies**

13. The total cost of a watch and a calculator is $50. The watch costs $20 more than the calculator. Find the cost of the calculator. **$15**

Getting Ready for the EOG Test

14. Jeff's team is selling raffle tickets to raise money for new uniforms. On which day were the most tickets sold? **B**
   A Monday   C Thursday
   B Wednesday   D Friday

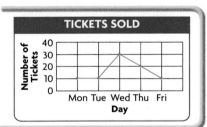

TICKETS SOLD

Chapter 16 **331**

North Carolina Standards 4.01 Collect, organize, analyze, and display data (including circle graphs and tables) to solve problems.

Independent Practice

Note that Exercises 12 and 13 are **multistep or strategy problems.** Assign Exercises 4–13.

Discuss each graph and the changes over time each one shows before students begin answering questions about the graphs independently.

Remind students of the abbreviations for months of the year.

SCAFFOLDED INSTRUCTION Use the prompts on Transparency 16 to guide instruction for the multistep or strategy problem in Exercise 13.

Transparency 16

4 ASSESS

Summarize the lesson by having students:

DISCUSS How is a line graph like a bar graph? How is it different from a bar graph? Possible answer: they both have a title, labels, and a scale; line graphs have points instead of bars; the points are connected with lines, but bars are not connected.

WRITE Explain why a line graph is a good choice for showing data about temperature. Give an example of other data that might be displayed in a line graph. Possible answers: Line graphs show change over time, and, in many places, temperature changes over time; a change in height, weight, or population.

LESSON QUIZ
For 1–2, use the Pencils Sold line graph on page 331.

Transparency 16.5

1. How many pencils were sold in August? 400 pencils

2. How many more pencils were sold in September than in November? 400 more

---

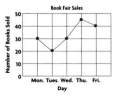

331

CHAPTER 16 Extra Practice

Purpose To provide extra practice for the skills presented in this chapter

The blue page references in each set of exercises refer to the lesson pages where each skill is taught.

Internet Resources

Visit **The Learning Site** at
www.harcourtschool.com
for a listing of practice activities.

Extra Practice

Set A (pp. 324–325)

For 1–5, use the bar graph.

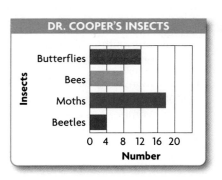

DR. COOPER'S INSECTS

1. What scale is used? scale of 4

2. How many moths are there? 18 moths

3. What is the total number of Dr. Cooper's insects? 42 insects

4. How many more butterflies are there than beetles? 8 more butterflies

5. How many fewer bees than moths are there? 10 fewer bees

Set B (pp. 328–329)

For 1–10, copy the grid. Locate each ordered pair. Draw a point. Label it with the letter. See answers on grid.

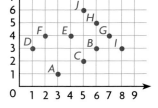

1. (3,1) **A**   2. (6,3) **B**

3. (5,2) **C**   4. (1,3) **D**

5. (4,4) **E**   6. (2,4) **F**

7. (7,4) **G**   8. (6,5) **H**

9. (8,3) **I**   10. (5,6) **J**

Set C (pp. 330–331)

For 1–3, use the line graph.

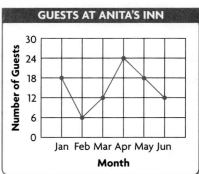

GUESTS AT ANITA'S INN

1. In what month did Anita's Inn have the most guests? In what month were there the fewest guests?
   most: April; fewest: February

2. How many guests stayed at Anita's Inn from January through June?
   90 guests

3. What trend do you see in the number of guests from February to April? The number of guests increases.

332

Review/Test

✓ CHECK VOCABULARY AND CONCEPTS

For 1–3, choose the best term from the box.

| bar graph |
| line graph |
| grid |
| trends |

1. A graph that uses bars to show data is a __?__. (p. 324)
   bar graph

2. The horizontal and vertical lines on a map make a __?__. (p. 328) **grid**

3. A graph that shows change over time is a __?__. (p. 330) **line graph**

4. How would you find (4,5) on a grid? (p. 328)
   Start at 0. Move 4 spaces to the right, then move 5 spaces up.

For 5–7, choose the letter that names each. (pp. 322–325; 330–331)

A. bar graph   **B.** pictograph   **C.** line plot   **D.** line graph

5. **B**
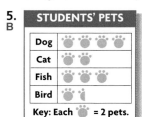
STUDENTS' PETS

Dog	🐾 🐾 🐾 🐾 🐾
Cat	🐾 🐾
Fish	🐾 🐾 🐾
Bird	🐾

Key: Each 🐾 = 2 pets.

6. **A**
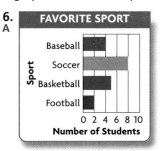
FAVORITE SPORT

7. **D**
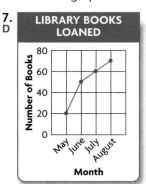
LIBRARY BOOKS LOANED

✓ CHECK SKILLS

For 8–9, use the bar graph above. (pp. 324–325)

8. What scale is used on this graph?
   scale of 2

9. How many students chose soccer?
   8 students

For 10–11, use the line graph above. (pp. 330–331)

10. In what month were the fewest books loaned?
    May

11. How many books were loaned from June through August?
    180 books

✓ CHECK PROBLEM SOLVING

For 12–15, use the pictograph above. (pp. 322–323)

12. What key is used on this graph?
    key of 2

13. How many pets does a 🐾 equal?
    1 pet

14. How many more dogs than cats do the students have? **4 more**

15. How many pets do the students have in all? **21 pets**

Chapter 16   **333**

Review/Test

Purpose To check understanding of concepts, skills, and problem solving presented in Chapter 16

Using the Page

The Chapter 16 Review/Test can be used as a **review** or a **test**.

- Items 1–7 check understanding of concepts and new vocabulary.
- Items 8–11 check skill proficiency.
- Items 12–15 check students' abilities to choose and apply problem solving strategies to real-life problems.

Suggest that students place the completed Chapter 16 Review/Test in their portfolios.

Using the Assessment Guide

- Multiple-choice format of Chapter 16 Posttest— See *Assessment Guide*, pp. AG101–102.
- Free-response format of Chapter 16 Posttest— See *Assessment Guide*, pp. AG103–104.

Using Student Self-Assessment

The How Did I Do? survey helps students assess what they have learned and how they learned it. This survey is available as a copying master in *Assessment Guide*, p. AGxvii.

Chapter 16 Test, page 1

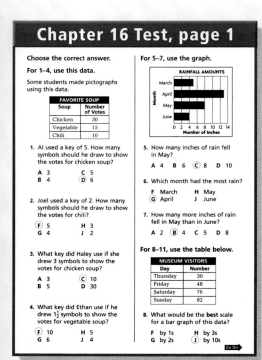

Chapter 16 Test, page 2

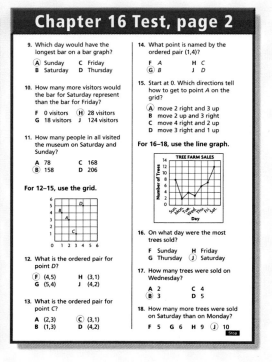

Analyze and Graph Data   333

CHAPTER 16

Getting Ready for the EOG Test

Chapters 1–16

Using the Pages

These pages may be used to help students get ready for the North Carolina EOG Test. The test items are written in the same style and arranged in the same format as those on the EOG Test.

The pages are cumulative. They cover the standards from the North Carolina Mathematics Standard Course of Study that have been taught up to this point in the text or in a previous grade. Each Getting Ready for the EOG Test also reviews the North Carolina mathematics strands shown below.

- Number and Operations
- Measurement
- Geometry
- Data Analysis and Probability
- Algebra

These pages can be assigned at the end of the chapter as classwork or as a homework assignment. You may want to have students use individual recording sheets presented in a multiple-choice (standardized) format. A Test Answer Sheet is available as a black-line master in the *Assessment Guide* (p. AGlii).

You may wish to have students describe how they solved each problem and share their solutions.

Getting Ready for the EOG Test

★ NUMBER AND OPERATIONS

1. Maura buys a pen for $1.89 and a card for $1.99. She pays with a $5 bill. How much change does she receive? D

   A $3.88   C $1.22
   B $2.12   D $1.12

2. Connie separates 24 marbles into 4 equal groups. Which array shows Connie's groups? C

   A

   B

   C

   D

3. A group of students will travel to the aquarium in 3 vans. Each van holds 9 students. How many students can be taken to the aquarium? C

   A 12   C 27
   B 18   D 36

4. **Explain It** Taro collected 378 stamps. He has 119 stamps from the United States. *About* how many stamps in Taro's collection are not from the United States? Explain your answer. **See page 335.**

★ MEASUREMENT AND GEOMETRY

5. Jake has a trumpet lesson at 1:15 P.M. The lesson lasts 1 hour. At what time will Jake be finished with his lesson? D

   A 12:15 P.M.
   B 1:30 P.M.
   C 1:45 P.M.
   D 2:15 P.M.

6. The clock shows the time when soccer practice ends. At what time does practice end? C

   A 6:30
   B 6:25
   C 5:30
   D 5:15

7. **Explain It** Cory identified this figure as a square pyramid. Explain whether you agree or disagree. **See page 335.**

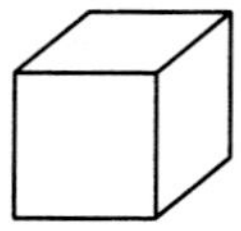

334

⭐ ALGEBRA

8. Emily wrote this number pattern. What number is missing? **C**

8, 16, 24, ▦, 40

A 28   **C** 32
B 30   **D** 36

9. There are 4 chairs at each table in the diner. If there are 32 chairs, what number sentence can you use to find the number of tables?
D
A $4 + 8 = 12$ **C** $32 + 4 = 36$
B $32 - 4 = 28$ **D** $32 \div 4 = 8$

> **TIP** **Eliminate choices.** See item 10. Since the difference between the numbers is 7, you can eliminate answer choices where the difference is greater than or less than 7.

10. The first four houses on Joan's block are numbered 11, 18, 25, and 32. What are the numbers on the next two houses? **D**

A 46 and 53   **C** 41 and 45
B 43 and 54   **D** 39 and 46

11. Explain It Mandy jogged on Sunday, Tuesday, Thursday, and Saturday. Predict what day Mandy will jog next. Explain your answer.
See below.

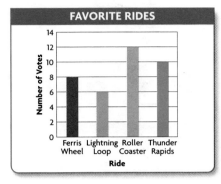

April						
Sun	Mon	Tue	Wed	Thu	Fri	Sat
	1	2	3	4	5	6
7	8	9	10	11	12	13
14	15	16	17	18	19	20
21	22	23	24	25	26	27
28	29	30				

⭐ DATA ANALYSIS AND PROBABILITY

12. Brad made this bar graph of his friends' favorite rides.

FAVORITE RIDES

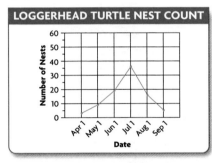

What scale did Brad use? **D**

A scale of 8   **C** scale of 4
B scale of 6   **D** scale of 2

13. Explain It The line graph shows the number of loggerhead turtle nests counted on the dates shown.

LOGGERHEAD TURTLE NEST COUNT

What do you notice about the number of nests counted between April 1 and September 1? On what date would you expect to find the *most* nests next year? Explain.
See below.

Chapter 16 335

Chapters 1–16

Item Analysis

You may wish to use the item analysis to determine which North Carolina standards need additional review.

Item	North Carolina Standard	Lesson
1	1.06	6.5
2	1.03	13.2
3	1.03	11.1
4	1.06	5.1
5	2.01	7.3
6	(2) 2.02	7.1
7	(1) Goal 3	Grade 1
8	5.01	9.3
9	Goal 5	12.3
10	5.01	9.3
11	5.01	9.3
12	4.01	16.2
13	4.01	16.5

SCORING RUBRIC
Explain It

2 Demonstrates a complete understanding of the problem and chooses an appropriate strategy to determine the solution

1 Demonstrates a partial understanding of the problem and chooses a strategy that does not lead to a complete and accurate solution

0 Demonstrates little understanding of the problem and shows little evidence of using any strategy to determine a solution

Explain It • Written Response

4. Possible answer: about 300 stamps; round 378 to 400 and 119 to 100. Subtract to find the estimated difference: $400 - 100 = 300$.

7. Disagree; possible answer: a square pyramid has 4 faces that are triangles and 1 face that is a square. This figure is a cube.

11. Monday; Possible answer: Mandy jogs every other day.

13. Possible answer: the number of nests increases from April 1 to July 1 and then decreases from July 1 to September 1. Based on this data, I would expect to find the most turtle nests on July 1 of next year.

Customary Units

NCTM Standards 2000

1. Number and Operations *Lessons 17.1–17.6*	6. Problem Solving *Lessons 17.1–17.6*
2. Algebra *Lessons 17.3, 17.4, 17.5*	7. Reasoning and Proof *Lessons 17.2, 17.3, 17.4, 17.5, 17.6*
3. Geometry	8. Communication *Lessons 17.2, 17.3, 17.4, 17.5, 17.6*
4. Measurement *Lessons 17.1, 17.2, 17.3, 17.4, 17.5, 17.6*	9. Connections *Lessons 17.1, 17.2, 17.4, 17.5, 17.6*
5. Data Analysis and Probability	10. Representation *Lesson 17.5*

Chapter Planner

Getting Ready for Chapter 17 • Assessing Prior Knowledge and INTERVENTION (See PE and TE page 337.)

LESSON	NORTH CAROLINA STANDARDS	PACING	VOCABULARY*	MATERIALS	RESOURCES AND TECHNOLOGY
17.1 **Length** pp. 338–341 Objective To estimate and measure length to the nearest inch and half inch	2.02b	1 Day	*Review* inch	*For each student* small paper clips, ruler	Reteach, Practice, Problem Solving, Challenge 17.1 ▫ Transparency 17.1 ⊚ **Intervention**, *Skill 52* (CD or Book) ⊚ **Harcourt Mega Math Ice Station Exploration**, *Linear Lab*
17.2 **Inch, Foot, Yard, and Mile** pp. 342–343 Objective To choose the appropriate unit and estimate length or distance	2.02b *also* 2.01b	1 Day	**foot (ft)** **yard (yd)** **mile (mi)**	*For Exercise 1* square tiles; *For Exercise 14* 1-inch grid paper	Reteach, Practice, Problem Solving, Challenge 17.2 ▫ Transparency 17.2 ⊚ **Intervention**, *Skill 52* (CD or Book) ⊚ **Harcourt Mega Math Ice Station Exploration**, *Linear Lab*
17.3 **Hands On: Capacity** pp. 344–345 Objective To estimate and measure capacity	2.02a *also* 2.01b	1 Day	**capacity** **cup (c)** **pint (pt)** **quart (qt)** **gallon (gal)**	*For each group* cup, pint, quart, gallon containers; water, rice, or beans	Reteach, Practice, Problem Solving, Challenge 17.3 ▫ Transparency 17.3 ⊚ **Intervention**, *Skill 63* (CD or Book)
17.4 **Hands On: Weight** pp. 346–347 Objective To estimate and measure weight	2.02c *also* 2.01b	1 Day	**ounce (oz)** **pound (lb)**	*For each group* simple balance, pennies, scale	Reteach, Practice, Problem Solving, Challenge 17.4 ▫ Transparency 17.4 ▫ Scaffolded Instruction Transparency 17 ▪ **Math Jingles® CD 3–4** ⊚ **Harcourt Mega Math Country Countdown**, *Harrison's Comparisons*
17.5 **Ways to Change Units** pp. 348–349 Objective To change units of measure	2.01b	1 Day			Reteach, Practice, Problem Solving, Challenge 17.5 ▫ Transparency 17.5 ⊚ **Intervention**, *Skill 63* (CD or Book) ⊚ **Harcourt Mega Math The Number Games**, *Tiny's Think Tank*
17.6 **Problem Solving Skill: Estimate or Measure** pp. 350–351 Objective To determine whether an estimate or a measured amount is needed to solve a problem	2.02	1 Day		▦	Reteach, Practice, Reading Strategy, Challenge 17.6 ▫ Transparency 17.6 ▫ Reading Transparency 17 ⊚ **Intervention • Problem Solving**, *Strategy/Skill 17* (CD or Book)

Ending Chapter 17 • Extra Practice, p. 352 • Chapter 17 Review/Test, p. 353 • Getting Ready for the EOG Test, p. 354–355

*Boldfaced terms are the key mathematical terms for the chapter. Other terms are review vocabulary.

Vocabulary Power

Review Vocabulary

To be ready for Chapter 17, students should know the following vocabulary term:

- **inch** (p. 337)—a customary unit used to measure length

Develop Key Chapter Vocabulary

The **boldfaced** words are the key vocabulary terms in the chapter.

- **foot** (p. 342)—a linear unit of measure equal to $\frac{1}{3}$ yard
- **yard** (p. 342)—a linear unit of measure equal to 3 feet
- **mile** (p. 342)—a linear unit of measure used for measuring long distances; 5,280 feet
- **capacity** (p. 344)—the amount a container can hold
- **cup** (p. 344)—a measure of capacity, equal to 8 ounces
- **pint** (p. 344)—a measure of capacity, equal to 2 cups
- **quart** (p. 344)—a measure of capacity, equal to 2 pints
- **gallon** (p. 344)—a measure of capacity, equal to 4 quarts
- **ounce** (p. 346)—a unit used to measure weight
- **pound** (p. 346)—a unit used to measure weight, equal to 16 ounces

Vocabulary Cards

Have students use the Vocabulary Cards on *Teacher's Resource Book* pages TR159–162 for the key terms in the chapter. The cards can be added to a file of mathematics terms.

Multimedia Math Glossary

For vocabulary support, visit **www.harcourtschool.com/mathglossary**

Math Journal

Have students define the key vocabulary terms: *foot, yard, mile, capacity, cup, pint, quart, gallon, ounce,* and *pound*. Have students use their own words and give an example of each.

M A T H Word Work

Objective To reinforce vocabulary concepts
Use after Lesson 17.4.

Materials *For the class* 3 large poster boards; *For each group* magazines, newspapers, art paper, crayons or pencils, glue

Label the posters **Length**, **Capacity**, and **Weight**. Divide the poster for Length into 3 sections labeled *feet, yards,* and *miles*. Divide the poster for Capacity into 4 sections labeled *cups, pints, quarts,* and *gallons*. Divide the poster for Weight into 2 sections labeled *ounces* and *pounds*.

For each unit of measure on the posters, have students work in small groups to find 2 things that would be measured in these units. Students can look for pictures or words in magazines and newspapers, or they can draw objects on art paper and cut them out. Have each group present their items to the class before gluing them to the posters.

MODIFYING INSTRUCTION You may wish to have cup, pint, and quart containers available for students to use as a reference.

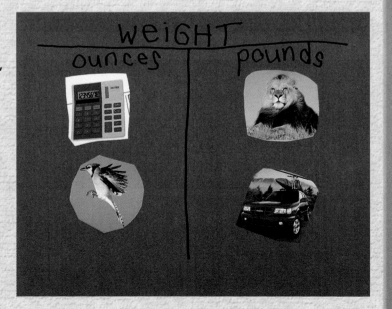

Mathematics Across the Grades

LOOKING BACK • Prerequisite Skills

To be ready for Chapter 17, students should have the following understandings and skills:

- **Measure to the Nearest Inch**—write lengths to the nearest inch

- **Find a Rule**—find a rule for number patterns

Check What You Know

Use page 337 to determine students' knowledge of prerequisite concepts and skills.

Intervention

Help students prepare for the chapter by using the intervention resources described on TE page 337.

LOOKING AT CHAPTER 17 • Essential Skills

Students will

- estimate and measure length to the nearest inch and half inch.

- choose the appropriate unit and estimate length or distance.

- estimate and measure capacity and weight.

- **convert units of measure.**

- use the problem solving skill *estimate or measure* to solve problems.

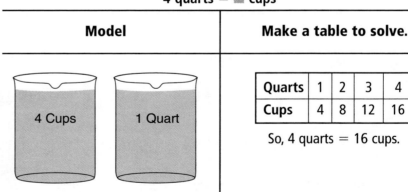

Example

4 quarts = ■ cups

Model	Make a table to solve.

4 Cups   1 Quart

Quarts	1	2	3	4
Cups	4	8	12	16

So, 4 quarts = 16 cups.

LOOKING AHEAD • Applications

Students will apply what they learn in Chapter 17 to the following new concepts:

- Estimate and Measure Length in Metric Units (Chapter 18)

- Find Mass in Metric Units (Chapter 18)

- Find Capacity in Metric Units (Chapter 18)

- Estimate and Find Volume (Chapter 22)

Differentiated Instruction

Meeting the Needs of All Learners

Extra Support	Activities for All	Enrichment
Alternative Teaching Strategy TE Lessons 17.1, 17.2, 17.3, 17.4, 17.5, 17.6 **Special Needs** TE Lesson 17.4 **ESOL/ESL** TE Lessons 17.1, 17.2, 17.3, 17.4, 17.5, 17.6	**Cross-Curricular Connections** **Career:** TE Lesson 17.2 **Language Arts:** TE Lesson 17.1 **Reading:** TE Lesson 17.6 **Science:** TE/PE Chapter Opener, TE Lesson 17.2 **Vocabulary:** TE p. 336B, PE p. 337, TE Lesson 17.6 **Writing:** TE Lessons 17.5, 17.6	**Advanced Learners** TE Lesson 17.4 **Early Finishers** TE Lessons 17.3, 17.5

Combination and Multi-age Classrooms

Grade 2	Grade 3	Grade 4
Skills Trace Across the Grades		
Measure to the nearest inch; measure length, capacity, and weight with non-standard units; review inches, feet, cups, pints, quarts, and pounds; introduce yards, gallons, and ounces.	**Measure to the nearest inch and half inch; estimate and measure length, capacity, and weight using appropriate units; convert from one unit of measurement to another.**	Choose the appropriate measurement unit; measure fractional parts; change linear units; measure capacity and weight.
Instructional Strategies		
Students on this level may require more time to build conceptual understanding. **Assignments** **Grade 3 Pupil Edition** • Have students work in small groups for Lessons 17.1, 17.3, and 17.4. • Have students skip Lessons 17.2, 17.5, and 17.6. **Grade 2 Pupil Edition**—pages 381–388 and 399–406	Students on this level should be able to complete all the lessons in the Pupil Edition and all the activities in the Teacher's Edition with minimal adjustments. **Assignment** **Grade 3 Pupil Edition**—pages 336–353	Students on this level will probably require less time to build conceptual understanding. **Assignments** **Grade 3 Pupil Edition** • Compact Lessons 17.1 and 17.2. • Extend Lesson 17.5 by challenging students to make tables to convert units of length, capacity, and weight. **Grade 4 Pupil Edition**—pages 518–531

Customary Units

Introducing the Chapter

Tell students that customary units are used to measure length, weight, capacity, and temperature. Have students focus on the graph and tell what customary unit of measurement is shown. feet

Using Data

To begin the study of this chapter, have students

* Find out how much greater the length of the space shuttle is than the length of Skylab. 4 feet

* Determine if the length of 3 space shuttles, placed end to end, would be greater than or less than the length of the Saturn Ⅴ rocket. The length of 3 space shuttles would be 3 feet greater than the length of a Saturn Ⅴ rocket.

* Compare the height of the Statue of Liberty in New York City, 305 feet, to the length of each spacecraft in the graph. 305 < 363; 305 > 122; 305 > 118

Problem Solving Project

Purpose To estimate and measure length in customary units

Grouping partners

Materials ruler or yardstick

Background The oldest moon rock brought back to Earth is more than 4 billion years old—about as old as the moon itself.

UNDERSTAND • PLAN • SOLVE • CHECK

Have students

* Record the estimates in feet and yards of the following: the height of the chalkboard and doorway, and the length and width of the hallway.

* Measure and record the actual heights, lengths, and widths to the nearest foot or yard.

* Compare the results with those of another pair of students. Check students' work.

Graphing Investigations
Begin Week 17.

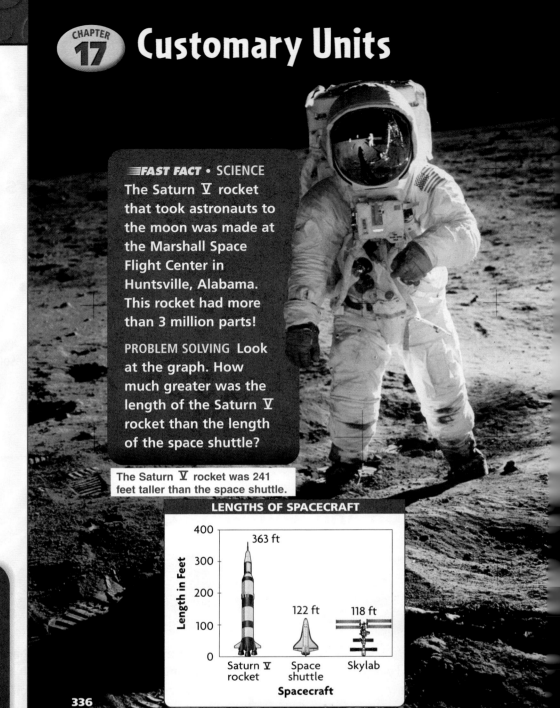

⚡FAST FACT • SCIENCE
The Saturn Ⅴ rocket that took astronauts to the moon was made at the Marshall Space Flight Center in Huntsville, Alabama. This rocket had more than 3 million parts!

PROBLEM SOLVING Look at the graph. How much greater was the length of the Saturn Ⅴ rocket than the length of the space shuttle?

The Saturn Ⅴ rocket was 241 feet taller than the space shuttle.

LENGTHS OF SPACECRAFT

363 ft

122 ft   118 ft

Length in Feet: 0, 100, 200, 300, 400

Saturn Ⅴ rocket   Space shuttle   Skylab

Spacecraft

336

WHY LEARN MATH? Astronauts use measurement to maneuver their spacecraft and conduct experiments. Ask: Besides temperatures, what might astronauts need to measure? Possible answer: lengths, weights, capacities

Family Involvement Activities

These activities provide:

* Letter to the Family
* Math Vocabulary
* Family Game
* Practice (Homework)

Family Involvement Activities, p. FA65

HARCOURT MATH
GRADE 3
Chapter 17
WHAT WE ARE LEARNING
Customary Units

VOCABULARY
Here are the vocabulary words we use in class:
Capacity The amount a container can hold
Inch (in.), foot (ft), yard (yd), mile (mi) Customary units used to measure length or distance
Cup (c), pint (pt), quart (qt), gallon (gal) Customary units used to measure capacity
Ounce (oz), pound (lb) Customary units used to measure weight

Name
Date

Dear Family,
Your child is learning about measurement using customary units.

We will learn to measure length, capacity, and weight. We will also learn how to change units. For example, to change 8 pints to quarts, your child will first decide how the units are related. Pints are smaller than quarts. 2 pints = 1 quart. Then he or she will use one of the following ways to find the answer.

One way: Solve by drawing.
Draw 8 pints. Circle groups of 2 to show quarts. There are 4 groups of 2 pints, so there are 4 quarts.

Another way: Make a table.
Put the larger measure on top.
Show 1 quart = 2 pints. Complete the table.

quarts	1	2	3	4
pints	2	4	6	8

The table shows that 4 quarts = 8 pints.

Use the activity that follows to help your child practice changing units. Encourage your child to do this activity with you and other members of your family.

Measuring in customary units is a real-life activity that builds confidence in using math.

Sincerely,

Family Involvement Activities FA65

CHECK WHAT YOU KNOW

Use this page to help you review and remember
important skills needed for Chapter 17.

✓ MEASURE TO THE NEAREST INCH

Write the length to the nearest inch.

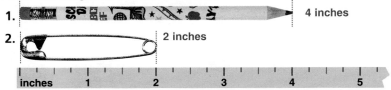

1. 4 inches

2. 2 inches

✓ FIND A RULE

Write a rule for the table. Then copy and complete
the table.

Multiply gloves by 5.

3.
gloves	1	2	3	4	5	6
fingers	5	10	15	■	■	■

20 25 30

Multiply rings by $3.

4.
rings	1	2	3	4	5	6
cost	$3	$6	$9	■	■	■

$12 $15 $18

5.
butterflies	1	5	3	4	7	9
wings	2	10	6	■	■	■

Multiply butterflies by 2. 8 14 18

6.
packs	3	2	7	5	1	8
crackers	21	14	49	■	■	■

Multiply packs by 7. 35 7 56

VOCABULARY POWER ✓

REVIEW

inch [inch] noun

When used as a noun, an *inch* is a
customary unit used to measure
length. When used as a verb, *inch*
means "to move by small amounts"
or "to move slowly." Write one
sentence using *inch* as a noun and
one sentence using *inch* as a verb.
Check students' sentences.

PREVIEW

foot (ft)	pint (pt)
yard (yd)	quart (qt)
mile (mi)	gallon (gal)
capacity	ounce (oz)
cup (c)	pound (lb)

GO ON-LINE www.harcourtschool.com/mathglossary

Assessing Prior Knowledge

Use the **Check What You Know** page to determine
whether your students have mastered the prerequisite skills critical for this chapter.

Intervention

- **Diagnose and Prescribe**
Evaluate your students' performance on this page
to determine whether intervention is necessary or
if enrichment is appropriate. Options that provide
instruction, practice, and a check are listed in the
chart below.

✓ CHECK WHAT YOU KNOW RESOURCES

Intervention Copying Masters or CD-ROMs

Enrichment Copying Masters

VOCABULARY POWER

For activities and information about the vocabulary in this chapter, see page 336B.

Were students successful with ✓ **CHECK WHAT YOU KNOW?**

IF ... **NO** THEN ... INTERVENE   **INTERVENTION OPTIONS**   IF ... **YES** THEN ... ENRICH

Skill/Items	Missed more than	Intervene with
Measure to the Nearest Inch, 1–2	0	• *Intervention*, Skill 52
Find a Rule, 3–6	1	• *Intervention*, Skill 63

Skill/Items	Missed fewer than	Enrich with
Measure to the Nearest Inch, 1–2	1	• *Intervention*, Enrichment p. IN361
Find a Rule, 3–6	2	• *Intervention*, Enrichment p. IN362

Lesson Planning

Objective To estimate and measure length to the nearest inch and half inch

Materials *For each student* small paper clips, ruler

NCTM Standards
1. Number and Operations
4. Measurement
6. Problem Solving
9. Connections

Math Background

Consider the following when introducing measuring length to the nearest inch and half inch.

- A measurement is a comparison.

- Each aspect of an object that can be measured is an attribute. The attribute length can be compared directly by placing one length in line with another.

- Estimate length by using objects that are about an inch long.

- Use a ruler when a more accurate measure is needed. Determine what accuracy is needed, such as to the nearest inch or half inch, and then make the measurement.

Warm-Up Resources

Number of the Day

Transparency **17.1**

Write two multiplication facts whose product is the number of sides in an octagon. Possible answers: $4 \times 2 = 8, 8 \times 1 = 8$

Daily Facts Practice

Have students practice multiplication and division facts by completing Set D of *Teacher's Resource Book*, p. TR95.

Transparency **17.1**

Problem of the Day

It took Silvia and Nick a total of 48 minutes to complete their homework. If it took Nick twice as long as Silvia, how long did it take each one? It took Nick 32 minutes and Silvia 16 minutes.

Solution Problem of the Day tab, p. PD17

Intervention and Extension Resources

Alternative Teaching Strategy

MATERIALS *For each student* lengths of string from 1 to 6 inches, ruler

Have students **estimate length using hands-on materials.** Have students arrange the strings from shortest to longest. Ask them to estimate the length of each string. Then have them check their estimate by measuring each string. Check students' work.

See also page 340.

KINESTHETIC

BODILY/KINESTHETIC

Multistep and Strategy Problems

The following multistep or strategy problem is provided in Lesson 17.1:

Page	Item
341	27

ESOL/ESL

MATERIALS *For each pair* magazines, scissors

Have students **estimate length** by looking through magazines to find pictures that are about 2 inches, 4 inches, and 6 inches in length. Have students cut out the pictures, label them, and share them with others. Check students' work.

VISUAL

VISUAL/SPATIAL

Language Arts Connection

Have students **discuss estimation.** Read *How Big Is a Foot?* by Rolf Myller. Then discuss these questions as a class: Answers will vary.

* Why did the first bed that the apprentice built turn out to be the wrong size?
* If you and a friend each made a bed to fit the size of your feet, would your beds be the same size? Explain your answer.
* How would a carpenter build a custom bed for you today?

AUDITORY

VERBAL/LINGUISTIC

Technology Link

💿 **Intervention,** *Skill 52*

💿 **Harcourt Mega Math Ice Station Exploration,** *Linear Lab,* Levels A, B, C, and D

GO The Harcourt Learning Site www.harcourtschool.com

Lesson 17.1 Organizer

Objective To estimate and measure length to the nearest inch and half inch

Materials *For each student* small paper clips, ruler

Vocabulary *Review* inch

---

1 INTRODUCE

QUICK REVIEW provides review of prerequisite skills.

WHY LEARN THIS? You will be able to look at an object and estimate its length close to the actual measurement. *Share the lesson objective with students.*

2 TEACH

Guided Instruction

- *Direct students' attention to the Remember box.* **If there is not a zero on a ruler, how would you know where to find the zero mark for the ruler?** Look for the first mark on the left end of the ruler.

- *Ask students to read the Learn section.* **REASONING Name an example of a time when you might estimate the length of something instead of measuring.** Possible answer: You might estimate how much string you would need to tie a package.
Which ribbon is longest? the blue ribbon
How do you find the number of inches when a ribbon does not line up exactly with an inch mark? Find the inch mark that is closest to the end of the ribbon.

MODIFYING INSTRUCTION After students measure and record information on the table, ask them to measure their pencils to the nearest half inch. To extend the activity, display an enlarged portion of a ruler and review the marks for $\frac{1}{2}$ inch and $\frac{1}{4}$ inch. Have volunteers measure their pencils to the nearest quarter inch.

338 Chapter 17

1 Length

Quick Review

1. $7 \times \blacksquare = 42$ $\underset{6}{}$ 2. $\blacksquare \times 5 = 45$ $\underset{9}{}$
3. $\blacksquare \times 8 = 32$ $\underset{4}{}$ 4. $6 \times \blacksquare = 48$ $\underset{8}{}$
5. $9 \times \blacksquare = 63$ $\underset{7}{}$

▶ Learn

HOW LONG? An estimate is an answer that is close to the actual answer. You can estimate length by using an item close to 1 inch, like a small paper clip or your knuckle.

Remember

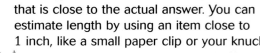

To use a ruler:

- line up one end of the object with the zero mark on the ruler.
- find the inch mark closest to the object's other end.

The ribbon is 2 inches long to the nearest inch.

HANDS ON Activity

MATERIALS: small paper clips, ruler

STEP 1

Copy the table.

LENGTHS OF RIBBONS		
Color	**Estimate**	**Measure**
green	about 1 inch	1 inch
blue		5 in.
yellow		2 in.
orange		4 in.
red		3 in.

STEP 2

Use paper clips to estimate the length of the blue ribbon. Record your estimate in your table. **Accept reasonable estimates.**

STEP 3

Use a ruler. Measure the length of the blue ribbon to the nearest inch. Record your measurement in your table.

STEP 4

Repeat Steps 2 and 3 for the yellow, orange, and red ribbons.

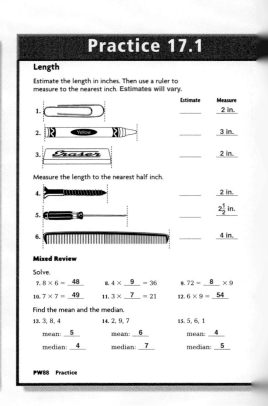

- Why does it make sense to use a small paper clip to estimate inches? A small paper clip has a length of about 1 inch.

338

Reteach 17.1

Length

Sometimes you want to know **about** how long an object is.

You can use a ruler to measure an object.
- Line up one end of the object with the left end of the ruler.
- Look at the other end of the object.

Find the closest inch mark.	When you need a measurement that is more accurate, you can measure to the nearest half inch.
The pencil is about 3 inches long, to the nearest inch.	The crayon is about $2\frac{1}{2}$ inches long, to the nearest half inch.

Use a ruler to measure to the nearest inch.

Measure

1. _____ **1** in.

2. _____ **3** in.

Use a ruler to measure the length to the nearest half inch.

3. _____ **4$\frac{1}{2}$** in.

4. _____ **3$\frac{1}{2}$** in.

RW88 Reteach

Practice 17.1

Length

Estimate the length in inches. Then use a ruler to measure to the nearest inch. Estimates will vary.

	Estimate	**Measure**
1.	_____	**2 in.**
2.	_____	**3 in.**
3.	_____	**2 in.**

Measure the length to the nearest half inch.

4.	**2 in.**
5.	**2$\frac{1}{2}$ in.**
6.	**4 in.**

Mixed Review

Solve.

7. $8 \times 6 = $ **48**   8. $4 \times$ **9** $= 36$ 9. $72 = $ **8** $\times 9$

10. $7 \times 7 = $ **49**   11. $3 \times$ **7** $= 21$ 12. $6 \times 9 = $ **54**

Find the mean and the median.

13. 3, 8, 4   14. 2, 9, 7   15. 5, 6, 1

mean: **5**   mean: **6**   mean: **4**

median: **4**   median: **7**   median: **5**

PW88 Practice

Measuring to the Nearest Half Inch

You can also measure to the nearest half inch.

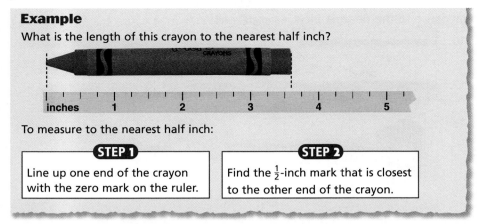

Example

What is the length of this crayon to the nearest half inch?

To measure to the nearest half inch:

STEP 1

Line up one end of the crayon with the zero mark on the ruler.

STEP 2

Find the $\frac{1}{2}$-inch mark that is closest to the other end of the crayon.

So, the length of the crayon to the nearest half inch is $3\frac{1}{2}$ inches.

▶ Check

1. Describe where you find $\frac{1}{2}$-inch marks on a ruler.

halfway between the inch marks

Estimate the length in inches. Then use a ruler to measure to the nearest inch. Estimates will vary.

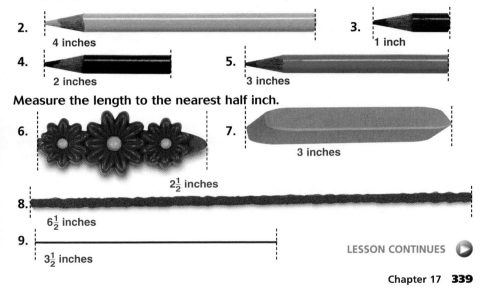

2. 4 inches

3. 1 inch

4. 2 inches

5. 3 inches

Measure the length to the nearest half inch.

6. $2\frac{1}{2}$ inches

7. 3 inches

8. $6\frac{1}{2}$ inches

9. $3\frac{1}{2}$ inches

LESSON CONTINUES ▶

Chapter 17 **339**

North Carolina Standards 2.02 Estimate and measure using appropriate units. b) Length

---

3 PRACTICE

Guided Practice

Do Check Exercises 1–9 with your students. Identify the students who are having difficulty and choose appropriate lesson resources to provide assistance.

///// **COMMON ERROR ALERT** /////

If students have difficulty making correct measurements, make sure they are lining up the left end or zero mark of the ruler with one end of the object they are measuring.

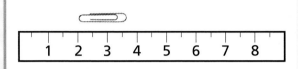

Challenge 17.1

No Rulers Allowed!

Measure and cut a 5-inch strip and a 2-inch strip from a piece of paper.

| 5 inches |

| 2 inches |

Use the two strips to measure the drawings in Problems 1–4 to the nearest half inch. Do **not** use a ruler.

Hints:

• If you fold each strip in half, you will have two more measuring strips. Half of the 5-inch strip will be $2\frac{1}{2}$ inches long. Half of the 2-inch strip will be ___1 inch long___.

• You can compare or combine the rulers to form different lengths.

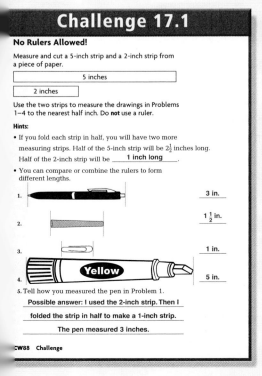

1. 3 in.

2. $1\frac{1}{2}$ in.

3. 1 in.

4. 5 in.

5. Tell how you measured the pen in Problem 1.

Possible answer: I used the 2-inch strip. Then I folded the strip in half to make a 1-inch strip. The pen measured 3 inches.

CW88 Challenge

Problem Solving 17.1

Length

Understand ▶ Plan ▶ Solve ▶ Check

Write the correct answer.

1. Ramses baked 63 cookies for his class party. If he made 9 batches, how many cookies did he make per batch?

7 cookies

2. Ms. Price chose 8 students from each third grade class to participate in the school musical, for a total of 32 students. How many classes participated?

4 classes

3. Estimate the length of this marker to the nearest inch.

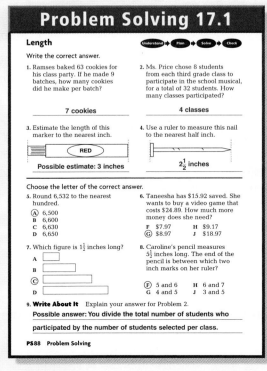

RED

Possible estimate: 3 inches

4. Use a ruler to measure this nail to the nearest half inch.

$2\frac{1}{2}$ inches

Choose the letter of the correct answer.

5. Round 6,532 to the nearest hundred.

Ⓐ 6,500
B 6,600
C 6,630
D 6,650

6. Taneesha has $15.92 saved. She wants to buy a video game that costs $24.89. How much more money does she need?

F $7.97   H $9.17
Ⓖ $8.97   J $18.97

7. Which figure is $1\frac{1}{2}$ inches long?

A
B
Ⓒ
D

8. Caroline's pencil measures $5\frac{1}{2}$ inches long. The end of the pencil is between which two inch marks on her ruler?

Ⓕ 5 and 6   H 6 and 7
G 4 and 5   J 3 and 5

9. Write About It Explain your answer for Problem 2.

Possible answer: You divide the total number of students who participated by the number of students selected per class.

PS88 Problem Solving

339

Independent Practice

Note that Exercise 27 is a **multistep or strategy problem.** Assign Exercises 10–30.

Direct students' attention to the directions preceding Exercise 15. Remind them that they will be measuring to the nearest half inch rather than to the nearest inch.

Vocabulary Power Discuss with students that packages of paper are labeled as *wide-rule* and *college-rule.* This refers to the distance in-between lines, or *rules,* on the paper. Discuss the difference between ruled and unruled paper.

Estimate the length in inches. Then use a ruler to measure to the nearest inch. Estimates will vary.

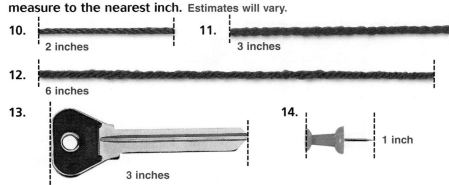

10. 2 inches
11. 3 inches
12. 6 inches
13. 3 inches
14. 1 inch

Measure the length to the nearest half inch.

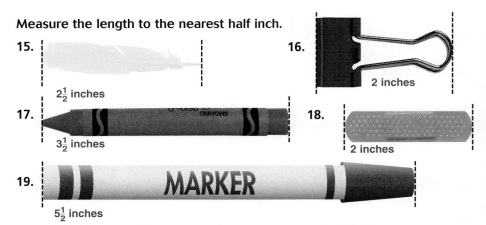

15. $2\frac{1}{2}$ inches
16. 2 inches
17. $3\frac{1}{2}$ inches
18. 2 inches
19. $5\frac{1}{2}$ inches

Use a ruler. Draw a line for each length. Check students' lines.

20. 1 inch
21. $2\frac{1}{2}$ inches
22. 4 inches
23. $5\frac{1}{2}$ inches

24. **≡FAST FACT • SCIENCE** The ruby-throated hummingbird is about 4 inches long. The brown pelican is about 40 inches long. The pelican is about how many times as long as the hummingbird?
about 10 times as long

25. **Vocabulary Power** The word *rule* comes from the Latin word *regula,* which means "straight stick." What math word is related to *rule* and could be described as a straight stick? **ruler**

26. Measure the classroom door from side to side to the nearest inch. Then measure a door at home in the same way. Which door has the greater measure?
Check students' answers.

340

Alternative Teaching Strategy   Scaffolded Instruction

PURPOSE Students use 1-inch paper strips to estimate and measure items.

MATERIALS *For each student* 2 paper ruler strips, p. TR55; scissors

In order to visually reinforce the length of a single inch, have each student cut apart one ruler strip into eight 1-inch sections.

Step 1

Give students several common items that are less than 8 inches in length, such as a pencil, a crayon, a stapler, or pieces of string. Ask students to estimate the length of each item they were given.

Step 2

Have students place individual inches of the ruler along the edge of the object to measure the actual length.

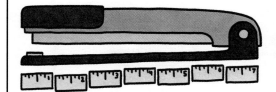

Step 3

Have students estimate the length of several other items and check their estimates using the same procedure.

Step 4

Invite students to use ruler strips to go on a "hunt" to find classroom items that measure about 2 inches, 4 inches, and 8 inches in length. They might locate items such as erasers, chalk, colored markers, and chalkboard erasers. Check students' work.

PROFESSIONAL DEVELOPMENT

27. Joyce used 72 beads to make 9 necklaces with an equal number of beads on each. How many beads were on 2 necklaces?
16 beads

28. A brush measures $6\frac{1}{2}$ inches. Between which two inch marks does the end of the brush lie? Explain. **between the 6-inch mark and the 7-inch mark; $6\frac{1}{2}$ in. is more than 6 in. but less than 7 in.**

29. Find two different-sized books. Measure the length of each cover to the nearest half inch. Use $<$ or $>$ to compare the measurements.
Check students' work.

30. Suppose you need at least 5 inches of yarn for an art project. Is this blue piece of yarn long enough? Explain. **See below.**

Getting Ready for the EOG Test

31. Mrs. Rogers used nails like the nail below when she built a birdhouse.

Which is the length of this nail to the nearest inch? **B**

A 1 inch   **C** 3 inches
B 2 inches   **D** 4 inches

32. Which is the *best* estimate for the length of a marker? **C**

A 1 inch
B 2 inches
C 5 inches
D 11 inches

30. Yes; this piece of yarn is $5\frac{1}{2}$ inches long, so it is enough yarn for the project.

Problem Solving — Thinker's Corner

You can measure lengths in more than one way. For example, use string to measure the line drawings.

MATERIALS: 2 pieces of string, each 1 ft long
2 different-colored markers

a. Start with one end of string on one end of line drawing A. Cover the line drawing with the string.

b. Make a mark on the string for the end of the line drawing.

c. Repeat for line drawing B.

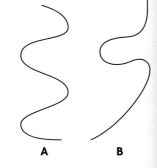

A   B

1. Which line drawing has the greater length? **B**

2. Measure the lengths marked on the pieces of string. Record the measurements.
A: 4 inches; B: 5 inches

Chapter 17 **341**

MULTISTEP OR STRATEGY PROBLEM To solve Exercise 27, students can divide $72 \div 9 = 8$. Since 8 beads are on each necklace, students can multiply $8 \times 2 = 16$ to find the number of beads on 2 necklaces.

Problem Solving — Thinker's Corner

• *Direct students' attention to the line drawings.* **Can you place a ruler next to line drawing A to find its length? Explain.** Possible answer: no; line drawing A is curved, and a ruler measures lengths that are straight.

4 ASSESS

Summarize the lesson by having students:

DISCUSS How can you estimate the length of your desk using a paper clip and then find the actual measure? Possible answer: Since a paper clip is about 1 inch long, line up paper clips along the length of the desk and count the paper clips. Then measure with a ruler.

WRITE Describe how you would measure the length of your math book to the nearest inch or half inch. Place the left end or zero mark of a ruler on the top edge of the book. Then look for the inch or half inch mark that is nearest to the bottom edge of the book.

LESSON QUIZ
Use a ruler. Draw a line for each length. Check students' work.

Transparency **17.1**

1. 4 inches

2. $5\frac{1}{2}$ inches

3. 2 inches

4. $6\frac{1}{2}$ inches

Lesson Planning

PROFESSIONAL DEVELOPMENT

Objective To choose the appropriate unit and estimate length or distance

Materials *For Exercise 1* square tiles; *For Exercise 14* 1-inch grid paper, p. TR57

NCTM Standards
1. **Number and Operations**
4. **Measurement**
6. **Problem Solving**
7. **Reasoning and Proof**
8. **Communication**
9. **Connections**

Math Background
Consider the following when helping students estimate length or distance.

- Deciding which unit to use depends upon what is being measured.
- Select the most efficient unit to express length or distance.

Vocabulary
foot (ft) a customary unit used to measure length and distance

yard (yd) a customary unit used to measure length and distance

mile (mi) a customary unit used to measure length and distance

Warm-Up Resources

Number of the Day
Transparency **17.2**

Measure the length of your shoe to the nearest inch. Use that number to write and solve five subtraction sentences. Answers will vary.

Daily Facts Practice

Have students practice multiplication and division facts by completing Set E of *Teacher's Resource Book*, p. TR95.

Transparency **17.2**

Problem of the Day

Katie, Jerry, and Adam each have a different colored pencil. The blue pencil is 5 inches long, and the red one is 6 inches long. Katie's yellow pencil is 2 inches longer than Jerry's pencil. Adam's pencil is 1 inch shorter than Katie's. How long is Katie's pencil? 7 inches long Who has the blue pencil? Jerry

Solution Problem of the Day tab, p. PD17

Intervention and Extension Resources

Alternative Teaching Strategy

MATERIALS paper clip, notebook paper, baseball bat

ESOL/ESL

Help students **recognize the length of customary units of measure** by observing and comparing real objects. Provide a paper clip, a sheet of notebook paper, and a baseball bat for students to observe and compare. Then have students use these objects to find other objects with lengths of about 1 inch, 1 foot, and 1 yard. Check students' work.

KINESTHETIC

BODILY/KINESTHETIC

Multistep and Strategy Problems

The following multistep or strategy problem is provided in Lesson 17.2:

Page	Item
343	15

Career Connection

Invite students to work in small groups to **brainstorm a list of careers for which measurement is essential.** For example, scientists who study animals use measurement to gather and share information. Have each group focus on one career and prepare a brief report on how measurement is used in that field. Have students share their results with the class. Check students' work.

VISUAL

INTERPERSONAL/SOCIAL

Science Connection

Have students **make animal fact cards that include units of measurement.**

Share the following: Walruses are large sea mammals. Their protective skin is about 1 inch thick. Their foreflippers are about 1–2 feet long. Their tusks grow to be about 1 yard long.

Have students research to find two animals and make a fact card for each, with measurement data about the animal. Have students share their animal fact cards with the class. Check students' work.

VISUAL

VERBAL/LINGUISTIC

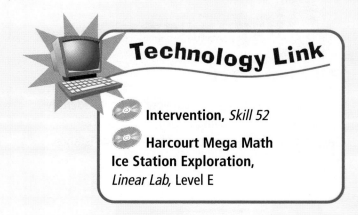

Technology Link

Intervention, *Skill 52*

Harcourt Mega Math
Ice Station Exploration,
Linear Lab, Level E

Lesson 17.2 Organizer

Objective To choose the appropriate unit and estimate length or distance

Vocabulary foot (ft), yard (yd), mile (mi)

Materials *For Exercise 1* square tiles; *For Exercise 14* 1-inch grid paper, p. TR57

1 INTRODUCE

QUICK REVIEW provides review of prerequisite skills.

WHY LEARN THIS? You will be able to estimate the lengths of objects or distances when measurements are not available. *Share the lesson objective with students.*

2 TEACH

Guided Instruction

MODIFYING INSTRUCTION Ask students to suggest other items that have the same length as the paper clip, notebook paper, baseball bat, and distance walked.

• *Point out that the abbreviation for inch (in.) has a period so that it is not confused with the word* in. **How can you decide which customary unit to use when measuring something?** by choosing a unit based on the size of the object or the distance

• *Review the information in the Table of Measures.* **Which unit would you use to measure the length of a rubber band? Explain.** inch; A rubber band is too short to measure in feet, yards, or miles.
What are some distances that you might measure in miles? Possible answers: distances between locations; distances you walk or run; distances traveled in cars, trains, or planes

3 PRACTICE

Guided Practice

Do Check Exercises 1–5 with your students. Identify students who are having difficulty and choose appropriate lesson resources to provide assistance.

---

2 Inch, Foot, Yard, and Mile

Quick Review
1. $41 + 52$ 93
2. $38 + 39$ 77
3. $12 + 34$ 46
4. $27 + 63$ 90
5. $12 + 12 + 12$ 36

VOCABULARY
foot (ft)
yard (yd)
mile (mi)

▶ **Learn**

CHOOSING UNITS   You know that an inch (in.) is used to measure length and distance. Other customary units used to measure length and distance are the **foot (ft)**, **yard (yd)**, and **mile (mi)**.

Examples

A paper clip is about 1 inch long.

A sheet of notebook paper is about 1 foot long.

A baseball bat is about 1 yard long.

You can walk 1 mile in about 20 minutes.

TABLE OF MEASURES
1 foot = 12 inches
1 yard = 3 feet = 36 inches
1 mile = 5,280 feet

• Explain which unit you would use to measure the length of your hand. inches; because my hand is less than 1 foot long

▶ **Check**

1. **Build** a 1-foot "ruler" using 1-inch square tiles. Use it to measure one side of a sheet of paper. **Check students' work.**

Choose the unit you would use to measure each. Write *inch, foot, yard,* **or** *mile*. **Possible answers are given.**

2. the length of a pencil inch
3. the length of a car foot or yard
4. the length of a parking lot yard
5. the distance a train goes in 30 minutes mile

A yardstick is 3 times as long as a 1-foot ruler.

342

Reteach 17.2

Inch, Foot, Yard, and Mile

The **inch (in.)**, **foot (ft)**, **yard (yd)**, and **mile (mi)** are customary units used to measure length or distance.

The length of a grasshopper is about 1 inch.   The length of Mr. Lee's boot is about 1 foot.   The height of Sara's little brother is about 1 yard.   The distance across Clear Lake is about 1 mile.

Complete each sentence. Write *more* **or** *less*.

1. The length of a jump rope is __more__ than 1 foot.
2. The length of a paintbrush is __more__ than 1 inch.
3. The distance you can throw a ball is __less__ than 1 mile.
4. The length of a ladybug is __less__ than 1 inch.
5. The length of a spoon is __less__ than 1 yard.
6. The height of a goat is __more__ than 1 foot.
7. The length of a classroom is __more__ than 1 yard.
8. The distance around a city is __more__ than 1 mile.

Choose the best unit to measure each item. Match by drawing a line.

9. the height of a door ——— inch
10. the distance across a football field ——— yard
11. the length of a carrot ——— mile
12. the distance between two towns ——— foot

Reteach   RW89

Practice 17.2

Inch, Foot, Yard, and Mile

Choose the unit you would use to measure each. Write *inch, foot, yard,* **or** *mile*. **Possible answers are given.**

1. the length of a table
   __foot__
2. the length of a pine cone
   __inch__
3. the length of a driveway
   __foot or yard__
4. the distance to the next town
   __mile__

Choose the best unit of measure. Write *inches, feet, yards,* **or** *miles*. **Possible answers are given.**

5. A pencil is about __5__ __inches__ long.
6. The distance from your home to the library is about 2 __miles__.
7. A bike is about __4__ __feet__ long.
8. The woman bought about __4__ __yards__ of fabric.
9. A sports card is about __3__ __inches__ long.
10. A man is about __6__ __feet__ tall.

Mixed Review

Find each product.

11. $7 \times 2 =$ __14__
12. __45__ $= 9 \times 5$
13. $6 \times 6 =$ __36__

Find each quotient.

14. $14 \div 2 =$ __7__
15. $27 \div 3 =$ __9__
16. __3__ $= 18 \div 6$
17. $24 \div 6 =$ __4__
18. __5__ $= 20 \div 4$
19. $8 \div 4 =$ __2__

Practice   PW89

Choose the unit you would use to measure each.
Write *inch, foot, yard,* or *mile*. Possible answers are given.

6. the height of a refrigerator **foot**

7. the length of your shoe **inch**

8. the length of the cafeteria **yard**

9. the distance between two cities **mile**

Choose the best unit of measure.
Write *inches, foot* or *feet, yards,* or *miles*.

10. Sal rides the bus 3 _?_ to school. **miles**

11. A football is about 1 _?_ long. **foot**

12. The distance between the floor and the doorknob is about 3 _?_ . **feet**

13. Sarah's math book is 11 _?_ long. **inches**

14. Cut a sheet of 1-inch grid paper into 6-inch strips. Use the strips and tape to make a 1-foot strip and a 1-yard strip. How many strips were needed for each? **2 strips; 6 strips**

15. Mitchell got 5 stickers from each of 6 friends. He bought 13 more stickers. How many stickers does Mitchell have in all? **43 stickers**

16. Angie thinks this grasshopper is about 4 inches long. Do you agree with her estimate? Measure to check and record the length. **disagree; 2 inches**

17. 📓 **Write About It** Estimate the distance from your desk to the classroom door in feet and in yards. Then measure the distance. Record your estimates and the actual measurement. **Check estimates and measurements.**

Getting Ready for the EOG Test

18. Which unit of measure would be the best choice for finding the length of this key? **A**

A inch
B foot
C yard
D mile

North Carolina Standards 2.02 Estimate and measure using appropriate units. b) Length (miles, ometers). *also* **2.01b**

Independent Practice

Note that Exercise 15 is a **multistep or strategy problem**. Assign Exercises 6–17.

Remind students that greater distances are usually measured in larger units of measure, and smaller units are used to measure lesser distances.

4 ASSESS

Summarize the lesson by having students:

Discuss Why is it important to have customary units of measure? Possible answer: so that everyone can find the same measure; so that we can talk about lengths and know what they are

📓 **Write** In your journal, list 4 customary units of measurement used in the United States to measure length or distance. List them in order from least to greatest and give an example of when you might use one of them to measure. inch, foot, yard, and mile; Answers will vary.

LESSON QUIZ
Choose the best unit of measure.
Write *inch, foot, yard,* or *mile*.

Transparency **17.2**

1. distance between Florida and North Carolina **mile**

2. height of a person **foot**

3. width of a chalkboard **yard**

4. thickness of your notebook **inch**

Challenge 17.2

Choose the Best Unit

1. What is the best unit for measuring each item on the quilt? Use the key to color each triangle on the quilt.
Check students' work.

Key	
inch	red
foot or yard	yellow
mile	green

length of earthworm **red**	height of cat **red**
length of driveway **y** / height of tree **y** / distance you can throw a baseball **y** / distance around a baseball diamond **y**	
green distance from New York City to San Francisco	green distance from Earth to the moon
distance you can bicycle in one hour **green** / distance across pond **y** / length of classroom **y**	distance from your house to the next town **green** / length of fence around garden **y** / length of dog leash **y**
distance around waist **red**	width of photograph **red**

2. In the top border of the quilt, write the name of an item to be measured in feet or yards. Color the top border yellow. Answers will vary. Check students' answers.

3. In the bottom border of the quilt, write the name of an item to be measured in miles. Color the bottom border green. Answers will vary. Check students' answers.

4. In each side border of the quilt, write the name of an item to be measured in inches. Color the side borders red. Answers will vary. Check students' answers.

Challenge **CW89**

Problem Solving 17.2

Inch, Foot, Yard, and Mile   Understand ► Plan ► Solve ► Check

Write the correct answer.

1. What unit would you use to measure the distance between towns? Write *inch, foot, yard,* or *mile*.
_____ **mile**

2. Compare the units of measure. Write <, >, or =.
4 feet ⬤ 1 yard
_____ **>**

3. Calvin has a yardstick and a 12-inch ruler. Which would be better to use to measure the length of a pencil?
_____ **the ruler**

4. A garden tool measures 11½ inches. The end of the tool is between which two inch marks?
_____ **11 and 12**

Choose the letter of the correct answer.

5. Which unit would you use to measure the length of your bedroom?

A inches   C yards
Ⓑ feet   D miles

6. Which would you **not** measure using inch, foot, yard, or mile?

F the distance from your house to school
G the length of a piece of chalk
H your height
Ⓙ your weight

7. What is the missing factor?
_?_ × 6 = 42

A 6   C 8
Ⓑ 7   D 9

8. Which number is twenty thousand three hundred and forty-six?

F 2,643   H 20,364
G 20,346   J 200,346

9. **Write About It** Explain your answer to Problem 3.
Possible answer: A ruler is smaller, so it would be easier to use to measure a pencil.

Problem Solving **PS89**

HANDS ON

Lesson Planning

PROFESSIONAL DEVELOPMENT

Objective To estimate and measure capacity

Materials *For each group* cup, pint, quart, gallon containers; water, rice, or beans

NCTM Standards
1. **Number and Operations**
2. **Algebra**
4. **Measurement**
6. **Problem Solving**
7. **Reasoning and Proof**
8. **Communication**

Math Background
These ideas will help students understand measuring capacity with customary units.

- To measure capacity, an indirect method is required, such as filling a container with beans and then pouring beans into another container.

- When estimating capacity, choose a benchmark unit, such as a cup of water, to determine whether small containers hold more than or less than a cup.

- Estimating capacity is a visual skill.

Vocabulary
capacity the amount a container can hold

cup (c) a customary unit used to measure capacity

pint (pt) a customary unit used to measure capacity

quart (qt) a customary unit used to measure capacity

gallon (gal) a customary unit used to measure capacity

Warm-Up Resources

Build Number Sense
3
2
1

Number of the Day

Transparency 17.3

The Number of the Day is 12—the number of items in a dozen. If a baker has 12 cups of flour and his muffin recipe calls for 3 cups of flour, how many batches of muffins can he bake? 4 batches

Review Basic Facts
8
+3

Daily Facts Practice

Have students practice subtraction facts by completing Set F of *Teacher's Resource Book*, p. TR95.

Solve a Problem

Transparency 17.3

Problem of the Day

Stan, Bruce, and Rita each measured a different item. Stan did not measure in inches. Neither Bruce nor Rita used a yardstick. Rita's measure was greater than Bruce's. Which of the following objects were measured in inches, feet, or yards and who measured each item?
a. a small table feet; Rita
b. an envelope inches; Bruce
c. a cafeteria yards; Stan

Solution Problem of the Day tab, p. PD17

Intervention and Extension Resources

Alternative Teaching Strategy

MATERIALS cup, pint, quart, gallon containers, and rice or beans

Help students **understand capacity** by having them pour contents from containers, rather than fill them. Have students fill a pint container with rice or beans. Then ask them to pour the contents into cup containers. Ask: How many cups could you fill with the contents of the pint container? 2 cups Continue the same activity with quart and gallon containers. Check students' work.

VISUAL, KINESTHETIC

BODILY/KINESTHETIC

Multistep and Strategy Problems

The following multistep or strategy problem is provided in Lesson 17.3:

Page	Item
345	8

ESOL/ESL

MATERIALS *For each pair* index cards

Help students **compare capacities**. Make a set of flashcards with a capacity pictured on each card, such as: 3 cups, 1 pint, or 2 quarts. Have pairs of students take turns drawing two cards and identifying the greater capacity. Tell students to phrase their answers in the form of a sentence: "Three cups is more than one pint." If they draw two cards with equal capacities, have them make a statement such as "Two cups equal one pint." Check students' work.

AUDITORY

VERBAL/LINGUISTIC

Early Finishers

MATERIALS *For each pair* index cards

Invite students to make a game to **identify equivalent capacities.**

- On pairs of index cards, have students write equivalent capacities, such as *2 cups* and *1 pint* or *4 quarts* and *1 gallon*. Have them make 6 pairs of cards using units of cups, pints, quarts, and gallons.
- Players shuffle the cards and place them face down.
- Students take turns trying to pick a pair of cards that shows equivalent capacities. Check students' work.

VISUAL

VISUAL/SPATIAL

Technology Link

Intervention, *Skill 63*

Lesson 17.3 Organizer

Objective To estimate and measure capacity

Vocabulary capacity, cup (c), pint (pt), quart (qt), gallon (gal)

Materials *For each group* cup, pint, quart, gallon containers; water, rice, or beans

---

1 INTRODUCE

QUICK REVIEW provides review of prerequisite skills.

WHY LEARN THIS? You can decide which customary units to use when measuring liquids. *Share the lesson objective with students.*

2 TEACH

Guided Instruction

- *Have students look at Step 1.*
Why does it make sense that your estimate must be more than 1 cup? Possible answer: the pint container is larger than the cup.

- *Direct students' attention to Steps 2–4.*
REASONING Do you predict that the number of cups in the table will increase or decrease? Explain. Possible answer: increase; the containers increase in size.

- *Use the data in the students' completed tables.*
How many cups are in 2 quarts? 8 cups
Are 2 quarts more than or less than 1 gallon? How do you know? less than; There are 8 cups in 2 quarts and 16 cups in 1 gallon.

MODIFYING INSTRUCTION You may wish to extend the lesson by including several containers that are nonstandard, irregular shapes and sizes. Have students estimate the capacity for each and then find the actual capacity and compare it to their estimates.

3 PRACTICE

Guided Practice

Complete Try It Exercises a–b with your students. Identify students who are having difficulty and choose appropriate lesson resources to provide assistance.

344 Chapter 17

LESSON
3

 **Capacity**

Quick Review
1. $2\overline{)8}$ 2. $4\overline{)16}$
3. $4\overline{)8}$ 4. $4\overline{)32}$
5. $2\overline{)16}$

▶ **Explore**

Capacity is the amount a container can hold. **Cup (c)**, **pint (pt)**, **quart (qt)**, and **gallon (gal)** are customary units for measuring capacity.

cup (c)   pint (pt)   quart (qt)   gallon (gal)

VOCABULARY
capacity   quart (qt)
cup (c)   gallon (gal)
pint (pt)

MATERIALS
cup, pint, quart, and gallon containers; water, rice, or beans

Activity

Copy the table to help find how many cups are in a pint, a quart, and a gallon.

NUMBER OF CUPS	Estimate	Measure
Cups in a pint?		
Cups in a quart?		
Cups in a gallon?		

STEP 1
Estimate the number of cups it will take to fill the pint container. Record your estimate.

STEP 2
Fill a cup and pour it into the pint container. Repeat until the pint container is full.

STEP 3
Record the actual number of cups it took to fill the pint container.

STEP 4
Repeat Steps 1–3 for the quart and the gallon containers.

Try It

a. How many pints does it take to fill a quart?
2 pints
b. How many pints does it take to fill a gallon?
8 pints

344

We are using pints to fill a quart. How many pints will it take?
2 pints

Reteach 17.3

Capacity
Capacity is the amount a container can hold.
Cup (c), **pint (pt)**, **quart (qt)**, and **gallon (gal)** are customary units used to measure capacity.

2 cups = 1 pint   2 pints = 1 quart   4 quarts = 1 gallon

Circle the unit of measure that is greater.
1. cup (pint) 2. (gallon) quart 3. (quart) pint

Complete each sentence. Write *more* or *less*.
4. A swimming pool contains ___more___ than 1 gallon.
5. A juice pitcher contains ___more___ than 1 cup.
6. A coffee mug contains ___less___ than 1 quart.

In each pair, circle the amount that is greater. Use the models above, or make your own to help you.
7. 2 quarts   (1 gallon)
8. (4 cups)   1 pint
9. (6 pints)   1 quart
10. 2 cups   (1 gallon)
11. 4 pints   (4 quarts)

RW90 Reteach

Practice 17.3

Capacity
Circle the better estimate.
1. 10 quarts or (10 gallons)
2. 2 cups or (2 quarts)

Compare. Write <, >, or = in each ○.
3. 3 cups (>) 1 pint
4. 1 gallon (=) 4 quarts
5. 3 pints (<) 2 quarts
6. 1 gallon (>) 10 cups
7. 7 pints (<) 1 gallon
8. 2 gallons (=) 16 pints

Mixed Review
9. $\begin{array}{r} 6 \\ \times 8 \\ \hline 48 \end{array}$
10. $\begin{array}{r} 9 \\ \times 9 \\ \hline 81 \end{array}$
11. $\begin{array}{r} 86 \\ -51 \\ \hline 35 \end{array}$
12. $\begin{array}{r} 99 \\ -83 \\ \hline 16 \end{array}$
13. $7\overline{)63}$ = 9
14. $5\overline{)40}$ = 8
15. $6\overline{)24}$ = 4
16. $1\overline{)12}$ = 12

17. Find the sum of 862 and 137.
999
18. Find the product of 6 and 9.
54

19. Which number is greater: 736 or 763.
763
20. Which number is less: 432 or 423.
423

21. What is 4×8?
32
22. What is $64 \div 8$?
8

PW90 Practice

Connect

How are cups, pints, quarts, and gallons related?

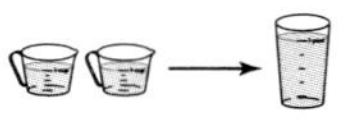

2 cups in 1 pint 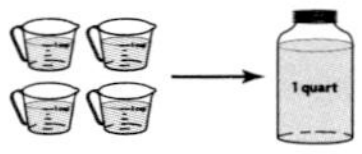 | 4 cups in 1 quart | 2 pints in 1 quart

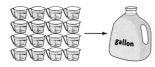  

16 cups in 1 gallon | 8 pints in 1 gallon | 4 quarts in 1 gallon

Practice and Problem Solving

Choose the better estimate.

1.

1 cup or
1 gallon?
1 gallon

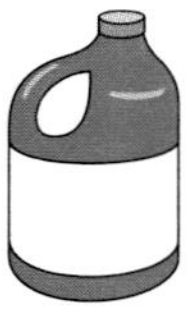

2.
3 cups or
3 quarts?
3 quarts

3.

2 cups or
2 quarts?
2 cups

4.

30 pints or
30 gallons?
30 gallons

Compare. Write <, >, or = for each ●.

5. 1 cup ● 3 pints
<

6. 1 gallon ● 3 quarts
>

7. 4 pints ● 1 quart
>

8. Alan had 6 boxes of cookies. Each box had 8 cookies. He sold 2 boxes. How many cookies does he have left? **32 cookies**

9. Write these units of capacity in order from least to greatest: *pint, cup, gallon, quart.*
cup, pint, quart, gallon

Getting Ready for the EOG Test

10. Mr. Williamson is making a pitcher of fruit punch for 4 guests. About how much should he make? **C**

A 4 ounces
B 1 cup
C 1 quart
D 3 gallons

Chapter 17 **345**

North Carolina Standards 2.02 Estimate and measure using appropriate units. a) Capacity (cups, ts, quarts, gallons, liters). *also* 2.01b

Independent Practice

Note that Exercise 8 is a **multistep or strategy problem.** Assign Exercises 1–9.

Summarize the lesson by having students:

DISCUSS What are some different units of measure you could use to measure the capacity of a kitchen sink? Possible answers: cup, pint, quart, gallon

Which unit of measure do you think would be the best choice to use? Explain. gallon; You need the fewest of them.

WRITE Eva is making a recipe that calls for 5 cups of milk. Milk is sold in quarts, half gallons, and gallons. Which quantity should Eva buy? Why? Possible answer: a half gallon or a gallon; A quart would not be enough because there are only 4 cups in a quart.

LESSON QUIZ
Compare. Write <, >, or = for each ●.

Transparency **17.3**

1. 3 cups ● 1 pint **>**

2. 2 cups ● 1 quart **<**

3. 3 pints ● 1 quart **>**

4. 4 quarts ● 1 gallon **=**

Challenge 17.3

Making Sense of Measurements

Each box below makes a statement about capacity. Circle the letter in the box if the statement could be true. Form the answer to the riddle by writing the circled letters in order on the blanks.

1. **A** A punch bowl holds 10 gallons.	2. ⓩ A medicine bottle holds less than 1 cup.	3. **O** A bathtub holds less than 3 quarts.
4. Ⓔ A tea kettle holds about 1 quart.	5. Ⓡ Beth drinks about 3 cups of milk a day.	6. **T** An eyedropper holds about 1 cup.
7. Ⓞ Sam bought 2 quarts of ice cream for his party.	8. **S** John's mug holds about 1 quart.	9. Ⓒ Mary and Liz shared a pint of juice.
10. **R** The sink holds 20 gallons of water.	11. Ⓤ Mrs. Frank made 2 quarts of soup.	12. **E** A car's gas tank holds less than 1 gallon.
13. Ⓟ Jane used 3 gallons of water to wash her lunch dishes.	14. Ⓢ Mr. Green made punch with 2 quarts of juice and 1 pint of sherbet.	15. **T** Sam poured 1 quart of milk into his glass.

How many cups of water can a funnel hold?

Z E R O   C U P S

W90 Challenge

Problem Solving 17.3

Capacity

Understand → Plan → Solve → Check

Write the correct answer.

1. Which unit would you use to measure juice in a glass? Write *cup, pint, quart,* or *gallon.*

cup

2. Choose the unit you would use to measure gas in a car. Write *cup, pint, quart,* or *gallon.*

gallon

3. Eli picked 3 cups of raspberries and a pint of strawberries. How many cups of fruit did he pick in all?

5 cups

4. Mia has one gallon of milk. Her mother bought one quart of milk. How many quarts do they have in all?

5 quarts

Choose the letter of the correct answer.

5. Which is *not* a customary unit for measuring capacity?

A cup
B pint
Ⓒ bucket
D quart

6. Which amount is less than $2.49?

F $3.29
G $2.95
H $2.84
Ⓙ $2.48

7. Which unit would be best to measure the eraser?

ERASER

Ⓐ inch
B yard
C mile
D foot

8. Heather began soccer practice at 2:30 P.M. and stopped at 4:15 P.M. How long was soccer practice?

F 1hr 15 min.
G 1hr 30 min.
Ⓗ 1hr 45 min.
J 1hr 55 min.

9. **Write About It** How did you solve Problem 3?

Possible answer: I know there are 2 c in a pt, so I added 3 c and 2 c to get 5 c.

PS90 Problem Solving

345

Weight

HANDS ON

Lesson Planning

PROFESSIONAL DEVELOPMENT

Objective To estimate and measure weight

Materials *For each group* simple balance, pennies, scale

NCTM Standards
1. **Number and Operations**
2. **Algebra**
4. **Measurement**
6. **Problem Solving**
7. **Reasoning and Proof**
8. **Communication**
9. **Connections**

Math Background
Consider the following when you teach the concept of weight.

- The density of an object, and not its size, determines its weight. For example, an ounce of feathers will take up more space than an ounce of lead.

- Later, students will learn that weight is the measure of the pull of gravity on an object.

Vocabulary
ounce (oz) a customary unit used to measure weight

pound (lb) a customary unit used to measure weight

Warm-Up Resources

Build Number Sense
3
2
1

Number of the Day

Transparency **17.4**

Write and solve 5 addition sentences using the number of months in one year. Possible answers: $6 + 6 = 12, 5 + 7 = 12, 10 + 2 = 12, 11 + 1 = 12, 12 + 0 = 12$

Review Basic Facts
8
+3

Daily Facts Practice

Have students practice multiplication facts by completing Set G of *Teacher's Resource Book*, p. TR95.

Solve a Problem

Transparency **17.4**

Problem of the Day

I am a 3-digit number. I am the sum of the number of inches in a foot, hours in a day, cups in a gallon, inches in a yard, and eggs in a dozen. What number am I? 100

Solution Problem of the Day tab, p. PD17

Intervention and Extension Resources

Alternative Teaching Strategy

Help students **make a table of equivalents** for ounces and pounds. Work with them to see that since 1 pound equals 16 ounces, then 2 pounds equal 16 + 16, or 32 ounces, and 3 pounds equal 32 + 16, or 48 ounces, and so on.

pounds	1	2	3	4	5
ounces	16	32	48	▪	▪

Ask: How many ounces equal 4 pounds? 5 pounds? 64 ounces; 80 ounces

VISUAL

VISUAL/SPATIAL

Multistep and Strategy Problems

The following multistep or strategy problem is provided in Lesson 17.4:

Page	Item
347	11

Special Needs

MATERIALS simple balance, common items

ESOL/ESL

Have students **estimate and compare items on a balance**. Gather several classroom items such as an eraser, a pair of scissors, a box of crayons, and a computer disc, as well as some snack foods such as an apple, a bunch of grapes, or a package of crackers. Have them predict which items are heavier than others. Then have them compare the items' weights on the balance and arrange the items from lightest to heaviest. Check students' work.

KINESTHETIC

BODILY/KINESTHETIC

Advanced Learners

MATERIALS *For each group* scale, common items to weigh

Challenge students to **find objects of different weights**. Have them make a two-column chart in which they list the weights in one column and objects that weigh about the same in the other.

Weight	Object
2 ounces	
$\frac{1}{4}$ pound	
$\frac{1}{2}$ pound	
12 ounces	
2 pounds	

Students can share and compare their results. Answers will vary.

KINESTHETIC

VISUAL/SPATIAL

Technology Link

Harcourt Mega Math Country Countdown, *Harrison's Comparisons,* Level G

Math Jingles® CD 3–4 • *Track 13*

Lesson 17.4 Organizer

Objective To estimate and measure weight

Vocabulary ounce (oz), pound (lb)

Materials *For each group* simple balance, pennies, scale

---

1 INTRODUCE

QUICK REVIEW provides review of prerequisite skills.

WHY LEARN THIS? You will use this information when buying things that are sold by weight, such as fruits and vegetables. *Share the lesson objective with students.*

2 TEACH

Guided Instruction

- *Have students read the Explore section and Step 1.*
  Why do you put 9 pennies on one side of the balance? Since 9 pennies weigh about 1 ounce, use them to find other objects that weigh about 1 ounce.
  Which objects weigh more than one ounce? Explain how you know. Answers will vary; possible answer: the balance will be tilted down on the side opposite from the pennies.

- *Have students complete Step 4.*
  REASONING How could you estimate and then weigh objects that are about ½ pound? Possible answer: to estimate, find objects that might weigh about one half as much as the items that weighed 1 pound; to weigh, place 72 pennies on one side of the balance.

REASONING Think about the different customary units of measure that you have learned. How many of these could you use to measure a book? Possible answer: Inches could be used to measure the length and width of the book. Ounces or pounds could be used to measure the weight of the book.

3 PRACTICE

Guided Practice

Do Try It Exercises a–d with your students. Identify students who are having difficulty and choose appropriate lesson resources to provide assistance.

LESSON 4

 **Weight**

Quick Review

Compare. Use <, >, or = for each ●.

1. 16 ÷ 8 ● 2 × 2 <
2. 10 ● 24 ÷ 3 >
3. 81 ÷ 9 ● 9 =
4. 18 ÷ 3 ● 10 ÷ 2 >
5. 13 ● 3 × 4 >

VOCABULARY
ounce (oz)   pound (lb)

MATERIALS
simple balance, pennies, scale

▶ Explore

An **ounce (oz)** and a **pound (lb)** are customary units for measuring weight.

9 pennies weigh about 1 ounce.

144 pennies weigh about 1 pound.

You can estimate and then weigh objects to decide if they weigh about 1 ounce or about 1 pound.

Activity

STEP 1
Place 9 pennies on one side of a balance to show 1 ounce. Find two objects that you think weigh about 1 ounce each. Weigh them to check.

STEP 2
Record what your objects are and whether they weigh more than, less than, or the same as 1 ounce.

STEP 3
Place 144 pennies on one side of the balance to show 1 pound. Find two objects that you think weigh about 1 pound each. Weigh them to check.

STEP 4
Record what your objects are and whether they weigh more than, less than, or the same as 1 pound.

Try It

Estimate the weight of each object in pounds. Then use a scale to measure to the nearest pound.
Check students' work.

a. dictionary   b. shoe
c. bottle of water   d. stapler

What is the weight of a dictionary in pounds?
Answers will vary.

346

Reteach 17.4

Weight

An **ounce (oz)** and a **pound (lb)** are customary units for measuring weight. Thinking about objects that weigh about 1 ounce or 1 pound can help you estimate the weight of other objects.

A large strawberry weighs about 1 ounce. A soccer ball weighs about 1 pound.

Complete each sentence. Write *more* or *less*.

1. A paper clip weighs __less__ than 1 ounce.
2. A cat weighs __more__ than 1 pound.
3. An apple weighs __more__ than 1 ounce.
4. A sheet of paper weighs __less__ than 1 ounce.
5. A watermelon weighs __more__ than 1 pound.
6. A pencil weighs __less__ than 1 pound.

Write the unit of measure you would use to weigh each. Write *ounce* or *pound*.

7. __pound__   8. __ounce__   9. __pound__
10. __pound__   11. __ounce__   12. __ounce__

Reteach RW91

Practice 17.4

Weight

Choose the unit you would use to weigh each. Write *ounce* or *pound*.

1. __pound__   2. __pound__   3. __ounce__
4. __ounce__   5. __pound__   6. __ounce__

Circle the better estimate.

7. 4 ounces or **4 pounds**
8. 10 ounces or **10 pounds**
9. 10 ounces or 10 pounds

Mixed Review

Write the numbers in order from least to greatest.
10. 234, 561, 144   __144, 234, 561__
11. 899, 998, 989   __899, 989, 998__
12. 1,482; 1,248; 1,842   __1,248; 1,482; 1,842__
13. 6,479; 8,372; 8,362   __6,479; 8,362; 8,372__

Write the missing factor.
14. 4 × __4__ = 16   15. 12 = 6 × __2__   16. 3 × __9__ = 27
17. 80 = __10__ × 8   18. __10__ × 3 = 30   19. 487 = __1__ × 487

Practice PW91

▶ Connect

How are pounds and ounces related?

These things each weigh about 1 ounce.

A loaf of bread weighs about 1 pound.

16 ounces = 1 pound

▶ Practice and Problem Solving

Choose the unit you would use to weigh each. Write *ounce* or *pound*.

1.
ounce

2.
pound

3.
pound

4.
ounce

Choose the better estimate.

5.
1 ounce or 1 pound?
1 pound

6.
3 ounces or 3 pounds?
3 ounces

7.
2 ounces or 2 pounds?
2 pounds

8.
2 ounces or 2 pounds?
2 ounces

Choose the better unit of measure. Write *ounces* or *pounds*.

9. A chair weighs about 12 __?__.
pounds

10. A plate weighs about 12 __?__.
ounces

11. REASONING Bill has 24 cookies divided equally into 6 bags. How many cookies are in 3 bags?
12 cookies

12. Write a problem about items from your home. Use pounds and ounces in your problem.
Check students' problems.

Getting Ready for the EOG Test

13. Which is the *best* estimate for the weight of a basketball? **C**

A 15 pounds **C** 1 pound
B 10 pounds **D** 1 ounce

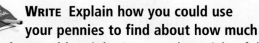

Chapter 17 **347**

North Carolina Standards 2.02 Estimate and measure using appropriate units. c) Mass (ounces, pounds, grams, kilograms). *also* **2.01b**

Independent Practice

Note that Exercise 11 is a **multistep or strategy problem.** Assign Exercises 1–12.

SCAFFOLDED INSTRUCTION Use the prompts on Transparency 17 to guide instruction for the multistep or strategy problem in Exercise 11.

Transparency **17**

4 ASSESS

Summarize the lesson by having students:

DISCUSS Explain what unit of measure you would use to describe the weight of a bag of oranges. Possible answer: use pound because a bag of oranges is much heavier than an ounce.

WRITE Explain how you could use your pennies to find about how much **2 apples would weigh.** Compare the weight of the apples with the weight of 9 pennies (1 ounce) and 144 pennies (1 pound): 2 apples weigh about a pound.

LESSON QUIZ
Choose the unit that you would use to weigh each. Write *ounce* or *pound*.

Transparency **17.4**

1. a dictionary pound **2.** a grape ounce
3. a pencil ounce **4.** a watermelon pound

Challenge 17.4

Balancing Toys

For 1–6, use the pictures to complete the sentences. Then use those sentences to answer problems 7–11.

1.
The whistle weighs **less** than the block.

2.
The car weighs **more** than the block.

3.
3 whistles weigh the same as 1 block.

4.
1 car weighs the same as **2** blocks.

5.
3 balls weigh the same as 2 blocks.

6.
1 pencil weighs **less** than the block.

7. How many whistles weigh the same as 1 car?
6 whistles

8. How many balls weigh the same as 1 car?
3 balls

1 block weighs 3 ounces. Write the weight of the other toys.

9.
1 ounce

10.
6 ounces

11.
2 ounces

Challenge CW91

Problem Solving 17.4

Weight

Understand ▸ Plan ▸ Solve ▸ Check

Write the correct answer.

1. Choose the better unit to weigh a quarter. Write *ounce* or *pound*.
ounce

2. Danny wants to weigh his pet hamster. Would he use ounces or pounds?
ounces

3. José deposited 563 cans into the recycling bin on Saturday. A week later, he deposited 278 more cans. How many cans were deposited in all?
841 cans

4. Abby wants to cut one pound of cheese into one-ounce cubes. How many cubes will she have?
16 cubes

Choose the letter of the correct answer.

5. If 9 pennies weigh about 1 ounce, about how much do 81 pennies weigh?
A about 8 oz **C** about 81 oz
(B) about 9 oz **D** about 1 lb

6. Which is *not* a customary unit for measuring length?
F inch **H** yard
G foot **(J)** ounce

7. Ami has 3 quarters and 1 dime. Matt has an equivalent set using dimes and nickels. Matt has 11 coins. How many dimes and nickels does he have?
A 5 dimes, 7 nickels
(B) 6 dimes, 5 nickels
C 7 dimes, 4 nickels
D 8 dimes, 3 nickels

8. Mary has 48 treats for 8 guests at her party. If they each get the same number of treats, how many will each guest get?
(F) 6 treats
G 7 treats
H 8 treats
J 10 treats

9. Write About It How did you choose the answer to Problem 1?
Possible answer: I know that ounces are used to weigh light objects, and a quarter is light.

Problem Solving PS91

347

Lesson Planning

PROFESSIONAL DEVELOPMENT

Objective To change units of measure

NCTM Standards
1. Number and Operations
2. Algebra
4. Measurement
6. Problem Solving
7. Reasoning and Proof
8. Communication
9. Connections
10. Representation

Math Background
These ideas will help students understand the concepts involved in changing units of length and capacity.

- Units of measure can be changed when you know how they relate to other units.

- Units of measure can be changed by drawing a picture or making a table.

Warm-Up Resources

Number of the Day

Transparency 17.5

The Number of the Day is the number of cups in two quarts. Write and solve 5 multiplication sentences using the number of cups as a factor. Possible answers: $8 \times 2 = 16$, $8 \times 4 = 32$, $8 \times 5 = 40$, $8 \times 8 = 64$, $8 \times 10 = 80$

Daily Facts Practice

Have students practice multiplication and division facts by completing Set A of *Teacher's Resource Book*, p. TR96.

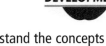
Transparency 17.5

Problem of the Day

Mr. Wren is building a tree house. He needs boards that are 42 inches long. He has boards that are 4 feet long. How many inches should he cut off each board? 6 inches

Solution Problem of the Day tab, p. PD17

Intervention and Extension Resources

Alternative Teaching Strategy

MATERIALS cup, pint, quart, and gallon containers; rice or water

ESOL/ESL

Help students **change units of capacity.** Some students may have difficulty visualizing the information in the Table of Measures on page 348. Have them change the units of capacity in the table using the appropriate measures and rice or water. Check students' work.

KINESTHETIC

BODILY/KINESTHETIC

Multistep and Strategy Problems

The following multistep or strategy problem is provided in Lesson 17.5:

Page	Item
349	11

Writing in Mathematics

Using the Table of Measures on page 348 as a reference, have students **write three word problems involving feet and inches, cups and quarts, and pints and gallons.** Have them exchange problems with a partner and solve. Check students' work.

Early Finishers

MATERIALS *For each group* tape measure or yardstick

Working with partners or in small groups, have students **use a tape measure or yardstick to measure** the following items:

- height of the classroom door
- length of their desk
- height of a window
- width of a bookshelf

Ask them to record these measurements in feet (with remaining inches) and in inches only. Check students' work.

KINESTHETIC

BODILY/KINESTHETIC

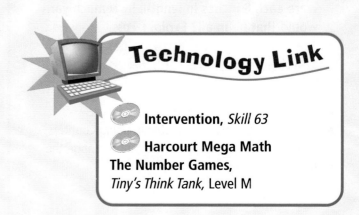

Technology Link

Intervention, *Skill 63*

Harcourt Mega Math
The Number Games,
Tiny's Think Tank, Level M

Lesson 17.5 Organizer

Objective To change units of measure

1 INTRODUCE

QUICK REVIEW provides review of prerequisite skills.

WHY LEARN THIS? You can describe a measured amount in more than one way. *Share the lesson objective with students.*

2 TEACH

Guided Instruction

- *Ask students to read the problem.*
  REASONING Why do you think it would be important to know how many quarts of juice the students need, rather than how many cups? Possible answer: juice isn't usually sold in cup containers.

- *Direct students' attention to Theresa's table.*
  What is a rule for Theresa's table? Possible answer: multiply the number of quarts by 4.
  REASONING How could division be used to solve the problem? Possible answer: since there are 4 cups in 1 quart, you could find 32 ÷ 4 to find the number of quarts that they should buy.
  What other method could either student use to find how many quarts are needed? Possible answers: skip-count or make a model

- *Direct students' attention to the Table of Measures.*
  ALGEBRAIC THINKING What is an expression that could be used to find the number of cups that are in one gallon? Explain. Possible answer: 4 + 4 + 4 + 4; 4 cups = 1 quart, and 4 quarts = 1 gallon, so you can add 4 four times to find the number of cups in a gallon.
  REASONING If you had 3 pieces of yarn that were each 8 inches in length, how much yarn would that be in all? Explain. Possible answer: 2 feet of yarn; 8 + 8 + 8 = 24; Since 1 foot is 12 inches and 24 = 12 + 12, there is a total of 2 feet of yarn.

MODIFYING INSTRUCTION Have students use manipulatives to solve the problem. Using counters to represent the 32 cups, have students arrange the counters in 8 groups of 4.

---

5 Ways to Change Units

Quick Review

Choose the smaller unit of measure in each.

1. pound, ounce   ounce
2. cup, pint   cup   3. quart, cup   cup
4. yard, foot   foot   5. pint, quart   pint

▷ **Learn**

CHANGE IT The students in Mrs. Lopez's class need 32 cups of juice for a picnic. How many quarts of juice should they buy?

To change cups into quarts, they must know how these units are related.

- A quart is larger than a cup.
- 4 cups = 1 quart

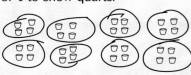

cup (c)   quart (qt)

Jake and Theresa used different ways to change cups into quarts.

Remember

Table of Measures

Length
12 inches = 1 foot
3 feet = 1 yard

Capacity
2 cups = 1 pint
4 cups = 1 quart
2 pints = 1 quart
8 pints = 1 gallon
4 quarts = 1 gallon

Weight
16 ounces = 1 pound

Jake
I'll draw 32 cups. I'll circle groups of 4 to show quarts.

There are 8 groups of 4 cups. So, 32 cups equals 8 quarts.

Theresa
I'll make a table.

Quarts	1	2	3	4	5	6	7	8
Cups	4	8	12	16	20	24	28	32

The table shows that 8 quarts equals 32 cups.

So, they should buy 8 quarts of juice.

MATH IDEA To change one unit into another, first decide how the units are related.

- Explain why Jake circled groups of 4 cups.
  Jake circled groups of 4 cups to show that there are 4 cups in 1 quart.

▷ **Check**

1. **Write** how many pints are in 2 gallons. Use the Table of Measures to help. **16 pints**

Technology Link

More Practice:
Harcourt Mega Math
The Number Games,
Tiny's Think Tank,
Level M

348

Reteach 17.5

Ways to Change Units

To change from one unit of measure to another, you must know how the units are related.

Table of Measures

Length	Capacity		
12 inches = 1 foot	2 cups = 1 pint	4 quarts = 1 gallon	
3 feet = 1 yard	4 cups = 1 quart	8 pints = 1 gallon	

How many cups are in 2 quarts?

1 quart   1 quart
1 quart = 4 cups
2 quarts = 4 + 4 or 8 cups

How many inches are in 3 feet?

1 foot   1 foot   1 foot
1 foot = 12 inches
2 feet = 12 + 12 or 24 inches
3 feet = 12 + 12 + 12 or 36 inches

Complete. Use the Table of Measures to help.

1. Change feet to inches.
   larger unit __feet__
   1 foot = __12 inches__

2. Change quarts to pints.
   larger unit __quarts__
   1 quart = __2 pints__

Change the units. Use the Table of Measures to help.

3. __4 cups__ = 1 quart
   __16 cups__ = 4 quarts

4. __12 inches__ = 1 foot
   __48 inches__ = 4 feet

5. __8 pints__ = 1 gallon

pints	8	16	24	32
gallons	1	2	3	4

__32 pints__ = 4 gallons

6. __3 feet__ = 1 yard

feet	3	6	9	12
yards	1	2	3	4

__9 feet__ = 3 yards

RW92 Reteach

Practice 17.5

Ways to Change Units

Table of Measures

Length	Capacity
12 inches = 1 foot	2 pints = 1 quart
3 feet = 1 yard	4 quarts = 1 gallon

Complete. Use the Table of Measures to help.

1. Change yards to feet.
   larger unit __yards__
   1 yard = __3 feet__

2. Change gallons to quarts.
   larger unit __gallons__
   1 gallon = __4 quarts__

Change the units. Use the Table of Measures to help.

3. __2__ pints = 1 quart
   __10__ pints = 5 quarts

4. __12__ inches = 1 foot
   __72__ inches = 6 feet

5. __4__ cups = 1 quart

cups	4	8	12	16
quarts	1	2	3	4

__12__ cups = 3 quarts

6. __3__ feet = 1 yard

feet	3	6	9	12
yards	1	2	3	4

__12__ feet = 4 yards

Mixed Review

Multiply.

7. 8 × 9 = __72__   8. 10 × 4 = __40__   9. 6 × 7 = __42__

Divide.

10. 18 ÷ 9 = __2__   11. 36 ÷ 4 = __9__   12. 40 ÷ 8 = __5__

PW92 Practice

Copy and complete. Use the Table of Measures to help.

2. Change gallons to pints.
larger unit: _?_ gallons

1 gallon = ■ pints **8**

3. Change feet to inches.
larger unit: _?_ feet

1 foot = ■ inches **12**

► **Practice and Problem Solving** Extra Practice, page 352, Set C

Copy and complete. Use the Table of Measures to help.

4. Change yards to feet.
larger unit: _?_ yards

1 yard = ■ feet **3**

5. Change quarts to gallons.
larger unit: _?_ gallons

■ quarts = 1 gallon **4**

Change the units. Use the Table of Measures to help.

6. ■ cups = 1 pint **2**

12 cups = ■ pints **6**

7. ■ inches = 1 foot **12**

feet	1	2
inches	12	■

■ inches = 2 feet **24**

Compare. Write <, >, or = for each ●.

8. 6 cups ● 2 quarts
<

9. 1 yard ● 36 inches
=

10. 20 ounces ● 1 pound
>

11. Neil bought 2 sandwiches. He paid with a $10 bill. He received $4 in change. How much did each sandwich cost? **$3 each**

12. Callie has 23 inches of yarn. Is this more than or less than 2 feet? Explain. **Less; 24 inches is 2 feet.**

13. ⭐ **What's the Error?** Dylan said that 24 pints equal 6 gallons. Describe his error. Draw a model to show your answer. **Dylan thought that 4 pints = 1 gallon, but 8 pints = 1 gallon. Check students' models. 24 pints = 3 gallons**

Getting Ready for the EOG Test

14. Mia bought 3 quarts of juice. How many cups of juice did she buy? **D**

  A 6 cups
  B 8 cups
  C 10 cups
  D 12 cups

 = =

4 cups   2 pints   1 quart

Chapter 17 **349**

* **North Carolina Standards 2.01** Solve problems using measurement concepts and procedures
olving: b) Equivalent measures within the same measurement system.

Challenge 17.5

How Much Do You Need?

Complete as much of each table as you need to solve each problem. Use the Table of Measures to help.

Table of Measures

Length	Capacity	Weight
12 inches = 1 foot 3 feet = 1 yard	2 cups = 1 pint 4 cups = 1 quart 2 pints = 1 quart 8 pints = 1 gallon 4 quarts = 1 gallon	16 ounces = 1 pound

1. You need 24 cups of punch for a party. How many quarts of punch do you need?

Quarts	1	2	3	4	5	6
Cups	4	8	12	16	20	24

6 quarts

2. You need 32 ounces of meat for hamburgers. How many pounds of meat do you need?

Pounds	1	2			
Ounces	16	32			

2 pounds

3. You need 12 feet of ribbon to make a banner. How many yards of ribbon do you need?

Yards	1	2	3	4	
Feet	3	6	9	12	

4 yards

4. You take 20 quarts of water on a camping trip. How many gallon jugs do you carry?

Gallons	1	2	3	4	5
Quarts	4	8	12	16	20

5 gallon jugs

W92 Challenge

Problem Solving 17.5

Ways to Change Units   Understand ➡ Plan ➡ Solve ➡ Check

Write the correct answer.

1. Vera's hair is 1 foot long. Gwen's hair is 8 inches long. Whose hair is longer?

Vera's

2. Which is a greater length, 2 feet or 36 inches?

36 in.

3. Estimate the length of this feather to the nearest inch.

Possible estimate: 2 inches

4. There are 2 cups in every pint. How many cups are in 8 pints?

16 cups

Choose the letter of the correct answer.

5. Which number is the same as three thousand fifty-two?

  A 3,000,052
  B 3,520
  C 3,502
  Ⓓ 3,052

6. Round 1,278 to the nearest ten.

  F 1,270
  Ⓖ 1,280
  H 1,290
  J 1,300

7. Which is a true sentence?

  A 1 foot = 10 inches
  B 1 foot = 24 inches
  C 1 inch = 12 feet
  Ⓓ 1 foot = 12 inches

8. Which of the following is the greatest unit of capacity?

  F quart
  G pint
  H cup
  Ⓙ gallon

9. Write About It Explain your answer for Problem 4.

Possible answer: Multiply the number of pints by 2.

PS92 Problem Solving

Guided Practice

Do Check Exercises 1–3 with your students. Identify students who are having difficulty and choose appropriate lesson resources to provide assistance.

For Exercises 2–3, students may wish to draw a picture or make a table to solve.

Independent Practice

Note that Exercise 11 is a **multistep or strategy problem.** Assign Exercises 4–13.

For Exercises 4–5, students may wish to draw a picture or make a table to solve.

Summarize the lesson by having students:

Discuss Rosa eats 1 cup of yogurt for lunch every day. Her dad bought her 2 quarts of yogurt. Will she have enough yogurt for the week? Explain. Yes; There are 4 cups in 1 quart and 8 cups in 2 quarts. After 7 days, she will have 1 cup left.

📓 **Write** Explain how to change 6 feet into inches. Possible answer: Make a table. Begin by showing there are 12 inches in a foot. Complete the table until you find how many inches are in 6 feet.

LESSON QUIZ   Transparency **17.5**

Copy and complete. Use the Table of Measures on page 348 to help.

1. Change inches to feet.
larger unit: _?_ feet

12 inches = ■ foot **1**

2. Change pints to cups.
larger unit: _?_ pints

1 pint = ■ cups **2**

349

Lesson 17.6

Problem Solving Skill

Estimate or Measure

Lesson Planning

PROFESSIONAL DEVELOPMENT

Objective To determine whether an estimate or a measured amount is needed to solve a problem

Lesson Resources Reading Transparency 17; Intervention • Problem Solving, Strategy/Skill 17

NCTM Standards

1. Number and Operations
4. Measurement
6. Problem Solving
7. Reasoning and Proof
8. Communication
9. Connections

Math Background

These ideas will help students determine whether an estimate or an actual measurement is needed.

- Students should read problems carefully; often there are clues in the problem, such as the word *about,* that tell them that only an estimate is needed.
- Understanding different real-life situations, such as using a recipe, will help students decide if an estimate or measurement is needed.

Warm-Up Resources

Build Number Sense

Number of the Day

Transparency 17.6

Write and solve a division sentence in which the dividend is the number of inches in one yard.
Possible answer: $36 \div 6 = 6$

Review Basic Facts

Daily Facts Practice

Have students practice division facts by completing Set B of *Teacher's Resource Book,* p. TR96.

Solve a Problem

Transparency 17.6

Problem of the Day

The left end of Natalie's ruler has broken off, so she starts measuring at the 3-inch mark. She measures a line that ends just past the halfway mark between 6 and 7 inches. How long is the line to the nearest half inch? $3\frac{1}{2}$ inches

Solution Problem of the Day tab, p. PD17

Intervention and Extension Resources

Alternative Teaching Strategy

Have students **decide when to estimate or measure**. On an overhead projector or on a chalkboard, draw a table with two headings: **Estimate, Measure**. Then discuss the following activities: making a recipe, using crepe paper to decorate a room for a party, building a birdhouse, watering a garden, filling in an order form, buying fabric for a costume, pouring popcorn into bowls. Discuss each activity and decide where each activity should be written in the table.

VISUAL

INTERPERSONAL/SOCIAL

Reading Strategy

Use Graphic Aids Explain that a table is a good way to find information. Discuss the following steps for reading a table.

1. Read the title to find out what the table is about.

2. Look at the headings at the top of the columns to see what kind of information is in each column.

3. Read each row to find exact information.

Have students review the tables that they made for the activity on page 338. Ask students to choose two of the ribbons and write a paragraph describing the information in their tables about those ribbons. Check students' work.

17 **Reading Transparency 17**

Multistep and Strategy Problems

The following multistep and strategy problems are provided in Lesson 17.6:

Page	Items
351	5–7

Vocabulary Strategy

Have students **review the meaning of** *estimate.* **ESOL/ESL** Have students go to **www.harcourtschool.com/ mathglossary** to review the noun and verb forms of *estimate.* Ask students to write a sentence using *estimate* as a noun and a sentence using *estimate* as a verb. Check students' work.

VISUAL

VERBAL/LINGUISTIC

Writing in Mathematics

 MATERIALS *For each student* articles from newspapers or magazines

Have students read articles to **find examples of when estimation is used and when actual measurements are made**. Have students write 3 or 4 sentences to explain why an estimate or an actual measure was used. Check students' work.

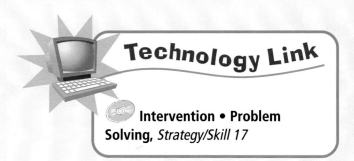

Technology Link

Intervention • Problem Solving, *Strategy/Skill 17*

Lesson 17.6 Organizer

Objective To determine whether an estimate or a measured amount is needed to solve a problem

Lesson Resources Reading Transparency 17; Intervention • Problem Solving, Strategy/Skill 17

1 INTRODUCE

QUICK REVIEW provides review of prerequisite skills.

WHY LEARN THIS? You can use this skill to decide when to estimate and when to measure. *Share the lesson objective with students.*

2 TEACH

Guided Instruction

• *Have students read the How Much? section.*
REASONING What if Ethan has a 1-pint pitcher to use for watering the plants? Can he still use an estimate? Explain. Possible answer: yes; there are 2 cups in a pint, so he can fill the pitcher with water and use about half of the water for one plant.
Give another example of when an amount of something does not need to be measured. Possible answer: when you pour juice into a glass, you don't need to measure the amount.

• *Discuss the Talk About It questions with students.*
What might happen if Ethan estimates the amount of water that he mixes with the paint powder? Possible answer: if there is not enough water mixed with the paint powder, the paint might not spread smoothly on students' papers. If there is too much water, the paint will be too thin and the color will be too light.

350 Chapter 17

Problem Solving Skill
Estimate or Measure

UNDERSTAND ▶ PLAN ▶ SOLVE ▶ CHECK

Quick Review
1. ■ inches = 1 foot 12
2. ■ cups = 1 pint 2
3. ■ ounces = 1 pound 16
4. 6 feet = ■ yards 2
5. 1 gallon = ■ quarts 4

HOW MUCH? Ethan's job is to water 4 plants in the classroom. Each plant needs about 1 cup of water. He has a 1-quart pitcher to use. Should Ethan estimate or measure the amount of water for each plant?

Each plant needs *about* 1 cup of water, so Ethan can use an estimate. There are 4 cups in 1 quart, so he can look at the pitcher and decide about how much to pour for 1 plant. He can use this as a benchmark.

What if Ethan's job is to mix water with the paint powder?

PAINT POWDER
Directions:
1. Pour one cup of water into the jar.
2. Stir for one minute.

Ethan needs to measure 1 cup of water to add to the jar. He should use a measuring cup because he needs a measured amount to mix the paint correctly.

Talk About It

• Why is an estimate close enough to use for watering the plants? **The plants need to be watered, but the amount of water could be a little more or less than a cup.**
• Why would Ethan need to measure the amount of water to mix with the paint powder? **The mixture of paint powder and water would need to be carefully measured so that the paint would be made correctly.**

350

Reteach 17.6

Problem Solving Skill

Estimate or Measure

Estimate to find the answer when you only need to know how many or about how much.

Measure when you need a certain amount.

Here are some examples.

Estimate to find the answer.	Measure to find the answer.
Problem There are 8 dogs at Mr. Wright's kennel. Each of the dogs' water bowls holds about 2 cups of water. How many quarts of water does Mr. Wright need to fill all the water bowls?	**Problem** Mr. Wright feeds each dog 12 ounces of dry food each day. How many pounds of dry food does he need each day for 8 dogs?
Estimate how much water is needed.	Find out how much food is needed.
8 × about 2 cups = about 16 cups 16 cups = 4 quarts	8 × 12 ounces = 96 ounces 96 ounces = 6 pounds
Mr. Wright needs about 4 quarts of water.	Mr. Wright needs 6 pounds of dry food each day.

Write whether you need an estimate or a measured amount. Then solve.

1. An apple weighs about 5 ounces. About how many apples would you expect to get in a 2-pound bag of apples?

   Estimate; 2 × 16 ounces = 32 ounces; 6 × 5 ounces = 30 ounces; about 6 apples

2. Ron has a rectangular garden that is 8 feet long and 4 feet wide. He wants to put fencing around all four sides. How many yards of fencing should he buy?

   Measured amount; 8 + 4 + 8 + 4 = 24 feet; 24 feet = 8 yards

Reteach RW93

Practice 17.6

Problem Solving Skill

Estimate or Measure

For 1–2, use the table. Tell if you need to measure or if an estimate will do.

SUPPLIES	
Item	**Size**
Fabric	5 yd piece
Fabric	10 yd piece
Fringe	4 ft roll
Fringe	3 yd roll

1. The Art Club is making 6 banners. For each banner, 4 feet of fabric is needed. Which piece of fabric should the Art Club buy? Explain.

   The 10 yd piece; possible answer: estimate; 24 ft is needed; more than 5 yds, or 15 ft, but less than 10 yds, or 30 ft is needed.

2. For each of the 6 banners, 2 feet of fringe is needed. What rolls of fringe should the Art club buy? Explain.

   Three 4 ft rolls; possible answer: measure; 12 ft of fringe is needed; 3 × 4 ft = 12 ft.

Mrs. Winters is buying rice to cook for a family dinner. Rice is packaged in 2-pound bags. She needs to make enough rice to serve 12 people.

3. For each serving, 4 ounces of rice are needed. How many bags of rice should Mrs. Winters buy?
   Ⓐ 2   C 4
   B 3   D 6

4. Which tool can Mrs. Winters use to measure the rice for one serving?
   F ruler   Ⓗ balance
   G yardstick   J thermometer

Mixed Review

5.   359
   + 264
   ─────
     623

6. 7,826
  + 1,358
  ───────
    9,184

7.   213
   − 156
   ─────
      57

8. 4,000
  − 2,479
  ───────
    1,521

Write <, >, or = in the ◯.

9. 326 ⊘< 362   10. 4,973 ⊜= 4,973   11. 17,824 ⊘> 17,631

Practice PW93

USE DATA For 1–2, use the table. Tell if you need to measure or if an estimate will do.

SUPPLIES	
Item	**Size**
Ribbon	20 ft roll
Ribbon	30 ft roll
Dried Beans	6 oz package
Dried Beans	1 lb package

1. Each student in Mrs. Garcia's class needs a 10-inch piece of ribbon for an art project. There are 20 students in the class. Which roll of ribbon should she buy? Explain. **See right.**

1. the 20 ft roll; Possible answer: estimate; Each student needs less than 1 ft of ribbon. 20 students would need less than 20 ft.

2. Coach Davis is making 8 bean bags. He needs 4 ounces of dried beans for each bean bag. What packages should he buy? Explain. **two 1 lb bags; Possible answer: measure; He needs 32 oz. 16 + 16 = 32, so 2 lb is how much he needs.**

Mr. Weston is buying soda water for a science activity. It is sold in 1-quart bottles. There are 6 groups of students in his class.

3. Each group needs 1 pint of soda water. How many bottles should Mr. Weston buy? **C**

A 1 C 3
B 2 D 4

4. Which tool should Mr. Weston use to measure the soda water for each group? **G**

F balance H ruler
G measuring cup J thermometer

Mixed Applications

USE DATA For 5–7, use the graph.

5. **? What's the Question?** The answer is 4 cups. **Possible question: How many cups are in 2 pints?**

6. Stacy mixed 3 cups of orange juice, 2 cups of pineapple juice, and 3 cups of cranberry juice. How many *pints* of fruit juice did she mix in all? **4 pints**

7. **REASONING** There are 2 pints in 1 quart. How many *cups* are there in *3 quarts*? **12 cups**

8. ✏ Write About It Give an example of when you would need to measure and an example of when an estimate would do. **Check students' responses.**

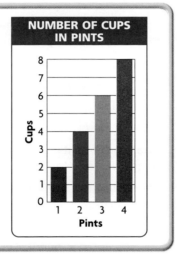

NUMBER OF CUPS IN PINTS

Chapter 17 **351**

---

* **North Carolina Standards 2.02** Estimate and measure using appropriate units.

Challenge 17.6

Estimated or Exact Relations

Complete each sentence. Circle *is about* or *equals* and write a whole number on the line. Use the Table of Measures for help.

Table of Measures		
Length	**Capacity**	**Weight**
12 inches = 1 foot 3 feet = 1 yard	2 cups = 1 pint 4 cups = 1 quart 2 pints = 1 quart 8 pints = 1 gallon 4 quarts = 1 gallon	16 ounces = 1 pound

1. 25 inches (is about)/ equals) __2__ feet.
2. 2 gallons (is about /(equals) __8__ quarts.
3. 15 feet (is about /(equals) __5__ yards.
4. 7 pints (is about)/ equals) __3 or 4__ quarts.
5. 3 pounds (is about /(equals) __48__ ounces.
6. 20 feet (is about)/ equals) __7__ yards.
7. 11 cups (is about)/ equals) __5 or 6__ pints.
8. 16 pints (is about /(equals)) __2__ gallons.
9. 30 ounces (is about)/ equals) __2__ pounds.
10. 5 gallons (is about /(equals)) __20__ quarts.
11. 23 cups (is about)/ equals) __6__ quarts.
12. 48 inches (is about /(equals)) __4__ feet.

Challenge **CW93**

Reading Strategy 17.6

Use Graphic Aids   Understand ➤ Plan ➤ Solve ➤ Check

Graphs, maps, tables, and charts are called **graphic aids**. Graphic aids organize information so it is easier to find and use.

Zach is using this map that shows some of the places in his town. He has hockey practice at the sports arena. After he finishes, he plans to go to the library. He wants to go by the shortest distance. Should he go past the park or past the fairgrounds?

1. What is the distance from the sports arena to the park and then to the library? **7 mi**

2. What is the distance from the sports arena to the fairgrounds and then to the library? **6 mi**

3. Which route should Zach take? **past the fairgrounds**

Use the map to solve.

4. Molly is at the zoo. She wants to visit the art museum and the science museum. She wants to travel the shortest distance. In what order should she visit the museums? Explain. **science museum then art museum; 8 miles < 11 miles**

5. Mike was at the library. He visited two other places of interest and rode exactly 8 miles. What places could he have visited? Explain. **the park and the zoo; 5 miles + 3 miles = 8 miles**

Reading Strategy **PS93**

---

3 PRACTICE

Guided Practice

Do Problem Solving Practice Exercises 1–4 with your students. Identify students who are having difficulty and choose appropriate lesson resources to provide assistance.

For Exercises 2 and 3, students may wish to use the Table of Measures on page 348.

Independent Practice

Note that Exercises 5–7 are **multistep or strategy problems.** Assign Exercises 5–8.

4 ASSESS

Summarize the lesson by having students:

DISCUSS Give an example of when you would need to measure. Explain why an estimate would not be good enough to use. Possible answer: When you are going to frame a picture, you need to measure the picture and the frame so that the picture will fit in the frame correctly.

📓 **WRITE** Suppose that you are planning a birthday party. Describe something that you would estimate for the party. Then describe something that you would need to measure for the party. Answers will vary.

LESSON QUIZ

Transparency 17.6

1. Mr. Connell is making a wooden picture frame. Can he estimate, or should he measure the pieces of wood that he cuts for the sides of the frame? Explain. He should measure the pieces of wood so that the frame will be the right size and shape.

2. Cathy is filling trays with soil so that she can plant flower seeds. Can she estimate, or should she measure the amount of soil for each tray? She can estimate by looking at how deep the soil is in the trays; the soil doesn't have to be a measured amount.

CHAPTER 17 Extra Practice

Purpose To provide extra practice for the skills presented in this chapter

The blue page references in each set of exercises refer to the lesson pages where each skill is taught.

Internet Resources

 Visit **The Learning Site** at **www.harcourtschool.com** for a listing of practice activities.

Extra Practice

Set A (pp. 338–341)

Measure the length to the nearest inch.

1. 2 in.

2. 2 in.

Measure the length to the nearest half inch.

3. $2\frac{1}{2}$ in.

4. 3 in.

5. $5\frac{1}{2}$ in.

Set B (pp. 342–343)

Choose the unit you would use to measure each.
Write *inch, foot, yard,* **or** *mile.* **Possible answers are given.**

1. the height of a 2-story house
   yard
2. the distance between 2 towns
   mile
3. the length of a hockey stick
   foot
4. the length of your thumb
   inch

Choose the best unit of measure.
Write *inches, feet, yards,* **or** *miles.*

5. A pen is about 6 _?_ long. **inches**
6. A car is about 4 _?_ long. **yards**
7. The distance from the school to the park is about 2 _?_. **miles**
8. The height of a chair is about 3 _?_. **feet**

Set C (pp. 348–349)

Change the units. Use the Table of Measures on page 348 to help.

1. ■ cups = 1 quart **4**

   16 cups = ■ quarts **4**

2. ■ feet = 1 yard **3**

feet	3	6		
yards	1	2	3	4

   ■ feet = 4 yards **12**

352

Review/Test

✓ CHECK CONCEPTS

Choose the better estimate. (pp. 346–347)

1.

1 ounce or
1 pound?
1 ounce

2.

2 ounces or
2 pounds?
2 pounds

3.

30 ounces or
30 pounds?
30 pounds

Choose the better estimate. (pp. 344–345)

4.

1 cup or
1 quart?
1 cup

5.

5 quarts or
5 gallons?
5 quarts

6.

1 cup or
1 quart?
1 cup

7.

4 pints or
4 gallons?
4 gallons

✓ CHECK SKILLS

Measure the length to the nearest inch. (pp. 338–341)

8.
   3 inches

9.
   1 inch

Choose the unit you would use to measure each.
Write inch, foot, yard, **or** mile. (pp. 342–343) **Possible answers are given.**

10. the length of a marker **inch**

11. the height of a wall **foot**

12. the distance a bus goes in 15 minutes **mile**

13. the distance between the classroom and the playground **yard**

✓ CHECK PROBLEM SOLVING (pp. 350–351)

14. Gail needs a piece of string to tie flowers together. Can she estimate the length of string or does she need to measure? Explain. **estimate; Possible answer: a certain length is not needed.**

15. Joe needs 2 cups of flour for a cookie recipe. Should he estimate or measure the amount of flour? Explain. **measure; Possible answer: a measured amount is needed for the cookies to turn out correctly.** **Chapter 17 353**

Review/Test

Purpose To check understanding of concepts, skills, and problem solving presented in Chapter 17

Using the Page

The Chapter 17 Review/Test can be used as a **review** or a **test**.

- Items 1–7 check understanding of new concepts.
- Items 8–13 check skill proficiency.
- Items 14–15 check students' abilities to choose and apply problem solving strategies to real-life measurement problems.

Portfolio ☐ Suggest that students place the completed Chapter 17 Review/Test in their portfolios.

Using the Assessment Guide

- Multiple-choice format of Chapter 17 Posttest— See Assessment Guide, pp. AG105–106.
- Free-response format of Chapter 17 Posttest— See Assessment Guide, pp. AG107–108.

Using Student Self-Assessment

The How Did I Do? survey helps students assess what they have learned and how they learned it. This survey is available as a copying master in Assessment Guide, p. AGxvii.

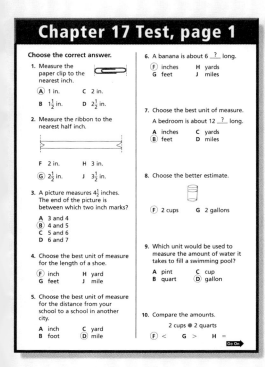

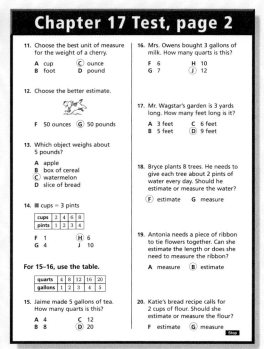

CHAPTER 17

Getting Ready for the EOG Test

Chapters 1–17

Using the Pages

These pages may be used to help students get ready for the North Carolina EOG Test. The test items are written in the same style and arranged in the same format as those on the EOG Test.

The pages are cumulative. They cover the standards from the North Carolina Mathematics Standard Course of Study that have been taught up to this point in the text or in a previous grade. Each Getting Ready for the EOG Test also reviews the North Carolina mathematics strands shown below.

- Number and Operations
- Measurement
- Geometry
- Data Analysis and Probability
- Algebra

These pages can be assigned at the end of the chapter as classwork or as a homework assignment. You may want to have students use individual recording sheets presented in a multiple-choice (standardized) format. A Test Answer Sheet is available as a blackline master in the *Assessment Guide* (p. AGlii).

You may wish to have students describe how they solved each problem and share their solutions.

Getting Ready for the ★EOG Test

★ NUMBER AND OPERATIONS

1. Lynn sold 8 bracelets at a craft fair. She charged $3 for each bracelet. Which operation should you use to find how much money she made at the fair? **C**

  A addition
  B subtraction
  C multiplication
  D division

2. Which division fact belongs to the same fact family as these multiplication facts? **B**

$$6 \times 4 = 24 \qquad 4 \times 6 = 24$$

  A $24 \div 8 = 3$
  B $24 \div 6 = 4$
  C $24 \div 3 = 8$
  D $24 \div 1 = 24$

3. Tara has 56 trading cards. She can put 8 cards on each page of her collection binder. Which of the following can be used to find the number of pages she needs for all of her cards? **C**

  A $56 - 8 = 48$ **C** $56 \div 8 = 7$
  B $56 + 8 = 64$ **D** $54 \div 9 = 6$

4. Explain It Dylan says the difference between 5,609 and 1,198 is *about* 3,000. Do you agree or disagree with Dylan's estimate? Explain. **See page 355.**

★ MEASUREMENT AND GEOMETRY

5. Which unit would be the most appropriate to determine the length of a football field? **C**

  A inch   **C** yard
  B foot   **D** mile

> **TIP** **Understand the problem.** See item 6. Each sports bottle holds one pint. Think about how many pints are in one gallon. Then multiply that number by 2 to find the number of pints in 2 gallons.

6. Coach Walton is filling sports bottles that each hold 1 pint. He has a water cooler with 2 gallons of water in it. How many bottles can he fill? **D**

  A 8
  B 10
  C 12
  D 16

7. Which would be *best* to measure the weight of a loaf of bread? **D**

  A inch   **C** ounce
  B quart   **D** pound

8. Explain It There are 2 cups in 1 pint. There are 2 pints in 1 quart. How many cups are in 1 quart? Explain. **See page 355.**

354

⭐ **ALGEBRA**

9. How many quarts are in 2 gallons? **c**

Gallons	1	2	3	4
Quarts	4	▦	12	16

A 5 quarts
B 6 quarts
C 8 quarts
D 10 quarts

10. Kendra wrote this number pattern:

40, 36, 32, 28

Which is a rule for her pattern? **D**

A Divide by 3.
B Add 3.
C Multiply by 4.
D Subtract 4.

11. Which number makes this equation true? **A**

$36 - ▦ = 28$

A 8   **C** 11
B 9   **D** 12

12. Explain It Angie thought of a number pattern and made this table. Explain how to find a rule for the table. Then use that rule to find the missing numbers.
See below.

In	2	4	6	8	10
Out	16	▦	▦	64	80

⭐ **DATA ANALYSIS AND PROBABILITY**

13. The line plot shows the high temperature for each day in April. How many days had a high temperature greater than 70°F?
D

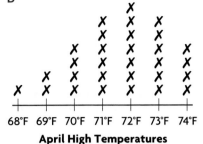

April High Temperatures

A 10   **C** 19
B 13   **D** 23

14. What are all of the possible outcomes for this spinner? **B**

A blue, green, yellow
B blue, red, yellow, blue
C yellow, blue, green
D red, yellow

15. Explain It Jared asked his classmates to name their favorite foods. These are the results.

FOOD	NUMBER OF VOTES
Pizza	卌 卌 l
Corn Dogs	ll
Hamburgers	卌 l

Jared says that pizza should be ordered for the class party. Do you agree or disagree? Explain.
See below.

Chapter 17   **355**

Chapters 1–17

Item Analysis

You may wish to use the item analysis to determine which North Carolina standards need additional review.

Item	North Carolina Standard	Lesson
1	1.03	13.5
2	1.03	12.4
3	1.03	14.3
4	1.02	5.1
5	2.02	17.2
6	2.01	17.5
7	2.02	17.4
8	2.01	17.5
9	5.02	17.5
10	5.01	11.2
11	5.04	4.6
12	5.01	11.2
13	4.01	15.5
14	(2) 4.02	Grade 2
15	4.01	15.2

SCORING RUBRIC
Explain It

2 Demonstrates a complete understanding of the problem and chooses an appropriate strategy to determine the solution

1 Demonstrates a partial understanding of the problem and chooses a strategy that does not lead to a complete and accurate solution

0 Demonstrates little understanding of the problem and shows little evidence of using any strategy to determine a solution

Explain It • Written Response

4. Possible answer: disagree; 5,609 rounds to 6,000 and 1,198 rounds to 1,000. 6,000 − 1,000 = 5,000.

8. 4 cups; Possible answer: you can draw a picture or make a table to show that 4 cups = 2 pints = 1 quart.

12. Possible answer: look at the pairs of numbers and see how they change from "in" to "out"; rule: multiply by 8; missing numbers: 32, 48.

15. Possible answer: agree; pizza had several more votes than either of the other foods.

CHAPTER 18
Metric Units and Temperature

Chapter Planner

Getting Ready for Chapter 18 • Assessing Prior Knowledge and INTERVENTION (See PE and TE page 357.)

LESSON	NORTH CAROLINA STANDARDS	PACING	VOCABULARY*	MATERIALS	RESOURCES AND TECHNOLOGY
18.1 **Length** pp. 358–361 **Objective** To estimate and measure length	2.02b *also* 2.01b	2 Days	**centimeter (cm)** **decimeter (dm)** **meter (m)** **kilometer (km)**	*For each student* centimeter ruler, centimeter grid paper, crayons, tape *For Thinker's Corner* centimeter ruler	Reteach, Practice, Problem Solving, Challenge 18.1 Worksheets Transparency 18.1 **Intervention,** *Skill 53* (CD or Book) **Harcourt Mega Math Ice Station Exploration,** *Linear Lab* Math Jingles® CD 3–4
18.2 **Problem Solving Strategy: Make a Table** pp. 362–363 **Objective** To use the problem solving strategy *make a table* to solve problems	2.01b *also* 1.06	1 Day			Reteach, Practice, Reading Strategy, Challenge 18.2 Worksheets Transparency 18.2 Scaffolded Instruction Transparency 18 Reading Transparency 18 **Intervention • Problem Solving,** *Strategy/Skill 18* (CD or Book)
18.3 **Hands On: Capacity** pp. 364–365 **Objective** To estimate and measure capacity	2.02a *also* 2.01b	1 Day	**milliliter (mL)** **liter (L)**	*For each group* plastic glass, liter container, large plastic pitcher, water	Reteach, Practice, Problem Solving, Challenge 18.3 Worksheets Transparency 18.3
18.4 **Hands On: Mass** pp. 366–367 **Objective** To estimate and measure mass	2.02c *also* 2.01b	1 Day	**gram (g)** **kilogram (kg)** **mass**	*For each group* classroom objects, small paper clips, simple balance, book with a mass of about 1 kilogram	Reteach, Practice, Problem Solving, Challenge 18.4 Worksheets Transparency 18.4 Math Jingles® CD 3–4
18.5 **Hands On: Fahrenheit and Celsius** pp. 368–369 **Objective** To estimate and measure temperature	2.02d	1 Day	**degrees Fahrenheit (°F)** **degrees Celsius (°C)**	*For each group* Celsius and Fahrenheit thermometers	Reteach, Practice, Problem Solving, Challenge 18.5 Worksheets Transparency 18.5 **Intervention,** *Skills 54–55* (CD or Book) Math Jingles® CD 3–4

Ending Chapter 18 • **Extra Practice,** p. 370 • **Chapter 18 Review/Test,** p. 371 • **Getting Ready for the EOG Test,** pp. 372–373

* **Boldfaced** terms are the key mathematical terms for the chapter.

Vocabulary Power

Review Vocabulary

To be ready for Chapter 18, students should know the following vocabulary term:

- **capacity** (p. 344)—the amount that a container can hold

Develop Key Chapter Vocabulary

The **boldfaced** words are the key vocabulary terms in the chapter.

- **centimeter** (p. 358)—a metric unit used to measure length
- **decimeter** (p. 358)—a metric unit used to measure length
- **meter** (p. 358)—a metric unit used to measure length or distance
- **kilometer** (p. 358)—a metric unit used to measure length or distance
- **milliliter** (p. 364)—a unit of capacity equal to one thousandth of a liter
- **liter** (p. 364)—a unit of capacity equal to a little more than one quart
- **gram** (p. 366)—a metric unit used to measure mass
- **kilogram** (p. 366)—a metric unit used to measure mass
- **mass** (p. 366)—the amount of matter in an object
- **degrees Fahrenheit** (p. 368)—a customary unit for measuring temperature
- **degrees Celsius** (p. 368)—a metric unit for measuring temperature

Vocabulary Cards

Have students use the Vocabulary Cards on *Teacher's Resource Book* pages TR161–166 for the key terms in the chapter. The cards can be added to a file of mathematics terms.

kilometer (km)

Multimedia Math Glossary

GO ON-LINE For vocabulary support, visit www.harcourtschool.com/mathglossary

Math Journal

Have students define the key vocabulary terms: *centimeter, decimeter, meter, kilometer, milliliter, liter, gram, kilogram, mass, degrees Fahrenheit,* and *degrees Celsius.* Have students use their own words and give an example of each.

M A T H Word Work

Objective To reinforce vocabulary concepts
Use after Lesson 18.4.

Materials *For each student* Vocabulary cards, pp. TR161–166

On their desks, have students place their cards face-up showing the metric units used to measure length, capacity, and mass. Tell students to hold up the card showing the best unit to use to measure each of the following as they are called out.

- capacity of a spoon **milliliter**
- distance from the classroom to the school office **meter**
- mass of an index card **gram**
- capacity of a bucket **liter**
- length of a shoe box **centimeter**
- distance from the school to the post office **kilometer**
- mass of a desk **kilogram**

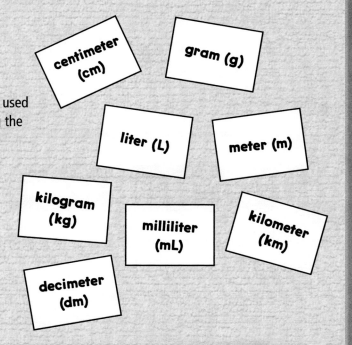

Metric Units and Temperature

Mathematics Across the Grades

LOOKING BACK • Prerequisite Skills

To be ready for Chapter 18, students should have the following understandings and skills:

- **Measure to the Nearest Centimeter**—measure length to the nearest centimeter

- **Read a Thermometer**—read temperatures at five-degree intervals

Check What You Know

Use page 357 to determine students' knowledge of prerequisite concepts and skills.

Intervention

Help students prepare for the chapter by using the intervention resources described on TE page 357.

LOOKING AT CHAPTER 18 • Essential Skills

Students will

- estimate and measure length.

- estimate and measure capacity.

- **estimate and measure mass.**

- use the problem solving strategy *make a table* to solve problems.

- estimate and measure temperature.

Example

Would a car be more likely to have a mass of 1,000 kilograms or 1,000 grams?

1kg   1g

1,000 g = 1 kg

So, a car would be more likely to have a mass of 1,000 kg.

LOOKING AHEAD • Applications

Students will apply what they learn in Chapter 18 to the following new concepts:

- Find Perimeter (Chapter 22)

- Use Algebra to Convert Units (Grade 4)

- Compare and Order Linear Measurements (Grade 4)

- Relate Benchmark Measurements (Grade 4)

Differentiated Instruction

Meeting the Needs of All Learners

Extra Support	Activities for All	Enrichment
Alternative Teaching Strategy TE Lessons 18.1, 18.2, 18.3, 18.4, 18.5 **ESOL/ESL** TE Lessons 18.1, 18.2, 18.3, 18.4, 18.5	**Cross-Curricular Connection** **Career:** TE Lesson 18.1 **Language Arts:** TE Lesson 18.4 **Reading:** TE Lesson 18.2 **Science:** TE/PE Chapter Opener **Vocabulary:** TE p. 356B, PE p. 357 **Writing:** TE Lesson 18.3	**Advanced Learners** TE Lessons 18.3, 18.5 **Early Finishers** TE Lessons 18.2, 18.4, 18.5

Combination and Multi-age Classrooms

Grade 2	Grade 3	Grade 4
Skills Trace Across the Grades		
Measure in metric units of length, capacity, and mass; read a Fahrenheit thermometer and a Celsius thermometer.	**Estimate and measure length, distance, capacity, and mass using metric units; estimate and measure temperature in degrees Fahrenheit and in degrees Celsius.**	Measure length, capacity, and mass using appropriate metric units; use algebraic equations to convert linear units; relate benchmark measurements.
Instructional Strategies		
Students on this level may require more time to build conceptual understanding. **Assignments** **Grade 3 Pupil Edition** • Provide students with additional hands-on opportunities for measuring in metric units. • Have them skip Lesson 18.2. **Grade 2 Pupil Edition**—pages 389–390 and 415–422	Students on this level should be able to complete all the lessons in the Pupil Edition and all the activities in the Teacher's Edition with minimal adjustments. **Assignment** **Grade 3 Pupil Edition**—pages 356–371	Students on this level will probably require less time to build conceptual understanding. **Assignments** **Grade 3 Pupil Edition** • Compact Lessons 18.1 and 18.2. **Grade 4 Pupil Edition**—pages 540–555

Metric Units and Temperature

Introducing the Chapter

Tell students that the metric system is a different type of measurement system than the customary system. In this chapter, they will learn about metric units used to measure length, capacity, and weight. They will also learn about measuring temperature in the customary system (degrees Fahrenheit) and in the metric system (degrees Celsius). Ask: If the temperature goes up, does that mean it has gotten warmer or cooler? warmer

Using Data

To begin the study of this chapter, have students

- Find which cities have a difference of less than 18°F between their average high and average low February temperatures. Boise and Grand Rapids

- Determine the difference between Birmingham's and Richmond's average high February temperatures. 8°F

Problem Solving Project

Purpose To graph temperatures using degrees Fahrenheit

Materials bar graph pattern, p. TR60 or TR61

Background The Fahrenheit scale and the Celsius scale were both developed in the 1700s. Although the United States uses the Fahrenheit scale, all other major countries in the world use the Celsius scale.

UNDERSTAND • PLAN • SOLVE • CHECK

Have students

- Make a bar graph that shows the high temperature for each city in the table. Write a title and labels for the graph.

- Use a scale of 10, and find about where each bar should end. Shade the bar to show the temperature.

- Write a question that a classmate can answer by using the graph.

Graphing Investigations
Begin Week 18.

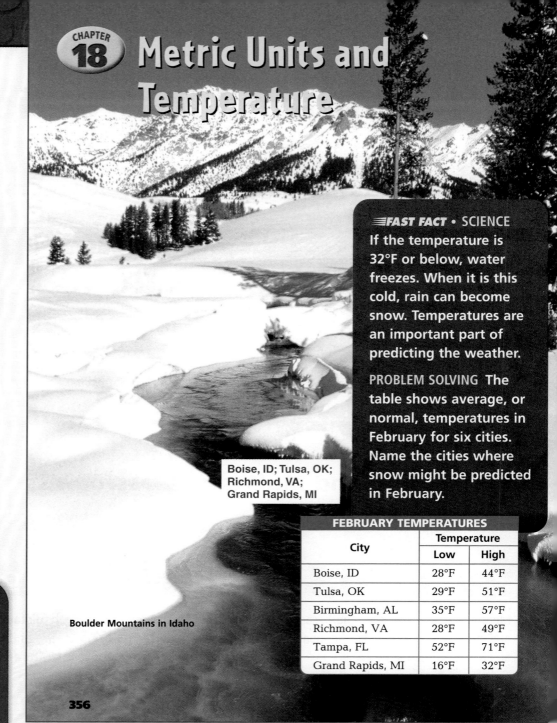

CHAPTER
18 Metric Units and Temperature

≡FAST FACT • SCIENCE
If the temperature is 32°F or below, water freezes. When it is this cold, rain can become snow. Temperatures are an important part of predicting the weather.

PROBLEM SOLVING The table shows average, or normal, temperatures in February for six cities. Name the cities where snow might be predicted in February.

Boise, ID; Tulsa, OK; Richmond, VA; Grand Rapids, MI

Boulder Mountains in Idaho

356

City	FEBRUARY TEMPERATURES	
	Temperature	
	Low	High
Boise, ID	28°F	44°F
Tulsa, OK	29°F	51°F
Birmingham, AL	35°F	57°F
Richmond, VA	28°F	49°F
Tampa, FL	52°F	71°F
Grand Rapids, MI	16°F	32°F

WHY LEARN MATH? Photographers often need to estimate distance when taking photographs. For example, for a certain setting on the camera, the photographer may need to be 1 meter away from the subject being photographed. Ask: In what other professions might someone use metric units? Possible answer: pharmacist, astronaut, chemist

Family Involvement Activities

These activities provide:

- Letter to the Family
- Math Vocabulary
- Family Game
- Practice (Homework)

Family Involvement Activities, p. FA69

CHECK WHAT YOU KNOW

Use this page to help you review and remember important skills needed for Chapter 18.

✓ MEASURE TO THE NEAREST CENTIMETER

Write the length to the nearest centimeter.

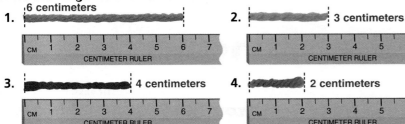

1. 6 centimeters

2. 3 centimeters

3. 4 centimeters

4. 2 centimeters

✓ READ A THERMOMETER

Write the temperature shown on each thermometer.

5. 40°F

6. 35°F

7. 15°C

VOCABULARY POWER

REVIEW

capacity [kə•pa′sə•tē] *noun*

Capacity is the amount that a container can hold. Look at different containers of juice at home or at the store. Write the capacity of each.
Check students' work.

PREVIEW

centimeter (cm)
meter (m)
kilometer (km)

liter (L)
gram (g)
kilogram (kg)

 www.harcourtschool.com/mathglossary

Chapter 18 **357**

Assessing Prior Knowledge

Use the **Check What You Know** page to determine whether your students have mastered the prerequisite skills critical for this chapter.

Intervention

- **Diagnose and Prescribe**
Evaluate your students' performance on this page to determine whether intervention is necessary or if enrichment is appropriate. Options that provide instruction, practice, and a check are listed in the chart below.

✓ CHECK WHAT YOU KNOW RESOURCES

Intervention Copying Masters or CD-ROMs

Enrichment Copying Masters

VOCABULARY POWER

For activities and information about the vocabulary in this chapter, see page 356B.

ADDITIONAL PREVIEW VOCABULARY

decimeter (dm), milliliter (mL), mass, degrees Fahrenheit (°F), degrees Celsius (°C)

Were students successful with ✓ CHECK WHAT YOU KNOW?

IF . . . NO
THEN . . . INTERVENE

INTERVENTION OPTIONS

IF . . . YES
THEN . . . ENRICH

Skill/Items	Missed more than	Intervene with
Measure to the Nearest Centimeter, 1–4	1	• *Intervention*, Skill 53
Read a Thermometer, 5–7	1	• *Intervention*, Skills 54–55

Skill/Items	Missed fewer than	Enrich with
Measure to the Nearest Centimeter, 1–4	2	• *Intervention*, Enrichment p. IN363
Read a Thermometer, 5–7	2	• *Intervention*, Enrichment p. IN364

Lesson Planning

PROFESSIONAL DEVELOPMENT

Objective To estimate and measure length

Materials *For each student* centimeter ruler, p. TR55; 1-centimeter grid paper, p. TR58; crayons; tape; *For Thinker's Corner* centimeter ruler

NCTM Standards
1. Number and Operations
4. Measurement
6. Problem Solving
7. Reasoning and Proof
8. Communication
9. Connections

Math Background
Consider the following when you introduce metric measurements of length or distance.

- The length of small objects is measured in centimeters.
- The length of larger objects is measured in decimeters or meters.
- Distances are measured in kilometers.
- Metric units are related based on multiples of ten.

Vocabulary
centimeter (cm) a metric unit that is used to measure length

decimeter (dm) a metric unit that is used to measure length

meter (m) a metric unit that is used to measure length or distance

kilometer (km) a metric unit that is used to measure length or distance

Warm-Up Resources

Build Number Sense

Number of the Day
Transparency 18.1

Take the number of feet in a mile. Write 4 number sentences that include this number.
Possible answers: 5,280 − 4,112 = 1,168; 5,000 + 200 + 80 = 5,280; 5,280 + 0 = 5,280; 5,280 − 110 = 5,170

Review Basic Facts

Daily Facts Practice

Have students practice division facts by completing Set C of *Teacher's Resource Book*, p. TR96.

Solve a Problem
Transparency 18.1

Problem of the Day

Mike drew a line twice as long as Penny's. Penny's line was 2 inches shorter than the one Cassandra drew. Cassandra's line was 20 inches long. How long were the lines Penny and Mike drew? Penny: 18 inches; Mike: 36 inches

Solution Problem of the Day tab, p. PD18

Intervention and Extension Resources

Alternative Teaching Strategy

MATERIALS *For each student* centimeter ruler or meter stick

Have students **measure objects**. Ask them to list three objects that they would measure by using each of the following metric units: centimeters, decimeters, meters. Then have them use a centimeter ruler or a meter stick to measure each object. Have them record their measurements in a table. Check students' work.

See also page 360.

KINESTHETIC

BODILY/KINESTHETIC

Multistep and Strategy Problems

The following multistep and strategy problems are provided in Lesson 18.1:

Page	Item
360	30, 32–33

ESOL/ESL

MATERIALS *For each student* meter stick, play money

ESOL/ESL

Help students **build understanding of lesson vocabulary**. Have students relate metric units and parts of a dollar. Use a meter stick and play money to demonstrate the following:

100 cm = 1 meter
100 cents = 1 dollar
10 dm = 1 meter
10 dimes = 1 dollar

VISUAL

VISUAL/SPATIAL

Career Connection

Have students **investigate careers that use metric measurements**. Suggest they consider fields like auto mechanics, medicine, optometry, rocket science, and food preparation. Have them share with the class how metric measurement is used in each career.

AUDITORY

VERBAL/LINGUISTIC

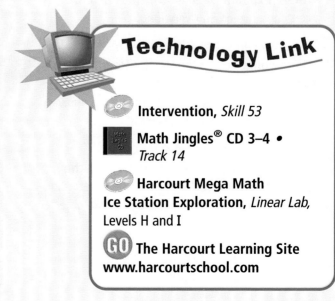

Technology Link

Intervention, *Skill 53*

Math Jingles® CD 3–4 • *Track 14*

Harcourt Mega Math Ice Station Exploration, *Linear Lab,* Levels H and I

GO The Harcourt Learning Site www.harcourtschool.com

Lesson 18.1 Organizer

Objective To estimate and measure length

Vocabulary centimeter (cm), decimeter (dm), meter (m), kilometer (km)

Materials *For each student* centimeter ruler, p. TR55; 1-centimeter grid paper, p. TR58; crayons; tape; *For Thinker's Corner* centimeter ruler

1 INTRODUCE

QUICK REVIEW provides review of prerequisite skills.

WHY LEARN THIS? The metric system is used throughout the world. *Share the lesson objective with students.*

2 TEACH

Guided Instruction

• *Discuss the vocabulary in the Learn section.*
Which measurement represents a distance that you cannot actually measure in your classroom? kilometer

MODIFYING INSTRUCTION Relate decimeter and centimeter to base-ten blocks. Use a rod to represent a decimeter and the length of a small cube to represent a centimeter. Students may use these as mental pictures to estimate length.

• *Have students look at the Activity.*
What classroom items could you measure using a centimeter ruler? Possible answers: book, pencil, chalk, eraser, paper, stapler
REASONING Would you choose to measure the height of the door using a centimeter ruler? Explain. No; the door is tall and the centimeter ruler isn't very long.

• *Direct students' attention to Step 3.*
How would you estimate the length of an object in centimeters? Possible answer: use your index finger and count about how many finger widths long each object is.

• *Have students read Step 4.*
How do you measure something "to the nearest centimeter"? Find the centimeter line that comes the closest to the end of the object.

Length

▶ **Learn**

MAKE IT METRIC In the metric system, **centimeter (cm)**, **decimeter (dm)**, **meter (m)**, and **kilometer (km)** are units used to measure length and distance.

VOCABULARY
centimeter (cm)
decimeter (dm)
meter (m)
kilometer (km)

A *centimeter* is about the width of your index finger.

A *decimeter* is about the width of an adult's hand.

Your armspan is about 1 *meter* long.

A *kilometer* is a little more than half a mile.

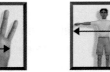

Activity
Materials: centimeter ruler

STEP 1
Copy the table.

LENGTH IN CENTIMETERS		
Object	Estimate	Measure

STEP 2
Write four objects that you would measure using centimeters.

STEP 3
Estimate the length of each object in centimeters. Record your estimates.

STEP 4
Use a centimeter ruler. Measure the length of each object to the nearest centimeter. Record your measurements.

358

Reteach 18.1

Length

• The width of your index finger is about 1 **centimeter (cm)**.
• The width of an adult's hand is about 1 **decimeter (dm)**.
• Your arm span is about 1 **meter (m)**.
• Five city blocks is about 1 **kilometer (km)**.

1. Record the unit you would use to measure each object. Then measure the lengths to the nearest *centimeter, decimeter, meter, or kilometer.* **Measurements will vary. Check students' tables.**

Object	Unit	Measurement
Shoe	dm	
Chalkboard	m	
Watch	cm	
Classmate's finger	cm	
Your classroom	m	
Crayon	cm	
Classmate's height	dm	

2. Order the items in your list from shortest to longest.
Possible order: finger, crayon, watch, shoe, height,
chalkboard, classroom

3. List 2 distances you would measure in kilometers.
Answers will vary.
a bike ride; distance between 2 cities

RW94 Reteach

Practice 18.1

Length

Estimate the length in centimeters. Then use a ruler to measure to the nearest centimeter. **Estimates may vary.**

1.
   9 cm

2.
   4 cm

3.
   6 cm

Choose the unit you would use to measure each. Write *cm, m,* or *km.* **Answers may vary.**

4. the length of your little finger
   cm

5. the distance between 2 towns
   km

6. the length of a chalkboard
   m

7. the length of your math book
   cm

8. the length of the Mississippi River
   km

9. the length of a poster
   cm

Mixed Review

10. $3.68
    − $1.79
    $1.89

11. 752
    + 134
    886

12. 54 ÷ **9** = 6

13. 8 × 0 = **0**

14. 5 ÷ **1** = 5

15. 7 × **8** = 56

Find the pattern and solve.

16. 64, 56, 48, 40, 32, **24**

17. 1, 3, 5, 7, 9, 11, **13**

18. 12, 18, 24, 30, **36**, 42

19. 37, 34, 31, 28, **25**, 22

PW94 Practice

Relating Units

Use the Table of Measures to find out how the metric units are related.

TABLE OF MEASURES
10 centimeters = 1 decimeter
100 centimeters = 1 meter
1,000 meters = 1 kilometer

Activity

MATERIALS: centimeter grid paper, crayons, tape

STEP 1	STEP 2
Use the Table of Measures to decide how many decimeters are in one meter.	Cut enough decimeter strips out of grid paper to make a 1-meter strip. Color each decimeter strip a different color.

STEP 3	STEP 4
Tape the decimeter strips together so that the edges do not overlap.	Estimate the length of your classroom. Then use your meter strip to find the actual measure. **Check students' work.**

• How did you decide how many decimeter strips were needed to make a meter strip? **Possible answer: 1 m = 100 cm and 10 cm = 1 dm. So, you can divide 100 cm by 10 cm. 100 ÷ 10 = 10**

▶ **Check**

1. **Explain** how to find the length in centimeters of objects that do not line up exactly with a centimeter mark.
Find the centimeter mark that is closest to the end of the object.

Estimate the length in centimeters. Then use a ruler to measure to the nearest centimeter.

Estimates will vary.

2.
5 cm

3.
2 cm

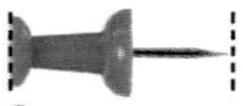

4.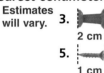
4 cm

5.
1 cm

Technology Link

More Practice:
Harcourt Mega Math
Ice Station
Exploration, *Linear Lab*, Levels H and I

Choose the unit you would use to measure each.
Write *cm, m,* or *km*. **Answers may vary.**

6. the length of a crayon **cm**
7. the length of a chalkboard **m**
8. the length of a carrot **cm**
9. the length of a playground **m**
10. the length of a highway **km**
11. the length of a butterfly **cm**

LESSON CONTINUES ▶

North Carolina Standards 2.02 Estimate and measure using appropriate units. b) Length (miles, meters). *also* 2.01b

---

• *Have students look at the Table of Measures on the top of page 359.*
Which is the greater length, 10 centimeters or 2 decimeters? Explain. 2 decimeters; 2 decimeters equals 20 centimeters.

MODIFYING INSTRUCTION For the activity, students can cut out the strips for base-ten rods found on p. TR7 to use as their decimeter strips.

After completing the activity, you may wish to have students estimate and then measure distances in meters, such as on the playground.

3 PRACTICE

Guided Practice

Do Check Exercises 1–11 with your students. Identify students who are having difficulty and choose appropriate lesson resources to provide assistance.

Challenge 18.1

Centimeter Estimation Game

Play with a partner.

Materials:
• table shown below for each player
• centimeter ruler

How to Play:

Step 1 Work with your partner to identify 10 objects or distances in the classroom that you will measure in centimeters. Record them in the first column of your tables.

Step 2 Work by yourself to estimate the length of each object or distance in centimeters. Record your estimates in the second column of your table.

Step 3 Work with your partner to measure the length of each object or distance to the nearest centimeter. Record these measurements in the third column of your tables.

Step 4 Work by yourself to find the difference between the estimated length and actual length of each object or distance. Record these differences in the fourth column of your table.

Step 5 Work by yourself to find the sum of the differences in the fourth column. The player with the lower sum wins!

Object/Distance	Estimated Length	Actual Length	Difference

W94 Challenge

Problem Solving 18.1

Length

Understand → Plan → Solve → Check

Write the correct answer.

1. Use a ruler to measure this line segment to the nearest centimeter.

6 centimeters

2. Which unit of measure would you use to measure the length of a fence that goes around a park? Write *centimeter, meter,* or *kilometer.*

meter

3. Tammy cut a 50-centimeter piece of yarn into 3 pieces. One piece was 12 centimeters and another was 8 centimeters. How long was the third piece of yarn?

30 centimeters

4. Michael has 8 dimes, 2 quarters, and 6 pennies. Does he have enough to buy a pen that costs $1.50? Write *yes* or *no.*

no

Choose the letter of the correct answer.

5. Choose the best estimate for the length of Garret's bedroom.

A 5 centimeters
B 5 decimeters
Ⓒ 5 meters
D 5 kilometers

6. Estimate the length of this line segment in centimeters.

F 1 centimeter
Ⓖ 3 centimeters
H 7 centimeters
J 100 centimeters

7. 643
+156

A 599
Ⓑ 799
C 893
D 899

8. Which figure is next in the pattern?

○□△○□△○□△

Ⓕ circle
G triangle
H square
J rhombus

9. **Write About It** How did you decide your answer to Problem 4?
Possible answer: Since 8 dimes is $0.80, 2 quarters is $0.50, and 6 pennies is $0.06, you know that Michael has $1.36. So, he has less than $1.50.

PS94 Problem Solving

359

Independent Practice

Note that Exercises 30, 32, and 33 are **multistep or strategy problems.** Assign Exercises 12–35.

MULTISTEP OR STRATEGY PROBLEM To solve Exercise 32, students can convert 2 decimeters into centimeters. 2 dm = 10 cm + 10 cm, so 2 dm = 20 cm. Then students can add 3 cm and 20 cm to see if it equals 23 cm.

Extra Practice, page 370, Set A

Practice and Problem Solving

Estimate the length in centimeters. Then use a ruler to measure to the nearest centimeter. **Estimates will vary.**

12.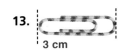
12 cm

13.
3 cm

14.
3 cm

15.
1 cm

Choose the unit you would use to measure each. Write *cm*, *m*, or *km*. **Answers may vary.**

16. the distance you can ride a bike in 30 minutes **km**

17. the distance from your classroom to the playground **m**

18. the length of a pencil **cm**

19. the length of your classroom **m**

Choose the better estimate.

20. Ali walked 4 _?_ in one hour. **A**
    A kilometers   B decimeters

21. Carole's ponytail is 1 _?_ long. **A**
    A decimeter   B kilometer

22. The wall is 3 _?_ high. **B**
    A centimeters   B meters

23. The paper clip is 3 _?_ long. **B**
    A decimeters   B centimeters

Compare. Write $<$ or $>$ for each ●. Use the Table of Measures on page 359 to help.

24. 5 cm ● 1 dm **<**

25. 1 m ● 50 cm **>**

26. 1 dm ● 10 m **<**

Use a ruler. Draw a line for each length. **Check students' lines.**

27. 2 centimeters

28. 1 decimeter

29. 14 centimeters

30. 📖 Write About It Choose 3 objects inside your classroom and 3 outside. Estimate and measure the lengths. Record the results. Tell what tool you used to measure each.
Check students' work.

31. **FAST FACT** • GEOGRAPHY Snake River Canyon in Idaho has a maximum depth of 2,400 meters. Write this number in word form and expanded form.
two thousand, four hundred; 2,000 + 400

32. **REASONING** Chad says 23 centimeters is the same as 2 decimeters plus 3 centimeters. Do you agree? Explain.
Yes; 2 dm = 20 cm; so 2 dm + 3 cm = 23 cm.

33. Adam was second in line. Susan stood behind Adam and in front of Jean. Tim was first in line. Who was fourth in line? **Jean**

360

Alternative Teaching Strategy Scaffolded Instruction

PURPOSE Students find that the metric system of measurement is based on multiples of ten.

MATERIALS *For each student* centimeter ruler, p. TR55

Explain to students that the metric system uses place value based on 10, just as our number system does.

• Display the following:
  10 centimeters = 1 decimeter

Ask students to tell how many centimeters are in 2 decimeters, 6 decimeters, and 10 decimeters. **20 cm, 60 cm, 100 cm**

• Display a meter stick and ask a volunteer to show 1 decimeter. As a group, count by tens to the end of the stick. Ask: How many groups of 10 centimeters are there in 1 meter? **10 groups** Since there are 10 groups of 10 centimeters in 1 meter, how many decimeters are in 1 meter? **10 dm** Write *10 decimeters = 1 meter.*

• To check students' understanding, have them complete as a group the following examples:
  _?_ centimeters = 3 decimeters **30**
  _?_ decimeters = 10 meters **100**

PROFESSIONAL DEVELOPMENT

34. **?** **What's the Error?** Nick said that the line below measures about 2 cm. Describe his error. Give the correct measure. **He should have measured to the closer centimeter mark. The line measures about 3 cm.**

35. Sarah drew this poster for her science project. What is the length of the bottom edge of her poster in decimeters? Explain. **4 dm long; Possible answer: Her poster is 40 cm long; 40 cm = 4 dm.**

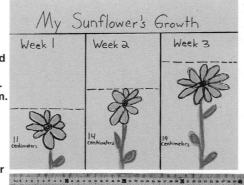

My Sunflower's Growth

| Week 1 | Week 2 | Week 3 |

36. Russell has 5 meters of string. How many centimeters of string does he have? **C**

- **A** 50 centimeters
- **B** 100 centimeters
- **C** 500 centimeters
- **D** 5,000 centimeters

37. Shawna used 125 centimeters of green ribbon and 175 centimeters of blue ribbon for an art poster. How many meters of ribbon did she use altogether? **A**

- **A** 3 meters
- **C** 10 meters
- **B** 5 meters
- **D** 25 meters

Problem Solving · Thinker's Corner

Measure the pieces of yarn and break the code! To find the correct letter for each blank, match the measurement and the color of the yarn.

W ▬▬▬▬▬▬▬
T ▬▬▬▬▬
T ▬▬▬▬▬▬
H ▬▬▬▬▬▬
S ▬▬▬▬▬
E ▬▬▬▬▬
C ▬▬▬▬▬▬
R ▬▬▬
A ▬▬▬
E ▬▬▬▬

What did the mother bird call the baby bird? **tweet heart**

?	?	?	?	?	?	?	?	?	?
3 cm	5 cm	2 cm	2 cm	4 cm	5 cm	2 cm	1 cm	1 cm	3 cm

Problem Solving · Thinker's Corner

- *Have students measure the pieces of yarn.* **How many pieces of yarn have a length of 2 cm?** 2 pieces **How many pieces of yarn have a length greater than 2 cm?** 6 pieces **What is the difference in length of the yarn for H and the yarn for S?** 1 cm

MODIFYING INSTRUCTION Tell students that not all of the pieces of yarn will be used and that some of the pieces of yarn may be used more than once.

4 ASSESS

Summarize the lesson by having students:

DISCUSS Why would it be better to measure the length of a chalkboard in meters rather than in centimeters? Possible answer: it would take fewer meters than centimeters.

WRITE Why is it important to have more than one unit of measure?
Possible answer: it makes it easier to measure objects of different sizes.

LESSON QUIZ

Choose the unit you would use to measure each. Write *cm, m,* or *km.* Answers may vary.

Transparency **18.1**

1. the length of a school bus m
2. the length of an eraser cm
3. the distance from one city to another city km
4. the length of a notebook cm

Lesson Planning

PROFESSIONAL
DEVELOPMENT

Objective To use the problem solving strategy *make a table* to solve problems

Lesson Resources Reading Transparency 18; Intervention • Problem Solving, Strategy/Skill 18

NCTM Standards
2. Algebra
4. Measurement
6. Problem Solving
7. Reasoning and Proof
8. Communication
9. Connections
10. Representation

Math Background

Consider these ideas when helping students use the strategy *make a table* to solve problems involving metric measurement.

- The problem should be analyzed to identify the question.

- A table can be used to organize information to solve problems.

- Making a table can help students visualize how metric measurements are related.

- As students use the strategy *make a table,* they will build skills needed for working with function tables.

Warm-Up Resources

Number of the Day

Transparency **18.2**

Write and solve five multiplication sentences using the number of decimeters in one meter. Possible answer: $10 \times 2 = 20$, $10 \times 4 = 40$, $10 \times 6 = 60$, $10 \times 8 = 80$, $10 \times 9 = 90$

Daily Facts Practice

Have students practice multiplication facts by completing Set D of *Teacher's Resource Book*, p. TR96.

Transparency **18.2**

Problem of the Day

Find the mystery metric fact.
- Take the number of centimeters in a meter.
- Divide it by 4.
- Subtract the product of 2 and 8.
- Round the number to the nearest ten.
The answer is the number of ___ in a ___. Possible answers: centimeters, decimeter; decimeters, meter

Solution Problem of the Day tab, p. PD18

Intervention and Extension Resources

Alternative Teaching Strategy

Help students **solve a problem.** For students who have difficulty understanding the problem on page 362, guide them through a simpler version of the same problem. Begin by asking students to figure out how much yarn would be needed for only 2 students. 400 cm, or 4 meters Then help them find how much yarn would be needed for 3 and then 4 students. 600 cm, or 6 meters; 800 cm, or 8 meters

VISUAL

LOGICAL/MATHEMATICAL

Reading Strategy

Choose Important Information Remind students that not all the information included in a problem may be important for solving the problem. Readers must determine what information is important and what information is not. Display the following problem. Ask students to identify the information that is not important.

Mrs. Chen is buying ribbon to make costumes. She needs 200 centimeters of ribbon for each costume. She wants to make 6 costumes. Each meter of ribbon costs $1.55. How many meters of ribbon will she need? Each meter of ribbon costs $1.55.

18 **Reading Transparency 18**

Multistep and Strategy Problems

The following multistep and strategy problems are provided in Lesson 18.2:

Page	Item
363	1–8

ESOL/ESL

Help students **understand the term** *table*. Some students may be confused by the term *table* because they might think of a piece of furniture. Explain that some English words have more than one meaning. Tell them that a table can also be a kind of chart. Draw a table on the chalkboard and point out the rows and columns.

ESOL/ESL

AUDITORY

VERBAL/LINGUISTIC

Early Finishers

MATERIALS newspapers, magazines, textbooks

Have students **identify and explain tables.** Invite students to look through newspapers, magazines, science textbooks, and social studies textbooks to locate examples of tables. Have them share their findings with the class, explaining the purpose of each table. Check students' work.

AUDITORY

INTERPERSONAL/SOCIAL

Technology Link

Intervention • Problem Solving, *Strategy/Skill 18*

Lesson 18.2 Organizer

Objective To use the problem solving strategy *make a table* to solve problems

Lesson Resources Reading Transparency 18; Intervention • Problem Solving, Strategy/Skill 18

1 INTRODUCE

QUICK REVIEW provides review of prerequisite skills.

WHY LEARN THIS? You'll know how to organize the information needed to solve problems in a table. *Share the lesson objective with students.*

2 TEACH

Guided Instruction

- *Direct students' attention to the Understand step.*
  Why is it important to think about whether the problem includes any information that is not needed to solve the problem? Possible answer: you can be confused by extra information you don't need.

- *Have students read Plan and discuss the table they will make to solve the problem.*
  How can making a table help you solve the problem? Possible answer: a table can help you see the relationships between units of measurement.

- *Ask students to study the table in the Solve section.*
  Why does the number of centimeters increase by 200 as you read across the table? Each student needs 200 centimeters, so each additional student increases the amount of yarn needed by 200 centimeters.
  REASONING How many meters of yarn would Ms. Tahn need if two students were absent?
  12 meters

- *Encourage students to think about the steps they followed to solve the problem.*
  Was making a table the best way to solve this problem? Explain. Answers will vary.

Problem Solving Strategy
Make a Table

Quick Review
1. 10×2 20
2. $200 + 200$ 400
3. $100 + 100$ 200
4. $400 + 400$ 800
5. $1,000 + 1,000$ 2,000

PROBLEM Each student in Ms. Tahn's art class needs 200 centimeters of yarn. If Ms. Tahn has 8 students, how many meters of yarn are needed?

UNDERSTAND
- What are you asked to find?
  how many meters of yarn are needed
- What information will you use?
  8 students each need 200 cm of yarn
- Is there any information you will not use? If so, what?
  No, you need all information given.

PLAN
- What strategy can you use to solve the problem?
  You can *make a table* to show how to change centimeters into meters.

SOLVE
- How can you use the strategy to solve the problem?

  Think: 100 cm = 1 m

Students	1	2	3	4	5	6	7	8
Centimeters	200	400	600	800	1,000	1,200	1,400	1,600
Meters	2	4	6	8	10	12	14	16

  The 8 students need 1,600 centimeters of yarn.

  1,600 centimeters = 16 meters

  So, 16 meters of yarn are needed.

CHECK
- How can you decide if your answer is correct?
  Possible answers: skip-count by 200 eight times; find how many hundreds are in 1,600.

362

Reteach 18.2

Problem Solving Strategy

Make a Table

Each student in Mr. Kinley's math class needs 300 centimeters of yarn to complete a project. If he has 5 students, how many meters of yarn does he need?

You can make a table to solve a problem. Remember: 100 centimeters = 1 meter.

Centimeters or Meters of Yarn Needed

Number of Students	Centimeters	Meters
1	300	3
2	600	6
3	900	9
4	1,200	12
5	1,500	15

Use the table to solve the problem.

1. Five students need 1,500 centimeters of yarn. So, 5 students need __15__ meters of yarn.

Make a table to solve.

2. What if Mr. Kinley had 7 students? How many meters of yarn would he need?
   __21 meters__

3. What if Mr. Kinley had 10 students? How many meters of yarn would he need? __30 meters__

Martin drove 3 kilometers. How many meters did he drive?

4. Which table could you use to help solve the problem? __A__

A
kilometers	1	2	3
meters	1,000	2,000	3,000

C
meters	1	2	3
decimeters	10	20	30

B
centimeters	100	200	300
meters	1	2	3

D
decimeters	1	2	3
centimeters	10	20	30

5. What is the solution to the problem? __3,000 meters__

6. Which table could you use to find how many decimeters are in 2 meters? How many decimeters equal 2 meters?
   __C; 20 decimeters__

Reteach RW95

Practice 18.2

Problem Solving Strategy

Make a Table

Complete this table.

1.
Meters	1	2	3	4	5	6	7	8	9	10
Centimeters	100	200	300	400	500	600	700	800	900	1,000

For 2–3, use the completed table above.

2. Gary needs 500 centimeters of space for a bookcase. How many meters of space does he need?
   __5 meters__

3. Kara needs 9 meters of string. How many centimeters of string does she need?
   __900 centimeters__

Jake drew a line that was 3 decimeters long. How many centimeters long was his line?

4. Which table helps solve the problem? __D__

A
Kilometers	1	2	3
Meters	1,000	2,000	3,000

C
Centimeters	100	200	300
Meters	1	2	3

B
Meters	1	2	3
Decimeters	10	20	30

D
Decimeters	1	2	3
Centimeters	10	20	30

5. What is the solution to the problem? __30 cm__

Mixed Review

Draw the next 3 shapes in the pattern.

6. ▽□△▽▽□△▽ ▽□△□ __▽□△__

7. ○○□○○○□○○□ __○○□__

Practice PW95

Strategies

Draw a Diagram or Picture
Make a Model or Act It Out
Make an Organized List
Find a Pattern
▶ Make a Table or Graph
Predict and Test
Work Backward
Solve a Simpler Problem
Write a Number Sentence
Use Logical Reasoning

Problem Solving

Use *make a table* to solve.

1. **What if** Ms. Tahn had 10 students? Use the table on page 362 to help decide how many meters of yarn are needed. **20 m**

2. Patty needs 150 centimeters of green yarn and 350 centimeters of white yarn. How many meters of yarn does she need in all? **5 m**

Barb jogged 3,000 meters. How many kilometers did she jog? (HINT: 1 km = 1,000 m)

3. Which table helps solve the problem? **A**

A
Kilometers	1	2	3
Meters	1,000	2,000	3,000

B
Centimeters	100	200	300
Meters	1	2	3

C
Meters	1	2	3
Decimeters	10	20	30

D
Decimeters	1	2	3
Centimeters	10	20	30

4. Which answers the question? **J**

F 3,000 km   **H** 30 km
G 300 km   **J** 3 km

Mixed Strategy Practice

USE DATA For 5–6, use the table.

5. Compare the heights of the mountain peaks. List them in order from the least to the greatest heights. **See right.**

6. Which two mountain peaks have a difference in height of 178 meters? **Borah Peak and Hyndman Peak**

7. **Write a problem** that uses kilometers, meters, decimeters, or centimeters. **Check students' problems.**

IDAHO MOUNTAIN PEAKS	
Peak	**Height**
Hyndman Peak	3,681 meters
Borah Peak	3,859 meters
Twin Peaks	3,152 meters

5. Twin Peaks, 3,152 m; Hyndman Peak, 3,681 m; Borah Peak, 3,859 m

8. Reece had some walnuts. He ate 3 walnuts. Then he gave 4 friends 5 walnuts each. He had 1 walnut left. How many walnuts did he start with? **24 walnuts**

Chapter 18 **363**

* **North Carolina Standards 2.01** Solve problems using measurement concepts and procedures
olving: b) Equivalent measures within the same measurement system. *also* 1.06

Challenge 18.2

What's the Order?

Order the lengths from least to greatest.

1. 305 cm, 31 km, 3 m, 35 dm

     3 m, 305 cm, 35 dm, 31 km

2. 295 cm, 2 m, 2 km, 2 dm

     2 dm, 2 m, 295 cm, 2 km

3. 15 km, 15 m, 15 dm, 51 cm

     51 cm, 15 dm, 15 m, 15 km

4. 8 m, 878 cm, 78 m, 87 dm

     8 m, 87 dm, 878 cm, 78 m

5. 355 cm, 5 m, 535 cm, 35 m

     355 cm, 5 m, 535 cm, 35 m

6. 986 cm, 98 km, 86 m, 89 dm, 9 m

     89 dm, 9 m, 986 cm, 86 m, 98 km

7. 92 km, 29 m, 9 dm, 290 cm, 229 dm

     290 cm, 92 dm, 229 dm, 29 m, 92 km

8. Think of two times when metric units of length might be used.

     Possible answers: in a science
     class; in sports

9. Write a problem using the measurements listed in one of the problems above. Solve.

     Check students' problems and solutions.

Reading Strategy 18.2

Choose Important Information

Understand → Plan → Solve → Check

A word problem may contain more information than is needed. You must decide what information you need to solve the problem.

Read the following problem:

The 10 students in Ms. Hurley's geography class are working on a project. The students are in groups of 2. Each group needs 600 centimeters of string for the project. How many meters does each group need?

1. Read each fact. If it contains information that is needed to solve the problem, write yes. If it does not, write no.

  a. There are 10 students in Ms. Hurley's class.   **no**
  b. The students are in groups of 2.   **no**
  c. Each group needs 600 centimeters of string.   **yes**

2. Solve the problem.

     600 centimeters = 6 meters

3. Describe the strategy you used.

Possible answer: I made a table. 100 centimeters = 1 meter

Draw a line through the fact or facts that are not needed to solve the problem. Then solve.

4. Henry drew 8 line segments on his paper. It took him 20 minutes in all. He drew one line segment that was 30 centimeters long. How many decimeters long was that line segment?

     3 decimeters

5. Fiona is cutting a piece of string into 9 pieces. She is also cutting some fabric into 7 squares. One piece of string is 300 centimeters long. How many meters long is that piece of string?

     3 meters

6. Tom is 3 years old. His favorite blanket is 1 meter long. How many centimeters long is his blanket?

     100 centimeters

7. Norma was third in line. The line was 8 meters long. How long was the line in centimeters?

     800 centimeters

---

3 PRACTICE

Guided Practice

Do Problem Solving Practice Exercises 1–4 with your students. Identify students who are having difficulty and choose appropriate lesson resources to provide assistance. Note that Exercises 1–4 are **multistep or strategy problems.**

Independent Practice

Note that Exercises 5–8 are **multistep or strategy problems.** Assign Exercises 5–8.

SCAFFOLDED INSTRUCTION Use the prompts on Transparency 18 to guide instruction for the multistep problem in Exercise 8.

Transparency **18**

4 ASSESS

Summarize the lesson by having students:

DISCUSS **When would you make a table to help you solve a problem?** Possible answer: when you need to change units of measurement.

 WRITE **Choose a problem that you solved using the *make a table* strategy. Explain how you completed the *Understand* step.** Answers will vary.

LESSON QUIZ

Use *make a table* to solve.

Transparency **18.2**

1. Judy is an electrician. She needs 1,200 centimeters of wire. How many meters of wire should she buy? **12 m**

2. Amal jogged 2 kilometers. How many meters did he jog? **2,000 m**

363

Lesson Planning

PROFESSIONAL DEVELOPMENT

Objective To estimate and measure capacity

Materials *For each group* plastic glass that holds about 250 mL, liter container, large plastic pitcher, water

NCTM Standards
4. Measurement
6. Problem Solving
7. Reasoning and Proof
8. Communication
9. Connections
10. Representation

Math Background
These ideas will help students understand measuring capacity in milliliters and liters.

- Smaller quantities are measured in milliliters.
- Larger quantities are measured in liters.
- One liter equals 1,000 milliliters.

Vocabulary
milliliter (mL) a metric unit that is used to measure capacity

liter (L) a metric unit that is used to measure capacity

Warm-Up Resources

Number of the Day
Transparency **18.3**

Write four number sentences that have a solution of 100. Possible answers: $200 - 100 = 100$, $50 + 50 = 100$, $10 \times 10 = 100$, $70 + 30 = 100$

Daily Facts Practice

Have students practice multiplication and division facts by completing Set E of *Teacher's Resource Book*, p. TR96.

Transparency **18.3**

Problem of the Day

A blue string is 11 cm long. A black string is 20 cm longer than the blue string. A green string is 10 cm shorter than the black string. A red string is 12 cm longer than the green string. List the strings and their lengths in order from shortest to longest. blue: 11 cm, green: 21 cm, black: 31 cm, red: 33 cm

Solution Problem of the Day tab, p. PD18

Intervention and Extension Resources

Alternative Teaching Strategy

MATERIALS 1-mL dropper, 250-mL container, 1-L bottle

ESOL/ESL

Help students **visualize metric units of capacity**. Provide real models of a 1-mL dropper, a 250-mL container, and a 1-L bottle. Have students estimate how much water each holds. Then fill the containers and compare the capacity of each with students' estimates. Reinforce the idea that a typical glass of milk or juice usually holds about 250 mL.

KINESTHETIC

VISUAL/SPATIAL

Multistep and Strategy Problems

The following multistep or strategy problem is provided in Lesson 18.3:

Page	Item
365	10

Writing in Mathematics

Have students **solve a problem.** Provide the following writing prompt. Ask students to write their answers in their journals.

Describe how you would find about how many milliliters of water are in a tray of ice cubes. Possible answer: Allow the ice to melt. Pour the water in a container showing milliliters, and read the number of milliliters of water in the container.

Advanced Learners

Challenge students to **identify metric measurements of capacity.** Have them make a list of containers of liquid that might be found in their homes. Next to each item, students should indicate whether the label on the container would show the measurement in milliliters or liters. Encourage students to share and compare their lists. Check students' work.

VISUAL

LOGICAL/MATHEMATICAL

Lesson 18.3 Organizer

Objective To estimate and measure capacity

Vocabulary milliliter (mL), liter (L)

Materials *For each group* plastic glass that holds about 250 mL, liter container, large plastic pitcher, water

1 INTRODUCE

QUICK REVIEW provides review of prerequisite skills.

WHY LEARN THIS? You can keep track of the amount of liquid you drink when preparing for an athletic event. *Share the lesson objective with students.*

2 TEACH

Guided Instruction

- *Have students study the three pictures.*
  Which container holds the greatest amount? the least amount? the liter bottle; the medicine dropper

MODIFYING INSTRUCTION Review the lesson on capacity in Chapter 17 to help students understand that capacity can be measured in different units.

- *Have students complete Steps 1–2.*
  What is something that is measured in milliliters? in liters? Possible answers: medicine; soft drinks

- *Check students' understanding.*
  REASONING How many milliliters of water would fill two 1-liter bottles? 2,000 mL

3 PRACTICE

Guided Practice

Do Try It Exercises a–b with your students. Identify students who are having difficulty and choose appropriate lesson resources to provide assistance.

LESSON 3 HANDS ON **Capacity**

 Explore

Capacity can be measured by using metric units such as the **milliliter (mL)** and **liter (L)**.

A dropper holds about 1 mL.

A glass holds about 250 mL.

A water bottle holds about 1 L.

Activity

Copy the table to help find the capacity of different containers.

STEP 1
Estimate the number of milliliters that are in 1 liter. Estimate the number of liters that will fill the pitcher.

STEP 2
Use the plastic water glass. Pour 250 mL of water into the liter container.

STEP 3
Repeat until the liter container is full. Record how many milliliters you poured.

STEP 4
Pour 1 liter of water at a time into the pitcher. Repeat until the pitcher is full. Record the number of liters.

FINDING CAPACITY		
How many:	Estimate	Measure
milliliters in a liter?		
liters in the pitcher?		

Try It

a. How many milliliters did it take to fill the liter container? **1,000 mL**

b. How many liters did you pour into the pitcher? **Check students' responses.**

364

 Quick Review

1. 300 + 400 700
2. 800 + 100 900
3. 2,000 + 2,000 4,000
4. 250 + 250 500
5. 900 + 200 1,100

VOCABULARY
milliliter (mL)
liter (L)

MATERIALS
plastic glass that holds about 250 mL, liter container, large plastic pitcher, water

---

Reteach 18.3

Capacity

Capacity is the amount a container will hold when it is filled. Capacity can be measured using the metric units **milliliter (mL)** and **liter (L)**.

1,000 mL = 1 L

1. The soccer coach has 8 L of sports drink. He wants to pour the drink into bottles that hold 1,000 mL each. How many bottles does he need?

   a. How many milliliters equal 1 liter? **1,000 mL**

   b. How many milliliters equal 8 liters? **8,000 mL**

   c. How many groups of 1,000 mL are in 8 L? **8**

   d. How many bottles does he need? **8**

2. Roy needs to put 4 liters of juice into a cooler. He has containers that hold 500 mL. How many containers of juice should he put into the cooler?

   a. How many milliliters equal 1 liter? **1,000 mL**

   b. How many milliliters equal 4 liters? **4,000 mL**

   c. How many groups of 500 are in 4,000? **8**

   d. How many containers of juice does he need? **8**

3. Tanya needs to put 6,000 mL of water into a tub. How many 1 L jugs should she fill?

   a. How many milliliters equal 1 liter? **1,000 mL**

   b. How many groups of 1,000 are in 6,000 mL? **6**

   c. How many liter containers should she fill? **6**

RW96 Reteach

Practice 18.3

Capacity

Circle the better estimate.

1. 1 mL or (1 L)   2. 4 mL or (4 L)   3. (15 mL) or 15 L

4. (250 mL) or 250 L   5. 2 mL or (2 L)   6. (3,000 mL) or 3,000 L

Choose the unit you would use to measure each. Write mL or L. **Answers may vary.**

7. a mug of hot chocolate   **mL**

8. water in a swimming pool   **L**

9. a glass of juice   **mL**

10. water for a flower garden   **L**

11. a can of soup   **mL**

12. 5 pitchers of lemonade   **L**

Mixed Review

13. 59 + 64 + 93 = **216**

14. 726 − 493 = **233**

Write <, >, or = in each ○.

15. 7 × 8 ⊜ 87 − 31

16. 56 ÷ 7 ⊘ 3 × 2

17. 40 ÷ 8 ⊘ 7

18. 9 × 2 ⊜ 6 × 3

Continue each pattern.

19. 8, 16, 24, 32, **40**

20. 4, 9, 14, 19, **24**, **29**

21. 2, 5, 8, 11, **14**, 17

22. 17, 15, 13, 11, **9**

PW96 Practice

Connect

How are liters and milliliters related?

1,000 milliliters = 1 liter

Liters	1	2	3	4
Milliliters	1,000	2,000	3,000	4,000

9. Possible response: a soup can; a spoon would have to be filled many more times than a soup can, so he could measure the capacity faster using a soup can.

1,000 mL, or 1 L

Independent Practice

Note that Exercise 10 is a **multistep or strategy problem**. Assign Exercises 1–10.

Practice and Problem Solving

Choose the better estimate.

1.
3 mL or 3 L? **3 L**

2.
400 mL or 400 L? **400 mL**

3.
2 mL or 2 L? **2 L**

4.
200 mL or 200 L? **200 mL**

Choose the unit you would use to measure the capacity of each. Write mL or L. Answers may vary.

5. **L**

6. **mL**

7. **mL**

8. **mL**

9. **REASONING** Rashad wants to measure the capacity of a bucket. Should he use a soup can or a spoon? Explain. **See above.**

10. **? What's the Question?** Jamal had some stamps. He gave away 2 stamps and then arranged the rest in 4 rows of 3. The answer is 14 stamps. **How many stamps did he start with?**

4 ASSESS

Summarize the lesson by having students:

DISCUSS What is the relationship of milliliters to liters? 1,000 milliliters = 1 liter

WRITE If a bottle's capacity is 4 L, how many milliliters does it hold? Explain how you found the answer. 4,000 mL; Possible answer: I made a table.

LESSON QUIZ

Choose the unit you would use to measure the capacity of each. Write mL or L.
Answers may vary.

1. a sink filled with water **L**

2. a bottle of syrup **mL**

3. a mug of soup **mL**

4. a jug of liquid laundry soap **L**

Transparency 18.3

Getting Ready for the EOG Test

11. Mr. Dawson put 3,000 milliliters of water in a bucket. How many liters of water is this? **B**

A 1 liter   C 10 liters
B 3 liters   D 30 liters

° North Carolina Standards 2.02 Estimate and measure using appropriate units. a) Capacity (cups, ...s, quarts, gallons, liters). *also* **2.01b**

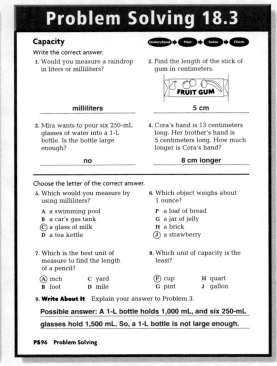

Challenge 18.3

Estimating and Comparing Capacity

Order the measurements from least to greatest capacity.

1. 5 L; 5,100 mL; 1,005 mL; 1 L

    1 L; 1,005 mL; 5L; 5,100 mL

2. 2,950 mL; 3,120 mL; 3 L; 21 L

    2,950 mL; 3 L; 3,120 mL; 21 L

3. 7,040 mL; 4,770 mL; 4 L; 7,400 mL

    4 L; 4,770 mL; 7,040 mL; 7,400 mL

4. 6,500 mL; 5 L; 5,600 mL; 6 L; 5,066 mL

    5 L; 5,066 mL; 5,600 mL; 6 L; 6,500 mL

5. List some containers that hold liquids. Record which metric unit would be better for measuring each container's capacity. **Check students' tables.**

Container	Milliliter (mL) or Liter (L)
Bottle of maple syrup	mL
Bottle of water	L

6. Write a problem using data from one of the problems above. Solve. **Check students' problems and solutions.**

N96 Challenge

Problem Solving 18.3

Capacity

Understand → Plan → Solve → Check

Write the correct answer.

1. Would you measure a raindrop in liters or milliliters?

    milliliters

2. Find the length of the stick of gum in centimeters.

    FRUIT GUM

    5 cm

3. Mira wants to pour six 250-mL glasses of water into a 1-L bottle. Is the bottle large enough?

    no

4. Cora's hand is 13 centimeters long. Her brother's hand is 5 centimeters long. How much longer is Cora's hand?

    8 cm longer

Choose the letter of the correct answer.

5. Which would you measure by using milliliters?

A a swimming pool
B a car's gas tank
C a glass of milk
D a tea kettle

6. Which object weighs about 1 ounce?

F a loaf of bread
G a jar of jelly
H a brick
J a strawberry

7. Which is the best unit of measure to find the length of a pencil?

A inch   C yard
B foot   D mile

8. Which unit of capacity is the least?

F cup   H quart
G pint   J gallon

9. **Write About It** Explain your answer to Problem 3.

Possible answer: A 1-L bottle holds 1,000 mL, and six 250-mL glasses hold 1,500 mL. So, a 1-L bottle is not large enough.

PS96 Problem Solving

Lesson Planning

PROFESSIONAL DEVELOPMENT

Objective To estimate and measure mass

Materials *For each group* classroom objects, small paper clips, simple balance, book with a mass of about 1 kilogram

NCTM Standards
4. Measurement
6. Problem Solving
7. Reasoning and Proof
8. Communication
9. Connections

Math Background
These ideas will help students understand metric measurement of mass.

- Grams and kilograms are units used for measuring mass.
- A kilogram is equivalent to 1,000 grams.
- Objects with the same size and dimensions do not necessarily have the same mass.
- Mass is the amount of matter something contains and weight is a measure of force of gravity upon an object.

Vocabulary
gram (g) a metric unit that is used to measure mass

kilogram (kg) a metric unit that is used to measure mass

mass the amount of matter in an object

Warm-Up Resources

Build Number Sense
3
2
1

Number of the Day

Transparency **18.4**

The number of the day is the number of nickels that equal the value of a quarter. Write and solve 2 number sentences using this number. Possible answer: $5 \times 5 = 25, 5 + 20 = 25$

Review Basic Facts
8
+3

Daily Facts Practice

Have students practice division facts by completing Set F of *Teacher's Resource Book*, p. TR96.

Solve a Problem

Transparency **18.4**

Problem of the Day

With their backpacks on, together Noah and Zack have a mass of 64 kilograms. Zack has a mass of 2 more kilograms than Noah. Each of their backpacks has a mass of 2 kilograms. What is the mass of each boy? Noah: 29 kilograms; Zack: 31 kilograms.

Solution Problem of the Day tab, p. PD18

Intervention and Extension Resources

Alternative Teaching Strategy

MATERIALS simple balance, objects to weigh

Have students work together using a simple balance to **measure a variety of objects to determine mass**. Suggest that students record their findings in a table. Check students' work.

KINESTHETIC

BODILY/KINESTHETIC

Multistep and Strategy Problems

The following multistep or strategy problem is provided in Lesson 18.4:

Page	Item
367	10

Language Arts Connection

Have students **identify items that can be measured in grams or kilograms**. Invite students to work individually or in pairs to write acrostic poems. Have them spell out the word *gram* or *kilogram*, and use words that name items that can be measured in that particular unit.

For example:
Gum wrapper
Raisin
Acorn
Marshmallow

Check students' work.

VISUAL

VERBAL/LINGUISTIC

Early Finishers

MATERIALS simple balance, objects of different masses

Have students **estimate and compare mass**. Provide them with a variety of objects of different masses. Have them predict which objects have about the same mass. Have them use the balance to test their predictions. Check students' work.

KINESTHETIC

BODILY/KINESTHETIC

Technology Link

Math Jingles® CD 3–4 •
Track 15

Lesson 18.4 Organizer

Objective To estimate and measure mass

Vocabulary gram (g), kilogram (kg), mass

Materials *For each group* classroom objects, small paper clips, simple balance, book with a mass of about 1 kilogram

---

1 INTRODUCE

QUICK REVIEW provides review of prerequisite skills.

WHY LEARN THIS? You can decide which metric unit to use to find the mass of an object. *Share the lesson objective with students.*

---

2 TEACH

Guided Instruction

- *Have students look at the pictures and captions at the top of the page.*
  Which unit measures more mass, 1 gram or 1 kilogram? 1 kilogram

- *Direct students' attention to Step 2 of the Activity.*
  What information do you have to help you decide what objects might have a mass of 10 grams? Possible answer: You know that 10 paper clips have a mass of about 10 grams, so you can compare the mass of other objects to the mass of 10 paper clips.

- *Direct students' attention to Step 3.*
  How many paper clips would you place on the balance to show 25 grams? 25 paper clips

MODIFYING INSTRUCTION If a metric scale is available, you may wish to have students measure the mass of several objects using this scale.

---

3 PRACTICE

Guided Practice

Complete Try It Exercises a–b with your students. Identify students who are having difficulty and choose appropriate lesson resources to provide assistance.

LESSON **4**

HANDS ON

Mass

▶ **Explore**

The **gram (g)** and the **kilogram (kg)** are metric units for measuring **mass**, or the amount of matter in an object.

A paper clip has a mass of about 1 gram.

A large book has a mass of about 1 kilogram.

VOCABULARY
gram (g)
kilogram (kg)
mass

MATERIALS
classroom objects, small paper clips, simple balance, book with a mass of about 1 kilogram

Activity

Find the mass of objects in your classroom.

STEP 1
Place 10 paper clips on one side of the simple balance to show 10 g.

STEP 2
Find an object that you think might equal 10 g. Use the balance to check.

STEP 3
Repeat Steps 1 and 2 for 25 g and 1 kg. Use the book to show 1 kg.

A nickel has a mass of about 5 grams. What things in your classroom have a mass of about 5 grams? Answers will vary.

Try It

Name an object that has a mass of each amount.

a. 5 grams
Possible answers: pencil; binder clip

b. 2 kilograms
Possible answers: a dictionary; a pair of boots

366

Reteach 18.4

Mass

The metric units for measuring mass are **gram (g)** and **kilogram (kg)**.

$1,000 \text{ g} = 1 \text{ kg}$

1. A box has a mass of 7 kg. What is the mass of the box in grams?
   a. How many grams equal 1 kilogram? ___1,000 g___
   b. What is the mass of the box in kilograms? ___7 kg___
   c. How many grams equal 7 kg? ___7,000 g___
   d. What is the mass of the box in grams? ___7,000 g___

2. A stack of books has a mass of 9,000 grams. What is the mass of the books in kilograms?
   a. How many grams equal 1 kilogram? ___1,000 g___
   b. What is the mass of the books in grams? ___9,000 g___
   c. How many kilograms equal 9,000 grams? ___9 kg___
   d. What is the mass of the books in kilograms? ___9 kg___

3. A suitcase has a mass of 12,000 grams. What is the mass of the suitcase in kilograms?
   a. How many grams equal 1 kilogram? ___1,000 g___
   b. How many groups of 1,000 are in 12,000? ___12___
   c. How many kilograms equal 12,000 grams? ___12 kg___
   d. What is the mass of the suitcase in kilograms? ___12 kg___

Reteach RW97

Practice 18.4

Mass

Circle the better estimate.

1. 6 g or 6 kg
2. 25 g or 25 kg
3. 22 g or 22 kg
4. 4 g or 4 kg
5. 6 g or 6 kg
6. 2 g or 2 kg

Choose the tool and unit to measure each.

Tools	Units
ruler	cm g
liter container	kg mL
simple balance	L m

7. the mass of a computer disk
   simple balance; g

8. the length of a desk
   ruler; cm

9. the capacity of a sink
   liter container; L

10. the mass of a sack of sugar
    simple balance; kg

11. the length of your hand
    ruler; cm

12. the mass of two bricks
    simple balance; kg

13. the mass of a feather
    simple balance; g

14. the mass of an eraser
    simple balance; g

Mixed Review

Solve.

15. $36 \div \underline{4} = 9$
16. $\underline{9} \times 6 = 54$
17. $4 \times \underline{7} = 28$
18. $\underline{12} \div 3 = 4$
19. $428 - 375 = \underline{53}$
20. $32 + 69 + 51 = \underline{152}$
21. $8 \times 0 = \underline{0}$
22. $10 \div 1 = \underline{10}$

Practice PW97

Connect

This cat has a mass of 5 kg. How many grams is that?

1,000 grams = 1 kilogram

Kilograms	1	2	3	4	5
Grams	1,000	2,000	3,000	4,000	5,000

So, the cat has a mass of 5,000 g.

11. No. Possible example: a pillow and a watermelon are about the same size, but the watermelon has a much greater mass.

Practice and Problem Solving

Choose the better estimate.

1.
200 g or 200 kg?
200 g

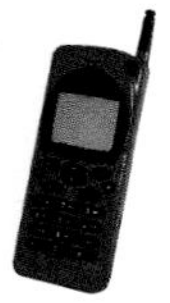

2.
18 g or 18 kg? **18 g**

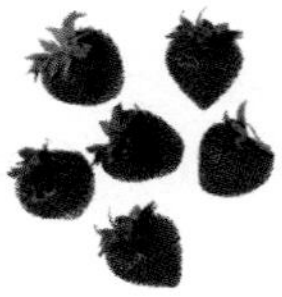

3.
9 g or 9 kg? **9 kg**

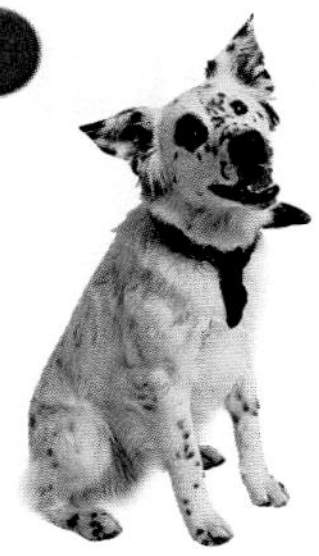

Choose the tool and unit to measure each.

4. length of a pencil
ruler; cm
5. mass of a grape
simple balance; g
6. capacity of a bucket
liter container; L
7. capacity of a tea kettle
liter container; L
8. mass of a flower
simple balance; g
9. length of a stamp
ruler; cm

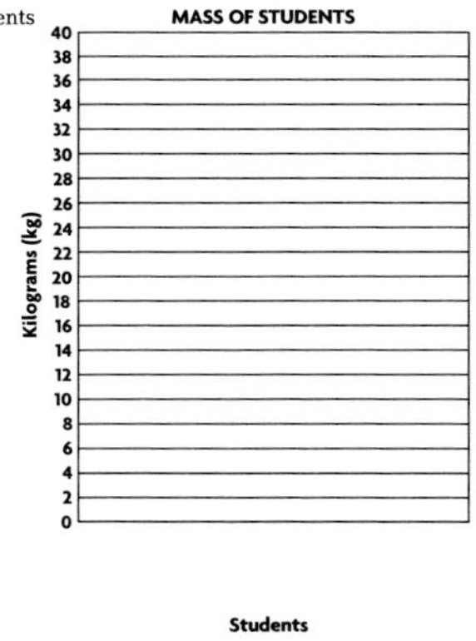

Tools	Units	
ruler	cm	g
liter container	kg	mL
simple balance	L	m

10. Sue had 3 red pens and 9 blue pens. She put the same number of pens into 2 cups. How many pens were in each cup? **6 pens**

11. 📖 **Write About It** Do objects of about the same size always have about the same mass? Give an example. **See above.**

Getting Ready for the EOG Test

12. Which unit of measure would be the most appropriate to find the mass of a strawberry? **D**

A centimeter
B kilogram
C milliliter
D gram

Chapter 18 **367**

North Carolina Standards 2.02 Estimate and measure using appropriate units. c) Mass (ounces, unds, grams, kilograms). *also* 2.01b

---

367

Fahrenheit and Celsius

HANDS ON

Lesson Planning

PROFESSIONAL DEVELOPMENT

Objective To estimate and measure temperature

Materials *For each group* Celsius and Fahrenheit thermometers

NCTM Standards
4. Measurement
6. Problem Solving
7. Reasoning and Proof
9. Connections
10. Representation

Math Background
These concepts will help students estimate and measure temperature.

- Degrees Celsius are metric units of measure for temperature, and degrees Fahrenheit are customary units of measure for temperature.

- Every Fahrenheit reading has a corresponding Celsius reading.

- The freezing and boiling points of each scale are useful benchmarks to help students understand temperatures in between.

Vocabulary
degrees Fahrenheit (°F) a standard unit for measuring temperature in the customary system

degrees Celsius (°C) a standard unit for measuring temperature in the metric system

Warm-Up Resources

Number of the Day

Transparency 18.5

Write two number sentences using the year you were born. Answers will vary.

Daily Facts Practice

Have students practice multiplication and division facts by completing Set G of *Teacher's Resource Book*, p. TR96.

Transparency 18.5

Problem of the Day

Last week Ms. Baker drank 2 cups of tea each morning except Saturday. How many pints of tea did she drink last week? 6 pints

Solution Problem of the Day tab, p. PD18

Intervention and Extension Resources

Alternative Teaching Strategy

MATERIALS *For teacher demonstration*
thermometer, a glass of cool water, hot water, ice

ESOL/ESL

Have students **practice measuring temperature**.
Place a thermometer (Fahrenheit or Celsius) in a glass
of cool water. Ask students to read the temperature. Change the
temperature of the water several times by adding ice or hot water
to give students additional practice in reading thermometers. Each
time you add hot water or ice, ask students to predict how the
temperature will change. Check students' work.

VISUAL

BODILY/KINESTHETIC

Multistep and Strategy Problems

The following multistep or strategy problem is provided in
Lesson 18.5:

Page	Item
369	12

Advanced Learners

MATERIALS number line, Celsius and Fahrenheit thermometers

Challenge students to **read negative temperatures**. Have students locate negative numbers on a number line. Have students practice reading temperatures below zero on Celsius and Fahrenheit thermometers. Check students' work.

VISUAL

BODILY/KINESTHETIC

Early Finishers

Have students **practice finding temperatures** by completing this table.

Day	High	Low	Difference
Mon	8°C	__°C 3	5°C
Tue	9°C	5°C	__°C 4
Wed	9°C	__°C 6	3°C
Thu	11°C	7°C	__°C 4
Fri	__°C 15	10°C	5°C

VISUAL

LOGICAL/MATHEMATICAL

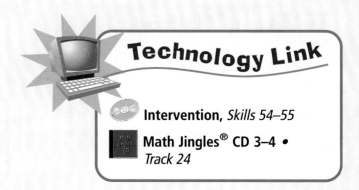

Technology Link

Intervention, *Skills 54–55*

Math Jingles® CD 3–4 •
Track 24

Lesson 18.5 Organizer

Objective To estimate and measure temperature

Vocabulary degrees Fahrenheit (°F), degrees Celsius (°C)

Materials *For each group* Celsius and Fahrenheit thermometers

---

1 INTRODUCE

QUICK REVIEW provides review of prerequisite skills.

WHY LEARN THIS? You'll be able to read the temperature on a Celsius or Fahrenheit thermometer and decide how to dress correctly for the weather outside. *Share the lesson objective with students.*

2 TEACH

Guided Instruction

• *Direct students' attention to the picture of the two scales on the thermometer.*
  How are these scales alike? How are they different? Possible answer: They both show numbers for every 10 degrees; they do not start and end with the same numbers.
  What is the temperature in degrees Celsius when the temperature is 50°F? How do you know? 10°C; read the two temperatures at the top of the red bar.

• *Check students' understanding.*
  What happens to water when the temperature is 32°F? It freezes.
  What Fahrenheit temperature is 10 degrees below the freezing point of water? 22°F
  REASONING If an outside thermometer showed the temperature to be 1°C, what might you be wearing? Possible answer: a jacket, hat, and mittens

3 PRACTICE

Guided Practice

Complete Try It Exercises a–d with your students. Identify students who are having difficulty and choose appropriate lesson resources to provide assistance.

368 Chapter 18

LESSON **5** HANDS ON

Fahrenheit and Celsius

VOCABULARY
degrees Fahrenheit (°F)
degrees Celsius (°C)

MATERIALS
Celsius and Fahrenheit thermometers

▷ **Explore**

Degrees Fahrenheit (°F) are customary units of temperature, and **degrees Celsius (°C)** are metric units of temperature.

Activity

STEP 1
Estimate the temperature outside the classroom in degrees Celsius and in degrees Fahrenheit. Record your estimates.

STEP 2
Measure the temperature outside the classroom using thermometers. Record the differences between your estimates and the actual measurements.

Try It

What is the temperature now?

a. The temperature was 71°F. It dropped 20°F. **51°F**

b. The temperature was 25°C. It dropped 3°C. **22°C**

c. The temperature was 58°F. It went up 15°F. **73°F**

d. The temperature was 17°C. It went up 4°C. **21°C**

368

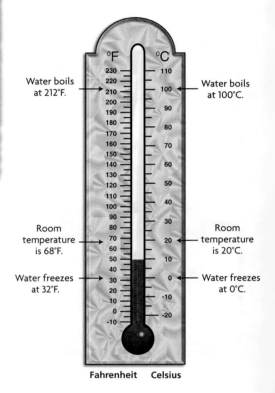

Water boils at 212°F. → Water boils at 100°C.

Room temperature is 68°F. → Room temperature is 20°C.

Water freezes at 32°F. → Water freezes at 0°C.

Fahrenheit   Celsius

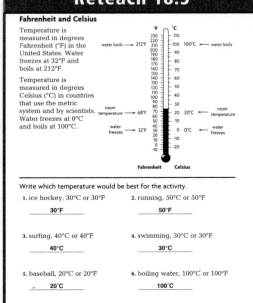

Reteach 18.5

Fahrenheit and Celsius

Temperature is measured in degrees Fahrenheit (°F) in the United States. Water freezes at 32°F and boils at 212°F.

Temperature is measured in degrees Celsius (°C) in countries that use the metric system and by scientists. Water freezes at 0°C and boils at 100°C.

water boils → 212°F — 100°C ← water boils
room temperature → 68°F — 20°C ← room temperature
water freezes → 32°F — 0°C ← water freezes

Fahrenheit   Celsius

Write which temperature would be best for the activity.

1. ice hockey, 30°C or 30°F   **30°F**

2. running, 50°C or 50°F   **50°F**

3. surfing, 40°C or 40°F   **40°C**

4. swimming, 30°C or 30°F   **30°C**

5. baseball, 20°C or 20°F   **20°C**

6. boiling water, 100°C or 100°F   **100°C**

RW98 Reteach

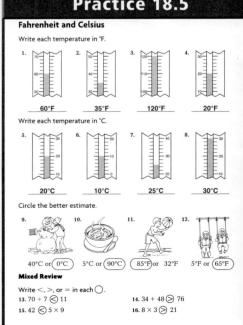

Practice 18.5

Fahrenheit and Celsius

Write each temperature in °F.

1.   2.   3.   4.
60°F   **35°F**   **120°F**   **20°F**

Write each temperature in °C.

5.   6.   7.   8.
20°C   **10°C**   **25°C**   **30°C**

Circle the better estimate.

9.   10.   11.   12.
40°C or **0°C**   5°C or **90°C**   **85°F** or 32°F   5°F or **65°F**

Mixed Review

Write <, >, or = in each ○.
13. 70 ÷ 7 ⊘ 11
14. 34 + 48 ⊘ 76
15. 42 ⊘ 5 × 9
16. 8 × 3 ⊘ 21

PW98 Practice

▶ **Connect**

On a thermometer, use the scale along each side like a number line. Then look at the top of the red bar. The thermometer on page 368 shows that the temperature is

50°F　**Read:** fifty degrees Fahrenheit
10°C　**Read:** ten degrees Celsius

▶ **Practice and Problem Solving**

Write each temperature in °F.

1. 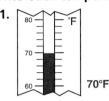 **70°F** 2. 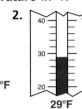 **29°F**

Write each temperature in °C.

3. 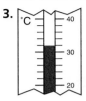 **32°C** 4. 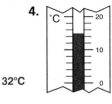 **15°C**

5. Look at the thermometer in Exercise 2. Is the temperature closer to 25°F or 30°F? **30°F**

6. Look at the thermometer in Exercise 3. Is the temperature closer to 30°C or 35°C? **30°C**

Choose the better estimate.

7.  25°F or 95°F? **95°F**
8.  56°F or 98°F? **56°F**
9.  8°C or 25°C? **25°C**
10.  0°C or 22°C? **0°C**

11. **Vocabulary Power** *Kilo-* means "one thousand" when used at the beginning of a word. What do you think *kiloliter* means? **A kiloliter is 1,000 liters.**

12. Sheli has 2 shelves with 10 books on each shelf. She has 4 books on her desk. How many books does she have in all? **24 books**

Getting Ready for the EOG Test

13. Lisa looked at the Fahrenheit thermometer on the porch. Which of the following is the temperature? **B**
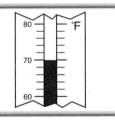
A 65°F　C 75°F
B 70°F　D 80°F

Chapter 18　**369**

North Carolina Standards 2.02 Estimate and measure using appropriate units. d) Temperature (Fahrenheit, Celsius).

Independent Practice

Note that Exercise 12 is a **multistep or strategy problem.** Assign Exercises 1–12.

Vocabulary Power Discuss with students how the metric units used to measure length, capacity, and mass are related by 10, 100, or 1,000. Brainstorm ideas of how students can remember the ways in which these units are related, such as with a mnemonic device or by drawing a picture.

4 ASSESS

Summarize the lesson by having students:

Discuss If you see an outdoor thermometer that shows the temperature is 93°, is the thermometer showing degrees Celsius or degrees Fahrenheit? Explain. degrees Fahrenheit; 93°C is much too hot for an outside temperature.

 Write Name a temperature in degrees Celsius or degrees Fahrenheit. Tell whether a room at that temperature would be comfortable or uncomfortable and explain why. Possible answer: 5°C; uncomfortable because it is close to freezing.

LESSON QUIZ　Transparency 18.5
1. If your ice cream were melting, would it be 30°F or 50°F? 50°F
2. If you were having a picnic, would it be 75°F or 35°F? 75°F
3. If you were ice-skating outside, would the temperature be 0°C or 15°C? 0°C

Challenge 18.5

A Cold Message

Circle the better answer for each problem. In the box below, shade all spaces that contain the answer you circled. You will find a cold day message. Some answers may be found more than once.

1. It's good to play ice hockey when it's (25°F)/ 75°F.
2. A room that is 70°C /(20°C) is comfortable.
3. Jump in the swimming pool when it's (30°C)/ 90°C.
4. A cup of soup is warm when it is 55°F /(110°F).
5. You may need a jacket when it's 60°C /(10°C) outside.
6. The snow should start to melt when the temperature rises above (0°C)/ 35°C.
7. Put on some shorts when the temperature is (80°F)/ 40°F.
8. In the summer, it sometimes cools down to 15°F /(60°F) at night.
9. The temperature was 53°F. It went up (17°F)/ 27°F to 70°F.
10. The temperature was 26°C. It dropped 44°C /(8°C) to 18°C.
11. The temperature was 12°C. It went up 3°C to 9°C /(15°C).
12. The temperature was (39°F)/ 49°F. It went up 25°F to 64°F.
13. The temperature was 24°C. It dropped 8°C to (16°C)/ 6°C.
14. The temperature was 44°F /(72°F) It dropped 14°F to 58°F.

CW98 Challenge

Problem Solving 18.5

Fahrenheit and Celsius　Understand → Plan → Solve → Check

Write the correct answer.

1. When practice began, the temperature was 22°C. At the end of practice, the temperature had dropped 4°C. What was the temperature at the end of practice? **18°C**

2. Mr. Torres gave 4 stickers to each of his 10 students. He also gave 21 stickers to another teacher. If he has 25 left, how many stickers did he start with? **86 stickers**

3. What is the value of the underlined digit? 5**8**,205 **8,000**

4. In the morning, the temperature outside was 57°F. In the afternoon, it was 73°F. How many degrees did the temperature rise? **16°F**

Choose the letter of the correct answer.

5. If the temperature was 21°C when the game started, and dropped 3°C during the game, what was the temperature at the end of the game?
A 3°C　C 21°C
(B) 18°C　D 24°C

6. Patricia is skip-counting on a hundred chart. If she starts on 2, and skip-counts by threes, which number will she **not** land on?
F 14　(H) 33
G 23　J 41

7. Elroy saved $4.38 last week, and $3.87 this week. How much did he save in the 2 weeks?
A $8.35　C $8.11
(B) $8.25　D $7.55

8. If someone is swimming in an outdoor pool, which temperature is it most likely to be?
F 25°F　H 38°F
G 5°C　(J) 83°F

9. **Write About It** Explain how you solved Problem 2. Possible answer: I multiplied 4 × 10 = 40. Next, I added 21 + 25 = 46. Finally, I added 40 + 46 = 86. So, he started with 86 stickers.

PS98 Problem Solving

369

CHAPTER 18 Extra Practice

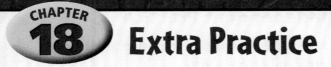

Purpose To provide extra practice for the skills presented in this chapter

The blue page references in each set of exercises refer to the lesson pages where each skill is taught.

Internet Resources

Visit **THE LEARNING SITE** at **www.harcourtschool.com** for a listing of practice activities.

Extra Practice

Set A (pp. 358–361)

Estimate the length in centimeters. Then use a ruler to measure to the nearest centimeter. Estimates may vary.

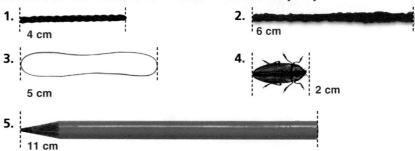

1. 4 cm

2. 6 cm

3. 5 cm

4. 2 cm

5. 11 cm

Choose the unit you would use to measure each. Write *cm, m,* **or** *km.* Answers may vary.

6. the length of a marker **cm**

7. the height of a two-story building **m**

8. the distance you can kick a ball **m**

9. the distance you can walk in half an hour **km**

Choose the better estimate.

10. Jana's math book is almost 3 _?_ long. **B**

   A meters
   B decimeters

11. Ed walked 1 _?_ to get to Jeff's house. **A**

   A kilometer
   B centimeter

12. The tree is about 6 _?_ high. **B**

   A kilometers
   B meters

13. The ant is 1 _?_ long. **B**

   A decimeter
   B centimeter

Solve.

14. Mathias has a piece of yarn that measures 13 centimeters. Is that more or less than 2 decimeters? Explain. **less; 1 dm = 10 cm, so 2 dm = 20 cm; 13 cm < 20 cm**

15. Alice had a ribbon 1 meter long. She cut 12 centimeters off of the ribbon. How many centimeters long is the ribbon now? **88 cm**

370

Review/Test

✔ CHECK VOCABULARY AND CONCEPTS

Choose the best term from the box.

1. Capacity can be measured by using metric units such as the __?__. (p. 364) **liter**

2. A metric unit for measuring mass is the __?__. (p. 366) **gram**

3. Customary units of temperature are __?__. (p. 368)
   degrees Fahrenheit

4. Metric units of temperature are __?__. (p. 368)
   degrees Celsius

> degrees Celsius
> degrees
>   Fahrenheit
> gram
> liter
> meter

Choose the better estimate. (pp. 364–365, 366–367, 368–369)

5.
   2 mL or 2 L? **2 L**

6.
   2 g or 2 kg? **2 kg**

7.
   30°F or 60°F? **30°F**

✔ CHECK SKILLS

Estimate the length in centimeters. Then use a ruler to measure to the nearest centimeter. (pp. 358–361) **Estimates will vary.**

8. ├───────┤ **2 cm**

9.
   7 cm

Choose the unit you would use to measure each. Write cm, m, or km. (pp. 358–361) **Answers may vary.**

10. the length of a pencil **cm**

11. the distance to the moon **km**

12. the length of a bee **cm**

13. the distance you run in 10 seconds **m**

✔ CHECK PROBLEM SOLVING

Use make a table to solve. (pp. 362–363)

14. Ashley has 5 meters of yarn. How many centimeters of yarn does she have? **500 cm**

15. Ray had 3 meters of string. Then he bought 400 centimeters more. How many meters does he have in all? **7 m**

Chapter 18 **371**

Review/Test

Purpose To check understanding of concepts, skills, and problem solving presented in Chapter 18

Using the Page

The Chapter 18 Review/Test can be used as a **review** or a **test**.

- Items 1–7 check understanding of concepts and new vocabulary.
- Items 8–13 check skill proficiency.
- Items 14–15 check students' abilities to choose and apply problem solving strategies to real-life measurement problems.

> **Portfolio** ✔ Suggest that students place the completed Chapter 18 Review/Test in their portfolios.

Using the Assessment Guide

- Multiple-choice format of Chapter 18 Posttest— See *Assessment Guide*, pp. AG109–110.
- Free-response format of Chapter 18 Posttest— See *Assessment Guide*, pp. AG111–112.

Using Student Self-Assessment

The How Did I Do? survey helps students assess what they have learned and how they learned it. This survey is available as a copying master in *Assessment Guide*, p. AGxvii.

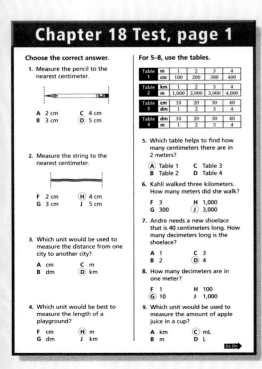

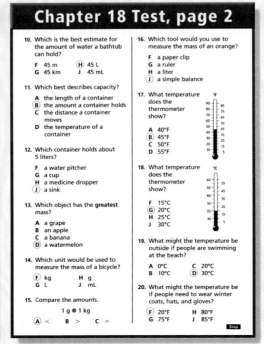

CHAPTER 18

Getting Ready for the EOG Test
Chapters 1–18

Using the Pages

These pages may be used to help students get ready for the North Carolina EOG Test. The test items are written in the same style and arranged in the same format as those on the EOG Test.

The pages are cumulative. They cover the standards from the North Carolina Mathematics Standard Course of Study that have been taught up to this point in the text or in a previous grade. Each Getting Ready for the EOG Test also reviews the North Carolina mathematics strands shown below.

- Number and Operations
- Measurement
- Geometry
- Data Analysis and Probability
- Algebra

These pages can be assigned at the end of the chapter as classwork or as a homework assignment. You may want to have students use individual recording sheets presented in a multiple-choice (standardized) format. A Test Answer Sheet is available as a black-line master in the *Assessment Guide* (p. AGlii).

You may wish to have students describe how they solved each problem and share their solutions.

Getting Ready for the EOG Test

⭐ NUMBER AND OPERATIONS

1. Elizabeth has 6 blue T-shirts, 8 red T-shirts, and 4 white T-shirts. How many T-shirts does she have altogether? **A**

   A 18   **C** 14
   B 16   **D** 10

2. Bob put $15.00 into a bank. He added $8.00 to the bank each week for 3 weeks. How much money is in his bank now? **C**

   A $23.00   **C** $39.00
   B $31.00   **D** $47.00

3. Terry bought 4 packs of markers. Each pack had 8 markers. Jim bought twice as many packs as Terry. Which expression shows how many markers Jim bought?
   C
   A $(4 + 8) + 2$ **C** $(4 \times 8) \times 2$
   B $(8 - 2) + 4$ **D** $(4 \times 4) \times 8$

4. **Explain It** The table shows the number of students in each grade. *About* how many students are in the third and fourth grades? Tell how you estimated. **See page 373.**

MAIN STREET SCHOOL	
Grade	Number of Students
Third	419
Fourth	487
Fifth	425

⭐ MEASUREMENT AND GEOMETRY

5. Which is the best unit to use to measure the length of a house?
   C
   A centimeter
   B inch
   C meter
   D pint

6. Which of these objects has a mass of about 5 kilograms? **B**

   A stamp
   B dog
   C banana
   D car

7. **Explain It** Alicia is drawing shapes on this grid.

   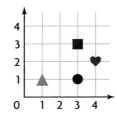

   She says that the circle is located at (3,1). Do you agree or disagree? Explain. **See page 373.**

⭐ ALGEBRA

TIP **Understand the problem.** See item 8. To find the pattern in the numbers on the lockers, see how the numbers change. Then find the missing number in the pattern.

8. The picture below shows the numbers on some lockers. What is the number for the open locker? **A**

A 12
B 11
C 10
D 8

9. Which rule could be used to complete the table? **C**

Dimes	1	2	3	4
Pennies	10	20	30	■

A Add 100.
B Subtract 100.
C Multiply by 10.
D Multiply by 100.

10. **Explain It** Write a story problem that could be solved using the number sentence $12 \div 4 = $ ■. Draw a picture to show what happens in your story. **See below.**

⭐ DATA ANALYSIS AND PROBABILITY

11. Look at the tally table. Which activity received exactly 8 votes? **B**

FAVORITE ACTIVITY	
Activity	**Tallies**
Kickball	卌 卌 ‖
Relay races	卌 ‖‖
Bowling	卌 ‖
Soccer	卌 卌 ‖‖‖

A kickball
B relay races
C bowling
D soccer

12. The table shows the low temperatures in some North Carolina cities on a day in September.

LOW TEMPERATURES	
City	**Temperature**
Cape Hatteras	72°F
Boone	45°F
Greensboro	61°F
Asheville	55°F

Which city had the warmest temperature? **A**

A Cape Hatteras
B Boone
C Greensboro
D Asheville

13. **Explain It** Look at the table above showing low temperatures. Explain how to find how much warmer Cape Hatteras was than Boone. **See below.**

Chapter 18   373

Chapters 1–18

Item Analysis

You may wish to use the item analysis to determine which North Carolina standards need additional review.

Item	North Carolina Standard	Lesson
1	1.02	1.4
2	1.06	11.5
3	1.06	11.3
4	1.02	4.1
5	2.02	18.1
6	2.02	18.4
7	3.02	16.4
8	5.02	2.5
9	5.01	11.2
10	5.04	13.2
11	4.01	15.2
12	4.01	15.2
13	4.01	15.2

SCORING RUBRIC
Explain It

2 Demonstrates a complete understanding of the problem and chooses an appropriate strategy to determine the solution

1 Demonstrates a partial understanding of the problem and chooses a strategy that does not lead to a complete and accurate solution

0 Demonstrates little understanding of the problem and shows little evidence of using any strategy to determine a solution

Explain It • Written Response

4. Possible answer: about 900 students; round 419 to 400 and 487 to 500; 400 + 500 = 900.

7. Agree; possible answer: if you start at 0, move 3 spaces to the right, and then move up 1 space, that is (3,1) on the grid, which is where the circle is.

10. Check students' problems and drawings. Possible answer: Doug divided a dozen bagels equally among 4 friends. Each friend got 3 bagels.

13. Possible answer: subtract the low temperature of Boone from the low temperature of Cape Hatteras; $72 - 45 = 27$, so the low temperature of Cape Hatteras is 27°F warmer.

UNIT 5

It's in the Bag
Stamp-o-Graph Math

Purpose To make stamps and use them to make graphs and locate points on a coordinate grid
Materials spools, water bottle lids, film canisters, precut foam shapes, colored ink pads or markers, grid paper, construction paper, scissors, glue, data

Using the Page

Preparing the Materials

- Assemble the materials needed for each student. Make sure there are enough spools, water bottle lids, and film canisters, since they are used as bases for the stamps. You may wish to have students glue the foam shapes onto the bases prior to doing the project.

Making the Project

- You may prefer to have students use washable markers or stamp pads.

- Have the class collect data on a subject of their choosing. Help students prepare the grids with labels and a scale. Make sure the grids are large enough for the pre-cut foam shapes they are using.

Extending the Project

- Have students work with a partner and use the stamps to explore measuring with nonstandard units. Direct students to draw lines of different lengths. Have them stamp images along the line to "measure" the line. Then using the same stamp as a unit of measurement, have students estimate the lengths of the other lines. Challenge students to use a larger or smaller stamp and estimate the lengths of the same lines using this stamp. Then direct students to measure with this stamp to check their estimates.

IT'S IN THE BAG

Stamp-O-Graph Math

PROJECT Make stamps, and use them to make a graph or locate points on a grid.

Materials

- Spools of all sizes
- Empty water bottle lids
- Film canisters
- Precut foam shapes
- Colored ink pads or markers
- Grid paper
- Construction paper
- Scissors and glue
- Data

Directions

1. Glue a piece of grid paper to construction paper to make a bar graph. Write a title and labels to match your data. Add a scale of numbers. *(Picture A)*

2. To make the stamps, glue the foam shapes onto the ends of spools, water bottle lids, or film canisters. Color the stamps with markers, or use rubber-stamp ink. *(Picture B)*

3. Use your data and the stamps to complete the bar graph. *(Picture C)*

4. Use another piece of grid paper and construction paper to make a grid for ordered pairs. Take turns with a partner locating points on the grid. Use a stamp to mark the position of each point.

Challenge

Read a Circle Graph

A **circle graph** shows data as parts of a whole circle.

The students at Tony's school were surveyed to find out what activities they could do to help raise money for a new school library. Tony made a circle graph to show the results of the survey. Which activity was the most popular?

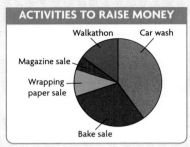

ACTIVITIES TO RAISE MONEY

Walkathon
Car wash
Magazine sale
Wrapping paper sale
Bake sale

The section for the car wash is larger than any other section. So, the car wash was the most popular activity.

Talk About It

• What activity did the fewest students choose?
magazine sale
• Do fewer students want to have a walkathon or sell wrapping paper? Explain. **Sell wrapping paper; the section for students who want to sell wrapping paper is smaller than the section for a walkathon.**

Try It

For 1–4, use the circle graph at the right.

FAVORITE SPORTS OF MYRA'S CLASSMATES

Basketball
Baseball
Soccer

1. What does the graph show?
the favorite sports named by Myra's classmates
2. Which sport was named by the fewest students?
soccer
3. What part of the class named baseball?
one half
4. Suppose another class was surveyed. Which sport do you think would be the most popular? Explain.
Baseball; possible answer: in Myra's class baseball was the most popular. So, it is likely that in a different class, baseball would also be the most popular.

Challenge
Read a Circle Graph

Objective To extend the concepts and skills of Chapters 15–18

Using the Page

• *Direct students' attention to the circle graph in the center of the page.*
Reasoning **How does the total number of students surveyed relate to the circle?** The whole circle represents the total number of students surveyed.
What is the purpose of the different colors on the graph? Possible answer: a different color is used to show each section.
Would changing the colors on the graph affect the data shown? Explain. No; changing the colors would not change the data represented.
Can you tell from this graph how much money might be raised for each activity? Explain. No; the graph only shows which activities the students are interested in doing.

Try It Before completing Exercises 1–4, remind students to carefully read the title of the graph and the labels.

Intervention and Extension Resources

Advanced Learners

To **reinforce the use of graphs as pictorial representations of data,** conduct a class survey. Divide the class into small groups. Have students write a survey question and then collect data and record it in tally or frequency tables. Then have students make pictographs, bar graphs, or circle graphs of the data. Ask each group to present its graph. Have students discuss why one type of graph was chosen over another. Display the graphs in the classroom.

VERBAL/LINGUISTIC

INTERPERSONAL

Study Guide and Review

Purpose To help students review concepts and skills presented in Chapters 15–18.

Using the Pages

✔ Assessment Checkpoint

The Study Guide and Review includes content from Chapters 15–18.

The blue page numbers in parentheses provided with each group of exercises indicate the pages on which the concept or skill was presented.

Study Guide and Review

VOCABULARY

Choose the best term from the box.

1. Information collected about people or things is called ___?___. (p. 302) **data**

2. A graph that uses a line to show how data change over time is a ___?___. (p. 330) **line graph**

> data
> survey
> bar graph
> line graph

STUDY AND SOLVE

Chapter 15

Classify data.

FAVORITE JUICE			
	Apple	Orange	Grape
Boys	6	8	3
Girls	5	4	6

How many boys voted in all?
Think: Find the sum. $6 + 8 + 3 = 17$
So, 17 boys voted in all.

For 3–5, use the table. (pp. 306–307)

3. How many more boys than girls voted? **2 more boys**

4. What is the most popular juice among the girls? **grape juice**

5. What is the most popular juice overall? Explain.
Orange juice, because 12 students chose it as their favorite. Only 11 chose apple juice and 9 chose grape juice.

Chapter 16

Read a bar graph.

How many students play soccer?

Step 1: Find the bar for soccer.
Step 2: Compare the height of the bar with the scale to find the number of students who play soccer.

So, 8 students play soccer.

For 6–7, use the bar graph. (pp. 324–325)

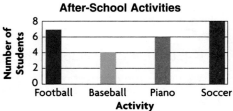

6. How many more students play soccer than play baseball?
4 more students

7. How many students play football?
7 students

Chapter 17

Change units.

There are 16 quarts of juice on the store shelf. How many gallons of juice is this?
Remember: 4 quarts = 1 gallon

Quarts	4	8	12	16
Gallons	1	2	3	4

So, there are 4 gallons of juice.

Change the units. (pp. 348–349)

Pints	1	2	3	4	5
Cups	2	4	6	8	10

8. 3 pints = ■ cups 6

9. ■ pints = 10 cups 5

10. ■ cups = 4 pints 8

Chapter 18

Estimate length and distance.

Choose the better estimate.

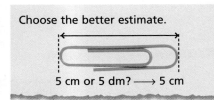

5 cm or 5 dm? ⟶ 5 cm

Choose the better estimate.
(pp. 358–361)

11. Your thumb: 5 dm or 5 cm? 5 cm

12. A lamp post: 3 dm or 3 m? 3 m

13. A pen: 15 cm or 15 dm? 15 cm

PROBLEM SOLVING PRACTICE

Solve. (pp. 308–309, 322–323, 350–351, 362–363)

14. Mr. Lind surveyed his customers to find out what to add to the menu. There were 20 votes for chili, 15 votes for ice cream, and 10 votes for pizza. Make a pictograph that shows the results of the survey. **Check students' graphs.**

16. Andre needs 2 cups of flour for a muffin recipe. Should he estimate or measure the amount of flour? Explain. **See above.**

16. measure; Possible answer: A recipe may not turn out right if you do not measure amounts called for.

15. Chris and Jill rolled 2 number cubes 15 times and recorded the sums. Their results were 6, 9, 5, 7, 7, 8, 7, 12, 3, 8, 2, 6, 4, 7, and 6. Make a table to find the sum rolled most often.
Check students' tables. 7 was rolled most often.

17. Philip made 4 gallons of iced tea. How many cups did he make?
(HINT: 16 cups = 1 gallon)
Check students' tables; 64 cups

Unit 5 • Chapters 15–18 377

✓ Assessment Checkpoint

Portfolio Suggestions The portfolio represents the growth, talents, achievements, and reflections of the mathematics learner. Students might spend a short time selecting work samples for their portfolios and completing A Guide to My Math Portfolio from *Assessment Guide*, page AGxix.

You may want to have students respond to the following questions:

- **What new understanding of math have I developed in the past several weeks?**
- **What growth in understanding or skills can I see in my work?**
- **What can I do to improve my understanding of math ideas?**
- **What would I like to learn more about?**

For information on how to organize, share, and evaluate portfolios, see *Assessment Guide*, page AGxviii.

Use the item analysis in the **Intervention** chart to diagnose students' errors. You may wish to reinforce content or remediate misunderstandings by using the text pages or lesson resources.

Unit Test

- Multiple-choice format of Unit 5 Posttest—See *Assessment Guide*, pp. AG113–116.
- Free-Response format of Unit 5 Posttest—See *Assessment Guide*, pp. AG117–120.

Study Guide and Review Intervention • How to Help Options

Items	Text Pages	Reteach and Practice Resources
3–5	306–307	Worksheets for Lesson 15.3
6–7	324–325	Worksheets for Lesson 16.2
8–10	348–349	Worksheets for Lesson 17.5
11–13	358–361	Worksheets for Lesson 18.1
14–17	308–309, 322–323, 350–351, 362–363	Worksheets for Lessons 15.4, 16.1, 17.6, 18.2

Performance Assessment

Purpose To provide performance assessment tasks for Chapters 15–18

Using the Page

- *Have students work individually or in pairs as an alternative to formal assessment.*

- *Use the performance indicators and work samples below to evaluate Tasks A–B.*

See *Performance Assessment* for

- a complete scoring rubric, PAx, for this unit.
- additional student work samples for this unit.
- copying masters for this unit.

Portfolio   You may suggest that students place completed Performance Assessment tasks in their portfolios.

Performance Indicators

Task A

A student with a Level 3 paper

✓ Completes a tally table.

✓ Completes a frequency table.

✓ Makes a pictograph, line plot, or bar graph.

Task B

A student with a Level 3 paper

✓ Estimates length to the nearest inch.

✓ Measures length to the nearest inch.

✓ Analyzes accuracy of measurements.

PERFORMANCE ASSESSMENT

TASK A • OUTDOOR FUN

You decide to write a report about your classmates' favorite outdoor game.

a. Take a survey to find your classmates' favorite outdoor game. Copy the tally table and the frequency table, and record their choices on both tables.
Answers will vary. Possible answers given.

b. Decide which type of graph would be best to display the data. Then make the graph. **Students' graphs should reflect data in tally table and frequency table.**

c. Write a question your classmates could answer by looking at your graph. **Possible question: Which game did most students say was their favorite?**

OUTDOOR GAMES	
Name	Tally
Freeze Tag	ℍℍ ℍℍ ℍℍ ℍℍ
T-ball	ℍℍ |||
Kickball	ℍℍ ℍℍ ||
Hopscotch	||||

OUTDOOR GAMES	
Name	Number
Freeze Tag	20
T-ball	8
Kickball	12
Hopscotch	4

TASK B • YARN DOLLS

Materials: ruler

Natalie is making yarn dolls. These pictures show the lengths of some of the pieces of yarn Natalie needs.

1. ━━━━━━━━━━━━━━━━━━━━━━━━

2. ━━━━━━━━━━━━━━━

3. ━━━━━━━━━

YARN MEASUREMENT	
Estimate	Actual
1.	
2.	
3.	

a. Copy and complete the table. Estimate the length of each piece of yarn to the nearest inch. Use a ruler to measure each piece of yarn to the nearest half inch.
Estimates will vary. 1. 6 in.; 2. 3 in.; 3. 2 in.

b. Compare each estimate to the measured length. Write *greater than, less than,* or *equal to.*
Answers will vary depending on students' estimates.

Work Samples for Task A and Task B

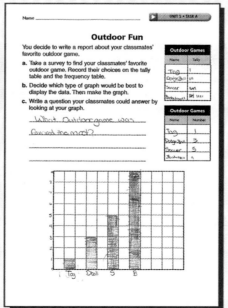

Level 3 This student shows a good understanding of making tables and graphs. All parts of the task are accurate and complete.

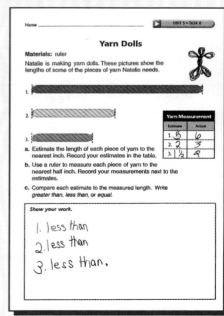

Level 3 The student shows understanding of the task. The student completes both the estimates and measurements in the table. Estimates are reasonable.

Technology Linkup

Enter Data on a Spreadsheet

Four friends recorded the number of miles they walked.

Lauren		Clark		Raul		Tina	
Week 1	7 mi	Week 1	6 mi	Week 1	9 mi	Week 1	5 mi
Week 2	10 mi	Week 2	8 mi	Week 2	10 mi	Week 2	8 mi
Week 3	12 mi	Week 3	9 mi	Week 3	12 mi	Week 3	10 mi

You can organize the data in a spreadsheet.

- Type the labels *Name, Week 1, Week 2,* and *Week 3.*

- Use the Tab or the arrow keys to enter each name and the number of miles each person walked.

- Use the spreadsheet to find who walked the greatest number of miles in Week 3.
  Both Raul and Lauren walked 12 miles in Week 3.

	A	B	C	D
1	Name	Week 1	Week 2	Week 3
2	Lauren	7	10	12
3	Clark	6	8	9
4	Raul	9	10	12
5	Tina	5	8	10

Practice and Problem Solving

1. Three friends recorded the number of pages they read each day for four days. Jake read 23, 25, 38, and 17 pages. Val read 14, 31, 29, and 22 pages. Emily read 25, 36, 21, and 10 pages. Enter the data on a spreadsheet. **Check students' work.**

2. George read 36, 22, 11, and 14 pages in four days. Add this data to the spreadsheet. **Check students' work.**

3. ✏ **Write a problem** Use the data on your spreadsheet to write a problem. Exchange problems with a classmate and solve. **Check students' work.**

GO ON-LINE **Multimedia Math Glossary** www.harcourtschool.com/mathglossary
Vocabulary Power Look up *mean* and *median* in the Multimedia Math Glossary. Are the mean and the median of a data set ever the same number? Explain.

Yes; possible explanation: in the data set, 2, 4, 6, 8, and 10, the mean is 6 and the median is 6.

Technology Linkup

Objective To practice entering data on a spreadsheet

Using the Page

Explain that displaying data in a spreadsheet is one way to organize data. When data is organized, it is simpler to make comparisons.

Using the Computer

- *Direct students' attention to the computer keyboard.*
  Locate the tab and arrow keys. Which hand is over these keys? The left hand is near the tab key and the right hand is near the arrow keys.

Reasoning Why is a spreadsheet simpler to read than data on separate pieces of paper? Possible answer: when the data is organized into rows and columns, you do not have to repeat Week 1, Week 2, and Week 3.

Practice and Problem Solving

Before assigning Exercises 1–3, briefly discuss with students the importance of entering the data consistently. Students should list the names in column A and the number of miles walked during the week in columns B, C, and D. Or have them list the names in columns B, C, and D and the number of miles walked during the week in column A.

Multimedia Math Glossary

Mean, median, and all other vocabulary words in this unit can be found in the Harcourt Multimedia Math Glossary.
www.harcourtschool.com/mathglossary

UNIT 5

Problem Solving
in North Carolina

Purpose To provide additional practice for concepts and skills in Chapters 15–18

Using the Page

GREENSBORO'S GARDENS

- *After students have completed Exercises 1–3, ask:*
  The crape myrtle tree is about how many times as tall as the blue heron? about 7 times as tall

- *Direct students' attention to the table.*
  What is the range of the temperatures? Explain. 20°F; 77°F − 57°F = 20°F
  Suppose you were asked to make a line graph to represent the temperature data. How many points would you plot? Explain.
  5; Each point represents a temperature at one of the five different times shown in the table.

Extension Challenge students to record the outdoor temperature at five different times during one school day. Then have them make a line graph to represent the data. Check students' work.

PROBLEM SOLVING IN NORTH CAROLINA

▲ North Carolina's state flower is the dogwood. Its pink or white blossoms can be seen from early spring into summer.

Greensboro

GREENSBORO'S GARDENS

The city of Greensboro has about 170 parks and 3 public gardens. Visitors to the Bog Garden can see native plants and animals from an elevated boardwalk through a swampland. The 17-acre Greensboro Arboretum serves as an outdoor classroom with its trails and butterfly garden. The Bicentennial Garden features colorful flower beds and a sculpture garden.

Choose the unit of measure. Write *inches, feet, yards,* **or** *miles.*

1. One crape myrtle tree in the Bicentennial Garden is
   20 _?_ tall. feet

2. The wingspan of an eastern tiger swallowtail butterfly in the Arboretum is about 6 _?_ . inches

3. A blue heron in the Bog Garden is about 3 _?_ tall. feet

USE DATA For 4–5, use the table.

GREENSBORO TEMPERATURES ON A FALL DAY					
Time	6:54 A.M.	9:54 A.M.	12:54 P.M.	3:54 P.M.	6:54 P.M.
Temperature	57°F	70°F	73°F	77°F	73°F

4. What is the median temperature? 73°F

5. 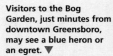 **Write a problem** using the information in the table. Exchange problems with a classmate, and solve. Check students' problems.

Visitors to the Bog Garden, just minutes from downtown Greensboro, may see a blue heron or an egret. ▼

NATURAL SCIENCE CENTER OF GREENSBORO

The Natural Science Center offers a hands-on museum, a zoo, a planetarium, and a nature trail. Families can learn about dinosaurs, view the sun in the solar observatory, feed and pet a burro, and see sharks or snakes in the Aquarium and Herpetarium.

1. Take a survey. Ask your classmates to choose what they would like to do at the Natural Science Center. Make a tally table and a frequency table of the data.
   Check students' tally and frequency tables.
2. **Write about it** Tell whether you think a tally table or a frequency table shows the data more clearly. Explain the reason for your choice. **See below.**

▲ Families can view the sun and each planet in its orbit in the Edward R. Zane Planetarium.

▲ Children can touch a dinosaur footprint in the Dinosaur Gallery.

Possible answer: A frequency table shows data more clearly because you can see the numbers immediately. You don't have to count the tally marks.

◀ The Aquarium's 1,500-gallon tank features sharks, a moray eel, and other sea creatures.

Using the Page

NATIONAL SCIENCE CENTER OF GREENSBORO

- *After students have completed Exercise 1, ask:*
  In what other ways can you display the data from your survey? Possible answers: a line plot, bar graph, or pictograph

- *Direct students' attention to Exercise 2.*
  Why is it helpful to make a tally table?
  Possible answer: Making a tally table helps you record data as you collect it.

Extension Provide students with the following frequency table:

PEOPLE IN PETTING AREA	
Time	Number
Early morning	25
Late morning	32
Early afternoon	33
Late afternoon	26

Ask students to make a bar graph of the data and to identify the range. Check students' bar graphs. The range of the data is 8.

Teaching Notes

Additional Ideas:

Good Questions to Ask:

Additional Resources:

Notes for Next Time:

Unit at a Glance

EXCERPTS FROM THE RESEARCH

"Direct instruction on words that are critical to new content produces the most powerful learning. The effects of vocabulary instruction are even more powerful when the words selected are those that students most likely will encounter when they learn new content." (Marzano, Pickering, and Pollock, 2001)

Assessment Options

Assessing Prior Knowledge

Determine whether students have the required prerequisite concepts and skills.

Check What You Know, PE pp. 383, 407, 423, 443

Test Preparation

Provide review and practice for chapter and standardized tests.

Getting Ready for the EOG Test, PE pp. 387, 389, 391, 395, 399, 404–405, 409, 411, 413, 415, 420–421, 427, 429, 431, 435, 440–441, 447, 449, 455, 458–459

Study Guide and Review, PE pp. 462–463

Formal Assessment

Assess students' mastery of chapter concepts and skills.

Chapter Review/Test, PE pp. 403, 419, 439, 457

Pretest and Posttest Options

Chapter Test, Form A
pp. AG121–122, 125–126, 129–130, 133–134

Chapter Test, Form B
pp. AG123–124, 127–128, 131–132, 135–136

Unit 6 Test • Chapters 19–22

Form A, pp. AG137–140

Form B, pp. AG141–144

Daily Assessment

Obtain daily feedback on students' understanding of concepts.

Quick Review, See the first page of each PE lesson.

Getting Ready for the EOG Test
See the last page of each PE skill lesson.

Number of the Day
See the first page of each TE lesson.

Problem of the Day
See the first page of each TE lesson.

Lesson Quiz
See the *Assess* section of each TE lesson.

Performance Assessment

Assess students' understanding of concepts applied to real-world situations.

Performance Assessment (Tasks A–B), PE p. 464; pp. PA48–49

Student Self-Assessment

Have students evaluate their own work.

How Did I Do?, p. AGxvii

A Guide to My Math Portfolio, p. AGxix

Math Journal
See *Write* in the *Assess* section of each TE lesson and TE pages 384B, 390B, 410B, 424B, 444B.

 Harcourt Assessment System

Make and grade chapter tests electronically.

This software includes:
- **multiple-choice items**
- **free-response items**
- **customizable tests**
- **the means to build your own tests from available items**
- **customizable student and class reports**

 Portfolio

Portfolio opportunities appear throughout the Pupil and Teacher's Editions.

Suggested work samples:

Problem Solving Project, TE pp. 382, 406, 422, 442

Write About It, PE pp. 386, 389, 391, 398, 409, 413, 415, 426, 431, 446, 454

Chapter Review/Test, PE pp. 403, 419, 439, 457

 KEY AG Assessment Guide   TE Teacher's Edition   PA Performance Assessment   PE Pupil Edition

LEARNING GOAL	TAUGHT IN LESSONS	CAT/ TERRA NOVA	CTBS/ TERRA NOVA	ITBS FORM A	MAT 8	STANFORD 10	NORTH CAROLINA STANDARDS
19A To identify and compare lines, line segments, line relationships, rays, and angles	19.1, 19.2	•	•	•	•	•	3.01
19B To identify, describe, and classify polygons, triangles, and quadrilaterals	19.3, 19.4, 19.5	•	•	•	•	•	3.01
19C To solve problems by using an appropriate strategy such as *draw a diagram*	19.6	•	•		•	•	3.01 maintains (2) 4.01
20A To identify and draw congruent and similar figures, lines of symmetry, and transformations of polygons	20.1, 20.2, 20.3, 20.4	•	•	•	•	•	3.01 maintains (2) 3.03
20B To solve problems by using an appropriate strategy such as *make a model*	20.5	•			•		3.01 maintains (2) 3.03
21A To identify solid figures and their properties and relationships with plane figures	21.1, 21.2	•	•	•	•	•	3.01
21B To combine plane figures to form patterns	21.3	•	•	•	•	•	3.01
21C To draw polygons using line segments	21.4	•	•			•	3.01
21D To solve problems by using an appropriate skill such as *identify relationships*	21.5	•		•	•	•	3.01
22A To estimate and measure perimeter and area using nonstandard and standard units	22.1, 22.2	•	•	•	•	•	
22B To solve problems by using an appropriate skill such as *make generalizations*	22.3	•		•			
22C To estimate volume using nonstandard and standard units	22.4	•				•	

Technology Links

 ## Harcourt Mega Math CD-ROM Series

The learning activities in this exciting, new comprehensive math software series complement, enrich, and enhance the Pupil Edition lessons.

Harcourt Mega Math Correlation		
Lesson	**Activity/Level**	**Skill**
19.1 & 19.2	Ice Station Exploration, Polar Planes, Levels A, B, and C	Line Segments, Angles, and Lines
19.3–19.5	Ice Station Exploration, Polar Planes, Levels D, E, and G	Classify Polygons
20.1 & 20.3	Ice Station Exploration, Polar Planes, Levels H and I	Congruent and Similar Figures
20.2	Ice Station Exploration, Polar Planes/Level J	Symmetry
20.4	Ice Station Exploration, Polar Planes, Level M	Slides, Flips, and Turns
21.1 & 21.2	Ice Station Exploration, Frozen Solids, Levels A, B, C, D, E, and F	Solid Figures
21.3	Ice Station Exploration, Polar Planes/Level N	Tessellations
22.1 & 22.2	Ice Station Exploration, Polar Planes, Levels P and Q	Perimeter and Area
22.4	Ice Station Exploration, Frozen Solids, Level J	Volume

The Harcourt Learning Site

www.harcourtschool.com

Visit **THE LEARNING SITE** at **www.harcourtschool.com** for a variety of activities and resources that can be used to explore, reinforce, practice, and extend the learning of the chapter.

- Multimedia Math Glossary
- Activities and instructional resources
- E-Lab activities
- Show Me math models

Intervention CD-ROMs

These CD-ROMs help you

- assess prerequisite concepts and skills for each chapter and assess problem-solving at point of use.

- diagnose to determine whether intervention is necessary or if enrichment is appropriate for a concept or skill.

- diagnose to determine whether intervention is necessary for a specific problem-solving strategy or skill.

- prescribe intervention for concepts, skills, and problem-solving strategies and skills.

- provide enrichment for students who mastered the prerequisite concepts and skills.

For the Student

The following technology can be used with students that need more instruction with skills or problem solving, and with students that will benefit from reinforcement, practice, and extension of skills from this chapter.

Intervention CD-ROMs

- Support and enrichment for prerequisite skills
- Support for problem solving

Harcourt Mega Math CD-ROMs

- Reinforcement, practice, and extension

Polar Planes
Skill Level G

Frozen Solids
Skill Level A

The Harcourt Learning Site
www.harcourtschool.com

- Multimedia Math Glossary
- E-Lab activities
- Show Me math models
- Games and activities

For the Teacher

Intervention CD-ROMs

- Diagnose and prescribe intervention for prerequisite skills.
- Provide enrichment for prerequisite skills.
- Diagnose and prescribe intervention for problem-solving strategies and skills.

Harcourt Mega Math CD-ROMs

- Customize additional practice for each student in your class.
- The leveled activities increase in difficulty as students progress.

The Harcourt Learning Site
www.harcourtschool.com

- Find activities and other resources.

Harcourt Assessment System

This software includes:

- Online test taking and automatic scoring
- A bank of items from which to build tests
- Immediate feedback on students' performance
- Correlation of items to textbook and state standards
- Comprehensive program management and class reporting
- Prescriptive reports

ePlanner

This on-line resource allows you to:

- Customize planning and pacing.
- Select resources for daily instruction.
- Reorder content to meet your state, district, or local needs.

For the Parent

The Harcourt Learning Site
www.harcourtschool.com

Encourage parents to visit the Math section of the Harcourt Learning Site to help them reinforce mathematics vocabulary, concepts, and skills with their children.

- Multimedia Math Glossary
- E-Lab interactive learning experiences
- Show Me math models
- Family Involvement tips and activities

Cross-Curricular Connections

Use these topics to help integrate mathematics into your daily planning.
See the pages indicated to find out more about each topic.

Art

- **Native American art,** PE p. 395
- **Making a mobile,** TE p. 396B
- **M. C. Escher,** PE p. 430
- **Tessellations in art,** TE p. 430B
- **Draw with plane figures,** TE p. 432B
- **Designing quilts,** TE p. 448B
- **Famous monuments,** PE p. 454

Social Studies

- **Traffic signs,** PE/TE p. 382
- **Ancient tile mosaics,** TE p. 408B
- **Williamsburg, Virginia,** PE/TE p. 422
- **Models of square pyramids,** TE p. 424B
- **The Olympics,** PE pp. 434, 435
- **History of tulips,** PE/TE p. 442
- **Architecture of Thomas Jefferson,** PE p. 447

Science

- **Geese,** PE p. 387
- **Classifying animals,** TE p. 400B
- **Starfish,** PE/TE p. 406
- **John Pennekamp Coral Reef State Park,** PE p. 411

Writing

- **Riddles,** TE pp. 384B, 410B
- **Compare and contrast,** TE p. 390B
- **Compare solid figures,** TE p. 424B
- **Word problems,** TE p. 444B

Language Arts/Reading

- **Vocabulary Strategy • Word origins,** TE p. 390B
- **Use graphic aids,** PE p. 399
- **Reading Strategy • Compare,** TE pp. 400B, 416B
- **Analogies,** PE p. 426
- **Reading Strategy • Make inferences,** TE p. 436B
- **Reading Strategy • Make generalizations,** TE p. 450B
- **Reading Strategy • Analyze information,** PE p. 455

Literature

- *The Greedy Triangle* by Marilyn Burns (Scholastic, Inc., 1994), TE p. 382G
- *Round Trip* by Ann Jonas (Greenwillow Books, 1983), TE p. 382G

Reaching All Learners

Differentiated Instruction

PURPOSE To draw lines of symmetry on plane figures

USING THE ACTIVITY WHEEL Have each student choose one activity to complete independently. *Use after Lesson 20.2.*

* The Activity Wheel provides each student with a choice, according to learning style, for practicing an important skill.

Check students' work.

ACTIVITY WHEEL*

Draw a unique shape with one line of symmetry. Include designs that match on both sides of the line of symmetry.

Draw the front of a building that has a line of symmetry. Draw windows, doors, and plants in such a way that the line remains a line of symmetry.

Trace two objects that have symmetry. Draw lines of symmetry on each. Cut the shapes out and use them as models to explain the meaning of symmetry.

Literature Connections

These books provide students with additional ways to explore geometry.

The Greedy Triangle by Marilyn Burns (Scholastic, Inc., 1994) is a story about a triangle who keeps changing its shape by increasing how many sides and angles it has.

- Have students look for the examples of each type of plane figure in the book and then name other real-life examples. *Use with Lesson 19.3.*

Round Trip by Ann Jonas (Greenwillow Books, 1983) The black-and-white illustrations will delight students, who can read the text forward and then upside down and backward.

- Have students trace figures in the book and draw a line of symmetry. *Use with Lesson 20.2.*

PRACTICE GAME

Right Angle Ramble

PURPOSE To identify right angles

MATERIALS *For each group of 3–5* game board, p. TR76; number cube, numbered 1–6, p. TR65; game markers

ABOUT THE GAME

- A player tosses the number cube and moves his or her marker the number of spaces indicated.

- When the player lands on a space with a letter, he or she must count the number of right angles in the space and the letter, and may then advance that many spaces.

- If the player lands on a space with a number, he or she must count the number of right angles and move back that many spaces.

Angles from A to...

Start A R K 5 N 8 P 9
5
3
M
6
W
2
X
Y
1
F C 4 7 E O H Z

- The first player to reach the end of the game board wins. *Use with Lesson 19.1.*

VISUAL, KINESTHETIC
BODILY/KINESTHETIC

Geometric Figures

NCTM Standards 2000

1. Number and Operations
Lesson 19.6
2. Algebra
3. Geometry
Lessons 19.1–19.6
4. Measurement
5. Data Analysis and Probability
Lesson 19.6

6. Problem Solving
Lessons 19.1–19.6
7. Reasoning and Proof
Lessons 19.1–19.6
8. Communication
Lessons 19.1–19.6
9. Connections
Lessons 19.1, 19.2, 19.4, 19.5
10. Representation
Lessons 19.1, 19.2, 19.3, 19.4, 19.5

Chapter Planner

Getting Ready for Chapter 19 • Assessing Prior Knowledge and INTERVENTION (See PE and TE page 383.)

LESSON	NORTH CAROLINA STANDARDS	PACING	VOCABULARY*	MATERIALS	RESOURCES AND TECHNOLOGY
19.1 Line Segments and Angles pp. 384–387 **Objective** To identify and draw lines, line segments, and rays, and to classify angles as right, acute, or obtuse	3.01	1 Day	**line**, **point** **line segment** **ray**, **angle** **right angle** **degree (°)** **acute angle** **obtuse angle**		Reteach, Practice, Problem Solving, Challenge 19.1 ▦ Transparency 19.1 ◉ **Intervention**, *Skills 56–57* (CD or Book) ◉ **Harcourt Mega Math Ice Station Exploration**, *Polar Planes*
19.2 Types of Lines pp. 388–389 **Objective** To identify intersecting, perpendicular, and parallel lines	3.01	1 Day	**intersecting lines** **perpendicular lines** **parallel lines**	*Optional* ruler, square dot paper	Reteach, Practice, Problem Solving, Challenge 19.2 ▦ Transparency 19.2 ◉ **Harcourt Mega Math Ice Station Exploration**, *Polar Planes*
19.3 Plane Figures pp. 390–391 **Objective** To identify, describe, classify, and draw plane figures	3.01	1 Day	**polygon** **quadrilateral** **pentagon** **hexagon** **octagon**		Reteach, Practice, Problem Solving, Challenge 19.3 ▦ Transparency 19.3 ◉ **Intervention**, *Skills 56–57* (CD or Book) ◉ **Harcourt Mega Math Ice Station Exploration**, *Polar Planes*
19.4 Triangles pp. 392–395 **Objective** To identify, describe, and classify triangles	3.01	1 Day	**equilateral** **isosceles** **scalene** **right triangle** **obtuse triangle** **acute triangle**	*For Linkup,* grid paper, pencil, crayons	Reteach, Practice, Problem Solving, Challenge 19.4 ▦ Transparency 19.4 ◉ **Harcourt Mega Math Ice Station Exploration**, *Polar Planes* ▣ **Math Jingles® CD 3–4**
19.5 Quadrilaterals pp. 396–399 **Objective** To identify, describe, and classify quadrilaterals	3.01	1 Day	**trapezoid** **parallelogram** **rhombus**		Reteach, Practice, Problem Solving, Challenge 19.5 ▦ Transparency 19.5 ◉ **Harcourt Mega Math Ice Station Exploration**, *Polar Planes*
19.6 Problem Solving Strategy: Draw a Diagram pp. 400–401 **Objective** To use the problem solving strategy *draw a diagram* to solve problems	3.01 maintains (2) 4.01	1 Day	**Venn diagram**	🖩	Reteach, Practice, Reading Strategy, Challenge 19.6 ▦ Transparency 19.6 ▦ Scaffolded Instruction Transparency 19 ▦ Reading Transparency 19 ◉ **Intervention • Problem Solving**, *Strategy/Skill 19* (CD or Book)

Ending Chapter 19 • Extra Practice, p. 402 • Chapter 19 Review/Test, p. 403 • Getting Ready for the EOG Test, pp. 404–405

****Boldfaced** terms are the key mathematical terms for the chapter.

Vocabulary Power

Review Vocabulary

To be ready for Chapter 19, students should know the following vocabulary terms:

- **circle**, **square**, **triangle**, and **rectangle**

Develop Key Chapter Vocabulary

The **boldfaced** words are the key vocabulary terms in the chapter.

- **line** (p. 384)—a straight path extending infinitely in both directions
- **point** (p. 384)—an exact location in space
- **line segment** (p. 384)—a part of a line with two endpoints
- **ray** (p. 384)—a part of a line with one endpoint that continues in one direction
- **angle** (p. 384)—two rays with a common endpoint
- **right angle** (p. 384)—an angle that measures 90°
- **degree (°)** (p. 385)—a unit of measure for angles
- **acute angle** (p. 385)—an angle less than 90°
- **obtuse angle** (p. 385)—an angle greater than 90° and less than 180°
- **intersecting lines** (p. 388)—lines that cross and form angles
- **perpendicular lines** (p. 388)—lines that cross to form right angles
- **parallel lines** (p. 388)—lines that never cross
- **polygon** (p. 390)—a closed plane figure with straight sides
- **quadrilateral** (p. 390)—a polygon with 4 sides
- **pentagon** (p. 390)—a polygon with 5 sides
- **hexagon** (p. 390)—a polygon with 6 sides
- **octagon** (p. 390)—a polygon with 8 sides
- **equilateral triangle** (p. 393)—a triangle with 3 equal sides
- **isosceles triangle** (p. 393)—a triangle with 2 equal sides
- **scalene triangle** (p. 393)—a triangle with 0 equal sides
- **right triangle** (p. 393)—a triangle with a right angle
- **obtuse triangle** (p. 393)—a triangle with 1 obtuse angle
- **acute triangle** (p. 393)—a triangle with 3 acute angles
- **trapezoid** (p. 396)—a quadrilateral with 1 pair of parallel sides
- **parallelogram** (p. 397)—a quadrilateral with 2 pairs of parallel sides
- **rhombus** (p. 397)—a quadrilateral with 2 pairs of parallel sides and 4 equal sides
- **Venn diagram** (p. 400)—a diagram that shows the relationships among sets

Vocabulary Cards

Have students use the Vocabulary Cards on *Teacher's Resource Book* pages TR165–172 for the key terms in the chapter. The cards can be added to a file of mathematics terms.

right angle

Multimedia Math Glossary

For vocabulary support, visit
www.harcourtschool.com/mathglossary

Math Journal

Have students define the key vocabulary terms in the chapter. Have students use their own words and give an example of each.

M A T H Word Work

Objective To reinforce vocabulary concepts *Use after Lesson 19.6.*

Display the 27 key vocabulary terms from the chapter. Tell students that they will each be writing a story and that they will choose one of the geometric terms to use as the main character. Students should use at least 4 of the vocabulary terms in their stories, but encourage them to use as many of the terms as they can. Have students include drawings with their stories.

MODIFYING INSTRUCTION You may wish to suggest a variety of alternative formats, such as a play, comic strip, song, or detective story.

The Missing Line Segment

Once upon a time, there was a line segment.

The line segment wanted to

Geometric Figures

Mathematics Across the Grades

LOOKING BACK • Prerequisite Skills

To be ready for Chapter 19, students should have the following understandings and skills:

- **Identify Plane Figures**—name plane figures

- **Sides and Vertices**—count sides and vertices of plane figures

Check What You Know

Use page 383 to determine students' knowledge of prerequisite concepts and skills.

Intervention

Help students prepare for the chapter by using the intervention resources described on TE page 383.

LOOKING AT CHAPTER 19 • Essential Skills

Students will

- identify and describe line segments, rays, angles, and types of lines.

- identify, describe, and classify plane figures.

- **identify, describe, and classify triangles.**

- identify, describe, and classify quadrilaterals.

- use the problem solving strategy *draw a diagram* to solve problems.

Example

Is this an *equilateral triangle,* an *isosceles triangle,* or a *scalene triangle*? Explain.

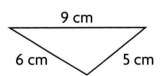

It is a scalene triangle because it has 0 equal sides.

LOOKING AHEAD • Applications

Students will apply what they learn in Chapter 19 to the following new concepts:

- Identify and Draw Congruent and Similar Figures (Chapter 20)

- Find Perimeter, Area, and Volume (Chapter 22)

- Identify and Draw Lines of Symmetry (Chapter 20)

- Measure Angles (Grade 4)

Differentiated Instruction

 Meeting the Needs of All Learners

Extra Support	Activities for All	Enrichment
Alternative Teaching Strategy TE Lessons 19.1, 19.2, 19.3, 19.4, 19.5, 19.6 **Special Needs** TE Lesson 19.2 **ESOL/ESL** TE Lessons 19.1, 19.2, 19.3, 19.4, 19.5, 19.6	**Cross-Curricular Connections** **Art:** TE Lesson 19.5 **Reading:** TE Lesson 19.6 **Science:** TE Lesson 19.6 **Social Studies:** TE/PE Chapter Opener **Vocabulary:** TE p. 382I, TE Lesson 19.3, PE p. 383 **Writing:** TE Lessons 19.1, 19.3	**Advanced Learners** TE Lessons 19.2, 19.4 **Early Finishers** TE Lesson 19.6

Combination and Multi-age Classrooms

Grade 2	Grade 3	Grade 4
Skills Trace Across the Grades		
Identify and sort plane shapes such as circles, squares, triangles, rectangles, and hexagons; combine and separate plane shapes.	**Classify types of lines and angles; identify and describe plane figures; classify triangles and quadrilaterals; sort polygons using a Venn diagram.**	Identify line relationships; measure angles; describe polygons as regular or not regular; classify triangles and quadrilaterals; identify and draw the parts of a circle.
Instructional Strategies		
Students on this level may require more time to build conceptual understanding. **Assignments** **Grade 3 Pupil Edition** • Have students work in pairs for Lessons 19.1, 19.2, and 19.3. • Have them skip Lessons 19.4 and 19.6. **Grade 2 Pupil Edition**—pages 317–326	Students on this level should be able to complete all the lessons in the Pupil Edition and all the activities in the Teacher's Edition with minimal adjustments. **Assignment** **Grade 3 Pupil Edition**—pages 382–403	Students on this level will probably require less time to build conceptual understanding. **Assignments** **Grade 3 Pupil Edition** • Compact Lessons 19.3, 19.4, and 19.5. • Challenge students to draw figures for each section of the Venn diagram on p. 400 in Lesson 19.6. **Grade 4 Pupil Edition**—pages 380–391

Geometric Figures

Introducing the Chapter

Tell students that polygons are closed plane figures with straight sides. Have students look at the photograph and tell whether or not the shapes they see are polygons. Ask them to explain their answers. All the shapes except the circle are polygons. All the shapes are closed figures, but the circle does not have straight sides.

Using Data

To begin the study of this chapter, have students

- Identify the shapes of the traffic signs shown on the page. Possible answer: rhombus, circle, rectangle, pentagon, triangle, octagon

- Name the shape that has exactly 3 sides. triangle

- Make a list of objects in their homes that have straight sides. Possible answers: table tops, rugs, towels

Problem Solving Project

Purpose To identify and classify polygons

Materials *For each student* rectangle or square pattern, p. TR38

Background The shape and color of a traffic sign are determined by the purpose of the sign. Warning signs are yellow. Guide signs, such as speed limit signs, are white. Information signs for parks and museums are brown.

UNDERSTAND • PLAN • SOLVE • CHECK

Have students

- Review their lists of signs that they saw on the way to school and tell which shapes are polygons.

- Record the number of sides of each sign.

- Choose a traffic sign that has exactly 4 sides and make a model of the sign. Check students' work.

Graphing Investigations
Begin Week 19.

≡FAST FACT • SOCIAL STUDIES Different shapes are used for different traffic signs. The stop sign is the only sign in the shape of an octagon. Signs for school zones are in the shape of a pentagon. Yield signs are triangles.

PROBLEM SOLVING Make a list of the traffic signs you see on your way to school. Tell what geometric shapes are used for the signs.

Answers will vary.   **Rockland County, New York**

382

WHY LEARN MATH? Graphic designers often design images on the computer to make a website more attractive. Many of the shapes they use in their designs are polygons. For example, an octagon could be used for an image of a stop sign on a website to help visitors navigate around the site. Ask students to explain how another polygon could be used for a web page. Possible answer: a triangle could be used to represent an arrow button that is clicked to move to the next or previous page.

Family Involvement Activities

These activities provide:

- Letter to the Family
- Math Vocabulary
- Family Game
- Practice (Homework)

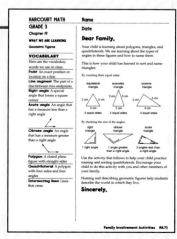

Family Involvement Activities, p. FA73

Use this page to help you review and remember
important skills needed for Chapter 19.

 IDENTIFY PLANE FIGURES

Choose the best term from the box.

circle
rectangle
square
triangle

1.
rectangle

2.
circle

3.
square

4.
triangle

5.
rectangle

6.
triangle

 SIDES AND VERTICES

Tell the number of sides and vertices in each figure.

7.
3 sides; 3 vertices

8.
4 sides; 4 vertices

9.
4 sides; 4 vertices

10.
3 sides; 3 vertices

11.
4 sides;
4 vertices

12.
6 sides;
6 vertices

13.
5 sides;
5 vertices

14.
4 sides;
4 vertices

 **VOCABULARY POWER**

REVIEW

triangle [trī′ang′gəl] *noun*

Tri- at the beginning of *triangle*
means "three." List some other
words that begin with *tri-*, and tell
how *three* is part of their meanings.
**Possible answers: tricycle, triceratops,
triple**

PREVIEW

point
line segment
right angle
acute angle

obtuse angle
intersecting lines
polygon
quadrilateral

GO ON-LINE www.harcourtschool.com/mathglossary

Chapter 19 **383**

Assessing Prior Knowledge

Use the **Check What You Know** page to determine
whether your students have mastered the prerequisite skills critical for this chapter.

Intervention

- **Diagnose and Prescribe**
  Evaluate your students' performance on this page
  to determine whether intervention is necessary or
  if enrichment is appropriate. Options that provide
  instruction, practice, and a check are provided in
  the chart below.

 CHECK WHAT YOU KNOW RESOURCES

Intervention Copying Masters or CD-ROMs

Enrichment Copying Masters

VOCABULARY POWER

For activities and information about the vocabulary in this chapter, see page 382I.

ADDITIONAL PREVIEW VOCABULARY line, ray,
angle, degree (°), perpendicular lines, parallel
lines, pentagon, hexagon, octagon, equilateral
triangle, isosceles triangle, scalene triangle,
right triangle, obtuse triangle, acute triangle,
trapezoid, parallelogram, rhombus, Venn
diagram

Were students successful with **CHECK WHAT YOU KNOW?**

IF . . . NO
THEN . . . INTERVENE

INTERVENTION OPTIONS

IF . . . YES
THEN . . . ENRICH

Skill/Items	Missed more than	Intervene with
Identify Plane Figures, 1–6	2	• *Intervention*, Skill 56
Sides and Vertices, 7–14	2	• *Intervention*, Skill 57

Skill/Items	Missed fewer than	Enrich with
Identify Plane Figures, 1–6	3	• *Intervention*, Enrichment p. IN366
Sides and Vertices, 7–14	3	• *Intervention*, Enrichment p. IN365

Lesson 19.1

Line Segments and Angles

Lesson Planning

PROFESSIONAL DEVELOPMENT

Objective **To identify and draw lines, line segments, and rays, and to classify angles as right, acute, or obtuse**

NCTM Standards

3. Geometry
6. Problem Solving
7. Reasoning and Proof
8. Communication
9. Connections
10. Representation

Math Background

These ideas will help students understand line segments and angles.

- A line is straight. It continues in both directions.
- A line segment is straight. It is part of a line, and it has two endpoints.
- A ray is a part of a line with one endpoint. It continues in one direction.
- An angle is formed when two rays share the same endpoint. An angle can be a right angle, an acute angle, or an obtuse angle.

Vocabulary

line a straight path extending in both directions with no endpoints

point an exact position or location

line segment a part of a line that has two endpoints

ray a part of a line that begins at one endpoint and continues in one direction

angle a figure formed by two rays that have the same endpoint

right angle an angle that forms a square corner

degree (°) a unit of measure used to measure angles

acute angle an angle that measures less than 90°

obtuse angle an angle that measures greater than 90°

Warm-Up Resources

Build Number Sense

Number of the Day

Transparency 19.1

Write and solve four division sentences using as one of the digits the number of vertices of a cube. Possible answers: $8 \div 2 = 4$; $64 \div 8 = 8$; $8 \div 1 = 8$; $32 \div 4 = 8$

Review Basic Facts

Daily Facts Practice

Have students practice multiplication facts by completing Set A of *Teacher's Resource Book*, p. TR97.

Solve a Problem

Transparency 19.1

Problem of the Day

You can use 6 toothpicks to build the number 6. Which numbers, 0–9, can you build using 5 toothpicks? 2, 3, and 5

Which number from 0–9 takes the most toothpicks to make? 8

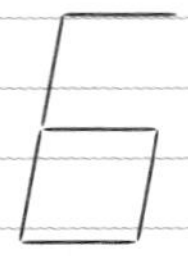

Solution Problem of the Day tab, p. PD19

Intervention and Extension Resources

Alternative Teaching Strategy

MATERIALS *for each group* paper, scissors

Help students **identify right angles, acute angles, and obtuse angles.** Have students cut out a circle, fold it on a line, and then fold this line on itself to create a square corner. They will have a right angle they can use to identify angles of various objects in the classroom. Have students list the objects in a table with the headings *Right Angles, Acute Angles,* and *Obtuse Angles.* Check students' work.

See also page 386.

KINESTHETIC

BODILY/KINESTHETIC

ESOL/ESL

Have students **practice using the terms *less than* and *greater than*.** Write sentence frames such as the following and have students fill in the terms *less than* or *greater than* to complete the sentences.

Twenty-five cents is _____ ten cents. greater than

Three is _____ five. less than

6 + 2 is _____ 2 + 4. greater than

VISUAL

VERBAL/LINGUISTIC

Multistep and Strategy Problems

The following multistep or strategy problem is provided in Lesson 19.1:

Page	Item
386	24

Writing in Mathematics

Have students **practice lesson vocabulary.** Ask them to write riddles that contain clues about the vocabulary words in the lesson. For example:

I am straight. I do not have any endpoints. What am I? a line

Check students' riddles, and then have them share their riddles with a partner.

Technology Link

Intervention, *Skills 56–57*

Harcourt Mega Math Ice Station Exploration, *Polar Planes,* Levels A and B

GO **The Harcourt Learning Site** www.harcourtschool.com

Lesson 19.1 Organizer

Objective To identify and draw lines, line segments, and rays, and to classify angles as right, acute, or obtuse

Vocabulary line, point, line segment, ray, angle, right angle, degree (°), acute angle, obtuse angle

1 INTRODUCE

QUICK REVIEW provides review of prerequisite skills.

WHY LEARN THIS? You'll be able to see line segments and angles in objects around you. *Share the lesson objective with students.*

2 TEACH

Guided Instruction

- *Check students' understanding of the definitions in the Learn section.*

  If you drew a straight mark between two points that are 2 inches apart, would you have drawn a line or a line segment? Explain. A line segment, because it is part of a line and has endpoints; a line does not end.

  How is a ray different from a line segment? A ray has one endpoint. A line segment has two endpoints.

- *Direct students' attention to the plane figure that Victor drew.*

  REASONING If Victor wanted to draw a bigger square on the grid paper, would he need to draw more points and line segments? Explain. No. He would still have 4 points, with longer line segments between them.

  What objects in the classroom have right angles? Possible answer: desks, doors, picture frames, sheets of paper, books

---

 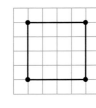

Line Segments and Angles

▶ **Learn**

POINT TO POINT Victor drew this plane figure by connecting points on grid paper. The sides of his figure are line segments. The terms below can help you describe figures in geometry.

Quick Review

Write the number of sides each figure has.

1. ▭ 2. ▢ 3. △
4 sides 4 sides 3 sides

4. ⬡ 5. ◺
4 sides 3 sides

VOCABULARY

line	right angle
point	degree (°)
line segment	acute angle
ray	obtuse angle
angle	

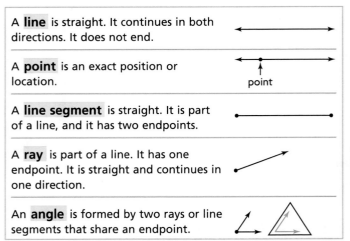

A **line** is straight. It continues in both directions. It does not end.

A **point** is an exact position or location.

A **line segment** is straight. It is part of a line, and it has two endpoints.

A **ray** is part of a line. It has one endpoint. It is straight and continues in one direction.

An **angle** is formed by two rays or line segments that share an endpoint.

- How many line segments did Victor draw? **4 line segments**

- **REASONING** How are lines and line segments alike? How are they different? **Possible answers: both are straight; a line continues in both directions; a line segment has 2 endpoints.**

Look at the angles in the plane figure that Victor drew. These four angles are right angles. A **right angle** is a special angle that forms a square corner. Use the corner of a sheet of paper to tell whether an angle is a right angle.

384

Naming Angles

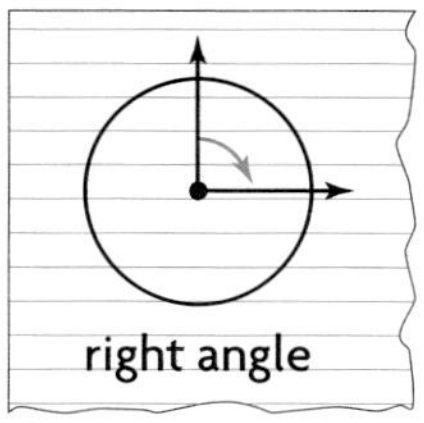

The unit used to measure an angle is a **degree (°)**. A right angle measures 90°. It can be shown as $\frac{1}{4}$ of a turn around a circle.

right angle

You can name angles by the size of the opening between the rays.

The measure of some angles is less than a right angle. These are **acute angles**.

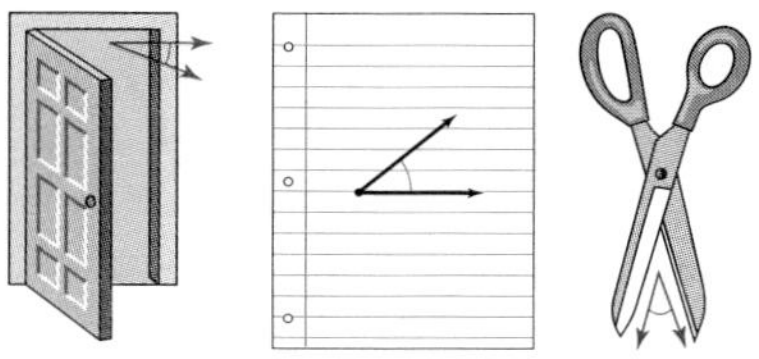

The measure of some angles is greater than a right angle. These are **obtuse angles**.

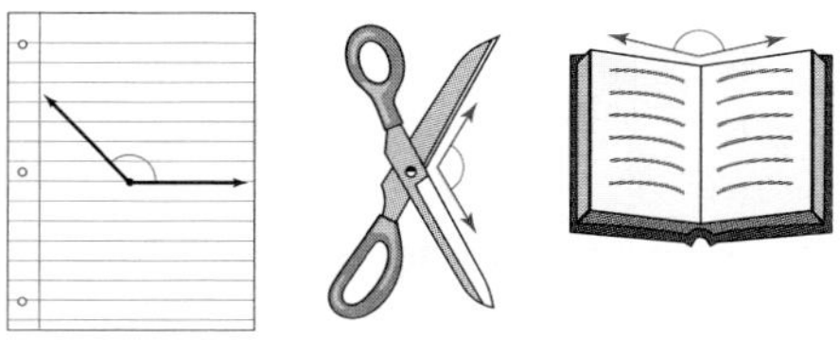

- **REASONING** The angle shown at the right is made up of two $\frac{1}{4}$ turns around the circle. Use what you know about right angles to find the degree measure of this angle. **Possible answer: since one $\frac{1}{4}$ turn measures 90°, you can add 90° + 90°; two $\frac{1}{4}$ turns measure 180°.**

MATH IDEA You can identify angles in plane figures. You can tell if an angle is a right angle, an acute angle, or an obtuse angle.

Check

1. **Draw** a triangle on grid paper like the one shown at the right. What kinds of angles does this triangle have? **Check students' work. There are 2 acute angles and 1 right angle.**

Name each figure.

2.
   line segment

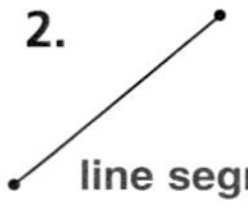

3.
   ray

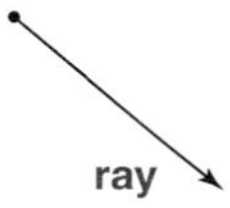

4.
   line

5.
   point

LESSON CONTINUES ▶

- **Ask students to read the Naming Angles section. REASONING** If you lifted the lid of a suitcase just a little bit, would you make an acute angle or an obtuse angle? acute angle

- Direct students' attention to the Reasoning question on page 385. Tell students that the angle pictured to the right of the Reasoning question is called a straight angle.
  REASONING Why do you suppose that this angle is called a *straight angle*? Possible answer: since the two rays form a straight line, the angle is called a straight angle.

MODIFYING INSTRUCTION Have students physically model $\frac{1}{4}$ turns. Begin with students standing and facing the front of the classroom. Have students turn so that they are facing to the right. Explain that this is a $\frac{1}{4}$ turn, which is also called a 90° turn. Have them continue $\frac{1}{4}$ turns until they have completed a full circle.

3 PRACTICE

Guided Practice

Do Check Exercises 1–5 with your students. Identify students who are having difficulty and choose appropriate lesson resources to provide assistance.

North Carolina Standards 3.01 Use appropriate vocabulary to compare, describe, and classify - and three-dimensional figures.

Challenge 19.1

What's the Angle?

Play with a partner.

Materials:
- 12 index cards, ruler

How to Play:
- Draw angles on the back of each index card. Be sure to have 4 that are *right* angles, 4 that are *acute* angles, and 4 that are *obtuse* angles.
- Shuffle the cards and lay them, face down, in 3 rows with 4 cards in each row.
- The object is to win cards by matching angles.
- The first player turns 2 cards over. If they are both the same type of angle, the player wins the cards. If they are not the same type, turn them back over and the next player takes a turn.
- The player with the most cards at the end wins.

Examples:

Not the same type

Same type

Not the same type

Same type

Not the same type

Same type

Challenge CW99

Problem Solving 19.1

Line Segments and Angles   Understand ▶ Plan ▶ Solve ▶ Check

Write the correct answer.

1. How many angles in this figure are obtuse angles?

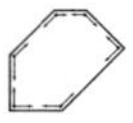

   four

2. Which types of angles make up this triangle?

   acute angles

3. An angle is formed by __?__ rays with the same endpoint.

   two

4. Chris sold 36 car wash tickets. If 9 people purchased an equal number of tickets, how many tickets did each person buy?

   4 tickets

Choose the letter of the correct answer.

5. A parking lot has 6 rows of cars. There are 8 cars in each row. How many cars are in the parking lot?

   A 2 cars
   B 14 cars
   Ⓒ 48 cars
   D 56 cars

6. Pete began reading at 10:30 A.M. He read 5 pages. Each page took him exactly 2 minutes to read. At what time did Pete finish reading?

   F 10:20 A.M.
   G 10:37 A.M.
   Ⓗ 10:40 A.M.
   J 11:00 A.M.

7. How many right angles does this figure have?

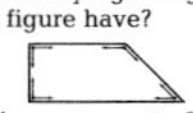

   A 1
   Ⓑ 2
   C 3
   D 4

8. Which of the following has two endpoints?

   F line
   Ⓖ line segment
   H ray
   J angle

9. **Write About It** Explain how you solved Problem 1.

   Possible answer: An obtuse angle is greater than a right angle.
   I found all the angles that were greater than that.

Problem Solving PS99

385

Independent Practice

Note that Exercise 24 is a **multistep or strategy problem.** Assign Exercises 6–27.

For Exercises 18–23, point out that not all the figures may contain all three items in the table.

MULTISTEP OR STRATEGY PROBLEM To solve Exercise 24, students can multiply 3 × 10 to find the number of stickers that Blanca bought in all. Then students can subtract 4 from the product to find how many stickers she will have left.

Name each figure.

6.  angle
7. 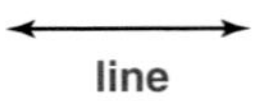 line
8.  ray
9.  line segment

Use a corner of a sheet of paper to tell whether each angle is a *right angle,* an *acute angle,* or an *obtuse angle.*

10. 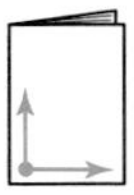 right angle
11. 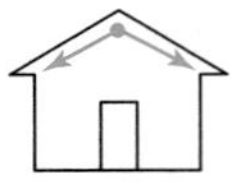 obtuse angle
12.  acute angle
13. 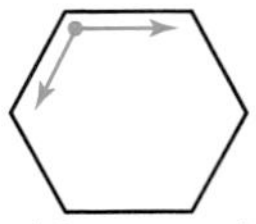 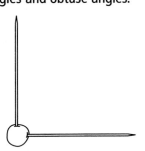 obtuse angle

Draw and label each figure. You may wish to use a ruler or straightedge. **Check students' work.**

14. line segment
15. ray
16. line
17. acute angle

Copy and complete the table.

Figure	Number of Line Segments	Number of Angles	Number of Right Angles
18. □	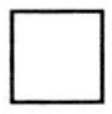 ▨ 4	▨ 4	▨ 4
19. ◇	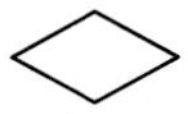 ▨ 4	▨ 4	▨ 0
20. △	 ▨ 3	▨ 3	▨ 0
21. ▭	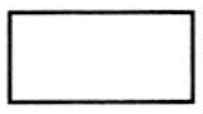 ▨ 4	▨ 4	▨ 4
22. ◺	 ▨ 3	▨ 3	▨ 1
23. ⬯	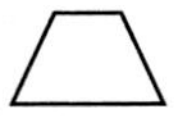 ▨ 4	▨ 4	▨ 0

24. Blanca bought 3 packs of stickers. Each pack has 10 stickers. If she gives 4 stickers to a friend, how many will she have left? **26 stickers**

25. ✏ Write About It Use a ruler or a straightedge to draw a triangle and a right angle. Describe the parts of each figure. **Check students' drawings and descriptions.**

386

Alternative Teaching Strategy   Scaffolded Instruction

PURPOSE Students model line segments, rays, and angles.

MATERIALS *For each student* two toothpicks and a small amount of modeling clay

Step 1

Draw a line. Point out the arrows on each end that indicate that the line does not end. Then have students look carefully at a single toothpick. Point out that it is pointed at each end, so it can represent a line.

Step 2

Have students form a line segment by placing a small ball of clay at each end of the line. Tell them that this is a line segment because it has two endpoints.

Step 3

Read aloud the definition of a ray. Tell students to represent a ray by removing one piece of clay.

Step 4

Show students how to place one end of both toothpicks in a single ball of clay to form a right angle. Have them move the

toothpicks to form acute angles and obtuse angles.

PROFESSIONAL DEVELOPMENT

Have students work in pairs as one student names a figure (line segment, ray, right angle, obtuse angle, acute angle) and the partner models the figure. **Check students' work.**

26. ≡**FAST FACT** • **SCIENCE** Geese fly in a "V" formation to save energy so that they can fly farther. What kind of angle describes this formation? **acute angle**

27. List at least 3 objects in the room that contain right angles. How can you be sure the angles are right angles? **Possible answers: book, door, table; compare angles to the square corner of a sheet of paper**

Getting Ready for the EOG Test

28. How many angles does a pentagon have? **C**

   A 3   **C** 5
   B 4   **D** 6

29. How many sides does a hexagon have? **D**

   A 3
   B 4
   C 5
   D 6

30. Complete to make the sentence correct.

This angle is _?_ . **A**

   A an acute angle
   B an obtuse angle
   C a right angle
   D a line

Problem Solving — Thinker's Corner

CLOCKS AND ANGLES Use what you learned in this lesson to describe the angles made by the hands of a clock.

Write whether each angle is a *right angle,* an *acute angle,* or an *obtuse angle.*

1.
7:45
acute angle

2.
11:15
obtuse angle

3.
9:00
right angle

4.
3:30
acute angle

5. REASONING The hour hand is between the 3 and 4. The minute hand is pointing to the 5. What time is it? Describe the angle made by the hands. **3:25; acute angle**

6. Joy left for school at 7:50 A.M. It took her 15 minutes to walk to school. What time is it? Describe the angle made by the hands. **8:05 A.M.; obtuse angle**

Chapter 19 **387**

Problem Solving — Thinker's Corner

• *Have students read the directions.*
REASONING Is there a time that can be shown on the clock in which no angle is formed by the hands? Explain. Possible answer: Yes; at 12:00 both hands are in the same position.

MODIFYING INSTRUCTION Have students use an analog clock with movable hands to form the angles shown on the clocks in Exercises 1–4 of the Thinker's Corner.

4 ASSESS

Summarize the lesson by having students:

DISCUSS How are line segments and angles used to make plane figures? Segments form the sides and come together to make angles.

 WRITE How do you know whether an angle is obtuse or acute? If the angle is less than a square corner, it is an acute angle. If the angle is greater than a square corner, it is an obtuse angle.

LESSON QUIZ
Name each figure.

Transparency **19.1**

1.   line segment

2.   obtuse angle

3.   ray

4.   line

Types of Lines

Lesson Planning

PROFESSIONAL DEVELOPMENT

Objective To identify intersecting, perpendicular, and parallel lines

Materials *Optional* ruler; square dot paper, p. TR30

NCTM Standards
3. Geometry
6. Problem Solving
7. Reasoning and Proof
8. Communication
9. Connections
10. Representation

Math Background
These ideas will help students understand the characteristics of intersecting, perpendicular, and parallel lines.

- Intersecting lines cross at one point to form angles.

- Parallel lines never cross and do not form angles.

- When two lines intersect, they form four angles. The opposite angles are equal.

- Opposite sides of a parallelogram are parallel.

- Perpendicular lines form right angles.

Vocabulary
intersecting lines lines that cross at exactly one point

perpendicular lines lines that cross to form right angles

parallel lines lines that never cross

Warm-Up Resources

Number of the Day

Transparency **19.2**

Write and solve three multiplication sentences using as one of the digits the number of right angles in a rectangle. Possible answers: $4 \times 4 = 16$; $4 \times 2 = 8$; $4 \times 5 = 20$

Daily Facts Practice

Have students practice multiplication and division facts by completing Set B of *Teacher's Resource Book*, p. TR97.

Transparency **19.2**

Problem of the Day

Mario drew a plane figure with 4 equal line segments and 4 right angles. Susana drew a plane figure with 3 line segments and 3 angles. Omar drew a plane figure with 0 line segments and 0 angles. What figure did each student draw? Possible answers: Mario, square; Susana, triangle; Omar, circle

Solution Problem of the Day tab, p. PD19

Intervention and Extension Resources

Alternative Teaching Strategy

MATERIALS index cards

ESOL/ESL

Have students **practice identifying parallel, perpendicular, and intersecting lines.** Draw several examples of intersecting (nonperpendicular), perpendicular, and parallel lines on individual index cards. Use them as flashcards, asking students to identify the type of lines pictured on each card. When intersecting lines are identified, ask whether they are perpendicular lines. Check students' work.

VISUAL

VISUAL/SPATIAL

Multistep and Strategy Problems

The following multistep and strategy problems are provided in Lesson 19.2:

Page	Item
389	14–15

Special Needs

Help students **remember the difference between parallel and intersecting lines.** Display the word *parallel*. Darken the 2 *l*'s in the middle of the word to draw attention to them. Point out that these lines never cross. Tell students to remember that the letters *ll* are parallel in the word *parallel*.

VISUAL

VISUAL/SPATIAL

Advanced Learners

Challenge students to **classify parallel, perpendicular, and intersecting lines.** Ask students to draw a map of an imaginary town.

- Tell them to draw parallel streets. Have them label the parallel streets with names beginning with *P*.
- Then have them add other streets that intersect the parallel streets. If the intersecting streets are perpendicular to the parallel streets, have students label those streets with names that begin with the letter *R*. If the intersecting streets are not perpendicular to the parallel streets, have them label those streets with names that begin with the letter *I*.
- Invite them to add features to the map such as rivers, ponds, and buildings. Have them share their maps with the class. Check students' work.

KINESTHETIC

VISUAL/SPATIAL

Technology Link

Harcourt Mega Math
Ice Station Exploration,
Polar Planes, Level C

Lesson 19.2 Organizer

Objective To identify intersecting, perpendicular, and parallel lines

Vocabulary intersecting lines, perpendicular lines, parallel lines

Materials *Optional* ruler; square dot paper, p. TR30

1 INTRODUCE

QUICK REVIEW provides review of prerequisite skills.

WHY LEARN THIS? You will be able to describe intersecting and parallel streets when giving directions. *Share the lesson objective with students.*

2 TEACH

Guided Instruction

- *Check students' understanding of the definitions in the Learn section.*
  Do all intersecting lines form right angles?
  Explain. No; they can also form acute angles and obtuse angles.

- *Direct students' attention to the example of perpendicular lines.*
  Which of these two lines is a horizontal line?
  the line that goes across, from side to side
  Which of these two lines is a vertical line?
  the line that goes up and down
  REASONING Can diagonal lines be perpendicular? Explain. Possible answer: Yes; If they intersect to form right angles, they are perpendicular.

MODIFYING INSTRUCTION Have students draw two squares on dot paper. In one square, have students draw a vertical line dividing the square in half, and a horizontal line that intersects this vertical line. In the other square, ask students to draw two diagonal lines (joining opposite corners). Have students use a corner of a sheet of paper to find out if the intersecting lines are perpendicular.

3 PRACTICE

Guided Practice

Do Check Exercises 1–4 with your students. Identify students who are having difficulty and choose appropriate lesson resources to provide assistance.

388 Chapter 19

---

2 Types of Lines

▶ Learn

GET IN LINE Here are some ways to describe the relationships between lines.

Lines that cross are **intersecting lines**. Intersecting lines form angles.

Intersecting lines that cross to form right angles are **perpendicular lines**.

Lines that never cross are **parallel lines**. Since parallel lines never cross, they do not form angles. They are always the same distance apart.

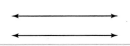

You may see models of intersecting, perpendicular, and parallel lines in the world around you.

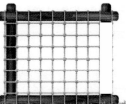

- Are the angles in the climbing net right angles? How can you check? Yes; possible answer: since the angles match the corner of a sheet of paper, they are right angles.
- **REASONING** Are intersecting lines always perpendicular lines? Explain. No; some lines that cross form angles that are not right angles.

▶ Check

1. **Explain** how to tell whether the swing chains are intersecting or parallel.
   You can tell they are parallel because they do not cross.

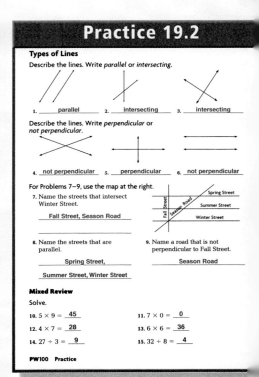

388

Quick Review

Write *right angle*, *obtuse angle*, or *acute angle*.

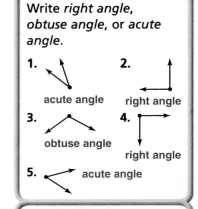

1. acute angle
2. right angle
3. obtuse angle
4. right angle
5. acute angle

VOCABULARY
intersecting lines
perpendicular lines
parallel lines

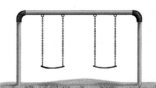

Reteach 19.2

Types of Lines

Lines that cross each other are **intersecting lines**. These lines intersect.

Lines that never cross are **parallel lines**. These lines are parallel.

Intersecting lines that cross to form right angles are called **perpendicular lines**. These lines are perpendicular.

In 1–3, draw intersecting lines. Check students' drawings.

1.   2.   3.

For 4–5, use the map.

4. Name the streets parallel to Foster Street. __Tufts St., Adams St.__

5. Name the streets that do not run perpendicular to Massachusetts Ave.
__Lake St., Broadway__

RW100 Reteach

Practice 19.2

Types of Lines

Describe the lines. Write *parallel* or *intersecting*.

1. __parallel__   2. __intersecting__   3. __intersecting__

Describe the lines. Write *perpendicular* or *not perpendicular*.

4. __not perpendicular__   5. __perpendicular__   6. __not perpendicular__

For Problems 7–9, use the map at the right.

7. Name the streets that intersect Winter Street.
__Fall Street, Season Road__

8. Name the streets that are parallel.
__Spring Street,__
__Summer Street, Winter Street__

9. Name a road that is not perpendicular to Fall Street.
__Season Road__

Mixed Review

Solve.

10. $5 \times 9 =$ __45__   11. $7 \times 0 =$ __0__

12. $4 \times 7 =$ __28__   13. $6 \times 6 =$ __36__

14. $27 \div 3 =$ __9__   15. $32 \div 8 =$ __4__

PW100 Practice

Describe the lines. Write *parallel* or *intersecting*.

2. 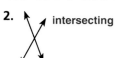 intersecting

3. parallel

4. intersecting

▶ **Practice and Problem Solving**   Extra Practice, page 402, Set B

Describe the lines. Write *parallel* or *intersecting*.

5.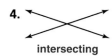
parallel

6.
intersecting

7.
parallel

Describe the intersecting lines. Write *perpendicular* or *not perpendicular*.

8.
perpendicular

9.
not perpendicular

10.
perpendicular

USE DATA For 11–13, use the map at the right.

11. Which street is parallel to Oak Street?
Elm Street

12. Is Oak Street perpendicular to Pine Street or
Maple Street? Explain. Maple Street; 4 right angles are
formed where Maple Street and Oak Street cross.

13. **What's the Question?** The answer is obtuse angle.
Possible question: What type of angle is formed by the
bicycle trail?

14. **REASONING** Use what you know about line
relationships to describe the sides of a rectangle.
Opposite sides are parallel, and sides that meet form right
angles.

15. **Write About It** Draw and label sets of
intersecting, parallel, and perpendicular lines. Use a
ruler to help. Describe the angles in each of your
drawings. Check students' drawings and descriptions.

Getting Ready for the EOG Test

16. Which kind of lines do the legs of the ironing
board model? **C**

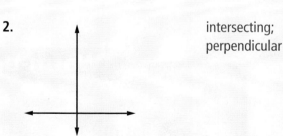

A parallel   **C** intersecting
B perpendicular **D** curved

☞ North Carolina Standards 3.01 Use appropriate vocabulary to compare, describe, and classify
two- and three-dimensional figures.

Independent Practice

Note that Exercises 14 and 15 are **multistep or
strategy problems.** Assign Exercises 5–15.

4 ASSESS

Summarize the lesson by having students:

**DISCUSS If someone tells you that two lines
intersect, do you know whether the lines form
right angles? Explain.** No; intersecting lines may
form different kinds of angles. Only some intersecting lines form right angles.

**WRITE Explain why two lines cannot be
both intersecting and parallel.** The lines
cannot be both intersecting and parallel because
parallel lines never cross, while intersecting lines
always cross.

LESSON QUIZ

Describe the lines. Write *parallel* or
intersecting. Write whether the
intersecting lines are *perpendicular* or
not perpendicular.

Transparency 19.2

1.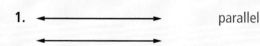
parallel

2.
intersecting;
perpendicular

3.
intersecting; not
perpendicular

Challenge 19.2

Mapmaker, Mapmaker, Make Me a Map!

Use the directions below and what you know about lines
and angles to label the streets on the map.

Check students' answers.

1. Label the first street to the north of and parallel to
   Main Street *River Road*.
2. Label the street to the north of and parallel to River
   Road *High Street*.
3. Label the street to the east of the bank and
   perpendicular to Main Street *Daisy Lane*.
4. Label the street to the west of the school *Pine
   Street*. It forms a right angle with Main Street and
   intersects High Street.
5. Label the street that meets Daisy Lane and
   High Street *Devine Drive*. It runs southwest
   and intersects Main Street east of the store.
6. Label the street that forms an obtuse angle on the
   south side of High Street *Last Road*. It intersects
   Main Street west of the bank.

Problem Solving 19.2

Types of Lines

Understand ▶ Plan ▶ Solve ▶ Check

Write the correct answer.

1. Write the name that best
   describes the line relationship:
   parallel or *intersecting*.

   parallel

2. Write the name that best
   describes the angle: *right angle,
   acute angle,* or *obtuse angle*.

   acute angle

3. Write *rays* or *lines* to describe
   the figures that form the angle
   in Problem 2.
   rays

4. Write *points, lines,* or *line
   segments* to describe the
   figures in Problem 1.
   lines

Choose the letter of the correct answer.

5. Which name describes the
   angle?

   A obtuse   C acute
   Ⓑ right   D parallel

6. Which name describes the
   figure?

   F ray   H point
   Ⓖ line segment J line

7. Emilio draws two parallel lines.
   Which statement about the
   lines is true?

   A They form two angles.
   B They form four angles.
   C They intersect.
   Ⓓ They do not intersect.

8. How many right angles are
   there in a square?

   F 1
   G 2
   H 3
   Ⓙ 4

9. **Write About It** Describe the strategy you used to solve Problem 8.
   **Possible Answer: I drew a picture of a square and counted four
   square corners, so I knew a square has four right angles.**

Plane Figures

Lesson Planning

Objective To identify, describe, classify, and draw plane figures

NCTM Standards
3. Geometry
6. Problem Solving
7. Reasoning and Proof
8. Communication
10. Representation

Math Background
These ideas will help students build understanding of polygons.

- Closed figures begin and end at the same point, and open figures have ends that do not meet.

- Polygons are closed figures made of line segments.

- The number of sides of a polygon equals the number of angles.

- All polygons are closed figures but not all closed figures are polygons.

- Polygons are two-dimensional figures because they can be measured in two dimensions: length and width.

Vocabulary
polygon   a closed plane figure with straight sides

quadrilateral   a polygon with 4 sides and 4 angles

pentagon   a polygon with 5 sides and 5 angles

hexagon   a polygon with 6 sides and 6 angles

octagon   a polygon with 8 sides and 8 angles

Warm-Up Resources

Number of the Day

Transparency **19.3**

Write four number sentences in which the answer is 90. Possible answers: $10 \times 9 = 90$, $900 \div 10 = 90$, $45 + 45 = 90$, $100 - 10 = 90$

Daily Facts Practice

Have students practice addition facts by completing Set C of *Teacher's Resource Book*, p. TR97.

Transparency **19.3**

Problem of the Day

John has 3 sisters and 1 brother. Susie has 1 sister and 3 brothers. Ashley has 2 sisters and 2 brothers. One of the girls is John's sister. Which one? Ashley

Solution Problem of the Day tab, p. PD19

Intervention and Extension Resources

Alternative Teaching Strategy

MATERIALS *For each student* scissors, 1-cm grid paper, p. TR58

ESOL/ESL

Have students **draw, sort, and identify polygons.**
Have students draw several polygons on their grid paper, cut them out, and trade them with another student. Ask students to sort them according to the number of sides and angles and write the name of the polygon on each figure. Check students' work.

VISUAL, KINESTHETIC

LOGICAL/MATHEMATICAL

Multistep and Strategy Problems

The following multistep or strategy problem is provided in Lesson 19.3:

Page	Item
391	20

Vocabulary Strategy

MATERIALS *For each pair* dictionary

Help students **understand the vocabulary in the lesson**. Share with students that many English words have a Greek or Latin origin. For example, *quadrilateral* comes from the Latin *quadri-*, meaning *"four,"* and *latus*, meaning *"side."* Have students work with a partner to find the roots and meanings for *pentagon, hexagon,* and *octagon.* Possible answer: *penta-:* five; *-gon:* angle; *hexa-:* six; *octa-:* eight

AUDITORY, VISUAL

VERBAL/LINGUISTIC

Writing in Mathematics

 Have students **compare and contrast quadrilaterals, pentagons, hexagons, and octagons.** Ask students to give real-life examples of each figure. Possible answer: Quadrilaterals, pentagons, hexagons, and octagons are all polygons. A quadrilateral has 4 sides and angles, a pentagon has 5, a hexagon has 6, and an octagon has 8. Examples: a piece of notebook paper; a school-crossing sign; shapes on wallpaper; stop sign

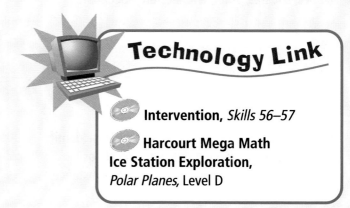

Technology Link

Intervention, *Skills 56–57*

Harcourt Mega Math
Ice Station Exploration,
Polar Planes, Level D

Lesson 19.3 Organizer

Objective To identify, describe, classify, and draw plane figures

Vocabulary polygon, quadrilateral, pentagon, hexagon, octagon

1 INTRODUCE

QUICK REVIEW provides review of prerequisite skills.

WHY LEARN THIS? You will be able to recognize and identify the shapes you see in road signs. *Share the lesson objective with students.*

2 TEACH

Guided Instruction

- *Have students read the Learn section and look at Figures A–D. Remind students that for a figure to be a polygon, two conditions must be met: it must be a closed figure with straight sides, and it must be made of line segments.*
  How are Figures C and D different? Possible answer: Figure C is open and has straight sides; Figure D is a closed figure with no straight sides.
  REASONING How could you change Figure C into a polygon? Draw a line segment to connect the two endpoints so that it becomes a closed figure.

- *Direct students' attention to the Examples of Polygons.*
  How are all octagons alike? How might they differ? They all have 8 sides and 8 angles; the sides may be different lengths.

- *Draw a 10-sided figure and label it* decagon.
  How many sides and angles are in a decagon? 10 sides and 10 angles

MODIFYING INSTRUCTION Have students form triangles, squares, and rectangles on a geoboard.

3 PRACTICE

Guided Practice

Do Check Exercises 1–6 with your students. Identify students who are having difficulty and choose appropriate lesson resources to provide assistance.

LESSON 3 Plane Figures

Quick Review

Write the number of sides each figure has.

1. ▽ 3 sides
2. ☐ 4 sides
3. ▯ 4 sides
4. ◇ 4 sides
5. ◺ 3 sides

VOCABULARY

polygon   hexagon
quadrilateral octagon
pentagon

▶ **Learn**

SHAPE UP!   A closed figure begins and ends at the same point. An open figure has ends that do not meet. A **polygon** is a closed plane figure with straight sides that are line segments. A circle is an example of a plane figure that has no straight sides.

polygons

A   B

not polygons

C   D

MATH IDEA You can name and sort polygons by the number of *sides* or *angles* they have.

Examples of Polygons

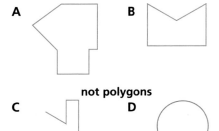

triangles	quadrilaterals	pentagons	hexagons	octagons
3 sides	4 sides	5 sides	6 sides	8 sides
3 angles	4 angles	5 angles	6 angles	8 angles

- What do you notice about the number of sides and the number of angles in polygons? **Possible answer: they have the same number of sides as angles.**

▶ **Check**

1. Explain why a circle is *not* a polygon.   **A circle does not have straight sides.**

390

Reteach 19.3

Plane Figures

A **closed figure** begins and ends at the same point.

An **open figure** has ends that do not meet.

closed figures   open figure

A **polygon** is a closed figure with straight sides that are line segments. You can name and sort polygons by the number of sides or angles they have.

triangle	quadrilateral	pentagon	hexagon	octagon
3 sides	4 sides	5 sides	6 sides	8 sides
3 angles	4 angles	5 angles	6 angles	8 angles

Tell if each figure is a polygon. Write *yes* or *no*.

1. no   2. yes   3. no   4. no   5. yes

Write the number of sides and angles each polygon has. Then name the polygon.

6. 4 sides / 4 angles / quadrilateral
7. 6 sides / 6 angles / hexagon
8. 3 sides / 3 angles / triangle
9. 5 sides / 5 angles / pentagon

Reteach RW101

Practice 19.3

Plane Figures

Tell if each figure is a polygon. Write *yes* or *no*.

1. yes   2. no   3. no   4. no   5. yes

Write the number of sides and angles each polygon has. Then name the polygon.

6. 5 sides; 5 angles; pentagon
7. 6 sides; 6 angles; hexagon
8. 4 sides; 4 angles; quadrilateral or trapezoid
9. 3 sides; 3 angles; triangle
10. 8 sides; 8 angles; octagon
11. 4 sides; 4 angles; quadrilateral or rhombus
12. 6 sides; 6 angles; hexagon
13. 5 sides; 5 angles; pentagon

Mixed Review

Decide if the number sentence is true or false. Write *true* or *false*.

14. $18 - 6 \neq 12$ false
15. $14 + 3 \neq 27$ true
16. $7 \times 6 = 42$ true
17. $18 \div 6 \neq 2$ true
18. $5 \times 7 = 12$ false
19. $36 \div 6 = 6$ true

Write +, −, ÷, or × in the ◯ to make the number sentence true.

20. $11 \;(+)\; 8 = 19$
21. $24 \;(+)\; 8 = 3$
22. $9 \;(\times)\; 9 = 81$
23. $35 \;(-)\; 5 = 30$
24. $11 \;(\times)\; 7 = 77$
25. $42 \;(-)\; 21 = 21$

Practice PW101

Tell if each figure is a polygon. Write *yes* or *no*.

2. yes

3. yes

4. no

5. yes

6. no

Practice and Problem Solving
 Extra Practice, page 402, Set C

Tell if each figure is a polygon. Write *yes* or *no*.

7. no

8. yes

9. no

10. no

11. yes

Write the number of sides and angles each polygon has. Then name the polygon.

12. 3 sides; 3 angles; triangle

13. 5 sides; 5 angles; pentagon

14. 4 sides; 4 angles; quadrilateral

15. 8 sides; 8 angles; octagon

16. 6 sides; 6 angles; hexagon

For 17–19, write the letters of the figures that answer the questions.

A   B   C   D   E

17. Which are polygons? **A, B, D**

18. Which is a quadrilateral? **B**

19. Which figures have some angles that are acute angles? **B, D**

20. Mr. Gomez delivered 3 cases of pasta to each of 3 stores. Each case had 8 boxes. How many boxes of pasta did he deliver? **72 boxes**

21. **Write About It** Draw polygons with 3, 4, 5, 6, and 8 sides. Then label each polygon.
Check students' drawings and labels.

Getting Ready for the EOG Test

22. Which statement is true about the figures in the group? **D**

A Three figures are polygons.
B All of the figures have 2 acute angles.
C Two figures are pentagons.
D One figure is a quadrilateral.

Chapter 19   **391**

★ **North Carolina Standards 3.01** Use appropriate vocabulary to compare, describe, and classify two- and three-dimensional figures.

Challenge 19.3

Polygon Puzzle

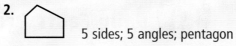

Answer the following questions and then follow the directions.

1. Write the numbers of the polygons that have 4 sides and 4 angles.
   1, 3, 5, 7, 9, 11, 13, 14, 15, 17

2. Write the numbers of the polygons that have 3 sides and 3 angles.
   2, 8, 12, 16

3. Write the numbers of the polygons that have 5 or more sides and 5 or more angles.
   4, 6, 10, 18, 19, 20

4. Use the chart to color the polygons.

5. Make your own design using polygons. Color the design. **Check students' designs.**

Numbers	Color
1, 15	Black
2, 16	Red
3, 14	Yellow
7, 13	Green
8, 12	Orange
5, 17	Purple
6, 19	Brown
10, 20	Blue
9, 11	Pink
4, 18	Light Blue

Challenge   CW101

Problem Solving 19.3

Plane Figures

Understand → Plan → Solve → Check

Write the correct answer.

1. Brad's teacher showed the class a figure with 5 sides and 5 angles. What was it?
   a pentagon

2. Is this figure a polygon? Write *yes* or *no*.
   no

3. Bethany told Jerry that a pentagon has 5 sides and 6 angles. Jerry told her why she was wrong. What did Jerry tell Bethany?
   A pentagon has 5 angles.

4. Manny has 415 marbles. He buys 2 more bags of 36 marbles each. How many marbles does he now have?
   487 marbles

Choose the letter of the correct answer.

5. How many sides does an octagon have?
   A 5
   B 6
   Ⓒ 8
   D 10

6. How many angles does a quadrilateral have?
   F 2
   G 3
   Ⓗ 4
   J 8

7. Which of the following is formed by two rays with the same endpoint?
   Ⓐ angle
   B line
   C ray
   D point

8. Which figure is a hexagon?
   F   H
   Ⓖ   J

9. **Write About It** Explain how the polygons in Problem 8 are different than solid figures.
   Possible answer: They are flat. Solid figures are not flat.

Problem Solving   PS101

COMMON ERROR ALERT

Students may lose count of the number of sides and angles for pentagons, hexagons, and octagons.

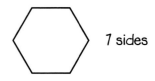 7 sides

Have them mark the first side or angle they count so they do not count it again.

Independent Practice

Note that Exercise 20 is a **multistep or strategy problem**. Assign Exercises 7–21.

For Exercise 21, suggest students use square dot paper, p. TR30, and a ruler to help them draw the polygons.

4 ASSESS

Summarize the lesson by having students:

Discuss How do you name and sort polygons?
by the number of sides and angles

Write Describe how you tell the difference between plane figures that are polygons and those that are not polygons.
Possible answer: Polygons are closed plane figures with straight sides. The sides and angles can be counted. Plane figures that are not polygons can be figures with curved lines.

LESSON QUIZ

Write the number of sides and angles each polygon has. Then name the polygon.

Transparency

19.3

1. 8 sides; 8 angles; octagon

2. 5 sides; 5 angles; pentagon

3. 6 sides; 6 angles; hexagon

4. 3 sides; 3 angles; triangle

391

Lesson Planning

PROFESSIONAL DEVELOPMENT

Objective To identify, describe, and classify triangles

Materials *For Link Up* grid paper, p. TR57; pencil, crayons

NCTM Standards
3. **Geometry**
6. **Problem Solving**
7. **Reasoning and Proof**
8. **Communication**
9. **Connections**
10. **Representation**

Math Background
Consider the following when introducing sorting triangles.

- Students can name triangles by their equal sides and by their angles.

- A triangle with 1 right angle is called a right triangle. A triangle with 1 angle that has a measure greater than a right angle and less than a straight angle (180°) is called an obtuse triangle. A triangle with 3 angles that each measure less than a right angle is called an acute triangle.

- Equilateral triangles have 3 equal sides. Isosceles triangles have 2 equal sides. Scalene triangles have no equal sides.

Vocabulary
equilateral triangle a triangle with 3 equal sides

isosceles triangle a triangle with 2 equal sides

scalene triangle a triangle in which all 3 sides have different lengths

right triangle a triangle with 1 right angle

obtuse triangle a triangle with 1 obtuse angle

acute triangle a triangle with 3 acute angles

Warm-Up Resources

Number of the Day

Transparency **19.4**

Write a multiplication sentence to find the number of sides on 9 quadrilaterals. Possible answer: $9 \times 4 = 36$

Daily Facts Practice

Have students practice subtraction facts by completing Set D of *Teacher's Resource Book*, p. TR97.

Transparency **19.4**

Problem of the Day

Diana drew 6 hexagons. Alex drew 9 triangles. Gina drew 10 pentagons. How many line segments did each student draw? Diana: 36, Alex: 27, Gina: 50 line segments

Solution Problem of the Day tab, p. PD19

Intervention and Extension Resources

Alternative Teaching Strategy

MATERIALS *For each student* centimeter ruler, p. TR55

Help students **identify equal sides of a triangle.** Some students may have difficulty deciding whether or not the sides of a triangle are equal. Suggest that students use a centimeter ruler. Demonstrate measuring and comparing the three sides of a given triangle. Remind students that triangles can have three equal sides, two equal sides, or no equal sides.

See also page 394.

VISUAL, KINESTHETIC

VISUAL/SPATIAL

Multistep and Strategy Problems

The following multistep or strategy problem is provided in Lesson 19.4:

Page	Item
394	19

Technology Link

Intervention, *Skills 56–57*

Harcourt Mega Math
Ice Station Exploration,
Polar Planes, Level E

Math Jingles® CD 3–4 •
Track 11

ESOL/ESL

MATERIALS *For each student* paper, ruler, 3 different-color crayons

ESOL/ESL

Help students **identify triangles.** Share that the first part of the word *triangle (tri-)* is used to describe things with three parts, such as a tricycle with three wheels. Explain that a triangle has 3 angles and 3 sides.

Have each student use a ruler to draw a triangle, using a different color crayon for each side. Encourage students to draw four more triangles, varying the lengths of the sides and the sizes of the angles. Have students write *triangles* at the top of their papers. Check students' work.

AUDITORY, VISUAL

VERBAL/LINGUISTIC

Advanced Learners

MATERIALS *For each student* straws cut into 10 pieces: one 2-cm, two 4-cm, three 6-cm, three 8-cm, and one 10-cm

Challenge students to **make triangles.** Have them use the straws to build as many different triangles as they can. Have them record each triangle in a table and determine if any combination of lengths is impossible to use.

3 equal sides   three 6-cm; three 8-cm

2 equal sides   4-, 4-, and 2-cm or 6-cm

6-, 6-, and 2-, 4-, 8-, or 10-cm; 8-, 8-, and 2-, 4-, 6-, or 10-cm

0 equal sides   4-, 6-, 8-cm; 6-, 8-, 10-cm; 4-, 8-, 10-cm

impossible   2-, 4-, 6-cm; 4-, 4-, 8-cm;
                     4-, 6-, 10-cm; 2-, 8-, 10-cm

KINESTHETIC

BODILY/KINESTHETIC

Lesson 19.4 Organizer

Objective To identify, describe, and classify triangles

Vocabulary equilateral triangle, isosceles triangle, scalene triangle, right triangle, obtuse triangle, acute triangle

Materials *For Link Up* grid paper, p. TR57; pencil, crayons

1 INTRODUCE

QUICK REVIEW provides review of prerequisite skills.

WHY LEARN THIS? You'll know how to identify different kinds of triangles commonly used in buildings, bridges, and other designs. *Share the lesson objective with students.*

2 TEACH

Guided Instruction

MODIFYING INSTRUCTION Before beginning the lesson, provide students with a variety of paper triangles. Have them sort them and explain their sorting method.

- *Ask students to examine the triangles at the top of the page.*
  Explain why Beverly and Armando couldn't sort the triangles by the number of sides or angles. All triangles have 3 sides and 3 angles.

- *Have students look at the triangles Armando sorted.*
  How can you check whether a triangle has a right angle? Use a corner of a sheet of paper.

4 Triangles

▶ Learn

TIME FOR TRIANGLES Beverly and Armando sorted these triangles in different ways.

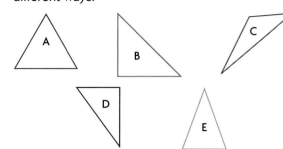

This is how Beverly sorted the triangles.

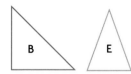

| All sides are equal. | Two sides are equal. | No sides are equal. |

This is how Armando sorted the triangles.

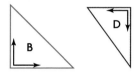 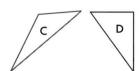

| One angle is a right angle. | One angle is an obtuse angle. | All angles are acute angles. |

- How did Beverly sort the triangles? How did Armando sort the triangles? **by the sides; by the angles**

- How can you check if an angle is an obtuse angle or an acute angle? **Possible answer: Use the corner of a sheet of paper to compare the angle to a right angle.**

392

Quick Review
Write if each angle is a *right angle, obtuse angle,* or *acute angle.*

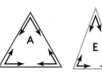

1. _____ 2. obtuse angle
acute angle
3. _____ 4. _____
5. _____ right angle acute angle
obtuse angle

VOCABULARY
equilateral triangle
isosceles triangle
scalene triangle
right triangle
obtuse triangle
acute triangle

Reteach 19.4

Triangles
You can name triangles by their equal sides.

| equilateral triangle | isosceles triangle | scalene triangle |

3 equal sides. 2 equal sides. 0 equal sides.

You can name triangles by their angles.

| right triangle | obtuse triangle | acute triangle |

1 right angle 1 obtuse angle 3 acute angles

For 1–4, use the triangles at the right. Write A, B, C, or D.

1. Which triangles are scalene? __A and C__
2. Which triangles have at least 2 equal sides? __B and D__
3. Which triangle has 3 acute angles? __D__
4. Which triangle is obtuse? __A__

For 5–9, write one letter from each box to describe each triangle.

a. equilateral triangle	d. right triangle
b. isosceles triangle	e. obtuse triangle
c. scalene triangle	f. acute triangle

5. __a, f__ 6. __b, d__ 7. __c, e__ 8. __c, d__ 9. __c, e__

RW102 Reteach

Practice 19.4

Triangles
For 1–3, use the triangles at the right. Write A, B, or C.

1. Which triangle is scalene? __C__
2. Which triangles have at least 2 equal sides? __A and B__
3. Which triangle has 1 angle that is greater than a right angle? __C__

Write one letter from each box to describe each triangle.

a. equilateral triangle	d. right triangle
b. isosceles triangle	e. obtuse triangle
c. scalene triangle	f. acute triangle

4. __b, f__ 5. __c, e__ 6. __c, d__ 7. __a, f__

Name each triangle. Write *equilateral, isosceles,* or *scalene.* Then write *right, obtuse,* or *acute.*

8. equilateral; acute 9. isosceles; acute 10. scalene; right 11. scalene; obtuse

Mixed Review

| 12. | 4,692
+ 8,403
13,095 | 13. | 9,721
+ 3,688
13,409 | 14. | 6,400
+ 7,211
13,611 | 15. | 4,209
+ 362
4,571 |

PW102 Practice

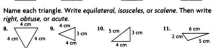

Name Triangles

You can name triangles by their equal sides.

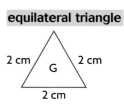
equilateral triangle

2 cm | 2 cm
G
2 cm

3 equal sides

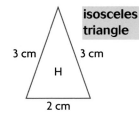
isosceles triangle

3 cm | 3 cm
H
2 cm

2 equal sides

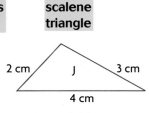
scalene triangle

2 cm | 3 cm
J
4 cm

0 equal sides

You can name triangles by their angles.

right triangle

K

1 right angle

obtuse triangle

L

1 obtuse angle

acute triangle

M

3 acute angles

- How are triangles J and M alike? How are they different? **Possible answers: Both have no right angles; triangle J has one obtuse angle and triangle M has 3 acute angles.**

 MATH IDEA You can name and sort triangles by their sides or their angles.

▶ Check

1. Describe triangle N by its sides. Then describe it by its angles.
   It has 2 equal sides. It is isosceles. It has a right angle. It is a right triangle.

N

For 2–5, use the triangles at the right. Write O, P, Q, or R.

2. Which triangles have 0 equal sides? **O and R**

3. Which triangle is an equilateral triangle? **Q**

4. Which triangles have 3 acute angles? **P and Q**

5. Which triangle is obtuse? **R**

3 cm | 5 cm
O
4 cm

3 cm | 7 cm
R
9 cm

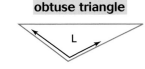
2 cm | 2 cm
P
1 cm

2 cm | 2 cm
Q
2 cm

LESSON CONTINUES ▶

Chapter 19 **393**

- *Discuss the strategies for sorting triangles.*
  How are triangles G and H alike? How are they different? Both have 3 acute angles; triangle G has 3 equal sides, while triangle H has 2 equal sides.
  REASONING Can a triangle have more than 1 right angle? Explain. No; if a figure had 2 right angles, it would have 3 sides that form an open figure, not a triangle.

- *Point out the Math Idea.*
  How can you name and sort triangles by their sides and by their angles? Determine if they have 3 equal sides, 2 equal sides, or 0 equal sides. Determine if they have 1 right angle, 1 obtuse angle, or 3 acute angles.

3 PRACTICE

Guided Practice

Do Check Exercises 1–5 with your students. Identify students who are having difficulty and choose appropriate lesson resources to provide assistance.

☞ **North Carolina Standards 3.01** Use appropriate vocabulary to compare, describe, and classify two- and three-dimensional figures.

Challenge 19.4

Triangle Tally

Do this activity with a partner. Check students' work.

Materials: 3 index cards, scissors, pencil, ruler, sheet of paper

- Each partner cuts one index card into 3 different triangles.
- Sort the triangles by the number of equal sides. Use a ruler to verify if the triangles have 0, 2, or 3 equal sides.
- Trace the 6 triangles on a sheet of paper.
- Tally your results in the table below.

SIDES OF THE TRIANGLES

0 equal sides	2 equal sides	3 equal sides

- Sort the triangles by their angles. Use the corner of the third index card to see if each triangle has one right angle, one obtuse angle, or three acute angles.
- Tally your results in the table below.

ANGLES OF THE TRIANGLES

1 right angle	1 obtuse angle	3 acute angles

CW102 Challenge

Problem Solving 19.4

Triangles

Understand ➡ Plan ➡ Solve ➡ Check

Write the correct answer.

1. John's teacher drew a triangle with 2 equal sides. What kind of triangle did she draw?
   _____isosceles triangle_____

2. What angle is made by the hands on the clock?
   _____obtuse angle_____

3. Vincent drew a line from one corner of this rectangle to another corner to make 2 triangles. Describe the 2 triangles he made.
   Possible answer: Each is a right triangle.

4. Is this figure a polygon? Write yes or no.
   _____yes_____

Choose the letter of the correct answer.

5. How many equal sides does a scalene triangle have?
   A 0   C 2
   B 1   D 3

6. Which triangle has only 2 acute angles?
   F   H
   G   J

7. Which triangle is an equilateral triangle?
   A   C
   B   D

8. Describe this triangle.
   F no sides equal, all angles less than a right angle
   G all sides equal, no right angle
   H 2 sides equal, one angle greater than a right angle
   J isosceles triangle with one right angle

9. **Write About It** Explain your answer to Problem 4.
   Possible answer: A polygon is a closed plane figure with straight sides.

PS102 Problem Solving

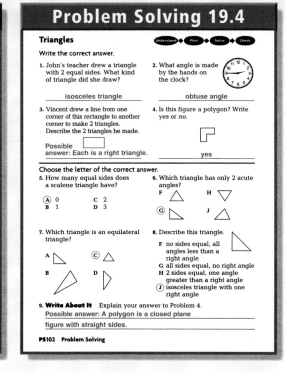

COMMON ERROR ALERT

Students may overlook triangles with right angles in different orientations. Have them mark a right angle in the corner of a self-stick note, using a brightly colored marker. They can stick the note on the page as a reminder or use it to test all three angles.

Independent Practice

Note that Exercise 19 is a **multistep or strategy problem**. Assign Exercises 6–22.

If students need assistance with Exercises 13–18, have them refer to the labeled triangles on page 393.

MULTISTEP OR STRATEGY PROBLEM To solve Exercise 19, students can add line segments AB + BC to find the length of the blue path, 12 feet. Then students can add AD + DE + EF + FC to find the length of the red path, 12 feet. Since 12 feet = 12 feet, both paths are the same length. Guide students to conclude that they must add all segments of each path before they can compare the lengths.

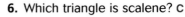

Practice and Problem Solving   Extra Practice, page 402, Set D

For 6–8, use the triangles at the right.
Write A, B, or C.

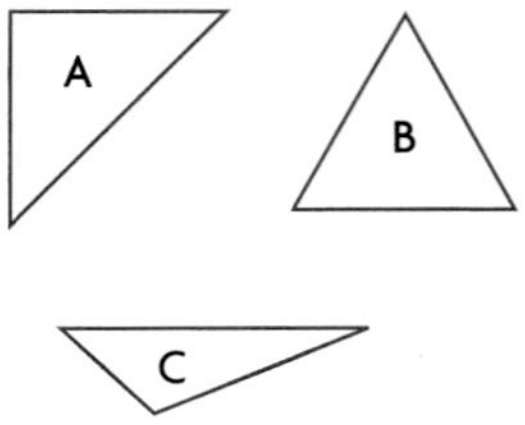

6. Which triangle is scalene? **C**

7. Which triangles have at least 2 equal sides? **A and B**

8. Which triangle has 1 obtuse angle? Which triangle has 3 acute angles? **C; B**

Write one letter from each box to describe each triangle.

a. equilateral triangle	d. right triangle
b. isosceles triangle	e. obtuse triangle
c. scalene triangle	f. acute triangle

9.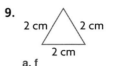
2 cm 2 cm
2 cm
a, f

10.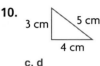
3 cm 5 cm
4 cm
c, d

11.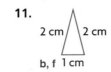
2 cm 2 cm
1 cm
b, f

12. 3 cm 2 cm
4 cm
c, e

Name each triangle. Write *equilateral, isosceles,* or *scalene.*

13. 4 cm 4 cm
4 cm
equilateral

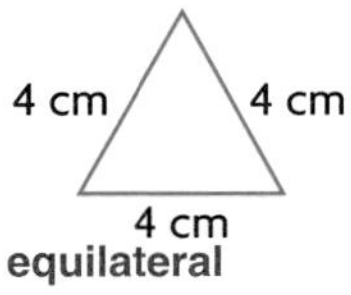

14. 4 cm 6 cm
8 cm
scalene

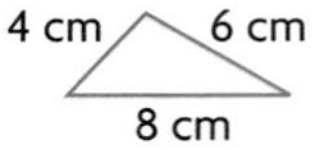

15. 2 cm 2 cm
3 cm
isosceles

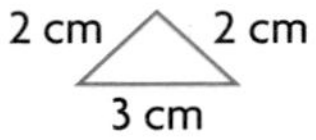

Name each triangle. Write *right, obtuse,* or *acute.*

16. 10 cm 6 cm
8 cm
right

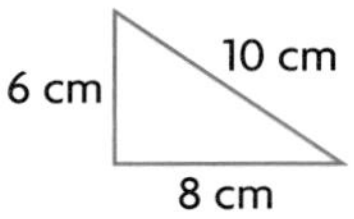

17. 4 cm 4 cm
3 cm
acute

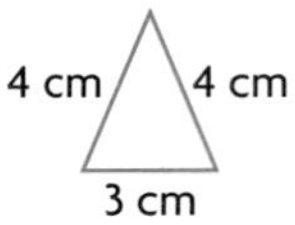

18. 3 cm 2 cm
4 cm
obtuse

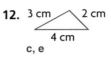

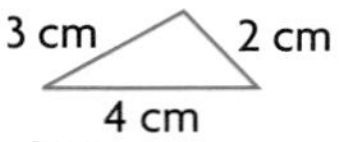

USE DATA For 19–20, use the diagram at the right.

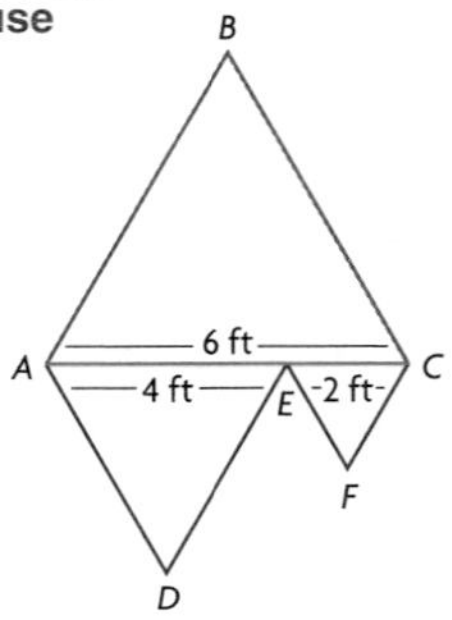

19. Mrs. Liu has a garden with paths that are equilateral triangles. The shortest path from *A* to *C* is the green path. Which path is longer: the blue path or the red path? Explain. **Both paths are the same distance. AB + BC = 12 ft. AD + DE + EF + FC = 12 ft**

20. **? What's the Question?** The answer is 4 feet longer. **Possible question: How much longer is the straight path from A to C than from E to C?**

394

Alternative Teaching Strategy   Scaffolded Instruction

PURPOSE Students classify triangles by using hands-on materials.

MATERIALS paper with a square corner; 1-cm grid paper, p. TR58; centimeter ruler, p. TR55; scissors

Step 1

Have students draw the triangles in Exercises 9–12 on grid paper and cut them out.

Step 2

Read the directions for Exercises 9–12 to students, emphasizing that they must choose one letter from each box to describe each triangle. Review the terms *equilateral trian-*

gle, isosceles triangle, scalene triangle, right triangle, obtuse triangle, and *acute triangle.*

Step 3

Have students look at Exercise 9. Ask: Does this triangle have equal sides? yes How many? 3 equal sides

Suggest students use a ruler to confirm their answers. Then have them write the letters of the appropriate names for the triangle.

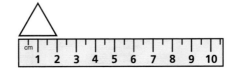

Step 4

Ask:
- Does the triangle in Exercise 9 have right angles? no
- Does it have 1 obtuse angle? no
- Does it have 3 acute angles? yes

Have students use paper with a square corner to confirm their answers.

Step 5

Repeat this procedure for Exercise 10. Then encourage students to follow this step-by-step approach for the remaining exercises. Check students' work.

PROFESSIONAL DEVELOPMENT

21. Vocabulary Power The word *parallel* comes from a Greek word, *parallelos,* which means "beside each other." How does this help explain the meaning of *parallel lines*? Possible answer: parallel lines never cross, so they are always beside each other.

22. Draw a triangle with 2 equal sides and one right angle. You may use grid paper to help. Name the triangle. Check students' drawings; right triangle or isosceles triangle

Getting Ready for the EOG Test

23. Which triangle has exactly 2 equal sides? D

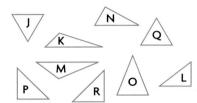

A B C D

24. Which triangle is obtuse? A

A B C D

25. Jen made a group with the triangles L, N, P, and R. How are these triangles alike? B

A All of their sides are equal.
B They all have right angles.
C They all have obtuse angles.
D They all are acute triangles.

Problem Solving LiNKUP ... to Art

Many artists use triangles in their works. The Native American blanket at the right uses different kinds of triangles. Find and name as many triangles on the blanket as you can.

MATERIALS: grid paper, pencil, crayons

1. Draw and color a blanket design on grid paper. Use different kinds of triangles in your design.

2. Trade designs with a classmate and describe the triangles you see. Check students' designs and descriptions.

Chapter 19 **395**

Reading Strategy

K-W-L CHART Before having students read the Link Up, have them look at the picture. Ask them to predict what the Link Up will be about. Then have students make a three-column chart headed *What I Know, What I Want to Know,* and *What I Learned.* Ask them to fill in the first two columns. Have them fill in the third column as they read the paragraph.

K-W-L Chart

What I Know	What I Want to Know	What I Learned

Vocabulary Power List some everyday objects that can be described using the word *parallel,* such as fence posts and railroad tracks. Ask students to name other examples.

Problem Solving LiNKUP ... to Art

- *Have students read the paragraph about Art.*
How can you identify an isosceles triangle? It has 2 equal sides.
In what other works of art might you see triangles? Possible answers: abstract paintings, sculptures, mosaics
REASONING Name two things that all the triangles you drew have in common. Possible answer: 3 sides, 3 angles

4 ASSESS

Summarize the lesson by having students:

DISCUSS Describe this triangle by its sides and its angles. It has 3 equal sides and 3 acute angles.

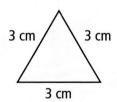

3 cm   3 cm

3 cm

 WRITE Draw an equilateral triangle, an isosceles triangle, a scalene triangle, a right triangle, an acute triangle, and an obtuse triangle, and describe each. Check students' work.

LESSON QUIZ
Use the triangles. Write *X, Y,* or *Z.*

Transparency **19.4**

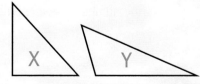

X   Y   Z

1. Which triangle is a right triangle? X

2. Which triangle is an isosceles triangle? Z

3. Which triangle is an obtuse triangle? Y

Lesson Planning

Objective To identify, describe, and classify quadrilaterals

NCTM Standards
3. Geometry
6. Problem Solving
7. Reasoning and Proof
8. Communication
9. Connections
10. Representation

Math Background
Consider the following when helping students understand how to identify quadrilaterals.

- An angle in a quadrilateral can be a right angle, an acute angle, or an obtuse angle.

- Some quadrilaterals have equal sides. Some quadrilaterals have parallel sides.

- All rhombuses, rectangles, and squares are parallelograms and all parallelograms are quadrilaterals. Not all quadrilaterals are parallelograms, rectangles, or squares.

- If a parallelogram has four right angles, it is either a square or a rectangle.

Vocabulary
trapezoid a quadrilateral with 1 pair of parallel sides
parallelogram a quadrilateral with opposite sides parallel and equal
rhombus a quadrilateral with 2 pairs of parallel sides and 4 equal sides

Warm-Up Resources

Number of the Day

Transparency **19.5**

Write and solve four multiplication sentences using the number of even numbers between 25 and 41.
Possible answers: $8 \times 4 = 32$, $8 \times 7 = 56$, $8 \times 6 = 48$, $8 \times 9 = 72$

Daily Facts Practice

Have students practice multiplication facts by completing Set E of *Teacher's Resource Book*, p. TR97.

Transparency **19.5**

Problem of the Day

Which term does not belong with the others? Explain. Possible answers are given.
1. product, divisor, dividend, quotient
   Product; it is not a division term.
2. quadrilateral, pentagon, circle, hexagon Circle; it is not a polygon.
3. cup, inch, pint, quart
   Inch; it is not a customary unit for measuring capacity.

Solution Problem of the Day tab, p. PD19

Intervention and Extension Resources

Alternative Teaching Strategy

Have students work with partners to **find examples of quadrilaterals** in printed materials such as textbooks, magazines, and newspaper ads. On a tally table, ask them to record how many parallelograms, rhombuses, rectangles, and squares they find. Check students' work.

See also page 398.

VISUAL

VISUAL/SPATIAL

Multistep and Strategy Problems

The following multistep and strategy problems are provided in Lesson 19.5:

Page	Item
398	24, 28

ESOL/ESL

MATERIALS *For each student* index cards

ESOL/ESL

Help students **understand terms such as quadrilateral, rectangle, square, parallelogram, parallel lines,** and **rhombus**. Have them use the Multimedia Math Glossary at **www.harcourtschool.com/mathglossary** for definitions and illustrations. Have students illustrate each word on one card and then write the corresponding definition on another card. Have them play a matching game with the cards. Check students' work.

VISUAL

VISUAL/SPATIAL, VERBAL/LINGUISTIC

Art Connection

MATERIALS square dot paper, p. TR30; crayons; scissors; coat hanger; string; tape

Have students **make a quadrilaterals mobile**.

- Have students use dot paper to draw and color several quadrilaterals including parallelograms, rhombuses, squares, and rectangles. Have them write the name on each quadrilateral after they have cut all of them out.
- Have students attach string and tie each shape to a coat hanger to make a mobile. Display students' mobiles in the classroom.

VISUAL

VISUAL/SPATIAL

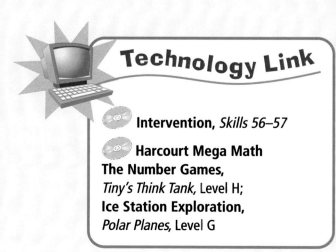

Technology Link

Intervention, *Skills 56–57*

Harcourt Mega Math
The Number Games,
Tiny's Think Tank, Level H;
Ice Station Exploration,
Polar Planes, Level G

Lesson 19.5 Organizer

Objective To identify, describe, and classify quadrilaterals

Vocabulary trapezoid, parallelogram, rhombus

1 INTRODUCE

QUICK REVIEW provides review of prerequisite skills.

WHY LEARN THIS? You'll be able to recognize and compare different kinds of quadrilaterals. *Share the lesson objective with students.*

2 TEACH

Guided Instruction

- *Discuss the Learn section.*
  What is a polygon? a closed plane figure with straight sides
  Explain why the three figures are labeled "not quadrilaterals." The first figure is not closed. The second one has 3 sides and 3 angles. The third figure has a curved side.

- *Direct students' attention to Examples A and B.*
  How are Examples A and B alike? They both have 4 sides and 4 angles.
  Which sides are parallel in Example A? the side on the top and the side on the bottom
  Which sides are parallel in Example B? the side on the top and the side on the bottom
  Which angles in Examples A and B are obtuse angles? Check students' responses.

396 Chapter 19

LESSON

5 Quadrilaterals

▶ Learn

LIMIT OF FOUR Polygons with 4 sides and 4 angles are quadrilaterals.

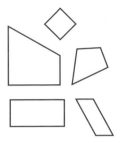

quadrilaterals   not quadrilaterals

A **trapezoid** is a special kind of quadrilateral. Trapezoids always have one pair of parallel sides, but the sizes of the angles are not always the same.

Technology Link
More Practice:
Harcourt Mega Math
Ice Station Exploration,
Polar Planes,
Level G

Examples of Trapezoids

Ⓐ
2 right angles
1 acute angle
1 obtuse angle
1 pair of parallel sides

Ⓑ
2 acute angles
2 obtuse angles
1 pair of parallel sides

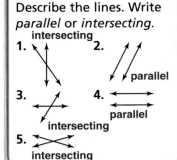

- How can you check if two sides of a quadrilateral are parallel? **Possible answer: think of the sides as lines and tell whether the lines would cross or not. Lines that never cross are parallel.**

396

Reteach 19.5

Quadrilaterals

Polygons with 4 sides and 4 angles are quadrilaterals.

quadrilaterals	not quadrilaterals

An angle in a quadrilateral can be a right angle, an obtuse angle, or an acute angle. The sides of a quadrilateral can be parallel.

Examples

A acute angle   parallel sides   obtuse angle   right angles

B right angle   parallel sides   right angle   parallel sides   right angle   right angle

Describe the angles and sides of each quadrilateral. Possible answers are given.

1. 2 pairs of parallel sides, 2 obtuse angles; 2 acute angles

2. 1 pair of parallel sides, 2 obtuse angles; 2 acute angles

3. 2 pairs of parallel sides, 4 right angles

Reteach   RW103

Practice 19.5

Quadrilaterals

For 1–3, use the quadrilaterals below. Write A, B, C, D, or E.

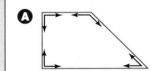

1. Which quadrilaterals have 2 pairs of equal sides? __A, B, E__
2. Which quadrilaterals have no right angles? __B, D, E__
3. How are quadrilaterals A and B alike? How are they different?
   Possible answers: Both figures have at least two pairs of parallel sides. Both have 4 equal sides and 4 angles. "A" has 4 right angles; "B" has no right angles.

For 4–7, write *all* the letters that describe each quadrilateral. Then write a name for each quadrilateral. Possible answers given.

a. It has 4 equal sides.   c. It has 4 right angles.
b. It has 2 pairs of parallel sides.   d. It has 2 pairs of equal sides.

4. b, c, d; rectangle, parallelogram
5. a, b, d; rhombus, parallelogram
6. a, b, c, d; parallelogram, square, rectangle
7. b, d; parallelogram

Mixed Review
8. 3 + 3 + 3 + 3 + 3 + 3 = __18__   9. 7 + 7 + 7 + 7 + 7 + 7 = __42__

Describe the lines. Write *intersecting* or *parallel*.
10. __parallel__   11. __intersecting__   12. __parallel__

Which number is less?
13. 4,375 or 4,735   14. 1,002 or 854   15. 2,014 or 2,004
__4,375__   __854__   __2,004__

Practice   PW103

Other Names for Quadrilaterals

Here are some quadrilaterals with pairs of parallel sides and pairs of equal sides.

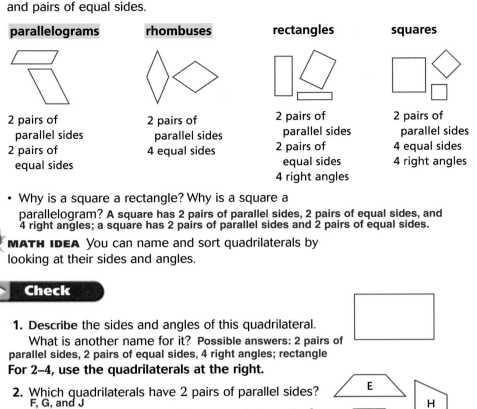

parallelograms	rhombuses	rectangles	squares
2 pairs of parallel sides	2 pairs of parallel sides	2 pairs of parallel sides	2 pairs of parallel sides
2 pairs of equal sides	4 equal sides	2 pairs of equal sides	4 equal sides
		4 right angles	4 right angles

- Why is a square a rectangle? Why is a square a parallelogram? **A square has 2 pairs of parallel sides, 2 pairs of equal sides, and 4 right angles; a square has 2 pairs of parallel sides and 2 pairs of equal sides.**

MATH IDEA You can name and sort quadrilaterals by looking at their sides and angles.

▶ Check

1. **Describe** the sides and angles of this quadrilateral. What is another name for it? **Possible answers: 2 pairs of parallel sides, 2 pairs of equal sides, 4 right angles; rectangle**

For 2–4, use the quadrilaterals at the right.

2. Which quadrilaterals have 2 pairs of parallel sides? **F, G, and J**
3. Which quadrilaterals have 2 or more right angles? **F, H, J**
4. How are quadrilateral E and quadrilateral G alike? How are they different? **Possible answers: both have parallel sides; E has 1 pair of parallel sides but G has 2 pairs of parallel sides.**

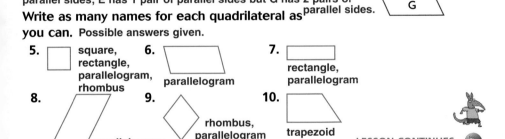

Write as many names for each quadrilateral as you can. Possible answers given.

5. **square, rectangle, parallelogram, rhombus**
6. **parallelogram**
7. **rectangle, parallelogram**
8. **parallelogram**
9. **rhombus, parallelogram**
10. **trapezoid**

LESSON CONTINUES ▶

Chapter 19 **397**

North Carolina Standards 3.01 Use appropriate vocabulary to compare, describe, and classify and three-dimensional figures.

- *Point out the illustrations and definitions of the four types of quadrilaterals with parallel sides at the top of page 397.*
  Which of these quadrilaterals have 4 right angles? the rectangles and the squares
  In what ways are squares and rhombuses alike? They both have four equal sides and two pairs of parallel sides.
  Is the following statement true or false? All of the quadrilaterals shown here have 2 pairs of parallel sides. true

- *Check students' understanding of the Math Idea.*
  How might the angles of various quadrilaterals differ? Possible answer: Some may have right angles. Others may not.

3 PRACTICE

Guided Practice

Do Check Exercises 1–10 with your students. Identify students who are having difficulty and choose appropriate lesson resources to provide assistance.

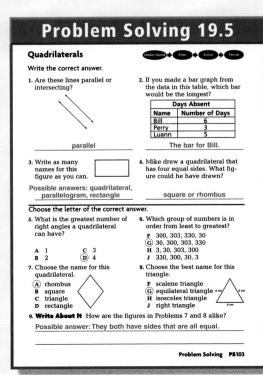

Challenge 19.5

Quadrilateral Puzzles

Read the clues. Color the figures. Write the name of each figure.

1. If a quadrilateral has 1 pair of parallel sides and 2 right angles, color it red.
2. If a quadrilateral has 4 right angles and 2 pairs of equal sides, color it blue.
3. If a quadrilateral has no equal sides and no right angles, color it green.
4. If a quadrilateral has 4 right angles and 4 equal sides, color it purple.
5. If a quadrilateral has one pair of parallel sides and no right angles, color it brown.
6. If a quadrilateral has 4 equal sides but has no right angles, color it orange.
7. If a quadrilateral has 6 right angles, color it black. There should be no quadrilaterals colored black.
8. If a quadrilateral has 2 pairs of parallel sides, no right angles, and 2 pairs of equal sides, color it pink.
9. If a quadrilateral has 1 right angle and 1 pair of parallel sides, color it gray. There should be no quadrilaterals colored gray.
10. If a quadrilateral has 4 right angles and no equal sides, color it yellow. There should be no quadrilaterals colored yellow.

blue rectangle · hexagon · pentagon · brown quadrilateral · red quadrilateral · orange rhombus · purple square · pink parallelogram · right triangle · octagon · green quadrilateral

Challenge CW103

Problem Solving 19.5

Quadrilaterals

Understand → Plan → Solve → Check

Write the correct answer.

1. Are these lines parallel or intersecting?

   parallel

2. If you made a bar graph from the data in this table, which bar would be the longest?

Days Absent	
Name	Number of Days
Bill	6
Perry	3
Luann	5

   The bar for Bill.

3. Write as many names for this figure as you can.

   Possible answers: quadrilateral, parallelogram, rectangle

4. Mike drew a quadrilateral that has four equal sides. What figure could he have drawn?

   square or rhombus

Choose the letter of the correct answer.

5. What is the greatest number of right angles a quadrilateral can have?

   A 1   C 3
   B 2   (D) 4

6. Which group of numbers is in order from least to greatest?

   F 300, 303, 330, 30
   (G) 30, 300, 303, 330
   H 3, 30, 303, 300
   J 330, 300, 30, 3

7. Choose the name for this quadrilateral.

   (A) rhombus
   B square
   C triangle
   D rectangle

8. Choose the best name for this triangle.

   F scalene triangle
   (G) equilateral triangle
   H isosceles triangle
   J right triangle

9. **Write About It** How are the figures in Problems 7 and 8 alike?

   Possible answer: They both have sides that are all equal.

Problem Solving PS103

Independent Practice

Note that Exercises 24 and 28 are **multistep or strategy problems.** Assign Exercises 11–30.

For Exercises 20–23, remind students that more than one letter may describe each quadrilateral.

MULTISTEP OR STRATEGY PROBLEM To solve Exercise 24, students can make a list of the ways they can identify quadrilaterals, in order to compare the 3 figures to figure G. Possible items might include the following: a quadrilateral is a polygon with 4 sides and 4 angles; an angle in a quadrilateral can be a right angle, an obtuse angle, or an acute angle; opposite sides of a quadrilateral can be parallel; opposite sides of a quadrilateral can be equal.

► **Practice and Problem Solving** Extra Practice, page 402, Set E

For 11–13, use the quadrilaterals at the right. Write A, B, C, D, and E.

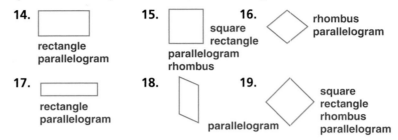

11. Which quadrilaterals have 2 pairs of equal sides?
A, B, and D

12. Which quadrilaterals have no right angles?
A, C, and E

13. How are quadrilateral A and quadrilateral D alike? How are they different? **Possible answers: both have 2 pairs of parallel sides; A has no right angles but D has 4 right angles.**

For 14–19, write as many names for each quadrilateral as you can. Possible answers given.

14.
rectangle
parallelogram

15.
square
rectangle
parallelogram
rhombus

16.
rhombus
parallelogram

17.
rectangle
parallelogram

18.
parallelogram

19.
square
rectangle
rhombus
parallelogram

For 20–23, write all the letters that describe each quadrilateral.

20.
a, b, c, d

21.
a, b, d

22.
b, d

23.
b, c, d

a. It has 4 equal sides.
b. It has 2 pairs of parallel sides.
c. It has 4 right angles.
d. It has 2 pairs of equal sides.

24. REASONING How is figure G like the figures to its right?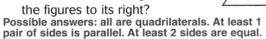
Possible answers: all are quadrilaterals. At least 1 pair of sides is parallel. At least 2 sides are equal.

25. I have 4 equal sides and 4 right angles. What am I? **square**

26. I have 5 sides and 5 angles. What am I? **pentagon**

27. **? What's the Error?** Colin said that a square is not a quadrilateral. Explain his error.
All quadrilaterals have 4 sides and 4 angles. Since a square has 4 sides and 4 angles, it is a quadrilateral.

28. ✎ **Write About It** Draw and label 4 different quadrilaterals on grid paper. Explain how each is different from the others. **Check students' drawings and explanations.**

398

Alternative Teaching Strategy   Scaffolded Instruction

PURPOSE Students use sides to sort quadrilaterals.

MATERIALS several paper squares, rectangles, rhombuses, and parallelograms of varying sizes

Step 1

Place all the quadrilaterals on a desk. Ask students to point to all the shapes that have 4 sides. squares, rectangles, rhombuses, parallelograms Help students draw the conclusion that all quadrilaterals have 4 sides.

Step 2

Ask students to point to all the quadrilaterals that have 4 equal sides. rhombuses, squares

Step 3

Ask students to point to all the quadrilaterals that have 2 pairs of equal sides. parallelograms, rectangles

Step 4

Ask students to point to all the quadrilaterals that have 2 pairs of parallel sides. rhombuses, squares, rectangles, parallelograms

PROFESSIONAL DEVELOPMENT

29. Akemi sees a tile with 4 right angles. She says it must be a square. Do you agree or disagree? Explain. Disagree; it could be a rectangle that is not a square.

30. Dante drew a quadrilateral with 4 right angles and 2 pairs of parallel sides. What could he have drawn? a square or a rectangle

Getting Ready for the EOG Test

31. Which figure has four equal sides? A

A   B   C   D

32. Which figure is a rhombus? D

A   B   C   D

33. Gina drew the figures U, W, and Y. How are these figures alike? B

  A They are all squares.
  B They each have four right angles.
  C They are all triangles.
  D They each have four equal sides.

Problem Solving LiNKUP . . . to Reading

STRATEGY • USE GRAPHIC AIDS Graphic aids, such as charts, diagrams, and maps, display information. Drawings and diagrams can be used to show how to build things, such as houses and bridges.

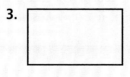

1. Possible answers: right angles, acute angles; rectangles, right triangles, equilateral triangles

2. Possible answers: obtuse angle; right angles, acute angles

1. Look at the drawing of the bridge. What kinds of angles do you see? What plane figures were used in the drawing? See above.

2. Look at the drawing of the house. What kind of angle was used for the roof? What other angles do you see in the drawing? See above.

Problem Solving LiNKUP . . . to Reading

• *Have students look at the diagrams in Exercises 1 and 2.*
  Why can drawings or diagrams sometimes be more helpful than written descriptions?
  Possible answer: How an object looks is easier to see in a drawing or diagram.

• *You may wish to have students make their own drawings after completing Exercises 1 and 2.*

4 ASSESS

Summarize the lesson by having students:

DISCUSS If a classmate told you that he or she drew a quadrilateral with four right angles, four equal sides, and two pairs of parallel sides, do you know for certain that the classmate drew a square? Explain. Yes; a square is the name for a quadrilateral with four right angles and four equal sides.

WRITE Describe how parallelograms and rhombuses are alike and how they are different. They both have 2 pairs of parallel sides. A parallelogram has 2 pairs of equal sides, but a rhombus has 4 equal sides.

LESSON QUIZ

Write *all* the letters that describe each quadrilateral below.

Transparency 19.5

  a. 4 equal sides   **b.** 2 pairs of parallel sides

  c. 4 right angles   **d.** 2 pairs of equal sides

1.

a, b, c, d

2.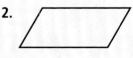

b, d

3.

b, c, d

4.

a, b, d

Lesson Planning

PROFESSIONAL DEVELOPMENT

Objective To use the problem solving strategy *draw a diagram* to solve problems

Lesson Resources Reading Transparency 19; Intervention • Problem Solving, Strategy/Skill 19

NCTM Standards
1. **Number and Operations**
3. **Geometry**
5. **Data Analysis and Probability**
6. **Problem Solving**
7. **Reasoning and Proof**
8. **Communication**

Math Background
These ideas will help students understand how to use a Venn diagram.

- A Venn diagram is used to show similarities and differences.

- Venn diagrams provide opportunities for students to practice comparing and contrasting figures.

- Geometric figures can be described by various characteristics.

Vocabulary
Venn diagram a diagram that shows relationships among sets of figures, objects, etc.

Warm-Up Resources

Number of the Day

Transparency **19.6**

The number of the day is the number of sides that a pentagon has. Multiply this number by 8. What is the product? 40

Daily Facts Practice

Have students practice division facts by completing Set F of *Teacher's Resource Book*, p. TR97.

Solve a Problem

Transparency **19.6**

Problem of the Day

I am a number less than 40 that can be divided equally into groups of 7. The sum of my digits is 8. What number am I? 35

Solution Problem of the Day tab, p. PD19

Intervention and Extension Resources

Alternative Teaching Strategy

MATERIALS *For each group* 2 large loops of yarn; index cards; several buttons, varying in size, color, and number of holes

 ESOL/ESL

Help students **learn to use a Venn diagram.** Have students begin by sorting the buttons by various characteristics. You may wish to make a list of these characteristics for students to refer to.

Give students labels that they can use for their Venn diagram, such as:

> **Buttons with 2 holes**
> **White buttons**

Have students make an index card for each label and place one label above each loop of yarn. Have students place buttons within the appropriate loops. Check students' work.

Have students make one Venn diagram with sets that intersect, and one Venn diagram with sets that do not intersect.

KINESTHETIC

VISUAL/SPATIAL, LOGICAL/MATHEMATICAL

Reading Strategy

Compare Explain to students that comparing objects means to look closely at them to decide how they are alike, and how they are different. Display the three figures below.

Tell students that one of the statements below describes how two of the figures are alike. Ask students to read the three statements and choose the statement that best describes the two figures that are alike. Have students indicate the two figures. b; the triangle
   and square
a. They both have curved lines.
b. They are both closed figures.
c. They are both open figures.

Transparency
19 **Reading Transparency 19**

Multistep and Strategy Problems

The following multistep and strategy problems are provided in Lesson 19.6:

Page	Item
401	1–7

Science Connection

Have students **use a Venn diagram** to show similarities and differences among animals. Share the following list with students: bee, owl, bat, eagle, butterfly, and penguin.

Have students work together in small groups. Have students use the following labels for the sets in their Venn diagram:

> **Birds**
> **Animals that can fly**

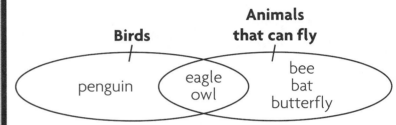

VISUAL
INTERPERSONAL/SOCIAL

Early Finishers

MATERIALS *For each group* large paper or poster, markers

Have students **make a large Venn diagram** for a bulletin board display. Have students use these labels:

> **First names that start with a consonant**
> **First names with 5 or more letters**

Have students include as many names as possible. Encourage students to use names that can be placed in the section where the sets overlap as well as names that can be placed in only one of the sets.

VISUAL

LOGICAL/MATHEMATICAL

Technology Link

Intervention • Problem Solving, *Strategy/Skill 19*

Lesson 19.6 Organizer

Objective To use the problem solving strategy *draw a diagram* to solve problems

Lesson Resources Reading Transparency 19; Intervention • Problem Solving, Strategy/Skill 19

Vocabulary Venn diagram

1 INTRODUCE

QUICK REVIEW provides review of prerequisite skills.

WHY LEARN THIS? You will be able to sort objects by deciding how they are alike and how they are different. *Share the lesson objective with students.*

2 TEACH

Guided Instruction

- *Have students read the Problem. Direct students' attention to the figures on the chalk board.*
  What are some ways to describe the figures?
  Possible answer: They are all polygons; Some of the figures have 4 sides; Some have 3, 5, or 6 sides; Some have right angles; Some have no right angles.

- *Have students look carefully at the Venn diagram in the Solve section.*
  What figures are in the set with the label *Quadrilaterals*? trapezoid, rhombus, parallelogram, quadrilateral (kite shape), square, and rectangle
  What figures are in the set with the label *Plane figures with 1 or more right angles*? square, rectangle, right triangle, pentagon, hexagon
  REASONING Why are the square and rectangle the only figures that are in the area where the sets overlap? Possible answer: The square and rectangle are the only figures that can be described both as "quadrilaterals" and as "plane figures with 1 or more right angles."

---

6 Problem Solving Strategy
Draw a Diagram

PROBLEM Mr. Carter drew some plane figures on a chalkboard. He asked his students to show how the figures were alike, and how they were different.

UNDERSTAND
- What are you asked to find?
  how figures are alike and different
- What information will you use?
  the plane figures on the chalkboard

PLAN
- What strategy can you use?
  You can *draw a diagram*.

SOLVE
- How can you show how the figures are alike and how they are different?
  You can *draw a Venn diagram*.

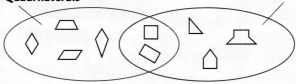

A **Venn diagram** shows relationships among sets of things. Each set in the diagram above has plane figures in it that are described by its label. The figures inside the area where the sets overlap are described by both labels.

CHECK
- What other strategy could you use?
  Possible answer: Make an organized list

400

Quick Review

Tell how many sides each figure has.

1. 3 sides   2. 5 sides

3. 4 sides   4. 4 sides

5. 6 sides

VOCABULARY
Venn diagram

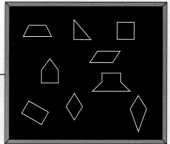

Reteach 19.6

Problem Solving Strategy

Draw a Diagram

When you are asked to show how things are alike and how things are different, it is sometimes helpful to draw a **Venn diagram**. Remember that a Venn diagram is made up of sets labeled for the items within each set.

The Venn diagram below has three parts:
- a part for triangles that are not shaded,
- a part for shaded figures that are not triangles, and
- a part where the sets overlap for triangles that are shaded.

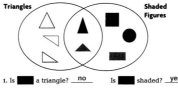

1. Is ■ a triangle? __no__   Is ■ shaded? __yes__
   In what part of the Venn diagram should you put ■?
   __In the part for shaded figures that are not triangles.__

2. Is ▲ a triangle? __yes__   Is ▲ shaded? __yes__
   In what part of the Venn diagram should you put ▲?
   __In the part where the sets overlap for shaded triangles.__

3. Is ◁ a triangle? __yes__   Is ◁ shaded? __no__
   In what part of the Venn diagram should you put ◁?
   __In the part for triangles that are not shaded.__

4. Draw the figures from Exercises 1–3 in the Venn diagram above.

RW104 Reteach

Practice 19.6

Problem Solving Strategy

Draw a Diagram

Describe where each figure should be in the Venn diagram. Explain.

1. 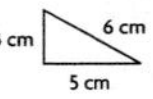 Possible answer: It should be in the part for triangles, but not in the part where the sets overlap because it is a right triangle but not an isosceles triangle.

2. 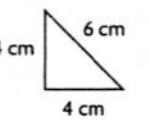 Possible answer: It should be in the part where the sets overlap because it is an isosceles triangle and a right triangle.

3. 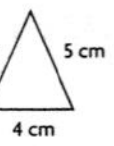 Possible answer: It should be in the part for isosceles triangles, but not in the part where the sets overlap, because it is an isosceles triangle but not a right triangle.

Mixed Review

Write whether each angle is a *right angle*, *acute angle*, or *obtuse angle*.

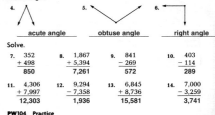

4. __acute angle__   5. __obtuse angle__   6. __right angle__

Solve.

7.	352 + 498 850	8.	1,867 + 5,394 7,261	9.	841 − 269 572	10.	403 − 114 289
11.	4,306 + 7,997 12,303	12.	9,294 − 7,358 1,936	13.	6,845 + 8,736 15,581	14.	7,000 − 3,259 3,741

PW104 Practice

Problem Solving Practice

1. **What if** the plane figure shown below was one of the figures on the chalkboard? Describe where it would be in the Venn diagram on page 400. **It would be in the part where the sets overlap because it has 4 sides and a right angle.**

2. Some Venn diagrams have sets that do not overlap. Explain why the sets in the diagram below do not overlap. **The sets do not overlap because no odd numbers are also even numbers, and no even numbers are also odd numbers.**

Even numbers

16 4
2 30 8
10

Odd numbers

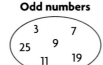

3 7
25 9
11 19

Marisa used the labels *multiples of 4* and *multiples of 6* for the sets in her Venn diagram.

3. Which number could be in the area where the sets overlap? **A**
   A 36   C 28
   B 32   D 26

4. Which number would *not* be in the area where the sets overlap? **H**
   F 12   H 30
   G 24   J 36

Mixed Strategy Practice

USE DATA For 5–7, use the bar graph.

5. Ms. Colmery's class filled 5 rows and 2 extra chairs in the museum auditorium. How many chairs were in each row?
   6 chairs in each row

6. **REASONING** Describe at least two ways chairs can be arranged in equal rows for Mr. Leong's class.
   See above.

7. How many students visited the museum in all? Write a number sentence and solve. **36 + 28 + 32 + 24 = 120; 120 students**

6. Possible answers: 3 rows of 8 chairs, 2 rows of 12 chairs

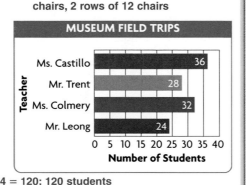

MUSEUM FIELD TRIPS

Ms. Castillo 36
Mr. Trent 28
Ms. Colmery 32
Mr. Leong 24

Number of Students

Chapter 19 **401**

* **North Carolina Standards 3.01** Use appropriate vocabulary to compare, describe, and classify - and three-dimensional figures. *also* maintains (2) 4.01

Challenge 19.6

Missing Labels

Label the sets in each Venn diagram below.
1. Figures That Have Straight Sides / Figures That Have Curved Sides

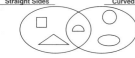

2. Multiples of 3 / Multiples of 4

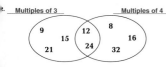

9 15 12 8 16
21 24 32

3. Intersecting Lines / Parallel Lines

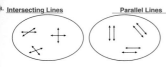

Draw your own Venn diagram, but do not label the sets. You may use geometric figures or numbers. Ask a classmate to label the sets.
Check students' diagrams.

W104 Challenge

Reading Strategy 19.6

Compare and Contrast

When you **compare** things, you decide how they are alike. When you **contrast** things, you decide how they are different. When you read some Venn diagrams, you may compare and contrast the geometric figures or numbers in the diagrams.

VOCABULARY compare contrast

Amanda sorted some shapes by placing them in a Venn diagram. Compare and contrast the shapes.

1. How is the shape in the overlapping area like the shapes in the rest of the circle labeled "Triangles"?
   All the shapes have 3 sides.

2. How is the shape in the overlapping area different from the shapes in the rest of the circle labeled "Triangles"?
   It is the only triangle with 3 equal sides.

3. Compare and contrast the shape in the overlapping area and the shapes in the rest of the circle labeled "Shapes with All Equal Sides."
   All the shapes have equal sides. The triangle has 3 sides, and the other shapes have more than 3 sides.

4. Compare and contrast the numbers in the Venn diagram.
   The numbers in the overlapping part are multiples of both 4 and 10. The numbers in the rest of the circle labeled "Multiples of 4" are not multiples of 10. The numbers in the rest of the circle labeled "Multiples of 10" are not multiples of 4.

PS104 Reading Strategy

PRACTICE

Guided Practice

Do Problem Solving Practice Exercises 1–4 with your students. Identify students who are having difficulty and choose appropriate lesson resources to provide assistance. Note that Exercises 1–4 are **multistep or strategy problems.**

For Exercises 3 and 4, you may wish to review the meaning of *multiple* with students. Students that are having difficulty can review this concept by looking at page 178 in their books.

Independent Practice

Note that Exercises 5–7 are **multistep or strategy problems.** Assign Exercises 5–7.

SCAFFOLDED INSTRUCTION Use the prompts on Transparency 19 to guide instruction for the multistep or strategy problem in Exercise 5.

Transparency **19**

ASSESS

Summarize the lesson by having students:

DISCUSS In what ways might a Venn diagram be useful? Possible answer: You could use it to sort various kinds of tools, toys, games, and so on.

WRITE Describe two sets of objects in which no members would overlap.
Possible answer: a set of triangles and a set of hexagons would not have any overlap.

LESSON QUIZ
Possible answers are given.

Transparency **19.6**

1. Describe where the figure below would be placed in the Venn diagram on page 400. **in the area where the sets overlap**

2. Describe where the figure below would be placed in the Venn diagram on page 400. **in the set of quadrilaterals, but not in the area where the sets overlap**

401

CHAPTER 19 Extra Practice

Purpose To provide extra practice for the skills presented in this chapter

The blue page references in each set of exercises refer to the lesson pages where each skill is taught.

Internet Resources

Visit **THE LEARNING SITE** at **www.harcourtschool.com** for a listing of practice activities.

Extra Practice

Set A (pp. 384–387)

Name each figure.

1. • point   2. ray   3. line segment   4. line

Write whether each angle is a *right angle,* an *acute angle,* or an *obtuse angle.*

5. obtuse angle   6. acute angle   7. right angle

Set B (pp. 388–389)

Describe the lines. Write *parallel* or *intersecting.* Tell whether the intersecting lines are *perpendicular* or *not perpendicular.*

1. parallel   2. intersecting; not perpendicular   3. parallel   4. intersecting; perpendicular

Set C (pp. 390–391)

Write the number of sides and angles each polygon has. Then name the polygon.

1. 4 sides; 4 angles; quadrilateral
2. 6 sides; 6 angles; hexagon
3. 3 sides; 3 angles; triangle
4. 5 sides; 5 angles; pentagon
5. 8 sides; 8 angles; octagon

Set D (pp. 392–395)

Name each triangle. Write *equilateral, isosceles,* or *scalene.*

1. 3 cm, 5 cm, 4 cm — scalene
2. 3 cm, 3 cm, 3 cm — equilateral
3. 1 cm, 2 cm, 2 cm — isosceles
4. 3 cm, 3 cm, 2 cm — isosceles
5. 4 cm, 2 cm, 3 cm — scalene

Set E (pp. 396–399)

Write as many names for each quadrilateral as you can. **Possible answers are given.**

2. square, rectangle, quadrilateral, parallelogram, rhombus

1.   2.   3.   4.   5.

1. rhombus, quadrilateral, parallelogram
3. rectangle, quadrilateral, parallelogram
4. quadrilateral, parallelogram
5. trapezoid, quadrilateral

402

Review/Test

✓ CHECK VOCABULARY

Choose the best term from the box.

| equilateral |
| line segment |
| perpendicular |
| angle |
| parallel |

1. An __?__ is formed by two rays with the same endpoint.
(p. 384) **angle**

2. Intersecting lines that cross to form right angles are __?__ lines. (p. 388) **perpendicular**

3. A triangle with 3 equal sides is __?__. (p. 393) **equilateral**

✓ CHECK SKILLS

20. Possible answer: it should be in the area where the sets overlap because it is a quadrilateral and it has 2 acute angles.

Write whether each angle is a *right angle*, an *acute angle*, or an *obtuse angle*. (pp. 384–387)

4. **obtuse angle**
5. **right angle**
6. **acute angle**
7. **right angle**

Write the number of sides and angles each polygon has. Then name the polygon. (pp. 390–391)

8. **5 sides; 5 angles; pentagon**
9. **8 sides; 8 angles; octagon**
10. **4 sides; 4 angles; quadrilateral**
11. **6 sides; 6 angles; hexagon**

Name each triangle. Write *equilateral, isosceles,* or *scalene.* (pp. 392–395)

12. 3 cm 3 cm 2 cm **isosceles**
13. 3 cm 3 cm 3 cm **equilateral**
14. 3 cm 4 cm 2 cm **scalene**
15. 3 cm 4 cm 5 cm **scalene**

Write as many names for each quadrilateral as you can. (pp. 396–399)
Possible answers given.
19. rectangle, parallelogram, rhombus, square

16. **parallelogram rhombus**
17. **parallelogram**
18. **rectangle parallelogram**
19. ◇

✓ CHECK PROBLEM SOLVING

20. Describe where the figure below should be in the Venn diagram. Explain. (pp. 400–401) **See above.**

Quadrilaterals — Plane figures with 1 or more acute angles

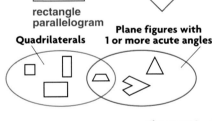

Chapter 19 **403**

Review/Test

Purpose To check understanding of concepts, skills, and problem solving presented in Chapter 19

Using the Page

The Chapter 19 Review/Test can be used as a **review** or a **test**.

- Items 1–3 check understanding of concepts and new vocabulary.
- Items 4–19 check skill proficiency.
- Item 20 checks students' abilities to choose and apply problem solving strategies to real-life geometry problems.

 Suggest that students place the completed Chapter 19 Review/Test in their portfolios.

Using the Assessment Guide

- Multiple-choice format of Chapter 19 Posttest— See *Assessment Guide*, pp. AG121–122.
- Free-response format of Chapter 19 Posttest— See *Assessment Guide*, pp. AG123–124.

Using Student Self-Assessment

The How Did I Do? survey helps students assess what they have learned and how they learned it. This survey is available as a copying master in *Assessment Guide*, p. AGxvii.

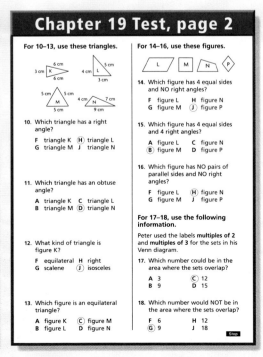

Chapter 19 Test, page 1

Choose the correct answer.

1. What is straight, continues in both directions, and does not end?
   A point   C line segment
   B line   D ray

2. What figure is formed by two rays with the same endpoint?
   F square   H triangle
   G angle   J circle

3. I am part of a line. I have one endpoint. I am straight and continue in one direction. What am I?
   A line   C line segment
   B ray   D angle

4. Emile's teacher drew this figure on the board. Which best describes the figure?
   F angle   H parallel lines
   G line   **J line segment**

5. The answer to a question asked by a teacher is, "Two lines that never cross." What could be the question?
   A What are parallel lines?
   B What is a line?
   C What is an angle?
   D What are intersecting lines?

6. What figure is shown?
   F intersecting lines
   G a ray
   H an angle
   J parallel lines

7. Which best describes the figure shown below?
   A point
   B line
   C parallel lines
   D intersecting lines

For 8–9, use the figures below.

8. Which figure is a quadrilateral?
   F figure A   H figure C
   G figure B   J figure D

9. Which figure is NOT a polygon?
   A figure A   C figure C
   B figure B   D figure D

Chapter 19 Test, page 2

For 10–13, use these triangles.

K 3 cm 6 cm 6 cm
L 5 cm 4 cm 3 cm
M 5 cm 5 cm 5 cm
N 4 cm 7 cm 9 cm

10. Which triangle has a right angle?
    F triangle K   **H triangle L**
    G triangle M   J triangle N

11. Which triangle has an obtuse angle?
    A triangle K   C triangle L
    B triangle M   **D triangle N**

12. What kind of triangle is figure K?
    F equilateral   **H right**
    G scalene   **J isosceles**

13. Which figure is an equilateral triangle?
    A figure K   C figure M
    B figure L   D figure N

For 14–16, use these figures.

L   M   N   P

14. Which figure has 4 equal sides and NO right angles?
    F figure L   H figure N
    G figure M   J figure P

15. Which figure has 4 equal sides and 4 right angles?
    A figure L   C figure N
    B figure M   D figure P

16. Which figure has NO pairs of parallel sides and NO right angles?
    F figure L   **H figure N**
    G figure M   J figure P

For 17–18, use the following information.
Peter used the labels **multiples of 2** and **multiples of 3** for the sets in his Venn diagram.

17. Which number could be in the area where the sets overlap?
    A 3   **C 12**
    B 9   D 15

18. Which number would NOT be in the area where the sets overlap?
    F 6   H 12
    G 9   J 18

Getting Ready for the EOG Test

Chapters 1–19

Using the Pages

These pages may be used to help students get ready for the North Carolina EOG Test. The test items are written in the same style and arranged in the same format as those on the EOG Test.

The pages are cumulative. They cover the standards from the North Carolina Mathematics Standard Course of Study that have been taught up to this point in the text or in a previous grade. Each Getting Ready for the EOG Test also reviews the North Carolina mathematics strands shown below.

- Number and Operations
- Measurement
- Geometry
- Data Analysis and Probability
- Algebra

These pages can be assigned at the end of the chapter as classwork or as a homework assignment. You may want to have students use individual recording sheets presented in a multiple-choice (standardized) format. A Test Answer Sheet is available as a blackline master in the *Assessment Guide* (p. AGlii).

You may wish to have students describe how they solved each problem and share their solutions.

Getting Ready for the EOG Test

⭐ NUMBER AND OPERATIONS

> **TIP** **Check your work.** See item 1. Multiply the number of cookies in each bag by the number of bags you think Barry used. Your answer should equal the number of cookies Barry made.

1. Barry made 36 cookies for a bake sale. He put 4 cookies in each bag. How many bags did he use? **C**

   A 6   **C** 9
   B 8   **D** 12

2. Mr. Dixon planted 8 rows of tomato plants in his garden. There are 6 plants in each row. How many tomato plants are in Mr. Dixon's garden? **D**

   A 14   **C** 24
   B 16   **D** 48

3. Which division sentence belongs to the same fact family as these multiplication sentences? **A**

   $6 \times 4 = 24$ $4 \times 6 = 24$

   A $24 \div 4 = 6$
   B $24 \div 3 = 8$
   C $24 \div 8 = 3$
   D $24 \div 1 = 24$

4. **Explain It** Ben has 1,109 stamps. Ali has 1,372 stamps. *About* how many more stamps does Ali have than Ben? Explain your answer.
   See page 405.

⭐ MEASUREMENT AND GEOMETRY

5. A garden is in the shape of a rhombus. Which figure below shows the shape of the garden? **A**

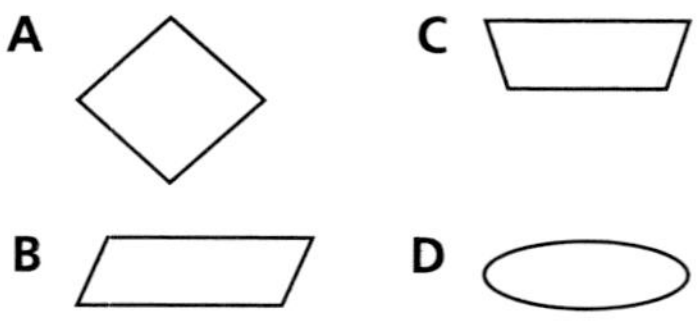

   A   **C**

   B   **D**

6. Jessica is making a design with this triangle.

   What kind of triangle is she using? **C**

   A obtuse   **C** right
   B acute   **D** equilateral

7. George wants to draw a pentagon. How many sides does he need to draw? **B**

   A 4   **C** 6
   B 5   **D** 8

8. **Explain It** Carla wants to put a ribbon border around this picture.

   7 inches
   5 inches   5 inches
   7 inches

   How many feet of ribbon will she need? How do you know?
   See page 405.

⭐ ALGEBRA

9. Which number sentence can be solved by using the picture below? **C**

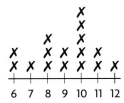

- **A** $12 \div 3 = $ ▨
- **B** $3 + 9 = $ ▨
- **C** $27 \div 3 = $ ▨
- **D** $9 - 3 = $ ▨

10. Pat has 24 photos to put into an album. She will put 4 photos on each page.

Which of the following can be used to find the number of pages that Pat will put photos on? **B**

- **A** $24 - 4 = $ ▨
- **B** $24 \div 4 = $ ▨
- **C** $24 + 4 = $ ▨
- **D** $24 \times 4 = $ ▨

11. Explain It Tyler collected 36 trading cards. He stacked the cards in 6 equal piles. How many cards were in each pile?

Write a number sentence to solve the problem. Tell how you decided what operation to use. **See below.**

⭐ DATA ANALYSIS AND PROBABILITY

12. The line plot below shows the number of books read by a third-grade class during the summer. Each X on the line plot stands for 1 student. How many students read more than 8 books? **D**

```
                X
                X
        X       X
 X     X X X X
 X X X X X X X
 +-+-+-+-+-+-+-
 6 7 8 9 10 11 12
```
Number of Books Read

- **A** 3   **C** 8
- **B** 6   **D** 10

13. Look at the line plot above. How many students read fewer than 10 books? **B**

- **A** 6   **C** 10
- **B** 8   **D** 12

14. Explain It Nicole made this bar graph to show the number of coins in her collection. Describe the data in the bar graph. **See below.**

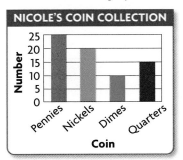

NICOLE'S COIN COLLECTION

Chapters 1–19

Item Analysis

You may wish to use the item analysis to determine which North Carolina standards need additional review.

Item	North Carolina Standard	Lesson
1	1.03	13.2
2	1.03	10.2
3	1.03	12.4
4	1.06	5.1
5	3.01	19.3
6	3.01	19.4
7	3.01	19.3
8	2.01	17.5
9	5.03	13.2
10	5.03	14.3
11	5.04	13.4
12	4.01	15.5
13	4.01	15.5
14	4.01	16.2

SCORING RUBRIC
Explain It

2 Demonstrates a complete understanding of the problem and chooses an appropriate strategy to determine the solution

1 Demonstrates a partial understanding of the problem and chooses a strategy that does not lead to a complete and accurate solution

0 Demonstrates little understanding of the problem and shows little evidence of using any strategy to determine a solution

Explain It • Written Response

4. About 300 more stamps; possible explanation: round each number to the nearest hundred. Then subtract: $1,400 - 1,100 = 300$.

8. 2 feet; possible explanation: add the lengths of the sides: $5 + 7 + 5 + 7 = 24$; 12 inches = 1 foot, so 24 inches = 2 feet.

11. $36 \div 6 = c$, $c = 6$ cards; possible explanation: Tyler put his cards into equal groups and division is used to make equal groups.

14. Possible response: she has 25 pennies, 20 nickels, 10 dimes, and 15 quarters in her collection. She has more pennies than any other coin.

Congruence and Symmetry

NCTM Standards 2000

1. Number and Operations
2. Algebra
3. Geometry
   Lessons 20.1, 20.2, 20.3, 20.4, 20.5
4. Measurement
5. Data Analysis and Probability

6. Problem Solving
   Lessons 20.1, 20.2, 20.3, 20.4, 20.5
7. Reasoning and Proof
   Lessons 20.1, 20.2, 20.3, 20.4, 20.5
8. Communication
   Lessons 20.1, 20.2, 20.3, 20.4, 20.5
9. Connections
10. Representation
    Lessons 20.1, 20.2, 20.3, 20.4, 20.5

Chapter Planner

Getting Ready for Chapter 20 • Assessing Prior Knowledge and INTERVENTION (See PE and TE page 407.)

LESSON	NORTH CAROLINA STANDARDS	PACING	VOCABULARY*	MATERIALS	RESOURCES AND TECHNOLOGY
20.1 Hands On: Congruent Figures pp. 408–409 Objective To identify and describe congruent figures	3.01 *also* maintains (2) 3.03	1 Day	**congruent**	*For each group* pattern blocks, triangle dot paper, crayons, grid paper	Reteach, Practice, Problem Solving, Challenge 20.1 Worksheets Transparency 20.1 **Intervention**, *Skill 58* (CD or Book) **Harcourt Mega Math Ice Station Exploration,** *Polar Planes*
20.2 Symmetry pp. 410–411 Objective To identify and draw lines of symmetry in plane figures	3.01 *also* maintains (2) 3.03	1 Day	**symmetry** **line of symmetry**	*For each student* pattern blocks, paper, scissors	Reteach, Practice, Problem Solving, Challenge 20.2 Worksheets Transparency 20.2 **Intervention**, *Skill 58* (CD or Book) **Harcourt Mega Math Ice Station Exploration,** *Polar Planes*
20.3 Similar Figures pp. 412–413 Objective To identify and draw similar figures	3.01	1 Day	**similar**	*For each group* 1-inch grid paper, 1-centimeter grid paper	Reteach, Practice, Problem Solving, Challenge 20.3 Worksheets Transparency 20.3 **Intervention**, *Skill 58* (CD or Book) **Harcourt Mega Math Ice Station Exploration,** *Polar Planes*
20.4 Hands On: Slides, Flips, and Turns pp. 414–415 Objective To identify and draw slides, flips, and turns		1 Day	**slide** **flip** **turn**	*For each group* pattern blocks, 1-centimeter grid paper	Reteach, Practice, Problem Solving, Challenge 20.4 Worksheets Transparency 20.4 **Intervention**, *Skill 58* (CD or Book) **Harcourt Mega Math Ice Station Exploration,** *Polar Planes*
20.5 Problem Solving Strategy: Make a Model pp. 416–417 Objective To use the problem solving strategy *make a model* to solve problems	3.01 *also* maintains (2) 3.03	1 Day			Reteach, Practice, Reading Strategy, Challenge 20.5 Worksheets Transparency 20.5 Scaffolded Instruction Transparency 20 Reading Transparency 20 **Intervention • Problem Solving,** *Strategy/Skill 20* (CD or Book)

Ending Chapter 20 • Extra Practice, p. 418 • Chapter 20 Review/Test, p. 419 • Getting Ready for the EOG Test, pp. 420–421

*Boldfaced terms are the key mathematical terms for the chapter.

Vocabulary Power

Review Vocabulary

To be ready for Chapter 20, students should know the following vocabulary terms:

- **half** (Grade 2)—either of two equal parts into which an object has been divided

Vocabulary Cards

Have students use the Vocabulary Cards on *Teacher's Resource Book* pages TR171–174 for the key terms in the chapter. The cards can be added to a file of mathematics terms.

Develop Key Chapter Vocabulary

The **boldfaced** words are the key vocabulary terms in the chapter.

- **congruent** (p. 408)—describes two figures that are the same size and shape

- **symmetry** (p. 410)—property of a figure that can be folded along a line so that the two parts match exactly

- **line of symmetry** (p. 410)—a line that divides a figure into halves that are mirror images of each other

- **similar** (p. 412)—describes two figures that have the same shape but may be different sizes

- **slide** (p. 414)—a movement of a figure to a new position without turning or flipping it

- **flip** (p. 414)—a move that involves flipping a figure over a line

- **turn** (p. 414)—a movement of a geometric figure around a specific point

Multimedia Math Glossary

GO ON-LINE For vocabulary support, visit **www.harcourtschool.com/mathglossary**

Math Journal

Have students define the key vocabulary terms: *congruent, symmetry, line of symmetry, similar, slide, flip,* and *turn.* Have students use their own words and give an example of each.

MATH Word Work

Objective To reinforce vocabulary concepts
Use after Lesson 20.4.

Materials *For each pair* pattern blocks; one 6-inch piece of yarn; paper; pencil; Vocabulary Cards, pp. TR171–174

One student chooses a vocabulary card. The other student demonstrates the meaning of the term. For example, Student 1 holds up the card for *congruent.* Student 2 may decide to show two congruent pattern blocks, build two congruent figures with multiple pattern blocks, or draw two congruent figures. Pairs should take turns until all vocabulary terms have been demonstrated.

MODIFYING INSTRUCTION Students may wish to use paper money for demonstrating flips and turns.

Congruence and Symmetry

Mathematics Across the Grades

LOOKING BACK • Prerequisite Skills

To be ready for Chapter 20, students should have the following understandings and skills:

- **Same Size, Same Shape** — decide if figures are the same size and the same shape

Check What You Know

Use page 407 to determine students' knowledge of prerequisite concepts and skills.

Intervention

Help students prepare for the chapter by using the intervention resources described on TE page 407.

LOOKING AT CHAPTER 20 • Essential Skills

Students will

- **identify and describe congruent figures.**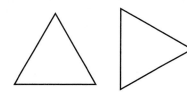
- identify and draw lines of symmetry.
- identify and draw similar figures.
- identify and draw slides, flips, and turns.
- use the problem solving strategy *make a model* to solve problems.

Example

Are the two figures below congruent? Explain.

Yes; they are the same size and shape, so they are congruent.

LOOKING AHEAD • Applications

Students will apply what they learn in Chapter 20 to the following new concepts:

- Congruent and Similar Figures (Grade 4)
- Transformations (Grade 4)
- Turns and Symmetry (Grade 4)
- Geometric Patterns (Grade 4)

Differentiated Instruction

Meeting the Needs of All Learners

Extra Support	Activities for All	Enrichment
Alternative Teaching Strategy TE Lessons 20.1, 20.2, 20.3, 20.4, 20.5 **ESOL/ESL** TE Lessons 20.1, 20.2, 20.3, 20.4, 20.5	**Cross-Curricular Connections** **Reading:** TE Lesson 20.5 **Science:** TE/PE p. 406 **Social Studies:** TE Lesson 20.1 **Vocabulary:** TE p. 406B, PE p. 407 **Writing:** TE Lesson 20.2	**Advanced Learners** TE Lesson 20.3 **Early Finishers** TE Lessons 20.2, 20.4, 20.5

Combination and Multi-age Classrooms

Grade 2	Grade 3	Grade 4
Skills Trace Across the Grades		
Explore concepts of congruence and symmetry, as well as slides, flips, and turns.	**Identify and draw congruent figures, similar figures, and lines of symmetry; identify, predict, and draw slides, flips, and turns.**	Identify rotational and line symmetry, congruent and similar figures, translations, reflections, and rotations.
Instructional Strategies		
Students on this level may require more time to build conceptual understanding. **Assignments** **Grade 3 Pupil Edition** • Have students work in pairs on Lessons 20.1, 20.2, and 20.5. **Grade 2 Pupil Edition**—pages 345–352	Students on this level should be able to complete all the lessons in the Pupil Edition and all the activities in the Teacher's Edition with minimal adjustments. **Assignment** **Grade 3 Pupil Edition**—pages 406–419	Students on this level will probably require less time to build conceptual understanding. **Assignments** **Grade 3 Pupil Edition** • Compact Lessons 20.2, 20.3, and 20.5. **Grade 4 Pupil Edition**—pages 398–403 and 406–409

Congruence and Symmetry

Introducing the Chapter

Explain that congruence means that two figures have the same size and shape, and that a line of symmetry is an imaginary line that divides a figure into congruent halves. Have students look at the photograph. Ask them whether the starfish has a line of symmetry, and have them explain their answers. Answers will vary.

Using Data

To begin the study of this chapter, have students

- Describe other plants or animals that have at least one line of symmetry. Have students identify the line of symmetry. Check students' work.

- Describe how to draw a shell congruent to the one in the photograph. Trace it exactly.

Problem Solving Project

Purpose To identify lines of symmetry

Background A starfish, or sea star, has hollow arms that have short spines. On the underside of the arms are rows of tube feet that may have suckers on their tips. Share the following information.

TYPE OF STARFISH	NUMBER OF ARMS
Solaster endeca	9–10
Spiny sun star	up to 14
Sunflower	15–24
Heliaster	up to 50
Crown-of-thorns	12–19

UNDERSTAND • PLAN • SOLVE • CHECK

Have students

- Draw any kind of starfish. Fold it to find its line or lines of symmetry.
- Draw a starfish with 9 arms so that it has 1 line of symmetry.
- Draw a starfish with 10 arms so that it has 2 lines of symmetry.

Check students' work.

Graphing Investigations
Begin Week 20.

≡FAST FACT • SCIENCE Many starfish have five arms, but some kinds have many more. These arms move, so you will see symmetry on a starfish some of the time. Symmetry can also be seen in other animals and objects.

PROBLEM SOLVING   Is the dashed line on the shell a line of symmetry? How do you know?

Yes; possible answer: if you cut out and fold the figure along the line, both sides match.

406

WHY LEARN MATH? Many artists use congruence and symmetry to make their works look attractive. What other people might use congruence and symmetry in their jobs? Possible answers: architects, interior designers, dancers

Family Involvement Activities

These activities provide:

- Letter to the Family
- Math Vocabulary
- Family Game
- Practice (Homework)

Family Involvement Activities, p. FA77

Use this page to help you review and remember important skills needed for Chapter 20.

SAME SIZE, SAME SHAPE

Tell whether the figures are the same size and shape. Write *yes* or *no*.

1.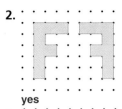
yes

2.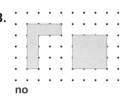
yes

3.
no

4.
yes

5.
no

6.
no

7.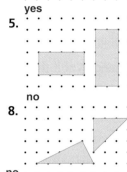
yes

8.
no

9.
yes

VOCABULARY POWER

REVIEW

half [haf] *noun*

The word *half* is sometimes used as part of a word or part of a phrase. Write a sentence using one of the following: **Check students' work.**

half dollar, half hour, half-moon, half note, halftime

PREVIEW

congruent   slide
symmetry   flip
line of symmetry   turn
similar

GO ON-LINE www.harcourtschool.com/mathglossary

Chapter 20 **407**

Assessing Prior Knowledge

Use the **Check What You Know** page to determine whether your students have mastered the prerequisite skills critical for this chapter.

Intervention

- **Diagnose and Prescribe**
  Evaluate your students' performance on this page to determine whether intervention is necessary or if enrichment is appropriate. Options that provide instruction, practice, and a check are listed in the chart below.

CHECK WHAT YOU KNOW RESOURCES

Intervention Copying Masters or CD-ROMs

Enrichment Copying Masters

VOCABULARY POWER

For activities and information about the vocabulary in this chapter, see page 406B.

Were students successful with ✓ CHECK WHAT YOU KNOW?

IF ... **NO**
THEN ... INTERVENE

INTERVENTION **OPTIONS**

IF ... **YES**
THEN ... ENRICH

Skill/Items	Missed more than	Intervene with
Same Size, Same Shape 1–9	2	• *Intervention*, Skill 58

Skill/Items	Missed fewer than	Enrich with
Same Size, Same Shape 1–9	3	• *Intervention*, Enrichment pp. IN367–368

Lesson Planning

Objective To identify and describe congruent figures

Materials *For each group* pattern blocks; triangle dot paper, p. TR29; crayons; grid paper, p. TR58

NCTM Standards
3. Geometry
6. Problem Solving
7. Reasoning and Proof
8. Communication
10. Representation

Math Background
These ideas will help students understand how to identify and describe congruent figures.

- Figures are congruent if they have the same size and shape.

- Figures can be in different positions and still be congruent.

- If the line segments and the angles of two figures are congruent, the figures are congruent.

- You can determine if two figures are congruent by tracing one figure and placing it over the second figure to see if they are exactly the same.

Vocabulary
congruent having the same size and shape

Warm-Up Resources

Number of the Day

Transparency **20.1**

The number of the day is your age. Write four number sentences using the number.
Possible answers: $9 - 4 = 5$; $9 \times 6 = 54$; $9 + 7 = 16$; $45 \div 5 = 9$

Daily Facts Practice

Have students practice multiplication and division facts by completing Set G of *Teacher's Resource Book*, p. TR97.

Transparency **20.1**

Problem of the Day

When Eddie drew a line from 1 corner of a figure to its opposite corner, he formed 2 triangles. What was his original figure? Possible answers: square or rectangle

Solution Problem of the Day tab, p. PD20

Intervention and Extension Resources

Alternative Teaching Strategy

MATERIALS *For each pair* 12 index cards, pattern blocks

Help students **identify congruent figures** by playing a concentration game. Have students trace different pattern blocks to make 6 pairs of congruent figures on the index cards and then lay the cards face down in a 3 × 4 array.

- Players take turns turning over 2 cards. If the figures are congruent, the player picks the cards up and plays again.
- If the figures are not congruent, the player turns the cards face down.
- Play continues until all pairs have been matched. The player with the greater number of cards is the winner. Check students' work.

VISUAL, KINESTHETIC

BODILY/KINESTHETIC

Multistep and Strategy Problems

The following multistep and strategy problems are provided in Lesson 20.1:

Page	Item
409	4–5

ESOL/ESL

MATERIALS *For each student* tracing paper, scissors, magazines, newspapers

ESOL/ESL

Help students **find congruent figures in different positions.** Have students look through magazines or newspapers for shapes they think might be congruent. Ask:

- Are the figures the same shape?
- Are they the same size?

Suggest that students find two figures, trace one, cut it out, and place it over the other figure to determine if the figures are congruent. Check students' work.

VISUAL, KINESTHETIC

VISUAL/SPATIAL

Social Studies Connection

MATERIALS *For each group* encyclopedia or reference books, posterboard

Invite students to **research the use of congruent figures in tiles and mosaics in ancient Greece and Rome.** Have students draw illustrations similar to those found on tiles and present them to the class. Check students' work.

VISUAL

VISUAL/SPATIAL

Technology Link

Intervention, *Skill 58*

Harcourt Mega Math
Ice Station Exploration,
Polar Planes, Level H

GO The Harcourt Learning Site
www.harcourtschool.com

Lesson 20.1 Organizer

Objective To identify and describe congruent figures

Vocabulary congruent

Materials *For each group* pattern blocks; triangle dot paper, p. TR29; crayons; grid paper, p. TR58

1 INTRODUCE

QUICK REVIEW provides review of prerequisite skills.

WHY LEARN THIS? You can identify congruent figures all around you. *Share the lesson objective with students.*

2 TEACH

Guided Instruction

• *Have students read the first paragraph and look at the pairs of figures.*

How do you know that the two rectangles are congruent? They are the same size and shape.

Why are the rectangle and the square not congruent? They are not the same shape.

• *Have students complete the activity on the page.*

How do you decide how many triangles you need to make a figure that is congruent to the hexagon? Put triangles on top of the hexagon until it is covered.

REASONING **What are some objects in the classroom that have the same shape and the same size?** Possible answers: chairs, markers, math books

MODIFYING INSTRUCTION Invite students to use geoboards to make congruent figures.

3 PRACTICE

Guided Practice

Discuss the Talk About It exercise with your students. Identify students who are having difficulty and choose appropriate lesson resources to provide assistance.

LESSON 1

Congruent Figures
HANDS ON

Quick Review

Write the number of sides and angles each polygon has.

1. 3 sides, 3 angles
2. 4 sides, 4 angles
3. 6 sides, 6 angles
4. 4 sides, 4 angles
5. 5 sides, 5 angles

VOCABULARY
congruent

MATERIALS
pattern blocks, triangle dot paper, crayons

 Explore

ARE THEY THE SAME? **Congruent** figures have the same *size* and *shape*. Figures can be in different positions and still be congruent.

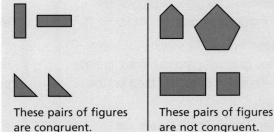

These pairs of figures are congruent. | These pairs of figures are not congruent.

Use pattern blocks to find and build congruent figures.

• Sort a group of pattern blocks. Look for blocks that are the same size and shape. Put congruent pieces together. **Check students' groupings.**

• Use only small green triangles to make a figure that is congruent to the yellow hexagon. On triangle dot paper, draw the figure you made. **Check students' figures.**

• Use any pattern blocks to make a different figure that is congruent to the yellow hexagon. Draw the figure you made. **Check students' figures.**

Talk About It

• How do you know that the figures you made are congruent? **The figures are the same size and shape.**

408

Technology Link
More Practice:
Harcourt Mega Math
Ice Station Exploration,
Polar Planes,
Level H

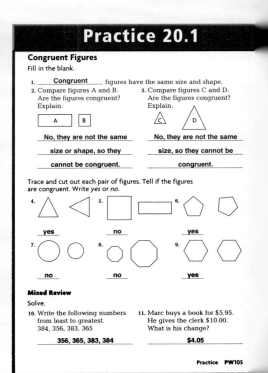

How many green triangles do I use to make a figure that is congruent to the yellow hexagon? 6

Reteach 20.1

Congruent Figures

Congruent figures have the same size and shape.

A   B   C   D

• Trace and cut out rectangle B.
• Place rectangle B over rectangle A.

The figures are the same size and shape.

So, rectangle A and rectangle B are congruent.

• Trace and cut out triangle D.
• Place triangle D over triangle C.

The figures are the same shape but not the same size.

So, triangle C and triangle D are not congruent.

For each pair, trace figure B. Place it over figure A. Write *yes* or *no* to tell if the shapes are congruent.

1. A   B   yes
2. A   B   no
3. A   B   yes
4. A   B   no

Reteach RW105

Practice 20.1

Congruent Figures

Fill in the blank.

1. **Congruent** figures have the same size and shape.

2. Compare figures A and B. Are the figures congruent? Explain.

A   B

No, they are not the same size or shape, so they cannot be congruent.

3. Compare figures C and D. Are the figures congruent? Explain.

C   D

No, they are not the same size, so they cannot be congruent.

Trace and cut out each pair of figures. Tell if the figures are congruent. Write *yes* or *no*.

4. yes
5. no
6. yes
7. no
8. no
9. yes

Mixed Review

Solve.

10. Write the following numbers from least to greatest. 384, 356, 383, 365

356, 365, 383, 384

11. Marc buys a book for $5.95. He gives the clerk $10.00. What is his change?

$4.05

Practice PW105

Connect

You can tell if two figures are congruent by tracing one figure and placing it over the second figure. If one figure covers the other exactly, they are congruent.

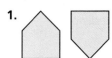

Trace and cut out rectangle A. Place it over rectangle B. Are rectangles A and B congruent? **yes**

Trace and cut out square C. Place it over square D. Are squares C and D congruent? **no**

 Practice and Problem Solving

Trace and cut out each pair of figures. Tell if the figures are congruent. Write *yes* or *no*.

1.
yes

2.
yes

3.
no

4. **REASONING** Joe says that the two figures below are congruent. Do you agree? Explain.

  Yes; Possible answer: they are the same size and shape. Even if they are in different positions, they are congruent.

5. **Write About It** Copy this figure on grid paper. Draw a congruent figure. Then explain how you know the figures are congruent.

Check students' drawings and explanations.

Getting Ready for the EOG Test

6. Which of the shapes is congruent to triangle T? **C**

A, B, C, D, T

Chapter 20 **409**

✱ North Carolina Standards **3.01** Use appropriate vocabulary to compare, describe, and classify two- and three-dimensional figures. *also maintains (2)* **3.03**

Independent Practice

Note that Exercises 4–5 are **multistep or strategy problems**. Assign Exercises 1–5.

4 ASSESS

Summarize the lesson by having students:

DISCUSS How can you tell if two figures are congruent? You can trace one figure and place it over the second figure. If the figures match, they are congruent.

WRITE Trace pattern blocks to draw two figures that are congruent. Explain how you know that they are congruent. Possible answer: since I traced the same pattern block for both figures, they have the same size and shape.

LESSON QUIZ
Tell if the figures are congruent. Write *yes* or *no*.

Transparency **20.1**

1. ○ ○ yes

2. □ ◇ yes

3. △ ▯ no

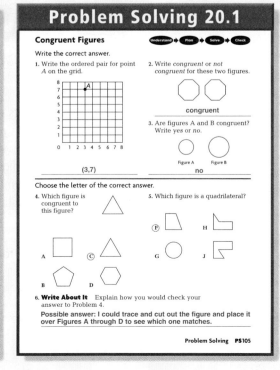

Challenge 20.1

Five Square

You can make several different shapes out of 5 congruent squares. At least 1 side of each square must touch the side of another square.

Look at the shapes. Shapes A and B are congruent. You can turn Shape A so it will fit on top of Shape B. Shapes C and D are not congruent.

A B

C D

Are the shapes congruent? Write *yes* or *no*.

1. yes 2. no 3. no

4. yes 5. yes 6. yes

You can make 12 different shapes with 5 congruent squares. At least 1 side of each square must touch the side of another square. The first 6 are done for you. Draw six more.

Challenge **CW105**

Problem Solving 20.1

Congruent Figures

Write the correct answer.

1. Write the ordered pair for point A on the grid.

2. Write *congruent* or *not congruent* for these two figures.

congruent

3. Are figures A and B congruent? Write *yes* or *no*.

Figure A Figure B

(3,7) no

Choose the letter of the correct answer.

4. Which figure is congruent to this figure?

5. Which figure is a quadrilateral?

F H

A C G J

B D

6. **Write About It** Explain how you would check your answer to Problem 4.

Possible answer: I could trace and cut out the figure and place it over Figures A through D to see which one matches.

Problem Solving **PS105**

409

Lesson Planning

Objective To identify and draw lines of symmetry in plane figures

Materials *For each student* pattern blocks, paper, scissors

NCTM Standards

3. Geometry
6. Problem Solving
7. Reasoning and Proof
8. Communication
10. Representation

Math Background

These ideas will help students understand how to identify and draw lines of symmetry in plane figures.

- A line of symmetry is an imaginary line that divides a figure in half.

- If you fold a figure along a line of symmetry, both sides match. One half of the figure is the mirror-image of the other half of the figure.

- Some figures have one or more lines of symmetry.

- Some figures have no lines of symmetry.

Vocabulary

symmetry quality of having halves that are mirror images of each other

line of symmetry an imaginary line that divides a figure into halves that match when the figure is folded along the line

Warm-Up Resources

Number of the Day

Transparency **20.2**

Find the number for each clue and add them together. The product of 8×6; the whole number that is 1 less than 13; the whole number that is 1 more than 19; the whole number between 30 and 32. 111

Daily Facts Practice

Have students practice multiplication and division facts by completing Set A of *Teacher's Resource Book,* p. TR98.

Transparency **20.2**

Problem of the Day

Simon wrote a 5-digit number. The sum of the digits was 31. Three of the digits were the same odd number. The other two digits were the same even number. Write a 5-digit number that could be Simon's number. Accept 5-digit numbers with the digits 5, 5, 5, 8, and 8 or the digits 9, 9, 9, 2, and 2 in any order.

Solution Problem of the Day tab, p. PD20

Intervention and Extension Resources

Alternative Teaching Strategy

MATERIALS *For each student* cutout shapes such as circles, squares, rectangles, and triangles

ESOL/ESL

Help students **identify lines of symmetry in plane figures.** Encourage students to fold the shapes into halves that match, unfold the shapes, and notice the lines of symmetry. When they understand the concept, suggest that students try to fold the shapes in half in different ways to see if the shapes have more than one line of symmetry. Check students' work.

KINESTHETIC

BODILY/KINESTHETIC

Multistep and Strategy Problems

The following multistep or strategy problem is provided in Lesson 20.2:

Page	Item
411	11

Writing in Mathematics

Have students **write riddles about symmetry.** Share the following example: "I am a plane figure. I have 4 equal sides and 4 equal angles. I have 4 lines of symmetry. What am I?" a square

Have students trade riddles with a classmate and solve. Check students' work.

Early Finishers

MATERIALS *For each student* mirror, pattern blocks or any small objects

Have students **find a line of symmetry.** Ask students to place a mirror where they think the line of symmetry is on one of the small objects. Tell students that if they can see the whole figure by using the image in the mirror, they have correctly identified the line of symmetry. Check students' work.

VISUAL, KINESTHETIC

BODILY/KINESTHETIC

Technology Link

Intervention, *Skill 58*

Harcourt Mega Math
Ice Station Exploration,
Polar Planes, Level J

Lesson 20.2 Organizer

Objective To identify and draw lines of symmetry in plane figures

Vocabulary symmetry, line of symmetry

Materials *For each student* pattern blocks, paper, scissors

---

1 INTRODUCE

QUICK REVIEW provides review of prerequisite skills.

WHY LEARN THIS? You will be able to recognize symmetry in nature, in art, and in common objects and symbols. *Share the lesson objective with students.*

---

2 TEACH

Guided Instruction

- *Have students read the first paragraph.*
  If you fold a figure in half, how many parts do you have? two
  What does it mean if both sides match? The figure has a line of symmetry.

- *Check students' understanding of the Math Idea.*
  Give an example of one figure with more than one line of symmetry and one with no line of symmetry. Possible answers: square; scalene triangle
  REASONING What are some objects on the playground that have at least one line of symmetry? Possible answers: a slide, a swing

- *Direct students' attention to the opened figure in Step 2.*
  Do both sides of your figure match? yes
  Where do you see the line of symmetry? in the middle

MODIFYING INSTRUCTION Have students hold the fold of the cutout figure to the edge of a small mirror. If they can see the whole figure by using the image in the mirror, then they know that the fold is a line of symmetry.

LESSON

2 Symmetry

▶ **Learn**

HALF AND HALF A figure has **symmetry** if it can be folded along a line so that the two parts match exactly. The line is called a **line of symmetry**.

MATH IDEA Some figures have one or more lines of symmetry. Some figures have no lines of symmetry.

1 line of symmetry	2 lines of symmetry	3 lines of symmetry	0 lines of symmetry

You can trace and fold a figure to find lines of symmetry.

Activity
MATERIALS: pattern blocks, paper, scissors

STEP 1
Trace a blue rhombus on a sheet of paper. Cut out the figure.

STEP 2
Fold the figure in half so that the two halves match. Draw a line along the fold.

STEP 3
Fold the figure in half in a different way so that the two halves match. Draw a line along this fold.

- How many lines of symmetry does the figure have?
  2 lines of symmetry
- Repeat the activity with an orange square and a red trapezoid.
  How many lines of symmetry does each figure have?
  orange square: 4 lines of symmetry; red trapezoid: 1 line of symmetry

410

Quick Review
Does each figure appear to be congruent to the figure at the right?
1.  no 2. no 3. yes
4. no 5. yes

VOCABULARY
symmetry   line of symmetry

Reteach 20.2

Symmetry

A **line of symmetry** is an imaginary line that divides a figure in half. If you fold a figure along a line of symmetry, the two sides match.

Materials: paper, pencil, scissors

You can follow these steps to make figures that have a line of symmetry.

Step 1
Fold a sheet of paper in half.

Step 2
Draw a figure on one side of the folded paper. Let the folded edge be one edge of your figure.

Step 3
Cut out the figure you drew. Do **not** cut the folded edge.

Step 4
Open up the figure you cut out. The new figure is symmetrical. The fold line is the line of symmetry.

Follow the steps above to make 3 different symmetrical figures.

RW106 Reteach

Practice 20.2

Symmetry

Draw the line or lines of symmetry.

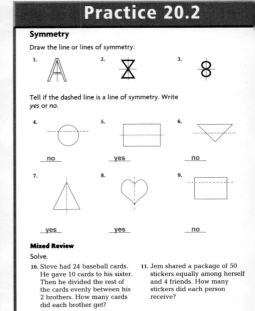

1.   2.   3.

Tell if the dashed line is a line of symmetry. Write *yes* or *no.*

4.   no   5.   yes   6.   no

7.   yes   8.   yes   9.   no

Mixed Review

Solve.

10. Steve had 24 baseball cards. He gave 10 cards to his sister. Then he divided the rest of the cards evenly between his 2 brothers. How many cards did each brother get?
    7 cards

11. Jem shared a package of 50 stickers equally among herself and 4 friends. How many stickers did each person receive?
    10 stickers

PW106 Practice

▶ Check

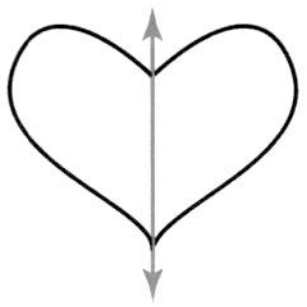

1. **Explain** how you know the blue line in the figure at the right is a line of symmetry.
   The line divides the figure into matching halves.

Tell if the blue line is a line of symmetry. Write *yes* or *no*.

2. 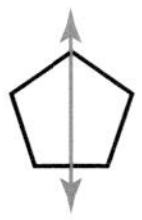 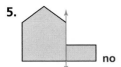 yes

3. 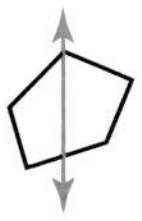 no

4. 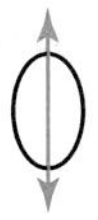 yes

▶ Practice and Problem Solving   Extra Practice, page 418, Set A

Tell if the blue line is a line of symmetry. Write *yes* or *no*.

5. no

6. 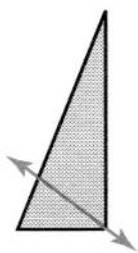 no

7. 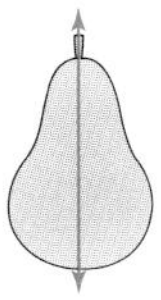 yes

Trace each figure. Then draw the line or lines of symmetry.

8.

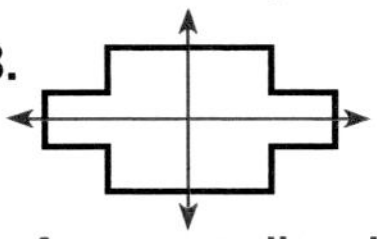

9.

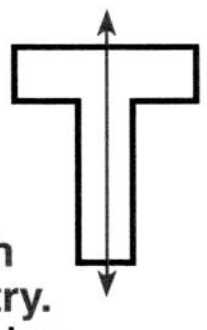

10.

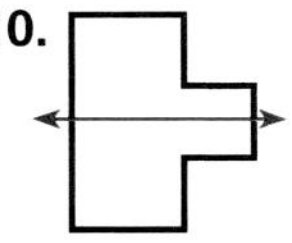

11. Agree; any line drawn through the center is a line of symmetry.

11. Jody says that a circle has too many lines of symmetry to count. Do you agree or disagree? Explain. See above.

12. 📖 **Write a problem** about a figure that has no lines of symmetry. Draw the figure on grid paper.
    Check students' work.

13. **Vocabulary Power** The word *figure* comes from a Latin word, *figura*, which means "to form or shape." List four geometric figures and draw a picture of each.
    Check students' names and drawings.

14. ▦**FAST FACT** • SCIENCE In 1959, John Pennekamp Coral Reef State Park in Florida became the first undersea park in the United States. How many years ago was this?
    Check students' work:
    [current year] − 1959

Getting Ready for the EOG Test

15. Which figure has only one line of symmetry? **D**

A 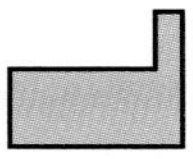   B 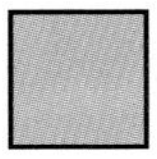   C 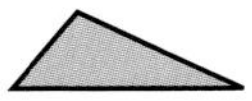   D

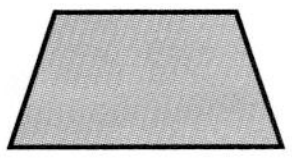

Chapter 20   **411**

North Carolina Standards 3.01 Use appropriate vocabulary to compare, describe, and classify two- and three-dimensional figures. *also* maintains (2) 3.03

Challenge 20.2

Symmetry

The picture at the right shows half of a figure that has a line of symmetry. You can complete the figure by thinking about what the mirror image would look like.

The second picture shows what the whole figure looks like.

Draw the other half of the figure.

1.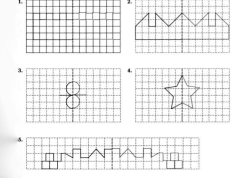

2.

3.

4.

5.

CW106 Challenge

Problem Solving 20.2

Symmetry   Understand → Plan → Solve → Check

Write the correct answer.

1. Is the dashed line a line of symmetry? Write *yes* or *no*.

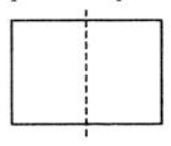

   yes

2. Are the figures congruent? Write *yes* or *no*.

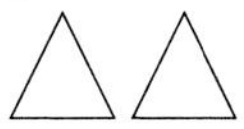

   yes

3. $36 \div 9 = \underline{?}$
   4

4. $3 \times \underline{?} = 21$
   7

Choose the letter of the correct answer.

5. Which of the following letters has a line of symmetry?
   A **L**   C **Q**
   B **G**   Ⓓ **U**

6. Which of the following numbers has a line of symmetry?
   F **5**   H **7**
   G **6**   J **8**

7. A television is on sale for $239. It was $349 before the sale. How much less expensive is it now?
   A $210   C $110
   B $200   D $100

8. How many sides does a pentagon have?
   F four   H six
   Ⓖ five   J eight

9. **Write About It** Explain how you found the answer to Problem 1.
   Possible answer: I traced the figure, cut it out, and folded it along that line to see if the sides matched.

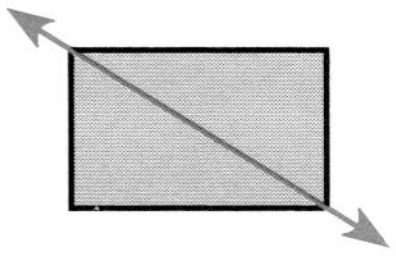

PS106 Problem Solving

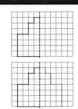
3 PRACTICE

Guided Practice

Do Check Exercises 1–4 with your students. Identify students who are having difficulty and choose appropriate lesson resources to provide assistance.

Independent Practice

Note that Exercise 11 is a **multistep or strategy problem**. Assign Exercises 5–14.

Vocabulary Power Ask a few students to draw plane figures on the board. Then have the rest of the class discuss how the figures' shapes are alike and how they are different.

4 ASSESS

Summarize the lesson by having students:

DISCUSS Describe the lines of symmetry that a square has. Possible answer: One is horizontal, one is vertical, and two are diagonal.

📓 **WRITE What strategy could you use to locate the lines of symmetry in a figure?**
Possible answer: Fold the shape in half, horizontally, vertically, and in other ways, to see if both halves match.

LESSON QUIZ

Tell if the blue line is a line of symmetry. Write *yes* or *no*.

Transparency
20.2

1. yes

2. no

3.  no

4. yes

411

Lesson Planning

Objective To identify and draw similar figures

Materials *For each group* 1-inch grid paper, p. TR57; 1-centimeter grid paper, p. TR58

NCTM Standards
3. Geometry
6. Problem Solving
7. Reasoning and Proof
8. Communication
10. Representation

Math Background
These ideas will help students understand the concept of similar figures.

- Similar figures have the same shape.
- Similar figures can differ in size and position.
- All congruent figures are similar, but not all similar figures are congruent.

Vocabulary
similar having the same shape and the same or different size

Warm-Up Resources

Number of the Day

Transparency **20.3**

Write and solve 2 addition and 2 subtraction sentences using the number of girls or boys in your class. Possible answers: $13 + 2 = 15$, $13 + 10 = 23$, $13 - 3 = 10$, $13 - 4 = 9$

Daily Facts Practice

Have students practice multiplication facts by completing Set B of *Teacher's Resource Book*, p. TR98.

Transparency **20.3**

Problem of the Day

Write the greatest and the least number using the digits 0, 1, 3, and 8. 8,310 and 1,038

Solution Problem of the Day tab, p. PD20

Intervention and Extension Resources

Alternative Teaching Strategy

MATERIALS *For each student* 1-cm grid paper, p. TR58

Help students **copy similar figures on grid paper**. Display a simple figure, such as a square, on 1-inch grid paper. Have students draw the figure on 1-cm grid paper. Help students see the one-to-one correspondence between the two drawings. Ask:

- How are the figures the same? They are the same shape.
- How are they different? They are different sizes.

Continue with several other shapes. Check students' work.

KINESTHETIC

LOGICAL/MATHEMATICAL

Multistep and Strategy Problems

The following multistep and strategy problems are provided in Lesson 20.3:

Page	Item
413	14–16

ESOL/ESL

Help students **understand the meaning of the term** *similar*. Explain that the dictionary definition of *similar* is "nearly but not exactly the same." Ask students to make a list of things that are similar, such as a basketball and a soccer ball or boots and shoes. Answers will vary. Then tell them that in math, the term *similar* has a more specific meaning. It describes plane figures that have exactly the same shape but may have different sizes or positions. Show students different sizes of art paper, posters, or note paper. Ask students to identify those that are similar. Have them explain why some are not similar. Answers will vary.

AUDITORY, VISUAL

VERBAL/LINGUISTIC

Advanced Learners

MATERIALS *For each pair* 1-inch grid paper, p. TR57; 1-cm grid paper, p. TR58

Challenge students to **draw similar figures on different sizes of grid paper**. Have one partner draw a plane figure such as a hexagon on 1-cm grid paper. Have the second partner draw the same plane figure on 1-inch grid paper. Have students compare their completed figures and check to see if they are similar. Students then reverse roles. Check students' work.

VISUAL

VISUAL/SPATIAL

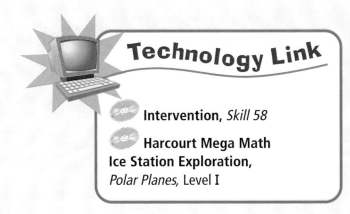

Technology Link

- Intervention, *Skill 58*
- **Harcourt Mega Math**
  Ice Station Exploration,
  Polar Planes, Level I

Lesson 20.3 Organizer

Objective To identify and draw similar figures

Vocabulary similar

Materials *For each group* 1-inch grid paper, p. TR57; 1-centimeter grid paper, p. TR58

---

1 INTRODUCE

QUICK REVIEW provides review of prerequisite skills.

WHY LEARN THIS? You will find that similar figures such as circles have the same shape but may have different sizes. *Share the lesson objective with students.*

---

2 TEACH

Guided Instruction

- *Check students' understanding of similar figures.*
  What must be the same about similar figures?
  They must have the same shape.
  What can be different about similar figures?
  They can have different sizes.

- *Ask students to look at the pairs of figures.*
  Look at the pair of squares. Are the squares similar? Explain. Yes; they have the same shape.
  Are the squares congruent? Explain. No; they are different sizes.

- *Have students discuss the Activity.*
  What do you know about congruent figures?
  They have the same size and the same shape.
  They can be in different positions.

- *Have students place their papers with similar figures side by side. Direct students to turn one of the figures upside down.*
  REASONING Are the figures similar? yes **How do you know?** Even though they are in different positions, the figures still have the same shape.

---

3 PRACTICE

Guided Practice

Do Check Exercises 1–4 with your students. Identify students who are having difficulty and choose appropriate lesson resources to provide assistance.

---

3 Similar Figures

▶ **Learn**

SIZE WISE Figures that have the same shape but may have different sizes are called **similar** figures.

These pairs of figures are similar. | These pairs of figures are not similar.

When you enlarge or reduce the size of a figure, the figure you make is similar to the first one.

 Activity

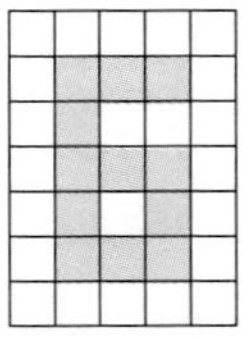

- Copy the figure at the right on 1-inch grid paper. Copy one square at a time.

- Is the figure you drew similar to the figure at the right? Is it congruent? Explain how you know.
  Yes; no; they are the same shape but different sizes, so they are similar but not congruent.

- Draw a figure on 1-centimeter grid paper. Copy the figure you drew, one square at a time, on 1-inch grid paper.

- Compare the two figures you drew. Tell what you know about the figures.

MATH IDEA Figures that are the same shape are similar, no matter what size they are or what position they are in.

1. Possible answer: the figures have the same shape, so they are similar. The figures are different sizes, so they are not congruent.

▶ **Check**

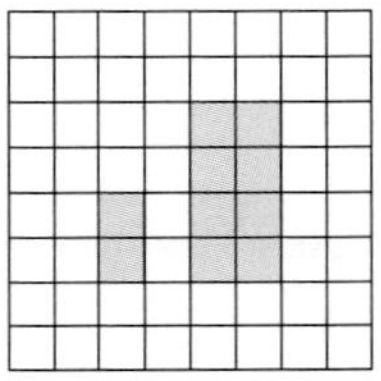

1. Explain whether or not these two figures are both similar and congruent.

412

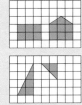

Tell if the blue line is a line of symmetry. Write *yes* or *no*.

1. no
2. yes
3. yes
4. yes
5. no

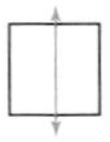

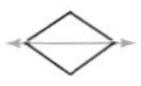

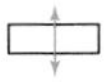

VOCABULARY
similar

MATERIALS
1-inch grid paper,
1-centimeter grid paper

Possible answers: the first figure is the same shape as the second figure; the figures are similar.

Reteach 20.3

Similar Figures

Similar figures do not have to be the same size, but they have to be the same shape. To change the size of a figure, follow these steps.

Step 1 Place points at each corner of the figure. Count the spaces between points.

Step 2 Count the same number of spaces on a smaller or larger grid. Place the points.

Step 3 Connect the points. Draw the sides between the points. This figure is similar to the first figure.

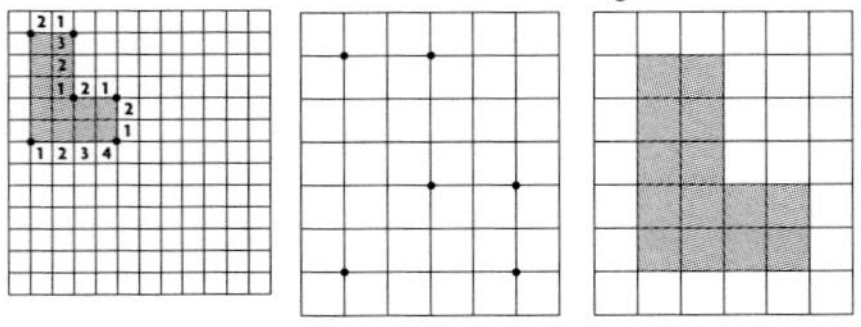

Change the size of each figure. Make a similar figure by using the grid below.

1.   2.   3.

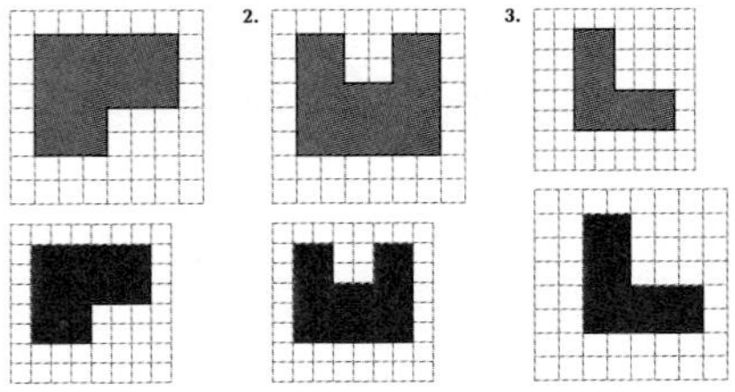

Reteach RW107

Practice 20.3

Similar Figures

Fill in the blank.

1. Figures that have the same shape but may have different sizes are called _____similar_____ figures.

For 2–3, draw a similar figure. Use the grids below.
Check students' drawings.

2.   3.

4. Draw a figure on one grid. Then draw a similar figure on the other grid.
Check students' drawings.

Mixed Review

Find the product.

5. $(2 \times 5) \times 6 =$ __60__   6. $(1 \times 7) \times 8 =$ __56__   7. $4 \times (3 \times 3) =$ __36__

Practice PW107

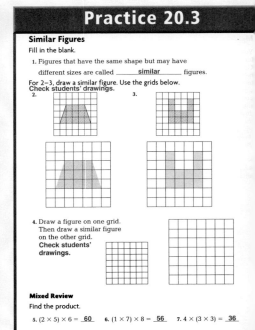

Tell if the figures appear to be similar. Write *yes* or *no*.

2. yes   3. no   4. yes

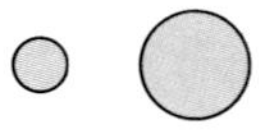

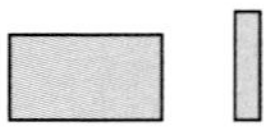

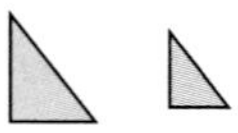

Practice and Problem Solving Extra Practice, page 418, Set B

Tell if the figures appear to be similar. Write *yes* or *no*.

5. yes   6. no   7. yes

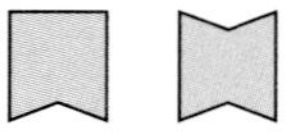

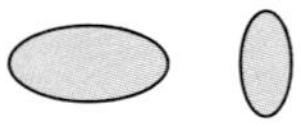

Draw a similar figure for each. Use 1-inch grid paper. Check students' drawings.

8.   9.   10.

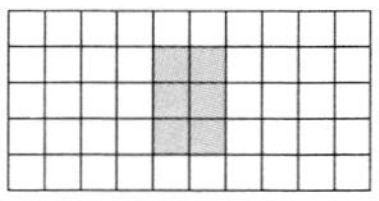

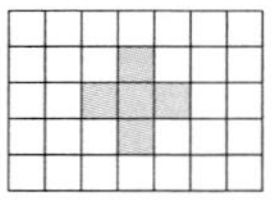

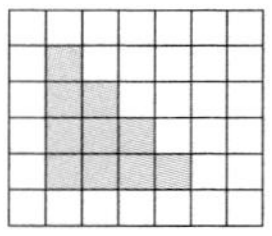

Draw a similar figure for each. Use 1-centimeter grid paper. Check students' drawings.

11.   12.   13.

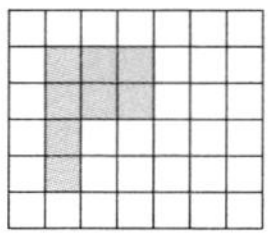

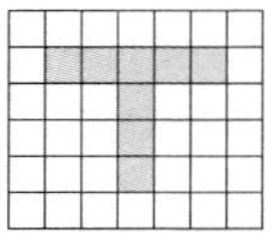

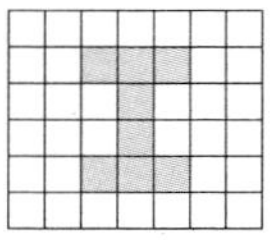

14. **REASONING** Do figures have to be in the same position for them to be similar? Explain. **No; as long as the figures have the same shape, they are similar.**

15. **REASONING** Are all rectangles similar? Draw pictures to explain. **Possible answer: no; not all rectangles are the same shape. If two rectangles are the same length, but one is wide and one is narrow, they are not similar. Check students' drawings.**

16. ✎ **Write About It** Draw a design on 1-inch grid paper. Have a classmate draw the design on 1-centimeter grid paper. Are the designs similar? How can you tell? **Possible answer: the designs are similar if they are the same shape.**

Getting Ready for the EOG Test

17. Which pair of swimming pool shapes appear to be similar? **A**

A   B   C   D

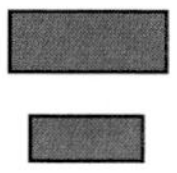

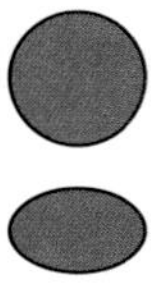

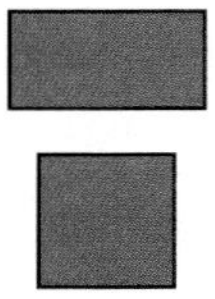

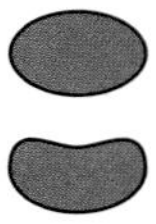

Chapter 20 **413**

North Carolina Standards 3.01 Use appropriate vocabulary to compare, describe, and classify - and three-dimensional figures.

Independent Practice

Note that Exercises 14–16 are **multistep or strategy problems.** Assign Exercises 5–16.

4 ASSESS

Summarize the lesson by having students:

DISCUSS How can you tell if 2 figures are similar? Possible answer: If the shapes of the figures are the same, they are similar.

📓 **WRITE** Find two triangles in Chapter 19 that are NOT similar. Trace both triangles and then explain why they are not similar. Check students' work.

LESSON QUIZ Transparency **20.3**

Draw a similar figure for each. Use 1-inch grid paper. Check students' work.

1.   2.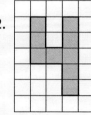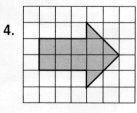

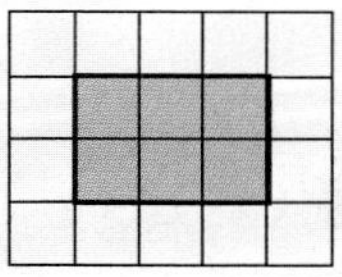

3. 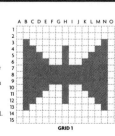   4.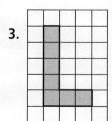

Challenge 20.3

Measurement

You can make a small drawing larger. Look at the design on Grid 1. The columns and rows have numbers and letters. Now look at the larger grid. It has the same numbers and letters. Put your finger on the letter B on the small grid. Move your finger down the column until you reach the number 5. Find the B-5 square on the large grid. Draw the same part of the design from the small grid onto the large grid.

Shade in the same design on the larger grid. Use the numbers and letters to help you.

GRID 1

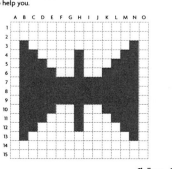

Challenge CW107

Problem Solving 20.3

Similar Figures Understand → Plan → Solve → Check

Write the correct answer.

1. Are the two figures similar? Write *yes* or *no*.

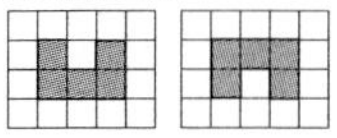

yes

2. Draw a figure similar to the following figure. Use the grid. **Check students' drawings**

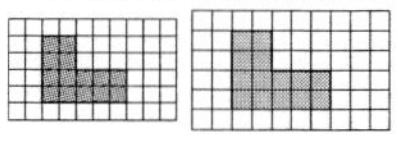

3. Look again at the two figures in problem 1. Are the figures congruent?

yes

4. Is Figure A similar to Figure B? Write *yes* or *no*.

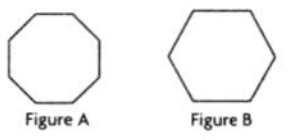

Figure A   Figure B

no

Choose the letter of the correct answer.

5. Which set of letters are similar?

A **R r**   C **A a**
B **Q q**   Ⓓ **S s**

6. On Saturday, Darius walked a total of 12 blocks to visit his friends. If he walked 4 blocks to Anesha's and 3 blocks to Xavier's, how many blocks did he walk to Yamilet's?

F 4   H 6
Ⓖ 5   J 7

7. Tasha arrived at the movie theater at 5:45 P.M. The movie started 25 minutes later. What time did the movie begin?

A 5:55 P.M.   Ⓒ 6:10 P.M.
B 6:05 P.M.   D 6:15 P.M.

8. To raise money for school, Adam sold 8 boxes of cards. Tina sold 5 boxes. Each box cost $4. How much money did they raise in all?

Ⓕ $52   G $45   H $32   J $25

9. **Write About It** Explain how you solved Problem 7. Possible answer: I know that in 15 minutes it will be 6:00 P.M. and 10 minutes more will be 6:10 P.M.

Problem Solving PS107

Slides, Flips, and Turns

Lesson Planning

PROFESSIONAL DEVELOPMENT

Objective To identify and draw slides, flips, and turns

Materials *For each group* pattern blocks; 1-centimeter grid paper, p. TR58

NCTM Standards
3. Geometry
6. Problem Solving
7. Reasoning and Proof
8. Communication
10. Representation

Math Background
These ideas will help students understand the concept of moving plane figures.

- You can describe a motion used to move a plane figure as a slide, a flip, or a turn.

- Slides, flips, and turns do not change the size or shape of a plane figure; they only change the location of a plane figure.

- Flips are also called reflections, turns are also called rotations, and slides are also called translations.

Vocabulary
slide a movement of a figure to a new position without turning or flipping it

flip a move that involves flipping a figure across an imaginary line

turn a move that involves rotating a figure

Warm-Up Resources

3 2 1 Build Number Sense

Number of the Day
Transparency 20.4

Add the number of letters in the words *slide* and *flip*. Then write and solve 5 multiplication sentences using that number. Possible answers: $9 \times 3 = 27$, $9 \times 5 = 45$, $9 \times 6 = 54$, $9 \times 8 = 72$, $9 \times 10 = 90$

Review Basic Facts
8 ÷ 3

Daily Facts Practice

Have students practice division facts by completing Set C of *Teacher's Resource* Book, p. TR98.

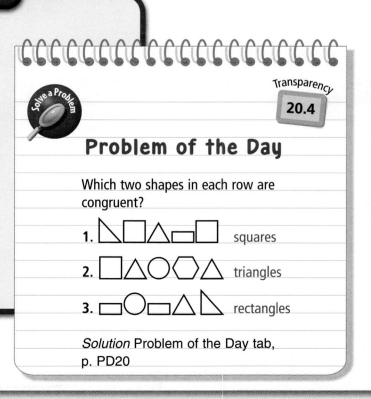

Solve a Problem

Transparency 20.4

Problem of the Day

Which two shapes in each row are congruent?

1. squares

2. triangles

3. rectangles

Solution Problem of the Day tab, p. PD20

Intervention and Extension Resources

Alternative Teaching Strategy

MATERIALS *For each student* 1 index card

Help students **model the motions** *slide, flip,* **and** *turn*.

- Have students place an index card on the left side of their desks and then slide it to the right side. Ask: What has changed? the location

- Next, tell students to place the card down and then turn it over. Ask: What has changed? Now I can see the reverse side.

- Then have students write the word *turn* on the card. Have students turn the card so that the word *turn* is upside down. Ask: What has changed? It is in a different position. Check students' work.

VISUAL

BODILY/KINESTHETIC

Multistep and Strategy Problems

The following multistep and strategy problems are provided in Lesson 20.4:

Page	Item
415	8–9

ESOL/ESL

Help students **practice using the terms** *slide, flip,* **and** *turn*. Begin by asking three students to use hand gestures to act out the meaning of each word. Then have students work in pairs to list examples of people or objects that slide, flip, and turn. Ask them to use each listed word in a sentence, such as:

- Skaters slide on the ice.

- Acrobats flip in the air.

- Car wheels turn.

Check students' work.

KINESTHETIC

VERBAL/LINGUISTIC

Early Finishers

MATERIALS *For each group* posterboard, number cube, pattern blocks

Have students **design a gameboard with a path that shows the result of sliding, flipping, or turning the figure drawn in the first space.** The first player tosses the number cube to see how many spaces to proceed along the path. If the player correctly identifies how the figure in the first space was moved, he or she advances to that space. Players take turns until one player reaches the end of the path. Check students' work.

VISUAL

VISUAL/SPATIAL

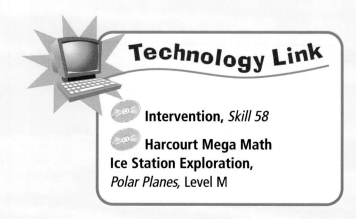

Technology Link

Intervention, *Skill 58*

Harcourt Mega Math
Ice Station Exploration,
Polar Planes, Level M

Lesson 20.4 Organizer

Objective To identify and draw slides, flips, and turns

Vocabulary slide, flip, turn

Materials *For each group* pattern blocks; 1-centimeter grid paper, p. TR58

---

1 INTRODUCE

QUICK REVIEW provides review of prerequisite skills.

WHY LEARN THIS? You will be able to recognize these motions in actions and in designs. *Share the lesson objective with students.*

2 TEACH

Guided Instruction

- *Direct students' attention to the diagrams that describe the motions of slides, flips, and turns.* **When you slide, flip, or turn an object, does its size or shape change in any way?** no **What changes?** the object's location or position

- *Have students read Steps 1 through 4. Remind students what a 180° turn is by demonstrating with a pencil or another object.* **Why is it important to trace the block before you slide, flip, or turn it?** so you can compare the figure before and after you move it

MODIFYING INSTRUCTION Have students put a colored dot in one corner of a figure to help identify whether it has been flipped or turned.

- *On a blank sheet of paper, ask students to draw a picture of a tree.* **Describe what your picture will look like if you slide it, flip it, or turn it.** Possible answer: slide: It will look the same. flip: The picture will be face down and you will see the blank side of the paper. turn: The tree will be upside down.

3 PRACTICE

Guided Practice

Discuss the Talk About It questions with your students. Identify students who are having difficulty and choose appropriate lesson resources to provide assistance.

Slides, Flips, and Turns

HANDS ON

Explore

A plane figure can be moved in different ways.

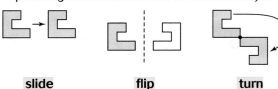

slide   flip   turn

Activity

Use a red trapezoid. Show different ways to move the block.

STEP 1
Trace the block on your paper.

STEP 2
Slide the block and trace it. Label the drawing "slide."
slide

STEP 3
Flip the block and trace it. Label the drawing "flip."
flip

STEP 4
Turn the block 180° and trace it. Label the drawing "turn."
turn

- Use a different pattern block. Repeat the steps above. **Check students' drawings.**

Talk About It

- Describe your drawings. Does a slide ever look like a flip? **Possible answer: using a square, a slide could look like a flip.**
- **REASONING** Does the size or shape of the block change when you slide, flip, or turn it? Explain. **No; whatever position it is in, it is still the same size and shape.**

414

Technology Link
More Practice:
Harcourt Mega Math
Ice Station Exploration,
Polar Planes, Level M

Quick Review

Does each figure appear to be congruent to the figure at the right?

1. [⎤ yes 2. ⌐⎤ no
3. ▭ no 4. ⎵ no
5. ⎵ yes

VOCABULARY
slide   flip   turn

MATERIALS
pattern blocks, paper

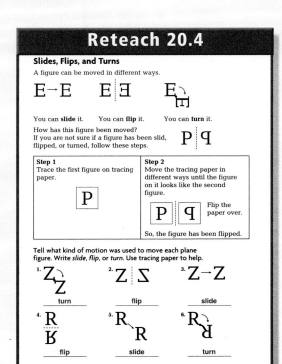

Reteach 20.4

Slides, Flips, and Turns

A figure can be moved in different ways.

E→E   E Ǝ   E

You can **slide** it. You can **flip** it. You can **turn** it.

How has this figure been moved? If you are not sure if a figure has been slid, flipped, or turned, follow these steps. P ꟼ

| Step 1 Trace the first figure on tracing paper. P | Step 2 Move the tracing paper in different ways until the figure on it looks like the second figure. P ꟼ Flip the paper over. |

So, the figure has been flipped.

Tell what kind of motion was used to move each plane figure. Write *slide*, *flip*, or *turn*. Use tracing paper to help.

1. Z Z — turn
2. Z Ƨ — flip
3. Z→Z — slide
4. R Я — flip
5. R R — slide
6. R Я — turn

RW108 Reteach

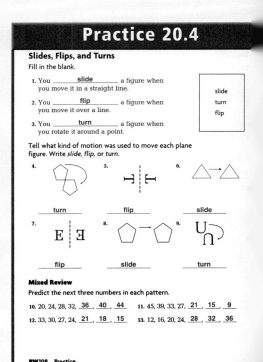

Practice 20.4

Slides, Flips, and Turns

Fill in the blank.

1. You _____slide_____ a figure when you move it in a straight line.
2. You _____flip_____ a figure when you move it over a line.
3. You _____turn_____ a figure when you rotate it around a point.

| slide |
| turn |
| flip |

Tell what kind of motion was used to move each plane figure. Write *slide*, *flip*, or *turn*.

4. turn
5. flip
6. slide

7. flip
8. slide
9. turn

Mixed Review

Predict the next three numbers in each pattern.

10. 20, 24, 28, 32, _36_, _40_, _44_
11. 45, 39, 33, 27, _21_, _15_, _9_
12. 33, 30, 27, 24, _21_, _18_, _15_
13. 12, 16, 20, 24, _28_, _32_, _36_

PW108 Practice

Think about how you use slides, flips, and turns to describe motions of real-life objects.

You can slide a dollar bill across a counter.

You can flip a postcard.

You can turn a puzzle piece.

MATH IDEA You can describe a motion used to move a plane figure as a slide, a flip, or a turn.

► **Practice and Problem Solving**

Tell what kind of motion was used to move each plane figure. Write *slide, flip,* **or** *turn.*

1. turn

2. flip

3.  slide

4. 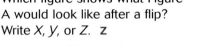 slide

5. 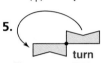 turn

6. flip

7. Which figure shows what Figure A would look like after a flip? Write *X, Y,* or *Z.* **Z**

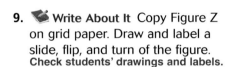

8. **REASONING** Draw a picture to predict the result of turning Figure A. What do you notice?
Check students' drawings and observations.

9. **Write About It** Copy Figure Z on grid paper. Draw and label a slide, flip, and turn of the figure.
Check students' drawings and labels.

Getting Ready for the EOG Test

10. Jackie saw this sign at the end of the street. Which term describes the shape of this sign? **B**

A hexagon   **C** quadrilateral
B octagon   **D** pentagon

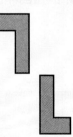

Chapter 20 **415**

Independent Practice

Note that Exercises 8–9 are **multistep or strategy problems.** Assign Exercises 1–9.

MODIFYING INSTRUCTION You may wish to have students use cards, books, and other objects to practice slides, flips, and turns.

ALGEBRAIC THINKING Understanding slides, flips, and turns is useful when students learn to perform transformations of plane figures on the coordinate plane.

4 ASSESS

Summarize the lesson by having students:

DISCUSS *Display these figures and ask:* **What motion could you use to move the first figure to the same place as the second? Explain.**

A turn; the figure is the same size and shape but is pointing in a different direction.

WRITE *Display the figure below.* **Draw what the figure will look like after it is flipped. How does it change? How does it stay the same?**

Possible answer: It is facing in a different direction; it has the same size and shape.

LESSON QUIZ
Tell what kind of motion was used to move each plane figure. Write *slide, flip,* or *turn.*

Transparency **20.4**

1. slide

2. flip

3. turn

Challenge 20.4

Turns

This figure has been turned 180°.

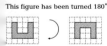

In Column B draw the figures in Column A as they would look after they have been turned 180°.

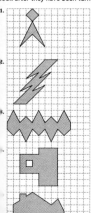

W108   Challenge

Problem Solving 20.4

Slides, Flips, and Turns   Understand ► Plan ► Solve ► Check

Write the correct answer.

1. What kind of motion was used? Write *slide, flip,* or *turn.*

flip

2. What kind of motion was used? Write *slide, flip,* or *turn.*

U → U
slide

3. When you slide a plane figure, does it change shape?

no

4. The difference between two numbers is 3. The product of the numbers is 88. What are the numbers?
8 and 11

Choose the letter of the correct answer.

5. What kind of motion was used to move the plane figure?

A slide   **C** turn
B flip   **D** flop

6. Which digit is in the thousands place?

235,461

F 2
G 4
H 5
J 6

7. Jared has 1 quarter, 2 dimes, 4 nickels, and 4 pennies in his pocket. How much money does Jared have?
A $0.54
B $0.59
C $0.64
D $0.69

8. Maria's CD case has 3 rows of 8 CD's. How many CDs are in the case?
F 12
G 24
H 48
J 36

9. **Write About It** What changes when you slide, flip, or turn a plane figure?
Possible answer: The only thing that changes is the position of the figure.

PS108   Problem Solving

415

Problem Solving Strategy
Make a Model

Lesson Planning

Objective To use the problem solving strategy *make a model* to solve problems

Lesson Resources Reading Transparency 20; Intervention • Problem Solving, Strategy/Skill 20

NCTM Standards
3. Geometry
6. Problem Solving
7. Reasoning and Proof
8. Communication
10. Representation

Math Background

Consider the following when you introduce the problem solving strategy *make a model*.

- You can make congruent figures by building models with pattern blocks.

- The strategy *make a model* can be used in conjunction with *draw a diagram* and *make a list* to solve geometry problems.

- Comparing geometric figures involves deciding how figures are alike and how they are different.

Warm-Up Resources

Number of the Day

Transparency
20.5

Write 2 multiplication and 2 division sentences using the number of lines of symmetry in a triangle that has three equal sides. Possible answers:
$3 \times 10 = 30$; $3 \times 7 = 21$; $27 \div 3 = 9$;
$15 \div 3 = 5$

Daily Facts Practice

Have students practice multiplication and division facts by completing Set D of *Teacher's Resource Book,* p. TR98.

Transparency
20.5

Problem of the Day

Craig traced the figure Paula had drawn. He erased one of the sides of the figure. Then he drew two more sides to make a symmetrical figure. His figure was a square. What was Paula's figure? a right triangle

Solution Problem of the Day tab, p. PD20

Intervention and Extension Resources

Alternative Teaching Strategy

MATERIALS *For each group* pattern blocks, paper, pencil

Have students **practice combining pattern blocks to make models.** Explain to students that they will use several pattern blocks to make different models of polygons. After they have made a model, ask students to trace the outside edges of the model and label the figure.

Have students make models of a rectangle, a pentagon, and an octagon. Check students' work.

VISUAL

VISUAL/SPATIAL

Reading Strategy

Compare Explain to students that when you compare figures, you decide how they are alike and how they are different. Have students use the figures below to choose the statement that best describes the relationship.

a. same shape but different size
b. same shape and same size
c. different shape and different size
d. different shape but same size

20 **Reading Transparency 20**

Multistep and Strategy Problems

The following multistep and strategy problems are provided in Lesson 20.5:

Page	Item
417	1–8

ESOL/ESL

Help students **understand the meaning of** *model.* Ask them to think of a model they may have at home: a train model or a doll house. Ask them to describe in what ways their models are like the real objects.

Lead students to conclude that making models is one way to solve problems.

AUDITORY

VERBAL/LINGUISTIC

Early Finishers

MATERIALS *For each group* books, magazines, newspapers, posterboard, markers

To help students **develop an awareness of the usefulness of models,** have them look through newspapers, magazines, and books to find examples of models.

● Have students make posters of the models they find.
● Have them share their posters with the class. Check students' work.

VISUAL

VISUAL/SPATIAL

Technology Link

Intervention • Problem Solving, *Strategy/Skill 20*

Lesson 20.5 Organizer

Objective To use the problem solving strategy *make a model* to solve problems

Lesson Resources Reading Transparency 20; Intervention • Problem Solving, Strategy/Skill 20

1 INTRODUCE

QUICK REVIEW provides review of prerequisite skills.

WHY LEARN THIS? You can compare figures to see if they are congruent. *Share the lesson objective with students.*

2 TEACH

Guided Instruction

• *Have students read the Problem.*
  How do you know if two figures are congruent? They must have the same size and the same shape.

• *Direct students' attention to the Plan section.*
  How can making a model help you solve the problem? Possible answer: I can try different combinations of pattern blocks until I have a model of a hexagon that is congruent to Tina's hexagon.

MODIFYING INSTRUCTION Have students trace the outline of the model of Tina's hexagon. Then students can place pattern blocks inside the outline.

ALGEBRAIC THINKING As students build another hexagon that is congruent to Tina's hexagon, you may wish to ask questions such as: What pattern block could be used in place of the 3 green triangles on the bottom of the hexagon? red trapezoid

416 Chapter 20

Problem Solving Strategy
Make a Model

Quick Review

Does each figure appear to be congruent to the figure at the right?

1. [triangle] no   2. [triangle] yes
3. [right triangle] no   4. [triangle] no
5. [triangle] yes

PROBLEM Tina combined pattern blocks to make one large polygon. She used 3 trapezoids and 7 triangles to make the hexagon at the right. What is another combination of pattern blocks that can be used to make a hexagon that is congruent to this one?

UNDERSTAND

• What are you asked to find? what other pattern blocks can be used to make a congruent hexagon
• What information will you use? the picture of the hexagon made with pattern blocks

PLAN

• What strategy can you use to solve the problem?
  You can *make a model.*

SOLVE

• How can you use the strategy to solve the problem?

  Make a model of Tina's hexagon. Then use some different blocks to make a hexagon that is congruent to Tina's hexagon. The hexagon shown at the right is congruent to Tina's hexagon.

  So, 1 hexagon, 1 rhombus, 1 trapezoid, and 5 triangles can be used to make the same shape.

CHECK

• How can you check your answer? Possible answer: you could trace both hexagons on paper, cut them out, and place one over the other.
• Are there any other possible models? Make a model to explain. **Yes; Check students' models.**

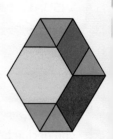

Tina's hexagon

416

Reteach 20.5

Problem Solving Strategy

Make a Model

Emily combined 1 hexagon and 3 triangle pattern blocks to make this large triangle. What other blocks could she have used to make a triangle congruent to this one?

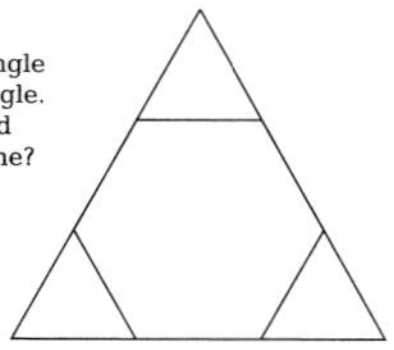

1. What are you asked to find?
   Another combination
   of pattern blocks that
   makes a congruent triangle

2. How will you do this?
   Possible answer: Figure out what other combination of pattern blocks makes a congruent triangle.

3. What information will you use?
   Emily used triangle and hexagon pattern blocks; the large triangle that Emily already made

You can make a model of the large triangle using pattern blocks. Try different combinations of blocks. Check that the triangle you make is congruent to the triangle Emily made. If not, revise your model and check again. **Possible solutions are given for 4–7.**

4. Solve the problem.
   2 triangles, 2 rhombuses,
   1 trapezoid

5. On paper, make a sketch of the model you made.

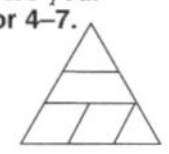

6. Find another combination of blocks.
   1 triangle, 1 rhombus,
   2 trapezoids

7. On paper, make a sketch of the model you made.

8. How could you check that the models you made are congruent to the large triangle Emily made first?
   Possible answer: Place my models on top of the drawing of Emily's model to see if they are the same size and shape.

Reteach **RW109**

Practice 20.5

Problem Solving Strategy

Make a Model

Make a model to solve.

For exercises 1 and 2, possible models are shown.

1. Jeff made the trapezoid shown at the right with pattern blocks. What is another combination of pattern blocks that can be used to make a trapezoid that is congruent to this one?

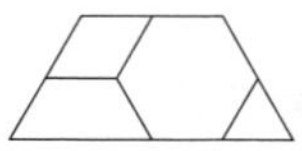

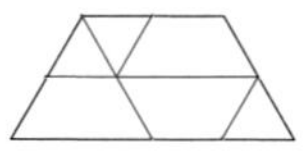

2. Use a different combination of pattern blocks to make another congruent trapezoid.

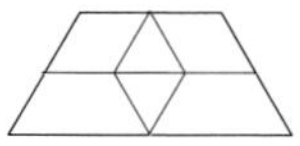

For 3–4, use pattern blocks to solve.

3. How many green triangles are needed to make a figure that is congruent to a yellow hexagon?
   A 3   C 6
   B 4   D 8

4. How many blue rhombuses are needed to make a figure that is congruent to a yellow hexagon?
   F 2   H 4
   G 3   J 5

Mixed Review

Tell if each figure is a polygon. Write *yes* or *no*.

5. 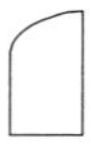 [figure] no   6.  [hexagon] yes   7. 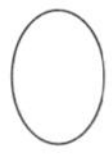 [oval] no

Practice **PW109**

Make a model to solve.

1. What if Tina used pattern blocks to make the rhombus shown at the right? What is another combination of pattern blocks that can be used to make a rhombus that is congruent to this one?

2. Use a different combination of pattern blocks to make another congruent rhombus.

Strategies

Draw a Diagram or Picture
▶ Make a Model or Act It Out
Make an Organized List
Find a Pattern
Make a Table or Graph
Predict and Test
Work Backward
Solve a Simpler Problem
Write a Number Sentence
Use Logical Reasoning

Problem Solving

For Exercises 1 and 2, some possible models are given:

For 3–4, use pattern blocks to solve.

3. How many green triangles are needed to make a figure that is congruent to a red trapezoid? **B**

A 2   C 4
B 3   D 5

4. How many red trapezoids are needed to make a figure that is congruent to a yellow hexagon? **F**

F 2   H 4
G 3   J 5

Mixed Strategy Practice

USE DATA For 5–6, use the line plot at the right.

5. Each *X* on the line plot stands for one student. How many students saw more than 4 movies last year?
12 students
6. What is the range for this set of data? What is the mode?
7 movies; 5 movies
7. There were 438 people on a train. At the station, 113 people got off and 256 people got on. How many people are on the train now? **581 people**

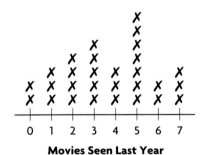

Movies Seen Last Year

8. Mimi bought a sandwich for $2.75 and a carton of milk for $1.25. She paid with a $5 bill. How much change should she get? **$1.00**

Chapter 20   **417**

North Carolina Standards **3.01** Use appropriate vocabulary to compare, describe, and classify
- and three-dimensional figures. *also* **maintains (2) 3.03**

Challenge 20.5

Tangrams

Tangrams are ancient Chinese puzzles. A square is divided into 7 pieces as shown below. Some or all of the pieces can be combined to make different shapes.

Trace the tangram puzzle. Then carefully cut apart the tangram pieces.

1. Use 2 pieces to make a square.

2. Use 3 pieces to make a parallelogram.

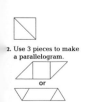

or

3. Use 6 pieces to make this fish.

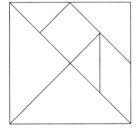

4. Try to put all 7 pieces back together again to make a square.

5. Make a shape with some or all of the tangram pieces. Draw the outline of the shape. Trade your outline for another student's and make the new shape.

Challenge   **CW109**

Reading Strategy 20.5

Compare and Contrast

When you **compare** things, you decide how they are alike. When you **contrast** things, you decide how they are different. As you read, you may compare and contrast characters, settings, and events. When you do math problems, you may compare and contrast numbers of items, colors, or sizes.

VOCABULARY
compare
contrast

Read the following problem.

Jason and Ella each built a figure with pattern blocks. How are the figures alike? How are they different?

Jason's Figure   Ella's Figure

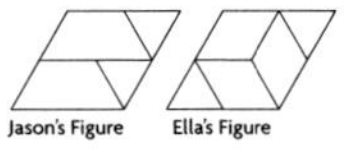

1. Complete the table to help you compare and contrast the two figures. The first row is done for you.

	Jason's Figure	Ella's Figure
What shape do the blocks make?	parallelogram	parallelogram
How many triangle blocks are used?	2	2
How many rhombus blocks are used?	0	3
How many trapezoid blocks are used?	2	0

2. How are the two figures alike? How are they different?

They are the same shape and both contain 2 triangles. Jason's figure is also made from 2 trapezoids. Ella's figure is also made from 3 rhombuses.

3. Describe the strategy you used to solve the problem.

Possible answer: I used a table to compare and contrast the types and numbers of blocks in the figures.

Make a table to help you compare and contrast the figures.

4. How are the figures alike? How are they different?

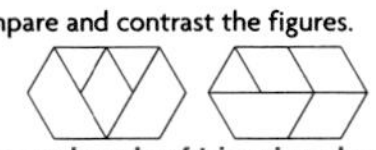

Both figures are hexagons and made of triangles, rhombuses, and trapezoids. One figure is made of 2 triangles, 1 rhombus, and 2 trapezoids. The other figure is made of 1 triangle, 3 rhombuses, and 1 trapezoid.

Reading Strategy   **PS109**

3 PRACTICE

Guided Practice

Do Problem Solving Practice Exercises 1–4 with your students. Identify students who are having difficulty and choose appropriate lesson resources to provide assistance. Note that Exercises 1–4 are **multistep or strategy problems.**

Independent Practice

Note that Exercises 5–8 are **multistep or strategy problems.** Assign Exercises 5–8.

SCAFFOLDED INSTRUCTION Use the prompts on Transparency 20 to guide instruction for the multistep or strategy problem in Exercise 8.

Transparency **20**

4 ASSESS

Summarize the lesson by having students:

DISCUSS How can making a model help you find two figures that are congruent? Possible answer: Making models can help you decide whether the figures are the same size and shape.

WRITE *Show students the figures below. Are the figures congruent? How do you know?* Yes; their outlines are the same size and shape.

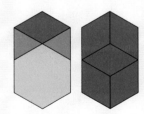

LESSON QUIZ
Use pattern blocks to solve.

Transparency **20.5**

1. How many green triangles are needed to make a figure that is congruent to a yellow hexagon? 6

2. Use a different combination of pattern blocks to make a figure that is congruent to the figure below.

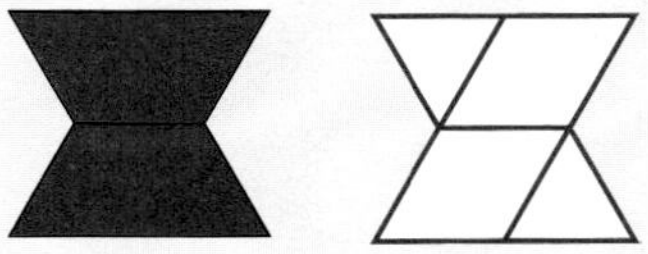

417

CHAPTER 20 Extra Practice

Purpose To provide extra practice for the skills presented in this chapter

The blue page references in each set of exercises refer to the lesson pages where each skill is taught.

Internet Resources

 Visit **THE LEARNING SITE** at **www.harcourtschool.com** for a listing of practice activities.

Extra Practice

Set A (pp. 410–411)

Tell if the blue line is a line of symmetry. Write *yes* or *no*.

1. 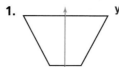 yes   2. 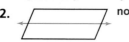 no   3. yes

Trace each figure. Then draw the line or lines of symmetry.

4. 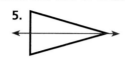   5. 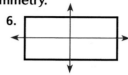   6.

7. Look at the letters in the word MATH. Which letters have one line of symmetry? Do any of the letters have more than one line of symmetry? Explain. **See right.**

8. On grid paper, draw a figure that has only one line of symmetry. Be sure to draw the line of symmetry on the figure. **Check students' work.**

7. The letters M, A, and T each have 1 line of symmetry. The letter H has 2 lines of symmetry.

Set B (pp. 412–413)

Tell if the figures appear to be similar. Write *yes* or *no*.

1.  yes   2.  yes   3.  no

4.  no   5. yes   6. no

7. Patty says that all squares are similar. Do you agree or disagree? Draw pictures to explain.
Possible answer: Agree: All squares are the same shape. Even if they are different sizes, they are the same shape. Check students' drawings.

418

Review/Test

✓ CHECK VOCABULARY AND CONCEPTS

Complete. Choose the best term from the box.

| symmetry |
| similar |
| congruent |

1. Figures that are the same size and shape are __?__ . (p. 408) **congruent**

2. A figure has __?__ if it can be folded along a line so that the two parts match exactly. (p. 410) **symmetry**

Tell what kind of motion was used to move each plane figure. Write *slide, flip,* or *turn*. (pp. 414–415)

3.
flip

4.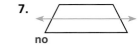
turn

5.
slide

✓ CHECK SKILLS

Tell if the blue line is a line of symmetry. Write *yes* or *no*. (pp. 410–411)

6.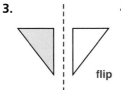
yes

7.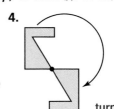
no

Tell if the figures appear to be similar. Write *yes* or *no*. (pp. 412–413)

8.
no

9.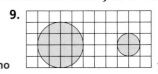
yes

✓ CHECK PROBLEM SOLVING

Solve. (pp. 416–417) **Some possible models are given.**

10. Make a model of this hexagon using pattern blocks. What is another combination of pattern blocks that can be used to make a hexagon that is congruent to this one?

Chapter 20 **419**

Review/Test

Purpose To check understanding of concepts, skills, and problem solving presented in Chapter 20

Using the Page

The Chapter 20 Review/Test can be used as a **review** or a **test**.

• Items 1–5 check understanding of concepts and new vocabulary.

• Items 6–9 check skill proficiency.

• Item 10 checks students' abilities to apply problem solving strategies to real-life congruency problems.

Portfolio Suggest that students place the completed Chapter 20 Review/Test in their portfolios.

Using the Assessment Guide

• Multiple-choice format of Chapter 20 Posttest— See *Assessment Guide*, pp. AG125–126.

• Free-response format of Chapter 20 Posttest— See *Assessment Guide*, pp. AG127–128.

Using Student Self-Assessment

The How Did I Do? survey helps students assess what they have learned and how they learned it. This survey is available as a copying master in *Assessment Guide*, p. AGxvii.

Chapter 20 Test, page 1

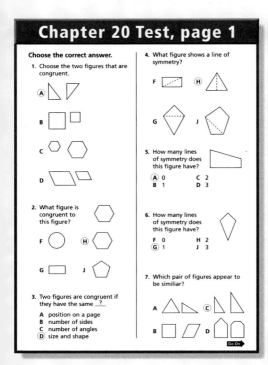

Chapter 20 Test, page 2

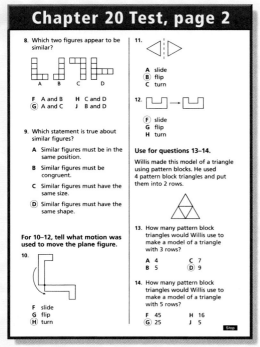

Congruence and Symmetry 419

CHAPTER 20

Getting Ready for the EOG Test

Chapters 1–20

Using the Pages

These pages may be used to help students get ready for the North Carolina EOG Test. The test items are written in the same style and arranged in the same format as those on the EOG Test.

The pages are cumulative. They cover the standards from the North Carolina Mathematics Standard Course of Study that have been taught up to this point in the text or in a previous grade. Each Getting Ready for the EOG Test also reviews the North Carolina mathematics strands shown below.

- Number and Operations
- Measurement
- Geometry
- Data Analysis and Probability
- Algebra

These pages can be assigned at the end of the chapter as classwork or as a homework assignment. You may want to have students use individual recording sheets presented in a multiple-choice (standardized) format. A Test Answer Sheet is available as a blackline master in the *Assessment Guide* (p. AGlii).

You may wish to have students describe how they solved each problem and share their solutions.

Getting Ready for the EOG Test

⭐ NUMBER AND OPERATIONS

1. Russ has 64 marbles. Tanika has 52 marbles. Anthony has 13 more marbles than Tanika. How many marbles do the three friends have in all? **B**

   A 193
   B 181
   C 142
   D 129

2. Which division sentence belongs to the same fact family as these multiplication sentences? **C**

   $5 \times 4 = 20$ $4 \times 5 = 20$

   A $20 \div 1 = 20$
   B $20 \div 2 = 10$
   C $20 \div 5 = 4$
   D $20 \div 10 = 2$

3. Which is the missing product in the table? **B**

×	3	4	5	6	7
9	27	36	▨	54	63

   A 39
   B 45
   C 48
   D 49

4. **Explain It** Tyler read 528 pages over the summer. Liz read 708 pages. About how many more pages did Liz read than Tyler? Explain how you estimated. **See page 421.**

420

⭐ MEASUREMENT AND GEOMETRY

5. Linda measured a piece of fabric for making a tablecloth. The length of the fabric was 18 feet. How many yards of fabric is this? **A**

   A 6 yards
   B 5 yards
   C 4 yards
   D 3 yards

6. Which of the following is the name for a polygon with exactly 4 sides? **D**

   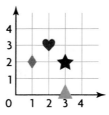

   A triangle
   B hexagon
   C pentagon
   D quadrilateral

7. **Explain It** What figure is found at (3,2) on the grid? Tell how you found the answer. **See page 421.**

⭐ DATA ANALYSIS AND PROBABILITY

8. The table shows the test scores for eight students. Which score occurred most often in the data? **D**

TEST SCORES	
Student	**Score**
Amy	94
Ben	96
Ellie	98
Chad	95
Tanya	96
Danny	97
Jung	92
Laney	96

A 93
B 94
C 95
D 96

9. Explain It Pedro asked his classmates about their pets. He found out that his classmates had 12 dogs, 9 cats, and 6 fish in all. Describe what Pedro should draw in his pictograph to show this data. **See below.**

PETS	
Dogs	
Cats	
Fish	

Key: ☺ = 3 animals.

⭐ ALGEBRA

10. Chris made a table of the money he earns working at the store. How much money does he earn if he works 7 hours? **C**

MONEY CHRIS EARNS	
Hours Worked	**Amount Earned**
4	$20
5	$25
6	$30
7	▨

A $12
B $32
C $35
D $40

> **TIP** **Eliminate choices.** See item 11. Substitute each answer choice in both equations. Eliminate answer choices that make one or both of the equations NOT true.

11. Which number makes both equations true? **B**

$$5 + \blacksquare = 6 \qquad 5 \times \blacksquare = 5$$

A 0   **C** 5
B 1   **D** 6

12. Explain It Describe the pattern of shapes below. Then name the next shape in this pattern.
See below.

Chapters 1–20

Item Analysis

You may wish to use the item analysis to determine which North Carolina standards need additional review.

Item	North Carolina Standard	Lesson
1	1.02	1.4
2	1.03	12.4
3	1.03	11.1
4	1.06	5.1
5	2.01	17.5
6	3.01	19.3
7	3.02	16.4
8	4.01	15.2
9	4.01	16.1
10	5.01	11.2
11	5.04	2.4
12	(2) 5.01	Grade 2

SCORING RUBRIC
Explain It

2 Demonstrates a complete understanding of the problem and chooses an appropriate strategy to determine the solution

1 Demonstrates a partial understanding of the problem and chooses a strategy that does not lead to a complete and accurate solution

0 Demonstrates little understanding of the problem and shows little evidence of using any strategy to determine a solution

Explain It • Written Response

4. Liz read about 200 more pages than Tyler. Possible answers: use front-end estimation: 700 − 500 = 200. Use rounding: 708 is about 700 and 528 is about 500. 700 − 500 = 200.

7. star; Possible answer: start at 0. Move 3 spaces to the right. Then move 2 spaces up.

9. Possible answer: he should draw 4 symbols for dogs since there are four 3s in 12, 3 symbols for cats since there are three 3s in 9, and 2 symbols for fish since there are two 3s in 6.

12. Possible answer: the pattern is a blue square followed by a red circle. The next shape will be a blue square.

Solid and Plane Figures

NCTM Standards 2000

1. Number and Operations	6. Problem Solving
2. Algebra	*Lessons 21.1, 21.2, 21.3, 21.4, 21.5*
Lesson 21.3	7. Reasoning and Proof
3. Geometry	*Lessons 21.1, 21.3, 21.5*
Lessons 21.1, 21.2, 21.3, 21.4, 21.5	8. Communication
4. Measurement	*Lessons 21.1, 21.2, 21.3, 21.4, 21.5*
5. Data Analysis and Probability	9. Connections
	Lessons 21.1, 21.2
	10. Representation
	Lessons 21.1, 21.2, 21.3, 21.4, 21.5

Chapter Planner

Getting Ready for Chapter 21 • Assessing Prior Knowledge and INTERVENTION (See PE and TE page 423.)

LESSON	NORTH CAROLINA STANDARDS	PACING	VOCABULARY*	MATERIALS	RESOURCES AND TECHNOLOGY
21.1 Solid Figures pp. 424–427 **Objective** To describe properties of solid figures and name the faces that make up solid figures	3.01	2 Days	**face** **edge** **vertex**	*For each group* solid figures, paper, crayons *For Thinker's Corner* connecting cubes	Reteach, Practice, Problem Solving, Challenge 21.1 Worksheets Transparency 21.1 **Intervention,** *Skill 59* (CD or Book) **Harcourt Mega Math Ice Station Exploration,** *Frozen Solids* **Math Jingles® CD 3–4**
21.2 Combine Solid Figures pp. 428–429 **Objective** To identify solid figures within complex solid objects	3.01	1 Day			Reteach, Practice, Problem Solving, Challenge 21.2 Worksheets Transparency 21.2 **Intervention,** *Skill 59* (CD or Book) **Harcourt Mega Math Ice Station Exploration,** *Frozen Solids*
21.3 Tessellations pp. 430–431 **Objective** To combine plane figures to form tessellations	3.01	1 Day	**tessellate** **tessellation**		Reteach, Practice, Problem Solving, Challenge 21.3 Worksheets Transparency 21.3 Scaffolded Instruction Transparency 21 **Harcourt Mega Math Ice Station Exploration,** *Polar Planes*
21.4 Draw Figures pp. 432–435 **Objective** To draw and classify polygons and solid figures	3.01	1 Day		*For each student* polygon worksheet, dot paper, ruler *For Linkup* paper clip, 2 pencils, ruler	Reteach, Practice, Problem Solving, Challenge 21.4 Worksheets Transparency 21.4 **Intervention,** *Skill 59* (CD or Book)
21.5 Problem Solving Skill: Identify Relationships pp. 436–437 **Objective** To use the problem solving skill *identify relationships* to identify solid figures from different perspectives	3.01	1 Day			Reteach, Practice, Reading Strategy, Challenge 21.5 Worksheets Transparency 21.5 Reading Transparency 21 **Intervention • Problem Solving,** *Strategy/Skill 21* (CD or Book)

Ending Chapter 21 • Extra Practice, p. 438 • Chapter 21 Review/Test, p. 439 • Getting Ready for the EOG Test, pp. 440–441

*****Boldfaced** terms are the key mathematical terms for the chapter.

Vocabulary Power

Review Vocabulary

To be ready for Chapter 21, students should know the following vocabulary terms:

- **cone**, **cube**, **cylinder**, **pyramid**, **rectangular prism** , and **sphere**

Vocabulary Cards

Have students use the Vocabulary Cards on *Teacher's Resource Book* pages TR173–176 for the key terms in the chapter. The cards can be added to a file of mathematics terms.

vertex

Develop Key Chapter Vocabulary

The **boldfaced** words are the key vocabulary terms in the chapter.

- **face** (p. 424)—a flat surface of a solid figure

- **edge** (p. 424)—the line segment formed where two faces meet

- **vertex** (p. 424)—a corner where three or more edges of a solid figure meet

- **tessellate** (p. 430)—to combine plane figures so they cover a surface without overlapping or leaving any space between them

- **tessellation** (p. 430)—a repeating pattern of plane figures that covers a surface with no gaps and no overlaps

Multimedia Math Glossary

For vocabulary support, visit
www.harcourtschool.com/mathglossary

Math Journal

Have students define the key vocabulary terms: *face, edge, vertex, tessellate,* and *tessellation*. Have students use their own words and give an example of each.

M A T H Word Work

Objective To reinforce vocabulary concepts
Use after Lesson 21.1.

Materials *For each student* solid figure patterns, pp. TR32–36; 4 different-colored markers; crayons; scissors; tape

For each solid figure pattern, have students use crayons to lightly shade all surfaces of the solid figures. Then have students use one marker to write *face* on each face of the cube, rectangular prism, and square pyramid. Have students use a second marker to write *curved surface* on the cone and cylinder.

Have students cut out each pattern, and then fold and tape them so that each makes a solid figure. With a third marker, have students darken the line for each edge of the cube, rectangular prism, and square pyramid. Then have students use a fourth marker to place a dot on each vertex of the figures. Display the figures. As an extension, have students build complex solid figures using several of the figures after completing Lesson 21.2.

Mathematics Across the Grades

LOOKING BACK • Prerequisite Skills

To be ready for Chapter 21, students should have the following understandings and skills:

- **Identify Solid Figures**—name solid figures

Check What You Know

Use page 423 to determine students' knowledge of prerequisite concepts and skills.

Intervention

Help students prepare for the chapter by using the intervention resources described on TE page 423.

LOOKING AT CHAPTER 21 • Essential Skills

Students will

- describe properties of solid figures and name the faces that make up solid figures.
- **identify solid figures within complex solid objects.**
- combine plane figures to form patterns.
- draw and classify polygons and solid figures.
- use the problem solving skill *identify relationships*.

Example

What solid figures were combined to make the figure below?	
Model	**Answer**
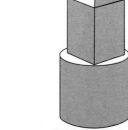	square pyramid, rectangular prism, cylinder

LOOKING AHEAD • Applications

Students will apply what they learn in Chapter 21 to the following new concepts:

- Find Perimeter, Area, and Volume (Chapter 22)
- Patterns for Solid Figures (Grade 4)
- Estimate and Find Volume of Prisms (Grade 4)
- Tessellations (Grade 4)

Differentiated Instruction

Meeting the Needs of All Learners

Extra Support	Activities for All	Enrichment
Alternative Teaching Strategy TE Lessons 21.1, 21.2, 21.3, 21.4, 21.5 **ESOL/ESL** TE Lessons 21.1, 21.2, 21.3, 21.4, 21.5	**Cross-Curricular Connections** **Art:** TE Lesson 21.4 **Fine Arts:** TE Lesson 21.3 **Reading:** TE Lesson 21.5 **Social Studies:** TE/PE Chapter Opener, TE Lesson 21.1 **Vocabulary:** TE p. 422B, PE p. 423 **Writing:** TE Lesson 21.1	**Advanced Learners** TE Lesson 21.4 **Early Finishers** TE Lessons 21.2, 21.5

Combination and Multi-age Classrooms

Grade 2	Grade 3	Grade 4
Skills Trace Across the Grades		
Identify plane shapes and solid figures; sort solid figures; compare solid figures and plane shapes.	**Identify solid figures and their properties; explore tessellations; draw plane and solid figures; recognize a solid figure from different perspectives.**	Classify polygons; explore tessellations with more than one shape; identify patterns for solid figures; find volume of prisms.
Instructional Strategies		
Students on this level may require more time to build conceptual understanding. **Assignments** **Grade 3 Pupil Edition** • Have students work in small groups to complete Lessons 21.1 and 21.5. • Have students use wood geo solids with Lesson 21.2. **Grade 2 Pupil Edition**—pages 331–338	Students on this level should be able to complete all the lessons in the Pupil Edition and all the activities in the Teacher's Edition with minimal adjustments. **Assignment** **Grade 3 Pupil Edition**—pages 422–439	Students on this level will probably require less time to build conceptual understanding. **Assignments** **Grade 3 Pupil Edition** • Compact Lessons 21.1, 21.2, and 21.3. • Challenge students to draw a variety of polygons after completing Lesson 21.4. **Grade 4 Pupil Edition**—pages 644–649

Solid and Plane Figures

Introducing the Chapter

Have students list the plane figures that they have learned. Then review the following solid figures: cube, rectangular prism, cone, pyramid, and cylinder. Have students look at the photo of the historic capitol building. Ask: Do you see any triangles or circles on the building? Possible answer: there are triangles above the windows on the top floor and there are some windows that are circles on the bottom floor.

Using Data

To begin the study of this chapter, have students

- Identify the plane shapes that are seen when looking at the bricks used for the building. rectangles

- Describe the solid figures that make up a school building on campus. Accept reasonable answers.

Problem Solving Project

Purpose To recognize plane figures and solid figures

Grouping small groups

Materials magazines and newspapers

Background The restoration of many Williamsburg buildings began in 1926 and continues today. More than half of the Williamsburg area has been affected by this restoration.

UNDERSTAND • PLAN • SOLVE • CHECK

Have students

- Look through magazines or newspapers to find pictures of buildings with identifiable solid figures and plane figures.

- Show pictures to other groups and describe the buildings by indicating the solid figures and the plane figures that are seen in the buildings.

Graphing Investigations
Begin Week 21.

≡FAST FACT • SOCIAL STUDIES
From 1699 to 1780, Williamsburg was the capital of the colony of Virginia. Many of the original buildings there have been restored to look as they did hundreds of years ago.

PROBLEM SOLVING Look at the historic capitol building. What plane figures do the windows form? What solid figures do you see?

Possible answers: rectangles, circles; cylinders, cones

Historic capitol building, Williamsburg

422

WHY LEARN MATH? A sculptor is an artist who carves or forms a substance like clay to make an image such as a statue. A sculptor often uses solid and plane figures in the process of making statues. For example, clay shaped as a cylinder could be formed to look like an arm. Ask: If a sculptor is making a small statue of an elephant, name some solid or plane shapes that could be used to make the statue. Possible answer: sphere: head; triangle: ear; cylinder: trunk

Family Involvement Activities

These activities provide:

- Letter to the Family
- Math Vocabulary
- Family Game
- Practice (Homework)

Family Involvement Activities, p. FA81

Use this page to help you review and remember
important skills needed for Chapter 21.

✓ IDENTIFY SOLID FIGURES

Choose the best term from the box.

cone	
cube	
cylinder	
pyramid	
rectangular prism	
sphere	

1.
cube

2.
cone

3.
cylinder

4.
cone

5.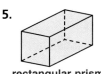
rectangular prism

6.
sphere

7.
pyramid

8.
cylinder

9.
cube

VOCABULARY POWER ✓

REVIEW

quadrilateral [kwä•drə•lat′ər•əl] *noun*

A quadrilateral is a polygon that has
four sides. Look in a dictionary for
quadruple. Is *four* part of its
definition? Explain. **Possible answer:
yes; quadruple means to make four
times as great.**

PREVIEW

face
edge
vertex
tessellate
tessellation

GO ON-LINE www.harcourtschool.com/mathglossary

Chapter 21 **423**

Assessing Prior Knowledge

Use the **Check What You Know** page to determine
whether your students have mastered the prerequisite skills critical for this chapter.

Intervention

- **Diagnose and Prescribe**

Evaluate your students' performance on this page
to determine whether intervention is necessary or
if enrichment is appropriate. Options that provide
instruction, practice, and a check are listed in the
chart below.

✓ CHECK WHAT YOU KNOW RESOURCES

Intervention Copying Masters or CD-ROMs

Enrichment Copying Masters

VOCABULARY POWER

For activities and information about the vocabulary in this chapter, see page 422B.

Were students successful with ✓ **CHECK WHAT YOU KNOW?**

IF . . . NO
THEN . . . INTERVENE

INTERVENTION OPTIONS

IF . . . YES
THEN . . . ENRICH

Skill/Items	Missed more than	Intervene with
Identify Solid Figures, 1–9	2	• *Intervention*, Skill 59

Skill/Items	Missed fewer than	Enrich with
Identify Solid Figures, 1–9	3	• *Intervention*, Enrichment pp. IN369–370

Lesson Planning

PROFESSIONAL DEVELOPMENT

Objective To describe properties of solid figures and name the faces that make up solid figures

Materials *For each group* solid figures, paper, crayons; *For Thinker's Corner* connecting cubes

NCTM Standards
3. Geometry
6. Problem Solving
7. Reasoning and Proof
8. Communication
9. Connections
10. Representation

Vocabulary

face a flat surface of a solid figure

edge the line segment formed where two faces of a solid figure meet

vertex a corner where three or more edges of a solid figure meet

Math Background

These ideas will help students understand the properties of solid figures.

- Solid figures may contain some or all of these parts: faces, edges, and vertices.

- The faces of solid figures can be described using the names of plane figures such as squares, rectangles, and triangles.

- Of the different types of pyramids, only the square pyramid is taught at this level. Students should begin calling it a square pyramid to help them distinguish it from other pyramids they will learn about later on.

- Solid figures are three-dimensional figures because they can be measured in three dimensions: length, width, and height.

Warm-Up Resources

Number of the Day

Transparency **21.1**

Write and solve 4 division sentences using the number of sides on a square. Possible answer: $16 ÷ 4 = 4, 20 ÷ 4 = 5, 24 ÷ 4 = 6, 0 ÷ 4 = 0$

Daily Facts Practice

Have students practice multiplication facts by completing Set E of *Teacher's Resource Book*, p. TR98.

Solve a Problem

Transparency **21.1**

Problem of the Day

Andrea has 1 coin. Simon has 4 more nickels than Pablo and 4 more coins than Andrea. They each have the same amount of money. What coins does each have? Andrea, 1 quarter; Simon, 5 nickels; Pablo, 2 dimes and a nickel

Solution Problem of the Day tab, p. PD21

Intervention and Extension Resources

Alternative Teaching Strategy

MATERIALS *For each group* solid figures, bag

ESOL/ESL

Have students **practice identifying solid figures**.

- Without students seeing what you place in the bag, put in one geometric solid.
- Have a volunteer feel inside the bag and try to identify the figure.
- Ask: What do you feel that gives you a clue to the figure's name?
- After the student has made a guess, take the figure out of the bag. Ask the group to name the faces and identify the solid.

Check students' work.

See also page 426.

KINESTHETIC

VISUAL/SPATIAL

Multistep and Strategy Problems

The following multistep or strategy problem is provided in Lesson 21.1:

Page	Item
427	19

Writing in Mathematics

Have students **compare solid figures**. Have them choose two solid figures and write how they are alike and how they are different. Encourage them to use the terms *face, edge*, and *vertex*. Check students' work.

Social Studies Connection

MATERIALS *For each group* construction paper, tape, scissors, encyclopedia or reference book

Have students **make models of square pyramids**. Encourage students to find out about the pyramids of Egypt or Mexico. Have them make models of the pyramids, noting the number of faces, edges, and vertices. Discuss how the ancient builders were able to make such large structures without modern machinery. Check students' work.

KINESTHETIC

BODILY/KINESTHETIC

Technology Link

Intervention, *Skill 59*

Harcourt Mega Math
Ice Station Exploration, *Frozen Solids,* Levels A, C, D, E, and F

Math Jingles® CD 3–4 • *Track 12*

GO The Harcourt Learning Site
www.harcourtschool.com

Lesson 21.1 Organizer

Objective To describe properties of solid figures and name the faces that make up solid figures

Vocabulary face, edge, vertex

Materials *For each group* solid figures, paper, crayons; *For Thinker's Corner* connecting cubes

---

1 INTRODUCE

QUICK REVIEW provides review of prerequisite skills.

WHY LEARN THIS? You can use this information to identify the shapes used in solid figures you see around you. *Share the lesson objective with students.*

---

2 TEACH

Guided Instruction

• *Introduce the lesson by having students look at the illustrations of solid figures.*

What everyday objects can you name that have the same shape as a cylinder? Possible answers: candle, roll of coins, can of dog food, jar

How are a sphere, a cylinder, and a cone alike and how are they different? They all have curved surfaces; a cylinder and a cone have flat surfaces and a sphere doesn't.

MODIFYING INSTRUCTION Tell students that the base of a solid figure is the bottom face of the figure. The term *square pyramid* means that this solid figure has a square base and has the shape of a pyramid.

• *Display the solid figure manipulatives.*

Which two solid figures have the same number of faces, edges, and vertices?
cube and rectangular prism

Where are the vertices on the square pyramid? Students should indicate the 4 corners of the square base and the point where the triangular faces meet.

▶ **Learn**

FIGURE IT OUT Use names of solid figures to describe objects around you.

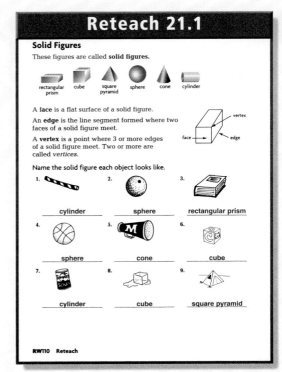

cube

rectangular prism

sphere

cylinder

square pyramid

cone

A **face** is a flat surface of a solid figure.

An **edge** is the line segment formed where two faces meet.

A **vertex** is a point where three or more edges meet. Two or more are called vertices.

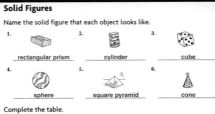

face

edge

vertex

A rectangular prism has 6 faces, 12 edges, and 8 vertices.

• How many edges does a cube have? **12 edges**

• **REASONING** Which solid figures will roll? Explain how you know. **Possible answers: spheres, cylinders, and cones; they have curved surfaces.**

424

Quick Review
Name each plane figure.

1.
circle

2.
triangle

3.
square

4.
rectangle

5.
triangle

VOCABULARY
face   edge   vertex

Technology Link
More Practice:
Harcourt Mega Math
Ice Station Exploration,
Frozen Solids,
Levels A, C, D, E, and F

Reteach 21.1

Solid Figures

These figures are called **solid figures.**

rectangular prism   cube   square pyramid   sphere   cone   cylinder

A **face** is a flat surface of a solid figure.

An **edge** is the line segment formed where two faces of a solid figure meet.

A **vertex** is a point where 3 or more edges of a solid figure meet. Two or more are called *vertices.*

vertex
face   edge

Name the solid figure each object looks like.

1. cylinder   2. sphere   3. rectangular prism

4. sphere   5. cone   6. cube

7. cylinder   8. cube   9. square pyramid

RW110   Reteach

Practice 21.1

Solid Figures

Name the solid figure that each object looks like.

1. rectangular prism   2. cylinder   3. cube

4. sphere   5. square pyramid   6. cone

Complete the table.

	Figure	Faces	Edges	Vertices
7.	Cube	6	12	8
8.	Rectangular prism	6	12	8
9.	Square pyramid	5	8	5

Mixed Review

Compare the numbers. Write <, >, or = in each ◯.

10. 3,535 ⊜ 3,355   11. 67,100 ⊜ 67,010
12. 53,701 ⊜ 53,701   13. 9,999 ⊜ 10,000

Find the quotient.

14. 25 ÷ 5 = **5**   15. 45 ÷ 9 = **5**   16. 35 ÷ 7 = **5**   17. 50 ÷ 10 = **5**

18. 49 ÷ 7 = **7**   19. 15 ÷ 5 = **3**   20. 81 ÷ 9 = **9**   21. 54 ÷ 6 = **9**

Find the difference.

22. 25 − 5 = **20**   23. 45 − 9 = **36**   24. 35 − 7 = **28**   25. 50 − 10 = **40**

26. 49 − 7 = **42**   27. 15 − 5 = **10**   28. 81 − 9 = **72**   29. 54 − 6 = **48**

PW110   Practice

Tracing Faces

Use names of plane figures to describe the faces of solid figures.

Activity

MATERIALS: solid figures (square pyramid, rectangular prism, cube), paper, crayons

Trace the faces of several solid figures. Then name the faces that make up each solid figure.

STEP 1

On a large sheet of paper, make a chart like the one below. Trace the faces of each solid figure.

Name of Figure	Faces	Names and Number of Faces
Square pyramid		

STEP 2

Record the names and number of faces for each solid figure.

Name of Figure	Faces	Names and Number of Faces
Square pyramid		1 square 4 triangles

Possible answers: all of the faces of a cube are squares. Some of the faces of the square pyramid are triangles. None of the faces of a square pyramid are circles.

- **REASONING** Use the words *all, some,* or *none* to describe the faces of the solid figures you traced.

MATH IDEA Some solid figures have faces, edges, and vertices. Faces of solid figures are plane figures such as squares, rectangles, and triangles.

▶ Check

1. Describe the faces of a cube.
The faces of a cube are 6 squares that are congruent.

Name the solid figure that each object looks like.

2.
sphere

3.
cone

4.
cylinder

5.
cube

LESSON CONTINUES ▶

Chapter 21 425

North Carolina Standards 3.01 Use appropriate vocabulary to compare, describe, and classify
- and three-dimensional figures.

- *Discuss the Activity.*
  How many faces does a cube have? 6 faces
  What shape are they? square

- *Have students read the Math Idea.* **Which can be stacked, a cone or a cylinder? Explain.**
  A cylinder; it has two flat surfaces.

3 PRACTICE

Guided Practice

Do Check Exercises 1–5 with your students. Identify students who are having difficulty and choose appropriate lesson resources to provide assistance.

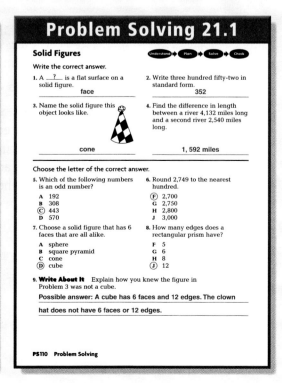

Challenge 21.1

Folding Solid Figures

You can make solid figures with paper. Look at the patterns on this page.

- Copy the patterns onto grid paper.
- Cut on the solid lines.
- Fold on the dotted lines.
- Use tape to hold your solid figure together.
- What figures did you make?

a rectangular prism and a cube

CV110 Challenge

Problem Solving 21.1

Solid Figures

Understand ▸ Plan ▸ Solve ▸ Check

Write the correct answer.

1. A __?__ is a flat surface on a solid figure.
face

2. Write three hundred fifty-two in standard form.
352

3. Name the solid figure this object looks like.
cone

4. Find the difference in length between a river 4,132 miles long and a second river 2,540 miles long.
1, 592 miles

Choose the letter of the correct answer.

5. Which of the following numbers is an odd number?
A 192
B 308
C 443
D 570

6. Round 2,749 to the nearest hundred.
F 2,700
G 2,750
H 2,800
J 3,000

7. Choose a solid figure that has 6 faces that are all alike.
A sphere
B square pyramid
C cone
D cube

8. How many edges does a rectangular prism have?
F 5
G 6
H 8
J 12

9. Write About It Explain how you knew that the figure in Problem 3 was not a cube.

Possible answer: A cube has 6 faces and 12 edges. The clown hat does not have 6 faces or 12 edges.

PS110 Problem Solving

425

Students may have difficulty distinguishing between cubes and non-cubical rectangular prisms. Have students trace one face of a cube and compare the tracing to the other faces. Repeat the process with a non-cubical rectangular prism to see the different sizes and shapes of the faces.

Independent Practice

Note that Exercise 19 is a **multistep or strategy problem**. Assign Exercises 6–20.

MULTISTEP OR STRATEGY PROBLEM To solve Exercise 19, students can add to find the total number of shells that Cindy has. Then students can divide by 4 to find how many groups she can make.

▶ Practice and Problem Solving · Extra Practice, page 438, Set A

Name the solid figure that each object looks like.

6.
square pyramid

7.
cube

8.
sphere

9.
rectangular prism

Which solid figure has the faces shown? Write *a, b,* or *c.*

10. b

11. a

12. c

a. rectangular prism
b. square pyramid
c. cube

Copy and complete the table.

FIGURE	FACES	EDGES	VERTICES
13. Rectangular prism	▓ 6	▓ 12	▓ 8
14. Cube	▓ 6	▓ 12	▓ 8
15. Square pyramid	▓ 5	▓ 8	▓ 5

16. **REASONING** An analogy is a comparison of similar features of objects. For example, *day* is to *light* as *night* is to *darkness.* Complete each analogy.

   a. A cereal *box* is to a *rectangular prism* as a *ball* is to a __?__ . **sphere**

   b. A *square* is to a *cube* as a *rectangle* is to a __?__ .
   rectangular prism

18. Josh painted a box shaped like a rectangular prism. Each face was a different color. How many colors did Josh use? **6 colors**

17. ✎ **Write About It** List objects you might find at a grocery store that look like each of the following solid figures. Think of at least two objects for each figure.
Check students' lists.
   a. sphere

   b. rectangular prism

   c. cylinder

426

Alternative Teaching Strategy · Scaffolded Instruction

PURPOSE Students use clay to identify faces in solid figures.

MATERIALS *For each group* cube, rectangular prism, square pyramid, clay, paper, pencil or crayon

Step 1

Explain to students that they can press the sides of solid objects into clay to see the faces, just as if they traced them.

Have students make a table with three columns labeled *Name of Figure, Number of Faces,* and *Names of Faces.*

Name of Figure	Number of Faces	Names of Faces

Step 2

Next, ask students to flatten their pieces of clay. Then have students press each face of the cube into the clay.

Step 3

Ask students to count the number of faces they have made in the clay. **6** Then ask them to identify the shape of the faces. **square**

Have students record this information in their tables.

PROFESSIONAL DEVELOPMENT

Step 4

Have students repeat the procedure with the rectangular prism and square pyramid. Encourage them to press all faces into the clay and then count the number and examine the shape of each face. **rectangular prism: 6 faces, 4 rectangles, 2 squares; square pyramid: 5 faces, 4 triangles, 1 square**

19. Cindy has 19 large shells and 17 small shells. How many groups of 4 shells can she make?
9 groups of 4 shells

20. Write a problem about a solid figure. Give clues about the figure. Exchange with a classmate and decide what the figure is.
Check students' work.

21. Which of the following is true about the figure below? **C**

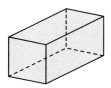

A It is a square pyramid.
B It has 8 faces.
C It has 12 edges.
D It has 6 vertices.

22. Carl built this figure with blocks. Which term *best* describes the figure that he made? **A**

A cube
B square pyramid
C cone
D cylinder

Problem Solving — Thinker's Corner ✦

VISUAL THINKING You can use connecting cubes or other blocks to model solid figures.

For 1–4, build and name the figure. **Check students' models.**

1. rectangular prism

2. cube

3. rectangular prism

4.

rectangular prism

5. Use 27 blocks to build a cube. Then use the same number of blocks to build a rectangular prism.

Check students' models. The cube has 3 layers of 3 rows of 3. The rectangular prism has 1 layer of 3 rows of 9.

Problem Solving — Thinker's Corner ✦

• *Discuss the activity with students.*
How can you decide how many cubes you will need to build each figure?
Possible answer: Look at the front and side of the picture of the figure to see how many cubes are in each layer.
REASONING How could you change the figure in Exercise 1 to make it a cube?
Possible answer: Add another layer with 3 rows of 3 cubes.

4 ASSESS

Summarize the lesson by having students:

DISCUSS Which solid figure has 6 faces that are the same? cube Which solid figures have curved surfaces? sphere, cylinder, and cone

 **WRITE** List the number of faces, edges, and vertices for the following solid figures: cube, rectangular prism, and square pyramid. cube: 6 faces, 12 edges, 8 vertices; rectangular prism: 6 faces, 12 edges, 8 vertices; square pyramid: 5 faces, 8 edges, 5 vertices

LESSON QUIZ
Name the solid figure that each object looks like.

Transparency
21.1

1. roll of pennies cylinder

2. marble sphere

3. shoe box rectangular prism

4. a ones block cube

427

Lesson Planning

PROFESSIONAL DEVELOPMENT

Objective To identify solid figures within complex solid objects

NCTM Standards
3. Geometry
6. Problem Solving
8. Communication
9. Connections
10. Representation

Math Background
Consider the following when introducing combining solid figures.

- Some objects are made by combining two or more solid figures.

- Provide models of solid figures for students to observe and handle.

- Encourage students to combine the solid figures to make their own complex objects.

Warm-Up Resources

Number of the Day

Transparency **21.2**

Write and solve four division sentences. Use the number of faces on a rectangular prism as either the quotient, dividend, or divisor. Possible answers: $6 \div 1 = 6$; $6 \div 3 = 2$; $18 \div 6 = 3$; $18 \div 3 = 6$

Daily Facts Practice

Have students practice multiplication facts by completing Set F of *Teacher's Resource Book*, p. TR98.

Solve a Problem

Transparency **21.2**

Problem of the Day

Carl's solid figure has 6 faces and 8 vertices. Anna's figure has 1 less face and 3 fewer vertices than Carl's. Name their figures. Anna—square pyramid; Carl—cube or rectangular prism

Solution Problem of the Day tab, p. PD21

Intervention and Extension Resources

Alternative Teaching Strategy

Have students **practice combining solid figures** by using class-room objects. Have students identify solid figures within the classroom, such as a pencil, desk, or box. Have them explore ways the objects can be combined and list the solid figures that were combined to make the complex objects. Check students' work.

KINESTHETIC

VISUAL/SPATIAL

Multistep and Strategy Problems

The following multistep or strategy problem is provided in Lesson 21.2:

Page	Item
429	14

ESOL/ESL

MATERIALS *For each pair* magazines, solid figures

ESOL/ESL

Have students look through magazines to **locate pictures of objects whose shapes could be built by combining solid figures**. When students find a picture of a complex object, they should complete the following sentence:

This shape could be made by combining _____ _____.

Students should then use the solid figures to make the shape. Check students' work.

VISUAL

VISUAL/SPATIAL

Early Finishers

MATERIALS *For each group* solid figures

Have students **make complex solid objects**. Give students the following solid figures: 4 cubes, 4 rectangular prisms, 3 square pyramids, 3 cylinders, and 2 cones. Ask them to make a structure, using all the figures. Allow time for students to compare their structures and determine different ways the figures can be combined. Check students' work.

KINESTHETIC

BODILY/KINESTHETIC

Technology Link

Intervention, *Skill 59*

Harcourt Mega Math
Ice Station Exploration,
Frozen Solids, Level B

Lesson 21.2 Organizer

Objective To identify solid figures within complex solid objects

---

1 INTRODUCE

QUICK REVIEW provides review of prerequisite skills.

WHY LEARN THIS? When you know how to identify solid figures, you'll notice them in objects around you. *Share the lesson objective with students.*

---

2 TEACH

Guided Instruction

- *Direct students' attention to the Learn section.*
  How is a cube different from a square?
  Possible answer: a cube is a solid figure; each face of a cube is a square.

- *Have students look at Examples A–C.*
  What real-life object does Example C look like? Possible answer: a bench
  How many solid figures are combined in each Example? Example A: 2, Example B: 4, Example C: 3

- *Discuss the questions following the Examples.*
  If you were building a model of a rocket from solid figures, what two figures might you use? Possible answer: a cylinder and a cone

- *Direct students' attention to the photo of the castle.*
  What solid figures do you see in the castle?
  Possible answer: cones, cylinders, rectangular prisms

MODIFYING INSTRUCTION Have students work in groups to construct and combine solid figures using pp. TR32–36.

---

3 PRACTICE

Guided Practice

Do Check Exercises 1–4 with your students. Identify students who are having difficulty and choose appropriate lesson resources to provide assistance.

LESSON 2 Combine Solid Figures

▶ Learn

PUT IT ALL TOGETHER Some objects are made up of two or more solid figures put together. Look at the house on the right. What solid figures make up the shape of the house?

Look at each part of the house separately. Think about the solid figures you know.

cube   square pyramid   rectangular prism

So, the house is made up of a cube, a square pyramid, and a rectangular prism.

⭐ **MATH IDEA** Solid figures can be combined to make different solid objects.

Examples

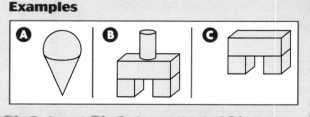
Ⓐ   Ⓑ   Ⓒ

- What solid figures are used to make Object A?
  a sphere and a cone
- What solid figures are used to make Object B?
  2 cubes, a rectangular prism, and a cylinder

▶ Check

1. **Explain** how you can make Object B look like Object C. **Remove the cylinder.**

428

▲ Craigievar Castle, near Alford, Scotland

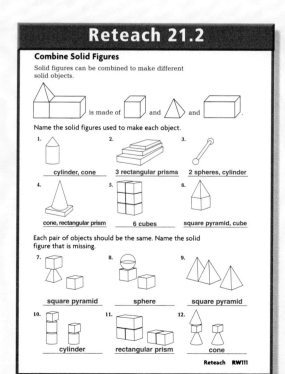

Reteach 21.2

Combine Solid Figures

Solid figures can be combined to make different solid objects.

_____ is made of _____ and _____ and _____.

Name the solid figures used to make each object.

1. cylinder, cone
2. 3 rectangular prisms
3. 2 spheres, cylinder
4. cone, rectangular prism
5. 6 cubes
6. square pyramid, cube

Each pair of objects should be the same. Name the solid figure that is missing.

7. square pyramid
8. sphere
9. square pyramid
10. cylinder
11. rectangular prism
12. cone

Reteach RW111

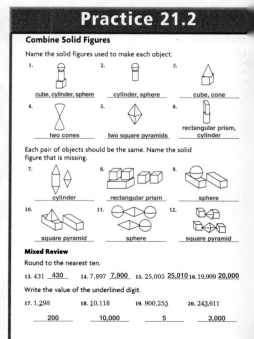

Practice 21.2

Combine Solid Figures

Name the solid figures used to make each object.

1. cube, cylinder, sphere
2. cylinder, sphere
3. cube, cone
4. two cones
5. two square pyramids
6. rectangular prism, cylinder

Each pair of objects should be the same. Name the solid figure that is missing.

7. cylinder
8. rectangular prism
9. sphere
10. square pyramid
11. sphere
12. square pyramid

Mixed Review

Round to the nearest ten.

13. 431 **430**
14. 7,897 **7,900**
15. 25,005 **25,010**
16. 19,999 **20,000**

Write the value of the underlined digit.

17. 1,298 **200**
18. 10,118 **10,000**
19. 900,255 **5**
20. 243,611 **3,000**

Practice PW111

Name the solid figures used to make each object.

2.  a cone,
a cylinder,
a sphere

3.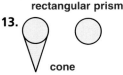
a rectangular prism, 4 cylinders

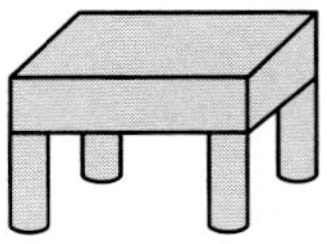

4.
2 square pyramids,
a cube

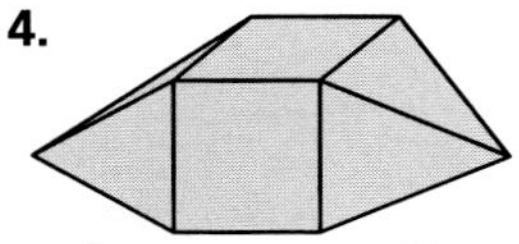

Practice and Problem Solving

Extra Practice, page 438, Set B

Name the solid figures used to make each object.

5.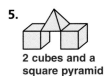
2 cubes and a
square pyramid

6.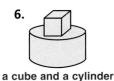
a cube and a cylinder

7.
a sphere, a cylinder, and a
rectangular prism

Each pair of objects should be the same. Name the
solid figure that is missing.

8.  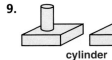 cone

9.
cylinder

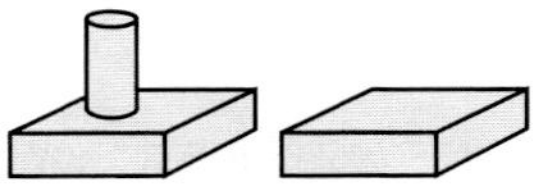

10.
rectangular prism

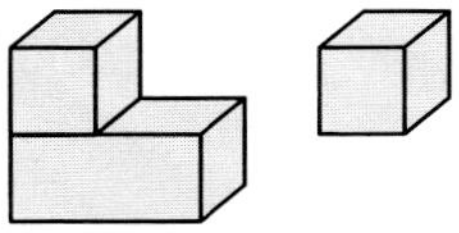

11.
square pyramid

12.
cube

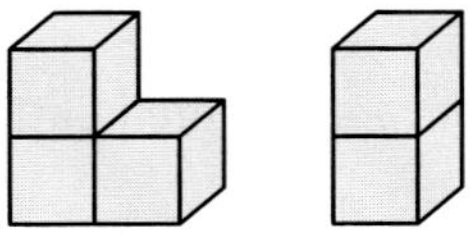

13.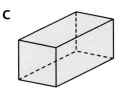
cone

14. Gwen had three $1 bills and 4 dimes. She paid $0.75 for a pen and $1.20 for a snack. How much money does she have left? $1.45

15. Vocabulary Power The word *polygon* comes from a Greek word that means "many angles." Draw a polygon. How many angles does it have? **Check students' responses.**

Getting Ready for the EOG Test

16. Which solid figure below has exactly 5 faces? **D**

A 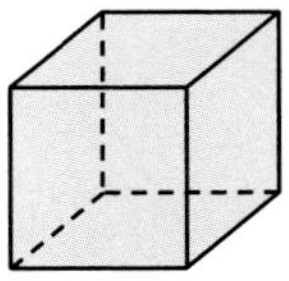 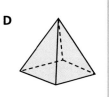 B 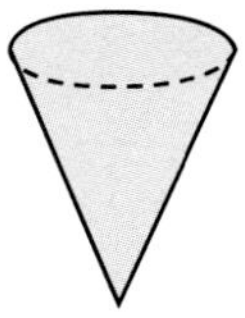   C 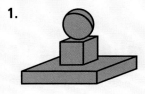 D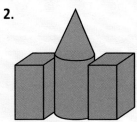

Chapter 21 **429**

* **North Carolina Standards 3.01** Use appropriate vocabulary to compare, describe, and classify
2- and three-dimensional figures.

Challenge 21.2

The Missing Half

Each figure below was once a cube, rectangular prism,
square pyramid, sphere, cone, or cylinder. Each has been
cut in half with one of the halves removed.
• Complete the solid figure.
• Name the solid figure. Check students' drawings.

1. 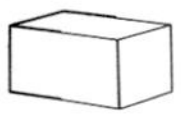 rectangular prism   2. 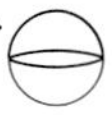 sphere
3.  square pyramid   4.  cylinder
5. 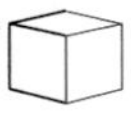 cube   6.  cone

Each figure below is made from two solids. One solid has   Check
been cut in half with one of the halves removed.   students' drawings.
Complete the figure. Name the solid figures.

7.  square pyramid; cube   8.  cone, cylinder

Challenge **CW111**

Problem Solving 21.2

Combine Solid Figures   Understand ➤ Plan ➤ Solve ➤ Check

Write the correct answer.

1. Which solid figures have at least one face that is a square?
   cube; square pyramid; some rectangular prisms

2. Name the solid figures used to make this figure. 
   square pyramid; rectangular prism

3. Name the solid figures used to make this object. 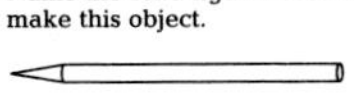
   cone; cylinder

4. Tammy keeps a monthly record of the number of books she reads. This month it shows:
   ⅢⅢⅢ II
   How many books has she read?
   12 books

Choose the letter of the correct answer.

5. What solid figure has four faces that are triangles?
   A cone   C square pyramid
   B sphere   D cylinder

6. Name the missing factor in the number sentence 6 × __ = 42.
   F 3   H 6
   G 4   J 7

7. Describe what the solid figure would look like if the cube were removed. 
   A sphere   C cone
   B square pyramid   D cube

8. What solid figures would you have if this figure were cut in half? 
   F sphere and a cylinder
   G two cylinders
   H cube and a cylinder
   J cone and a cylinder

9. **Write About It** Explain how you selected your answer to Problem 8.
   Possible answer: The object is a cylinder. A cylinder cut in half
   is just 2 cylinders.

Problem Solving **PS111**

COMMON ERROR ALERT

Watch for students who have difficulty visualizing the solid figures that make up each complex object. Have students use geometric solids to construct the complex objects to determine the solid figures used to make each object.

Independent Practice

Note that Exercise 14 is a **multistep or strategy problem**. Assign Exercises 5–15.

Vocabulary Power Ask students to name some polygons that end in *–gon*. Discuss the number of angles that each of these polygons has. Point out that the beginning of each of these names is a clue that tells how many angles the polygon has.

4 ASSESS

Summarize the lesson by having students:

Discuss Which solid figures could you use to model a set of stair steps? Explain how you could combine the figures to build the steps.
Possible answers: You could place a cube on top of a rectangular prism; you could use 2 cubes as a base and place 1 cube on top.

Write Explain how to combine a cube and a square pyramid to make a solid figure that looks like a house. Place the square pyramid on top of the cube so that it looks like the roof of a house.

LESSON QUIZ   Transparency **21.2**

Name the solid figures used to make each object.

1.
sphere, rectangular prism, cube

2.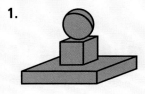
cone, cylinder,
2 rectangular prisms

429

Lesson Planning

PROFESSIONAL DEVELOPMENT

Objective To combine plane figures to form tessellations

NCTM Standards
2. Algebra
3. Geometry
6. Problem Solving
7. Reasoning and Proof
8. Communication
10. Representation

Math Background
These ideas will help students understand combining plane figures to form tessellations.

- Plane figures tessellate if they combine to cover a surface without overlapping or leaving any space between them.

- Tessellations are repeated patterns formed by plane figures.

- Not all plane figures can be combined to form tessellations.

Vocabulary
tessellate to cover a surface by repeating a plane figure without overlapping or leaving any space between the figures

tessellation a repeating pattern formed by plane figures that covers a surface without gaps or overlaps

Warm-Up Resources

Build Number Sense
3 2 1

Number of the Day
Transparency **21.3**

Write and solve four division sentences using the number of minutes between 4:18 P.M. and 4:38 P.M. as the dividend. Possible answers: 20 ÷ 4 = 5, 20 ÷ 5 = 4, 20 ÷ 10 = 2, 20 ÷ 2 = 10

Review Basic Facts
8 +3

Daily Facts Practice

Have students practice multiplication facts by completing Set G of *Teacher's Resource Book*, p. TR98.

Solve a Problem

Transparency **21.3**

Problem of the Day

Sara drew a plane figure with 4 equal sides and 4 right angles. Luz drew a plane figure with no straight sides and no angles inside Sara's figure. Ali drew a plane figure with 3 sides and 3 angles on top of Sara's figure. How did the design look? Possible answer: Sara drew a square, Luz drew a circle inside the square, and Ali drew a triangle on top of the square.

Solution Problem of the Day tab, p. PD21

Intervention and Extension Resources

Alternative Teaching Strategy

MATERIALS *For each group* pattern blocks

Have students **make tessellations by using pattern blocks**.

- Give each group four triangles and ask them to fit them together so they do not overlap and there is no space between them.
- Repeat the same directions with four square blocks and then six hexagon blocks.
- Ask: What do you observe about the pattern blocks? Possible answer: All of the blocks tessellate because they do not overlap and there is no space between them.

KINESTHETIC

BODILY/KINESTHETIC

Multistep and Strategy Problems

The following multistep or strategy problem is provided in Lesson 21.3:

Page	Item
431	15

ESOL/ESL

Help students **understand the difference between** *tessellate* **and** *tessellation*. Display the words *tessellate* and *tessellation*. Explain that *tessellate* is a verb used to tell what plane figures do when they combine to cover a surface without overlapping or leaving any space between them. A *tessellation* is the repeating pattern formed by the combined figures. To form the word *tessellation* from *tessellate*, drop the final *e* and add *ion* to the end of the word. Explain that this ending often turns a verb, or action word, into a noun. Say the words *celebrate, graduate,* and *communicate*. Have students turn each word into a noun by dropping the final *e* and adding *ion*. Then ask them to use each noun in a sentence. Check students' work.

AUDITORY, VISUAL

VERBAL/LINGUISTIC

Fine Arts Connection

MATERIALS *For each group* art books

Encourage students to **identify tessellations in artwork**. In addition to using art books, encourage students to find artwork using approved Internet resources. Have each group select a favorite piece of artwork to present to the class. Ask them to share the title of the piece and name of the artist and to identify the plane figures and tessellations. Check students' work.

VISUAL

VISUAL/SPATIAL

Technology Link

Harcourt Mega Math
Ice Station Exploration,
Polar Planes, Level N

Lesson 21.3 Organizer

Objective To combine plane figures to form tessellations

Vocabulary tessellate, tessellation

---

1 INTRODUCE

QUICK REVIEW provides review of prerequisite skills.

WHY LEARN THIS? You'll be able to recognize tessellations in artwork. *Share the lesson objective with students.*

---

2 TEACH

Guided Instruction

- *Check students' understanding of tessellation.*
  What is meant by *without overlapping*?
  Possible answer: not crossing over or covering part of another figure

- *Direct students' attention to the row of figures that tessellate.*
  What are the names of the figures that tessellate? square, hexagon, triangle

- *Have students look at the row of figures that do not tessellate.*
  What is the difference between figures that tessellate and figures that do not tessellate?
  Possible answer: When you place the figures that tessellate next to each other, they fit together without leaving any spaces. The circles and pentagons leave gaps between them.

MODIFYING INSTRUCTION Have students trace two or more figures on *Teacher's Resource Book* p. TR39 and combine them in a tessellation. Then have students use the same combined figures to make a different tessellation by flipping and turning them.

---

3 PRACTICE

Guided Practice

Do Check Exercises 1–5 with your students. Identify students who are having difficulty and choose appropriate lesson resources to provide assistance.

LESSON

3 Tessellations

Quick Review
Name each figure.
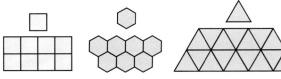
1. trapezoid 2. triangle pentagon
3. rectangle 4. octagon 5.

VOCABULARY
tessellate
tessellation

▶ Learn

TWIST AND TURN M. C. Escher, a Dutch artist, created many works of art by combining figures in a special way.

When plane figures combine to cover a surface without overlapping or leaving any space between them, those figures **tessellate**. The repeating pattern formed by the figures is called a **tessellation**.

These figures tessellate.

 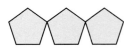

These figures do not tessellate.

- Describe the figure in the art by M. C. Escher. Does the figure tessellate? How do you know? **Possible answers: a person; yes; there is no space between the figures.**

MATH IDEA Some plane figures can be combined to form tessellations.

▶ Check

1. **Explain** how you know that circles do not tessellate.
   Possible answer: when placed side by side, circles leave gaps between them, so they do not tessellate.

430

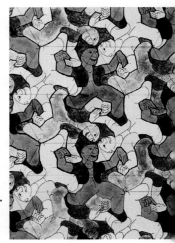

▲
Symmetry Drawing E21 by M. C. Escher. ©2000 Cordon Art-Baarn-Holland. All rights reserved.

Reteach 21.3

Tessellations

When you combine plane figures so that they cover a surface without overlapping or leaving a space between them, you are making a **tessellation**.

Not all figures tessellate.

The squares tessellate.	The octagons do not tessellate.
The parallelograms tessellate.	The circles do not tessellate.

Tell if each figure will tessellate. Write *yes* or *no*.

1. yes   2. no   3. yes   4. no

Trace and cut out each figure. Use each figure to make a tessellation. You may color your design. **Check students' drawings.**

5.

6.

RW112 Reteach

Practice 21.3

Tessellations

Tell if each figure will tessellate. Write *yes* or *no*.

1. yes   2. yes   3. no   4. yes

Trace and cut out each figure. Use each figure to make a tessellation. You may color your design. **Check students' designs.**

5.   6.

Mixed Review

Write each number in standard form.

7. 20,000 + 800 + 5   8. 30,000 + 6,000 + 10   9. 50,000 + 7,000 + 3
   20,805   36,010   57,003

Estimate each sum. **Possible estimates are given.**

10. 874	11. 952	12. 892	13. 352	14. 925
+ 635	+ 411	+ 999	+ 429	+ 659
1,500	1,400	1,900	800	1,600

Write the number of sides and angles each plane figure has.

15. hexagon   16. octagon   17. pentagon
    6; 6   8; 8   5; 5

PW112 Practice

Tell if each figure will tessellate. Write *yes* or *no*.

2.
no

3.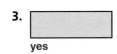
yes

4.
yes

5.
no

Practice and Problem Solving
Extra Practice, page 438, Set C

Tell if each figure will tessellate. Write *yes* or *no*.

6.
yes

7.
yes

8.
no

9.
no

Trace and cut out each figure. Use each figure to make a tessellation. You may color your design. **Check students' designs.**

10.

11.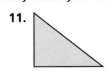

12.

13. Is this a tessellation? Explain why or why not. **No, there is space between the figures.**

14. 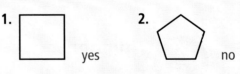 **Write About It** Explain how you know that this figure will not tessellate. **Possible answer: when you place 2 or more figures side by side, there are gaps between them.**

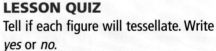

15. Pilar wants to buy 6 pencils. Store A sells 6 pencils for $0.49. Store B's price is $0.09 each. Where should Pilar buy her pencils in order to spend the least amount of money? Explain. **Store A; Store B's pencils cost $0.54 in all.**

Getting Ready for the EOG Test

16. Which solid figure has exactly 5 vertices? **B**

A cube
B square pyramid
C cylinder
D rectangular prism

17. How many faces does a cube have? **C**

A 4
B 5
C 6
D 8

Chapter 21 **431**

North Carolina Standards 3.01 Use appropriate vocabulary to compare, describe, and classify two- and three-dimensional figures.

Independent Practice

Note that Exercise 15 is a **multistep or strategy problem.** Assign Exercises 6–15.

SCAFFOLDED INSTRUCTION Use the prompts on Transparency 21 to guide instruction for the multistep or strategy problem in Exercise 15.

Transparency **21**

4 ASSESS

Summarize the lesson by having students:

DISCUSS How can you tell whether a figure can tessellate? Possible answer: if you can combine several of the same figure without overlapping or leaving any space between them, then the figure can tessellate.

WRITE Draw a tessellation pattern in your journal. Tell what plane figure or figures you drew and why your pattern is a tessellation. Check students' work.

LESSON QUIZ
Tell if each figure will tessellate. Write *yes* or *no*.

Transparency **21.3**

1.
yes

2.
no

3.
yes

4.
no

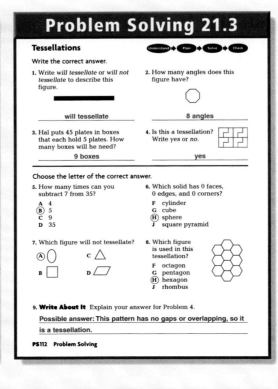

Lesson Planning

PROFESSIONAL DEVELOPMENT

Objective To draw and classify polygons and solid figures

Materials *For each student* polygon worksheet, p. TR31; square dot paper, p. TR30; ruler; *For Linkup* paper clip, 2 pencils, ruler

NCTM Standards
3. Geometry
6. Problem Solving
8. Communication
10. Representation

Math Background
These ideas will help students draw and classify plane and solid figures.

● All polygons are closed figures made up of line segments that share end points.

● Students can classify polygons by the number of sides and angles.

● Students can classify solid figures by the number of sides, edges, and vertices.

● Drawing figures gives students an opportunity to apply their knowledge of polygons and solid figures.

Warm-Up Resources

Number of the Day

Transparency **21.4**

The number of the day is the number of days in one week. Multiply this number by the number of dimes in one dollar. What is the product? 70

Daily Facts Practice

Have students practice multiplication and division facts by completing Set A of *Teacher's Resource Book*, p. TR99.

Transparency **21.4**

Problem of the Day

Luis and Jenna each had the same amount of money. Luis had three quarters. Jenna had 10 coins. What coins did Jenna have? Possible answers: 5 dimes and 5 nickels; 1 half-dollar, 4 nickels, and 5 pennies

Solution Problem of the Day tab, p. PD21

Intervention and Extension Resources

Alternative Teaching Strategy

MATERIALS *For each student* pattern blocks, paper, pencil

ESOL/ESL

Have students **draw polygons.** Tell students to trace several different pattern blocks. Below each drawing, have students label the polygon and write the number of sides and angles.

See also page 434.

KINESTHETIC

VISUAL/SPATIAL

Art Connection

MATERIALS *For each student* ruler, pencil, markers or crayons

Have students **draw pictures by combining plane figures.** Suggest that students try a variety of things, such as an airplane, a traffic light, a dog, or a robot. Encourage students to draw in pencil first and then draw over the pencil lines with markers or crayons.

VISUAL

INTRAPERSONAL/INTROSPECTIVE

Multistep and Strategy Problems

The following multistep or strategy problem is provided in Lesson 21.4:

Page	Item
435	17

Advanced Learners

MATERIALS *For each student* dot paper, p. TR30; ruler; pencil

Have students **draw several polygons** with 6, 8, and 10 sides. Encourage students to darken the dots that are endpoints shared by the line segments of the polygon.

VISUAL

VISUAL/SPATIAL

Technology Link

Intervention, *Skill 59*

Lesson 21.4 Organizer

Objective To draw and classify polygons and solid figures

Materials *For each student* polygon worksheet, p. TR31; square dot paper, p. TR30; ruler; *For Linkup* paper clip, 2 pencils, ruler

1 INTRODUCE

QUICK REVIEW provides review of prerequisite skills.

WHY LEARN THIS? You can draw many different figures and objects with line segments. *Share the lesson objective with students.*

2 TEACH

Guided Instruction

- *Discuss Step 1 with students.*
  Suppose that you only drew a line segment from A to B and from B to C. Would this be a polygon? Explain. No; it can only be a polygon if it is a closed figure.
  What is formed when two line segments share one endpoint? an angle

- *Direct students' attention to the Reasoning question.*
  How do you know if either of these line segments is a line of symmetry? Possible answer: You can check each line segment by folding the rectangle in half along each line segment. If the sides match exactly, then the line segment is a line of symmetry.

4 Draw Figures

LESSON

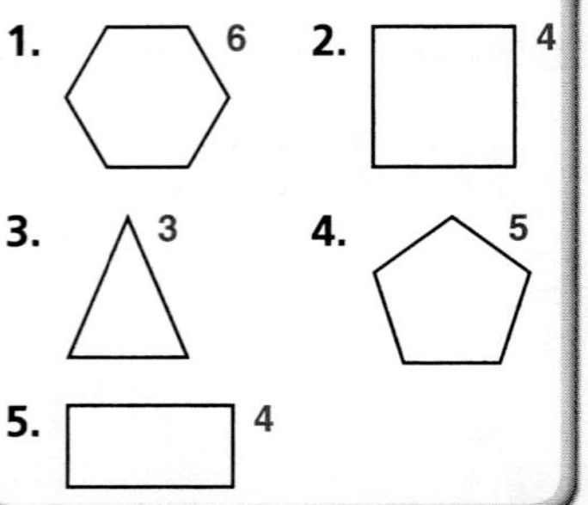

▶ Learn

DRAW IT You can draw polygons using line segments. Since a polygon is a closed figure, it will begin and end at the same point.

Activity 1 Draw plane figures.

MATERIALS: polygon worksheet, pencil, ruler

STEP 1
On your worksheet, use a ruler to draw line segments from A to B, from B to C, and from C to A.

STEP 2
Use a ruler to draw line segments from D to E, E to F, F to G, G to H, H to I, and I to D.

STEP 3
Use a ruler to draw line segments from J to K, K to L, L to M, and M to J.

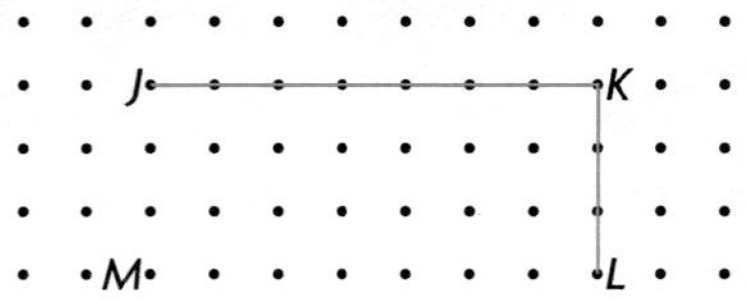

- What polygons did you draw? How many sides and angles does each polygon have? **triangle, hexagon, and rectangle; triangle: 3 sides and 3 angles; hexagon: 6 sides and 6 angles; rectangle: 4 sides and 4 angles**
- Describe the angles in each polygon that you drew. **triangle: 3 acute angles; hexagon: 2 right angles, 4 obtuse angles; rectangle: 4 right angles**
- **REASONING** Can a line segment be drawn on a rectangle to form 2 congruent triangles? to form 2 congruent rectangles? Draw pictures on dot paper to explain. **Yes; yes; check students' drawings.**

432

Quick Review

Write the number of sides each figure has.

1. 6
2. 4
3. 3
4. 5
5. 4

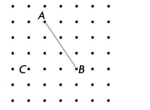

Reteach 21.4

Draw Figures

You can use line segments on dot paper to draw polygons and solid figures.

Draw a rectangular prism.

Draw the front face.	Draw slanted line segments from 3 corners.	Connect the slanted segments to complete the top and one face.	Draw dotted line segments to show the faces that can't be seen.

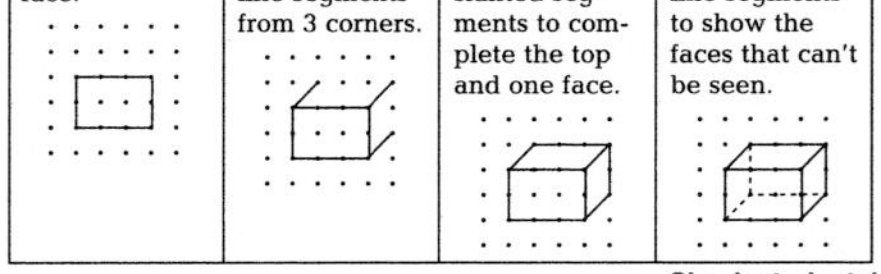

Check students' drawings.

Follow the steps above to draw each solid figure.

1. a rectangular prism that is 4 units wide and 2 units high
2. a cube that is 3 units wide

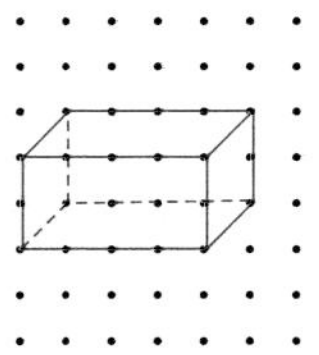

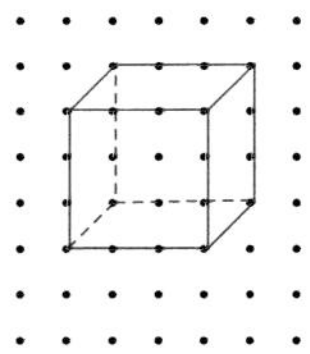

Reteach   RW113

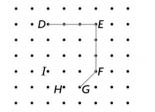

Practice 21.4

Draw Figures

Write the number of line segments needed to draw each figure.

1. square ___4___   2. pentagon ___5___   3. trapezoid ___4___

Copy the solid figure. Name the figure.

4.

square pyramid

Draw the missing line segments so that each figure matches its label. Possible answers are shown.

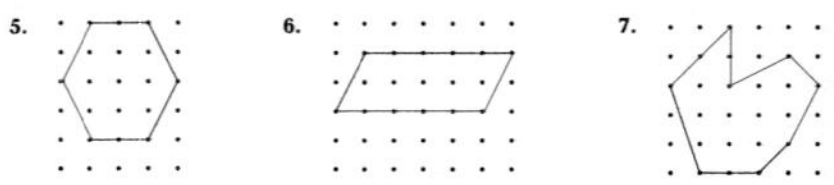

5. hexagon   6. parallelogram   7. octagon

8. Trace the figure shown at the right. Cut out the figure along the solid lines. Then fold along the dotted lines. Tape the edges of the figure together. What solid figure do you have?

___rectangular prism___

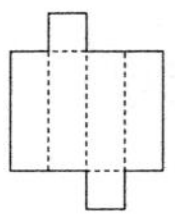

Mixed Review

Find the missing factor.

9. $7 \times$ ___3___ $= 21$ 10. ___1___ $\times 4 = 4$ 11. $6 \times$ ___8___ $= 48$

12. $9 \times$ ___0___ $= 0$ 13. ___5___ $\times 7 = 35$ 14. ___7___ $\times 9 = 63$

Practice   PW113

Draw a Solid Figure

The faces of solid figures are polygons. Look to see where these faces meet to find edges and vertices.

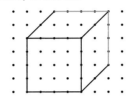

Activity 2
MATERIALS: dot paper, pencil, ruler

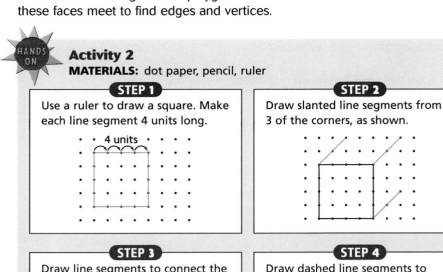

STEP 1
Use a ruler to draw a square. Make each line segment 4 units long.

4 units

STEP 2
Draw slanted line segments from 3 of the corners, as shown.

STEP 3
Draw line segments to connect the endpoints of the slanted line segments, as shown.

STEP 4
Draw dashed line segments to show the faces that cannot be seen.

• How many faces does a cube have? How many edges and vertices does a cube have? **6 faces; 12 edges, 8 vertices**

▶ Check

1. **Explain** what a vertex is. Compare the number of vertices of a cube and a square pyramid. **A vertex is a corner where three or more edges meet; square pyramid: 5; cube: 8; 5 < 8, so a square pyramid has fewer vertices than a cube.**

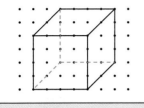

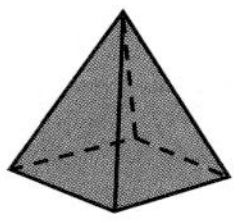

For 2–4, draw each figure on dot paper. Then, write the number of line segments needed to draw each figure.
Check students' drawings.

2. pentagon **5**   3. rectangle **4**   4. hexagon **6**

LESSON CONTINUES

🏴 North Carolina Standards 3.01 Use appropriate vocabulary to compare, describe, and classify o- and three-dimensional figures.

• *Have students complete Activity 2.*
What plane figures are the faces of a cube?
squares
REASONING How are a square and a cube different? Accept reasonable descriptions.

• *Direct students' attention to the figure in Step 4.*
Are the solid line segments edges of the cube? yes **Are the dashed line segments edges of the cube?** yes **How many vertices of the cube can be seen in the drawing?**
8 vertices

3 PRACTICE

Guided Practice

Do Check Exercises 1–4 with your students. Identify students who are having difficulty and choose appropriate lesson resources to provide assistance.

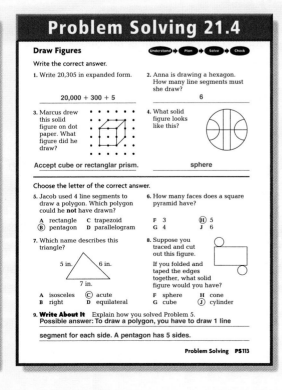

Challenge 21.4

Nets

Materials: ruler, scissors, tape

The figure at the right is called a **net**. It shows all the faces of a square pyramid. If you cut it out and folded it along the dotted lines, you can tape it together to make a square pyramid. On the dot paper below, draw a net for a cube or for a rectangular prism.

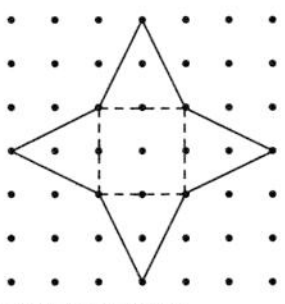

Check your work. Trace your net. Then cut it out and fold it. Tape the edges together. Does it make a cube or a rectangular prism? **Check students' nets.**

Challenge **CW113**

Problem Solving 21.4

Draw Figures

Understand → Plan → Solve → Check

Write the correct answer.

1. Write 20,305 in expanded form.

20,000 + 300 + 5

2. Anna is drawing a hexagon. How many line segments must she draw?

6

3. Marcus drew this solid figure on dot paper. What figure did he draw?

Accept cube or rectanglar prism.

4. What solid figure looks like this?

sphere

Choose the letter of the correct answer.

5. Jacob used 4 line segments to draw a polygon. Which polygon could he **not** have drawn?

A rectangle   C trapezoid
B pentagon   D parallelogram

6. How many faces does a square pyramid have?

F 3   H 5
G 4   J 6

7. Which name describes this triangle?

5 in.   6 in.
7 in.

A isosceles   C acute
B right   D equilateral

8. Suppose you traced and cut out this figure.

If you folded and taped the edges together, what solid figure would you have?

F sphere   H cone
G cube   J cylinder

9. **Write About It** Explain how you solved Problem 5. Possible answer: To draw a polygon, you have to draw 1 line segment for each side. A pentagon has 5 sides.

Problem Solving **PS113**

Independent Practice

Note that Exercise 17 is a **multistep or strategy problem**. Assign Exercises 5–18.

Note that for Exercises 10, 11, and 14 students may draw a variety of correct answers. Tell students to count the number of sides to be sure each answer is correct.

MULTISTEP OR STRATEGY PROBLEM To solve Exercise 17, students should determine how many angles each of the polygons in the problem has. Students will then add the number of angles of each polygon that Rex drew to find the total number of angles. Next, they will add to find the total number of angles that Alicia drew. Finally, students will compare the two totals.

Practice and Problem Solving   Extra Practice, page 438, Set D

For 5–7, draw each figure on dot paper. Then, write the number of line segments needed to draw each figure.
Check students' drawings.
  5. parallelogram 4   **6.** octagon 8   **7.** triangle 3

For 8, copy the solid figure on dot paper. Name the figure.
Check students' drawings; rectangular prism
  8.

For 9–14, copy each figure on dot paper. Draw the missing line segments so that the figure matches its label.
For Exercises 10, 11, and 14, more than 1 correct drawing is possible.

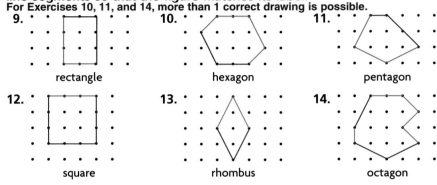

  9. rectangle   **10.** hexagon   **11.** pentagon

  12. square   **13.** rhombus   **14.** octagon

15. **FAST FACT • SOCIAL STUDIES** The Olympic flag was first used at the 1920 Summer Olympics. There were 2,669 athletes taking part. At the 1992 Summer Olympics, there were 9,367 athletes. Which Olympics had more athletes? How many more?
the 1992 Summer Olympics; 6,698 more athletes

16. Trace the figure shown at the right. Cut out the figure along the solid lines. Then fold along the 4 dotted lines. Tape the edges of the figure together. What solid figure do you have?
Check students' work; square pyramid.

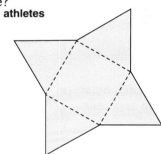

434

Alternative Teaching Strategy

Scaffolded Instruction

PURPOSE To practice drawing quadrilaterals

MATERIALS square dot paper, p. TR30; ruler; pencil; red crayon

Before beginning the activity, remind students that the distance from one point to the next point is referred to as one unit. Have students look at the illustration in Step 1 of Activity 2 on page 433.

Step 1

Students will begin by drawing a rectangle. Have students choose a dot in the top left-hand corner of their paper and mark the dot with a crayon. Using a ruler and a pencil,

have students draw a horizontal line segment (toward the right) that is 4 units long. Have students mark the second endpoint with a crayon.

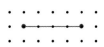

Step 2

Have students draw a vertical line segment that is 6 units long extending toward the bottom of the paper from each of the endpoints. Have students mark the new endpoints in the same way and draw the final side of the rectangle.

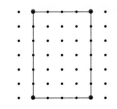

Step 3

Have students draw another rectangle that is 5 units long and 2 units wide, following the same procedure.

You may wish to have students try drawing a trapezoid. Remind them to draw one pair of parallel sides.

434   Chapter 21

17. Rex drew 2 quadrilaterals and 2 hexagons. Ali drew an octagon, 2 pentagons, and a triangle. Who drew more angles? Explain. **Ali; Rex: 4 + 4 + 6 + 6 = 20; Ali: 8 + 5 + 5 + 3 = 21; 20 < 21**

18.  **What's the Error?** The lengths of the sides of a triangle are 3 inches, 3 inches, and 2 inches. Justin said it is an equilateral triangle. Describe his error. **Possible answer: the triangle is an isosceles triangle because only 2 sides are equal.**

Getting Ready for the Test

19. James drew the figure below. **D**

Which names the figure that James drew?

A rectangle   **C** hexagon
B triangle   **D** pentagon

20. Lori drew the figure below. **A**

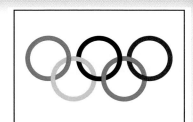

How many right angles does this figure have?

A 0   **C** 2
B 1   **D** 4

Problem Solving LINKUP ... to Social Studies

The 5 circles on the Olympic flag represent the 5 regions of the world that join together for the Olympic Games. A circle is a plane figure made of points that are the same distance from a center point.

Follow the directions to draw a circle.

MATERIALS: paper clip, 2 pencils, ruler

1. Draw a point. Draw a circle by placing the pencils in the ends of the paper clip. The pencil on the point should not move.

2. Place three points on top of the circle that you drew. Measure the distance from the center point to each of the points on the circle. Are they the same distance from the center? **Yes; they are the same distance from the center of the circle.**

Chapter 21 **435**

Reading Strategy

K-W-L CHART Before having students read the Linkup, have them look at the flag. Then have students make a three-column chart headed *What I Know, What I Want to Know,* and *What I Learned.* Ask them to fill in the first two columns. Have them fill in the third column as they read the paragraph.

K-W-L Chart

What I Know	What I Want to Know	What I Learned

- *Have students read the paragraph.*
  Where is another place that you have seen circles? Possible answers: clock face, traffic light

- *Read the activity directions.*
  REASONING Will it make any difference where you place the 3 points on the circle? No; all points on the circle will be the same distance from the center.

4 ASSESS

Summarize the lesson by having students:

DISCUSS What do you know about the sides of any polygon? Possible answer: the sides are line segments, and these sides form a closed figure.

 WRITE Describe how you would draw a quadrilateral. Possible answer: I would use 4 line segments that make a closed figure with 4 angles.

LESSON QUIZ
For 1–3, draw each figure on dot paper. Then, write the number of line segments needed to draw each figure. Check students' drawings.

Transparency **21.4**

1. square   4

2. right triangle   3

3. rectangle   4

435

Lesson Planning

Objective To use the problem solving skill *identify relationships* to identify solid figures from different perspectives

Lesson Resources Reading Transparency 21; Intervention • Problem Solving, Strategy/Skill 21

NCTM Standards
3. Geometry
6. Problem Solving
7. Reasoning and Proof
8. Communication
10. Representation

Math Background
These ideas will help students identify relationships between plane and solid figures.

- The flat surfaces of solid figures are plane figures.

- Recognizing the different faces of a solid figure is a key step to understanding solid figures.

- Different solid figures may have some of the same plane figures as flat surfaces.

Warm-Up Resources

Number of the Day

Transparency **21.5**

The number of the day is 20. Write four multiplication sentences with 20 as the product. Possible answer: $4 \times 5 = 20$; $2 \times 10 = 20$; $10 \times 2 = 20$; $1 \times 20 = 20$

Daily Facts Practice

Have students practice multiplication and division facts by completing Set B of *Teacher's Resource Book,* p. TR99.

Transparency **21.5**

Problem of the Day

For every 4 seeds Tammy planted, only 1 sprouted. If 9 seeds sprouted, how many seeds did Tammy plant? 36 seeds

Solution Problem of the Day tab, p. PD21

Intervention and Extension Resources

Alternative Teaching Strategy

MATERIALS *For the whole group* solid figure manipulatives

Help students **identify the relationships between plane and solid figures.** Have a volunteer hold up a solid figure and point to one of the flat surfaces. Ask the group to identify the face as a plane figure. Have students take turns showing flat surfaces of solid figures and identifying them as plane figures.

KINESTHETIC, VISUAL

VISUAL/SPATIAL

Reading Strategy

Make Inferences Have students read the following riddles and decide what solid figures are being described.

I am a solid figure with 6 faces. My faces are not all the same size. What am I? rectangular prism

I am a solid figure that has a circle on both ends. I also have a curved surface. What am I? cylinder

 21 **Reading Transparency 21**

Multistep and Strategy Problems

The following multistep and strategy problems are provided in Lesson 21.5:

Page	Item
437	7–8

ESOL/ESL

MATERIALS *For each student* tracing paper, pencil, scissors, tape, 8 index cards

Have students **make flash cards of plane figures.** Have students fold the tracing paper into 8 small sections and then cut the paper on the folds. Have students find examples of plane figures in their math books. Have them trace one plane figure on each piece of tracing paper and then tape the piece of tracing paper onto an index card. Have students write a label for the figure on the index card. Encourage students to trace more than one type of triangle and quadrilateral to reinforce the more specific vocabulary terms.

VISUAL

VERBAL/LINGUISTIC

Early Finishers

MATERIALS *For each student* solid figure patterns, pp. TR32–36; crayons; scissors; tape

To reinforce students' understanding of the faces of solid figures, have them **make models of solid figures.** For each solid figure pattern, have students shade each face or surface a different color. Then have students cut out the pattern and tape the edges together so that it is in the shape of a solid figure.

KINESTHETIC

VISUAL/SPATIAL, BODILY/KINESTHETIC

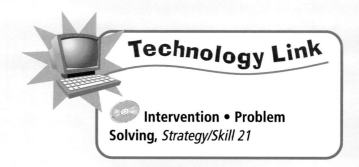

Technology Link

Intervention • Problem Solving, *Strategy/Skill 21*

Lesson 21.5 Organizer

Objective To use the problem solving skill *identify relationships* to identify solid figures from different perspectives

Lesson Resources Reading Transparency 21; Intervention • Problem Solving, Strategy/Skill 21

1 INTRODUCE

QUICK REVIEW provides review of prerequisite skills.

WHY LEARN THIS? You can recognize solid figures from different views. *Share the lesson objective with students.*

2 TEACH

Guided Instruction

- *Have students read the first paragraph.*
  What do you know about solid figures that could help you answer the question? the different plane figures that are the flat surfaces of solid figures

- *After discussing the figures that this top view could be of, have students look at the square again.*
  REASONING Which solid figures could this be if it is the bottom view? cube, rectangular prism, square pyramid

MODIFYING INSTRUCTION When discussing the Talk About It question, you may wish to display a cone on a table or desktop and have students look down at the cone.

436 Chapter 21

LESSON **5**

Problem Solving Skill
Identify Relationships

UNDERSTAND > PLAN > SOLVE > CHECK

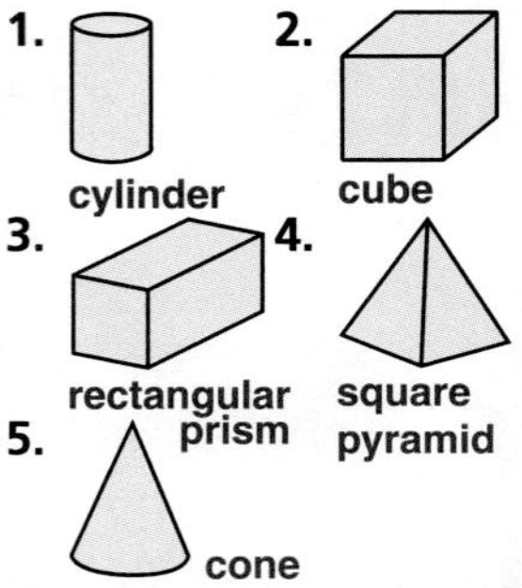

DIFFERENT VIEWS Mrs. Pine is teaching her students about solid figures. The students looked at the different views of solid figures. Which solid figures could this be?

top view

All of the faces of a cube are squares. So, this could be a cube.

Some rectangular prisms have two faces that are squares. So, this could be a rectangular prism.

Which solid figures could this be?

bottom view

The bottom of a cone is a circle. So, this could be a cone.

The bottom of a cylinder is a circle. So, this could be a cylinder.

The view of a sphere from *any* direction looks like a circle. So, this could be a sphere.

Talk About It

- The figure at the right is the top view of a cone. Explain what you see when you look at the top of a cone. **Possible answer: You would see a point in the middle where the cone comes to a point, and a circle that is the flat surface at the bottom of the cone.**

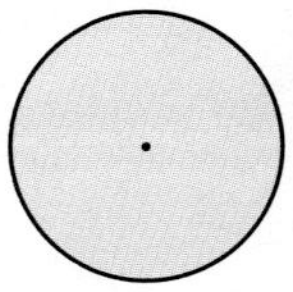

436

Reteach 21.5

Problem Solving Skill
Identify Relationships

When you look at different views of solid figures, you may see different shapes. The different shapes you can see when looking at one rectangular prism are shown.

Rectangular Prism	Top View— square	Bottom View— square	Side View— rectangle

Draw and name the shapes you would see if you looked at different views of these solid figures. Check students' drawings.

Solid Figure	Top View	Bottom View	Side View
1.	square	square	square
2.	circle	circle	rectangle
3.	circle	circle	circle
4.	square with dot	square	triangle

RW114 Reteach

Practice 21.5

Problem Solving Skill
Identify Relationships

1. Look at the side of this rectangular prism. What plane figure describes the shape you see? _____ rectangle

For 2–5, use the figures below.

Figure K   Figure L   Figure M   Figure N

2. Which figure is the side view of a square pyramid?
   A Figure K   **C Figure M**
   B Figure L   D Figure N

3. Which figure is the side view of a cube?
   F Figure K   H Figure M
   G Figure L   J Figure N

4. Which figure is the top view of a sphere?
   A Figure K   C Figure M
   B Figure L   D Figure N

5. Which figure is the bottom view of a cylinder?
   F Figure K   H Figure M
   G Figure L   J Figure N

Mixed Review

Choose the unit you would use to measure each.
Write *inch*, *foot*, *yard*, or *mile*. Possible answers are given.

6. the height of a chair _____ foot
7. the length of a river _____ mile
8. the length of your arm _____ inch
9. the length of your classroom _____ yard

PW114 Practice

Problem Solving Practice

1. What if Mrs. Pine's class looked at the side view of a square pyramid? What plane figure could be used to describe the shape that the students would see? **triangle**

2. Look at the cylinder. Even though the side of the cylinder is a curved surface, a plane figure can be used to describe the side view. Name this plane figure. **rectangle**

For 3–4, use the figures below.

| Figure Q | Figure R | Figure S | Figure T |

3. Which figure is the top view of a cylinder? **A**

A Figure Q   C Figure S
B Figure R   D Figure T

4. Which figure is the bottom view of a square pyramid? **G**

F Figure Q   H Figure S
G Figure R   J Figure T

Mixed Applications

USE DATA For 5–8, use the bar graph.

5. How many more members are in the Music Club than in the Swimming Club? **4 more members**

6. How many members are in the four clubs altogether?
72 members

7. List the clubs in order from the greatest number of members to the least number of members. **See above.**

8. ✎ **Write a problem** using the data in the bar graph. Explain how to find the answer. **Check students' work.**

7. Running (24), Music (20), Swimming (16), Art (12)

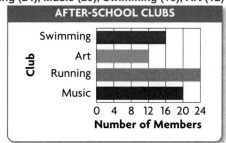
AFTER-SCHOOL CLUBS

9. Possible question: how many faces, edges, and vertices does a square pyramid have?

9. ❓ **What's the Question?** The answer is 5 faces, 8 edges, and 5 vertices. **See above.**

Chapter 21 **437**

North Carolina Standards 3.01 Use appropriate vocabulary to compare, describe, and classify two- and three-dimensional figures.

PRACTICE

Guided Practice

Do Problem Solving Practice Exercises 1–4 with your students. Identify students who are having difficulty and choose appropriate lesson resources to provide assistance.

Independent Practice

Note that Exercises 7 and 8 are **multistep or strategy problems.** Assign Exercises 5–9.

ASSESS

Summarize the lesson by having students:

DISCUSS What are some everyday objects that have a bottom view that is a circle? Possible answer: a can, a drinking glass

 WRITE Describe what a box of cereal looks like from the top, bottom, and side. Possible answer: The top looks like a rectangle, the bottom looks like the same size rectangle as the top, and the side looks like a larger rectangle than the top or bottom.

LESSON QUIZ
For 1–3, use the figures below.

Transparency
21.5

A   B   C

1. Which figure is the top view of a cylinder? figure A

2. Which figure is the side view of a cube? figure C

3. Which figure is the bottom view of a rectangular prism? figure B

Challenge 21.5

Different Views

You can put cubes together in many different ways to make new solid figures. When you do this, the top, front, and side views of the new figure may be different.

Sketch the top, bottom, and side views of each figure. If you need help, build the figure out of cubes and look at it from different views.

	Top View	Front View	Side View
1.			
2.			
3.			
4.			

CW114 Challenge

Reading Strategy 21.5

Form Mental Images

Sometimes it helps to understand what you are reading if you form a picture of it in your mind. For example, when you read a story, you probably form a mental picture of what your favorite character looks like. You can also form mental pictures of the information in math problems.

► Kim drew a line through the center of a square. She made two congruent figures. What figures did she make?

1. Picture Kim's drawing in your mind. Describe the picture.
   Possible response: A square with a line going from opposite corners.

2. Solve the problem.
   Possible answer: two triangles

Form a mental picture for each problem. Then solve.

3. Mary has a card with a capital M on it. She turned the card upside down. What letter does it look like the card has on it now?
   W

4. Lee planted a garden that is 20 feet long and 12 feet wide. It has 4 square corners. What shape is Lee's garden?
   rectangle

5. Bethany drew a triangle. She was able to draw one line of symmetry on it. What kind of triangle did Bethany draw?
   isosceles

6. Martin's school is located at the corner of Pine Street and Main Street. Are Pine Street and Main Street intersecting or parallel streets?
   intersecting

PS114 Reading Strategy

437

Purpose To provide extra practice for the skills presented in this chapter

The blue page references in each set of exercises refer to the lesson pages where each skill is taught.

Internet Resources

Visit **THE LEARNING SITE** at **www.harcourtschool.com** for a listing of practice activities.

Extra Practice

Set A (pp. 424–427)

Name the solid figure that each object looks like.

1.
cone

2.
cylinder

3.
rectangular prism

4.
sphere

Set B (pp. 428–429)

Name the solid figures used to make each object.

1. cone, sphere, cube

2. cube, cylinder, square pyramid

3. rectangular prism, cube, square pyramid

Set C (pp. 430–431)

Tell if each figure will tessellate. Write _yes_ or _no_.

1. no   **2.** no   **3.** yes   **4.** yes

5. Use grid paper and pattern blocks to make a design. Repeat your design to make a tessellation.
Check students' designs.

Set D (pp. 432–435)

For 1–3, draw each figure on dot paper. Then, write the number of line segments needed to draw each figure.
Check students' drawings.
1. rhombus 4   **2.** hexagon 6   **3.** quadrilateral 4

For 4–6, copy each figure on dot paper. Draw the missing line segments so that the figure matches its label.
For Exercises 5 and 6, more than 1 correct drawing is possible.

4.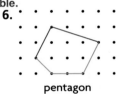
triangle

5. trapezoid

6. pentagon

438

Review/Test

✓ CHECK VOCABULARY AND CONCEPTS

For 1–2, choose the best term from the box.

tessellation	
face	
edge	

1. A flat surface of a solid figure is a __?__. (p. 424)
face

2. The line segment formed where two faces meet is called an __?__. (p. 424) **edge**

3. A solid figure has 6 square faces. What is it? (pp. 424–427) **cube**

4. A solid figure has 6 rectangular faces. What is it? (pp. 424–427)
rectangular prism

✓ CHECK SKILLS

For 5–6, name the solid figures used to make each object. (pp. 428–429)

5.
rectangular prism, cube, cone

6.
rectangular prism, 2 cylinders, cube

Tell if each figure will tessellate. Write *yes* or *no*. (pp. 430–431)

7.
yes

8.
no

9.
yes

10.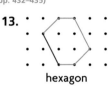
no

For 11–13, copy each figure on dot paper. Draw the missing line segments so that the figure matches its label. (pp. 432–435)
For Exercise 12, more than 1 correct drawing is possible.

11.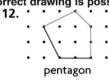
rectangle

12.
pentagon

13.
hexagon

✓ CHECK PROBLEM SOLVING

For 14–15, use the figures at the right. (pp. 436–437)

14. Which figure is the bottom view of a cone? **Figure A**

15. Which figure is the side view of a cube? **Figure C**

Figure A   Figure B   Figure C

Chapter 21   **439**

Review/Test

Purpose To check understanding of concepts, skills, and problem solving presented in Chapter 21

Using the Page

The Chapter 21 Review/Test can be used as a **review** or a **test**.

- Items 1–4 check understanding of concepts and new vocabulary.
- Items 5–13 check skill proficiency.
- Items 14–15 check students' abilities to choose and apply problem solving strategies to geometry problems.

Portfolio   Suggest that students place the completed Chapter 21 Review/Test in their portfolios.

Using the Assessment Guide

- Multiple-choice format of Chapter 21 Posttest—See *Assessment Guide*, pp. AG129–130.
- Free-response format of Chapter 21 Posttest—See *Assessment Guide*, pp. AG131–132.

Using Student Self-Assessment

The How Did I Do? survey helps students assess what they have learned and how they learned it. This survey is available as a copying master in *Assessment Guide*, p. AGxvii.

Chapter 21 Test, page 1

Choose the correct answer.

1. What solid figure has a shape like a box of cereal?
   A rectangular prism
   B cylinder
   C sphere
   D cone

2. How many edges does a rectangular prism have?
   F 6   H 12
   G 8   J 14

3. I am a solid figure. I look like a bowling ball. What figure am I?
   A a cube
   B a sphere
   C a cylinder
   D a cone

4. Which best describes the faces of a cube?
   F pentagons
   G circles
   H triangles
   J squares

5. What solid figure has 5 faces, 8 edges, and 5 vertices?
   A cube
   B square pyramid
   C sphere
   D rectangular prism

6. What solid figures are used to make the object?
   F cone, cylinder
   G cone, sphere
   H cone, square pyramid
   J cylinder, sphere

7. What solid figures are used to make the object?
   A cone, cube
   B square pyramid, cone
   C sphere, cube
   D cube, square pyramid

8. What solid figures are used to make the object?
   F cube, cylinder
   G cube, rectangular prism
   H cube, sphere
   J cone, cube

Go On ➡

Chapter 21 Test, page 2

9. Which figure will NOT tessellate?
   A ◯   C △
   B ▢   D ⬡

10. Which figure will tessellate?
    F ◇   H ◯
    G   J

11. Which figure will NOT tessellate?
    A △   C ◯
    B ▭   D ⬡

12. Which figure will NOT tessellate?
    F ⬡   H △
    G   J ⬠

13. How many line segments are needed to draw an octagon?
    A 8   C 6
    B 7   D 5

14. Which figure can be drawn with 4 line segments?
    F hexagon   H pyramid
    G rectangle J cylinder

15. How many angles does a pentagon have?
    A 8   C 5
    B 7   D 2

16. How many vertices does a parallelogram have?
    F 8   H 5
    G 6   J 4

Use this figure for 17 and 18.

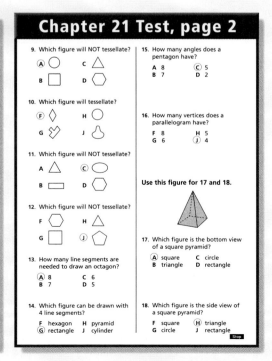

17. Which figure is the bottom view of a square pyramid?
    A square   C circle
    B triangle D rectangle

18. Which figure is the side view of a square pyramid?
    F square   H triangle
    G circle   J rectangle

Stop

Solid and Plane Figures   **439**

CHAPTER 21

Getting Ready for the EOG Test
Chapters 1–21

Using the Pages

These pages may be used to help students get ready for the North Carolina EOG Test. The test items are written in the same style and arranged in the same format as those on the EOG Test.

The pages are cumulative. They cover the standards from the North Carolina Mathematics Standard Course of Study that have been taught up to this point in the text or in a previous grade. Each Getting Ready for the EOG Test also reviews the North Carolina mathematics strands shown below.

- Number and Operations
- Measurement
- Geometry
- Data Analysis and Probability
- Algebra

These pages can be assigned at the end of the chapter as classwork or as a homework assignment. You may want to have students use individual recording sheets presented in a multiple-choice (standardized) format. A Test Answer Sheet is available as a blackline master in the *Assessment Guide* (p. AGlii).

You may wish to have students describe how they solved each problem and share their solutions.

Getting Ready for the EOG Test

⭐ NUMBER AND OPERATIONS

1. Marci has 8 tomato plants in each of 4 rows in her garden. How many tomato plants are in her garden in all? **C**

   A 10   **C** 32
   B 12   **D** 36

2. Toshi and 6 teammates want to buy a shirt for their coach. The shirt costs $42. If each player pays the same amount, how much will Toshi pay? **C**

   A $8   **C** $6
   B $7   **D** $5

3. Mr. Grant drives a delivery truck. He drove 367 miles on Monday and 252 miles on Tuesday. How many miles did he drive in the two days in all? **A**

   A 619 miles   **C** 519 miles
   B 615 miles   **D** 515 miles

   > **TIP** **Understand the problem.** See item 4. The word *about* tells you that you need an estimate rather than an exact answer.

4. **Explain It** A school band uses 129 instruments. There are 57 wind instruments. About how many instruments are not wind instruments? Explain how you found your answer. **See page 441.**

⭐ MEASUREMENT AND GEOMETRY

5. Victor made a model of a solid figure that has 4 faces that are triangles and 1 face that is a square. Which solid figure could he have made? **D**

   A cube
   B cylinder
   C rectangular prism
   D square pyramid

6. A sidewalk in front of a park is 9 yards long. What is the length of the sidewalk in feet? **B**

   A 18 feet
   B 27 feet
   C 30 feet
   D 45 feet

7. Shannon drew a polygon that had exactly 5 sides. Which polygon did she draw? **B**

   A hexagon
   B pentagon
   C quadrilateral
   D octagon

8. **Explain It** Gwen pressed the bottom of a solid figure into clay. It left the outline of a circle. Can you tell for certain which solid figure Gwen used? Explain why or why not. **See page 441.**

440

⭐ ALGEBRA

9. Henry wrote the pattern below.

8, 13, 18, 23, 28

Which statement is the **best** description of how the numbers in the pattern are related? **D**

A Each number is two times the number before it.

B Each number is 5 less than the number before it.

C Each number is 6 more than the number before it.

D Each number is 5 more than the number before it.

10. Which figure comes next in this pattern? **C**

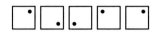

A

B

C

D

11. Explain It Mrs. Turner waters her plants once every three days. This week, she watered the plants on Tuesday and Friday. What are the next two days when she will water her plants? Explain how you found your answer. **See below.**

⭐ DATA ANALYSIS AND PROBABILITY

12. The table shows the number of books the students read. How many more books did the girls read than the boys? **A**

BOOKS READ BY OUR CLASS		
	Fiction	**Nonfiction**
Girls	29	34
Boys	24	37

A 2
B 3
C 4
D 5

13. Explain It Mr. Clark made a bar graph to show the amount of bird seed that he sold in the beginning of the summer.

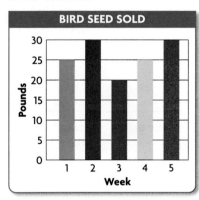

If Mr. Clark made a pictograph of this data, how many pounds should each symbol stand for? Explain your answer, and tell how many symbols would be used for each week. **See below.**

Chapters 1–21

Item Analysis

You may wish to use the item analysis to determine which North Carolina standards need additional review.

Item	North Carolina Standard	Lesson
1	1.03	10.2
2	1.03	14.1
3	1.02	4.3
4	1.06	5.1
5	3.01	21.1
6	2.01	17.5
7	3.01	19.3
8	3.01	21.1
9	5.01	2.5
10	(2) 5.01	Grade 2
11	5.01	2.5
12	4.01	15.3
13	4.01	16.1

SCORING RUBRIC
Explain It

2 Demonstrates a complete understanding of the problem and chooses an appropriate strategy to determine the solution

1 Demonstrates a partial understanding of the problem and chooses a strategy that does not lead to a complete and accurate solution

0 Demonstrates little understanding of the problem and shows little evidence of using any strategy to determine a solution

Explain It • Written Response

4. Possible answer: about 70 instruments; 129 rounded to the nearest ten is 130 and 57 rounded to the nearest ten is 60. 130 − 60 = 70.

8. No; it could have been either a cone, a sphere, or a cylinder.

11. Monday and Thursday; possible answer: Mrs. Turner waters once every 3 days. Since the last day she watered was Friday, count on 3 days to Monday and another 3 days to Thursday.

13. Possible answer: each symbol should stand for 5 pounds because all of the amounts can be divided into groups of 5. Week 1: 5 symbols; Week 2: 6 symbols; Week 3: 4 symbols; Week 4: 5 symbols; Week 5: 6 symbols.

Perimeter, Area, and Volume

NCTM Standards 2000

1. Number and Operations *Lessons 22.1, 22.2, 22.3, 22.4*	6. Problem Solving *Lessons 22.1, 22.2, 22.3, 22.4*
2. Algebra *Lessons 22.1, 22.3, 22.4*	7. Reasoning and Proof *Lessons 22.1, 22.2, 22.3, 22.4*
3. Geometry *Lessons 22.1, 22.3, 22.4*	8. Communication *Lessons 22.1, 22.2, 22.3, 22.4*
4. Measurement *Lessons 22.1, 22.2, 22.3, 22.4*	9. Connections *Lessons 22.2, 22.3*
5. Data Analysis and Probability	10. Representation *Lessons 22.1, 22.2, 22.3, 22.4*

Chapter Planner

Getting Ready for Chapter 22 • Assessing Prior Knowledge and INTERVENTION (See PE and TE page 443.)

LESSON	NORTH CAROLINA STANDARDS	PACING	VOCABULARY*	MATERIALS	RESOURCES AND TECHNOLOGY
22.1 **Perimeter** pp. 444–447 Objective To estimate and find the perimeter of an object or plane figure		1 Day	**perimeter**	*For each student* toothpicks, paper clips, centimeter ruler	Reteach, Practice, Problem Solving, Challenge 22.1 Worksheets Transparency 22.1 **Intervention,** *Skill 9* (CD or Book) **Harcourt Mega Math Ice Station Exploration,** *Polar Planes* **Math Jingles® CD 3–4**
22.2 **Hands On: Area** pp. 448–449 Objective To find the area of a plane figure		1 Day	**square unit area**	*For each group* square tiles, 1-inch grid paper	Reteach, Practice, Problem Solving, Challenge 22.2 Worksheets Transparency 22.2 **Intervention,** *Skills 26–28* (CD or Book) **Harcourt Mega Math Ice Station Exploration,** *Polar Planes*
22.3 **Problem Solving Skill: Make Generalizations** pp. 450–451 Objective To apply the problem solving skill *make generalizations* to solve problems		1 Day			Reteach, Practice, Reading Strategy, Challenge 22.3 Worksheets Transparency 22.3 Scaffolded Instruction Transparency 22 Reading Transparency 22 **Intervention • Problem Solving,** *Strategy/Skill 22* (CD or Book)
22.4 **Volume** pp. 452–455 Objective To estimate and measure volume		2 Days	**volume cubic unit**	*For each group* color cubes, small box *For Linkup* connecting cubes, grid paper	Reteach, Practice, Problem Solving, Challenge 22.4 Worksheets Transparency 22.4 **Intervention,** *Skills 26–28* (CD or Book) **Harcourt Mega Math Ice Station Exploration,** *Frozen Solids*

Ending Chapter 22 • Extra Practice, p. 456 • Chapter 22 Review/Test, p. 457 • Getting Ready for the EOG Test, pp. 458–459

Ending Unit 6 • **It's in the Bag,** p. 460; **Challenge,** p. 461; **Study Guide and Review,** pp. 462–463; **Performance Assessment,** p. 464; **Technology Linkup,** p. 465; **Problem Solving in North Carolina,** pp. 466–467

*****Boldfaced** terms are the key mathematical terms for the chapter.

Vocabulary Power

Vocabulary Cards

Have students use the Vocabulary Cards on *Teacher's Resource Book* pages TR175–176 for the key terms in the chapter. The cards can be added to a file of mathematics terms.

area

Develop Key Chapter Vocabulary

The **boldfaced** words are the key vocabulary terms in the chapter.

- **perimeter** (p. 444)—the distance around a figure
- **square unit** (p. 448)—a square with a side length of 1 unit
- **area** (p. 448)—number of square units needed to cover a flat surface
- **volume** (p. 452)—the amount of space occupied by a solid figure
- **cubic unit** (p. 452)—a cube with a side length of 1 unit used to measure volume

Multimedia Math Glossary

GO ON-LINE For vocabulary support, visit **www.harcourtschool.com/mathglossary**

Math Journal

Have students define the key vocabulary terms: *perimeter, square unit, area, volume,* and *cubic unit.* Have students use their own words and give an example of each.

M A T H Word Work

Objective To reinforce vocabulary concepts
Use after Lesson 22.2.

Materials *For each student* 1-inch grid paper, p. TR57; 1-centimeter grid paper, p. TR58; 2 colors of crayons or markers

Have students choose one color crayon or marker to use for perimeter and one color crayon or marker to use for area. Tell students that they will be drawing different polygons, and that all sides of the polygons must be on the lines of the grid paper.

Have students begin with the 1-inch grid paper. Tell them to draw a figure with a perimeter that is less than 10 inches. (Note: Students may wish to first draw the perimeter in pencil, then use the crayon or marker that they chose to use for perimeter.) Have them shade in the area of the figure using the crayon or marker chosen for area. Below the figure, have students record the perimeter and the area. Next, have students repeat these steps for a figure that has a perimeter of exactly 16 inches.

Have students use the 1-centimeter grid paper to draw a figure with a perimeter of less than 20 centimeters and a figure with a perimeter of exactly 32 centimeters. Have students label the perimeter and area for each.

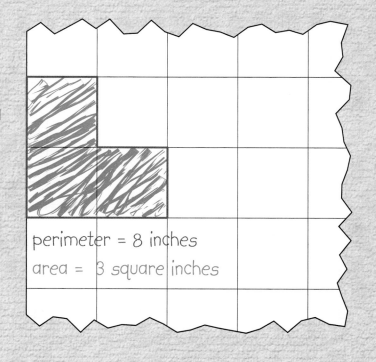

perimeter = 8 inches
area = 3 square inches

Mathematics Across the Grades

 LOOKING BACK • Prerequisite Skills

To be ready for Chapter 22, students should have the following understandings and skills:

- **Column Addition**—adding columns of 1-digit numbers
- **Multiplication Facts**—multiplication facts to 10

Check What You Know

Use page 443 to determine students' knowledge of prerequisite concepts and skills.

Intervention

Help students prepare for the chapter by using the intervention resources described on TE page 443.

 LOOKING AT CHAPTER 22 • Essential Skills

Students will

- **estimate and find the perimeter of an object or plane figure.**
- **find the area of a plane figure.**
- apply the problem solving skill *make generalizations* to solve a problem involving finding perimeter and area.
- **estimate and measure volume.**

Example

Find the area and the perimeter of this figure.

1 ft

6 ft

Perimeter	Area
6 ft + 1 ft + 6 ft + 1 ft = 14 feet	6 ft × 1 ft = 6 square feet
So, the perimeter is 14 feet.	So, the area is 6 square feet.

 LOOKING AHEAD • Applications

Students will apply what they learn in Chapter 22 to the following new concepts:

- Find the Perimeter of Polygons Using a Formula (Grade 4)
- Find the Area of Polygons (Grade 4)
- Relate Area and Perimeter (Grade 4)
- Find the Volume of Rectangular Prisms (Grade 4)

Differentiated Instruction

Meeting the Needs of All Learners

Extra Support	Activities for All	Enrichment
Alternative Teaching Strategy TE Lessons 22.1, 22.2, 22.3, 22.4 **Special Needs** TE Lesson 22.4 **ESOL/ESL** TE Lessons 22.1, 22.2, 22.3, 22.4	**Cross-Curricular Connections** **Art:** TE Lesson 22.2 **Reading:** TE Lesson 22.3 **Social Studies:** TE/PE Chapter Opener **Vocabulary:** TE p. 442B, PE p. 443 **Writing:** TE Lesson 22.1	**Advanced Learners** TE Lesson 22.1 **Early Finishers** TE Lessons 22.3, 22.4

Combination and Multi-age Classrooms

Grade 2	Grade 3	Grade 4
Skills Trace Across the Grades		
Find perimeter of shapes in centimeters; find area using square tiles; estimate the number of cubes that fill a space.	**Estimate and measure perimeter and area using nonstandard and standard units; estimate and find volume of rectangular prisms made of cubes.**	Find perimeter using various methods including using a formula; estimate and find area of polygons; relate perimeter and area; estimate and find volume of prisms.
Instructional Strategies		
Students on this level may require more time to build conceptual understanding. **Assignments** **Grade 3 Pupil Edition** • Have students work in pairs for Lessons 22.1 and 22.2. • Have students use square tiles to model the activities in Lesson 22.3. **Grade 2 Pupil Edition**—pages 431–438	Students on this level should be able to complete all the lessons in the Pupil Edition and all the activities in the Teacher's Edition with minimal adjustments. **Assignment** **Grade 3 Pupil Edition**—pages 442–457	Students on this level will probably require less time to build conceptual understanding. **Assignments** **Grade 3 Pupil Edition** • Compact Lessons 22.3 and 22.4. **Grade 4 Pupil Edition**—pages 612–617, 620–621, and 628–635

Perimeter, Area, and Volume

Introducing the Chapter

Tell students that the distance around a figure is called its perimeter. Have students focus on the diagram of the garden and tell what unit of measure is used to describe the lengths of the sides. feet

Using Data

To begin the study of this chapter, have students

- Find the length of the shortest side of the garden. 2 feet

- Find the difference in length between the shortest side and the longest side of the garden. 4 feet

- Restate the perimeter of the garden, 22 feet, in yards and feet. 7 yd 1 ft

Problem Solving Project

Purpose To use connecting cubes to make solid figures

Grouping small groups

Materials *For each group* connecting cubes

Background Tulips were first grown in Turkey. The name *tulip* is from a Turkish word that means *turban*. A turban is a headpiece made from a twisted scarf or sash.

UNDERSTAND • PLAN • SOLVE • CHECK

Have students

- Construct a rectangular prism that is 4 cubes long and 2 cubes wide and count the number of cubes they used. 8 cubes

- Construct a figure that is 6 cubes long and 6 cubes wide and count the number of cubes they used. 36 cubes

- Construct a cube that is 4 cubes long, 4 cubes wide, and 4 cubes high and count the number of cubes they used. 64 cubes

Graphing Investigations
Begin Week 22.

≡**FAST FACT** • SOCIAL STUDIES People have grown flowers for thousands of years. In the 1600s, tulips in Holland were so valuable that the bulbs were used as money!

PROBLEM SOLVING Look below at the diagram of a garden. How can you find how many feet of fencing you would need to go around this garden?

Add the lengths of the sides;
5 + 3 + 3 + 3 + 2 + 6 = 22 ft.

442

WHY LEARN MATH? Landscape gardeners use measurement to help them plan and design the outside areas for homes and businesses. Gardeners often need to know the area of a garden so that they can order the proper amount of mulch or fertilizer. Ask: What other professions need to know how to find area? Possible answers: carpenter, carpet salesperson, house painter, glass cutter

Family Involvement Activities

These activities provide:

- Letter to the Family
- Math Vocabulary
- Family Game
- Practice (Homework)

Family Involvement Activities, p. FA87

Use this page to help you review and remember
important skills needed for Chapter 22.

✔ COLUMN ADDITION

Find each sum.

1.
$$\begin{array}{r} 3 \\ 7 \\ +5 \\ \hline 15 \end{array}$$

2.
$$\begin{array}{r} 2 \\ 4 \\ +8 \\ \hline 14 \end{array}$$

3.
$$\begin{array}{r} 1 \\ 3 \\ +9 \\ \hline 13 \end{array}$$

4.
$$\begin{array}{r} 6 \\ 2 \\ +9 \\ \hline 17 \end{array}$$

5.
$$\begin{array}{r} 6 \\ 7 \\ +3 \\ \hline 16 \end{array}$$

6.
$$\begin{array}{r} 4 \\ 9 \\ +3 \\ \hline 16 \end{array}$$

7.
$$\begin{array}{r} 5 \\ 5 \\ +7 \\ \hline 17 \end{array}$$

8.
$$\begin{array}{r} 9 \\ 8 \\ +1 \\ \hline 18 \end{array}$$

9. $4 + 3 + 3 + 5$ 15

10. $8 + 3 + 2 + 9$ 22

11. $5 + 6 + 2 + 5$ 18

12. $9 + 2 + 9$ 20

✔ MULTIPLICATION FACTS

Find each product.

13. $7 \times 4 = \blacksquare$ 28

14. $3 \times 6 = \blacksquare$ 18

15. $2 \times 5 = \blacksquare$ 10

16. $4 \times 9 = \blacksquare$ 36

17. $7 \times 2 = \blacksquare$ 14

18. $6 \times 6 = \blacksquare$ 36

19. $9 \times 8 = \blacksquare$ 72

20. $10 \times 3 = \blacksquare$ 30

21. $4 \times 5 = \blacksquare$ 20

VOCABULARY POWER ✔

REVIEW

square [skwâr] *noun*

A square is a quadrilateral that has
4 right angles and 4 equal sides.
On grid paper, draw 2 squares that
are different sizes. Include labels
showing the lengths of the sides.
Check students' work.

PREVIEW

perimeter   volume

square unit   cubic unit

area

 GO ON-LINE   www.harcourtschool.com/mathglossary

Chapter 22 **443**

Assessing Prior Knowledge

Use the **Check What You Know** page to determine
whether your students have mastered the prerequisite skills critical for this chapter.

Intervention

• **Diagnose and Prescribe**
Evaluate your students' performance on this page
to determine whether intervention is necessary or
if enrichment is appropriate. Options that provide
instruction, practice, and a check are listed in the
chart below.

✔ CHECK WHAT YOU KNOW RESOURCES

Intervention Copying Masters or CD-ROMs

Enrichment Copying Masters

VOCABULARY POWER

For activities and information about the vocabulary in this chapter, see page 442B.

Were students successful with ✔ **CHECK WHAT YOU KNOW?**

IF . . . **NO** THEN . . . **INTERVENE**   **INTERVENTION OPTIONS**   IF . . . **YES** THEN . . . **ENRICH**

Skill/Items	Missed more than	Intervene with
Column Addition, 1–12	3	• *Intervention*, Skill 9
Multiplication Facts, 13–21	2	• *Intervention*, Skills 26–28

Skill/Items	Missed fewer than	Enrich with
Column Addition, 1–12	4	• *Intervention*, Enrichment p. IN371
Multiplication Facts, 13–21	3	• *Intervention*, Enrichment p. IN372

Perimeter

Lesson Planning

PROFESSIONAL DEVELOPMENT

Objective To estimate and find the perimeter of an object or plane figure

Materials *For each student* toothpicks; paper clips; centimeter ruler, p. TR55

NCTM Standards
1. Number and Operations
2. Algebra
3. Geometry
4. Measurement
6. Problem Solving
7. Reasoning and Proof
8. Communication
10. Representation

Math Background
These ideas will help students understand how to estimate and find the perimeter of objects and plane figures.

- Estimate the perimeter of an object before measuring it.
- Measure to find the perimeter. Then compare the actual measurement to the estimate.
- Find the perimeter of a figure by adding the lengths of each of the sides.

Vocabulary
perimeter the distance around a figure

Warm-Up Resources

Number of the Day

Transparency **22.1**

Find the number of letters in the word *perimeter*. Write and solve 5 multiplication or division sentences using that number. Possible answer:
$9 \times 5 = 45, 54 \div 6 = 9, 3 \times 3 = 9, 9 \times 7 = 63, 81 \div 9 = 9$

Daily Facts Practice

Have students practice multiplication and division facts by completing Set C of *Teacher's Resource Book*, p. TR99.

Transparency **22.1**

Problem of the Day

Bert made 6 different rectangles using toothpicks. He used 24 toothpicks for each rectangle. How wide and long was each rectangle in toothpicks? Which one was a square? 1 by 11, 2 by 10, 3 by 9, 4 by 8, 5 by 7, 6 by 6; 6 by 6 was a square

Solution Problem of the Day tab, p. PD22

Intervention and Extension Resources

Alternative Teaching Strategy

MATERIALS *For each pair* self-stick notes or index cards

ESOL/ESL

Help students **find the perimeter of the chalkboard** by using objects of varying sizes. Give each pair of students a different kind of object to use as a unit of measure, such as self-stick notes or index cards. Have students present their results to the class. Check students' work.

See also page 446.

KINESTHETIC

BODILY/KINESTHETIC

Multistep and Strategy Problems

The following multistep or strategy problem is provided in Lesson 22.1:

Page	Item
446	13

Writing in Mathematics

Help students **apply their understanding of perimeter to write a math problem.** Display the following story starter.

Judy needed to find the perimeter of her garden.

Ask students to continue the story. Have them include the reason why Judy needed to find the garden's perimeter and the process she used. Check students' work.

Advanced Learners

MATERIALS *For each student* sheets of $8\frac{1}{2} \times 11$ paper

Challenge students to **find the perimeter of the classroom** using the longer side of sheets of $8\frac{1}{2} \times 11$ paper. Give them fewer sheets of paper than they need. Ask: What measurement strategies could you use? Possible answers: reuse the sheets of paper after measuring 1 side, estimate, make a benchmark of 10 sheets and skip-count.

Have students use their strategies to measure and compare their results. Answers will vary.

KINESTHETIC

BODILY/KINESTHETIC

Technology Link

Intervention, *Skill 9*

Harcourt Mega Math
Ice Station Exploration,
Polar Planes, Level P

Math Jingles® CD 3–4 •
Track 16

GO The Harcourt Learning Site
www.harcourtschool.com

Lesson 22.1 Organizer

Objective To estimate and find the perimeter of an object or plane figure

Vocabulary perimeter

Materials *For each student* toothpicks; paper clips; centimeter ruler, p. TR55

1 INTRODUCE

QUICK REVIEW provides review of prerequisite skills.

WHY LEARN THIS? You'll know how to estimate and find the distance around something, such as a picture frame or a poster, by using different methods. *Share the lesson objective with students.*

2 TEACH

Guided Instruction

- *Ask students to read Step 1 of the Activity.* **How would you estimate the perimeter?** Possible answer: by looking at the paper clips, guessing how many clips would line up along each edge of the book, then adding the 4 numbers. I would do the same with the toothpicks.

- *Direct students' attention to the table.* **What is the difference between an *estimate* and an *actual measurement*?** An estimate is what you think the measurement will be. The measurement is the actual number you get when you measure with the toothpicks or paper clips.

LESSON

1 Perimeter

▶ Learn

AROUND AND AROUND The distance around a figure is called its **perimeter**.

You can estimate the perimeter of your math book.

Activity
MATERIALS: toothpicks, paper clips

STEP 1
Copy the table. Estimate the perimeter of your math book in paper clips and in toothpicks. Record your estimates.

STEP 2
Use paper clips. Record how many paper clips it takes to go around all the edges of your math book.

STEP 3
Use toothpicks. Record how many toothpicks it takes to go around all the edges of your math book.

PERIMETER OF MY MATH BOOK

	Estimate	Measurement
Number of paper clips		
Number of toothpicks		

- How does your estimate compare with your actual measurement? Answers will vary.
- Did it take more paper clips or more toothpicks to measure the perimeter of your math book? Explain. See above right.

Possible answer: More paper clips were needed because the toothpicks were longer than the paper clips.

- **REASONING** Would it be better to measure the perimeter of your math book with paper clips or with your shoe? Explain. Possible answer: paper clips; A shoe is much bigger, and it would be more difficult to get a close measure of the book's perimeter with something so big.

444

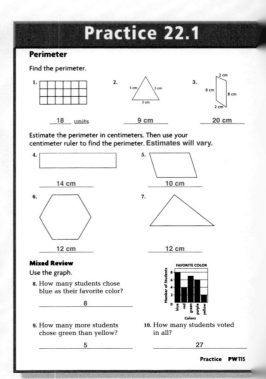

Quick Review
1. $2 + 3 + 3 = \blacksquare$ 8
2. $5 + 6 + 7 = \blacksquare$ 18
3. $7 + 3 + 6 = \blacksquare$ 16
4. $4 + 2 + 9 = \blacksquare$ 15
5. $10 + 4 + 4 + 2 = \blacksquare$
  20

VOCABULARY
perimeter

Reteach 22.1

Perimeter

Perimeter is the distance around a figure. You can add the lengths of the sides of a figure to find the perimeter.

$1 \text{ cm} + 3 \text{ cm} + 1 \text{ cm} + 3 \text{ cm} = 8 \text{ cm}$
The perimeter is 8 centimeters.

$3 \text{ ft} + 4 \text{ ft} + 5 \text{ ft} = 12 \text{ ft}$
The perimeter is 12 feet.

Use a centimeter ruler to measure the length of each side. Then add the lengths of the sides to find the perimeter.

1.
$3 \text{ cm} + 3 \text{ cm} + 3 \text{ cm} + 3 \text{ cm}$
$= 12 \text{ cm}$

2.
$2 \text{ cm} + 6 \text{ cm} + 2 \text{ cm} + 6 \text{ cm}$
$= 16 \text{ cm}$

3.
$3 \text{ cm} + 3 \text{ cm} + 3 \text{ cm}$
$= 9 \text{ cm}$

4.
$5 \text{ cm} + 2 \text{ cm} + 3 \text{ cm} + 2 \text{ cm}$
$= 12 \text{ cm}$

Find the perimeter of each figure.

5. 10 m, 5 m, 10 m, 5 m
30 m

6. 4 ft, 3 ft, 3 ft, 4 ft
14 ft

7. 4 in., 3 in., 5 in., 8 in.
20 in.

Reteach RW115

Practice 22.1

Perimeter

Find the perimeter.

1. 18 units
2. 3 cm, 3 cm, 3 cm — 9 cm
3. 2 cm, 8 cm, 8 cm, 2 cm — 20 cm

Estimate the perimeter in centimeters. Then use your centimeter ruler to find the perimeter. Estimates will vary.

4. 14 cm
5. 10 cm
6. 12 cm
7. 12 cm

Mixed Review
Use the graph.

8. How many students chose blue as their favorite color?
8

9. How many more students chose green than yellow?
5

10. How many students voted in all?
27

FAVORITE COLOR

Practice PW115

444 Chapter 22

Other Ways to Find Perimeter

You can count the units to find the perimeter.

Examples Count the units to find the perimeter.

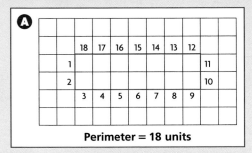

Perimeter = 18 units

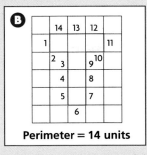

Perimeter = 14 units

You can add the lengths of the sides to find the perimeter.

More Examples Find the perimeter.

C
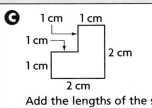

Add the lengths of the sides:
1 cm + 2 cm + 2 cm + 1 cm +
1 cm + 1 cm = 8 cm
The perimeter is 8 cm.

D

Use a ruler to find the length of each side in centimeters.

Add the lengths of the sides to find the perimeter.
3 cm + 2 cm + 3 cm + 2 cm = 10 cm
The perimeter is 10 cm.

- **REASONING** Explain how to find the perimeter of a square if the length of one side is 5 inches. **Possible answer: All 4 sides of a square have the same length, so you can add 5 + 5 + 5 + 5 = 20; so, the perimeter is 20 inches.**

▶ Check

1. Explain how you could measure only 2 sides to find the perimeter in Example D. **Possible answer: Rectangles have 2 pairs of equal sides. If you know the length of 1 side from each pair, then you know the length of the other 2 sides without measuring them.**

Find the perimeter.

2.
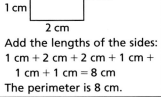
8 units

3.

3 cm ... 3 cm
11 cm   5 cm

LESSON CONTINUES ▶

Chapter 22 **445**

Direct students' attention sidebar

- *Direct students' attention to Examples A and B.* **What do the numbers around each figure stand for?** The numbers show how each unit of the perimeter of the figure is counted.

- *Ask students to look at Example C.* **Why are there 6 addends in this number sentence instead of 4?** This figure has 6 sides. **REASONING Could you measure only one side of a triangle to find its perimeter? Explain.** Yes, if you were finding the perimeter of an equilateral triangle

SPECIAL NOTE: Have students begin collecting and recording the daily outdoor temperature. This data will be used for an activity in Chapter 24.

3 PRACTICE

Guided Practice

Do Check Exercises 1–3 with your students. Identify students who are having difficulty and choose appropriate lesson resources to provide assistance.

445

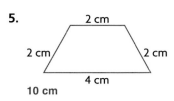
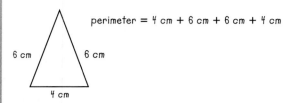

COMMON ERROR ALERT

Some students may measure a side of an object more than once.

perimeter = 4 cm + 6 cm + 6 cm + 4 cm

6 cm   6 cm

4 cm

To correct, have them set a paper clip on the side where they began measuring.

Independent Practice

Note that Exercise 13 is a **multistep or strategy problem.** Assign Exercises 4–16.

MULTISTEP OR STRATEGY PROBLEM To solve Exercise 13, have students add the lengths of side A and side B together, and then subtract the total from the perimeter, 8 cm, to find the length of side C. Guide students to conclude that they could also subtract the lengths of side A and side B from the perimeter to find the length of side C, 3 cm.

Find the perimeter.

4.

14 units

5.

2 cm

2 cm   2 cm

4 cm

10 cm

6.

3 cm

1 cm   1 cm

3 cm

8 cm

7.

12 units

8.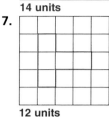

1 cm

2 cm   2 cm

1 cm

6 cm

9.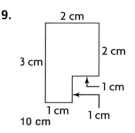

2 cm

3 cm   2 cm

1 cm

1 cm   1 cm

10 cm

Estimate the perimeter in centimeters. Then use your centimeter ruler to find the perimeter. Estimates will vary.

10.

16 cm

11.

6 cm

12. USE DATA The drawing at the right shows the size of Mrs. Gibson's vegetable garden. She wants to put a fence around her garden. Use the scale to find how many yards of fencing she will need.
12 yards of fencing

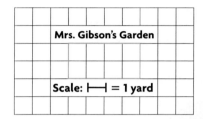

Mrs. Gibson's Garden

Scale: ⊢—⊣ = 1 yard

13.  This triangle has a perimeter of 8 cm. How long is Side C?

3 cm
Side B
3 cm
Side A
2 cm
Side C
☐ cm

14. ✏ **Write About It** Choose an object. Explain how to estimate and measure its perimeter. Then use a ruler to measure its perimeter in inches.
Check students' work.

446

Alternative Teaching Strategy   Scaffolded Instruction

PURPOSE Students use increasingly larger units to estimate the perimeters of various-sized objects.

MATERIALS *For each group* paper clips, markers, paintbrushes, broom, magazine, poster board

Step 1

Discuss with students how they would estimate the perimeter of a magazine in paper clips. Then have them place the paper clips around the edges of the magazine to check their estimates.

Step 2

Have students estimate the perimeter of a piece of poster board in markers. Then have them place the markers along the edge of

the poster board to check their answers. Ask: Would you need more or less paper clips than markers to estimate the perimeter of the poster board? Explain. more; The markers are longer than the paper clips.

PROFESSIONAL DEVELOPMENT

Step 3

Continue the estimation and measuring process by having students estimate the perimeter of their desks in paintbrushes and the perimeter of the classroom in brooms. Then have them compare their estimates to their measurements. Check students' work.

15. Use grid paper. Draw a rectangle with a perimeter of 12 units.
Check students' drawings.

16. Jana's beach towel is 5 feet long and 3 feet wide. What is its perimeter? **16 feet**

17. Mr. Thompson is making a wooden frame for his poster. How many feet of wood will he need to go around the poster? **D**

← 3 feet →

4 feet | 4 feet

← 3 feet →

A 7 feet   **C** 11 feet
B 10 feet   **D** 14 feet

18. Susan drew this design for the center of a quilt. What is the distance around the design? **B**

A 18 units
B 16 units
C 14 units
D 12 units

Problem Solving 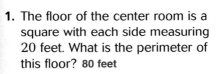 ... to Social Studies

In 1806, Thomas Jefferson built a house in the Blue Ridge Mountains of Virginia. In the center of the house, Jefferson built a special room that is a perfect cube. This room is 20 feet long, 20 feet wide, and 20 feet tall. Jefferson's granddaughter would draw in this room because a large window called a skylight was in the ceiling.

1. The floor of the center room is a square with each side measuring 20 feet. What is the perimeter of this floor? **80 feet**

2. Around the house, Jefferson built a circular road that measured 540 yards. Write an expression to find how many feet this is. Find the value of the expression.
540 + 540 + 540; 1,620 feet

Chapter 22   **447**

Reading Strategy

K-W-L CHART Before having students read the Link Up, have them look at the photo. Ask them to predict what the Link Up will be about. Then have students make a three-column chart headed *What I Know, What I Want to Know,* and *What I Learned.* Ask them to fill in the first two columns. Have them fill in the third column as they read the paragraph.

K-W-L Chart

What I Know	What I Want to Know	What I Learned

Problem Solving ... to Social Studies

• *Direct students' attention to Exercise 1.*
How do you find the perimeter of the floor?
Possible answer: by adding the lengths of the 4 sides of the square: 20 + 20 + 20 + 20 = 80 feet

REASONING There are 32 panes of glass in the center room skylight. What is the perimeter of the skylight if the length of each pane of glass measures 1 foot and the panes are arranged in 2 rows of 16? **36 feet** in 4 rows of 8? **24 feet**

4 ASSESS

Summarize the lesson by having students:

DISCUSS How do you find the perimeter of an object when you don't know the lengths of the sides? by using a ruler to measure each side, then adding the lengths of the sides

WRITE Explain how you could draw a rectangle that has a perimeter of 16 cm. Possible answer: by drawing two sides that are 3 cm in length and two that are 5 cm in length

LESSON QUIZ
Find the perimeter.

Transparency **22.1**

1. The length of one side of a square is 8 cm. What is its perimeter? 32 cm

2. A rectangle is 8 feet long and 6 feet wide. What is its perimeter? 28 feet

Area

Lesson Planning

Objective To find the area of a plane figure

Materials *For each group* square tiles; 1-inch grid paper, p. TR57

NCTM Standards
1. Number and Operations
4. Measurement
6. Problem Solving
7. Reasoning and Proof
8. Communication
9. Connections
10. Representation

Math Background
These ideas will help students understand how to find the area of a plane figure.

- Find the area by counting the number of square units needed to cover a surface.

- To find the area of a rectangle, multiply the number of rows times the number of square units in each row.

Vocabulary
square unit a square with a side length of 1 unit

area number of square units needed to cover a flat surface

Warm-Up Resources

Number of the Day

Transparency **22.2**

Use the number of inches in a foot to write one number sentence with three addends. Possible answer: 12 + 8 + 10 = 30

Daily Facts Practice

Have students practice division facts by completing Set D of *Teacher's Resource Book*, p. TR99.

Transparency **22.2**

Problem of the Day

One side of Dot's triangle and the length of Bob's rectangle are 4 cm. Another side of Dot's triangle is as long as a side of Dave's square. The perimeter of each figure is 12 cm. How long are the sides of each figure? square: 3 cm by 3 cm; rectangle: 4 cm by 2 cm; triangle: 3 cm by 4 cm by 5 cm

Solution Problem of the Day tab, p. PD22

Intervention and Extension Resources

Alternative Teaching Strategy

MATERIALS *For each student* 1-cm grid paper, p. TR58

Help students **find the area of plane figures by drawing them on grid paper**. Have students draw rectangles with the following dimensions: 2 rows, 6 in each row; 4 rows, 7 in each row; 5 rows, 8 in each row. Encourage them to count the number of rows and the number of squares in each row. Have students multiply to find the area and then count the squares to check their work. 12 square centimeters; 28 square centimeters; 40 square centimeters

VISUAL

VISUAL/SPATIAL

Multistep and Strategy Problems

The following multistep and strategy problems are provided in Lesson 22.2:

Page	Item
449	7, 9

ESOL/ESL

ESOL/ESL

Help students **understand the difference between** *perimeter* **and** *area.*

Have students make a 3-column chart.

- In the first column, have them write the words *perimeter, square unit*, and *area.*
- In the second column, have them write the definition of each word.
- In the third column, have them illustrate each word with a drawing. Check students' work.

VISUAL

VISUAL/SPATIAL

Art Connection

Help students **reinforce the concept of finding perimeter and area** by designing a quilt.

Have students decide the perimeter and area of each square. Ask: If each student makes one square, what will the perimeter and area of the completed class quilt be? Answers will vary.

VISUAL

VISUAL/SPATIAL, LOGICAL/MATHEMATICAL

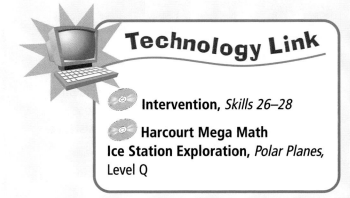

Technology Link

Intervention, *Skills 26–28*

Harcourt Mega Math
Ice Station Exploration, *Polar Planes,* Level Q

Lesson 22.2 Organizer

Objective To find the area of a plane figure

Vocabulary square unit, area

Materials *For each group* square tiles; 1-inch grid paper, p. TR57

---

1 INTRODUCE

QUICK REVIEW provides review of prerequisite skills.

WHY LEARN THIS? You can find out how much area a plane figure, such as a bulletin board, covers. *Share the lesson objective with students.*

---

2 TEACH

Guided Instruction

• *Ask students to read the definitions of* square unit *and* area.
  What are some examples of flat surfaces?
  Possible answers: desktop, tabletop, floor

• *Discuss Step 1 with students.*
  Do you think you will use the same number of square tiles as the other students? Explain.
  Yes, the front of the book is the same size.

• *Ask students to work in pairs. Then have students read and complete Steps 2 and 3.*
  Why is drawing a picture helpful? Possible answer: it is helpful when counting the square units.

• *Have students read the Math Idea.*
  How can you find the area of a book cover if you run out of tiles? Possible answer: find the number of tiles in one row. Then make one column of tiles to find the total number of rows. Multiply the number of rows by the number of tiles in each row.

---

3 PRACTICE

Guided Practice

Do Try It Exercises a–b with your students. Identify students who are having difficulty and choose appropriate lesson resources to provide assistance.

448 Chapter 22

Quick Review
1. $5 \times 8 = \blacksquare$ 2. $7 \times 6 = \blacksquare$
         40   42
3. $3 \times 3 = \blacksquare$ 4. $2 \times 8 = \blacksquare$
         9   16
5. $6 \times 4 = \blacksquare$
         24

▶ **Explore**

A **square unit** is a square with a side length of 1 unit. You use square units to measure area. **Area** is the number of square units needed to cover a flat surface.

1 square unit:
1 unit / 1 unit / 1 unit / 1 unit

VOCABULARY
square unit
area

MATERIALS
square tiles
grid paper

Activity

Use square tiles to find the area of your math book cover.

STEP 1
Estimate how many squares will cover your math book. Then place square tiles in rows on the front of your math book. Cover the whole surface.

STEP 2
Use grid paper. Draw a picture to show how you covered the math book.

STEP 3
Count and record the number of square tiles you used. This number is the book cover's area in square units.

MATH IDEA You can find the area of a surface by counting the number of square units needed to cover the surface.
• Look at the picture you made. How could you use multiplication to find the area? Possible answer: You could multiply the number in each row times the number of rows.

Try It

Use square tiles to find the area of each.
Check students' work.
a. an index card   b. a sheet of paper

How many rows of tiles do I need to cover an index card?

448

Reteach 22.2

Area

The **area** of a figure is the number of square units needed to cover a flat surface.

This is a square unit. ☐   Count the number of square units to find the area. The area of the figure is 6 square units.

Find the area of each figure. Write the area in square units.

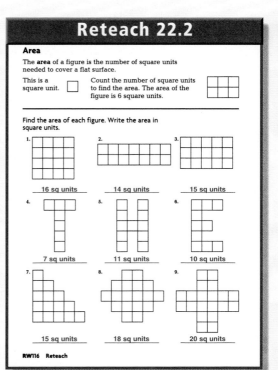

1. 16 sq units   2. 14 sq units   3. 15 sq units
4. 7 sq units   5. 11 sq units   6. 10 sq units
7. 15 sq units   8. 18 sq units   9. 20 sq units

RW116   Reteach

Practice 22.2

Area

Find the area of each figure. Write the area in square units.

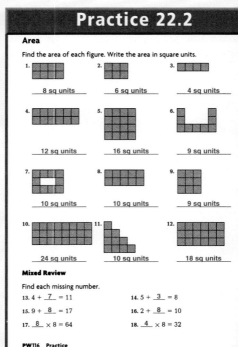

1. 8 sq units   2. 6 sq units   3. 4 sq units
4. 12 sq units   5. 16 sq units   6. 9 sq units
7. 10 sq units   8. 10 sq units   9. 9 sq units
10. 24 sq units 11. 10 sq units 12. 18 sq units

Mixed Review

Find each missing number.
13. $4 + \underline{7} = 11$ 14. $5 + \underline{3} = 8$
15. $9 + \underline{8} = 17$ 16. $2 + \underline{8} = 10$
17. $\underline{8} \times 8 = 64$ 18. $\underline{4} \times 8 = 32$

PW116   Practice

▶ Connect

To find the area of a rectangle, multiply the number of rows times the number in each row.

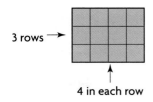

3 rows →

4 in each row

number of rows	number in each row	area
↓	↓	↓
3	× 4	= 12 square units

▶ Practice and Problem Solving

Find the area of each figure. Write the area in square units.

1.

9 square units

2.

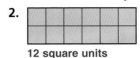

12 square units

3.

8 square units

4.

24 square units

5.

8 square units

6.

10 square units

7. REASONING For which of the figures in Exercises 1–6 could you use multiplication to find the area? Explain. **See above.**

7. Figures in Exercises 1, 2, 3, and 4; you can multiply the number of rows by the number of units in each row.

8. ❓ **What's the Question?** Rachel's blanket is 6 feet wide and 4 feet long. The answer is 24 square feet. **What's the area of the blanket?**

9. Copy the figure at the right on grid paper. Show the perimeter in red, and show the area in blue. Record the perimeter and area of the figure. **Check students' drawings. Perimeter: 18 units; Area: 10 square units**

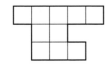

Getting Ready for the EOG Test

10. Joshua made the figure at the right with square tiles. How many tiles did he use? **C**

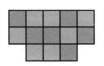

A 16 square tiles   C 13 square tiles
B 15 square tiles   D 12 square tiles

Chapter 22   **449**

COMMON ERROR ALERT

Students may confuse the terms *perimeter* and *area*. Have students look up both terms in their glossaries, write the definitions in their math journals, and draw pictures that will help them remember the meanings of both words.

Independent Practice

Note that Exercises 7 and 9 are **multistep or strategy problems.** Assign Exercises 1–9.

4 ASSESS

Summarize the lesson by having students:

DISCUSS How could you find the area of your desktop? Possible answer: by covering it with square tiles and counting the tiles

📓 **WRITE How can you use multiplication to find area?** Possible answer: by multiplying the number of rows by the number in each row

LESSON QUIZ

Find the area of each figure. Write the area in square units.

Transparency **22.2**

1.   16 square units

2.   18 square units

3.   18 square units

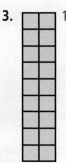

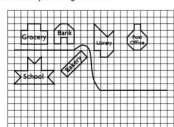
449

Lesson Planning

Objective To apply the problem solving skill *make generalizations* to solve problems

Lesson Resources Reading Transparency 22; Intervention • Problem Solving, Strategy/Skill 22

NCTM Standards
1. **Number and Operations**
2. **Algebra**
3. **Geometry**
4. **Measurement**
6. **Problem Solving**
7. **Reasoning and Proof**
8. **Communication**
9. **Connections**
10. **Representation**

Math Background
Consider the following when making generalizations about the perimeter and area of rectangles and squares.

- Rectangles that have different shapes may have the same perimeter but have different areas.

- When comparing the areas of rectangles with the same perimeter, a square will always have the greatest area.

Warm-Up Resources

Number of the Day

Transparency 22.3

Write 5 division sentences using the number of letters in a friend's first name as the divisor.
Answers will vary.

Daily Facts Practice

Have students practice division facts by completing Set E of *Teacher's Resource Book*, p. TR99.

Transparency 22.3

Problem of the Day

Draw each figure and find its perimeter and area.
1. 3 units wide, 6 units long 18 units; 18 square units
2. 8 units wide, 5 units long 26 units; 40 square units
3. 7 units wide, 7 units long 28 units; 49 square units

Solution Problem of the Day tab, p. PD22

Intervention and Extension Resources

Alternative Teaching Strategy

MATERIALS *For each group* geoboard, rubber bands

Have students **compare the areas of different shapes that have the same perimeter.**

- In the top left corner of the geoboard, have students make a rectangle that is 3 units wide and 1 unit long. Ask: What is the perimeter of this rectangle? 8 units What is the area? 3 square units

- In the bottom right corner of the geoboard, have students make a square that has sides that are each 2 units long. Ask: What is the perimeter of the square? 8 units What is the area? 4 square units

Ask: What do you notice about the perimeters and areas of the two figures? Possible answer: the perimeters are the same, but the area of the square is greater than the area of the rectangle.

KINESTHETIC

BODILY/KINESTHETIC

Reading Strategy

Make Generalizations Tell students that a generalization is a broad conclusion based on given or known information that they can apply to similar situations.

Ask: What generalization can be made from Lesson 3? If a square and a rectangle have the same perimeter, the square will always have the greater area.

Transparency
22 **Reading Transparency 22**

Multistep and Strategy Problems

The following multistep and strategy problems are provided in Lesson 22.3:

Page	Item
451	1–8

ESOL/ESL

Help students **build understanding of the terms** *least area* **and** *greatest area.* Display 3 different-sized rectangles. While comparing the rectangles, point to the figure with the greatest area while saying "greatest area." Then point to the figure with the least area while saying "least area." Now repeat the exercise using other rectangles or rectangular classroom objects, such as different-sized book covers or tabletops. Have students draw similar objects and ask them to identify the items with the greatest area and those with the least area. Check students' work.

ESOL/ESL

VISUAL

VERBAL/LINGUISTIC

Early Finishers

MATERIALS *For each pair* toothpicks

Help students **find areas of rectangles and squares.** Have one student construct a rectangle of any size with toothpicks. Have the partner measure the length and width of the rectangle, then calculate the area of the rectangle. Have students trade tasks and continue with other rectangles or squares. Check students' work.

KINESTHETIC

BODILY/KINESTHETIC, INTERPERSONAL/SOCIAL

Technology Link

Intervention • Problem Solving, *Strategy/Skill 22*

Lesson 22.3 Organizer

Objective To apply the problem solving skill *make generalizations* to solve problems

Lesson Resources Reading Transparency 22; Intervention • Problem Solving, Strategy/Skill 22

1 INTRODUCE

QUICK REVIEW provides review of prerequisite skills.

WHY LEARN THIS? You'll be able to make generalizations that will help you solve similar problems. *Share the lesson objective with students.*

2 TEACH

Guided Instruction

• *After they read the introduction, have students look at Maura's drawings.*
Why are these the only rectangles and square that Maura could make? These are the only ones that have a perimeter of 12 feet.

• *Ask students to look at the number sentences under Maura's first drawing.*
What does the number sentence 1 + 5 + 1 + 5 = 12 feet show? It shows how Maura added the lengths of the 4 sides of the rectangle to find the perimeter.

• *Direct students' attention to Talk About It.*
What generalization could you make about the figures? Possible answer: when comparing the areas of rectangles and squares with the same perimeter, squares always have the greatest area.
How will this generalization help you solve similar problems in the future? Possible answer: I will know that the square with the same perimeter as other rectangles has the greatest area without having to find the areas of all the rectangles.

450 Chapter 22

---

3 Problem Solving Skill
Make Generalizations

Quick Review

1. $4 + 2 + 4 + 2 = \blacksquare$ 12

2. $8 + 3 + 8 + 3 = \blacksquare$ 22

3. $3 \times 4 = \blacksquare$ 12

4. $7 \times 3 = \blacksquare$ 21

5. $8 \times 4 = \blacksquare$ 32

UNDERSTAND > PLAN > SOLVE > CHECK

DON'T FENCE ME IN   Maura plans to plant a flower garden and put a fence around it. She has 12 feet of fencing to make a square or rectangular garden. If she wants to have the greatest area possible, should her fence be a square or a rectangle?

Maura draws a picture to show all the square and rectangular gardens she can make.

1 ... 5

2 ... 4

3 ... 3

Perimeter:
$1 + 5 + 1 + 5 = 12$ feet
Area:
$1 \times 5 = 5$ square feet

Perimeter:
$2 + 4 + 2 + 4 = 12$ feet
Area:
$2 \times 4 = 8$ square feet

Perimeter:
$3 + 3 + 3 + 3 = 12$ feet
Area:
$3 \times 3 = 9$ square feet

Order the areas: $5 < 8 < 9$

9 square feet is the greatest area.

So, Maura's fence should be a square.

Talk About It

• **Describe** how the area changes when rectangles with the same perimeter change from long and thin to square.
Possible answer: The area increases.
• **What if** Maura had 20 feet of fencing? To have the greatest area, should her fence be a square or a rectangle?
square

450

Reteach 22.3

Problem Solving Skill

Make Generalizations

A **generalization** is a statement that tells how things are alike in some way. Words like *many, most, usually,* and *generally* often signal generalizations.

Look at the areas and perimeters of these squares. What generalization can you make?

perimeter: 12 units   **perimeter:** 20 units   **perimeter:** 28 units
area: 9 square units   **area:** 25 square units   **area:** 49 square units

Generalization: Usually the number in the area of a square is greater than the number in the perimeter of the square.

Find the perimeter and area for each of the following rectangles.

perimeter: __20__ units   **perimeter:** __20__ units   **perimeter:** __20__ units
area: __16__ square units   **area:** __21__ square units   **area:** __24__ square units

Circle the generalization that you can make about the rectangles above.

The perimeter of a rectangle is measured in square units.

Rectangles with the same perimeters and different areas always have the same shape.

As rectangles with the same perimeters become more like squares in shape, their areas usually increase.

Reteach   **RW117**

Practice 22.3

Problem Solving Skill

Make Generalizations

1. A laundry room is shaped like a rectangle. The area of the room is 6 square yards. The perimeter is 10 yards. The room is longer than it is wide. How wide is the room? How long is the room?

2 yd wide; 3 yd long

2. Mark has a piece of string that is 12 inches long. He shapes the string into a rectangle that has an area of 5 square inches. Can Mark make a shape that has a greater area with the string? If so, what is the area?
Yes. Possible answers: 8 sq in., 9 sq in.

3. The perimeter of a table is 24 feet. The table is twice as long as it is wide. How long and how wide is the table?

4 ft; 8 ft;

4. Mrs. Brown put a wallpaper border around a room that is 10 feet long and 9 feet wide. How long is the wallpaper border? What is the area of the floor in the room?

38 ft; 90 sq ft

Mixed Review

Solve.

5. The time shown on Mario's watch is 10:45. He has just finished raking leaves for 30 minutes. Before that, he played basketball for 1 hour. At what time did he start playing basketball?

9:15

6. Carrie is swimming in the middle lane of the pool. She waves to her father, who is swimming 3 lanes away, in the end lane. How many lanes does the pool have?

7 lanes

7. $\begin{array}{r} 9 \\ \times 6 \\ \hline 54 \end{array}$ 8. $\begin{array}{r} 5 \\ \times 7 \\ \hline 35 \end{array}$ 9. $\begin{array}{r} 7 \\ \times 7 \\ \hline 49 \end{array}$ 10. $\begin{array}{r} 8 \\ \times 3 \\ \hline 24 \end{array}$ 11. $\begin{array}{r} 4 \\ \times 6 \\ \hline 24 \end{array}$

Practice   **PW117**

Problem Solving Practice

Hop-along trail
Snacks

1. What if Maura had 8 feet of fencing to make a rectangle or square with the greatest possible area? How long should it be? How wide should it be? **2 feet long and 2 feet wide**

2. Kyle used 16 feet of fencing to make a square play yard for his rabbit. What was the length of each side? What was the area of the play yard? **4 feet; 16 square feet**

Jane drew some figures on grid paper.

3. Which figure has a perimeter of 16 units? **C**

A

B

C

D

4. Which figure has an area of 15 square units? **J**

F

G

H

J

Mixed Applications

5. Abe bought 3 muffins for $1 each and 2 cartons of milk for $0.50 each. How much did he spend in all? **$4**

6. Ted eats 1 sandwich and drinks 2 glasses of milk each day. How many glasses of milk does he drink in one week? **14 glasses of milk**

7. **REASONING** I am a 2-digit number less than 20. I can be divided evenly into groups of 4. I cannot be divided evenly into groups of 3. What number am I? **16**

8. Write a problem about the perimeter and area of a rectangle. Use square tiles to make the rectangle. Then draw a picture of your rectangle. **Check students' problems and drawings.**

Chapter 22 451

---

③ PRACTICE

Guided Practice

Do Problem Solving Practice Exercises 1–4 with your students. Identify students who are having difficulty and choose appropriate lesson resources to provide assistance. Note that Exercises 1–4 are **multistep or strategy problems.**

Independent Practice

Note that Exercises 5–8 are **multistep or strategy problems.** Assign Exercises 5–8.

SCAFFOLDED INSTRUCTION Use the prompts on Transparency 22 to guide instruction for the multistep or strategy problem in Exercise 5.

Transparency 22

④ ASSESS

Summarize the lesson by having students:

DISCUSS Can you make more different rectangular fences with a perimeter of 30 feet than rectangular fences with a perimeter of 24 feet? **Explain.** Yes, there are more combinations of factors of 30 than 24.

WRITE What generalization can you make about squares and rectangles that have the same perimeter? Give an example. The square will always have a greater area than any other rectangle. A square with 6-inch sides has a greater area but the same perimeter as a rectangle 10 inches long and 2 inches wide and a rectangle 8 inches long and 4 inches wide. The perimeter of each is 24 inches.

LESSON QUIZ

Transparency 22.3

1. Heather has 20 feet of lumber to build a pen with the greatest area for her rabbit. How long should it be? 5 feet long How wide should it be? 5 feet wide

2. Fran has 24 inches of string. She made a rectangle 8 inches long and 4 inches wide. Could she have made a shape with a larger area? Explain. Yes, she could have made a square with sides of 6 inches and an area of 36 square inches. The rectangle she made has an area of only 32 square inches.

Challenge 22.3

Painting Project

Amanda and her father are painting the walls of a playroom. One of the walls has a window. Another wall has a door, which they are not painting.

Find the area that needs to be painted on each of the four walls. All measurements are given in feet.

1.
8 / 10
area = **80** square feet

2.
8 / 9
area = **72** square feet

3.
8 / 10
7 / 3
area = **59** square feet

4.
8 / 9
3 / 4
area = **60** square feet

5. What is the total area that needs to be painted?
271 sq ft

6. The label on the can of paint says that 1 quart covers about 100 square feet. How many quarts of paint will Amanda and her father need to paint the walls with 2 coats of paint?
6 qt

7. Amanda wants to put a wallpaper border around the room near the ceiling. How many feet of wallpaper border does she need to go all the way around the room?
38 ft

Challenge CW117

Reading Strategy 22.3

Paraphrase  Understand → Plan → Solve → Check

Sometimes it is helpful to **paraphrase**, or tell again in your own words, what a problem is asking you to do. This helps you better understand the problem. Many ideas, words, and problems in math can be paraphrased.

Read the following problem.

▶ Mr. Wilson will let Jamie display her antique dollhouse furniture along with his model planes at the model show. Her space has a perimeter of 14 feet and an area of 12 square feet. How long is it? How wide is it?

1. Use your own words to paraphrase the problem.
Answers will vary.

2. Solve the problem.
Possible answer: An array of 12 squares can be 2 × 6, 3 × 4, or 1 × 12. Only the 3 × 4 array has a perimeter of 14.
3 + 4 + 3 + 4 = 14

3. Describe the problem solving strategy you used. **Possible answer:** I acted it out using square tiles to make arrays of 12. Then I found the perimeter of each array.

Solve.

4. Mrs. Chung asked Jeff to paint a design on a tile. The perimeter is 18 in. The area is 18 square inches. How long is the tile? How wide is it?
6 × 3 = 18 sq in.; 6 + 3 + 6 + 3 = 18 in.; 6 in. long; 3 in. wide

5. Dave and Lisa have a garden. The perimeter is 20 feet. The area is 16 square feet. How long is the garden? How wide is it?
8 × 2 = 16 sq ft; 8 + 2 + 8 + 2 = 20 ft; 8 ft long; 2 ft wide

Reading Strategy PS117

451

Lesson Planning

PROFESSIONAL DEVELOPMENT

Objective To estimate and measure volume

Materials *For each group* color cubes, small box; *For Linkup* connecting cubes; grid paper, p. TR58

NCTM Standards
1. **Number and Operations**
2. **Algebra**
3. **Geometry**
4. **Measurement**
6. **Problem Solving**
7. **Reasoning and Proof**
8. **Communication**
10. **Representation**

Math Background
Consider the following when you introduce estimating and measuring volume.

- Volume is the amount of space a solid figure takes up.
- Volume is measured in cubic units.
- To measure the volume of a solid, find the number of cubic units needed to fill the solid.
- Instead of counting each cube, find the number of cubes in one layer and multiply by the number of layers to find the volume.

Vocabulary
volume the amount of space a solid figure takes up

cubic unit a cube with a side length of 1 unit used to measure volume

Warm-Up Resources

Number of the Day

Transparency **22.4**

Find today's date on the calendar. Use that number to write three number sentences using at least two different operations. Check students' work.

Daily Facts Practice

Have students practice multiplication and division facts by completing Set F of *Teacher's Resource Book,* p. TR99.

Transparency **22.4**

Problem of the Day

The perimeter of each face of a solid figure is 32 units. The area of each face is 64 square units. What plane figure forms each face? What is the name of the solid figure? square; cube

Solution Problem of the Day tab, p. PD22

Intervention and Extension Resources

Alternative Teaching Strategy

MATERIALS *For each student* connecting cubes

ESOL/ESL

Help students **build understanding of the volume of a figure.** Rather than placing color cubes in a box, have students use connecting cubes to build a rectangular prism. In this way, students can see the connecting cubes in the faces of the figure, as well as the number of layers in the figure. Check students' work.

See also page 454.

VISUAL, KINESTHETIC

VISUAL/SPATIAL, BODILY/KINESTHETIC

Multistep and Strategy Problems

The following multistep or strategy problem is provided in Lesson 22.4:

Page	Item
454	17

Special Needs

MATERIALS *For each group* color cubes, 2–4 boxes

Help students **estimate the volume of different-sized boxes.** Have students estimate which box has the greatest volume and which box has the least volume.

- Have students estimate the number of cubes that will be needed to show the volume of each box.
- Have them test their estimates by placing cubes inside or next to each box until they match its volume.
- Have students count the total cubes to find the volume of each box and compare. Check students' work.

VISUAL, KINESTHETIC

VISUAL/SPATIAL, BODILY/KINESTHETIC

Early Finishers

MATERIALS *For each pair* color cubes

Have students **find the volume of solids made of color cubes.** Ask one student to make a rectangular prism or a cube using the color cubes. Then have the partner make a table in which the length, width, and height of the figure are recorded. Students can exchange tables with other pairs of students and have them build the solid figures and find the volume. Check students' work.

VISUAL, KINESTHETIC

VISUAL/SPATIAL, BODILY/KINESTHETIC

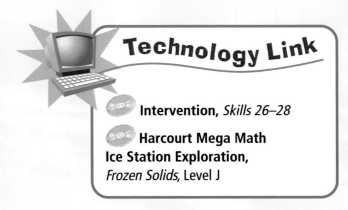

Technology Link

- **Intervention,** *Skills 26–28*
- **Harcourt Mega Math Ice Station Exploration,** *Frozen Solids,* Level J

Lesson 22.4 Organizer

Objective To estimate and measure volume

Vocabulary volume, cubic unit

Materials *For each group* connecting cubes, small box; *For Linkup* connecting cubes; grid paper, p. TR58

1 INTRODUCE

QUICK REVIEW provides review of prerequisite skills.

WHY LEARN THIS? You will be able to determine how much a container such as a box can hold. *Share the lesson objective with students.*

2 TEACH

Guided Instruction

• *Introduce the vocabulary terms.*
What is meant by the words *amount of space a solid figure takes up*? the space inside the figure

MODIFYING INSTRUCTION Have students use boxes of various sizes to estimate and find volume. If large boxes are used, have students work in small groups.

• *Have students complete Step 2.*
How many cubes did you use to fill the bottom of the box? How many layers of cubes did you make? Answers will vary.

• *To check understanding, have students read the Math Idea.*
Explain the Math Idea in your own words.
Possible answer: to measure the volume of a solid figure, fill it with cubes and count the number of cubes you used.

LESSON

▶ Learn

FILL IT UP **Volume** is the amount of space a solid figure takes up.

A **cubic unit** is used to measure volume. A cubic unit is a cube with a side length of 1 unit. You can use connecting cubes to show cubic units.

1 cubic unit

Activity
Use connecting cubes to find the volume of a box.

MATERIALS: connecting cubes, small box

STEP 1
Estimate how many cubes it will take to fill the box. Record your estimate.

STEP 2
Count the cubes you use. Place the cubes in rows along the bottom of the box. Then continue to make layers of cubes until the box is full.

STEP 3
Record how many cubes it took to fill the box. This is the volume of the box in cubic units.

• How does your estimate compare with the actual volume? **Answers will vary.**

MATH IDEA To measure the volume of a solid, find the number of cubic units needed to fill the solid.

452

Quick Review

1. $1 \times 4 \times 2 = \blacksquare$ 8
2. $2 \times 3 \times 2 = \blacksquare$ 12
3. $5 \times 1 \times 2 = \blacksquare$ 10
4. $3 \times 2 \times 8 = \blacksquare$ 48
5. $4 \times 2 \times 3 = \blacksquare$ 24

VOCABULARY
volume
cubic unit

Technology Link
More Practice:
Harcourt Mega Math
Ice Station Exploration,
Frozen Solids, **Level J**

Reteach 22.4

Volume

When you measure **volume**, you measure the amount of space a solid figure takes up.

To measure the volume of a solid figure, find the number of cubic units needed to fill the solid.

1 unit
1 unit
1 unit
1 cubic unit

Here are two ways to find the volume of a rectangular prism.

You can count and add.

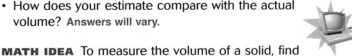

Count the number of cubes in one layer. Then add the number of cubes in each layer.

$10 + 10 + 10 = 30$ cubic units

You can count and multiply.

Count the number of cubes in one layer. Then multiply by the number of layers.

3 layers $\times$ 10 cubes = 30 cubic units

1.
__3__ layers $\times$ __8__ cubes = __24__ cubic units

2.
__5__ layers $\times$ __6__ cubes = __30__ cubic units

3.
__2__ layers $\times$ __9__ cubes = __18__ cubic units

RW118 Reteach

Practice 22.4

Volume

Use cubes to make each solid. Then write the volume in cubic units.

1.
volume: __36 cu units__

2.
volume: __48 cu units__

3.
volume: __20 cu units__

4.
volume: __16 cu units__

Find the volume of each solid. Write the volume in cubic units.

5.
volume: __63 cu units__

6.
volume: __72 cu units__

7.
volume: __49 cu units__

8.
volume: __100 cu units__

Mixed Review

Add.

9.	10.	11.	12.
532	158	851	936
+ 196	+ 270	+ 653	+ 498
728	428	1,504	1,434

PW118 Practice

Find the Volume

When you cannot count each cube, you can think about layers to find the volume.

Example

Find the volume of each solid.

Since you cannot see each cube, look at the top layer of cubes. For a rectangular prism,
number of layers × number of cubes in each layer = volume.

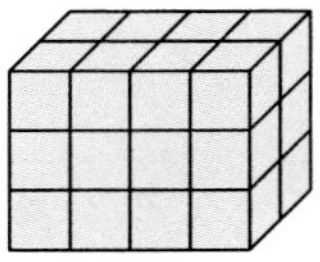

3 layers × 8 cubes per layer =
24 cubic units
So, the volume is 24 cubic units.

2 layers × 6 cubes per layer =
12 cubic units
So, the volume is 12 cubic units.

▶ Check

1. **Explain** how you would find the volume of a box that has 4 layers and each layer is 3 cubes long and 2 cubes wide. **Answers may vary. The volume is 24 cubic units.**

Use cubes to make each solid. Then write the volume in cubic units.

2.

18 cubic units

3.

6 cubic units

4.

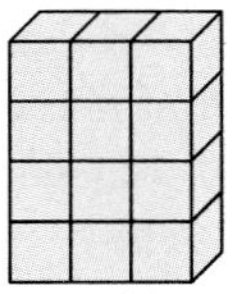

12 cubic units

5.

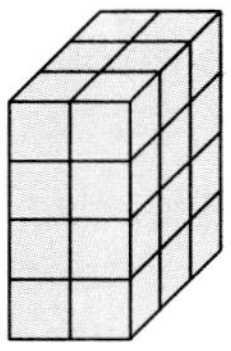

24 cubic units

6.

9 cubic units

7.

27 cubic units

LESSON CONTINUES ▶

Chapter 22 **453**

• *Have students look at the figures in the example.* **If you flipped the figure on the left so that the face with 6 cubes showing was on top, would the volume change? Explain.** No; the figure still has the same number of cubes. **If each layer of the figure on the right has 6 cubes, and there are 2 layers, what is the volume?** 12 cubic units

3 PRACTICE

Guided Practice

Do Check Exercises 1–7 with your students. Identify students who are having difficulty and choose appropriate lesson resources to provide assistance.

Challenge 22.4

Combining Volumes

Some solids are made by combining two or more rectangular prisms. To find the volume of these solids, first find the volume of each prism. Then add the volumes.

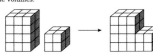

3 layers × 6 cubes = 24 cubic units

2 layers × 4 cubes = 8 cubic units

24 + 8 = 32 cubic units

Find the volume of each solid. Write the volume in cubic units.

1.

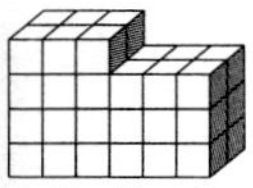

42 cubic units

2.

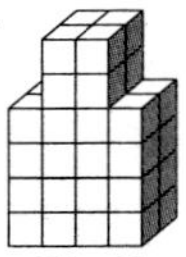

40 cubic units

3.

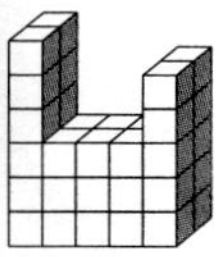

40 cubic units

4.

72 cubic units

118   Challenge

Problem Solving 22.4

Volume

Understand ▸ Plan ▸ Solve ▸ Check

Write the correct answer.

1. Find the total area of this figure.

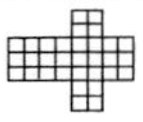

32 square units

2. Find the volume of this solid.

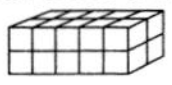

20 cubic units

3. A box is 4 cubes long and 2 cubes wide. Its volume is 32 cubic units. What is the height of the box?

4 cubes

4. Ruth wants to save 5 dollars worth of pennies. How many pennies must she save?

500 pennies

Choose the letter of the correct answer.

5. Find the area of this figure.

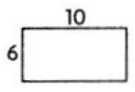

10
6

Ⓐ 60 square units
B   32 square units
C   26 square units
D   16 square units

6. Find the volume of this solid.

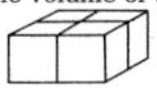

Ⓕ 4 cubic units
G   16 cubic units
H   20 cubic units
J   24 cubic units

7. There are 81 chairs in 9 equal rows. How many chairs are in each row?

A   12   C   10
B   11   Ⓓ 9

8. Nona fit 3 rows of 3 cubes in the bottom of a box. She put in 7 more layers. How many cubes did Nona fit in the box?

F   14 cubes   Ⓗ 72 cubes
G   17 cubes   J   114 cubes

9. **Write About It** How can you check that your answer to Problem 3 is correct?

Possible answer: I can multiply the length by the height by the width to get 32. 4 × 2 = 8; 8 × 4 = 32.

PS118   Problem Solving

453

Independent Practice

Note that Exercise 17 is a **multistep or strategy problem**. Assign Exercises 8–21.

Vocabulary Power Name some everyday examples of perimeter, such as the perimeter of a building or of a baseball field. Discuss each example and decide when it would be helpful to know the perimeter.

MULTISTEP OR STRATEGY PROBLEM To solve Exercise 17, students must divide 32 by 4 to get 8, and then divide 8 by 4 to find the height of the box. Guide students to conclude that the division must be done twice to find the height of 2 cubes.

ALGEBRAIC THINKING For Exercise 18, have students write a number sentence to show how many cubes are in one layer. Then have them write a number sentence using the product as one of the factors of 12.

Use cubes to make each solid. Then write the volume in cubic units.

8.
32 cubic units

9.
8 cubic units

10.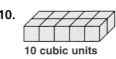
10 cubic units

Find the volume of each solid. Write the volume in cubic units.

11.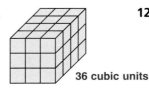
36 cubic units

12.
16 cubic units

13.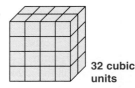
32 cubic units

14. **Vocabulary Power** The word *perimeter* comes from the Greek words *peri*, which means "around," and *metron*, which means "measure." Describe how to find the perimeter of a poster.
Possible answer: Measure all the way around the outer edge of the poster.

15. **? What's the Error?** Justin found the volume of this solid. He said the volume was 16 cubic units. Describe his error. Give the correct volume. 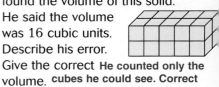 **He counted only the cubes he could see. Correct volume is 20 cubic units.**

16. Sam's box is 2 cubes long, 2 cubes wide, and 3 cubes high. What is the volume of his box? **12 cubic units**

17. Todd's box is 4 cubes long and 4 cubes wide. It has a volume of 32 cubic units. What is the height of the box? **2 cubes**

18. **ALGEBRA** Each layer of Andrew's prism is 6 cubic units. Its volume is 12 cubic units. How many layers are in the prism? You may use cubes to help. **2 layers**

19. **FAST FACT • ART** The St. Louis Gateway Arch is 630 feet high. It is 325 feet taller than the Statue of Liberty. What is the height of the Statue of Liberty? **305 feet**

20. **Write About It** How is finding the area of a figure different from finding the volume of a solid?
Possible answer: To find the area you cover the surface, and to find the volume you fill the space inside.

21. Look at the figure in Exercise 13. Write a multiplication sentence to find the volume of the figure.
Possible answer: 8 [cubic units] × 4 [layers] = 32 cubic units

454

Alternative Teaching Strategy   Scaffolded Instruction

PURPOSE Students use cubes and a box to find volume.

MATERIALS *For each group* color cubes, empty box

Step 1

Have students put cubes in a row along the longest edge of the box. Ask: How many cubes are in a row? Check students' work. Explain that this number is the *length*.

Step 2

Have students add more rows to cover the bottom of the box. Ask: How many rows are in the bottom layer? Check students' work. Explain that this number is the *width*.

Step 3

Have students add layers of cubes to fill the box. Ask: How many layers are there? Check students' work. Explain that this number is the *height*.

Step 4

Ask students to count all the cubes. Then ask: How many cubes did it take to fill the box? Check students' work. Tell students that this number is the *volume*.

PROFESSIONAL DEVELOPMENT

Step 5

Have students make a four-column table. The title of the table is *Volume*, and the titles of the columns are *Length, Width, Height,* and *Volume*. Then have students record the information about their boxes in the table.

Volume			
Length	Width	Height	Volume
4	2	3	24

---

22. Jane looks into this box filled with cubes. There are 4 layers of cubes. In each layer there are 2 rows of 5 cubes. How many cubes are in the box? **A**

A 40 cubes
B 35 cubes
C 20 cubes
D 11 cubes

Problem Solving **LiNKUP** . . . to Reading

STRATEGY • ANALYZE INFORMATION To solve some problems, you need to *analyze*, or look carefully at, each part.

Analyze these drawings to identify the solid figure. Notice that the drawings of the top, side, and front views are plane shapes, not solid figures.

So, the solid figure looks like this.

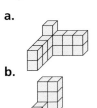

Choose the solid figure that each set of drawings shows.

1. b
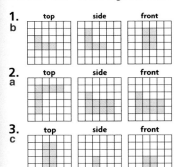

a.

2. a

b.

3. c

c.

4. Build a figure with connecting cubes. Then use grid paper and draw its top, side, and front views. **Check students' work.**

Chapter 22 **455**

Problem Solving **LiNKUP** . . . to Reading

- *Have students look at the figure in the introduction.*
  How many cubes are used to make this solid figure? 12 cubes

- *Have students look at Exercises 1–3.*
  Which of the figures from Exercises 1–3 has the greatest volume? What is its volume? *a* has the greatest volume; 15 cubes.
  REASONING How do the different views help you decide how to match each set of drawings with a solid face? Possible answer: by comparing the different views of each figure to see if they match, you can match the solid figures with the views.

4 ASSESS

Summarize the lesson by having students:

DISCUSS How can you find the volume of a shoe box? Place cubes in rows in the bottom of the box. Continue to make layers of cubes until the box is full. Multiply the number of cubes in each layer by the number of layers to get the total volume.

WRITE Todd has a box that is 4 cubes long and 4 cubes wide. The box has a volume of 48 cubes. What is the height of the box? Explain. 3 cubes; each layer has 16 cubes. $16 + 16 + 16 = 48$

LESSON QUIZ
Find the volume of each solid. Write the volume in cubic units.

Transparency **22.4**

1. 12 cubic units

2.  10 cubic units

3. 27 cubic units

455

CHAPTER 22 Extra Practice

Purpose To provide extra practice for the skills presented in this chapter

The blue page references in each set of exercises refer to the lesson pages where each skill is taught.

Internet Resources

 Visit **THE LEARNING SITE** at **www.harcourtschool.com** for a listing of practice activities.

Extra Practice

Set A (pp. 444–447)

Find the perimeter.

1.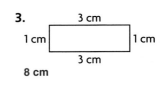
5 cm
2 cm / 2 cm
5 cm
14 cm

2.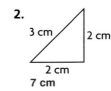
3 cm / 2 cm
2 cm
7 cm

3.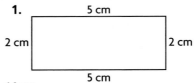
3 cm
1 cm / 1 cm
3 cm
8 cm

Estimate the perimeter in centimeters. Then use your centimeter ruler to find the perimeter. Estimates will vary.

4.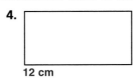
12 cm

5.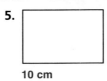
10 cm

6.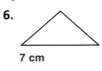
7 cm

Set B (pp. 452–455)

Find the volume of each solid. Write the volume in cubic units.

1.
2 cubic units

2.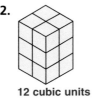
12 cubic units

3.
6 cubic units

4.
4 cubic units

5.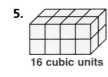
16 cubic units

6.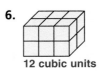
12 cubic units

7.
6 cubic units

8.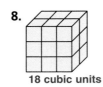
18 cubic units

9.
18 cubic units

456

Review/Test

CHECK VOCABULARY AND CONCEPTS

Choose the best term from the box.

area
cubic units
perimeter

1. To measure volume, you use __?__ . (p. 452) **cubic units**

2. The distance around a figure is called its __?__ . (p. 444) **perimeter**

Find the perimeter of each figure.
(pp. 444–447)

  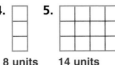

3. 8 units
4. 8 units
5. 14 units

Write the area in square units.
(pp. 448–449)

15 square units

6. 8 square units
7.

CHECK SKILLS

Find the perimeter. (pp. 444–447)

8. 1 cm / 1 cm / 1 cm / 3 cm

9. 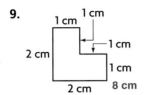 1 cm 1 cm 1 cm 2 cm 1 cm 2 cm 8 cm

10. 3 cm 2 cm 2 cm 10 cm 3 cm

Write the volume in cubic units. (pp. 452–455)

 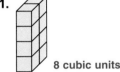  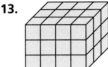 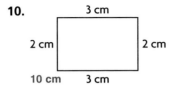

11. 8 cubic units
12. 18 cubic units
13. 36 cubic units

CHECK PROBLEM SOLVING

Solve. (pp. 450–451)

14. Pedro has 20 inches of string. He wants to make a rectangle or square with the greatest possible area. How wide should it be? How long should it be? **5 in. wide, 5 in. long**

15. Nora has 16 inches of ribbon. She wants to make a rectangle or square with the greatest possible area. How long should it be? How wide should it be? **4 inches long; 4 inches wide**

Chapter 22 457

Review/Test

Purpose To check understanding of concepts, skills, and problem solving presented in Chapter 22

Using the Page

The Chapter 22 Review/Test can be used as a **review** or a **test**.

- Items 1–7 check understanding of concepts and new vocabulary.
- Items 8–13 check skill proficiency.
- Items 14–15 check students' abilities to choose and apply problem solving strategies to real-life measurement problems.

Portfolio Suggest that students place the completed Chapter 22 Review/Test in their portfolios.

Using the Assessment Guide

- Multiple-choice format of Chapter 22 Posttest— See *Assessment Guide*, pp. AG133–134.
- Free-response format of Chapter 22 Posttest— See *Assessment Guide*, pp. AG135–136.

Using Student Self-Assessment

The How Did I Do? survey helps students assess what they have learned and how they learned it. This survey is available as a copying master in *Assessment Guide*, p. AGxvii.

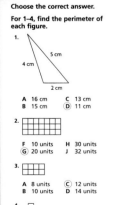
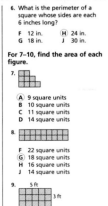
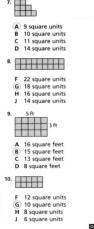
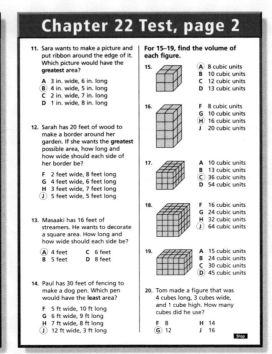

Chapter 22 Test, page 1

Choose the correct answer.

For 1–4, find the perimeter of each figure.

1. 5 cm 4 cm 2 cm
   A 16 cm   C 13 cm
   B 15 cm   (D) 11 cm

2.
   F 10 units   H 30 units
   (G) 20 units   J 32 units

3.
   A 8 units   (C) 12 units
   B 10 units   D 14 units

4.
   F 6 units   H 12 units
   G 10 units   (J) 16 units

5. What is the perimeter of a rectangle that is 4 inches long and 3 inches wide?
   A 7 in.   C 21 in.
   (B) 14 in.   D 28 in.

6. What is the perimeter of a square whose sides are each 6 inches long?
   F 12 in.   (H) 24 in.
   G 18 in.   J 30 in.

For 7–10, find the area of each figure.

7.
   (A) 9 square units
   B 10 square units
   C 11 square units
   D 14 square units

8.
   F 22 square units
   (G) 18 square units
   H 16 square units
   J 14 square units

9. 5 ft 3 ft
   A 16 square feet
   (B) 15 square feet
   C 13 square feet
   D 8 square feet

10.
   F 12 square units
   (G) 10 square units
   H 8 square units
   J 6 square units

Go On

Chapter 22 Test, page 2

11. Sara wants to make a picture and put ribbon around the edge of it. Which picture would have the greatest area?
    A 3 in. wide, 6 in. long
    (B) 4 in. wide, 5 in. long
    C 2 in. wide, 7 in. long
    D 1 in. wide, 8 in. long

12. Sarah has 20 feet of wood to make a border around her garden. If she wants the greatest possible area, how long and how wide should each side of her border be?
    F 2 feet wide, 8 feet long
    G 4 feet wide, 6 feet long
    H 3 feet wide, 7 feet long
    (J) 5 feet wide, 5 feet long

13. Masaaki has 16 feet of streamers. He wants to decorate a square area. How long and how wide should each side be?
    (A) 4 feet   C 6 feet
    B 5 feet   D 8 feet

14. Paul has 30 feet of fencing to make a dog pen. Which pen would have the **least** area?
    F 5 ft wide, 10 ft long
    G 6 ft wide, 9 ft long
    H 7 ft wide, 8 ft long
    (J) 12 ft wide, 3 ft long

For 15–19, find the volume of each figure.

15.
   (A) 8 cubic units
   B 10 cubic units
   C 12 cubic units
   D 13 cubic units

16.
   F 8 cubic units
   G 10 cubic units
   (H) 16 cubic units
   J 20 cubic units

17.
   A 10 cubic units
   B 13 cubic units
   (C) 36 cubic units
   D 54 cubic units

18.
   F 16 cubic units
   G 24 cubic units
   H 32 cubic units
   (J) 64 cubic units

19.
   A 15 cubic units
   B 24 cubic units
   C 30 cubic units
   (D) 45 cubic units

20. Tom made a figure that was 4 cubes long, 3 cubes wide, and 1 cube high. How many cubes did he use?
    F 8   H 14
    (G) 12   J 16

Stop

Perimeter, Area, and Volume 457

CHAPTER 22

Getting Ready for the EOG Test

Chapters 1–22

Using the Pages

These pages may be used to help students get ready for the North Carolina EOG Test. The test items are written in the same style and arranged in the same format as those on the EOG Test.

The pages are cumulative. They cover the standards from the North Carolina Mathematics Standard Course of Study that have been taught up to this point in the text or in a previous grade. Each Getting Ready for the EOG Test also reviews the North Carolina mathematics strands shown below.

- Number and Operations
- Measurement
- Geometry
- Data Analysis and Probability
- Algebra

These pages can be assigned at the end of the chapter as classwork or as a homework assignment. You may want to have students use individual recording sheets presented in a multiple-choice (standardized) format. A Test Answer Sheet is available as a black-line master in the *Assessment Guide* (p. AGlii).

You may wish to have students describe how they solved each problem and share their solutions.

Getting Ready for the EOG Test

★ NUMBER AND OPERATIONS

1. What is the value of the digit 5 in 5,468? **A**

  A 5,000
  B   500
  C   50
  D   5

> **TIP** **Understand the problem.** See item 2. You are asked to find the number of boxes sold *in all*. You must decide which operation to use to find the answer.

2. The table shows how many boxes of cookies Austin, Taylor, and Caroline sold.

COOKIES SOLD	
Name	**Number of Boxes**
Austin	68
Taylor	56
Caroline	60

How many boxes of cookies did they sell in all? **B**

  A 174
  B 184
  C 190
  D 204

3. **Explain It** In October, 6 classes went on a field trip. There were 18 students in each class. *About* how many students went on the trip? Tell how you estimated. See page 459.

★ MEASUREMENT AND GEOMETRY

4. Mrs. Lee displayed this poster.

Which polygon describes the shape of the poster? **D**

  A triangle   **C** octagon
  B pentagon   **D** hexagon

5. Antonio is putting a fence around a square garden. One side of the garden is 4 feet long. How many feet of fencing are needed in all? **D**

  A 8 feet   **C** 12 feet
  B 10 feet   **D** 16 feet

6. **Explain It** What kind of polygon is shown below?

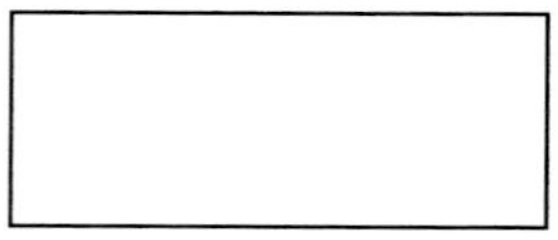

Describe the sides and angles of this polygon. See page 459.

458

⭐ ALGEBRA

7. The table below shows the number of note cards in boxes. Which number is missing in the table? **A**

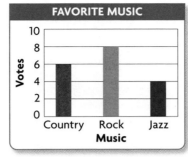

Boxes	1	2	3	4
Cards	12	24	▦	48

A 36
B 34
C 32
D 30

8. Robin wrote this number pattern.

   24, 21, 18, 15, 12

Which rule could she have used to make the pattern? **B**

A Add 4.
B Subtract 3.
C Multiply by 2.
D Divide by 3.

9. Explain It Michael had 136 coins. He gave some coins to his brother. Now Michael has 119 coins.

Write a number sentence with a variable for the number of coins Michael gave to his brother. Then explain how you can find the number that the variable stands for. **See below.**

⭐ DATA ANALYSIS AND PROBABILITY

10. The bar graph below shows the number of votes for favorite kinds of music.

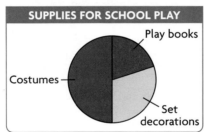

FAVORITE MUSIC

How many votes for favorite kinds of music were there in all? **C**

A 12   **C** 18
B 16   **D** 20

11. Explain It Mr. Anderson made a circle graph to show how he spent money on supplies for the school play. List the supplies in order from the *least* amount spent to the *greatest* amount spent. Explain how you decided in what order to list the supplies. **See below.**

SUPPLIES FOR SCHOOL PLAY

Play books
Costumes
Set decorations

Chapters 1–22

Item Analysis

You may wish to use the item analysis to determine which North Carolina standards need additional review.

Item	North Carolina Standard	Lesson
1	1.01	2.3
2	1.02	1.4
3	1.06	4.1
4	3.01	19.3
5	2.02	22.1
6	3.01	19.3
7	5.02	9.3
8	5.01	9.3
9	5.04	5.4
10	4.01	16.2
11	4.01	15.5

SCORING RUBRIC
Explain It

2 Demonstrates a complete understanding of the problem and chooses an appropriate strategy to determine the solution

1 Demonstrates a partial understanding of the problem and chooses a strategy that does not lead to a complete and accurate solution

0 Demonstrates little understanding of the problem and shows little evidence of using any strategy to determine a solution

Explain It • Written Response

3. Possible answer: about 120 students; round 18 to 20. Then add: 20 + 20 + 20 + 20 + 20 + 20 = 120.

6. Possible answer: quadrilateral; it has 2 pairs of parallel sides and 4 right angles.

9. Possible answer: 136 − 119 = c; start with the number of coins Michael had. Subtract the number of coins that he has left. The variable stands for 17, which is the number of coins Michael gave to his brother.

11. Play books, set decorations, costumes; possible answer: I looked at the size of each part of the circle graph. The smallest part of the circle graph shows that the least amount was spent on play books, and the largest part shows that the greatest amount was spent on costumes.

It's in the Bag
Pocketful of Polygons

Purpose To make polygons and describe them

Materials *For each student* construction paper; tape; polygon worksheets, pp. TR188–193; scissors; crayons

Using the Page

Preparing the Materials

- Make copies of the polygon worksheets for each student. Gather all other materials needed for the project. If there are not enough supplies, students may work in pairs.

Making the Project

- Have students use the construction paper to make a pocket for holding their polygons. You may wish to have students complete Step 1 on one day and Steps 2–4 on a different day.

Extending the Project

- Challenge students to draw and cut out their own polygons. Encourage students to use a ruler for drawing the sides and to make the polygons large enough to write labels and descriptions on them.

IT'S IN THE BAG

Pocketful of Polygons

PROJECT Make polygons and describe them.

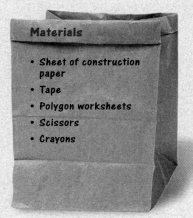

Materials

- **Sheet of construction paper**
- **Tape**
- **Polygon worksheets**
- **Scissors**
- **Crayons**

Directions

1. Fold the sheet of construction paper in half. Tape the left and right sides closed, leaving the top of the pocket open. *(Picture A)* Decorate the front of your pocket.

2. On the worksheets, complete the sentences to describe each polygon. *(Picture B)*

3. Use crayons to color your polygons. Then cut out the polygons. *(Picture C)*

4. Share your descriptions with classmates. Store your polygons in the pocket that you made.

460 Unit 6 • It's in the Bag

Challenge

Measure with Degrees

You can use a circle to measure angles in degrees.

A $\frac{1}{4}$ turn around a circle measures 90°.

A $\frac{1}{2}$ turn measures 180°.

A full turn measures 360°.

 Activity

MATERIALS: circle pattern, pencil, tracing paper

Measure the angle at the right.

STEP 1	**STEP 2**	**STEP 3**
Trace the circle pattern onto tracing paper. Fold it in half 3 times. Open up the circle and mark the center. 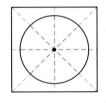	Label each fold with the measures shown. 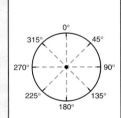	Place the center of the circle on the vertex of the angle. Line up one ray with the 0° mark. Read the measure at the other ray. 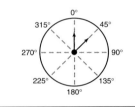

So, the angle measures 45°.

Try It

Use your circle to measure each angle.

1. 90°
2. 225°
3. 135°
4. 270°

  Intervention and Extension Resources

Advanced Learners

MATERIALS *For each group* protractor, paper

Extend the concept of measuring with degrees by having students use protractors to measure angles. Give each group a protractor and point out the mark on the protractor that shows where to align the vertex. Have students draw angles on a sheet of paper and use the protractor to measure the angles. Discuss the similarities and differences between the protractor and the circle used in the activity on the page.

KINESTHETIC

LOGICAL/MATHEMATICAL

Challenge
Measure with Degrees

Objective To extend the concepts and skills of Chapters 19–22

Materials *For each student* circle pattern, p. TR38; pencil; tracing paper

Using the Page

- *Direct students' attention to the circles at the top of the page.*

  What is a name for the angle that measures 90°? right angle

  Reasoning Why is there only one ray on the third circle? It shows that the ray has turned all the way around the circle.

  Algebraic Thinking What do you think the measure of a $\frac{3}{4}$ turn would be? A $\frac{3}{4}$ turn would measure 270°.

Try It Before completing Try It Exercises 1–4, have students estimate the measure of each angle.

Study Guide and Review

Study Guide and Review

Purpose To help students review concepts and skills presented in Chapters 19–22

Using the Pages

✔ Assessment Checkpoint

The Study Guide and Review includes content from Chapters 19–22.

Chapter 19

19.1 Line Segments and Angles

19.2 Types of Lines

19.3 Plane Figures

19.4 Triangles

19.5 Quadrilaterals

19.6 Problem Solving Strategy: *Draw a Diagram*

Chapter 20

20.1 Hands On: Congruent Figures

20.2 Symmetry

20.3 Similar Figures

20.4 Hands On: Slides, Flips, and Turns

20.5 Problem Solving Strategy: *Make a Model*

Chapter 21

21.1 Solid Figures

21.2 Combine Solid Figures

21.3 Tessellations

21.4 Draw Figures

21.5 Problem Solving Skill: *Identify Relationships*

Chapter 22

22.1 Perimeter

22.2 Hands On: Area

22.3 Problem Solving Skill: *Make Generalizations*

22.4 Volume

The blue page numbers in parentheses provided with each group of exercises indicate the pages on which the concept or skill was presented.

VOCABULARY

Choose the best term from the box.

| face |
| polygon |
| vertex |

1. A closed plane figure with straight sides is a ? . (p. 390) **polygon**
2. A corner of a solid figure where three or more edges meet is called a ? . (p. 424) **vertex**

STUDY AND SOLVE

Chapter 19

Classify angles.

This angle is a **right angle**. It forms a square corner.

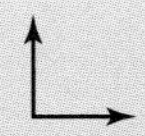

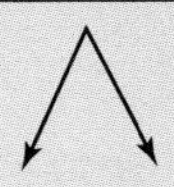

This angle is an **acute angle**.  This angle is an **obtuse angle**.

Write whether the angle is a *right angle,* an *obtuse angle,* or an *acute angle.* (pp. 384–387)

3. 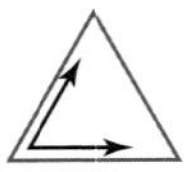 **acute angle**

4. 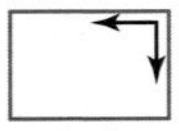 **right angle**

5. 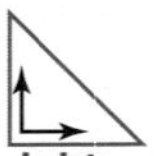 **right angle**

6. 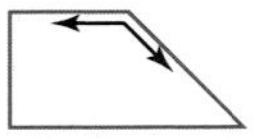 **obtuse angle**

Classify polygons.

Which figure is a pentagon?

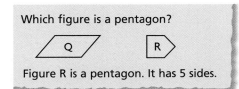

Figure R is a pentagon. It has 5 sides.

For 7–8, use the figures. (pp. 390–391)

7. Which is a quadrilateral? **C**

8. Which is a hexagon? **A**

Chapter 20

Identify lines of symmetry.

When a figure is folded along a line of symmetry, the two parts match exactly.

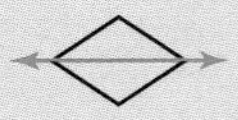

For 9–10, tell if the blue line is a line of symmetry. Write *yes* or *no.* (pp. 410–411)

9.  **no**

10.  **yes**

Chapter 21

Describe solid figures.

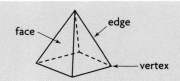

This square pyramid has 5 faces, 8 edges, and 5 vertices. One face is a square, and the other four faces are triangles.

For 11–13, use the figure. (pp. 424–427)

11. How many faces, edges, and vertices does the figure have?
6 faces; 12 edges; 8 vertices
12. What shape are the faces of this figure? **rectangles**
13. What is this figure called?
rectangular prism

Chapter 22

Find perimeter and area.

Add the lengths of the sides to find the perimeter.
$3 + 5 + 3 + 5 = 16$
So, the perimeter is 16 units.
Multiply the number of rows times the number in each row to find the area.
$3 \times 5 = 15$
So, the area is 15 square units.

Find the perimeter. (pp. 444–447)

14.
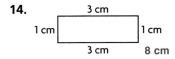

Write the area in square units.
(pp. 448–449)

15.

6 square units

16.

12 square units

PROBLEM SOLVING PRACTICE

Solve. (pp. 416–417, 450–451)

17. Use pattern blocks to make a quadrilateral. Then use a different combination of pattern blocks to make a figure that is congruent to your quadrilateral.
Check students' models.

18. Jed makes a rectangle with the greatest possible area using 16 inches of string. What are the length and width of his rectangle?
length: 4 in.; width: 4 in.

Unit 6 • Chapters 19–22   463

Portfolio **Portfolio Suggestions** The portfolio represents the growth, talents, achievements, and reflections of the mathematics learner. Students might spend a short time selecting work samples for their portfolios and completing A Guide to My Math Portfolio from *Assessment Guide*, page AGxix.

You may want to have students respond to the following questions:

• **What new understanding of math have I developed in the past several weeks?**

• **What growth in understanding or skills can I see in my work?**

• **What can I do to improve my understanding of math ideas?**

• **What would I like to learn more about?**

For information on how to organize, share, and evaluate portfolios, see *Assessment Guide*, page AGxviii.

Use the item analysis in the **Intervention** chart to diagnose students' errors. You may wish to reinforce content or remediate misunderstandings by using the text pages or lesson resources.

Unit Test

• Multiple-choice format of Unit 6 Posttest–See *Assessment Guide*, pp. AG137–140.

• Free-Response format of Unit 6 Posttest–See *Assessment Guide*, pp. AG141–144.

Study Guide and Review Intervention • How to Help Options

Items	Text Pages	Reteach and Practice Resources
3–6	384–387	Worksheets for Lesson 19.1
7–8	390–391	Worksheets for Lesson 19.3
9–10	410–411	Worksheets for Lesson 20.2
11–13	424–427	Worksheets for Lesson 21.1
14	444–447	Worksheets for Lesson 22.1
15–16	448–449	Worksheets for Lesson 22.2
17, 18	416–417, 450–451	Worksheets for Lessons 20.5, 22.3

Performance Assessment

Purpose To provide performance assessment tasks for Chapters 19–22

Using the Page

- *Have students work individually or in pairs as an alternative to formal assessment.*

- *Use the performance indicators and work samples below to evaluate Tasks A–B.*

See *Performance Assessment* for

- a complete scoring rubric, p. PAx, for this unit.
- additional student work samples for this unit.
- copying masters for this unit.

You may suggest that students place completed Performance Assessment tasks in their portfolios.

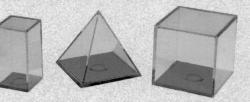

PERFORMANCE ASSESSMENT

TASK A • ART CLASS

Matthew is learning how to draw these solid figures in art class.

triangle	point
square	line segment
polygon	angle
rectangle	perpendicular
quadrilateral	right angle
parallelogram	parallel

a. Choose one of the solid figures. Tell how many faces, edges, and vertices it has. **See above.**

b. Draw each plane figure that is a face of the solid figure you chose. Label each plane figure with its name. **Possible answer: The faces drawn are a square and a triangle.**

c. Write at least three sentences to describe one of the faces. Use as many of the terms from the box at the top of the page as you can. **Possible answer: It is a polygon, a quadrilateral, and a square. It has 4 line segments and 4 right angles. It has 2 pairs of parallel sides.**

a. Possible answer: A square pyramid has 5 faces, 8 edges, and 5 vertices.

b. Possible answer: My design has 3 lines of symmetry since it is an equilateral triangle. If you fold it along the lines, both sides would match.

TASK B • MATH T-SHIRTS

Materials: pattern blocks, ruler

The math club members want to design special T-shirts to wear on meeting days. These are the rules for the design.

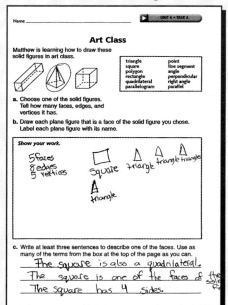

Design Rules

1. The design must be made of pattern-block shapes.
2. The design must be in the shape of a triangle.
3. One side of the triangle must be at least 6 inches long.
4. Congruent shapes must be the same color.

a. Follow all the design rules listed in the box. First, use pattern blocks to make a design for the T-shirt. Then, draw your design. **Check students' designs.**

b. Explain whether your design has any lines of symmetry. **See above.**

c. Explain how you would enlarge the design for a poster. **Possible answer: I could copy my design on 1-inch grid paper and then copy it on 2-inch grid paper to enlarge it.**

464 Unit 6 • Performance Assessment

Performance Indicators

Task A

A student with a Level 3 paper

✓ Identifies the number of faces, edges, and vertices of a solid figure.

✓ Draws and names each plane figure face of a solid figure.

✓ Writes three sentences describing attributes of one plane figure face of a solid figure.

Task B

A student with a Level 3 paper

✓ Uses pattern blocks to make a triangle with one side at least 6 inches long.

✓ Recognizes congruent shapes.

✓ Recognizes figures with lines of symmetry.

✓ Explains how to enlarge a figure or design.

Work Samples for Task A and Task B

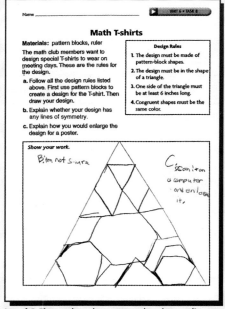

Level 3 This student shows good understanding of the task. Answers are complete and accurate. The sentences make sense and are complete.

Level 3 The student demonstrated understanding of the task. The triangle is about the correct size. Answer to part *c* is acceptable, although it is not the expected response.

Technology Linkup

Symmetry

Computers can help you draw geometric figures. Use drawing tools on a computer to draw a square. Draw one line of symmetry on the square.

STEP 1

Open a computer application that has drawing tools. Choose the tool to make a square.

STEP 2

Go to the place on the screen where you want to draw the figure. Use the tool to draw a square.

STEP 3

Choose the line tool. Use the tool to draw a line of symmetry on the square.

Practice and Problem Solving

Use computer drawing tools to draw each figure.
For Exercises 1–7, check students' drawings.

1. square
2. rectangle
3. triangle
4. circle

5. Draw a rectangle. Draw two lines of symmetry on the rectangle.

6. Draw a circle. Draw two lines of symmetry on the circle.

7. **STRETCH YOUR THINKING** Make a figure by combining at least two different geometric figures.

GO ON-LINE

Multimedia Math Glossary www.harcourtschool.com/mathglossary
Vocabulary Power Look up *congruent figures* in the Multimedia Math Glossary. Draw two figures that are congruent. Then draw the line or lines of symmetry on each. **Check students' drawings.**

Technology Linkup

Objective To use a computer to draw plane figures and lines of symmetry

Using the Page

- *Direct students' attention to Step 1.*
  How do you find the menu of the different drawing tools? Possible answer: move the mouse so that the arrow is on the icon and click on the icon to get the menu.

Encourage students to make the square large enough so that they can easily draw the line of symmetry on the square.

- *Direct students' attention to Step 3.*
  How can you tell where the middle of the square is? Possible answer: you can look at the ruler toolbar above or to the right of your page.
  Describe another line of symmetry that could be drawn on the square. Possible answer: a diagonal line from the top left corner to the bottom right corner

Using the Computer

Many drawing tools will allow you to draw a square by holding down the shift key when using a rectangle tool. Likewise, you can draw a circle by holding down the shift key when using an oval tool.

Practice and Problem Solving

You might want to model selecting some of the AutoShapes and extending them before students try it on their own. For the Vocabulary Power item, the congruent figures can be drawn by hand or on the computer.

Multimedia Math Glossary

Congruent figures and all other key vocabulary terms in this unit can be found in the Harcourt Multimedia Math Glossary.
www.harcourtschool.com/mathglossary

Problem Solving
in North Carolina

Purpose To provide additional practice for concepts and skills in Chapters 19–22

Using the Page

HIGH POINT

- *Direct students' attention to the photo at the top of the page.*
What solid figure best describes the shape of the World's Largest Chest of Drawers? rectangular prism
How many faces, edges, and vertices does this solid figure have? 6 faces, 12 edges, and 8 vertices
Do you see any parallel lines? Do you see any perpendicular lines? Possible answer: yes; the edges along the bottom of the drawers are parallel; the side edges of the drawers are perpendicular to the bottom edges of the drawers.

Extension Challenge students to design the front of a building that looks like a chest of drawers. Have them write a description of the building using key vocabulary terms from this unit. Check students' work.

▲ In 1996, the Chest of Drawers was rebuilt into a chest with socks hanging from a drawer.

High Point

HIGH POINT

High Point is famous for the furniture that is made there. More than half of all furniture that is made in the United States is made within 200 miles of High Point.

USE DATA For 1–2, use the photographs.

1. Find examples of polygons and trace them. Write as many vocabulary terms for the polygons as you can. **Check students' work.**
2. Look at the polygons that you traced. Are any of the figures similar? Are any of the figures congruent? **Check students' work.**
3. The original World's Largest Chest of Drawers, built in 1926, was 20 feet tall. Write this height in yards and feet. **6 yd 2 ft**

▲ The World's Largest Chest of Drawers was built in 1926 to be the town's Bureau of Information.

466 Unit 6 • Problem Solving in North Carolina

▲ There are many dollhouses to see at the Angela Peterson Doll and Miniature Museum.

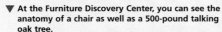

◄ Angela Peterson collected hundreds of dolls from around the world.

▼ At the Furniture Discovery Center, you can see the anatomy of a chair as well as a 500-pound talking oak tree.

FURNITURE OF DIFFERENT SIZES

At the Angela Peterson Doll and Miniature Museum, visitors can see dolls, dollhouses, and dollhouse furniture. At the Furniture Discovery Center, visitors can learn how furniture is made.

USE DATA For 1, use the photograph above.

1. Use the names of solid and plane figures to describe one of the dollhouses. **Check students' responses.**

2. Use dot paper. Draw a polygon to show a floor plan for one room of a dollhouse. Describe the polygon. **Check students' drawings.**

3. **STRETCH YOUR THINKING** The Furniture Discovery Center has more than 8,000 square feet of exhibit space. Suppose one room is 30 feet long and 24 feet wide. What is the area of the room in square yards? Explain. 80 sq yd; possible explanation: 3 ft = 1 yd, so 30 ft = 10 yd and 24 ft = 8 yd. Multiply to find the area: 10 × 8 = 80.

Using the Page

FURNITURE OF DIFFERENT SIZES

- *Have students read the introductory paragraph.* **Reasoning** **What math skills do you think would be used when making furniture? Explain.** Possible answer: measurement would be used to make sure materials like wood are the right size so that pieces fit together correctly. Geometry would be used when designing the shapes of pieces of furniture.

- *Have students complete Exercise 2.* **Does the floor plan that you drew have a line of symmetry?** Check students' responses.

Extension Have students look around the classroom or school for examples of similar and congruent figures. Have them draw diagrams and label their examples. Check students' work.

EOG TEST HANDBOOK

The tips and the problems on the following pages will help you succeed on the EOG Test.

Tips for Success on the EOG Test H2

Before working on the Getting Ready for the EOG Test problems and before taking the EOG Test, sharpen your test-taking skills by reviewing these pages. Here you can find tips such as how to get ready for the test, how to understand the directions, and how to keep track of time.

Getting Ready for the EOG Test H6

The problems in this section cover the strands of the North Carolina Mathematics Standard Course of Study. Use these problems to build your test-taking skills and to prepare for EOG success.

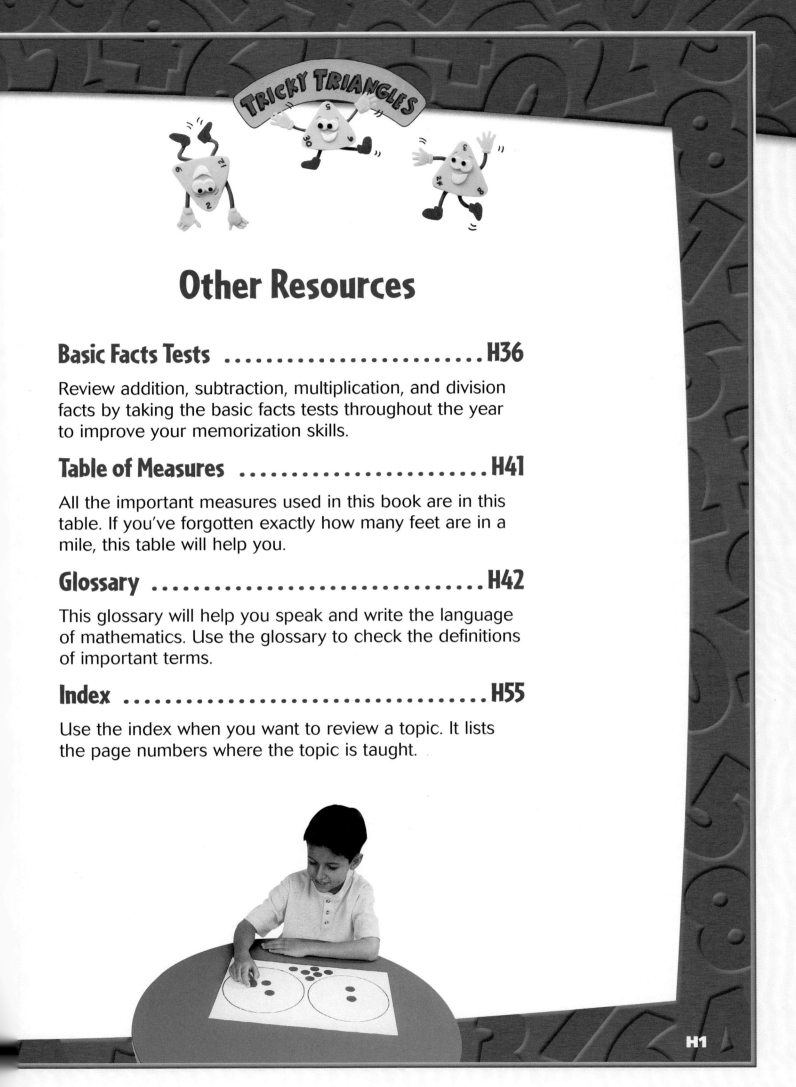

Other Resources

Basic Facts Tests H36

Review addition, subtraction, multiplication, and division facts by taking the basic facts tests throughout the year to improve your memorization skills.

Table of Measures H41

All the important measures used in this book are in this table. If you've forgotten exactly how many feet are in a mile, this table will help you.

Glossary H42

This glossary will help you speak and write the language of mathematics. Use the glossary to check the definitions of important terms.

Index H55

Use the index when you want to review a topic. It lists the page numbers where the topic is taught.

Tips for Success on the EOG Test

Being a good test-taker is like being a good problem solver. When you answer test questions, you are solving problems. Remember to UNDERSTAND, PLAN, **SOLVE**, and CHECK.

UNDERSTAND

Read the problem.

- Look for math terms and recall their meanings.
- Reread the problem and think about the question.
- Use the details in the problem and the question.

1. The sum of the digits of a number is 14. Both the digits are odd. The ones digit is 4 less than the tens digit. What is the number?

A 59 C 86
B 77 D 95

TIP! Understand the problem.
Remember the meanings of *sum*, *digits*, and *odd*. Reread the problem to compare the details to the answer choices. Since all choices have a sum of 14, look for the odd digits. Then look for a ones digit that is 4 less than the tens digit. The answer is **D**.

- Each word is important. Missing a word or reading it incorrectly could cause you to get the wrong answer.
- Pay attention to words that are in **bold italic** type.

2. Kent bought 3 pens at $0.98 each and 4 notebooks at $1.89 each. **About** how much did he pay for all of the items?

A $3 C $11
B $7 D $15

TIP! Look for important words.
The word *about* is an important word. It tells you to estimate the total amount. Round each money amount to the nearest dollar and then multiply by the number of each item. Find the sum of the products. The answer is **C**.

PLAN

Think about how you can solve the problem.

- See if you can solve the problem with the information given.
- Pictures, charts, tables, and graphs may have the information you need.
- You may need to think about information you already know.

3. Soccer practice started at 12:00. The clock shows the time practice ended. How long was soccer practice?

A 10 minutes
B 20 minutes
C 35 minutes
D 50 minutes

TIP! Get the information you need.
Use the clock to find how long soccer practice lasted. You can find out how much time passed by counting by fives. The answer is **D**.

- You may need to write a number sentence and solve it.
- Some problems have two steps or more.
- In some problems you need to look at relationships instead of computing an answer.
- If the path to the solution isn't clear, choose a problem solving strategy and use it to solve the problem.

4. June always has 30 days. Mary takes swimming lessons every three days in June, starting on June 3. How many times will she have lessons?

A 5 C 12
B 10 D 30

TIP! Decide on a plan.
"Lessons every three days" sounds like a pattern. Use the strategy *find a pattern*. Count by threes beginning with June 3 until you reach 30. You name 10 numbers, so the answer is **B**.

SOLVE

Follow your plan, working logically and carefully.

- Estimate your answer. Look for unreasonable answer choices.
- Use reasoning to find the most likely choices.
- Solve all steps needed to answer the problem.
- If your answer does not match any answer choice, check your numbers and your computation.

5. The cafeteria served 76 lunches each day for a week. How many lunches were served in 5 days?

A 76
B 353
C 380
D 1,380

TIP! Eliminate choices.
Estimate the product (5 × 80). The only reasonable answers are B and C. Since 5 times the ones digit 6 is 30, the answer must end in zero. If you are still not certain, multiply and check your answer against B and C. The answer is **C**.

- If your answer still does not match, look for another form of the number, such as a decimal instead of a fraction.
- If answer choices are given as pictures, look at each one by itself while you cover the other three.
- Read answer choices that are statements and relate them to the problem one by one.
- If your strategy isn't working, try a different one.

6. Mr. Rodriguez is putting a wallpaper border around a room. The room is 9 feet wide and 12 feet long. How many feet of border does he need?

A 21 feet C 84 feet
B 42 feet D 108 feet

TIP! Choose the answer.
The border goes around all four walls, two that are 9 feet and two that are 12 feet. Add the lengths of the four walls (9 + 9 + 12 + 12). Find the answer choice that shows this sum. The answer is **B**.

CHECK

Take time to catch your mistakes.

- Be sure you answered the question asked.
- Check for important words you might have missed.
- Did you use all the information you needed?
- Check your computation by using a different method.
- Draw a picture when you are unsure of your answer.

7. Katy is buying 3 books. Their prices are $4.95, $3.25, and $7.49. What is the total cost of the books?

A $14.59 C $15.59
B $14.69 D $15.69

TIP! Check your work.
To check column addition, write the numbers in a different order. Then you will be using different basic facts. For example, add $7.49 + $3.25 + $4.95. The answer is **D**.

Don't Forget!

Before the test

- Listen to the teacher's directions and read the instructions.
- Write down the ending time of the test.
- Know where and how to mark your answers.
- Know whether you should write on the test page or use scratch paper.
- Before the test begins, ask any questions you may have.

During the test

- Work quickly but carefully. If you are unsure how to answer a question, leave it blank and return to it later.
- If you cannot finish on time, read the questions that are left. Answer the easiest ones first. Then answer the others.
- Fill in each answer space carefully. Erase completely if you change an answer. Erase any stray marks.
- Check that the answer number matches the question number, especially if you have skipped a question.

NUMBER AND OPERATIONS

1 Jody wrote this number.

$2,000 + 500 + 8$

What is this number in standard form? C

A 2,850
B 2,580
C 2,508
D 258

2 Which figure is divided into fourths? A

A

B

C

D

3 The Seascape Amusement Park had three hundred twenty-nine visitors one day. How is the number of visitors written in standard form? D

A 3,290
B 3,029
C 392
D 329

Study and Review	
Item	Lesson Pages
1	24–27
2	516–519
3	22–23

NUMBER AND OPERATIONS

4 Robert placed 28 matchbox cars on 4 shelves. Each shelf has the same number of cars. How many cars are on 3 shelves? C

A 7
B 14
C 21
D 28

5 Ruth's book is 243 pages long. Tyler's book is 198 pages long. How many more pages does Ruth's book have than Tyler's book? D

A 441
B 155
C 55
D 45

6 One truck has 6 wheels. If Brian counts 48 wheels in all, how many trucks are there? A

A 8
B 12
C 42
D 56

Study and Review	
Item	Lesson Pages
4	260–261
5	96–97
6	274–277

NUMBER AND OPERATIONS

7 Harry wants to know if he has enough money to buy these items.

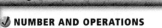

Round each amount to the nearest dollar. *About* how much will all of the items cost? B

A about $4.00
B about $8.00
C about $10.00
D about $12.00

8 Which of the following numbers is odd? D

A 752
B 934
C 106
D 643

9 What fraction of the whole figure is shaded? A

A $\frac{3}{8}$

B $\frac{1}{2}$

C $\frac{5}{8}$

D $\frac{6}{8}$

Study and Review	
Item	Lesson Pages
7	120–121
8	20–21
9	516–519

Number and Operations

ITEM ANALYSIS	
North Carolina Standard	Items
1.01	1, 3
1.02	5
1.03	4, 6
1.05	2, 9
(2) 1.06	8
1.06	7

✓ NUMBER AND OPERATIONS

10 Which list shows these fractions in order from *least* to *greatest*? C

A $\frac{1}{2}, \frac{1}{3}, \frac{1}{4}, \frac{1}{6}$

B $\frac{1}{4}, \frac{1}{3}, \frac{1}{6}, \frac{1}{2}$

C $\frac{1}{6}, \frac{1}{4}, \frac{1}{3}, \frac{1}{2}$

D $\frac{1}{6}, \frac{1}{4}, \frac{1}{2}, \frac{1}{3}$

11 Jose planted 4 seeds in each of 6 containers. How many seeds did Jose plant in all? D

A 2
B 10
C 20
D 24

12 Which figure shows 2×7? A

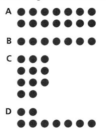

Study and Review	
Item	Lesson Pages
10	526–529
11	194–195
12	162–163

✓ NUMBER AND OPERATIONS

13 What mixed number names the shaded parts? C

A $1\frac{1}{6}$

B $2\frac{1}{2}$

C $2\frac{1}{6}$

D $2\frac{1}{3}$

14 Karlene went to the store. She bought a sweater for $24 and a pair of shorts for $9. How much more did the sweater cost than the shorts? C

A $43
B $33
C $15
D $5

15 Which of these fractions does not equal one fourth? D

A

B

C

D

Study and Review	
Item	Lesson Pages
13	532–533
14	10–11
15	522–525

✓ NUMBER AND OPERATIONS

16 Which expression shows how to estimate $489 + 238$ by rounding to the nearest hundred? D

A $400 + 200$
B $500 + 300$
C $400 + 300$
D $500 + 200$

17 Which of these figures is made with an odd number of circles? B

A

B

C

D

18 James wrote this number.

6,098

Which shows the number in expanded form? B

A $6{,}000 + 900 + 80$
B $6{,}000 + 90 + 8$
C $600 + 90 + 8$
D $6 + 9 + 8$

Study and Review	
Item	Lesson Pages
16	68–69
17	20–21
18	24–27

Number and Operations

ITEM ANALYSIS	
North Carolina Standard	Items
1.01	18
1.02	14, 16
1.03	11–12
1.05	10, 13, 15
(2) 1.06	17

NUMBER AND OPERATIONS

19 Mrs. Clark gave each student 3 pencils and 2 pens on the first day of school. There were 9 students in her class. How many pens did she give to her students? B

A 11
B 18
C 27
D 35

20 There were 24 students sitting on the bleachers. Six teachers sat with them. Then, half of the teachers left. Which number sentence shows how to find the number of people still on the bleachers? A

A $24 + 6 - 3 = 27$
B $24 - 6 - 3 = 15$
C $24 + 6 - 12 = 18$
D $24 + 6 - 6 = 24$

21 There are 8 people at the skate park. Each person wants 3 slices of pizza. Each pizza has 6 slices. How many pizzas are needed for the people at the skate park? B

A 3
B 4
C 6
D 8

Study and Review	
Item	Lesson Pages
19	212–215
20	222–223
21	274–277

MEASUREMENT AND GEOMETRY

1 Which of the following figures contains a right angle? C

A

B

C

D

2 Justin needs to cut an 8 inch piece of wood, but he does not have a ruler. Which of the following would be the *best* way to decide how long to cut the wood? C

A Guess how long it is.
B Look at another piece of wood.
C Measure with a paper clip.
D Ask the price of the wood.

3 Mrs. Perez is making cocoa for 7 family members. Each family member wants 2 cups of cocoa. *About* how much cocoa will she need? A

A 1 gallon
B 1 quart
C 1 cup
D 1 ounce

Study and Review	
Item	Lesson Pages
1	384–387
2	338–341
3	344–345

MEASUREMENT AND GEOMETRY

4 Which of these figures has only flat surfaces? C

A

B

C

D

5 Which figure has a square face? B

A  C

B   D

6 Louis is trying to determine how wide his bedroom door is. Which of these is the *best* estimate of how wide the door is? C

A 3 quarts
B 3 inches
C 3 feet
D 3 yards

Study and Review	
Item	Lesson Pages
4	424–427
5	424–427
6	338–341, 358–361

Number and Operations

ITEM ANALYSIS	
North Carolina Standard	Items
1.03	19
1.06	20–21

Measurement and Geometry

ITEM ANALYSIS	
North Carolina Standard	Items
2.02	2–3, 6
3.01	1, 4–5

7 Which letter has only one line of symmetry? B

A H
B M
C P
D X

8 What is the name of this figure? A

A cone
B cylinder
C pyramid
D rectangular prism

9 Which drawing shows how a soup can would look when viewed from above? D

A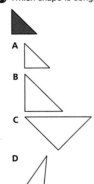

B

C

D

Study and Review

Item	Lesson Pages
7	410–411
8	424–427
9	436–437

---

10 Lucia has 9 blocks. Which figure can she build? B

A   C

B   D

11 Which shape is congruent to the shaded figure? A

A

B

C

D

12 What is the *best* estimate for the weight of a wooden baseball bat? B

A 2 ounces
B 2 pounds
C 20 pounds
D 2 feet

Study and Review

Item	Lesson Pages
10	452–453
11	408–409
12	346–347, 366–367

---

13 If you wanted to know how much water your bathtub holds, which unit of measure would you use? D

A cup
B pint
C quart
D gallon

14 Mica has 16 coins that total $0.65. What coins could he have? B

A 2 quarters, 3 dimes, 4 nickels, 7 pennies
B 1 quarter, 1 dime, 4 nickels, 10 pennies
C 2 quarters, 1 dime, 4 nickels, 9 pennies
D 1 quarter, 2 dimes, 5 nickels, 8 pennies

15 What is the length of the eraser to the nearest centimeter? A

A 3 centimeters
B 7 centimeters
C 8 centimeters
D 12 centimeters

Measurement and Geometry

ITEM ANALYSIS	
North Carolina Standard	Items
2.01	14
2.02	12–13, 15
3.01	8–10
(2) 3.03	7, 11

Study and Review

Item	Lesson Pages
13	344–345
14	110–113
15	358–361

Getting Ready for the EOG Test

✓ MEASUREMENT AND GEOMETRY

16 Sheila wants to make a frame for this poster. What is the distance around the poster? **B**

|←——— 1 meter ———→|

1 meter

Reading is fun!

A 2 meters   C 8 meters
B 4 meters   D 10 meters

17 Which object looks like a rectangular prism? **C**

A   C
B   D

18 Which sentence *best* describes the ice cream cone? **C**

A It is made with a cone and a cube.
B It is made with a sphere and a cylinder.
C It is made with a cone and a sphere.
D It is made with a sphere and a pyramid.

Study and Review	
Item	Lesson Pages
16	444–447
17	424–427
18	428–429

✓ MEASUREMENT AND GEOMETRY

19 The clock shows the time Tina starts making lunch. What time does the clock show? **C**

A 12:32   C 11:32
B 11:35   D 11:22

20 Which figures are congruent? **A**

A

B

C

D

21 Riley looks at the thermometer.

Fahrenheit

°F

What temperature is shown? **B**

A 80°F   C 90°F
B 85°F   D 98°F

Study and Review	
Item	Lesson Pages
19	128–131
20	408–409
21	368–369

Getting Ready for the EOG Test

✓ MEASUREMENT AND GEOMETRY

22 Which of the following is true about this figure? **C**

A It has no lines of symmetry.
B It has one line of symmetry.
C It has two lines of symmetry.
D It has four lines of symmetry.

23 What is located at (3,2) on the coordinate grid? **B**

A swing set   C sandbox
B slide   D water fountain

24 Which of the following is the *best* estimate for the height of your front door? **B**

A 20 centimeters
B 2 meters
C 20 meters
D 2 kilometers

Study and Review	
Item	Lesson Pages
22	410–411
23	328–329
24	358–361

Measurement and Geometry

ITEM ANALYSIS	
North Carolina Standard	Items
Goal 2	16, 19
2.02	21, 24
3.01	17–18
3.02	23
(2) 3.03	20, 22

1 The table shows how many pages Tyson read each day. If the pattern continues, how many pages will Tyson read Thursday? C

PAGES TYSON READ	
Day	Number of Pages
Monday	9
Tuesday	12
Wednesday	15

A 12
B 16
C 18
D 45

2 What is the next figure in this pattern? C

A △△△

B △△△
△△

C △△△△
△△△△

D △△△△△
△△△△△

3 What is the next number in this pattern? C

4, 8, 12, 16, ▨

A 17
B 18
C 20
D 24

Study and Review	
Item	Lesson Pages
1	476–477
2	474–475
3	476–477

✔ **ALGEBRA**

4 Trains leave the station on a regular schedule. Trains leave at 2:30 P.M., 4:30 P.M., 6:30 P.M, and 8:30 P.M. What time is the next train scheduled to leave? D

A 7:30 P.M.
B 9:30 P.M.
C 10:00 P.M.
D 10:30 P.M.

5 Brooke made a pattern with beads.

How many beads will Brooke have used in all if she stops her pattern after putting down 6 orange beads? D

A 12 beads
B 20 beads
C 28 beads
D 40 beads

6 James had 16 baseball cards. He received some more as gifts. Now James has 28 cards. Which number sentence can you use to find the number of baseball cards James received as gifts? B

A $16 + 28 = $ ▨
B $16 + $ ▨ $ = 28$
C $28 + $ ▨ $ = 16$
D $16 + $ ▨ $ = 18$

Study and Review	
Item	Lesson Pages
4	134–135, 480–481
5	470–473
6	4–5

✔ **ALGEBRA**

7 What figure comes next in the pattern? A

△ □ ⬠

A ⬡

B △

C ▭

D ⬭

8 Jason made this table.

Number of Wagons	Number of Wheels
1	4
2	8
3	12
▨	▨

Which two numbers should come next? B

A 4, 13
B 4, 16
C 4, 20
D 6, 24

9 What is a rule for this pattern? D

4, 3, 7, 6, 10, 9, 13, 12

A Subtract 1, and then add 3.
B Add 1, and then subtract 4.
C Add 4, and then subtract 1.
D Subtract 1, and then add 4.

Study and Review	
Item	Lesson Pages
7	470–473
8	216–217
9	180–181

Algebra

ITEM ANALYSIS	
North Carolina Standard	Items
5.01	5, 7, 9
5.02	1–4, 8
5.03	6

✓ **ALGEBRA**

10 What is the next figure in the pattern? **C**

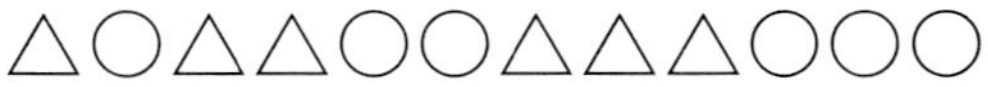

△○△△○○△△△○○○

A circle
B square
C triangle
D rectangle

11 Annette drew this pattern. What figure is missing? **C**

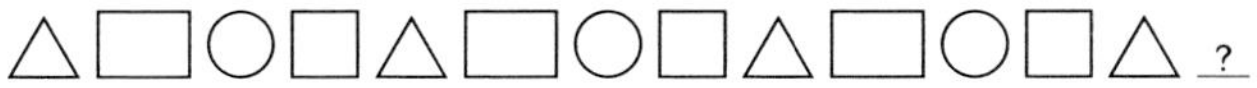

△□○□△□○□△□○□△ ?

A ○
B △
C □ 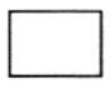
D □

12 Which number would complete this pattern? **A**

32, 40, 48, ■, 64, 72

A 56
B 55
C 54
D 53

Study and Review	
Item	Lesson Pages
10	470–473
11	470–473
12	476–477

✓ **ALGEBRA**

13 Karen drew this pattern.

Which rule matches her pattern? **D**

A Multiply the number of hearts by 2.
B Add 2 hearts.
C Multiply the number of hearts by 3.
D Add 3 hearts.

14 Frank wrote this pattern.

7, 12, 10, 15, 13, 18, 16

What is a rule for Frank's pattern? **B**

A Add 2, and then subtract 1.
B Add 5, and then subtract 2.
C Add 5, and then subtract 3.
D Add 6, and then subtract 2.

15 Which number pattern describes this pattern? **D**

A 2, 4, 6, 12
B 10, 8, 4, 2
C 2, 4, 6, 8
D 2, 4, 8, 16

Study and Review	
Item	Lesson Pages
13	474–475
14	180–181
15	474–475

✓ **ALGEBRA**

16 Michelle saves $6.00 each week. How much money will she save in 5 weeks? **C**

Week	1	2	3	4	5
Total Saved	$6	$12	$18	$24	■

A $26
B $28
C $30
D $32

17 Mrs. Artie planted flowers in a pattern: red, yellow, pink, red, yellow, pink, red, yellow, pink. If the pattern continues, what color will the twelfth flower be? **A**

A pink
B red
C yellow
D white

18 What number is missing from the table? **B**

In	Out
1	6
3	8
5	10
■	12

A 6
B 7
C 8
D 9

Study and Review	
Item	Lesson Pages
16	216–217
17	470–473
18	216–217

Algebra

ITEM ANALYSIS	
North Carolina Standard	Items
5.01	10–11, 13–15, 17
5.02	12, 16, 18

ALGEBRA

19 Kelly used number cards to create the pattern below.

| 24 | 12 | 6 | 3 |

What is a rule for her pattern? B

A Multiply by 2.
B Divide by 2.
C Subtract 12.
D Subtract 6.

20 Kendra is making a design. There are 6 stars in the first row, 12 stars in the second row, and 18 stars in the third row. How many stars could be in the sixth row if the pattern continues? C

A 24
B 30
C 36
D 42

21 Sandra swam 3 laps on Monday, 5 laps on Tuesday, 4 laps on Wednesday, 6 laps on Thursday, 5 laps on Friday, 7 laps on Saturday, and 6 laps on Sunday. If her pattern continues, how many laps will she swim on Monday? B

A 6 laps
B 8 laps
C 9 laps
D 10 laps

Study and Review	
Item	Lesson Pages
19	216–217
20	474–475
21	180–181

DATA ANALYSIS AND PROBABILITY

1 The graph below shows the average monthly temperatures in Charlotte, North Carolina. What month is usually the warmest? B

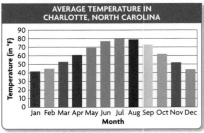

AVERAGE TEMPERATURE IN CHARLOTTE, NORTH CAROLINA

A June   C August
B July   D December

2 The graph at the right shows the results of a survey of a group of students. Which type of food got the most votes? D

FAVORITE LUNCH FOODS

A chicken
B hamburger
C hot dog
D pizza

3 There are 7 blocks in a bag. Three of the blocks are blue and the rest are red. One block is picked without looking. Which *best* describes the chance that a red block will be picked? B

A certain   C impossible
B likely   D unlikely

Study and Review	
Item	Lesson Pages
1	324–325
2	324–325
3	488–489

DATA ANALYSIS AND PROBABILITY

4 The Venn diagram shows figures sorted by equal sides and four sides. How many figures have both four sides and equal sides? B

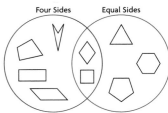

Four Sides   Equal Sides

A 1
B 2
C 3
D 4

5 From which box is it certain that a ball will be picked? D

A   C
B   D

6 Maura is placing a science book, a math book, and a social studies book on her shelf. How many ways can Maura arrange her books? B

A 3
B 6
C 9
D 12

Study and Review	
Item	Lesson Pages
4	400–401
5	488–489
6	498–499

Algebra

ITEM ANALYSIS	
North Carolina Standard	Items
5.01	19, 21
5.02	20

Data Analysis and Probability

ITEM ANALYSIS	
North Carolina Standard	Items
4.01	1–2
(2) 4.01	4
(2) 4.02	3, 5
4.02	6

✓ DATA ANALYSIS AND PROBABILITY

7 Which list shows all of the different ways you can make a 3-digit number using the digits 2, 4, and 6? D

   A 246, 426, 624
   B 264, 462, 642
   C 246, 264, 426, 624, 642
   D 246, 264, 426, 462, 624, 642

8 Which event is certain? A

   A There will be 30 days in September.
   B There will be sunshine on July 4.
   C It will rain on April 1.
   D September 2 will come after September 3.

9 Jordan made a spinner for a game he invented.

The pointer of the spinner is most likely to land on which number? B

   A 1
   B 2
   C 3
   D 4

Study and Review	
Item	Lesson Pages
7	498–499
8	488–489
9	492–495

✓ DATA ANALYSIS AND PROBABILITY

10 The third-grade class collected data about favorite hobbies.

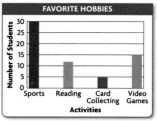

How many more students chose sports than video games? B

   A 5   **C** 30
   B 15   **D** 45

11 Use the graph above. Which activity received 7 more votes than card collecting? B

   A sports   **C** card collecting
   B reading   **D** video games

12 Keith is making a pictograph of the data in the table.

FAVORITE SPORTS	
Sport	Number of Votes
Soccer	15
Basketball	10
Field Hockey	5
Softball	20

If each symbol is equal to 5 votes, how many symbols should Keith use to show votes for basketball? A

   A 2   **C** 10
   B 3   **D** 15

Study and Review	
Item	Lesson Pages
10	324–325
11	324–325
12	322–323

✓ DATA ANALYSIS AND PROBABILITY

13 Corwin drew a time line to show his day.

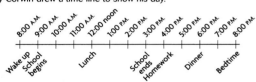

How many hours was Corwin at school? B

   A 5 hours
   B 6 hours
   C 7 hours
   D 8 hours

14 Julian counted the number of birds he saw at the bird feeder each morning. He saw 5 birds on Monday, 7 birds on Tuesday, 5 birds on Wednesday, and 6 birds on Thursday. On which days did he see the same number of birds? C

   A Tuesday and Wednesday
   B Monday and Tuesday
   C Monday and Wednesday
   D Tuesday and Thursday

15 There are 8 marbles in a bag. Five of the marbles are green, and the rest are red. Which *best* describes the chance that a red marble will be picked? B

   A impossible
   B unlikely
   C likely
   D certain

Study and Review	
Item	Lesson Pages
13	142–143
14	302–303
15	488–489

Data Analysis and Probability

ITEM ANALYSIS	
North Carolina Standard	Items
4.01	10–14
(2) 4.02	8–9, 15
4.02	7

DATA ANALYSIS AND PROBABILITY

16 Tracey is deciding what outfit to wear. She can wear a T-shirt or a blouse, with either a skirt or a pair of pants. How many different outfits does Tracey have to choose from? D

A 1 **C** 3
B 2 **D** 4

17 Lori has a cube. Two sides are blue, one side is red, and three sides are green. Which of the following statements is *true*? B

A Lori is most likely to roll blue.
B It is impossible for Lori to roll purple.
C Lori is least likely to roll green.
D It is certain that Lori will roll green.

18 Jesse counted the number of students in the library. On Monday she counted 25 people. On Tuesday she counted 41 people. On Wednesday she counted 33 people. Which table shows Jesse's data? A

A
Day	Mon	Tues	Wed
Students	25	41	33

B
Day	Mon	Tues	Wed
Students	25	33	41

C
Day	Mon	Tues	Wed
Students	33	25	41

D
Day	Mon	Tues	Wed
Students	41	25	33

Study and Review	
Item	Lesson Pages
16	498–499
17	492–495
18	302–303

 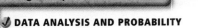

DATA ANALYSIS AND PROBABILITY

19 How many different ways can you arrange the letters M, A, T, and H? C

A 8 **C** 24
B 18 **D** 40

20 Connie recorded the number of students in her class each day for 2 weeks. She made a line plot. What is the mode of this data? B

Students in Class

A 21 **C** 25
B 23 **D** 26

21 The pointer of the spinner is *least likely* to land on which number? D

A 1 **C** 3
B 2 **D** 4

Study and Review	
Item	Lesson Pages
19	498–499
20	310–313
21	492–495

DATA ANALYSIS AND PROBABILITY

22 Elena made a pictograph to show her classmates' votes for class president.

VOTES FOR CLASS PRESIDENT

Elena	☺☺☺☺
James	☺☺
Pete	☺(
Lea	☺☺(
Jorge	☺☺☺(

Each ☺ = 2 votes.

How many more votes did Elena receive than Lea? C

A 1 **C** 3
B 2 **D** 4

23 Grant counted the number of crayons that each person in Shannon's group had at the table.

How many crayons in all do Shannon and Eric have? C

A 14 **C** 16
B 15 **D** 18

SHANNON'S GROUP

Name	Number of Crayons
Thomas	9
Kate	6
Eric	7
Pamela	7
Shannon	9

24 The pointer on the spinner is equally likely to land on which colors? A

A red, blue, green **C** white, red
B yellow, green **D** blue, green, yellow

Study and Review	
Item	Lesson Pages
22	322–323
23	304–305
24	490–491

Data Analysis and Probability

ITEM ANALYSIS	
North Carolina Standard	Items
4.01	18, 20, 22–23
(2) 4.02	17, 21, 24
4.02	16, 19

	K	L	M	N	O	P	Q	R
A	3 + 2 = 5	0 + 6 = 6	2 + 4 = 6	5 + 9 = 14	6 + 1 = 7	2 + 5 = 7	3 + 10 = 13	4 + 4 = 8
B	8 + 9 = 17	0 + 7 = 7	3 + 5 = 8	9 + 6 = 15	6 + 7 = 13	2 + 8 = 10	3 + 3 = 6	7 + 10 = 17
C	4 + 6 = 10	9 + 0 = 9	7 + 8 = 15	4 + 10 = 14	3 + 7 = 10	7 + 7 = 14	4 + 2 = 6	7 + 5 = 12
D	5 + 7 = 12	3 + 9 = 12	8 + 1 = 9	9 + 5 = 14	10 + 5 = 15	9 + 8 = 17	2 + 6 = 8	8 + 7 = 15
E	7 + 4 = 11	0 + 8 = 8	3 + 6 = 9	6 + 10 = 16	5 + 3 = 8	2 + 7 = 9	8 + 2 = 10	9 + 9 = 18
F	2 + 3 = 5	1 + 7 = 8	6 + 8 = 14	5 + 2 = 7	7 + 3 = 10	4 + 8 = 12	10 + 10 = 20	6 + 6 = 12
G	8 + 3 = 11	7 + 2 = 9	7 + 0 = 7	8 + 5 = 13	9 + 1 = 10	4 + 7 = 11	8 + 4 = 12	10 + 8 = 18
H	7 + 9 = 16	5 + 6 = 11	8 + 10 = 18	6 + 5 = 11	8 + 6 = 14	9 + 4 = 13	0 + 9 = 9	7 + 1 = 8
I	4 + 3 = 7	5 + 5 = 10	6 + 4 = 10	10 + 2 = 12	7 + 6 = 13	8 + 0 = 8	6 + 9 = 15	9 + 2 = 11
J	5 + 8 = 13	1 + 9 = 10	5 + 4 = 9	8 + 8 = 16	6 + 2 = 8	6 + 3 = 9	9 + 7 = 16	9 + 10 = 19

	K	L	M	N	O	P	Q	R
A	9 − 1 = 8	10 − 4 = 6	7 − 2 = 5	6 − 4 = 2	20 − 10 = 10	7 − 0 = 7	8 − 3 = 5	13 − 9 = 4
B	9 − 9 = 0	13 − 4 = 9	7 − 1 = 6	11 − 5 = 6	9 − 7 = 2	6 − 3 = 3	15 − 10 = 5	6 − 2 = 4
C	10 − 2 = 8	8 − 8 = 0	16 − 8 = 8	6 − 5 = 1	18 − 10 = 8	8 − 7 = 1	13 − 3 = 10	15 − 6 = 9
D	11 − 7 = 4	9 − 5 = 4	12 − 8 = 4	8 − 1 = 7	15 − 8 = 7	18 − 9 = 9	14 − 10 = 4	9 − 4 = 5
E	9 − 2 = 7	7 − 7 = 0	10 − 3 = 7	8 − 5 = 3	16 − 9 = 7	11 − 9 = 2	14 − 8 = 6	12 − 6 = 6
F	7 − 3 = 4	12 − 10 = 2	17 − 9 = 8	6 − 0 = 6	9 − 6 = 3	11 − 8 = 3	10 − 9 = 1	12 − 2 = 10
G	15 − 7 = 8	8 − 4 = 4	13 − 6 = 7	7 − 5 = 2	11 − 2 = 9	12 − 3 = 9	14 − 6 = 8	11 − 4 = 7
H	7 − 6 = 1	13 − 5 = 8	12 − 9 = 3	10 − 5 = 5	13 − 8 = 5	11 − 3 = 8	16 − 10 = 6	14 − 7 = 7
I	5 − 0 = 5	10 − 8 = 2	11 − 6 = 5	9 − 3 = 6	14 − 5 = 9	5 − 4 = 1	7 − 7 = 0	14 − 9 = 5
J	15 − 9 = 6	9 − 8 = 1	13 − 7 = 6	8 − 2 = 6	7 − 4 = 3	13 − 10 = 3	10 − 6 = 4	16 − 7 = 9

MULTIPLICATION FACTS TEST

	K	L	M	N	O	P	Q	R
A	2 ×7 = 14	0 ×6 = 0	6 ×6 = 36	9 ×2 = 18	8 ×3 = 24	3 ×4 = 12	2 ×8 = 16	6 ×1 = 6
B	7 ×7 = 49	5 ×9 = 45	2 ×2 = 4	7 ×5 = 35	2 ×3 = 6	10 ×8 = 80	4 ×10 = 40	8 ×4 = 32
C	4 ×5 = 20	5 ×1 = 5	7 ×0 = 0	6 ×3 = 18	3 ×5 = 15	6 ×8 = 48	7 ×3 = 21	9 ×9 = 81
D	0 ×9 = 0	6 ×4 = 24	6 ×10 = 60	1 ×6 = 6	9 ×8 = 72	4 ×4 = 16	3 ×2 = 6	9 ×3 = 27
E	0 ×7 = 0	9 ×4 = 36	1 ×7 = 7	9 ×7 = 63	2 ×5 = 10	7 ×9 = 63	5 ×6 = 30	5 ×8 = 40
F	4 ×3 = 12	6 ×9 = 54	1 ×9 = 9	7 ×6 = 42	7 ×10 = 70	6 ×0 = 0	2 ×9 = 18	10 ×3 = 30
G	5 ×3 = 15	1 ×5 = 5	7 ×1 = 7	3 ×8 = 24	3 ×6 = 18	8 ×10 = 80	3 ×9 = 27	6 ×7 = 42
H	7 ×4 = 28	7 ×2 = 14	3 ×7 = 21	2 ×4 = 8	7 ×8 = 56	4 ×7 = 28	5 ×10 = 50	8 ×6 = 48
I	4 ×6 = 24	5 ×5 = 25	5 ×7 = 35	3 ×3 = 9	9 ×6 = 54	8 ×0 = 0	4 ×9 = 36	8 ×8 = 64
J	8 ×9 = 72	6 ×2 = 12	4 ×8 = 32	9 ×5 = 45	5 ×4 = 20	0 ×5 = 0	10 ×6 = 60	9 ×10 = 90

H38 Facts Tests

DIVISION FACTS TEST

	K	L	M	N	O	P	Q	R
A	1)1 → 1	3)9 → 3	2)6 → 3	2)4 → 2	1)6 → 6	3)12 → 4	5)15 → 3	7)21 → 3
B	6)24 → 4	8)56 → 7	5)40 → 8	6)18 → 3	6)30 → 5	7)42 → 6	9)81 → 9	5)45 → 9
C	5)30 → 6	2)16 → 8	3)21 → 7	7)35 → 5	3)15 → 5	9)9 → 1	8)16 → 2	9)63 → 7
D	4)32 → 8	9)90 → 10	4)8 → 2	8)48 → 6	9)54 → 6	3)18 → 6	10)50 → 5	6)48 → 8
E	7)28 → 4	3)0 → 0	5)20 → 4	4)24 → 6	7)14 → 2	3)6 → 2	5)50 → 10	10)60 → 6
F	9)18 → 2	4)36 → 9	5)25 → 5	7)63 → 9	1)5 → 5	8)32 → 4	9)45 → 5	6)54 → 9
G	2)14 → 7	8)24 → 3	4)4 → 1	5)40 → 8	3)9 → 3	4)12 → 3	7)56 → 8	8)72 → 9
H	5)35 → 7	1)4 → 4	8)64 → 8	5)10 → 2	8)40 → 5	2)12 → 6	6)42 → 7	10)70 → 7
I	7)49 → 7	9)27 → 3	10)90 → 9	3)27 → 9	9)36 → 4	4)20 → 5	9)72 → 8	8)80 → 10
J	8)0 → 0	4)28 → 7	2)10 → 5	7)70 → 10	1)3 → 3	10)80 → 8	6)60 → 10	10)100 → 10

Student Handbook **H39**

MULTIPLICATION AND DIVISION FACTS TEST

	K	L	M	N	O	P	Q	R
A	2)18 → 9	8 ×4 = 32	5)15 → 3	10 ×6 = 60	8 ×1 = 8	3)24 → 8	6)12 → 2	5 ×8 = 40
B	8 ×2 = 16	7)56 → 8	9)81 → 9	4 ×10 = 40	7 ×9 = 63	1)6 → 6	8)80 → 10	4 ×9 = 36
C	6)36 → 6	8 ×5 = 40	7 ×7 = 49	10)90 → 9	5)45 → 9	6 ×7 = 42	8)16 → 2	9 ×9 = 81
D	10 ×2 = 20	4)32 → 8	9)54 → 6	7 ×8 = 56	9 ×3 = 27	9)90 → 10	6)54 → 9	9 ×4 = 36
E	8 ×10 = 80	7 ×6 = 42	8)64 → 8	2)20 → 10	9 ×0 = 0	10 ×10 = 100	3)36 → 12	10)100 → 10
F	4)40 → 10	8 ×3 = 24	8 ×6 = 48	9 ×6 = 54	7)49 → 7	9)45 → 5	10 ×3 = 30	9 ×7 = 63
G	8)48 → 6	6)60 → 10	9 ×2 = 18	5 ×9 = 45	7)42 → 6	4)36 → 9	5 ×10 = 50	9 ×8 = 72
H	6 ×5 = 30	8 ×8 = 64	9)72 → 8	5)50 → 10	6 ×9 = 54	8 ×5 = 40	9)36 → 4	7)63 → 9
I	8)56 → 7	10)80 → 8	7 ×8 = 56	10 ×9 = 90	5)50 → 10	9 ×5 = 45	10 ×8 = 80	10)70 → 7
J	6 ×8 = 48	10 ×9 = 90	4)40 → 10	7)35 → 5	3 ×6 = 18	8)56 → 7	9 ×8 = 72	7 ×5 = 35

H40 Student Handbook

Basic Facts

Background

The Pupil Edition pages and the ideas described below have two purposes: to help students memorize basic facts and to reinforce and review the facts that students know. To make the most of practice sessions, do the following:

- Begin practice as soon as students show an understanding of a fact's meaning and symbols.
- Before students drill, be sure they realize that their goal is memorization—not just getting an answer.

- Vary the practice to keep the interest of students.
- Keep practice sessions short and frequent. Schedule practice sessions almost every day.
- Motivate students by sharing your enthusiasm for practice activities. Reward efforts with praise.

Activity Ideas

BOARD GAMES Students generate two numbers by using number cubes, spinners, number cards, or fact cards. Then students add, subtract, multiply, or divide the numbers to determine their moves on a game board.

TARGET GAMES Each student in a group generates three digits by using a spinner, rolling a number cube, or drawing cards from a box. The winner is the student who comes closest to a target number by combining the digits in an expression, such as $7 + 5 - 4$. During each turn, students make mental computations to find the best combination of digits.

CONCENTRATION Students make an array of cards face down and take turns trying to turn over pairs of cards that match. Matching cards might have the same answer ($4 + 7$ and $8 + 3$) or they might be related ($24 \div 8$ and 3×8).

WHAT'S THE QUESTION? Students place a set of numbered cards face down in rows. They take turns turning over a card and naming an expression equal to the number on the card.

Practice Ideas

ORAL PRACTICE Have students read aloud and answer the exercises in one row or column.

QUICK QUIZ Students record their answers for one or more rows or columns on lettered strips of paper.

WHOLE PAGE Students draw a lettered grid on their papers, like the grid on the pupil page, to record their answers. To prevent skipping exercises, they slide a paper or ruler beneath the rows or alongside the columns of exercises.

SELF-CHECK Each time students repeat a set of facts, they record the number correct on a table or graph. They set personal goals for weekly progress.

TIMED PRACTICE FOR AUTOMATICITY Students repeat a set of exercises over several days, using immediate recall to increase speed and accuracy.

HORIZONTAL FORMATS The addition, subtraction, and multiplication facts are shown in a vertical format. The division facts are shown in the "house" format. Students practice basic facts by rewriting and solving them in a horizontal format.

BASIC FACT STRATEGIES Students review the basic fact strategies for addition: *counting on, doubles* and *doubles plus one*, and *make a ten*. Students repeat with the strategies for subtraction: *counting back* and *doubles* and *doubles minus one*.

INVERSE OPERATIONS Students write the related subtraction fact for each addition fact and the related addition fact for each subtraction fact. They do the same for the multiplication and division facts.

FLASH CARDS AND OTHER GRAPHIC AIDS Students record the facts they miss and make flash cards to use for memorization. Students work in pairs to review those facts. As students read the cards and complete the facts, they separate the cards into facts they know and facts they do not know. They shuffle the do-not-know cards and continue until all the cards are in the do-know pile.

DESK SHEET Students make a desk sheet of a test by highlighting missed facts and taping the sheet to their desks. Students say each missed fact with the correct answer every time they sit down at their desks.

FACT FAMILIES Given one addition or subtraction fact or one multiplication or division fact, students write the other facts in the fact family.

MULTIPLICATION TABLES Students go through the multiplication facts and find all of the facts for 1, 2, 3, and so on. They fill in any missing facts. Then they rewrite all of the facts in their own multiplication table.

METRIC | CUSTOMARY

Length

METRIC	CUSTOMARY
1 decimeter (dm) = 10 centimeters	1 foot (ft) = 12 inches (in.)
1 meter (m) = 100 centimeters	1 yard (yd) = 3 feet, or 36 inches
1 meter (m) = 10 decimeters	1 mile (mi) = 1,760 yards, or 5,280 feet
1 kilometer (km) = 1,000 meters	

Mass/Weight

METRIC	CUSTOMARY
1 kilogram (kg) = 1,000 grams (g)	1 pound (lb) = 16 ounces (oz)

Capacity

METRIC	CUSTOMARY
1 liter (L) = 1,000 milliliters (mL)	1 pint (pt) = 2 cups (c)
	1 quart (qt) = 2 pints
	1 gallon (gal) = 4 quarts

TIME

1 minute (min) = 60 seconds (sec)	1 year (yr) = 12 months (mo), or about 52 weeks
1 hour (hr) = 60 minutes	
1 day = 24 hours	1 year = 365 days
1 week (wk) = 7 days	1 leap year = 366 days

MONEY

1 penny = 1 cent (¢)
1 nickel = 5 cents
1 dime = 10 cents
1 quarter = 25 cents
1 half dollar = 50 cents
1 dollar ($) = 100 cents

SYMBOLS

< is less than
> is greater than
= is equal to
≠ is not equal to
°F degrees Fahrenheit
°C degrees Celsius
(2,3) ordered pair

GLOSSARY

A

acute angle [ə·kyōōt′ ang′gəl] An angle that has a measure less than a right angle (p. 385)
Example:

acute triangle [ə·kyōōt′ trī′ang·gəl] A triangle that has three acute angles (p. 393)

addend [a′dend] Any of the numbers that are added (p. 4)
Example: 2 + 3 = 5
↑ ↑
addend addend

addition [ə·dish′ən] The process of finding the total number of items when two or more groups of items are joined; the opposite operation of subtraction (p. 2)

A.M. [ā em] The hours between midnight and noon (p. 132)

angle [ang′gəl] A figure formed by two rays or line segments that share an endpoint (p. 384)
Example:

Word History

When the letter "g" is replaced with the letter "k" in the word *angle*, the word becomes *ankle*. Both words come from the same Latin root, *angulus*, which means "a sharp bend."

area [âr′ē·ə] The number of square units needed to cover a flat surface (p. 448)
Example:

area = 15 square units

array [ə·rā′] An arrangement of objects in rows and columns (p. 162)
Example:

column
↓
row →

3 × 4 = 12

Associative Property of Addition
See Grouping Property of Addition.

Associative Property of Multiplication
[ə·sō′shē·ā·tiv prä′pər·tē əv mul·tə·plə·kā′shən] The property that states that when the grouping of factors is changed, the product remains the same (p. 218)
Example:
(3 × 2) × 4 = 24
3 × (2 × 4) = 24

B

bar graph [bär graf] A graph that uses bars to show data (p. 324)
Example:

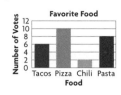

Favorite Food
Number of Votes
Tacos Pizza Chili Pasta
Food

benchmark numbers [bench′märk num′bərz] Numbers that help you estimate the number of objects without counting them, such as 25, 50, 100, 1,000 (p. 40)

C

calendar [ka′lən·dər] A chart that shows the days, weeks, and months of a year (p. 138)

capacity [kə·pa′sə·tē] The amount a container can hold (p. 344)

center [sen′tər] A point in the middle of a circle that is the same distance from anywhere on the circle (p. 435)
Example:

center

centimeter (cm) [sen′tə·mē·tər] A metric unit that is used to measure length or distance (p. 358)
Example:

1 cm

certain [sûr′tən] An event is certain if it will always happen. (p. 488)

circle [sər′kəl] A closed figure made up of points that are the same distance from the center (p. 435)

circle graph [sər′kəl graf] A graph in the shape of a circle that shows data as a whole made up of different parts (p. 313)
Example:

Black
Red
Blonde Brown

Classmates' Hair Color

classify [kla′sə·fī] To group pieces of data according to how they are the same; for example, you can classify data by size, color, or shape. (p. 306)

clockwise [klok′wīz] In the same direction in which the hands of a clock move (p. 131)

closed figure [klōzd fi′gyər] A shape that begins and ends at the same point (p. 390)
Examples:

Commutative Property of Addition
See Order Property of Addition.

Commutative Property of Multiplication
[kə·myōō·tə·tiv prä′pər·tē əv mul·tə·plə·kā′shən] The property that states that you can multiply two factors in any order and get the same product (p. 163)
Examples: 2 × 4 = 8
4 × 2 = 8

compare [kəm·pâr′] To describe whether numbers are equal to, less than, or greater than each other (p. 42)

---

cone [kōn] A solid, pointed figure that has a flat, round base (p. 424)
Example:

congruent [kən·grōō′ənt] Figures that have the same size and shape (p. 408)
Example:

counterclockwise [koun′tər·klok′wīz] In the opposite direction in which the hands of a clock move (p. 131)

counting back [koun′ting bak] A way to find the difference when you subtract 1, 2, or 3
Example: 8 − 3 = ▦ Count: 8 . . . 7, 6, 5

counting on [koun′ting on] A way to find the sum when one of the addends is 1, 2, or 3
Example: 5 + 2 = ▦ Count: 5 . . . 6, 7

counting up [koun′ting up] A way to find the difference by beginning with the smaller number
Example: 7 − 4 = ▦

Count: 4 . . . 5, 6, 7 ← 3 is the difference.

cube [kyōōb] A solid figure with six congruent square faces (p. 424)
Example:

cubic unit [kyōō′bik yōō′nət] A cube with a side length of one unit; used to measure volume (p. 452)

cup (c) [kup] A customary unit used to measure capacity (p. 344)

cylinder [sil′in·dər] A solid or hollow object that is shaped like a can (p. 424)
Example:

D

data [dā′tə] Information collected about people or things (p. 302)

decimal [de′sə·məl] A number with one or more digits to the right of the decimal point (p. 558)

decimal point [de′sə·məl point] A symbol used to separate dollars from cents in money and to separate the ones place from the tenths place in decimals (p. 110)
Example: 4.5
└decimal point

decimeter (dm) [de′sə·mē·tər] A metric unit that is used to measure length or distance; 1 decimeter = 10 centimeters (p. 358)

degree (°) [di·grē′] The unit used to measure angles and temperature (p. 385)

degree Celsius (°C) [di·grē′ sel′sē·əs] A metric unit for measuring temperature (p. 368)

degree Fahrenheit (°F) [di·grē′ far′ən·hīt] A customary unit for measuring temperature (p. 368)

denominator [di·nä′mə·nā·tər] The part of a fraction below the line, which tells how many equal parts there are in the whole or in the group (p. 516)
Example: $\frac{3}{4}$ ←denominator

difference [dif′rən(t)s] The answer in a subtraction problem (p. 10)
Example: 6 − 4 = 2
└difference

digits [di′jəts] The symbols 0, 1, 2, 3, 4, 5, 6, 7, 8, and 9 (p. 22)

Word History

The word *distributive* comes from the Latin word *distribuere* which means "to divide up." When you use the Distributive Property, you *divide up* one factor and multiply each part by the other factor.

Distributive Property [di·strib′yə·tiv prä′pər·tē] The property that states that multiplying a sum by a number is the same as multiplying each addend by the number and then adding the products (p. 220)
Examples:
3 × (4 + 2) = (3 × 4) + (3 × 2)
3 × 6 = 12 + 6
18 = 18

divide [di·vīd′] To separate into equal groups; the opposite operation of multiplication (p. 238)

dividend [di′və·dend] The number that is to be divided in a division problem (p. 242)
Example: 35 ÷ 5 = 7
└dividend

divisor [di·vī′zər] The number that divides the dividend (p. 242)
Example: 35 ÷ 5 = 7
└divisor

E

edge [ej] A line segment formed where two faces meet (p. 424)
Example:

edge

elapsed time [i·lapst′ tīm] The amount of time that passes from the start of an activity to the end of that activity (p. 134)

equal sign (=) [ē′kwəl sīn] A symbol used to show that two numbers have the same value (p. 42)
Example: 384 = 384

equal to (=) [ē′kwəl tōō] Having the same value (p. 42)
Example: 4 + 4 is equal to 3 + 5

equally likely [ē′kwəl·lē lī′klē] Having the same chance of happening (p. 490)

equation [i·kwā′zhən] A number sentence that uses the equal sign to show that two amounts are equal (p. 242)
Examples:
3 + 7 = 10
4 − 1 = 3
12 + n = 21

equilateral triangle [ē·kwə·lat′ər·əl trī′ang·gəl] A triangle that has three equal sides (p. 393)
Examples:

equivalent [ē·kwiv′ə·lənt] Two or more sets that name the same amount (p. 111)

equivalent fractions [ē·kwiv′ə·lənt frak′shənz] Two or more fractions that name the same amount (p. 522)
Example:

$\frac{3}{4} = \frac{6}{8}$

estimate [es′tə·māt] *verb*: To find about how many or how much (p. 68)

estimate [es′tə·mit] *noun*: A number close to an exact amount (p. 68)

even [ē′vən] A whole number that has a 0, 2, 4, 6, or 8 in the ones place (p. 20)

event [i·vent′] Something that happens (p. 488)

expanded form [ik·spand′id fôrm] A way to write numbers by showing the value of each digit (p. 22)
Example: 7,201 = 7,000 + 200 + 1

experiment [ik·sper′ə·mənt] A test that is done in order to find out something (p. 492)

expression [ik·spre′shən] The part of a number sentence that combines numbers and operation signs, but doesn't have an equal sign (p. 80)
Example: 5 × 6

F

face [fās] A flat surface of a solid figure (p. 424)
Example:

face

fact family [fakt fam'ə•lē] A set of related addition and subtraction, or multiplication and division, number sentences (pp. 2, 246)
Example:

$$4 \times 7 = 28 \qquad 28 \div 7 = 4$$
$$7 \times 4 = 28 \qquad 28 \div 4 = 7$$

factor [fak'tər] A number that is multiplied by another number to find a product (p. 160)
Example: $3 \times 8 = 24$

factor   factor

flip [flip] A movement of a figure to a new position by flipping the figure over a line (p. 414)
Example:

foot (ft) [fŏot] A customary unit used to measure length or distance; 1 foot = 12 inches (p. 342)

fraction [frak'shən] A number that names part of a whole or part of a group (p. 516)
Example:

  $\frac{1}{3}$

Word History

A *fraction* is a part of a whole, or a whole that is broken into pieces. *Fraction* comes from the Latin word *frangere,* which means "to break".

frequency table [frē'kwen•sē tā'bəl] A table that uses numbers to record data (p. 302)
Example:

FAVORITE COLOR	
Color	Number
blue	10
red	7
green	8
yellow	4

front-end estimation [frunt-end es•tə•mā'shən] A method of estimating a sum or difference by using the front digit of the number and adding zeros for the other digits (p. 68)
Example:

$$\begin{array}{r} 4,496 \rightarrow 4,000 \\ +3,745 \rightarrow +3,000 \\ \hline 7,000 \end{array}$$

G

gallon (gal) [ga'lən] A customary unit for measuring capacity; 1 gallon = 4 quarts (p. 344)

gram (g) [gram] A metric unit that is used to measure mass (p. 366)

greater than (>) [grā'tər than] A symbol used to compare two numbers, with the greater number given first (p. 42)
Example: 6 > 4

grid [grid] Horizontal and vertical lines on a map (p. 328)

Grouping Property of Addition [grōō'ping prä'pər•tē əv ə•dish'ən] A rule stating that you can group addends in different ways and still get the same sum (p. 6)
Example:

$$4 + (2 + 5) = 11 \text{ and}$$
$$(4 + 2) + 5 = 11$$

Grouping Property of Multiplication [grōō'ping prä'pər•tē əv mul•tə•pla•kā'shən] The property that states that when the grouping of factors is changed, the product remains the same (p. 218)
Example:

$$3 \times (4 \times 1) = 12 \text{ and}$$
$$(3 \times 4) \times 1 = 12$$

H

half hour [haf our] 30 minutes (p. 129)
Example: Between 4:00 and 4:30 is one half hour.

hexagon [hek'sə•gän] A polygon with six sides (p. 390)
Examples:

horizontal bar graph [hôr•ə•zän'tal bär graf] A bar graph in which the bars go from left to right (p. 324)

hour (hr) [our] A unit used to measure time; in one hour, the hour hand on a clock moves from one number to the next; 1 hour = 60 minutes (p. 129)

hour hand [our hand] The short hand on an analog clock (p. 128)

hundredth [hun'drədth] One of one hundred equal parts (p. 562)
Example:

└─hundredth

I

Identity Property of Addition [i•den'tə•tē prä'pər•tē əv ə•dish'ən] The property that states that when you add zero to a number, the result is that number (p. 6)
Example: 24 + 0 = 24

Identity Property of Multiplication [i•den'tə•tē prä'pər•tē əv mul•tə•pla•kā'shən] The property that states that the product of any number and 1 is that number (p. 220)
Example: $5 \times 1 = 5$
$1 \times 8 = 8$

impossible [im•pä'sə•bəl] An event that will never happen (p. 488)

inch (in.) [inch] A customary unit used for measuring length or distance (p. 338)
Example:

←—1 inch—→

intersecting lines [in•tər•sek'ting linz] Lines that cross (p. 388)
Example:

inverse operations [in'vərs ä•pə•rā'shənz] Opposite operations, or operations that undo each other, such as addition and subtraction or multiplication and division (pp. 2, 242)

isosceles triangle [i•sos'ə•lēz tri'ang•gəl] A triangle that has two equal sides (p. 393)
Example:

10 in.   10 in.
7 in.

K

kilogram (kg) [kil'ə•gram] A metric unit for measuring mass; 1 kilogram = 1,000 grams (p. 366)

kilometer (km) [kə•lä'mə•tər] A metric unit for measuring length or distance; 1 kilometer = 1,000 meters (p. 358)

L

less than (<) [les than] A symbol used to compare two numbers, with the lesser number given first (p. 42)
Example: 3 < 7

like fractions [lik frak'shənz] Fractions that have the same denominator (p. 540)
Example: $\frac{3}{8}$ and $\frac{7}{8}$

likely [lik'lē] An event is likely if it has a good chance of happening (p. 488)

---

line [lin] A straight path extending in both directions with no endpoints (p. 384)
Example:

Word History

The word *line* comes from *linen,* a thread spun from the fibers of the flax plant. In early times thread was held tight to mark a straight line between two points.

line graph [lin graf] A graph that uses a line to show how data change over time (p. 330)
Example:

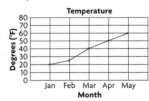
Temperature
Degrees (°F)
80 70 60 50 40 30 20 10
Jan Feb Mar Apr May
Month

line of symmetry [lin əv sim'ə•trē] An imaginary line on a figure that when the figure is folded on this line, the two parts match exactly (p. 410)
Example:

line of symmetry

line plot [lin plöt] A graph that records each piece of data on a number line (p. 310)
Example:

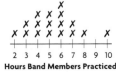
Hours Band Members Practiced

line segment [lin seg'mənt] A part of a line that includes two points, called endpoints, and all of the points between them (p. 384)
Example:

liter (L) [lē'tər] A metric unit for measuring capacity; 1 liter = 1,000 milliliters (p. 364)

M

mass [mas] The amount of matter in an object (p. 366)

mean [mēn] The number found by dividing the sum of a set of numbers by the number of addends (p. 314)
Example:
Find the mean for: 2, 3, 5, 5, 6, and 9
$$2 + 3 + 5 + 5 + 6 + 9 = 30$$
$$30 \div 6 = 5$$
The mean is 5.

median [mē'dē•ən] The middle number in an ordered list of numbers (p. 314)

1, 3, 4, 6, 7
└median

meter (m) [mē'tər] A metric unit for measuring length or distance; 1 meter = 100 centimeters (p. 358)

midnight [mid'nit] 12:00 at night (p. 132)

mile (mi) [mil] A customary unit for measuring length or distance; 1 mile = 5,280 feet (p. 342)

milliliter (mL) [mi'lə•lē•tər] A metric unit for measuring capacity (p. 364)

minute (min) [min'it] A unit used to measure short amounts of time; in one minute, the minute hand moves from one mark to the next (p. 128)

minute hand [mi'nət hand] The long hand on an analog clock (p. 128)

mixed number [mikst num'bər] A number represented by a whole number and a fraction (p. 532)
Example: $4\frac{1}{2}$

mode [mōd] The number or item found most often in a set of data (p. 310)

multiple [mul'tə•pəl] A number that is the product of a given number and a whole number (p. 178)
Example:

$$\begin{array}{cccc} 10 & 10 & 10 & 10 \\ \underline{\times 1} & \underline{\times 2} & \underline{\times 3} & \underline{\times 4} \\ 10 & 20 & 30 & 40 \end{array} \leftarrow \text{multiples of 10}$$

multiply [mul'tə•pli] When you combine equal groups, you can multiply to find how many in all; the opposite operation of division. (p. 158)

multistep problem [mul'tē•step prä'bləm] A problem with more than one step (p. 222)

N

noon [nōōn] 12:00 in the day (p. 132)

not equal to (≠) [not ē'kwal tōō] A number or set of numbers that is not equal to another number or set of numbers (p. 80)
Examples:

$$4 \neq 5$$
$$3 + 3 \neq 3 + 8$$
$$217 \neq 271$$

number sentence [num'bər sen'təns] A sentence that includes numbers, operation symbols, and a greater than or less than symbol or an equal sign (p. 80)
Example:
$5 + 3 = 8$ is a number sentence.

numerator [nōō'mə•rā•tər] The part of a fraction above the line, which tells how many parts are being counted (p. 516)
Example: $\frac{3}{4}$ ←numerator

O

obtuse angle [əb•t(y)ōōs' ang'gəl] An angle that has a measure greater than a right angle (p. 385)
Example:

obtuse triangle [əb•t(y)ōōs' tri'ang•gəl] A triangle that has 1 obtuse angle (p. 393)

octagon [äk'tə•gän] A polygon with eight sides (p. 390)
Example:

odd [od] A whole number that has a 1, 3, 5, 7, or 9 in the ones place (p. 20)

open figure [ō•pən fi'•gyər] A figure that does not begin and end at the same point (p. 390)
Examples:

Order Property of Addition [ôr'dər prä'pər•tē əv ə•dish'ən] The property that states that you can add two numbers in any order and get the same sum (p. 6)
Example: 6 + 7 = 13
7 + 6 = 13

Order Property of Multiplication [ôr'dər prä'pər•tē əv mul•tə•pla•kā'shən] The property that states that you can multiply two factors in any order and get the same product (p. 163)
Example: $4 \times 2 = 8$
$2 \times 4 = 8$

ordered pair [ôr'dərd pâr] A pair of numbers that names a point on a grid (p. 328)
Example: (3,4)

5 4 3 2 1
0 1 2 3 4 5

H46–H49   Glossary

ounce (oz) [ouns] A customary unit for measuring weight (p. 346)

outcome [out′kum] A possible result of an experiment (p. 490)

parallel lines [par′ə•lel linz] Lines that never cross; lines that are always the same distance apart (p. 388)
Example:

parallelogram [par•ə•lel′ə•gram] A quadrilateral with 2 pairs of parallel sides and 2 pairs of equal sides (p. 397)
Example:

pattern [pat′ərn] An ordered set of numbers or objects; the order helps you predict what will come next. (p. 30)
Examples:
2, 4, 6, 8, 10

pattern unit [pat′ərn yōō′nət] The part of a pattern that repeats (p. 470)
Example:

pattern unit

pentagon [pen′tə•gän] A polygon with five sides (p. 390)
Example:

perimeter [pə•ri′mə•tər] The distance around a figure (p. 444)
Example:

perpendicular lines [pûr•pən•dik′yə•lər linz] Lines that intersect to form right angles (p. 388)
Example:

pictograph [pik′tə•graf] A graph that uses pictures to show and compare information (p. 198)
Example:

HOW WE GET TO SCHOOL	
Walk	✸ ✸
Ride a Bike	✸ ✸ ✸
Ride a Bus	✸ ✸ ✸ ✸ ✸
Ride in a Car	✸
Key: Each ✸ = 10 students.	

pint (pt) [pint] A customary unit for measuring capacity; 1 pint = 2 cups (p. 344)

place value [plās val′yōō] The value of each digit in a number, based on the location of the digit (p. 22)

plane [plāne] A flat surface that goes on and on
Example:

part of a plane

plane figure [plāne fi′•gyər] A closed figure in a plane that is formed by lines that are curved, straight, or both (p. 390)
Example:

P.M. [pē em] The hours between noon and midnight (p. 132)

point [point] An exact position or location (p. 384)

polygon [pol′ē•gän] A closed plane figure with straight sides that are line segments (p. 390)
Examples:

Word History

Did you ever notice that a *polygon* looks like a bunch of knees that are bent? This is how the term got its name. *Poly-* is from the Greek root, *poli*, that means "many". The ending *-gon* is from the Latin, *gonus*, which means "to bend the knee".

possible outcome [pos′ə•bəl out′kəm] Something that has a chance of happening (p. 490)

pound (lb) [pound] A customary unit for measuring weight; 1 pound = 16 ounces (p. 346)

predict [pri•dikt′] To make a reasonable guess about what will happen (p. 490)

probability [prä•bə•bil′ə•tē] The chance that a given event will occur (p. 488)
Example:

probability of red = one out of four

product [prä′dəkt] The answer in a multiplication problem (p. 160)
Example: 3 × 8 = 24
∟product

Q

quadrilateral [kwa•drə•lat′ər•əl] A polygon with four sides (p. 390)
Example:

quart (qt) [kwôrt] A customary unit for measuring capacity; 1 quart = 2 pints (p. 344)

quarter hour [kwôr•tər our] 15 minutes (p. 129)
Example: Between 4:00 and 4:15 is one quarter hour.

quotient [kwō′shənt] The number, not including the remainder, that results from division (p. 242)
Example: 8 ÷ 4 = 2
∟quotient

R

range [rānj] The difference between the greatest number and the least number in a set of data (p. 310)

ray [rā] A part of a line, with one endpoint, that is straight and continues in one direction (p. 384)
Example:

rectangle [rek′tang•gəl] A quadrilateral with 2 pairs of parallel sides, 2 pairs of equal sides, and 4 right angles (p. 397)
Example:

---

rectangular prism [rek•tan′gyə•lər pri′zəm] A solid figure with six faces that are all rectangles (p. 424)
Example:

regroup [rē•grōōp′] To exchange amounts of equal value to rename a number (p. 8)
Example: 5 + 8 = 13 ones or 1 ten 3 ones

remainder [ri•mān′dər] The amount left over when a number cannot be divided evenly (p. 618)

results [ri•zults′] The answers from a survey (p. 304)

rhombus [räm′bəs] A quadrilateral with 2 pairs of parallel sides and 4 equal sides (p. 397)
Example:

right angle [rit ang′gəl] A special angle that forms a square corner; a right angle measures 90° (p. 384)
Example:

right triangle [rit tri′ang•gəl] A triangle with one right angle (p. 393)
Example:

rounding [roun′ding] Replacing a number with another number that tells about how many or how much (p. 50)

S

scale [skāl] The numbers on a bar graph that help you read the number each bar shows (p. 324)

scalene triangle [skā′lēn tri′ang•gəl] A triangle in which no sides are equal (p. 393)
Example:

schedule [ske′•jōōl] A table that lists activities or events and the times they happen (p. 136)

sequence [sē′kwəns] To write events in order (p. 142)

similar [si′mə•lər] Having the same shape and the same or different size (p. 412)
Example:

simplest form [sim′pləst fôrm] When a fraction is modeled with the largest fraction bar or bars possible (p. 542)

slide [slīd] A movement of a figure to a new position without turning or flipping it (p. 414)
Example:

sphere [sfir] A solid figure that has the shape of a round ball (p. 424)
Example:

square [skwâr] A quadrilateral with 2 pairs of parallel sides, 4 equal sides, and 4 right angles (p. 397)
Example:

square pyramid [skwâr pir′ə•mid] A solid, pointed figure with a flat base that is a square (p. 424)
Example:

---

square unit [skwâr yōō′nət] A square with a side length of one unit; used to measure area (p. 448)

standard form [stan′dərd fôrm] A way to write numbers by using the digits 0–9, with each digit having a place value (p. 22)
Example: 345 ← standard form

subtraction [səb•trak′shən] The process of finding how many are left when a number of items are taken away from a group of items; the process of finding the difference when two groups are compared; the opposite operation of addition (p. 10)

sum [sum] The answer to an addition problem (p. 4)

survey [sər′vā] A method of gathering information (p. 304)

symmetry [sim′ə•trē] A figure has symmetry if it can be folded along a line so that the two parts match exactly; one half of the figure looks like the mirror image of the other half (p. 410)

T

tally table [ta′lē tā′bəl] A table that uses tally marks to record data (p. 302)
Example:

FAVORITE SPORT	
Sport	**Number**
Soccer	⊪⊪ ⦙⦙⦙
Baseball	⦙⦙⦙
Football	⊪⊪
Basketball	⊪⊪ ⦙

tenth [tenth] One of ten equal parts (p. 558)
Example:

∟tenth

tessellate [tes′ə•lāt] To combine plane figures so they cover a surface without overlapping or leaving any space between them (p. 430)

tessellation [tes•sə•lā′shən] A repeating pattern of closed figures that covers a surface with no gaps and no overlaps (p. 430)
Example:

time line [tīm līn] A drawing that shows when and in what order events took place (p. 142)

trapezoid [trap′ə•zoid] A quadrilateral with one pair of parallel sides (p. 396)
Example:

tree diagram [trē dī′ə•gram] An organized list that shows all possible outcomes of an event (p. 498)
Example:

tan pants — blue shirt / red shirt / white shirt
black pants — blue shirt / red shirt / white shirt

trends [trendz] Areas on a graph where data increase, decrease, or stay the same over time (p. 330)

triangle [trī′ang•gəl] A polygon with three sides (p. 392)
Examples:

turn [tûrn] A movement of a figure to a new position by rotating the figure around a point (p. 414)
Example:

U

unit cost [yoo′nit kôst] The cost of one item when several items are sold for a single price (p. 297)

unlikely [ən·līk′lē] An event is unlikely if it does not have a good chance of happening. (p. 488)

V

variable [vâr′ē·ə·bəl] A symbol or a letter that stands for an unknown number (p. 243)

> **Word History**
>
> **Variable** The word *vary* comes from the Latin, *variabilis*, meaning "changeable." At first the word applied to changes of color, as in the speckled fur of animals. Eventually the word was used for things that involve change of any kind.

Venn diagram [ven dī′ə·gram] A diagram that shows relationships among sets of things (p. 400)
Example:

2-Digit Numbers   Even Numbers

35	12	8
17	10	6
29		4

vertex [vûr′teks] The point at which two or more line segments meet in a plane figure or where three or more edges meet in a solid figure (p. 424)
Examples:

vertical bar graph [vûr′ti·kəl bär graf] A bar graph in which the bars go up from bottom to top (p. 324)

volume [väl′yəm] The amount of space a solid figure takes up (p. 452)

W

whole number [hōl nəm′bər] One of the numbers 0, 1, 2, 3, 4, ... The set of whole numbers goes on without end.

word form [wûrd form] A way to write numbers by using words (p. 22)
Example: The word form of 212 is two hundred twelve.

Y

yard (yd) [yärd] A customary unit for measuring length or distance; 1 yard = 3 feet (p. 342)

Z

Zero Property of Multiplication [zir′ō prä′pər·tē əv mul·tə·plə·kā′shən] The property that states that the product of zero and any number is zero (p. 220)
Example: $0 \times 6 = 0$

HARCOURT

Math

Problem of the Day

This section provides complete solutions for the **Problem of the Day** in each lesson plan. The problems include all types—one-step, multi-step, applied, process, nonroutine, open-ended, and puzzle problems—and provide options for students to develop their ability to use logical reasoning to choose and apply problem-solving strategies to varied and interesting situations.

The **Problem of the Day** for a lesson is also available on the Daily Transparency.

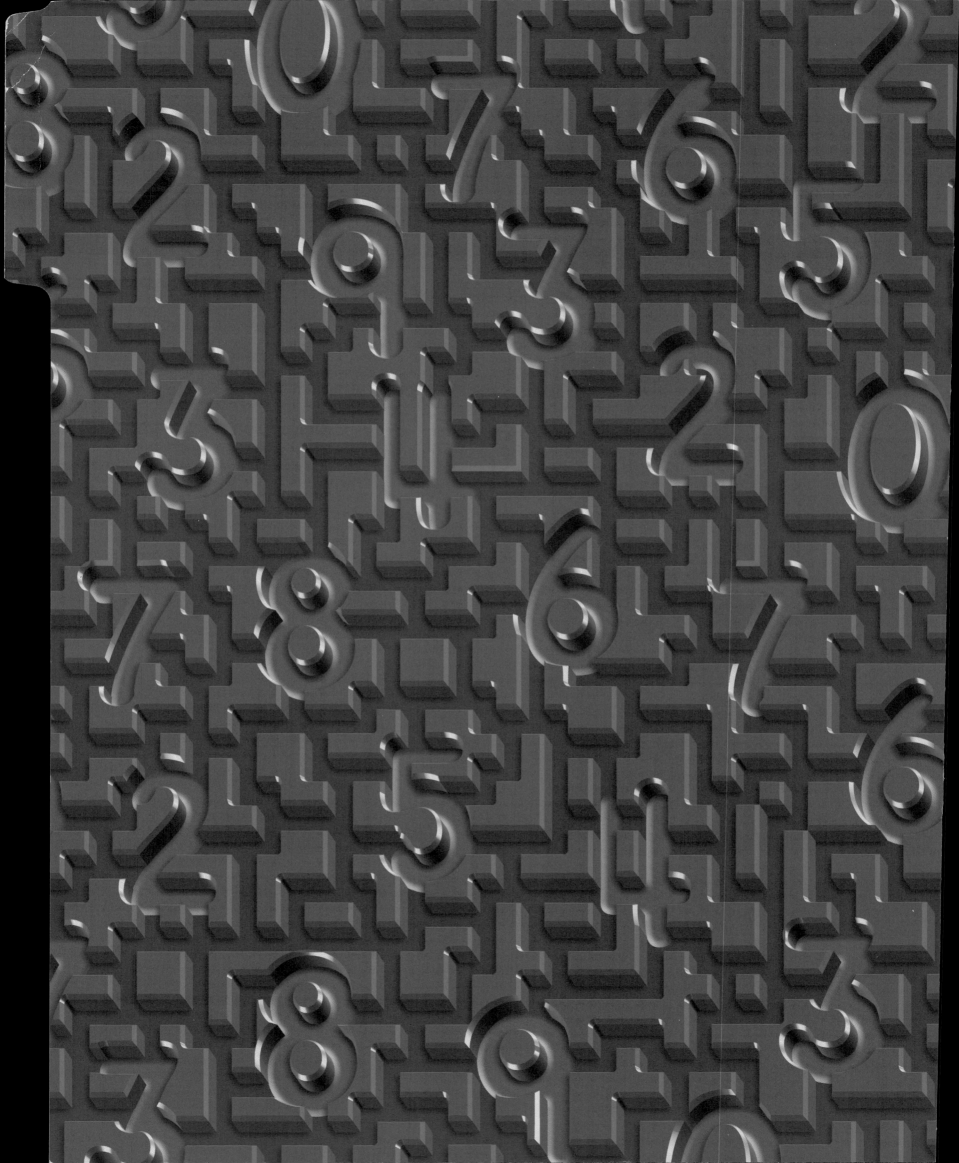

Chapter 12 Answer Key

Lesson 12.1

Problem

Rudy is saving $6 a week to buy a computer game that costs $24. Al is saving $4 a week to buy the same game. Who will be able to buy the game sooner? How much sooner?

Solution

Strategy: Write an Equation

Rudy: $24 \div 6 = 4$ weeks

Al: $24 \div 4 = 6$ weeks

Rudy will be able to buy the game 2 weeks sooner than Al.

Lesson 12.2

Problem

Krista has 8 dimes and 20 pennies. She divides them equally among 3 friends and herself. How many dimes does each get? How many pennies does each get? How much money does each person have?

Solution

Strategy: Write an Equation

$3 + 1 = 4$ people

$8 \div 4 = 2$ dimes each

$20 \div 4 = 5$ pennies each

2 dimes + 5 pennies = 25 cents

2 dimes; 5 pennies; 25¢

Lesson 12.3

Problem

Replace each ■ with a digit from 1 to 9. Use each digit only once. Make a true number sentence.

1. $36 \div ■ = ■$
2. $■ \times ■ = 30$
3. $11 - ■ = ■$
4. $■ + ■ + ■ = 10$

Solution

Strategy: Predict and Test

Possible answers:

1. $36 \div 4 = 9$
2. $6 \times 5 = 30$
3. $11 - 8 = 3$
4. $1 + 2 + 7 = 10$

Lesson 12.4

Problem

Find the two numbers whose product is 6 and quotient is 6. What is the sum and difference of the two numbers?

Solution

Strategy: Write an Equation

Students can use a multiplication table to find the numbers whose product and quotient are 6.

$6 \times 1 = 6$ $6 \div 1 = 6$

$6 + 1 = 7$ $6 - 1 = 5$

6, 1; 7, 5

Lesson 12.5

Problem

Alicia is twice as old as Jon. Tina is twice as old as Alicia. Tina is 12 years old. What is the difference between Tina's age and Jon's?

Solution

Strategy: Write an Equation

$? \times 2 = 12$ or $12 \div 2 = 6$ Alicia is 6 years old.

$? \times 2 = 6$ or $6 \div 2 = 3$ Jon is 3 years old.

$12 - 3 = 9$

9 years; Tina is 12 years old, Alicia is 6 years old, and Jon is 3 years old

Chapter 13 Answer Key

Lesson 13.1

Problem

Find the number that does not belong in each group.

1. 12, 16, 10, 5, 8
2. 45, 18, 20, 15, 50
3. 24, 35, 56, 63, 42
4. 32, 40, 24, 48, 23
5. 38, 24, 15, 12, 28

Solution

Strategy: Use Logical Reasoning

1. 5   The others are multiples of 2.
2. 18   The others are multiples of 5.
3. 24   The others are multiples of 7.
4. 23   The others are multiples of 8.
5. 15   The others are multiples of 2.

Lesson 13.2

Problem

All of the even numbers less than 9 are factors of me. Who am I?

Solution

Strategy: Use a Multiplication Table
Since the number is even, 2 is a factor.
The other numbers can be found using the table.
One solution: I am the number 24.
Other solutions: 48, 72, . . .

Lesson 13.3

Problem

Jannelle has 50 pennies. How many pennies will she put in a group if she wants to exchange them for nickels? for dimes? for quarters?

Solution

Strategy: Act It Out
Students may use coins to model each exchange.
Jannelle will exchange 5 pennies for each nickel, 10 pennies for each dime, and 25 pennies for each quarter.

Lesson 13.4

Problem

Joey wants to plant 4 rows of beans with 5 bean seeds in each row. He also plans to plant 3 pepper seeds in each of the 4 rows. How many seeds will he need in all?

Solution

Strategy: Write an Equation
$4 \times 5 = 20$ bean seeds
$3 \times 4 = 12$ pepper seeds
$20 + 12 = 32$
Joey needs a total of 32 seeds.

Lesson 13.5

Problem

Billy's mother cut each of 2 pizzas into 6 pieces. Billy and 3 of his friends shared the pieces equally. How many pieces did each of them get?

Solution

Strategy: Write an Equation
Multiply to find the number of pieces in all.
$2 \times 6 = 12$ pieces
Add to find how many people got pizza.
$3 + 1 = 4$
Divide to find how many pieces each person got.
$12 \div 4 = 3$
Each got 3 pieces.

Chapter 14 Answer Key

Lesson 14.1

Problem

Mrs. Martin baked some cupcakes. She put 8 chocolate chips and 4 nuts on each. If she used 48 chocolate chips, how many nuts did she use?

Solution

Strategy: Use Logical Reasoning/Write a Number Sentence

Since Mrs. Martin used 48 chocolate chips and put 8 chips on each cupcake, divide to find the number of cupcakes: $48 \div 8 = 6$.

Then multiply the number of nuts she put on each cupcake, 4, by the number of cupcakes, 6: $4 \times 6 = 24$.

So, she used 24 nuts.

Lesson 14.2

Problem

If you divide this number by 2, the quotient is 8. What is the quotient if the number is divided by 4?

Solution

Strategy: Predict and Test

Try 16. $16 \div 2 = 8$. 16 is the number.

The quotient of 16 divided by 4 is 4.

Lesson 14.3

Problem

Two sisters and two brothers need to share $36 equally. How much money will each person get?

Solution

Strategy: Write a Number Sentence

Two sisters and two brothers make a total of 4 people.

$36 \div 4 = 9

Each person will get $9.

Lesson 14.4

Problem

Ben, Carl, and Evan are each less than 15 years old. Last year, Evan was 10 years older than Ben. Next year, Evan will be 3 times as old as Carl. How old are the children now?

Solution

Strategy: Use Logical Reasoning/Write a Number Sentence

If Evan was 10 years older than Ben last year, then Evan must have been 11, 12, or 13. If next year Evan will be 3 times as old as Carl, Evan will be 15 then, and Carl will be 5 ($3 \times 5 = 15$).

So, this year Evan must be 14, Carl is 4, and Ben is 4 ($14 - 10 = 4$).

Lesson 14.5

Problem

Rachel has 40 trading cards. She wants to share them equally among herself and 4 friends. How many cards does each friend get?

Solution

Strategy: Write a Number Sentence

Rachel wants to divide the cards among 4 friends and herself, which makes a total of 5 people.

$40 \div 5 = 8$

Each friend gets 8 cards.

Problem of the Day

Chapter 15 Answer Key

Lesson 15.1

Problem

The survey of Kathy's class of 32 students showed that 6 students have birthdays in the shortest month of the year. In each of the months with only 30 days, there were 3 students who have birthdays. In each of the other months, the same number of students have birthdays. Tell the number of students who have birthdays in each month of the year.

Solution

Strategy: Make a Model

Use a calendar to determine the shortest month (February). So there are 6 birthdays in February. Using the calendar, students can determine that there are 4 months with 30 days. $4 \times 3 = 12$

Since there are 12 months in a year, students can subtract. $12 - 4 = 8$

$8 - 1 = 7$

There are 7 months left over. There are a total of 32 students. We have accounted for 18, leaving 14 students with birthdays in the remaining 7 months. 14 divided by 7 is 2. Therefore there are 2 students with birthdays in each month with 31 days. Jan, 2; Feb, 6; March, 2; April, 3; May, 2; June, 3; July, 2; Aug, 2; Sept, 3; Oct, 2; Nov, 3; Dec, 2

Lesson 15.2

Problem

Rashana asked her 28 classmates which flavor of yogurt they like best—lemon, vanilla, or strawberry. The number of tallies she recorded for lemon was 2 more than the number for strawberry but 3 less than the number for vanilla. How many students said they like vanilla best?

Solution

Strategy: Make an Organized List

Strawberry	Lemon	Vanilla	Total
1	3	6	10
2	4	7	13
3	5	8	16
4	6	9	19
5	7	10	22
6	8	11	25
7	9	12	28

12 students like vanilla best.

Lesson 15.3

Problem

Thirty students answered a survey about 3 favorite recess games. Two more liked kickball than tag, and two more liked tag than hide and seek. What numbers appeared for each recess game on the frequency table?

Solution

Strategy: Predict and Test

Kickball	Tag	Hide and Seek	Total	Notes
10	8	6	24	too low
14	12	10	36	too high
12	10	8	30	

12 for kickball; 10 for tag; 8 for hide and seek.

Lesson 15.4

Problem

Show this data in a table. In Ali's class, 3 girls have long, straight, blond hair, and 1 has short, straight, blond hair. The only redhead has long, straight hair. No girls have long, curly hair. The only girls with short, curly hair are 3 whose hair is brown. Of the 3 other brown-haired girls, 2 have long, straight hair, and one has short, straight hair. Find the types of hair that are most common.

Solution

Strategy: Make a Table

	Long		Short	
	Curly	Straight	Curly	Straight
Blond	0	3	0	1
Brown	0	2	3	1
Red	0	1	0	0

The most common types of hair are long, straight, blond, and short, curly, brown.

Chapter 15 Answer Key

Lesson 15.5

Problem

Three students made 3 graphs. The boy who made the horizontal bar graph was not Jeff. Amy did not make the vertical bar graph. Paul did not make the pictograph. Which of the 3 graphs did each student make?

Solution

Strategy: Use Logical Reasoning

Jeff was not the boy who made the horizontal bar graph, so Paul was the boy who made the horizontal bar graph. Amy did not make the vertical bar graph, so Jeff made the vertical bar graph. The only graph left is the pictograph, so Amy made the pictograph.

Lesson 15.6

Problem

Graham saved for 5 weeks to buy a train set that cost $29.56. About how much did he set aside each week?

Solution

Strategy: Solve a Simpler Problem

Since $30 is close to $29.56, divide $30 by 5 weeks to find about how much Graham saved each week. $30 ÷ 5 = $6. He saved about $6.00 per week.

Chapter 16 Answer Key

Lesson 16.1

Problem

The third graders at Lincoln School are trying to collect 100 soup cans for a food drive. Each time they collect 4 cans of soup they make a tally mark. There are 6 tally marks for Mrs. Blake's class, 4 tally marks for Mr. Wu's class, and 5 tally marks for Ms. Carr's class. How many more soup cans do students need to collect?

Solution

Strategy: Write a Number Sentence
$4 \times 6 = 24$; $4 \times 4 = 16$; $4 \times 5 = 20$;
$24 + 16 + 20 = 60$; $100 - 60 = 40$
Students need to collect 40 more cans.

Lesson 16.2

Problem

The numbers in Alicia's table are 16, 26, 32, 12, and 22, and those in Ian's table are 20, 8, 36, 24, and 40. What number could they both use for the key of their pictographs? Is there another number that Ian could use?

Solution

Strategy: Use Logical Thinking
All their numbers are even numbers (multiples of 2), so both could use 2 in their keys. Ian could use 4 because all his numbers are also multiples of 4. If he used 4 in the key, he would not have to draw as many pictures.

Lesson 16.3

Problem

Nathan marked the scale on his bar graph by skip-counting by 6's. If he drew a bar graph to show 28 flowers, between what two numbers should he end the bar?

Solution

Strategy: Draw a Picture
Write the numbers from 1 to 36. Underline the multiples of 6.
1, 2, 3, 4, 5, <u>6</u>, 7, 8, 9, 10, 11, <u>12</u>, 13, 14, 15, 16, 17, <u>18</u>, 19, 20, 21, 22, 23, <u>24</u>, 25, 26, 27, 28, 29, <u>30</u>, 31, 32, 33, 34, 35, <u>36</u> 28 is between 24 and 30, but closer to 30, so he should make the bar on the graph between 24 and 30, but closer to 30.

Lesson 16.4

Problem

A bar graph showed that Barb read twice as many library books as Lisa. Mike read 25 more books than Lisa, but 15 fewer than Barb. How many books did each read?

Solution

Strategy: Predict and Test

Lisa's books	Mike's books	Barb's books
$1 + 25 =$	$26 + 15 =$	41

but 2 x 1 does not equal 41.

$10 + 25 =$	$35 + 15 =$	50

but 2 x 10 does not equal 50.

$20 + 25 =$	$45 + 15 =$	60

but 2×20 does not equal 60.

$40 + 25 =$	$65 + 15 =$	80

and 2×40 does equal 80.

Lisa read 40 books, Mike read 65 books, and Barb read 80 books.

Lesson 16.5

Problem

The streets and avenues on a map are one block apart. Stan's house is at 4th Avenue and 6th Street (4,6). His grandmother's house is at 7th Avenue and 2nd Street (7,2). How many blocks is it from his house to his grandmother's house?

Solution

Strategy: Draw a Diagram
Students draw a grid and locate the ordered pairs (4,6) and (7,2). They then count the number of squares over and down (or down and over).

It is 7 blocks from Stan's house to his grandmother's.

Chapter 17 Answer Key

Lesson 17.1

Problem

It took Silvia and Nick a total of 48 minutes to complete their homework. If it took Nick twice as long as Silvia, how long did it take each one?

Solution

Strategy: Predict and Test
Try Nick: 22, Silvia: 11 $22 + 11 = 33$, not 48
Try Nick: 32, Silvia: 16 $32 + 16 = 48$

So, it took Nick 32 minutes and Silvia 16 minutes.

Lesson 17.2

Problem

Katie, Jerry, and Adam each have a different colored pencil. The blue pencil is 5 inches long, and the red one is 6 inches long. Katie's yellow pencil is 2 inches longer than Jerry's pencil. Adam's pencil is 1 inch shorter than Katie's. How long is Katie's pencil? Who has the blue pencil?

Solution

Strategy: Make an Organized List
Fill in the list as you read each detail.

Name	Color	Length
Jerry	blue	5 in.
Adam	red	6 in.
Katie	yellow	7 in.

Katie's pencil is 7 in. long and Jerry has the blue pencil.

Lesson 17.3

Problem

Stan, Bruce, and Rita each measured a different item. Stan did not measure in inches. Neither Bruce nor Rita used a yardstick. Rita's measure was greater than Bruce's. Which of the following objects were measured in inches, feet, or yards and who measured each of them?
a. a small table
b. an envelope
c. a cafeteria

Solution

Strategy: Use Logical Reasoning
Since Stan did not measure in inches, he probably measured the cafeteria in yards. Since Rita's measure was greater than Bruce's, her measurement was in a larger unit so she must have been measuring in feet and Bruce in inches.
Rita measured the small table in feet, Bruce measured the envelope in inches, and Stan measured the cafeteria in yards.

Lesson 17.4

Problem

I am a 3-digit number. I am the sum of the number of inches in a foot, hours in a day, cups in a gallon, inches in a yard, and eggs in a dozen. What number am I?

Solution

Strategy: Write an Equation
$12 + 24 + 16 + 36 + 12 = 100$
I am the number 100.

Lesson 17.5

Problem

Mr. Wren is building a tree house. He needs boards that are 42 inches long. He has boards that are 4 feet long. How many inches should he cut off each board?

Solution

Strategy: Write an Equation
There are 12 inches in a foot, so
$4 \times 12 = 48$
$48 - 42 = 6$
There are 48 inches in 4 feet, so he should cut 6 inches off each board.

Lesson 17.6

Problem

The left end of Natalie's ruler has broken off, so she starts measuring at the 3-inch mark. She measures a line that ends just past the halfway mark between 6 and 7 inches. How long is the line to the nearest half inch?

Solution

Strategy: Write an Equation
If the ruler were not broken the line would be $6\frac{1}{2}$ inches long. Since she starts at 3 inches, subtract.
$6\frac{1}{2} - 3 = 3\frac{1}{2}$ $3\frac{1}{2}$ inches

Chapter 18 Answer Key

Lesson 18.1

Problem

Mike drew a line twice as long as Penny's. Penny's line was 2 inches shorter than the one Cassandra drew. Cassandra's line was 20 inches long. How long were the lines Penny and Mike drew?

Solution

Strategy: Write a Number Sentence
Penny   20 in. − 2 in. = 18 in.
Mike   18 in. × 2 = 36 in.
Penny, 18 in.; Mike, 36 in.

Lesson 18.2

Problem

Find the mystery metric fact.
• Take the number of centimeters in a meter.
• Divide it by 4.
• Subtract the product of 2 and 8.
• Round the number to the nearest ten.
The answer is the number of _____ in a _____.

Solution

Strategy: Write a Number Sentence
There are 100 cm in a meter.
100 ÷ 4 = 25
2 × 8 = 16
25 − 16 = 9, and 9 rounds to 10.
Possible answers: centimeters, decimeter; decimeters, meter.

Lesson 18.3

Problem

A blue string is 11 cm long. A black string is 20 cm longer than the blue string. A green string is 10 cm shorter than the black string. A red string is 12 cm longer than the green string. List the strings and their lengths in order from shortest to longest.

Solution

Strategy: Make an Organized List/Write a Number Sentence
Blue   11 cm
Black   31 cm (20 + 11)
Green   21 cm (31 − 10)
Red   33 cm (21 + 12)
11 cm, 21 cm, 31 cm, 33 cm

Lesson 18.4

Problem

With their backpacks on, together Noah and Zack have a mass of 64 kilograms. Zack's mass is 2 more kilograms than Noah's. Each of their backpacks has a mass of 2 kilograms. What is the mass of each boy?

Solution

Strategy: Write a Number Sentence/Predict and Test
2 + 2 = 4   (the mass of 2 backpacks)
64 − 4 = 60   (the mass of 2 boys)
Predict and test to find a number that, when added to itself plus 2, is equal to 60.
29 + 31 = 60
Noah's mass is 29 kg and Zack's mass is 31 kg.

Lesson 18.5

Problem

Last week Ms. Baker drank 2 cups of tea each morning except Saturday. How many pints of tea did she drink last week?

Solution

Strategy: Write a Number Sentence
2 cups = 1 pint
7 days − 1 day = 6 days
6 days × 2 cups = 12 cups
12 cups = 6 pints
Ms. Baker drank 6 pints of tea last week.

Chapter 19 Answer Key

Lesson 19.1

Problem

You can use 6 toothpicks to build the number 6. Which numbers, 0–9, can you build using 5 toothpicks? Which number from 0–9 takes the most toothpicks to make?

Solution

Strategy: Make a Model

Students use 5 toothpicks to show the numbers 2, 3, and 5. Making the number 8 takes the most toothpicks.

Lesson 19.2

Problem

Mario drew a plane figure with 4 equal line segments and 4 right angles. Susana drew a plane figure with 3 line segments and 3 angles. Omar drew a plane figure with 0 line segments and 0 angles. What figure did each student draw?

Solution

Strategy: Use Logical Reasoning

Omar's figure could be a circle; circles are plane figures with 0 line segments and 0 angles. Susana must have drawn a triangle, since triangles have 3 line segments and 3 angles. Mario must have drawn a square. Squares have 4 equal line segments and 4 right angles.

Mario, square; Susana, triangle; Omar, circle

Lesson 19.3

Problem

John has 3 sisters and 1 brother. Susie has 1 sister and 3 brothers. Ashley has 2 sisters and 2 brothers. One of the girls is John's sister. Which one?

Solution

Strategy: Use Logical Reasoning

Since Susie has 3 brothers, John would have to have 2 brothers for Susie to be his sister. Ashley has 2 brothers and 2 sisters and John has 3 sisters and 1 brother, each has a family with a total of 3 girls and 2 boys.

Ashley is John's sister.

Lesson 19.4

Problem

Diana drew 6 hexagons. Alex drew 9 triangles. Gina drew 10 pentagons. How many line segments did each student draw?

Solution

Strategy: Write a Number Sentence

A hexagon has 6 line segments. $6 \times 6 = 36$
A triangle has 3 line segments. $3 \times 9 = 27$
A pentagon has 5 line segments. $5 \times 10 = 50$
Diana: 36, Alex: 27, Gina: 50 line segments

Lesson 19.5

Problem

Which term does not belong with the others? Explain.
1. product, divisor, dividend, quotient
2. quadrilateral, pentagon, circle, hexagon
3. cup, inch, pint, quart

Solution

Strategy: Find a Pattern

Product is a multiplication term, therefore it does not belong.
Quadrilaterals, pentagons, and hexagons are all polygons. A circle is not, therefore it does not belong.
Cup, pint, and quart are all customary units for measuring capacity. An inch is a customary unit for measuring length and does not belong.

Lesson 19.6

Problem

I am a number less than 40 that can be divided equally into groups of 7. The sum of my digits is 8. What number am I?

Solution

Strategy: Use Logical Reasoning

The numbers less than 40 that can be divided equally into groups of 7 are 7, 14, 21, 28, and 35. Of these numbers, only one has digits with a sum of 8.
35

Chapter 20 Answer Key

Lesson 20.1

Problem

When Eddie drew a line from 1 corner of a figure to the opposite corner, he formed 2 triangles. What was his original figure?

Solution

Strategy: Draw a Picture

Students may try drawing different plane figures to find the solution. Check student's drawings.

The figure was a square or a rectangle.

Lesson 20.2

Problem

Simon wrote a 5-digit number. The sum of the digits was 31. Three of the digits were the same odd number. The other digits were the same even number. Write a 5-digit number that could be Simon's number.

Solution

Strategy: Use Logical Reasoning

Find all possible sums of three 1-digit odd numbers.

Odd digit	1	3	5	7	9
Sum of 3 digits	3	9	15	21	27

Find all possible sums of two 1-digit even numbers

Even digit	2	4	6	8
Sum of 2 digits	4	8	12	16

Find combinations of sums that total 31: $27 + 4 = 31$ and $15 + 16 = 31$. Write a 5-digit number using 3 odd digits and 2 even digits that total 31.

Accept 5-digit numbers with three 5s and two 8s or three 9s and two 2s in any order.

Lesson 20.3

Problem

Write the greatest and least number using the digits 0, 1, 3, and 8.

Solution

Strategy: Use Logical Reasoning

For the greatest number, write the digits in order from greatest to least so that the greatest digit is in the greatest place-value position. You could write the digits in the opposite order for the least number, but you cannot begin a number with 0; so, use 1 in the thousands place, 0 in the hundreds place, and continue the digits in ascending value.

8,310 and 1,038

Lesson 20.4

Problem

What two shapes in each row are congruent?

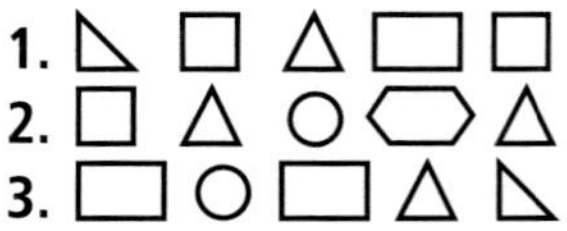

1. ◺ ☐ △ ☐☐ ☐
2. ☐ △ ○ ⬡ △
3. ☐ ○ ☐ △ ◺

Solution

Strategy: Predict and Test

Cut out the figures in each row and place each figure on top of the other figures until you find two that are the same size and the same shape.

The squares are congruent, the triangles are congruent, and the rectangles are congruent.

Lesson 20.5

Problem

Craig traced the figure Paula had drawn. He erased one of the sides of the figure. Then he drew two more sides to make a symmetrical figure. His figure was a square. What was Paula's figure?

Solution

Strategy: Draw a Picture

Paula's picture was half of Craig's and her figure had exactly 3 sides. If you draw a line from 1 corner to the opposite corner of a square, you have 2 right triangles.

Paula's figure was a right triangle.

Chapter 21 Answer Key

Lesson 21.1

Problem

Andrea has 1 coin. Simon has 4 more nickels than Pablo and 4 more coins than Andrea. They each have the same amount of money. What coins does each have?

Solution

Strategy: Predict and Test

Andrea has 1 quarter.

Simon has 5 nickels.

Pablo has 2 dimes and a nickel.

Lesson 21.2

Problem

Carl's solid figure has 6 faces and 8 vertices. Anna's figure has 1 less face and three fewer vertices than Carl's. Name their figures.

Solution

Strategy: Use Logical Reasoning

A square pyramid is the only solid figure with 5 faces and 8 vertices. Carl has a cube or rectangular prism because his figure has 6 faces. A cube or rectangular prism has 6 faces and 8 vertices.

Anna — square pyramid; Carl — cube or rectangular prism

Lesson 21.3

Problem

Sara drew a plane figure with 4 equal sides and 4 right angles. Luz drew a plane figure with no straight sides and no angles inside Sara's figure. Ali drew a plane figure with 3 sides and 3 angles on top of Sara's figure. How did the design look?

Solution

Strategy: Use Logical Reasoning

A figure with 4 equal sides and 4 right angles is a square. A figure with no straight sides or angles could be a circle. A figure with 3 sides and 3 angles is a triangle.

Possible answer: Sara drew a square, Luz drew a circle inside the square, and Ali drew a triangle on top of the square.

Lesson 21.4

Problem

Luis and Jenna each had the same amount of money. Luis had three quarters. Jenna had 10 coins. What coins did Jenna have?

Solution

Strategy: Make a Table

Luis has 75 cents. Make a table to show all possible combinations of coins that total 75 cents. Find combinations that use exactly 10 coins.

H	Q	D	N	P
I	I			
I		2	I	
I		2		5
I			4	5

Possible answers: 5 dimes and 5 nickels; 1 half dollar, 4 nickels, and 5 pennies

Lesson 21.5

Problem

For every 4 seeds Tammy planted, only 1 sprouted. If 9 seeds sprouted, how many seeds did Tammy plant?

Solution

Strategy: Make a Table

Make a table showing the number of seeds planted and the number of seeds sprouted. Find a pattern and extend it to find the number of seeds for 9 sprouts.

Seeds	4	8	12	16	20	24	28	32	36
Sprouts	1	2	3	4	5	6	7	8	9

36 seeds

Chapter 22 Answer Key

Lesson 22.1

Problem
Bert made 6 different rectangles using toothpicks. He used 24 toothpicks for each rectangle. How wide and long was each rectangle in toothpicks? Which one was a square?

Solution
Strategy: Make a Model
Students could use 24 unit cubes to model rectangles with these dimensions:
1 by 11, 2 by 10, 3 by 9, 4 by 8, 5 by 7, 6 by 6; 6 by 6 was a square.

Lesson 22.2

Problem
One side of Dot's triangle and the length of Bob's rectangle are 4 cm. Another side of Dot's triangle is as long as a side of Dave's square. The perimeter of each figure is 12 cm. How long are the sides of each figure?

Solution
Strategy: Make a Model
If needed, give this hint: Find the sides of Dave's figure first.

Dave's: Students arrange unit blocks to form a square with a perimeter of 12. It will be 3 x 3. (One side of Dot's triangle will be 3.)

Bob's: They arrange unit blocks to form a rectangle with a perimeter of 12 and one side of 4. The other side will be 2.

Dot's: Students draw a triangle and write 4 on one side, 3 on another. The perimeter is 12, so the missing side is 5.

Dave's square: 3 cm by 3 cm
Bob's rectangle: 4 cm by 2 cm
Dot's triangle: 3 cm by 4 cm by 5 cm

Lesson 22.3

Problem
Draw each figure and find its perimeter and area.
1. 3 units wide, 6 units long
2. 8 units wide, 5 units long
3. 7 units wide, 7 units long

Solution
Strategy: Draw a Picture/Write a Number Sentence

1. $P = 3 + 3 + 6 + 6 = 18$ units
$A = 3 \times 6 = 18$ square units

2.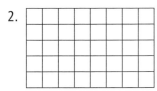
$P = 5 + 5 + 8 + 8 = 26$ units
$A = 5 \times 8 = 40$ square units

3.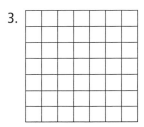
$P = 7 + 7 + 7 + 7 = 28$ units
$A = 7 \times 7 = 49$ square units

Lesson 22.4

Problem
The perimeter of each face of a solid figure is 32 units. The area of each face is 64 square units. What plane figure forms each face? What is the name of the solid figure?

Solution
Strategy: Predict and Test
If faces are squares and the perimeter of each face is 32 units, then each edge of the squares will be 8 units. The area would then be square 64 units.
Each face is a square. The solid figure is a cube.

Math

Bibliography and Index

The following bibliography contains references to:

- **Fiction and nonfiction books for students**
- **Technology resources**
- **Professional books and magazines**

These materials will assist you in creating an interesting learning environment. The references to literature are provided to help you work through your media center to acquire literature selections that you can use with *Harcourt Math*. The math activities developed to correlate to these books will help you build a math curriculum to meet the needs of all students.

The index contains information for both the Pupil Edition and Teacher Edition. The italicized entries are found in the Teacher Edition.

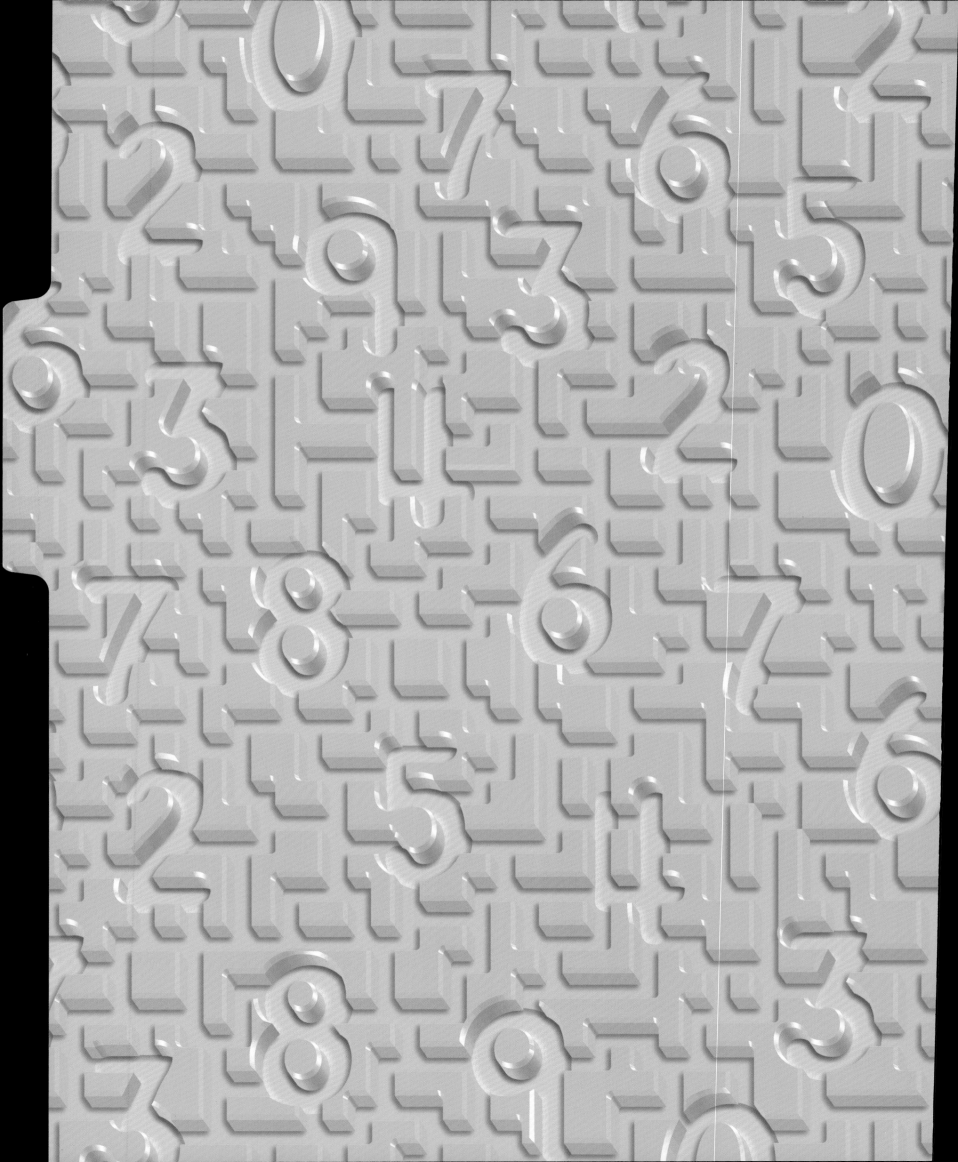

Bibliography

Books for Students

The Alaska Purchase. Cohen, Daniel. Millbrook, 1996.

Amanda Bean's Amazing Dream. Neuschwander, Cindy. Scholastic, 1998.

American History Math: 50 Problem-Solving Activities That Link Math to Key Events in U.S. History. Glasthal, Jacqueline B. Scholastic, 1996.

Anno's Mysterious Multiplying Jar. Anno, Masaichiro and Mitsumasa. Putnam, 1983.

Apollo 11. Stein, Conrad R. Children's Press, 1995.

Arithmetricks: 50 Easy Ways to Add, Subtract, Multiply, and Divide Without a Calculator. Julius, Edward H. Wiley & Sons, 1995.

A Bag Full of Pups. Gackenbach, Dick. Houghton Mifflin, 1983.

Bats, Bugs, and Biodiversity: Adventures in the Amazonian Rain Forest. Goodman, Susan E. Atheneum, 1995.

Beach Feet. Reiser, Lynn. William Morrow & Company, 1981.

Bicycle Race. Crews, Donald. Greenwillow Books, 1985.

Charlie and the Great Glass Elevator. Dahl, Roald. Puffin Books, 1998.

Chibi. Brenner, Barbara, and Julia Takaya. Clarion, 1996.

Class President. Hurwitz, Johanna. Scholastic, 1991.

A Cloak for the Dreamer. Friedman, Aileen. Scholastic, 1995.

Cool Math: Math Tricks, Amazing Math Activities, Cool Calculations, Awesome Math Factoids and More. Maganzini, Christi. Price Stern Sloan, Inc., 1997.

Counting on Frank. Clement, Rod. Gareth Stevens Publishing, 1991.

The Cuckoo Child. King-Smith, Dick. Hyperion Books for Children, 1993.

Discovering Graph Secrets. Markle, Sandra. Atheneum, 1997.

Discovering Math: Multiplication. Stienecker, David L. Benchmark Books, 1996.

Divide and Ride. Murphy, Stuart J. HarperCollins, 1997.

Do You Wanna Bet? Your Chance to Find Out About Probability. Cushman, Jean. Houghton Mifflin, 1991.

The Doorbell Rang. Hutchins, Pat. Greenwillow Books, 1986.

Each Orange Had 8 Slices. Giganti, Paul, Jr. Greenwillow Books, 1992.

Early Schools. Kalman, Bobbie D. Crabtree, 1982.

Earthquakes. Branley, Franklyn. Trophy Press, 1994.

Eating Fractions. McMillan, Bruce. Scholastic, 1991.

Exploring the Night Sky. Dickinson, Terence. Camden House, 1987.

Flatland. Abbott, Edwin A. Dover Publications, Inc., 1952.

Fourscore and 7: Investigating Math in American History. Franco, Betsy. Good Year Books, 1999.

Fraction Action. Leedy, Loreen. Holiday House, 1994.

Fraction Fun. Adler, David A. Holiday House, 1996.

Frogs, Toads, Lizards, and Salamanders. Parker, Nancy Winslow. Greenwillow Books, 1990.

Funny and Fabulous Fraction Stories. Greenberg, Dan. Scholastic, 1996.

G is for Googol. Schwartz, David M. Tricycle Press, 1998.

A Grain of Rice. Pittman, Helena Clare. Hastings House, 1986.

Grandfather Tang's Story. Tompert, Ann. Crown Publishers, 1990.

The Grapes of Math: Mind Stretching Math Riddles. Tang, Greg. Scholastic Press, 2001.

The Greedy Triangle. Burns, Marilyn. Scholastic, Inc., 1994.

Hey, New Kid! Duffey, Betsy. Viking, 1996.

How Big Is a Foot? Myller, Rolf. Young Yearling, 1991.

How Big Were the Dinosaurs? Most, Bernard. Harcourt Brace & Company, 1994.

How Many Days to America? Bunting, Eve. Clarion, 1988.

How Many Snails? Giganti, Paul, Jr. William Morrow & Company, 1996.

If You Made a Million. Schwartz, David M. Lothrop, Lee & Shepard, 1989.

Jigsaw Jackson. Birchman, David F. Lothrop, Lee & Shepard, 1996.

Keeping Time. Branley, Franklyn M. Houghton Mifflin, 1993.

Kids' Money Book. Godfrey, Neale S. Simon & Schuster, 1998.

The King's Equal. Paterson, Katherine. HarperCollins, 1992.

Lemonade for Sale. Murphy, Stuart J. HarperCollins, 1998.

The Librarian Who Measured the Earth. Lasky, Kathryn. Little, Brown and Company, 1994.

Lilly and Miss Liberty. Stevens, Carla. Little Apple, 1993.

The Man Who Counted: A Collection of Mathematical Adventures. Tahan, Malba. W. W. Norton & Company, 1993.

The Math Chef. D'Amico, Joan, and Karen Eich Drummond. John Wiley & Sons, 1997.

Math Counts: Capacity. Pluckrose, Henry. Children's Press, 1995.

Math Counts: Time. Pluckrose, Henry. Children's Press, 1995.

Math Curse. Scieszka, Jon. Penguin, 1995.

Math Mini Mysteries. Markle, Sandra. Atheneum, 1993.

Math Mysteries. Silbert, Jack. Scholastic, 1995.

Millions of Cats. Gág, Wanda. Sandcastle Books, 1988.

My Place in Space. Hirst, Robin and Sally. Orchard Books, 1992.

Nearer Nature. Arnosky, Jim. Midaya Press, 1996.

Nine for California. Levitin, Sonia. Orchard Books, 1996.

The Noonday Friends. Stolz, Mary. HarperCollins, 1995.

Old Home Day. Hall, Donald. Harcourt Brace & Company, 1996.

One Hundred Hungry Ants. Pinczes, Elinor J. Houghton Mifflin Company, 1993.

Paperboy. Kroeger, Mary Kay. Houghton Mifflin, 1996.

A Picture Book of Jesse Owens. Adler, David A. Holiday House, 1992.

Probability Pistachio. Murphy, Stuart S. Harper Trophy, 2001.

Pyramid. Macaulay, David. Houghton Mifflin, 1975.

The Quilt-Block History of Pioneer Days: With Projects Kids Can Make. Cobb, Mary. Millbrook, 1995.

Ready, Set, Hop! Murphy, Stuart J. HarperCollins, 1996.

Round Trip. Jonas, Ann. Greenwillow Books, 1983.

Selina and the Bear Paw Quilt. Smucker, Barbara. Dragonfly Books, 1999.

Shake, Rattle, and Roll!: Cool, and Educational, Things to Do With Dice. Onyshko, Dan. Penguin, 1997.

Shape Up! Adler, David. Holiday House, 1998.

Shaping the Earth. Patent, Dorothy Hinshaw. Clarion Books, 2000.

Sir Cumference and the First Round Table: A Math Adventure. Neuschwander, Cindy. Charlesbridge Publishing, 1997.

The Story of Maps and Navigation. Ganeri, Anita. Oxford University Press, 1997.

Summer Ice: Life Along the Antarctic Peninsula. McMillan, Bruce. Houghton Mifflin, 1995.

The Tarantula in My Purse. George, Jean Craighead. HarperCollins, 1996.

Too Many Kangaroo Things to Do! Murphy, Stuart J. HarperCollins, 1996.

The Toothpaste Millionaire. Merrill, Jean. Houghton Mifflin, 1972.

The Trading Game. Slote, Alfred. Harper Trophy, 1990.

The Trumpet of the Swan. White, E. B. HarperCollins, 1987.

Weather & Climate. Watt, Fiona, and Francis Wilson. EDC Publishing, 1992.

What Are You Figuring Now? A Story About Benjamin Banneker. Ferris, Jeri. Carolrhoda Books, 1988.

What Is a Wall, After All? Allen, Judy. Candlewick Press, 1993.

What's Faster Than a Speeding Cheetah? Wells, Robert E. Albert Whitman & Company, 1997.

Where Am I? The Story of Maps and Navigation. Smith, A. G. Stoddart Kids, 1997.

Zoo. Gibbons, Gail. Trophy Press, 1991.

Math Software

TITLE	PUBLISHER	DESCRIPTION	SYSTEM REQUIREMENTS
Harcourt Mega Math: Country Countdown	Harcourt	This program teaches students the concepts, facts, and thinking skills necessary to build math confidence and develop a strong, lasting understanding of math. **Math Topics** • Place Value • Comparing Number Sets • Addition • Time • Subtraction • Graphing	**PC:** Pentium II; Windows® 98, ME, XP Pro, 2000; 64MB RAM (128MB for Windows 2000) and XP SVGA; Sound Blaster® 16 or compatible sound card; 4X CD-ROM; 50 MB free hard drive space; Internet Explorer 5.5; Adobe Acrobat Reader 5.0 **Macintosh:** Macintosh G3; OS 8.6-9.2.2 or OS X 10.2.2; 64MB RAM with virtual memory enabled (128 for OS X); 800 × 600 resolution, thousands of color; 4X CD-ROM; 50 free hard drive space; Internet Explorer 5.5; Adobe Acrobat Reader 5.0
Harcourt Mega Math: The Number Games	Harcourt	This program teaches students the concepts, facts, and thinking skills necessary to build math confidence and develop a strong, lasting understanding of math. **Math Topics** • Money • Division • Patterns • Graphing • Multiplication	**PC:** Pentium II; Windows® 98, ME, XP Pro, 2000; 64MB RAM (128MB for Windows 2000) and XP SVGA; Sound Blaster® 16 or compatible sound card; 4X CD-ROM; 50 MB free hard drive space; Internet Explorer 5.5; Adobe Acrobat Reader 5.0 **Macintosh:** Macintosh G3; OS 8.6-9.2.2 or OS X 10.1.2; 64MB RAM with virtual memory enabled (128 for OS X); 800 × 600 resolution, thousands of color; 4X CD-ROM; 50 MB free hard drive space; Internet Explorer 5.5; Adobe Acrobat Reader 5.0
Harcourt Mega Math: Ice Station Exploration	Harcourt	This program teaches students the concepts, facts, and thinking skills necessary to build math confidence and develop a strong, lasting understanding of math. **Math Topics** • Plane Geometry • Linear Measurement • Solid Geometry • Algebra	**PC:** Pentium II; Windows® 98, ME, XP Pro, 2000; 64MB RAM (128MB for Windows 2000) and XP SVGA; Sound Blaster® 16 or compatible sound card; 4X CD-ROM; 50 MB free hard drive space; Internet Explorer 5.5; Adobe Acrobat Reader 5.0 **Macintosh:** Macintosh G3; OS 8.6-9.2.2 or OS X 10.1.2; 64MB RAM with virtual memory enabled (128 for OS X); 800 × 600 resolution, thousands of color; 4X CD-ROM; 50 MB free hard drive space; Internet Explorer 5.5; Adobe Acrobat Reader 5.0
Harcourt Mega Math: Fraction Action	Harcourt	This program teaches students the concepts, facts, and thinking skills necessary to build math confidence and develop a strong, lasting understanding of math. **Math Topics** • Fraction Concepts • Fraction Operations • Decimal Concepts • Probability	**PC:** Pentium II; Windows® 98, ME, XP Pro, 2000; 64MB RAM (128MB for Windows 2000) and XP SVGA; Sound Blaster® 16 or compatible sound card; 4X CD-ROM; 50 MB free hard drive space; Internet Explorer 5.5; Adobe Acrobat Reader 5.0 **Macintosh:** Macintosh G3; OS 8.6-9.2.2 or OS X 10.1.2; 64MB RAM with virtual memory enabled (128 for OS X); 800 × 600 resolution, thousands of color; 4X CD-ROM; 50 MB free hard drive space; Internet Explorer 5.5; Adobe Acrobat Reader 5.0
JumpStart Adventures 3rd Grade: Mystery Mountain	Knowledge Adventure	Students apply lessons in math and other curriculum areas while trying to defeat the schemes of a villain who is trying to use a time machine to alter the past. **Math Topics** • Addition • Estimation • Subtraction • Measurement • Multiplication • Problem Solving	**PC:** Windows 3.1/ 95/98, 486 DX2/ 66 MHz PC or higher; 16 MB RAM, 9 MB available on hard drive; quad-speed CD-ROM drive; 256-colors; Windows-compatible sound card **Macintosh:** Motorola 68040 40 MHz or Power PC Processor; System 7.5, 8 MB RAM, 9 MB available on hard drive; double-speed CD-ROM drive, 256-colors
JumpStart Adventures 4th Grade: Haunted Island	Knowledge Adventure	Students apply lessons in math and other curriculum areas to rescue 13 lost friends before they turn into freakish fiends forever! **Math Topics** • Equations • Division • Multiplication • Addition • Subtraction • Decimals • Fractions • Units of Measure	**PC:** Windows 95/98 486 DX2/66 MHz; 8 MB available, 9 MB available on hard drive; double-speed CD-ROM drive; SVGA 256-color graphics; MPC-compatible sound card **Macintosh:** 68040 40 MHz or Power PC Processor; System 7.1; 8 MB RAM, 9 MB available on hard drive; double-speed CD-ROM drive; 256-colors, 13" monitor

Math Software

TITLE	PUBLISHER	DESCRIPTION	SYSTEM REQUIREMENTS
JumpStart Adventures 5th Grade: Jo Hammet, Kid Detective	Knowledge Adventure	While visiting the museum on a field trip, Jo Hammet uncovers a sinister plot to destroy all of the city's factories! Her mission (with student help) is to find clues leading to the capture of the mad genius, Dr. X. **Math Topics** • Fractions • Decimals • Equations • Division • Multiplication • Geometry • Ratios	**PC:** Windows 3.1/95/98, 486 DX/2 66; 16 MB RAM, 15 MB available on hard drive; double speed CD-ROM drive; 256-color SVGA graphics; MPC-compatible sound card **Macintosh:** Motorola 68040 25 MHz or Power Macintosh; System 7.1; 8 MB RAM, 15 MB available on hard drive; double-speed CD-ROM drive; 256-color graphics
The ClueFinders 5th Grade Adventure	The Learning Company	A sudden tsunami has shipwrecked the gang on an uncharted volcanic island, and Owen and Leslie have disappeared! Students collect the mysterious Cryp Tiles to solve the mystery before the volcano blows! **Math Topics** • Multiplication • Division • Geometry	**PC:** Pentium® 166 MHz or faster (Pentium® II 300 MHz or faster for XP); Windows® 95/98/Me/2000/XP 100 MB available on hard disk; 32 MB RAM (128 MB RAM for XP); 8X CD-ROM; High Color, 16-bit; Windows-compatible Sound card and speakers; mouse; Internet Access Printer recommended **Macintosh:** Power PC 180 MHz or faster; Mac OS 8.6-9x; 100 MB available on hard disk; 32 MB RAM; 8X CD-ROM; thousands color; 16-bit; sound card and speakers; mouse; Internet Access Printer
Carmen Sandiego Math Detective	The Learning Company	The program includes three levels of over 250 activities with thousands of math problems, as well as over 400 word problems and customizable problem sets. **Math Topics** • Numeration • Geometry • Measurement • Problem Solving	**PC:** Windows® 3.1; 486/66Mhz or better; 8MB RAM; 80MB Hard Drive; 256-colors; 2X CD-ROM; Windows compliant sound device; mouse **PC:** Windows® 95/98; 486/66Mhz or better, 16 MB RAM; 80MB Hard Drive; Super VGA (640 × 480) 256-colors; 4X CD-ROM; Windows compliant sound device **PowerMac™:** 16MB RAM, 20 MB Hard Drive; 256-colors, 4X CD-ROM; requires a 100 Mhz PowerPC or better
Community Construction Kit	Tom Snyder Productions	An opportunity for students to develop and create their own communities by designing historically accurate buildings and landscaping. **Math Topics** • Geometry • Map Skills • 3-D Concepts	**PC:** Windows 3.1/95/98/2000: IBM-compatible 486, 16 MB RAM, 256-colors; 640 × 480 resolution **Macintosh:** 68030 processor; Mac OS 7.1-9.x and OSX (classic mode), 8 MB, 256-colors; 640 × 480 resolution
Cornerstone ATS 3.2: Mathematics—Level B	The Learning Company	The process includes: Warm-up, Review, Quiz, Take Five, and Worksheet to demonstrate, guide, test, reinforce, and provide extra practice of concepts. **Math Topics** • Number Concepts • Percents • Whole Number Computation • Estimation • Fractions • Decimals • Data and Graphs	**PC:** Windows 95/98/2000, ME, NT 4.0 with Service Pack 5; 32 MB RAM; 4X CD-ROM; 640 × 480, 256-colors; hard disk; mouse; Windows compatible sound device and printer (optional). Supported Networks: Win NT 4.0 w/SP5, Novell NetWare 4.11, 5.0 **Macintosh:** PowerPC processor; Mac OS 7.5.5 or higher; 4X CD-ROM; 32 MB RAM (48 MB RAM if running an internet browser) plus virtual memory; 640 × 480, 256-colors; mouse; Macintosh compatible printer (optional). Supported Networks: Appleshare 6.3
The Cruncher 2.0	Knowledge Adventure	Program features include a full-featured spreadsheet, step-by-step animated tutorials, twenty cross-curricular projects and templates, colorful charts, and graphs. **Math Topics** • Spreadsheets • Graphs • Statistics • Surveys • Investments	**PC:** Windows 95/98; 486 66 MHz; 16 MB RAM; quad-speed CD-ROM; 640 × 480, 256-color SVGA graphics; Windows-compatible sound card **Macintosh:** Power Mac; System 7.5.1; 16 MB RAM; quad-speed CD-ROM drive; 14" monitor; 640 × 480, 256-colors
Equivalent Fractions	Tenth Planet	Uses engaging multicultural themes to help students understand that fractions can be named in different but equivalent ways. **Math Topics** • Equivalent Fractions • Compare Fractions	**PC:** Windows 95/98, 486 or higher; OS 3.1 or higher; 16 MB RAM; 2 MB storage; CD-ROM required; 256 colors; incompatible with 2000 NP and XP **Macintosh:** 68040 processor or faster; OS 7.5 or higher; 8 MB RAM; 640 × 480 color monitor; 256-colors; Ethernet or faster network protocol

Math Software

TITLE	PUBLISHER	DESCRIPTION	SYSTEM REQUIREMENTS
Fraction Operations	Tenth Planet	Fraction Operations combines hands-on techniques with multimedia technology. Math concepts are presented in a variety of ways to accommodate a range of learning styles and ability levels. **Math Topics** • Common Denominators • Addition • Equivalent Fractions • Subtraction • Dividing Fractions • Multiplication	**PC:** Windows 95/98, 486 or higher; OS 3.1 or higher; 16 MB RAM; 2 MB storage; CD-ROM required; 256-colors; incompatible with 2000 NP and XP **Macintosh:** OS 7.5 or higher; 68040 processor or faster; 8 MB RAM; 640 × 480 color monitor; 256-colors; Ethernet or faster network protocol
Geometer's Sketchpad	Key Curriculum Press	The software allows students to create geometric figures that can be manipulated, transformed, and distorted while preserving geometric relationships. The software includes specific lessons for investigations, explorations, demonstrations, and constructions. **Math Topics** • Geometry • Visualization • Analysis • Informal Deduction	**PC:** Pentium®-based system or equivalent, Windows 95, NT 4 or later; 16MB RAM, CD-ROM drive **Macintosh:** Power Mac™-based system, Mac OS 8.6 or later; 16MB RAM, CD-ROM drive
The Graph Club	Tom Snyder Productions	The Graph Club is an easy-to-use graphing tool that can be used for self-directed exploration, lessons, and presentations, or creative class projects. **Math Topics** • Gather, Sort, and Classify • Interpret Tables and Graphs • Analyze Data and Graphs	**PC:** Windows 98/2000/NT/XP, Pentium 300MHz; 64 MB RAM; thousands of colors; 800 × 600 resolution; Network CD available **Macintosh:** PowerPC 100MHz; OS 8.6-9.X and OSX (native mode); 64 MB RAM; thousands of colors; 800 × 600 resolution; Network CD available
Graph Master	Tom Snyder Productions	Graph Master is a more powerful graphing program appropriate for students in grade 4 and up. The program allows students to analyze data by providing 9 different types of graphs, and many tools for comparing, filtering, and sorting data. **Math Topics** • Gather, Sort, and Classify • Interpret Tables and Graphs • Analyze Data and Graphs • Statistics	**PC:** Windows 95/98/2000/XP, IBM-compatible Pentium, 100 MHz; 32 MB RAM, 64 MB RAM is recommended; 256-colors, 800 × 600 resolution; Network CD available **Macintosh:** Power PC, 100 MHz; Mac OS 8.1-9.x and OSX (classic mode); 32 MB RAM, 64 MB RAM is recommended; 256-colors, 800 × 600 resolution; Network CD available
Math Blaster Ages 7-9	Knowledge Adventure	The program includes over 300 math lessons and 1000 math problems that focus on fundamental math skills, logic and problem-solving, and math confidence. Tracks student progress. **Math Topics** • Computation • Percents • Fractions • Estimation • Decimals • Number Patterns	**PC:** Windows 95/98; Pentium 90 MHz; 16 MB RAM (32 MB RAM recommended); 256-color SVGA graphics; quad-speed CD-ROM drive; Windows-compatible sound card **Macintosh:** Power Mac; system 7.5.3; 32 MB RAM; 640 × 480, 256-colors
Math Blaster Ages 9-12	Knowledge Adventure	Includes over 50,000 problems with 3 levels of play and 10 areas of skill development covering advanced math skills. **Math Topics** • Computation • Fractions • Estimation • Patterns • Integers	**PC:** Windows 95/98; Pentium 90 MHz; 16 MB RAM (32 MB RAM recommended); 16-bit high color graphics; 14″ monitor; quad-speed CD-ROM drive; 16-bit sound card **Macintosh:** Power Mac; system 7.5.3; 32 MB RAM; quad-speed CD-ROM drive; 10MB available on hard drive; thousands of colors; 14″ monitor; 16-bit sound card
Math Blaster Cross Terrain Challenge	Knowledge Adventure	Five critical-thinking activities focus on logical- and critical-thinking skills. **Math Topics** • Problem Solving • Numerical Coordinates • Decision Making • Directional Coordinates	**PC:** Windows 95/98/ME/2000; Pentium 200 MHz or higher; 32 MB RAM; high color 16-bit 800 × 600; 12X CD-ROM; Windows-compatible sound card **Macintosh:** G3 processor; Mac OS 8.1. 8.6, 9.1 (or higher); 64 MB RAM; 12X CD-ROM; thousands of colors, 800 × 600
Math Blaster Pre-Algebra	Knowledge Adventure	Earth's inhabitants are being "zapped" of their mathematical abilities by the magnetic brain invented by Dr. Dabble, the mad scientist. Students solve word problems involving pre-algebra and logical-thinking skills as they attempt to locate the disembodied brain in Dr. Dabble's mansion. **Math Topics** • Decimals • Factors • Integers • Fractions • Prime Numbers • Multiples • Percents	**PC:** Windows 95/98; 486 DX 33 MHz; 16 MB RAM; quad-speed CD-ROM drive; 640 × 480 256-colors SVGA graphics; 14″ monitor; 16-bit sound card **Macintosh:** Power Mac; system 7.5; 16 MB RAM; quad-speed CD-ROM drive; 8MB available on hard drive; 256-colors; 14″ monitor

Math Software

TITLE	PUBLISHER	DESCRIPTION	SYSTEM REQUIREMENTS
Math for the Real World	Knowledge Adventure	Students solve practical real-world problems as they travel the country with an up-and-coming rock band. **Math Topics** • Time • Money • Fractions • Logic • Charts	**PC:** Windows 95/98; 486/66 MHz or faster; 16 MB RAM; 4X CD-ROM drive; 256-colors; Windows-compatible sound card **Macintosh:** Power Mac; system 7.5.1; 16 MB RAM, 4X CD-ROM; hard drive; 256-colors; 14" monitor
Math Workshop Deluxe	The Learning Company	Interface divides activities into beginning (downstairs) and more advanced (upstairs). Custom play option allows teachers to create their own "problem sets." **Math Topics** • Computation • Estimation • Logical Reasoning • Fractions • Spatial Visualization	**PC:** Windows 3.1 or 95; 486SX/33MHz; 8MB RAM; 4MB hard disk space; 2X CD-ROM; 640 × 480, 256-colors; Win-compatible sound card **Macintosh:** PowerPC; System 7.1.2; 12MB RAM (5MB free); 2.6MB hard disk space; 2X CD-ROM; 640 × 480, 256-colors; 13" monitor
Thinkin' Things Collection 2	Edmark	Students are led to use logical reasoning and creative imagination as they perform various tasks in this engaging program. **Math Topics** • Critical Thinking • Spatial Awareness • Problem Solving • Perspective	**PC:** Windows 95/98, 486, Pentium or better, 33 MHZ or faster; 8 MB RAM, 12 MB available disk space; 2X CD-ROM; SVGA, 640 × 480, 16-bit color; Win-compatible sound card, Edmark TouchWindow, Microphone **Macintosh:** 68030, 68040 or PowerPC; OS 7.5.6-9.X, 4 MB, 5 MB for OS 7.5 or later; 8 MB recommended RAM, 12 MB RAM available disk space; 2X CD-ROM; 640 × 480, 256-colors; Edmark TouchWindow, Microphone
Thinkin' Things Collection 3	Edmark	This program allows students to use logical reasoning to solve various activities. They are encouraged to be creative in their solutions. **Math Topics** • Logical Reasoning • Analyze and Synthesize Information	**PC:** Windows 95/98, 486, Pentium® or better, 33 MHz or faster recommended; Hard disk with 2 MB free, 8 MB RAM required; 2X or faster CD-ROM drive; Super VGA graphics, 640 × 480, 256-colors; Windows-compatible sound card; Optional: Microphone, Edmark TouchWindow® **Macintosh:** 68030, 68040, or PowerPC; Mac 7.5.6-9.X; 4 MB RAM, 1900K unused, 5 MB for System 7.5 or later, 8 MB RAM recommended; 2X or faster CD-ROM drive; 256 or more colors, 13" monitor or larger, Optional: Microphone, Edmark TouchWindow®
MindTwister Math	Edmark	MindTwister Math engages 1 to 3 players in a fast-paced format that involves both competition and cooperation. Best played with multiple players, the software provides an extensive review of third grade math skills. **Math Topics** • Place Value • Time and Money • Computation • Problem Solving • Geometry • Estimation and Mental Math • Fractions and Decimals • Patterns	**PC:** Win 95/98; Pentium or better (66 MHz recommended); Hard Disk with 40 MB free; 16 MB RAM; 2X CD-ROM drive; 640 × 480, 256-colors; Windows-compatible sound card **Macintosh:** Power Mac; OS 7.5.6-9.x or better; 12 MB RAM; Hard disk with 40 MB free; 2X CD-ROM drive; 640 × 480, 256-colors monitor
Stickybear Math II Deluxe	Optimum Resource	Designed to help students learn multiplication and division, from basic facts through multi-digit with regrouping. Visual aids are available to students, and the program offers a wide array of customization features for teachers. **Math Topics** • Multiplication • Division	**PC:** Pentium II 166 Mhz, Windows 95/98/2000*, XP*; 32 MB RAM, 4X CD-ROM drive or higher; 800 × 600 resolution, 256-colors **Macintosh:** Power PC or higher, System 7.6.1 through OS X; 16 MB RAM; 4X CD-ROM; 800 × 600 resolution, 256-colors *2000 and XP as Power User or Administrator only*
Stickybear's Math Splash	Optimum Resource	Four activities provide practice in computation. The program offers a number of customization features, including level of difficulty, optional auto-advance, and selection of problem types. **Math Topics** • Addition • Multiplication • Subtraction • Division	**PC:** Windows 486/66MHz, 16MB RAM; 2X CD-ROM drive; 800 × 600 resolution, 256-colors **Macintosh:** 68040 or Power PC; System 7.6.1 through OS X; 8 MB RAM; 2X CD-ROM; 800 × 600 resolution, 256-colors
Math Munchers Deluxe	The Learning Company	Students help the Math Munchers dodge a crew of troublesome troggles. Reinforces computation skills and math thinking skills. **Math Topics** • Computation • Math Thinking • Whole Numbers	**PC:** Win 3.1/95; 486SX/50MHz; 4MB RAM (8MB for Win95); 2X CD-ROM; 640 × 480, 256 colors; Win-compatible sound card **Macintosh:** 68040/20MHz/PowerPC; System 7.1; 5MB RAM; 2X CD-ROM; 13" monitor, 640 × 480, 256-colors

Baratta-Lorton, M. *Mathematics Their Way: An Activity-Centered Mathematics Program for Early Childhood Education.* Addison-Wesley, 1995.

Baratta-Lorton, R. *Mathematics: A Way of Thinking.* Addison-Wesley, 1977.

Benson, D. *The Moment of Proof: Mathematical Epiphanies.* Oxford University Press, 1999.

Berk, L., and A. Winsler. *Scaffolding Children's Learning: Vygotsky and Early Childhood Education.* National Association for the Education of Young Children, 1995.

Bloomer, A., and P. Carlson. *Activity Math: Using Manipulatives in the Classroom.* Addison-Wesley, 1993.

Bresser, R., and C. Holtzman. *Developing Number Sense—Grades 3–6.* Math Solutions Publications, 1999.

Bright, G., and J. Harvey. *Basic Math Games.* Dale Seymour Publications, 1987.

Brodie, J. P. *Constructing Ideas About Large Numbers.* Creative Publications, 1995.

Burk, D., A. Snider, and P. Symonds. *Box It or Bag It Mathematics: Teachers' Resource Guide, First–Second.* The Math Learning Center, 1988.

Burns, M. *About Teaching Mathematics.* Math Solutions Publications, 1993.

Burns, M. *About Teaching Mathematics: A K–8 Resource.* Math Solutions Publications, 1992.

Burns, M. *A Collection of Math Lessons from Grades 6–8.* Math Solutions Publications, 1990.

Burns, M. *Math and Literature (K–3).* Math Solutions Publications, 1992.

Burns, M. *Math By All Means: Division, Grades 3 and 4.* Math Solutions Publications, 1994.

Burns, M. *Math By All Means: Multiplication, Grade 3.* Math Solutions Publications, 1994.

Burns, M. *Math By All Means: Probability, Grades 3 and 4.* Math Solutions Publications, 1994.

Burns, M. *MATH: Facing an American Phobia.* Math Solutions Publications, 1998.

Burns, M. *Probability, Grades 2–3.* Math Solutions Publications, 1994.

Burns, M. *This Book Is About Time.* Yolla Bolly Press, 1978.

Burton, G. *Towards a Good Beginning: Teaching Early Childhood Mathematics.* Addison-Wesley, 1985.

Burton, G., D. Clements, et al. *Addenda Series, Grades K–6.* NCTM, 1991–1992.

Burton, G., et al. *Addenda Series, Grades K–6, Number Sense and Operations.* NCTM, 1993.

Butterworth, B. *The Mathematical Brain.* Macmillan, 1999.

Caine, R. and G. *Unleashing the Power of Perceptual Change: The Potential of Brain-Based Teaching.* ASCD, 1997.

Carpenter, T., E. Fennema, M. Franke, L. Levi, and S. Empson. *Children's Mathematics—Cognitively Guided Instruction.* Heinemann, 1999.

Cathcart. W., Y. Pothier, J. Vance, and N. Bezuk. *Learning Mathematics in Elementary and Middle Schools.* Merrill, 2000.

Childs, L., and L. Choate. *Nimble with Numbers.* Dale Seymour Publications, 1999.

Clapham, C. *Concise Dictionary of Mathematics.* Oxford University Press, 1996.

Coates, G., and J. Stenmark. *Family Math for Young Children.* Lawrence Hall of Science, 1997.

Coburn, T., et al. *Addenda Series, Grades K–6, Patterns.* NCTM, 1993.

Cohen, J. "The First 'R': Reflective Capacities." *Educational Leadership,* Vol. 57, ASCD, September 1999.

Cooney, M., ed. *Celebrating Women in Mathematics and Science.* NCTM, 1996.

Copley, J., ed. *Mathematics in the Early Years.* NCTM, 1999.

Cowan, T., and J. Maguire. *Timelines of African-American History: 500 Years of Black Achievement.* Berkley Publishing Group, 1994.

Crawford, M., and M. Witte. "Strategies for Mathematics: Teaching in Context." *Educational Leadership,* Vol. 57, ASCD, November 1999.

Curcio, F. "Developing Number Sense in the Middle Grades," *Addenda Series.* NCTM, 1991.

Curcio, F., and N. Bezuk, et al. *Addenda Series, Grades 5–8, Understanding Rational Numbers and Proportions.* NCTM, 1994.

Danielson, C., and L. Abrutyn. *An Introduction to Using Portfolios in the Classroom.* ASCD, 1997.

Del Grande, J., and L. Morrow. *Addenda Series, Grades K–6, Geometry and Spatial Sense.* NCTM, 1993.

Drake, S. *Planning Integrated Curriculum.* ASCD, 1993.

Eby, J., and E. Kujawa. *Reflective Planning, Teaching and Evaluation: K–12.* Merrill, 1994.

Elliott, P., ed. *Communication in Mathematics, K–12 and Beyond (1996 Yearbook).* NCTM, 1996.

Fennell, F., and D. Williams. "Decimal Dash," in *The Arithmetic Teacher.* NCTM, 1986.

Ferrini-Mundy, J., K. Graham, L. Johnson, and G. Mills, eds. *Making Change in Mathematics Education: Learning from the Field.* NCTM, 1998.

Flournoy, V., et al. *The Patchwork Quilt.* Scholastic, 1996.

Forte, I., and S. Schurr. *Interdisciplinary Units and Projects for Thematic Instruction.* Incentive Publications Inc., 1994.

Franco, B., et al. "Geometry Concentration," in *Understanding Geometry.* Great Source Education Group, 1998.

Franco, B., et al. *Understanding Geometry.* Great Source Education Group, 1998.

Fuson, K. C., and Y. Kwon. "Korean Children's Understanding of Multidigit Addition and Subtraction." *Child Development,* Vol. 63, 491–506, 1992.

Garland, T. *Fibonacci Fun: Fascinating Activities with Intriguing Numbers.* Dale Seymour Publications, 1998.

Geary, D. C. *Children's Mathematical Development: Research and Practical Applications.* American Psychological Association, Washington, D.C., 1994.

Geary, D. C. "Reflections of Evolution and Culture in Children's Cognition: Implications for Mathematics Development and Mathematics Instruction." *American Psychologist,* Vol. 50, 24–27, 1995.

Geary, D. C., C. C. Bow-Tomas, and Y. Yao. "Counting Knowledge and Skill in Cognitive Addition: A Comparison of Normal and Mathematically Disabled Children." *Journal of Experimental Child Psychology,* Vol. 54, 372–91,1992.

Geary, D. C., et al. "A Biocultural Model of Academic Development," in *Global Prospects for Education: Development, Culture, and Schooling.* Edited by S. G. Paris and H. M. Wellman, Washington, D.C.: American Psychological Association, 1998.

Geary, D. C., et al. "Development of Arithmetical Competencies in Chinese and American Children: Influence of Age, Language, and Schooling." *Child Development,* Vol. 67, 2022–44, 1996.

Geary, D. C., and K. F. Widamin. "Numerical Cognition: On the Convergence of Componential and Psychometric Models." *Intelligence,* Vol. 16, 47–80, 1992.

Geddes, D., et al. *Addenda Series, Grades 5–8, Geometry in the Middle Grades.* NCTM, 1992.

Geddes, D., et al. *Addenda Series, Grades 5–8, Measurement in the Middle Grades.* NCTM, 1994.

Gelfand, I., and A. Shen. *Algebra.* Birkhauser, 1993.

Glassman, B., ed. *Macmillan Visual Almanac.* Blackbirch Press, 1996.

Glatzer, D., and J. Glatzer. *Math Connections.* Dale Seymour Publications, 1989.

Goldsmith, L., and J. Mark. "What Is Standards-Based Mathematics Curriculum?" *Educational Leadership,* Vol. 57, ASCD, November 1999.

Greenes, C., and G. Immerzeel. *Problem Solving Focus: Time and Money.* Dale Seymour Publications, 1993.

Grouws, D., ed. *Handbook of Research on Mathematics Teaching and Learning.* Macmillan, 1992.

Han, S. T., and B. Ford. *The Master Revealed—A Journey with Tangrams.* Cuisenaire, 1990.

Heaton, R. *Teaching Mathematics to the New Standards: Relearning the Dance.* Teachers College Press, 2000.

Henderson, J. *Reflective Teaching: Becoming an Inquiring Educator.* Macmillan, 1992.

Hiebert, J., T. Carpenter, E. Fennema, K. Fuson, D. Wearne, H. Murray, A. Olivier, and P. Humam. *Making Sense: Teaching and Learning Mathematics with Understanding.* Heinemann, 1997.

Hoffman, P. *The Man Who Loved Only Numbers: The Story of Paul Erdos and the Search for Mathematical Truth.* Hyperion, 1998.

House, P., and A. Coxford. *Connecting Mathematics Across the Curriculum.* NCTM, 1995.

Hynes, M. E., ed. *Mission Mathematics: K–6.* NCTM, 1997.

Irvin, J., ed. *What Current Research Says to the Middle Level Practitioner.* National Middle School Association, 1997.

Jacobs, H. *Interdisciplinary Curriculum: Design and Implementation.* ASCD, 1989.

Jurgens, H., E. Maletsky, H.O. Peitgen, T. Perciante, D. Saupe, and L. Yunker. *Fractals for the Classroom: Strategic Activities, Vols. 1 & 2.* NCTM. Copublished with Springer-Verlag, 1991-1992.

Kamii, C., and L. Housman. *Young Children Reinvent Arithmetic: Implications of Piaget's Theory.* Teachers College Press, 1999.

Kaplan, J. *Basic Decimals.* Educational Design, Inc., 1996.

Kaplan, J. *Basic Fractions.* Educational Design, Inc., 1996.

Kaplan, J. *Strategies for Solving Math Word Problems.* Educational Design, Inc., 1996.

Kenney, P., and E. Silver. *Results from the Sixth Mathematics Assessment of the National Assessment of Educational Progress.* NCTM, 1997.

Krause, M. *Multicultural Mathematics Materials.* NCTM, 1993.

Lamancusa, J. *Kid Cash: Creative Money-Making Ideas.* TAB Books, 1993.

Lee, M., and M. Miller. *Great Graphing.* Scholastic Professional Books, 1993.

Leutzinger, L., ed. *Mathematics in the Middle.* NCTM. Copublished with the National Middle School Association, 1998.

Levia, M., et al. "Oh How We've Changed!" in *Addenda Series: Fourth Grade.* NCTM, 1992.

Lindquist, M., et al. *Making Sense of Data. Addenda Series, Grades K–6.* NCTM, 1992.

Ma, Liping. *Knowing and Teaching Elementary Mathematics.* Lawrence Erlbaum Associates, 1999.

Madfes, T., project director. *Learning from Assessment: Tools for Examining Assessment through Standards.* (Includes PBS Mathline Video). NCTM, 1999.

Maletsky, E. *Teaching with Student Math Notes.* NCTM, 1993.

Mamchur, C. *A Teacher's Guide to Cognitive Type Theory and Learning Style.* ASCD, 1996.

The Math Learning Center. "Fractions on a Geoboard," in *Opening Eyes to Mathematics, Volume 3.* 1995.

McIntosh, A., B. Reys, R. Reys, and J. Hope. *Number SENSE: Simple Effective Number Sense Experiences, Grades 4–6.* Dale Seymour Publications, 1997.

Means, B., C. Chelener, and M. Knapp. *Teaching Advanced Skills to At-Risk Students.* Jossey-Bass Inc., 1991.

Mendlesohn, E. *Teaching Primary Math with Music.* Dale Seymour Publications, 1990.

Merrill, W. *A Calculator Tutorial.* Dale Seymour Publications, 1996.

Miller, D., and A. McKinnon. *The Beginning School Mathematics Project.* ASCD, 1995.

Miller, E. *Read It! Draw It! Solve It! Problem Solving for Primary Grades.* Dale Seymour Publications, 1997.

Morrison, P., and P. Morrison. *Powers of Ten.* W. H. Freeman and Company, 1982.

Morrow, L., ed. *The Teaching and Learning of Algorithms in School Mathematics (1998 Yearbook).* NCTM, 1998.

Moses, B. *Algebraic Thinking, Grades K–12: Readings from NCTM's School-Based Journals and Other Publications.* NCTM, 1999.

Myren, C. *Posing Open-Ended Questions in the Primary Classroom.* Teaching Resource Center, 1997.

Newman, V. *Math Journals, Grades K–5.* Teaching Resource Center, 1994.

Newman, V. *Numbercises—A Fitness Program: Strategies for Addition and Subtraction.* Teaching Resource Center, 1998.

Norton-Wolf, S. *Base-Ten Block Activities.* Learning Resources, 1990.

O'Connor, V., and M. Hynes. *Mission Mathematics: 5–8.* NCTM, 1997.

Ohanian, S. *Garbage, Pizza, Patchwork Quilts, and Math Magic.* W. H. Freeman and Company, 1992.

Olson, A. *Mathematics Through Paper Folding.* NCTM, 1975.

Pappas, T. *Fractals, Googols and Other Mathematical Tales.* Wild World Publishing/Tetra, 1993.

Pappas, T. *The Magic of Mathematics—Discovering the Spell of Mathematics.* Wild World Publishing/Tetra, 1994.

Parker, M., ed. *She Does Math!—Real-Life Problems from Women on the Job.* The Mathematical Association of America, 1995.

Perrone, V., ed. *Expanding Student Assessment.* ASCD, 1991.

Phillips, E., et al. *Addenda Series, Grades 5–8, Patterns and Functions.* NCTM, 1991.

Phillips, L. M., ed. *Mathematics: Teacher Resource Handbook.* Kraus International Publications, 1993.

Piccirilli, R. *Mental Math: Computation Activities for Anytime.* Scholastic Professional Books, 1996.

Pohl, V. *How to Enrich Geometry Using String Designs.* NCTM, 1986.

Pollard, J. *Building Toothpick Bridges.* Dale Seymour Publications, 1985.

Project AIMS. *AIMS Activities.* AIMS Educational Foundation, 1988–1995.

Reys, B., et al. *Addenda Series, Grades 5–8.* NCTM, 1991.

Rich, D. *MegaSkills.* Houghton Mifflin, 1992.

Richardson, K. *Developing Number Concepts: Book 1, Counting, Comparing and Patterns.* Dale Seymour Publications, 1999.

Richardson, K. *Developing Number Concepts: Book 2, Addition and Subtraction.* Dale Seymour Publications, 1999.

Richardson, K. *Developing Number Concepts: Book 3, Place Value, Multiplication, and Division.* Dale Seymour Publications, 1998.

Ringenberg, L. *A Portrait of 2.* NCTM, 1995.

Rommel, Carol A. *Integrating Beginning Math & Literature.* Incentive Publications, Inc., 1991.

Satariano, P. *Storytime, Mathtime: Math Explorations in Children's Literature.* Dale Seymour Publications, 1997.

Schechter, B. *My Brain Is Open: The Mathematical Journeys of Paul Erdos.* Simon & Schuster, 1998.

Scheidt, T. *Fantasy Baseball.* Giant Step Press, 1994.

Schifter, D., and C. Fosnot. *Reconstructing Mathematics Education: Stories of Teachers Meeting the Challenge of Reform.* Teachers College Press, 1993.

Schoenfeld, A. "When Good Teaching Leads to Bad Results: The Disasters of Well-Taught Mathematics Courses." *Educational Psychologist,* Vol. 23, 145–66, 1998.

Schullman, D., and E. Rebeka. *Growing Mathematical Ideas in Kindergarten.* Math Solutions Publications, 1999.

Schultz, K., et al. *Mathematics for Every Young Child.* Merrill, 1990.

Seymour, D. *Getting Smarter Every Day.* Prentice Hall, 1999.

Seymour, D. *Probability Model Masters.* Dale Seymour Publications, 1990.

Sheffield, L. *Developing Mathematically Promising Students.* NCTM, 1999.

Silverman, R., W. Welty, and S. Lyon. *Case Studies for Teacher Problem Solving.* McGraw-Hill, Inc., 1992.

Singer, Margie, et al. *Between Never and Always*. Dale Seymour Publications, 1997.

Skinner, P. *It All Adds Up!* Math Solutions Publications (Adapted by permission of Addison-Wesley Longman, Australia), 1999.

Skinner, P. *What's Your Problem? Posing and Solving Mathematical Problems, K–2.* Heinemann, 1990.

Slavin, R. E., N. L. Karweit, and B. A. Wasik, eds. *Preventing Early School Failure: Research, Policy, and Practice.* Allyn and Bacon, 1994.

Sobel, M., and E. Maletsky. *Teaching Mathematics: A Sourcebook of Aids, Activities, and Strategies.* Allyn & Bacon, 1998.

Sonnabend, T. *Mathematics for Elementary Teachers—An Interactive Approach.* Saunders College Publishing, Harcourt Brace College Publishers, 1993.

Steen, L., ed. *On the Shoulders of Giants—New Approaches to Numeracy.* National Research Council, 1990.

Steen, L., ed. *Why Numbers Count—Quantitative Literacy for Tomorrow's America.* NCTM, 1997.

Stenmark, J., V. Thompson, and R. Cossey. *Family Math.* University of California, 1986.

Stenmark, J., ed. *Mathematics Assessment: Myths, Models, Good Questions, and Practical Suggestions.* NCTM, 1991.

Sternberg, R., and W. Williams. *How to Develop Student Creativity.* ASCD, 1996.

Stevenson, F. *Exploratory Problems in Mathematics.* NCTM, 1992.

Stewart, K., and K. Walker. *20 Thinking Questions for Base-Ten Blocks, Grades 3–6.* Creative Publications, 1995.

Stiff, L., and F. Curcio, eds. *Developing Mathematical Reasoning in Grades K–12 (1999 Yearbook).* NCTM, 1999.

Sylvester, R. *A Celebration of Neurons—An Educator's Guide to the Human Brain.* ASCD, 1995.

A Teacher's Guide to Performance-Based Learning and Assessment. Educators in Connecticut's Pomperaug Regional School District 15. ASCD, 1996.

Thiessen, D., and M. Mathias. *The Wonderful World of Mathematics: A Critically Annotated List of Children's Books in Mathematics.* NCTM, 1992.

Thornton, C., and N. Bley, eds. *Windows of Opportunity: Mathematics for Students with Special Needs.* NCTM, 1994.

Threewit, F. *Estimation Destinations.* Cuisenaire, 1994.

Tomlinson, Carol Ann. *How to Differentiate Instruction in Mixed-Ability Classrooms.* ASCD, 1995.

Trafton, P., and D. Thiessen. *Learning Through Problems: Number Sense and Computational Strategies/A Resource for Teachers.* Heinemann, 1999.

Van Cleave, J. "Graphing," *Math for Every Kid: Easy Activities That Make Learning Math Fun.* Wiley, 1991.

Van Cleave, J. *Math for Every Kid: Easy Activities That Make Learning Math Fun.* Wiley, 1991.

Van de Walle, J. *Elementary and Middle School Mathematics: Teaching Developmentally, Third Edition.* Dale Seymour Publications, 1997.

Walter, M. *Boxes, Squares, and Other Things.* NCTM, 1995.

Webb, N., and T. Romberg. *Reforming Mathematics Education in America's Cities: The Urban Mathematics Collaborative Project.* Teachers College Press, 1994.

Welchman-Tischler, R. *How to Use Children's Literature to Teach Mathematics.* NCTM, 1992.

Wu, H. "The 1997 Mathematics Standards War in California," in *What Is at Stake at the K–12 Standards Wars?* Edited by S. Stotsky. New York: Peter Lang Publishers, 1999.

Zaslavsky, C. *Fear of Math—How to Get Over It and Get On with Your Life.* Rutgers University Press, 1994.

Zaslavsky, C. *Multicultural Math: Hands-On Math Activities from Around the World.* Scholastic Professional Books, 1994.

Zawojewski, J., et al. *Addenda Series, Grades 5–8, Dealing with Data and Chance.* NCTM, 1991.

Zemelman, S., H. Daniels, and A. Hyde. *Best Practice: New Standards for Teaching and Learning in America's Schools.* Heinemann, 1998.

BIBLIOGRAPHY FOR EXCERPTS FROM THE RESEARCH

Burton, G. M. "Patterning: Powerful Play," *School Science and Mathematics,* Vol. 82, 39–44, 1982.

Carpenter, T. P., J. M. Moser, and H. C. Bebout. "Representation of Addition and Subtraction Word Problems," *Journal for Research in Mathematics Education,* Vol. 24, 345–357, 1988.

Choate, L. D., and J. K. Okey. "Graphically Speaking: Primary-level Graphing Experiences. In A. P. Shulte and J. R. Smart (Eds.), *Teaching Statistics and Probability: 1981 Yearbook* (pp. 33–41). Reston, VA: National Council of Teachers of Mathematics, 1981.

Kilpatrick, J., J. Swafford, and F. Bradford, Eds. *Adding It Up: Helping Children Learn Mathematics.* Center for Education, Division of Behavioral and Social Sciences and Education, National Research Council. Washington, DC: National Academy Press, 2001.

Marzano, R. J., D. J. Pickering, and J. E. Pollock. *Classroom Instruction that Works: Research-Based Strategies for Increasing Student Achievement.* Alexandria, VA: Association for Supervision and Curriculum Development, 2001.

Van de Walle, J. A., and K. B. Watkins. "Early Development of Number Sense." In R. Jensen (Ed.), *Research Ideas for the Classroom: Early Childhood Mathematics* (pp. 127–150). New York: Macmillan, 1993.

A.M., 132–133

Activities

Family Involvement Activities, xxvi, 18, 38, 66, 86, 108, 126, 156, 174, 192, 210, 236, 256, 272, 300, 320, 336, 356, 382, 406, 422, 442, 468, 486, 514, 538, 556, 574, 598, 616

Literature Connections, xxviG, 66G, 156G, 236G, 300G, 382G, 468G, 514G, 598G

Practice Game, xxviG, 66G, 156G, 236G, 300G, 382G, 468G, 514G, 598G

Acute angle, 385–386

Acute triangle, 393–395

Addends, 1, 4–5, 68, 69

missing, 73, 78, 94

Addition

to check subtraction, 94, 98

estimating sums, 68–69, 72–73

fact families, 2–3

four-digit numbers, 72–73

fractions, 540–541, 542–543

greater numbers, 72–73

grouping addends, 68

Grouping Property of, 6–7, 68–69

Identity Property, 6–7

inverse operation of subtraction, 2–3

mental math and, 77

modeling for

simple fractions, 540

whole numbers, 70

of money, 120–121, 580–583

of more than two addends, 68–69

and multiplication, 158–159

of one-digit numbers, 68–69, 158–159, 175

order of addends, 68

Order Property of, 6–7

properties of, 6–7

regrouping, 70–73, 76–79

repeated, 158–159

three-digit numbers, 70–73

three or more addends, 68–69

two-digit numbers, 8–9, 69

Addition strategies

predicting and testing, 74–75

Advanced Learners. See Reaching All Learners

Algebra

add/subtract money, 120–121

addition of like fractions, 540–543

connecting addition and multiplication, 158–159

equations, 264–266

expressions, 80–81, 264–265

comparing, 121, 263

evaluating, 197, 204, 446, 454, 551, 582

writing, 80–81, 264–265

extending linear pattern by its rules, 180–181, 212–213, 216–217, 259, 261

fact families, 2–3, 246–249

find a rule, 216–217

find the cost, 284–285

functional relationships, 113, 276, 284–285

inequalities, 44, 47–49, 201, 263, 282

inverse operations of addition and subtraction, 2–3

inverse operations of multiplication and division, 242–248

missing addend, 4–5, 73, 78, 94, 276

missing digit, 261, 276, 622

missing factors, 186–187,195, 201, 204, 211, 213, 219, 221, 244, 248, 259, 261,274–276, 281, 604

missing operation symbol, 241, 279

multiply with three factors, 218–219

number sentences, 80–81, 622

patterns, 216–217, 470–473,474–475, 476–477, 478–479, 480–481, 518

practice the facts, 202–205

recording division of two-digit numbers, 621–623

recording multiplication of two-digit numbers, 603–605

relating multiplication and division, 242–243

solving unit cost problems, 284–285

subtraction of greater numbers, 98–101, 104

subtraction of like fractions, 544–549

Algebraic Thinking, 25, 44, 51, 73, 75, 78, 81, 94, 97, 111, 114, 164, 197, 204, 219, 244, 259, 265, 276, 282, 285, 304, 324, 328, 348, 415, 416, 454, 480, 489, 499, 547, 558, 576, 578, 601, 604

Alternative Teaching Strategy, 2B, 4B, 6B, 8B, 10B, 12B, 20B, 22B, 24B, 26, 28B, 30B, 32B, 40B, 42B, 44, 46B, 48B, 50B, 52B, 68B, 70B, 72B, 74B, 76B, 78, 80B, 88B, 90B, 92B, 94, 96B, 98B, 100, 102B, 110B, 112, 114B, 116B, 118B, 120B, 128B, 130, 132B, 134B, 136B, 138B, 140, 142B, 158B, 160B, 162B, 164B, 166, 168B, 176B, 178B, 180B, 182B, 184, 186B, 194B, 196B, 198B, 200B, 202B, 204, 212B, 214, 216B, 218B, 220B, 222B, 238B, 240B, 242B, 244, 246B, 248, 250B, 258B, 260B, 262B, 264B, 266B, 274B, 276, 278B, 280B, 282, 284B, 286B, 302B, 304B, 306B, 308B, 310B, 312, 314B, 322B, 324B, 326B, 328B, 330B, 340, 342B, 344B, 346B, 348B, 350B, 358B, 360, 362B, 364B, 366B, 368B, 384B, 386, 388B, 390B, 392B, 394, 396B, 398, 400B, 408B, 410B, 412B, 414B, 416B, 424B, 426, 428B, 430B, 432B, 434, 436B, 444B, 446, 448B, 450B, 452B, 454, 470B, 472, 474B, 476B, 478B, 480B, 488B, 490B, 492B, 494, 496B, 498B, 500B, 516B, 518, 520B, 522B, 524, 526B, 528, 530B, 532B, 540B, 542B, 544B, 546B, 548, 550B, 558B, 560B, 562B, 564B, 566B, 568B, 576B, 578B, 580B, 582, 584B, 600B, 602B, 604, 606B, 608B, 610, 618B, 620B, 622, 624B, 626B, 628B

Angles, 384–385

acute, 385, 386, 387

measured in degrees, 385

naming, 385

obtuse, 385, 386, 387

in polygons, 390–391

in quadrilaterals, 396–399

L

M

geometric wood solids, 425–426, 436–437

grid paper, 412–413, 448, 451, 602

hundred chart, 21, 215

multiplication tables, 178, 280, 281

number cards, 79

number cube, 309

number lines, 164–166, 240, 311, 517, 532–533, 566, 567

pattern blocks, 408–409, 410, 414–415, 416–417, 470, 478–479

place-value chart, 24, 32, 43, 566, 567

play money, 109–113, 116–119, 575–578

ruler, 338–341, 358–361, 445, 446

scale, 346

spinners, 308, 488, 491, 492–494

tiles, 162–163, 182–184, 194, 196, 200, 201–202, 218, 242, 243, 275, 276, 280–282, 448, 493, 494

time line, 142

yardstick, 342

Mass, 366–367

Math Background, *2A, 4A, 6A, 8A, 10A, 12A, 20A, 22A, 24A, 28A, 30A, 32A, 40A, 42A, 46A, 48A, 50A, 52A, 68A, 70A, 72A, 74A, 76A, 80A, 88A, 90A, 92A, 96A, 98A, 102A, 110A, 114A, 116A, 118A, 120A, 128A, 132A, 134A, 136A, 138A, 142A, 158A, 160A, 162A, 164A, 168A, 176A, 178A, 180A, 182A, 186A, 194A, 196A, 198A, 200A, 202A, 212A, 216A, 218A, 220A, 222A, 238A, 240A, 242A, 246A, 250A, 258A, 260A, 262A, 264A, 266A, 274A, 278A, 280A, 284A, 286A, 302A, 304A, 306A, 308A, 310A, 314A, 322A, 324A, 326A, 328A, 330A, 342A, 344A, 346A, 348A, 350A, 358A, 362A, 364A, 366A, 368A, 384A, 388A, 390A, 392A, 396A, 400A, 408A, 410A, 412A, 414A, 416A, 424A, 428A, 430A, 432A, 436A, 444A, 448A, 450A, 452A, 470A, 474A, 476A, 478A, 480A, 488A, 490A, 492A, 496A, 498A, 500A, 516A, 520A, 522A, 526A, 530A, 532A, 540A, 542A, 544A, 546A, 550A, 558A, 560A, 562A, 564A, 566A, 568A, 576A, 578A, 580A, 584A, 600A, 602A, 606A, 608A, 618A, 620A, 624A, 626A, 628A*

Math Connection, *92B, 116B, 212B, 522B*

Math Jingles® CD 3–4, *22B, 52B, 118B, 134B, 160B, 164B, 180B, 182B, 202B, 212B, 218B, 242B, 246B, 258B, 260B, 262B, 280B, 284B, 310B, 328B, 346B, 358B, 366B, 368B, 392B, 424B, 444B, 470B, 516B, 546B, 562B, 578B, 602B, 628B*

Math Journal, *3, 5, 7, 9, 11, 13, 21, 23, 27, 29, 31, 33, 41, 45, 47, 49, 51, 53, 69, 71, 73, 75, 79, 81, 89, 91, 95, 97, 101, 103, 113, 115, 117, 119, 121, 131, 133, 135, 137, 141, 143, 159, 161, 163, 167, 169, 177, 179, 181, 185, 187, 195, 197, 199, 201, 205, 215, 217, 219, 221, 223, 239, 241, 245, 249, 251, 259, 261, 263, 265, 267, 277, 279, 283, 285, 287, 303, 305, 307, 309, 313, 315, 323, 325, 327, 329, 331, 341, 343, 345, 347, 349, 351, 361, 363, 365, 367, 369, 387, 389, 391, 395, 399, 401, 409, 411, 413, 415, 417, 427, 429, 431, 435, 437, 447, 449, 451, 455, 473, 475, 477, 479, 481, 489, 491, 495, 497, 499, 501, 519, 521, 525, 529, 531, 533, 541, 543, 545, 549, 551, 559, 561, 563, 565, 567, 569, 577, 579, 583, 585, 601, 605, 607, 611, 619, 623, 625, 627, 629. See also Writing in Mathematics*

Math Word Work, *xxvii, 18B, 38B, 66I, 86B, 108B, 126B, 156I, 174B, 192B, 210B, 236I, 256B, 272B, 300I, 320B, 336B, 356B, 382I, 406B, 422B, 442B, 468I, 486B, 514I, 538B, 556B, 574B, 598I, 616B*

Mathematics Across the Grades, *xxviJ, 18C, 38C, 66J, 86C, 108C, 126C, 156J, 174C, 192C, 210C, 236J, 256C, 272C, 300J, 320C, 336C, 356C, 382J, 406C, 422C, 442C, 468J, 486C, 514J, 538C, 556C, 574C, 598J, 616C*

Mean, 314–315

Measurement

of angles in degrees, 385, 461

area, 448–449

capacity, 344–345

changing units, 348–349

choosing a reasonable unit, 348–349, 358, 359, 364–367

choosing an appropriate measuring tool, 338, 348–349, 358, 359, 364–367

customary units

cups, 344–345

feet, 339–343

gallons, 344–345

inches, 337–343

miles, 342–343

ounces, 346–347

pints, 344–345

pounds, 346–347

quarts, 344–345

yards, 342–343

degrees Celsius, 368–369

degrees Fahrenheit, 368–369

estimating

capacity, 364–365

length, 340–341

volume, 350–351, 452–453

weight/mass, 346–347, 366–367

half inch, 339

length, 338–343, 358–361

liquid volume, 344–345, 364–365

mass, 366–367

metric units

centimeters, 358–361

decimeters, 358–361

grams, 366–367

kilograms, 366–367

kilometers, 358–361

liters, 364–365

meters, 358–361

milliliters, 364–365

to nearest half inch, 339–340

to nearest inch, 337–341

in nonstandard units, 338, 346, 365, 366, 444

perimeter of polygon, 444–445

relating units, 359

square units, 448

Table of Measures, 342, 348, 359

temperature, 368–369

time

day, 138, 139

hour, 128–135

minute, 128–135

month, 138, 139

week, 138, 139

year, 138

Multimedia Math Glossary, *xxvil,* 1, *18B,* 19, *38B,* 39, 63, *63, 66l,* 67, *86B,* 87, *108B,* 109, *126B,* 127, 153, *153, 156l,* 157, *174B,* 175, *192B,* 193, *210B,* 211, 233, *233, 236l,* 237, *256B,* 257, *272B,* 273, 297, *297, 300l,* 301, *320B,* 321, *336B,* 337, *356B,* 357, 379, *379, 382l,* 383, *406B,* 407, 423, *442B,* 443, 465, *465, 468l,* 469, *486B,* 487, 511, *511, 514l,* 515, *538B,* 539, *556B,* 557, *574B,* 575, 595, *595, 598l,* 599, *616B,* 617, 639, *639*

Multiple, 178, 600–601

Multiple Intelligences

bodily/kinesthetic, 8B, 10B, 20B, 22B, 24B, 28B, 40B, 42B, 46B, 52B, 70B, 72B, 76B, 90B, 92B, 96B, 114B, 116B, 118B, 132B, 134B, 138B, 142B, 158B, 160B, 162B, 164B, 176B, 178B, 180B, 186B, 194B, 196B, 200B, 212B, 218B, 220B, 238B, 242B, 258B, 260B, 262B, 264B, 278B, 284B, 286B, 304B, 306B, 314B, 322B, 328B, 338B, 342B, 344B, 346B, 348B, 358B, 366B, 368B, 384B, 392B, 408B, 410B, 414B, 424B, 428B, 430B, 436B, 444B, 450B, 452B, 461, 470B, 474B, 480B, 488B, 492B, 496B, 520B, 522B, 540B, 546B, 558B, 562B, 576B, 578B, 584B, 591B, 602B, 620B, 624B, 628B

interpersonal/social, 6B, 8B, 10B, 12B, 30B, 70B, 72B, 74B, 76B, 88B, 102B, 110B, 116B, 128B, 136B, 178B, 180B, 182B, 220B, 250B, 258B, 266B, 302B, 310B, 314B, 322B, 324B, 342B, 350B, 362B, 375, 400B, 450B, 488B, 500B, 522B, 526B, 530B, 532B, 540B, 550B, 564B, 568B

intrapersonal/introspective, 90B, 132B, 142B, 182B, 220B, 238B, 474B, 544B

logical/mathematical, 2B, 4B, 6B, 8B, 10B, 12B, 20B, 22B, 28B, 30B, 32B, 48B, 68B, 70B, 74B, 80B, 90B, 92B, 96B, 98B, 102B, 110B, 114B, 116B, 120B, 132B, 134B, 136B, 158B, 160B, 168B, 180B, 182B, 186B, 198B, 212B, 216B, 218B, 220B, 222B, 242B, 246B, 250B, 258B, 260B, 262B, 274B, 284B, 314B, 362B, 364B, 368B, 390B, 400B, 412B, 448B, 461, 474B, 476B, 478B, 480B, 498B, 500B, 522B, 530B, 542B, 560B, 562B, 566B, 568B, 600B, 606B, 608B

musical/rhythmic, 128B, 180B, 240B, 470B, 478B, 516B

verbal/linguistic, 2B, 12B, 24B, 32B, 40B, 46B, 50B, 72B, 74B, 76B, 80B, 88B, 96B, 102B, 128B, 134B, 138B, 176B, 178B, 180B, 182B, 186B, 194B, 196B, 198B, 200B, 220B, 246B, 250B, 258B, 260B, 262B, 264B, 266B, 280B, 304B, 308B, 314B, 326B, 328B, 330B, 338B, 342B, 344B, 350B, 358B, 362B, 366B, 384B, 390B, 392B, 396B, 412B, 414B, 416B, 430B, 436B, 450B, 470B, 474B, 476B, 478B, 488B, 490B, 492B, 496B, 507, 516B, 540B, 542B, 550B, 560B, 562B, 578B, 580B, 584B, 606B, 618B, 624B, 626B, 628B, 635

visual/spatial, 22B, 28B, 30B, 40B, 42B, 48B, 50B, 52B, 68B, 72B, 74B, 76B, 88B, 92B, 98B, 102B, 138B, 142B, 158B, 162B, 164B, 168B, 176B, 178B, 182B, 186B, 194B, 196B, 200B, 202B, 220B, 222B, 229, 240B, 258B, 260B, 262B, 264B, 266B, 274B, 278B, 280B, 284B, 286B, 302B, 306B, 308B, 310B, 322B, 324B, 326B, 338B, 344B, 346B, 358B, 364B, 388B, 392B, 396B, 400B, 408B, 412B, 414B, 416B, 424B, 428B, 430B, 432B, 436B, 448B, 452B, 470B, 474B, 480B, 488B, 490B, 520B, 526B, 530B, 532B, 544B, 546B, 558B, 560B, 564B, 566B, 576B, 578B, 580B, 584B, 602B, 608B, 620B, 626B

Multiplication

and addition, 158–159

Associative Property of, 218–219, 220–221

checking division with, 258–259

Commutative Property of, 162–167, 182–183, 202–203, 220–221

Distributive Property of, 220–221

and division, 242–245

fact families, 246–249

factors, 160

    zero, 176–177

    one, 176–177

    two, 160–161

    three, 164–165

    four, 178–179

    five, 160–161

    six, 194–195

    seven, 200–201

    eight, 196–197

    nine, 212–213

    ten, 212–213

    eleven, 229

    twelve, 229

Grouping Property of, 218–219, 220–221

Identity Property of, 220–221

as inverse of division, 242–243, 626

model, 158–159, 160–161, 162–163, 164–165, 176, 182–183, 194, 196, 200, 202, 218, 220

multiples of ten and one hundred, 600–601

Order Property of, 162–167, 182–183, 202–203, 220–221

product, 160

Property of One, 220–221

skip-counting in, 157, 182–185, 212

three-digit numbers, 635

with three factors, 218–219

two-digit numbers, 602–605, 608–611

Zero Property, 220–221

Multiplication facts, 156–235

through eleven and twelve, 229

through five, 174–175, 193

through ten, 212–215

Multiplication table, 178–179

to find missing factor, 186, 281

to five, 258

to nine, 178, 183, 186, 202, 260

to six, 247

to ten, 212, 281

Multistep problems

At least one multistep problem is provided in every exercise set. Some examples are 8, 9, 10, 11, 20, 46, 48, 69, 70, 71, 72, 76, 90, 91, 92, 93, 94, 95, 98, 100, 101, 120, 121, 122, 159, 179, 184, 185, 187, 194, 195, 197, 200, 201, 202, 212–215, 222–223, 238, 246–248, 258–261, 266, 274–285, 302–303, 314, 326–327, 338, 344, 346, 358, 359, 361, 363, 364, 365, 366, 368, 425, 432, 433, 444, 448, 449, 450, 452, 490, 492, 493, 496, 522, 523, 527, 540, 542, 544, 550, 560, 561, 568, 569, 578, 580, 581, 606–607, 608–609, 619, 620, 621, 622, 623, 626

Multistep and Strategy Problems. *Specific problems are referenced in the Teacher's Edition in the Independent Practice section of each lesson.*

Music Connection, *302B, 470B*

NCTM Standards, *2A, 4A, 6A, 8A, 10A, 12A, 20A, 22A, 24A, 28A, 30A, 32A, 40A, 42A, 46A, 48A, 50A, 52A, 68A, 70A, 72A, 74A, 76A, 80A, 88A, 90A, 92A, 96A, 98A, 102A, 110A, 114A, 116A, 118A, 120A, 128A, 132A, 134A, 136A, 138A, 142A, 158A, 160A, 162A, 164A, 168A, 176A, 178A, 180A, 182A, 186A, 194A, 196A, 198A, 200A, 202A, 212A, 216A, 218A, 220A, 222A, 238A, 240A, 242A, 246A, 250A, 258A, 260A, 262A, 264A, 266A, 274A, 278A, 280A, 284A, 286A, 302A, 304A, 306A, 308A, 310A, 314A, 322A, 324A, 326A, 328A, 330A, 342A, 344A, 346A, 348A, 350A, 358A, 362A, 364A, 366A, 368A, 384A, 388A, 390A, 392A, 396A, 400A, 408A, 410A, 412A, 414A, 416A, 424A, 428A, 430A, 432A, 436A, 444A, 448A, 450A, 452A, 470A, 474A, 476A, 478A, 480A, 488A, 490A, 492A, 496A, 498A, 500A, 516A, 520A, 522A, 526A, 530A, 532A, 540A, 542A, 544A, 546A, 550A, 558A, 560A, 562A, 564A, 566A, 568A, 576A, 578A, 580A, 584A, 600A, 602A, 606A, 608A, 618A, 620A, 624A, 626A, 628A*

NCTM Standards Correlations, *NA1–NA7*

Nickel, 109–113, 118–119

Noon, 132

North Carolina EOG Test Handbook, H1–H35

Not equal to, 80–81
    symbol for, 80

Number
    benchmark, 40–41
    comparing, 42–45
    even or odd, 20–21
    expanded form, 22–23, 25, 26, 32–33, 564, 565
    hundred thousands, 32–33
    mixed, 532–533
    ordering, 42, 46–47
    patterns, 30–31, 476–477, 478–479, 480–481
    rounding, 50, 52
    sentences, 80–81, 250–251
    size of, 40–41
    standard form, 22–23, 25–26, 32–33
    to ten thousand, 32–33
    word form, 22–24, 32–33

Number line
    comparing numbers on, 42, 43
    decimals on, 566–567, 570, 591
    to find product, 164–166
    finding a pattern on, 180
    fractions on, 516–519, 591
    mixed numbers on, 532–533
    multiplication, 164–165
    ordering numbers, 39, 42, 46–47, 566–567
    patterns on, 180
    in rounding, 50, 52
    skip-counting on, 182, 212

Number of the Day, *2A, 4A, 6A, 8A, 10A, 12A, 20A, 22A, 24A, 28A, 30A, 32A, 40A, 42A, 46A, 48A, 50A, 52A, 68A, 70A, 72A, 74A, 76A, 80A, 88A, 90A, 92A, 96A, 98A, 102A, 110A, 114A, 116A, 118A, 120A, 128A, 132A, 134A, 136A, 138A, 142A, 158A, 160A, 162A, 164A, 168A, 176A, 178A, 180A, 182A, 186A, 194A, 196A, 198A, 200A, 202A, 212A, 216A, 218A, 220A, 222A, 238A, 240A, 242A, 246A, 250A, 258A, 260A, 262A, 264A, 266A, 274A, 278A, 280A, 284A, 286A, 302A, 304A, 306A, 308A, 310A, 314A, 322A, 324A, 326A, 328A, 330A, 342A, 344A, 346A, 348A, 350A, 358A, 362A, 364A, 366A, 368A, 384A, 388A, 390A, 392A, 396A, 400A, 408A, 410A, 412A, 414A, 416A, 424A, 428A, 430A, 432A, 436A, 444A, 448A, 450A, 452A, 470A, 474A, 476A, 478A, 480A, 488A, 490A, 492A, 496A, 498A, 500A, 516A, 520A, 522A, 526A, 530A, 532A, 540A, 542A, 544A, 546A, 550A, 558A, 560A, 562A, 564A, 566A, 568A, 576A, 578A, 580A, 584A, 600A, 602A, 606A, 608A, 618A, 620A, 624A, 626A, 628A*

Number Sense
    adding
        decimals, 580–585
        fractions, 540–541, 542–543
        multidigit whole numbers, 68–81
    benchmarks, 40–41
    checking division with multiplication, 258, 278, 626
    comparing and ordering
        decimals, 566–567
        fractions, 526–531
        whole numbers, 42–47, 48–49
    connecting addition and multiplication, 158–159
    counting whole numbers, 20–29
    dividing multidigit numbers, 618–622, 626–629
    estimation, 68–69, 88–89, 96–97, 102–103
    Grouping, or Associative, Property of Multiplication, 220–221
    Grouping Property of Addition, 2–3, 68–69
    identify place value, 19, 22–23, 24–26, 32–33, 46–47, 50–53
    Identity Property of Addition, 6–7
    Identity Property of Multiplication, 176–177, 220–221
    inverse, 2–3, 242–248, 258–261, 274–279, 281, 622
    memorize division facts, 258–263, 274–283
    memorize multiplication facts, 158–167, 176–179, 182–187, 194–197, 200–205, 212–215, 218–219, 220–221
    modeling fractions, 516–519, 520–525
    money, 110–121, 580–585
    multiply multidigit numbers, 602–607, 608–611
    Order, or Commutative, Property of Multiplication, 162–163, 164–165, 202
    Order Property of Addition, 6–7
    reading and writing
        decimals, 558–568
        fractions, 516–519, 520
        whole numbers, 20–27
    relating addition and multiplication, 158–159
    relating decimals and money, 578–579
    relating fractions and money, 576–577
    relating multiplication and division, 242–246
    relating subtraction and division, 240–241
    relating whole numbers, fractions, and decimals, 516–531, 558–565
    rounding, 50–53, 68–69
    subtracting
        decimals, 580–585
        fractions, 544–549
        multidigit whole numbers, 90–101

unit cost, 284–285
using expanded notation, 22–23, 25, 26–33, 564–565
Zero Property, 176–177, 204, 262, 263
Number sentence
expressions in, 264
as problem solving strategy, 250–251
true/false, 80, 81
writing, 250–251
Numerator, 516–519, 520–521, 539

Obtuse angle, 385–386
Obtuse triangle, 393–395
Octagons, 390–391
Odd numbers, 20–21
Ones
division by, 262–263
multiplying by, 176–177
place value and, 19
Open figure, 390
Operation
choosing, 266–267, 606–607
symbols for, 80–81, 264–265
Order Property of Addition, 6–7
Order Property of Multiplication. *See Commutative Property of Multiplication*
Ordered pair, 328–329
Ordering
decimals, 566–567
fractions, 527–529
on number line, 39, 42, 46–47, 566–567
numbers, 42, 46–47, 48–49
Ounce, 346–347
Outcomes
possible, 490–491
predicting, 490–491, 496–497
recording, 490–491, 492–494

P.M., 132–133
Pacing. *See the Chapter Planner for each chapter*
Parallel lines, 388–389, 396–399
Parallelogram, 396–399
Parts of a group, 520–521
Parts of a whole, 516–519
Pattern Finding strategy, 180–181, 480–481
Patterns
colors, 507

create, 478–479
describe, 180–181, 216–217, 470–481
even/odd numbers, 21
extend, 180–181, 216–217, 470–477, 478–479
finding, 180–181, 216–217, 480–481
geometric, 470–472
identify missing parts in, 470, 476, 480
make, 478–479
with multiples, 194, 196, 212, 600–601
number, 30–31, 476–481
with number line, 180
with pattern blocks, 470, 478–479
place value, 30–31
plane figures, 430–431, 470–472
in problem solving, 180–181, 480–481
repeating, 180–181, 216–217
and tessellation, 430–431
translating, 471
units, 470–472
visual, 473, 474–475
write a rule, 216–217, 474–481
Penny, 109–115, 118–119
Pentagons, 390–391
Performance Assessment, *xxviB,* 62, *62, 66B,* 152, *152, 156B,* 232, *232, 236B,* 296, *296, 300B,* 378, *378, 382B,* 464, *464, 468B,* 510, *510, 514B,* 594, *594, 598B,* 638, *638*
Perimeter
estimate, 444
find, 442, 444–447
Permutations. *See Arrangements*
Perpendicular lines, 388
Physical Education/Health Connection, *488B, 602B*
Pictographs, 2, 13, 18, 26, 29, 79, 140, 156, 174, 181, 198, 207, 210, 223, 267, 320–321, 322–323
Pint, 344–345
Place value
chart, 22, 24, 32, 43–44
comparing numbers, 44
decimal use of, 558–559
five- and six-digit numbers, 32–33
four-digit numbers, 24–25
in hundred thousands, 32–33
hundreds, 22–23
multiply nine and ten, 212–215
ordering numbers, 46–47
patterns, 30–31
ten thousands, 32–33
thousands, 24–27
three-digit numbers, 22–23
Plane figures, 390–391
area of, 448–449, 450–451
combine, 430–431
identifying, 390–391, 392–395, 396–399, 425
patterns with, 470–472

to nearest ten, 50–51
to nearest thousand, 52–53
rules for, 52
using number line, 50–51, 52

Rule
finding, 216–217
for patterns, 474–475, 476–477

Rulers
using customary, 337–341
using metric, 358–361, 445–446

Scaffolded Instruction
Alternative Teaching Strategy, 26, 44, 78, 94, 100, 112, 130, 140, 166, 184, 204, 214, 244, 248, 276, 282, 312, 340, 360, 386, 394, 398, 426, 434, 446, 454, 472, 494, 518, 524, 528, 548, 582, 604, 610, 622
Problem Solving, 7, 33, 53, 75, 103, 115, 143, 163, 187, 197, 214, 251, 261, 279, 309, 331, 347, 363, 401, 417, 431, 451, 481, 494, 524, 551, 569, 585, 604, 622

Scale of a graph, 324–327

Scale, measuring weight, 346

Scalene triangle, 393–395

Schedules, 136–137

Science Connection, 10B, 48B, 196B, 198B, 250B, 274B, 342B, 400B, 496B, 546B, 600B, 626B

Scope and Sequence, SC1–SC28

Sequence events, 142–143

Sides
and angles, 390–391
of polygons, 390–391, 396–399
sorting triangles by, 392–395

Similar figures, 412–413

Simplest form of fraction, 542–543, 546–548

Skills Trace Across the Grades, xxviK, 18D, 38D, 58D, 66K, 86D, 108D, 126D, 174D, 192D, 210D, 236K, 256D, 272D, 300K, 320D, 336D, 356D, 382K, 406D, 442D, 468K, 486D, 514K, 538D, 556D, 574D, 598K, 616D

Skills Trace for Grade 3, xxviK, 18D, 38D, 58D, 66K, 86D, 108D, 126D, 174D, 192D, 210D, 236K, 256D, 272D, 300K, 320D, 336D, 356D, 382K, 406D, 442D, 468K, 486D, 514K, 538D, 556D, 574D, 598K, 616D

Skip-count
by fives, 21, 157
by fours, 321
by tens, 21, 157, 211, 212
by threes, 157, 164–167, 182, 321
by twos, 21, 157, 321
on hundred chart, 21

Slide, 414–415

Social Studies Connection, 12B, 32B, 102B, 118B, 128B, 138B, 149, 240B, 262B, 408B, 424B, 474B, 488B, 560B, 578B

Solid figures
combining, 428–429
identifying, 424–427

Solve a Simpler Problem strategy, 584–585

Special Needs. See Reaching All Learners, Special Needs

Sphere, 424–426, 436

Square pyramid, 424–429, 436–437

Square unit, 448–449, 450–451

Squares, 396–399

Standard form, 22–26, 564, 565

Standardized Test Correlations. See Correlations to Standardized Tests

Statistics
bar graph, 49, 55, 94, 108, 166, 278, 325, 326, 327, 343, 351, 401, 437, 447, 492, 494, 528, 569, 623
line graph, 330–331
line plot, 310–313
pictograph, 2, 13, 18, 26, 29, 79, 140, 156, 174, 181, 198, 207, 210, 223, 267, 320, 322–323
survey, 302–305, 311

Study Guide and Review, 60–61, 150–151, 230–231, 294–295, 376–377, 462–463, 508–509, 592–593, 636–637

Subtraction
across zeros, 92–95
addition and, 2–3, 94, 96, 98, 100
basic facts, 10–11
decimals, 580–583
and division, 240–241
estimation and, 88–89
fact families, 2–3
fractions, 544–549
greater numbers, 96–101
inverse operation of addition, 2–3
with money, 120–121
regrouping, 90–91, 92–97, 98–100
repeated, 240–241, 280–282
three- and four-digit numbers, 90–95, 96–97
two-digit numbers, 10–11

Sum. *See Addition*

Summarize. See the Discuss and Write questions in the Assess section of each TE lesson

Survey, 304–305, 311–312, 327

Symbols
equal to, 42–43
finding missing operation symbol, 80–81, 104–105, 265, 279
greater than, 42–43
less than, 42–43
not equal to, 80–81

Symmetry, 410–411
line of, 410–411

Table of Measures, 139, 342, 348, 359, H41

Tables and charts

analyzing data from, 11, 22, 49, 51, 53, 75, 78, 100, 103, 115, 121, 122, 143, 158, 169, 199, 204, 272, 300, 307, 327, 351, 356, 501, 601, 607, 610

bar graphs from, 327

classifying data from, 306–307

completing, 9, 11, 73, 119, 195, 197, 201, 214, 217, 426, 526

division, 259, 261, 275, 276, 278, 279

frequency, 302, 305

grouping data in, 342, 358, 444, 578

making, 275, 276, 306, 348

as problem solving strategy, 114–115, 308–309, 362–363

multiplication, 202, 212, 239, 276, 278, 279

schedules, 136–137

tally, *See* Tally table

writing rules, 216, 217

Tally table, 302, 303, 304, 305, 308, 310, 311, 321, 487, 490, 492, 497

Technology

ePlanner, xxviE, 66E, 156E, 236E, 300E, 382E, 468E, 514E, 598E

Harcourt Assessment System, xxviB, 66B, 156B, 236B, 300B, 382B, 468B, 514B, 598B

Harcourt Learning Site, 2B, 14, 20B, 34, 40B, 68B, 82, 88B, 104, 110B, 122, 128B, 144, 158B, 170, 176B, 188, 194B, 206, 212B, 224, 238B, 252, 258B, 268, 274B, 302B, 316, 322B, 338B, 352, 358B, 370, 384B, 402, 408B, 418, 424B, 438, 444B, 470B, 482, 488B, 502, 516B, 534, 540B, 558B, 570, 576B, 586, 600B, 612, 618B, 630

Harcourt Mega Math Software, xxviD–xxviE, 66D–66E, 156D–156E, 236D–236E, 300D–300E, 382D–382E, 468D–468E, 514D–514E, 598D–598E

Country Countdown, 2B, 8B, 10B, 22B, 24B, 42B, 70B, 90B, 128B, 134B, 138B, 158B, 160B, 162B, 238B, 258B, 346B

Fraction Action, 30B, 42B, 50B, 52B, 488B, 490B, 492B, 496B, 516B, 520B, 522B, 526B, 540B, 542B, 544B, 546B, 560B, 562B, 564B, 566B

Ice Station Exploration, 4B, 80B, 212B, 216B, 242B, 246B, 280B, 338B, 342B, 358B, 384B, 388B, 390B, 392B, 396B, 408B, 410B, 412B, 414B, 424B, 428B, 430B, 444B, 448B, 452B

The Number Games, 30B, 76B, 96B, 110B, 118B, 120B, 134B, 178B, 182B, 198B, 200B, 212B, 260B, 274B, 278B, 310B, 314B, 324B, 326B, 328B, 330B, 348B, 396B, 470B, 476B, 580B, 600B, 602B, 618B, 620B, 626B

Intervention CD-ROMs, xxviD–xxviE, 2B, 4B, 6B, 8B, 10B, 12B, 20B, 22B, 24B, 28B, 30B, 32B, 40B, 42B, 46B, 48B, 50B, 52B, 66D–66E, 68B, 70B, 72B, 74B, 76B, 80B, 88B, 90B, 92B, 96B, 98B, 102B, 110B, 114B, 116B, 118B, 120B, 128B, 132B, 134B, 136B, 138B, 142B, 156D–156E, 158B, 160B, 162B, 164B, 168B, 176B, 178B, 180B, 182B, 186B, 194B, 196B, 198B, 200B, 202B, 212B, 216B, 218B, 220B, 222B, 236D–236E, 238B, 240B, 242B, 246B, 250B, 258B, 260B, 262B, 266B, 274B, 278B, 280B, 284B, 286B, 300D–300E, 302B, 304B, 306B, 308B, 310B, 314B,

322B, 324B, 326B, 328B, 330B, 338B, 342B, 344B, 346B, 348B, 350B, 358B, 362B, 368B, 382D–382E, 384B, 390B, 392B, 396B, 400B, 408B, 410B, 412B, 414B, 416B, 424B, 428B, 432B, 436B, 444B, 448B, 450B, 452B, 468D–468E, 470B, 474B, 476B, 478B, 480B, 488B, 490B, 492B, 496B, 500B, 514D–514E, 516B, 520B, 522B, 526B, 530B, 532B, 540B, 542B, 544B, 546B, 550B, 558B, 560B, 562B, 564B, 566B, 568B, 576B, 578B, 580B, 584B, 598D–598E, 600B, 602B, 606B, 608B, 618B, 620B, 624B, 626B, 628B

Math Jingles® CD 3–4, 22B, 52B, 118B, 134B, 160B, 164B, 180B, 182B, 202B, 212B, 218B, 242B, 246B, 258B, 260B, 262B, 280B, 284B, 310B, 328B, 346B, 358B, 366B, 368B, 392B, 424B, 444B, 470B, 516B, 546B, 562B, 578B, 602B, 628B

Multimedia Glossary, xxviI, 18B, 38B, 66I, 86B, 108B, 126B, 156I, 174B, 192B, 210B, 236I, 256B, 272B, 300I, 320B, 336B, 356B, 382I, 406B, 422B, 442B, 468I, 486B, 514I, 538B, 556B, 574B, 598I, 616B

Technology Link, xxviD, 2B, 4B, 6B, 8B, 10B, 12B, 20B, 22B, 24B, 28B, 30B, 32B, 40B, 42B, 46B, 48B, 50B, 52B, 63, 66D, 68B, 70B, 72B, 74B, 76B, 80B, 88B, 90B, 92B, 96B, 98B, 102B, 110B, 114B, 116B, 118B, 120B, 128B, 132B, 134B, 136B, 138B, 142B, 153, 156D, 158B, 160B, 162B, 164B, 168B, 176B, 178B, 180B, 182B, 186B, 194B, 196B, 198B, 200B, 202B, 212B, 216B, 218B, 220B, 222B, 233, 236D, 238B, 240B, 242B, 246B, 250B, 258B, 260B, 262B, 264B, 266B, 274B, 278B, 280B, 284B, 286B, 297, 300D, 302B, 304B, 306B, 308B, 310B, 314B, 322B, 324B, 326B, 328B, 330B, 338B, 342B, 344B, 346B, 348B, 350B, 358B, 362B, 364B, 366B, 368B, 379, 382D, 384B, 388B, 390B, 392B, 396B, 400B, 408B, 410B, 412B, 414B, 416B, 424B, 428B, 430B, 432B, 436B, 444B, 448B, 450B, 452B, 465, 468D, 470B, 474B, 476B, 478B, 480B, 488B, 490B, 492B, 496B, 498B, 500B, 511, 514D, 516B, 520B, 522B, 526B, 530B, 532B, 540B, 542B, 544B, 546B, 550B, 558B, 560B, 562B, 564B, 566B, 568B, 576B, 578B, 580B, 584B, 595, 598D, 600B, 602B, 606B, 608B, 618B, 620B, 624B, 626B, 628B, 639

Technology Link

Harcourt Mega Math, 2, 8, 22, 25, 43, 70, 77, 91, 111, 119, 158, 162, 182, 200, 213, 216, 242, 247, 261, 274, 281, 311, 325, 330, 489, 493, 547, 580, 603, 619

Technology Linkup, 63, 153, 233, 297, 379, 465, 511, 595, 639

Temperature

degrees Celsius, 368–369

degrees Fahrenheit, 368–369

measuring, 368–369

Ten thousand

numbers to, 24–29

understanding, 32–33

Tens, place value and, 20

Tenths

adding and subtracting, 580–583

modeling, 560–561

relating fractions and decimals, 558–559

Tessellation, 430–431

Thinker's Corner, 27, 45, 79, 101, 131, 141, 167, 185, 205, 245, 249, 283, 341, 361, 387, 427, 473

Thousands

comparing, 43

multiples of, 24–28
numbers to, 24–29
place value of, 24, 28
rounding, 52–53
understanding, 25

Three-digit numbers
adding, 70–73
division of, 626–627
estimating with, 88–89
multiplying, 600–611
rounding, 50
subtracting, 90–93

Three-dimensional figures. *See* Solid figures

Time
A.M., 132–133
analog clocks, 128–131, 132–133, 134–135
calendars, 138–140
days, 138, 139, 140
digital clocks, 128, 129, 131, 133
elapsed, 134–135, 136–137, 138–140
hour, 128
midnight, 132
minute, 128
months, 138, 139
noon, 132
P.M., 132–133
schedules, 136–137
telling, 128–130, H8
units of, 139
weeks, 138–140
years, 138–139

Time line, 142, 143

Tips for Success on the EOG Test, H2–H5

Too Much/Too Little Information, 168–169, 568–569

Trapezoid, 396–398

Tree diagram, 498–499

Trend, 330–331

Triangles
acute, 392–395
attributes of, 392–395
classifying, 392–395
equilateral, 392–395
as face of solid figure, 424–427
isosceles, 392–393
naming, 392–393
obtuse, 392–395
right, 392–395
scalene, 392–395
sorting, 392–395

Turn, 414–415

Two-digit numbers
addition, 8–9, 36, 69
multiplication with, 600–611

record division of, 621–623
subtraction, 10–11, 87

Two-dimensional figures. *See* Plane figures

Unit at a Glance, *xxviA, 66A, 156A, 235A, 300A, 382A, 468A, 514A, 598A*

Unit cost, finding, 284–285

Units, changing, 348–349

Universal Access
Advanced Learners 4B, 6B, 20B, 22B, 28B, 42B, 50B, 59, 68B, 70B, 90B, 98B, 110B, 120B, 134B, 136B, 160B, 162B, 168B, 182B, 186B, 202B, 216B, 218B, 220B, 246B, 258B, 280B, 284B, 304B, 308B, 310B, 314B, 324B, 330B, 346B, 364B, 368B, 375, 388B, 392B, 412B, 432B, 444B, 461, 476B, 490B, 498B, 520B, 526B, 530B, 532B, 540B, 550B, 558B, 564B, 566B, 580B, 606B, 608B, 618B, 624B

Alternative Teaching Strategy 2B, 4B, 6B, 8B, 10B, 12B, 20B, 22B, 24B, 26, 28B, 30B, 32B, 40B, 42B, 44, 46B, 48B, 50B, 52B, 68B, 70B, 72B, 74B, 76B, 78, 80B, 88B, 90B, 92B, 94, 96B, 98B, 100, 102B, 110B, 112, 114B, 116B, 118B, 120B, 128B, 130, 132B, 134B, 136B, 138B, 140, 142B, 158B, 160B, 162B, 164B, 166, 168B, 176B, 178B, 180B, 182B, 184, 186B, 194B, 196B, 198B, 200B, 202B, 204, 212B, 214, 216B, 218B, 220B, 222B, 238B, 240B, 242B, 244, 246B, 248, 250B, 258B, 260B, 262B, 264B, 266B, 274B, 276, 278B, 280B, 282, 284B, 286B, 302B, 304B, 306B, 308B, 310B, 312, 314B, 322B, 324B, 326B, 328B, 330B, 340, 342B, 344B, 346B, 348B, 350B, 358B, 360, 362B, 364B, 366B, 368B, 384B, 386, 388B, 390B, 392B, 394, 396B, 398, 400B, 408B, 410B, 412B, 414B, 416B, 424B, 426, 428B, 430B, 432B, 434, 436B, 444B, 446, 448B, 450B, 452B, 454, 470B, 472, 474B, 476B, 478B, 480B, 488B, 490B, 492B, 494, 496B, 498B, 500B, 516B, 518, 520B, 522B, 524, 526B, 528, 530B, 532B, 540B, 542B, 544B, 546B, 548, 550B, 558B, 560B, 562B, 564B, 566B, 568B, 576B, 578B, 580B, 582, 584B, 600B, 602B, 604, 606B, 608B, 610, 618B, 620B, 622, 624B, 626B, 628B

Art Connection, 30B, 160B, 180B, 328B, 396B, 430B, 432B, 448B, 470B, 474B

Career Connection, 128B, 246B, 342B, 358B, 474B, 584B, 628B

Differentiated Instruction, xxviG, xxviK, 18D, 38D, 66G, 66K, 86D, 108D, 126D, 156G, 156K, 174D, 192D, 210D, 236G, 236K, 256D, 272D, 300G, 300K, 320D, 336D, 356D, 382G, 382K, 406D, 422D, 442D, 468G, 468K, 486D, 514G, 514K, 538K, 556D, 574D, 598G, 598K, 616D

Early Finishers, 2B, 8B, 24B, 46B, 52B, 72B, 74B, 88B, 90B, 96B, 132B, 142B, 158B, 164B, 176B, 178B, 194B, 200B, 212B, 222B, 238B, 260B, 262B, 264B, 266B, 278B, 284B, 286B, 306B, 322B, 326B, 344B, 348B, 362B, 366B, 368B, 400B, 410B, 414B, 416B, 428B, 436B, 450B, 452B, 480B, 492B, 522B, 542B, 544B, 562B, 568B, 576B, 584B, 620B

ESOL/ESL, 2B, 4B, 6B, 8B, 10B, 12B, 20B, 22B, 24B, 28B, 32B, 40B, 42B, 46B, 48B, 50B, 52B, 68B, 70B, 72B, 74B, 76B, 80B, 88B, 90B, 92B, 96B, 98B, 102B, 110B, 114B, 116B, 118B, 120B, 128B, 132B, 134B, 136B, 138B, 142B, 158B, 160B, 162B, 164B, 168B, 176B, 178B, 180B, 182B, 186B, 194B, 196B, 198B, 200B, 202B, 212B, 216B, 218B, 220B,

Teaching Notes

Additional Ideas:

Good Questions to Ask:

Additional Resources:

Notes for Next Time:

HARCOURT

Math

NCTM Standards Correlations

This section contains the following:

- **Correlations to the NCTM Standards and Expectations**

These correlations demonstrate how *Harcourt Math* supports and aligns with the NCTM Content Standards. The chart indicates the lessons and chapters that correlate to each standard for the appropriate grade span.

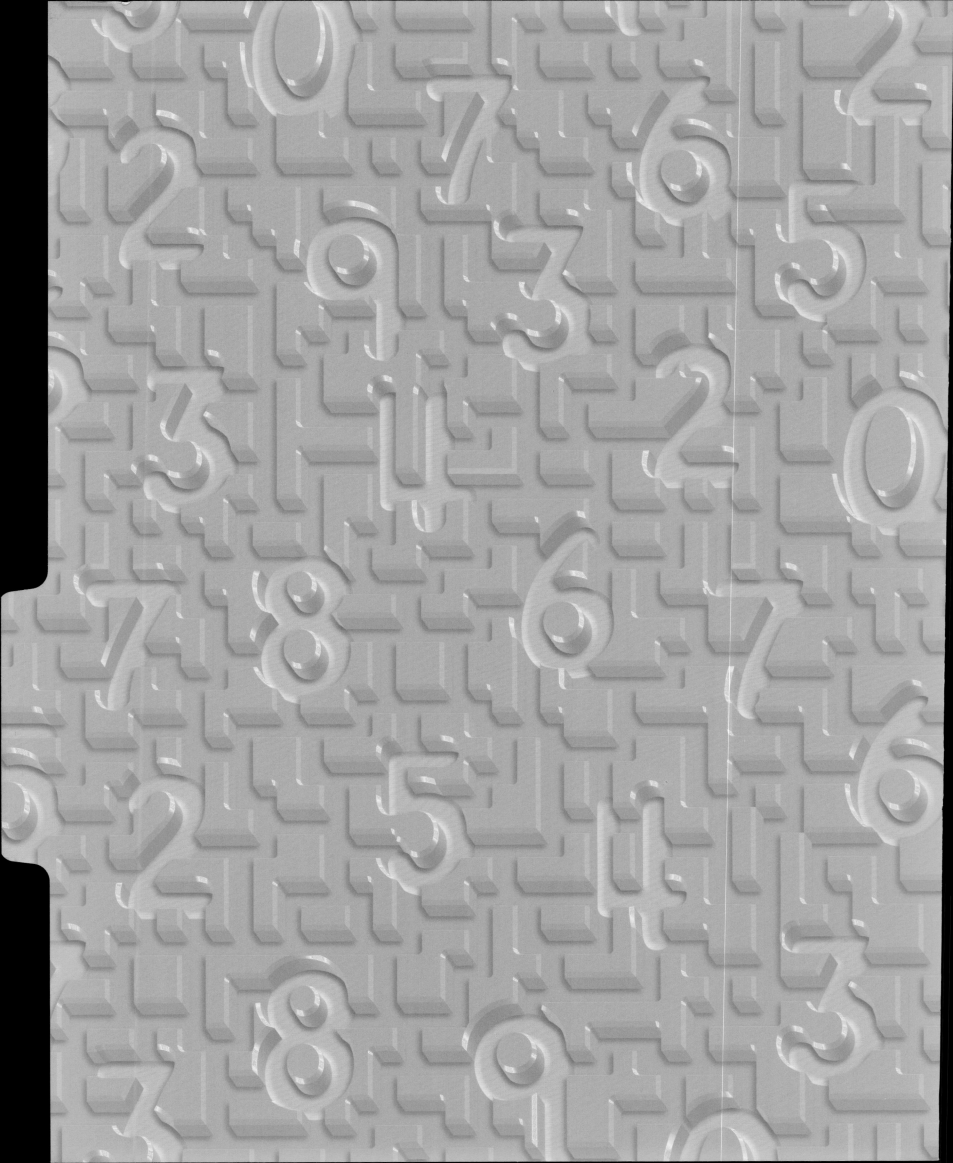

Correlations to NCTM Standards

STANDARD	GRADES 3–5 EXPECTATIONS	CORRELATION TO NCTM STANDARDS
Instructional programs from prekindergarten through grade 12 should enable all students to—	*In grades 3–5 all students should—*	
1. NUMBER AND OPERATIONS		
Understand numbers, ways of representing numbers, relationships among numbers, and number systems	• Understand the place-value structure of the base-ten number system and be able to represent and compare whole numbers and decimals; • recognize equivalent representations for the same number and generate them by decomposing and composing numbers; • develop understanding of fractions as parts of unit wholes, as parts of a collection, as locations on number lines, and as divisions of whole numbers; • use models, benchmarks, and equivalent forms to judge the size of fractions; • recognize and generate equivalent forms of commonly used fractions, decimals, and percents; • explore numbers less than 0 by extending the number line and through familiar applications; • describe classes of numbers according to characteristics such as the nature of their factors.	Lessons 1.1, 1.2, 1.3, 1.4, 1.5, 1.6, 2.1, 2.2, 2.3, 2.5, 2.6, 3.1, 3.2, 3.3, 3.4, 3.5, 3.6, 4.1, 4.2, 4.3, 4.4, 4.5, 4.6, 5.1, 5.2, 5.3, 5.4, 5.5, 5.6, 6.1, 6.2, 6.3, 6.4, 6.5, 7.1, 7.3, 7.4, 7.5, 7.6, 8.1, 8.2, 8.3, 8.4, 8.5, 9.1, 9.2, 9.3, 9.4, 9.5, 10.1, 10.2, 10.3, 10.4, 10.5, 11.1, 11.2, 11.3, 11.4, 11.5, 12.1, 12.2, 12.3, 12.4, 12.5, 13.1, 13.2, 13.3, 13.4, 13.5, 14.1, 14.2, 14.3, 14.4, 14.5, 15.1, 15.2, 15.3, 15.4, 15.5, 15.6, 16.1, 16.2, 16.3, 16.5, 17.1, 17.2, 17.3, 17.4, 17.5, 17.6, 18.1, 19.6, 22.1, 22.2, 22.3, 22.4, 23.3, 23.4, 23.5, 24.2, 24.3, 24.4, 24.5, 25.1, 25.2, 25.3, 25.4, 25.5, 25.6, 26.1, 26.2, 26.3, 26.4, 26.5, 27.1, 27.2, 27.3, 27.4, 27.5, 27.6, 28.1, 28.2, 28.3, 28.4, 29.1, 29.2, 29.3, 29.4, 30.1, 30.2, 30.3, 30.4, 30.5
Understand meanings of operations and how they relate to one another	• understand various meanings of multiplication and division; • understand the effects of multiplying and dividing whole numbers; • identify and use relationships between operations, such as division as the inverse of multiplication, to solve problems; • understand and use properties of operations, such as the distributivity of multiplication over addition.	
Compute fluently and make reasonable estimates	• develop fluency with basic number combinations for multiplication and division and use these combinations to mentally compute related problems, such as 30×50; • develop fluency in adding, subtracting, multiplying, and dividing whole numbers; • develop and use strategies to estimate the results of whole-number computations and to judge the reasonableness of such results; • develop and use strategies to estimate computations involving fractions and decimals in situations relevant to students' experience; • use visual models, benchmarks, and equivalent forms to add and subtract commonly used fractions and decimals;	

STANDARD	GRADES 3–5 EXPECTATIONS	CORRELATION TO NCTM STANDARDS
Instructional programs from prekindergarten through grade 12 should enable all students to—	*In grades 3–5 all students should—*	

1. NUMBER AND OPERATIONS *(continued)*

	• select appropriate methods and tools for computing with whole numbers from among mental computation, estimation, calculators, and paper and pencil according to the context and nature of the computation and use the selected method or tool.	

2. ALGEBRA

Understand patterns, relations, and functions	• describe, extend, and make generalizations about geometric and numeric patterns; • represent and analyze patterns and functions, using words, tables, and graphs.	Lessons 1.1, 1.2, 1.3, 1.6, 2.5, 3.2, 4.3, 4.4, 4.5, 4.6, 5.3, 5.4, 5.5, 6.3, 6.5, 8.1, 8.2, 8.3, 8.4, 8.5, 9.1, 9.2, 9.3, 9.4, 9.5, 10.1, 10.2, 10.3, 10.4, 10.5, 11.2, 11.3, 11.4, 12.2, 12.3, 12.4, 12.5, 13.4, 14.1, 14.2, 14.3, 14.4, 15.3, 16.2, 16.4, 17.3, 17.4, 17.5, 18.2, 21.3, 22.1, 22.3, 22.4, 23.1, 23.2, 23.3, 23.4, 23.5, 24.1, 24.5, 25.1, 25.3, 27.4, 27.6, 28.1, 28.2, 28.3, 28.4, 29.1, 30.2
Represent and analyze mathematical situations and structures using algebraic symbols	• identify such properties as commutativity, associativity, and distributivity and use them to compute with whole numbers; • represent the idea of variable as an unknown quantity using a letter or a symbol; • express mathematical relationships using equations.	
Use mathematical models to represent and understand quantitative relationships	• model problem situations with objects and use representations such as graphs, tables, and equations to draw conclusions.	
Analyze change in various contexts	• investigate how a change in one variable relates to a change in a second variable; • identify and describe situations with constant or varying rates of change and compare them.	

STANDARD	GRADES 3–5 EXPECTATIONS	CORRELATION TO NCTM STANDARDS
Instructional programs from prekindergarten through grade 12 should enable all students to—	*In grades 3–5 all students should—*	

3. GEOMETRY

STANDARD	GRADES 3–5 EXPECTATIONS	CORRELATION TO NCTM STANDARDS
Analyze characteristics and properties of two- and three-dimensional geometric shapes and develop mathematical arguments about geometric relationships	• identify, compare, and analyze attributes of two- and three-dimensional shapes and develop vocabulary to describe the attributes; • classify two- and three-dimensional shapes according to their properties and develop definitions of classes of shapes such as triangles and pyramids; • investigate, describe, and reason about the results of subdividing, combining, and transforming shapes; • explore congruence and similarity; • make and test conjectures about geometric properties and relationships and develop logical arguments to justify conclusions.	Lessons 19.1, 19.2, 19.3, 19.4, 19.5, 19.6, 20.1, 20.2, 20.3, 20.4, 20.5, 21.1, 21.2, 21.3, 21.4, 21.5, 22.1, 22.3, 22.4, 23.1, 23.2, 23.4
Specify locations and describe spatial relationships using coordinate geometry and other representational systems	• describe location and movement using common language and geometric vocabulary; • make and use coordinate systems to specify locations and to describe paths; • find the distance between points along horizontal and vertical lines of a coordinate system.	
Apply transformations and use symmetry to analyze mathematical situations	• predict and describe the results of sliding, flipping, and turning two-dimensional shapes; • describe a motion or series of motions that will show that two shapes are congruent; • identify and describe line and rotational symmetry in two- and three-dimensional shapes and designs.	
Use visualization, spatial reasoning, and geometric modeling to solve problems	• build and draw geometric objects; • create and describe mental images of objects, patterns, and paths; • identify and build a three-dimensional object from two-dimensional representations of that object; • identify and build a two-dimensional representation of a three-dimensional object; • use geometric models to solve problems in other areas of mathematics, such as number and measurement; • recognize geometric ideas and relationships and apply them to other disciplines and to problems that arise in the classroom or in everyday life.	

STANDARD	GRADES 3–5 EXPECTATIONS	CORRELATION TO NCTM STANDARDS
Instructional programs from prekindergarten through grade 12 should enable all students to—	*In grades 3–5 all students should—*	

4. MEASUREMENT

Understand measurable attributes of objects and the units, systems, and processes of measurement	• understand such attributes as length, area, weight, volume, and size of angle and select the appropriate type of unit for measuring each attribute; • understand the need for measuring with standard units and become familiar with standard units in the customary and metric systems; • carry out simple unit conversions, such as from centimeters to meters, within a system of measurement; • understand that measurements are approximations and understand how differences in units affect precision; • explore what happens to measurements of a two-dimensional shape such as its perimeter and area when the shape is changed in some way.	Lessons 7.1, 7.2, 7.3, 7.4, 7.5, 7.6, 17.1, 17.2, 17.3, 17.4, 17.5, 17.6, 18.1, 18.2, 18.3, 18.4, 18.5, 22.1, 22.2, 22.3, 22.4
Apply appropriate techniques, tools, and formulas to determine measurements	• develop strategies for estimating the perimeters, areas, and volumes of irregular shapes; • select and apply appropriate standard units and tools to measure length, area, volume, weight, time, temperature, and the size of angles; • select and use benchmarks to estimate measurements; • develop, understand, and use formulas to find the area of rectangles and related triangles and parallelograms; • develop strategies to determine the surface areas and volumes of rectangular solids.	

STANDARD	GRADES 3–5 EXPECTATIONS	CORRELATION TO NCTM STANDARDS
Instructional programs from prekindergarten through grade 12 should enable all students to—	*In grades 3–5 all students should—*	

5. DATA ANALYSIS AND PROBABILITY

STANDARD	GRADES 3–5 EXPECTATIONS	CORRELATION TO NCTM STANDARDS
Formulate questions that can be addressed with data and collect, organize, and display relevant data to answer them	• design investigations to address a question and consider how data-collection methods affect the nature of the data set; • collect data using observations, surveys, and experiments; • represent data using tables and graphs such as line plots, bar graphs, and line graphs; • recognize the difference in representing categorical and numerical data.	Lessons 3.2, 3.4, 3.5, 3.6, 6.2, 9.3, 10.3, 15.1, 15.2, 15.3, 15.4, 15.5, 15.6, 16.1, 16.2, 16.3, 16.4, 16.5, 19.6, 24.1, 24.2, 24.3, 24.4, 24.5, 24.6
Select and use appropriate statistical methods to analyze data	• describe the shape and important features of a set of data and compare related data sets, with an emphasis on how the data are distributed; • use measures of center, focusing on the median, and understand what each does and does not indicate about the data set; • compare different representations of the same data and evaluate how well each representation shows important aspects of the data.	
Develop and evaluate inferences and predictions that are based on data	• propose and justify conclusions and predictions that are based on data and design studies to further investigate the conclusions or predictions.	
Understand and apply basic concepts of probability	• describe events as likely or unlikely and discuss the degree of likelihood using such words as *certain, equally likely,* and *impossible*; • predict the probability of outcomes of simple experiments and test the predictions; • understand that the measure of the likelihood of an event can be represented by a number from 0 to 1.	

STANDARD	GRADES 3–5 EXPECTATIONS	CORRELATION TO NCTM STANDARDS
6. PROBLEM SOLVING		
Instructional programs from prekindergarten through grade 12 should enable all students to—	• Build new mathematical knowledge through problem solving • Solve problems that arise in mathematics and in other contexts • Apply and adapt a variety of appropriate strategies to solve problems • Monitor and reflect on the process of mathematical problem solving	Lessons 1.1, 1.2, 1.3, 1.4, 1.5, 1.6, 2.1, 2.2, 2.3, 2.4, 2.5, 2.6, 3.1, 3.2, 3.3, 3.4, 3.5, 3.6, 4.1, 4.2, 4.3, 4.4, 4.5, 4.6, 5.1, 5.2, 5.3, 5.4, 5.5, 5.6, 6.1, 6.2, 6.3, 6.4, 6.5, 7.1, 7.2, 7.3, 7.4, 7.5, 7.6, 8.1, 8.2, 8.3, 8.4, 8.5, 9.1, 9.2, 9.3, 9.4, 9.5, 10.1, 10.2, 10.3, 10.4, 10.5, 11.1, 11.2, 11.3, 11.4, 11.5, 12.1, 12.2, 12.3, 12.4, 12.5, 13.4, 13.5, 14.1, 14.2, 14.3, 14.4, 14.5, 15.1, 15.2, 15.3, 15.4, 15.5, 15.6, 16.1, 16.2, 16.3, 16.4, 16.5, 17.1, 17.2, 17.3, 17.4, 17.5, 17.6, 18.1, 18.2, 18.3, 18.4, 18.5, 19.1, 19.2, 19.3, 19.4, 19.5, 19.6, 20.1, 20.2, 20.3, 20.4, 20.5, 21.1, 21.2, 21.3, 21.4, 21.5, 22.1, 22.2, 22.3, 22.4, 23.1, 23.2, 23.3, 23.4, 23.5, 24.1, 24.2, 24.3, 24.4, 24.5, 24.6, 25.1, 25.2, 25.3, 25.4, 25.5, 25.6, 26.1, 26.2, 26.3, 26.4, 26.5, 27.1, 27.2, 27.3, 27.4, 27.5, 27.6, 28.1, 28.2, 28.3, 28.4, 29.1, 29.2, 29.3, 29.4, 30.1, 30.2, 30.3, 30.4, 30.5
7. REASONING AND PROOF		
Instructional programs from prekindergarten through grade 12 should enable all students to—	• Recognize reasoning and proof as fundamental aspects of mathematics • Make and investigate mathematical conjectures • Develop and evaluate mathematical arguments and proofs • Select and use various types of reasoning and methods of proof	Lessons 1.1, 1.2, 1.3, 1.5, 1.6, 2.1, 2.2, 2.3, 2.4, 2.6, 3.1, 3.2, 3.3, 3.4, 3.5, 3.6, 4.1, 4.2, 4.3, 4.4, 4.6, 5.2, 5.3, 5.4, 5.5, 5.6, 6.1, 6.2, 6.3, 6.4, 7.1, 7.2, 7.5, 7.6, 8.1, 8.2, 8.3, 8.4, 8.5, 9.1, 9.2, 9.3, 9.4, 10.1, 10.2, 10.4, 10.5, 11.2, 11.3, 11.4, 12.1, 12.2, 12.3, 12.4, 12.5, 13.1, 13.2, 13.3, 14.1, 14.2, 14.3, 14.4, 14.5, 15.1, 15.2, 15.3, 15.4, 15.6, 16.1, 16.2, 16.4, 17.2, 17.3, 17.4, 17.5, 17.6, 18.1, 18.2, 18.3, 18.4, 18.5, 19.1, 19.2, 19.3, 19.4, 19.5, 19.6, 20.1, 20.2, 20.3, 20.4, 20.5, 21.1, 21.3, 21.5, 22.1, 22.2, 22.3, 22.4, 23.1, 23.5, 24.1, 24.2, 24.3, 24.4, 24.5, 24.6, 25.1, 25.3, 25.4, 25.5, 25.6, 26.1, 26.2, 26.4, 26.5, 27.1, 27.2, 27.3, 27.4, 27.5, 28.1, 28.2, 28.3, 28.4, 29.1, 29.2, 29.3, 29.4, 30.2, 30.4, 30.5

8. COMMUNICATION

Instructional programs from prekindergarten through grade 12 should enable all students to—

- Organize and consolidate their mathematical thinking through communication
- Communicate their mathematical thinking coherently and clearly to peers, teachers, and others
- Analyze and evaluate the mathematical thinking and strategies of others
- Use the language of mathematics to express mathematical ideas precisely

Lessons 1.1, 1.2, 1.3, 1.4, 1.5, 1.6, 2.1, 2.2, 2.3, 2.4, 2.5, 2.6, 3.1, 3.2, 3.3, 3.4, 3.5, 3.6, 4.1, 4.2, 4.3, 4.4, 4.5, 4.6, 5.2, 5.3, 5.4, 5.5, 5.6, 6.1, 6.2, 6.3, 6.4, 6.5, 7.1, 7.2, 7.3, 7.4, 7.5, 7.6, 8.1, 8.2, 8.3, 8.4, 8.5, 9.1, 9.3, 10.1, 10.2, 10.4, 10.5, 11.1, 11.2, 11.3, 11.4, 11.5, 12.2, 12.3, 12.4, 12.5, 13.1, 13.2, 13.3, 13.4, 13.5, 14.1, 14.2, 14.3, 14.4, 14.5, 15.1, 15.2, 15.3, 15.4, 15.5, 15.6, 16.1, 16.2, 16.3, 16.4, 16.5, 17.2, 17.3, 17.4, 17.5, 17.6, 18.1, 18.2, 18.3, 18.4, 19.1, 19.2, 19.3, 19.4, 19.5, 19.6, 20.1, 20.2, 20.3, 20.4, 20.5, 21.1, 21.2, 21.3, 21.4, 21.5, 22.1, 22.2, 22.3, 22.4, 23.1, 23.2, 23.3, 24.1, 24.2, 24.3, 24.4, 24.5, 25.1, 25.2, 25.3, 25.4, 25.5, 25.6, 26.1, 26.2, 26.3, 26.4, 26.5, 27.1, 27.3, 27.4, 27.5, 27.6, 28.1, 28.2, 28.3, 28.4, 29.1, 29.2, 29.3, 29.4, 30.1, 30.2, 30.3, 30.4, 30.5

9. CONNECTIONS

Instructional programs from prekindergarten through grade 12 should enable all students to—

- Recognize and use connections among mathematical ideas
- Understand how mathematical ideas interconnect and build on one another to produce a coherent whole
- Recognize and apply mathematics in contexts outside of mathematics

Lessons 1.2, 1.3, 1.4, 1.5, 1.6, 2.1, 2.2, 2.3, 2.4, 2.6, 3.1, 3.2, 3.3, 3.4, 3.5, 3.6, 4.2, 4.3, 4.4, 5.1, 5.3, 5.4, 5.5, 6.1, 7.4, 7.5, 7.6, 8.1, 8.4, 8.5, 9.4, 10.1, 10.2, 10.4, 10.5, 12.1, 12.2, 12.3, 12.4, 14.1, 14.2, 14.3, 14.4, 15.1, 15.2, 15.3, 15.4, 15.5, 15.6, 16.2, 16.4, 16.5, 17.1, 17.2, 17.4, 17.5, 17.6, 18.1, 18.2, 18.3, 18.4, 18.5, 19.1, 19.2, 19.4, 19.5, 21.1, 21.2, 22.2, 22.3, 23.5, 24.1, 24.2, 24.3, 24.4, 25.1, 25.2, 25.3, 25.4, 25.5, 25.6, 26.2, 26.3, 26.4, 26.5, 27.1, 27.2, 27.3, 27.4, 27.5, 27.6, 28.1, 28.2, 28.3, 29.1, 29.2, 29.3, 29.4

10. REPRESENTATION

Instructional programs from prekindergarten through grade 12 should enable all students to—

- Create and use representations to organize, record, and communicate mathematical ideas
- Select, apply, and translate among mathematical representations to solve problems
- Use representations to model and interpret physical, social, and mathematical phenomena

Lessons 1.2, 1.3, 2.1, 2.2, 2.3, 2.4, 2.5, 2.6, 3.5, 3.6, 4.2, 4.3, 4.4, 4.5, 4.6, 5.2, 5.3, 5.6, 6.1, 6.2, 6.3, 6.4, 6.5, 7.2, 7.3, 7.4, 7.5, 7.6, 8.4, 9.2, 9.3, 9.4, 10.1, 10.2, 10.3, 10.4, 10.5, 11.1, 11.2, 11.3, 11.4, 11.5, 12.1, 12.3, 12.4, 12.5, 14.1, 14.2, 14.3, 14.4, 14.5, 15.1, 15.2, 15.3, 15.4, 15.5, 15.6, 16.1, 16.2, 16.3, 16.4, 16.5, 17.5, 18.2, 18.5, 19.1, 19.2, 19.3, 19.4, 19.5, 20.1, 20.2, 20.3, 20.4, 20.5, 21.1, 21.2, 21.3, 21.4, 21.5, 22.1, 22.2, 22.3, 22.4, 24.3, 24.4, 24.5, 24.6, 25.1, 25.2, 25.3, 25.4, 25.5, 25.6, 26.1, 26.2, 26.3, 26.4, 26.5, 27.1, 27.2, 27.3, 27.4, 27.5, 28.1, 28.3, 29.1, 29.2, 29.3, 29.4, 30.1, 30.2, 30.3

Teaching Notes

Additional Ideas:

Good Questions to Ask:

Additional Resources:

Notes for Next Time:

HARCOURT

Math

North Carolina Mathematics Standard Course of Study Correlations

This section contains the following:

- **Correlations to the North Carolina Mathematics Standard Course of Study**

These correlations demonstrate how *Harcourt Math* supports and aligns with the North Carolina Mathematics Standard Course of Study. Page references for the Pupil and Teacher Editions follow each Objective.

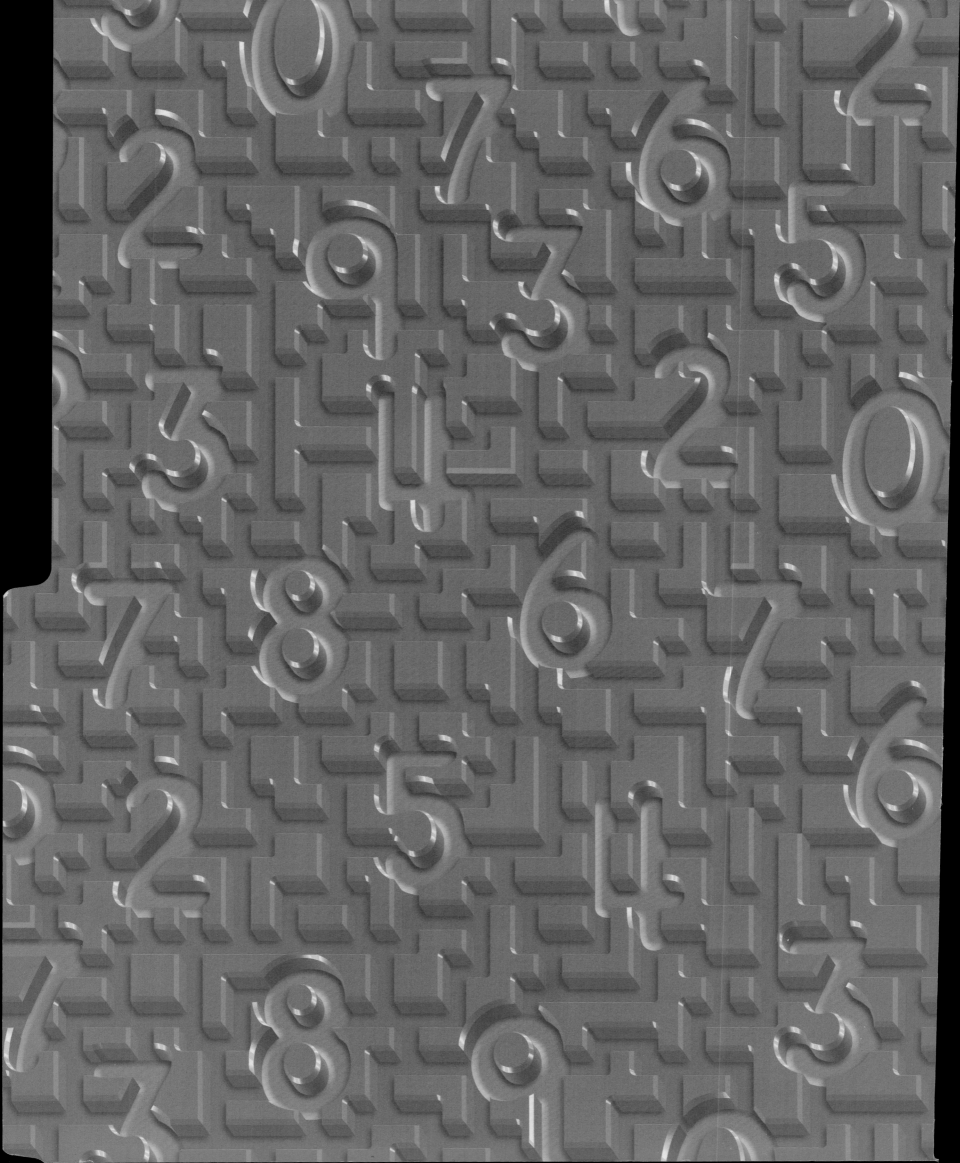

Correlations to the North Carolina Mathematics Standard Course of Study

OBJECTIVE	PUPIL EDITION AND TEACHER EDITION PAGES
NUMBER AND OPERATIONS	
Competency Goal 1: The learner will model, identify, and compute with whole numbers through 9,999.	
1.01 Develop number sense for whole numbers through 9,999.	22–23, 24–27, 32–33, 40–41, 42–45, 46–47, 48–49, 50–51, 52–53, 116–117
a) Connect model, number word, and number using a variety of representations.	22–23, 24–27
b) Build understanding of place value (ones through thousands).	22–23, 24–27, 32–33
c) Compare and order.	42–45, 46–47, 48–49, 116–117
1.02 Develop fluency with multi-digit addition and subtraction through 9,999 using:	2–3, 4–5, 6–7, 8–9, 10–11, 12–13, 68–69, 70–71, 72–73, 88–89, 92–95, 96–97, 98–101, 102–103, 120–121
a) Strategies for adding and subtracting numbers.	2–3, 4–5, 6–7, 8–9, 10–11, 12–13, 92–95, 96–97, 120–121
b) Estimation of sums and differences in appropriate situations.	68–69, 88–89, 102–103
c) Relationships between operations.	2–3, 4–5
1.03 Develop fluency with multiplication from 1×1 to 12×12 and division up to two-digit by one-digit numbers using:	158–159, 160–161, 162–163, 164–167, 168–169, 176–177, 178–179, 182–185, 186–187, 194–195, 196–197, 198–199, 200–201, 202–205, 212–215, 216–217, 218–219, 220–221, 238–239, 240–241, 242–245, 246–249, 258–259, 260–261, 262–263, 274–277, 278–279, 280–283, 284–285, 600–601, 602–605, 608–611, 618–619, 620–623, 624–625
a) Strategies for multiplying and dividing numbers.	162–163, 178–179, 194–195, 212–213, 220–221, 600–601, 602–605
b) Estimation of products and quotients in appropriate situations.	608–611, 628–629, 635
c) Relationships between operations.	158–159, 240–241, 242–245
1.04 Use basic properties (identity, commutative, associative, order of operations) for addition, subtraction, multiplication, and division.	6–7, 164–167, 176–177, 218–219, 220–221

Source for North Carolina Mathematics Standard Course of Study: North Carolina Department of Public Instruction

OBJECTIVE	PUPIL EDITION AND TEACHER EDITION PAGES
NUMBER AND OPERATIONS	
1.05 Use area or region models and set models of fractions to explore part-whole relationships.	516–519, 520–521, 522–525, 526–529, 530–531, 532–533, 558–559, 560–561, 562–563, 564–565, 576–577, 578–579
a) Represent fractions concretely and symbolically (halves, fourths, thirds, sixths, eighths).	516–519, 520–521
b) Compare and order fractions (halves, fourths, thirds, sixths, eighths) using models and benchmark numbers (zero, one-half, one); describe comparisons.	526–529, 530–531
c) Model and describe common equivalents, especially relationships among halves, fourths, and eighths, and thirds and sixths.	522–525
d) Understand that the fractional relationships that occur between zero and one also occur between every two consecutive whole numbers.	532–533, 564–565
e) Understand and use mixed numbers and their equivalent fraction forms.	532–533
1.06 Develop flexibility in solving problems by selecting strategies and using mental computation, estimation, calculators or computers, and paper and pencil.	6–7, 12–13, 68–69, 76–79, 98–101, 168–169, 180–181, 222–223, 250–251, 266–267, 286–287, 362–363, 568–569, 584–585, 606–607, 608–611
MEASUREMENT	
Competency Goal 2: The learner will recognize and use standard units of metric and customary measurement.	
2.01 Solve problems using measurement concepts and procedures involving:	110–113, 114–115, 134–135, 136–137, 348–349
a) Elapsed time.	134–135, 136–137, 138–141, 142–143
b) Equivalent measures within the same measurement system.	110–113, 114–115, 348–349
2.02 Estimate and measure using appropriate units.	338–341, 342–343, 344–345, 346–347, 350–351, 358–361, 362–363, 364–365, 366–367, 368–369
a) Capacity (cups, pints, quarts, gallons, liters).	344–345, 364–365
b) Length (miles, kilometers).	338–341, 342–343, 358–361, 362–363
c) Mass (ounces, pounds, grams, kilograms).	346–347, 366–367
d) Temperature (Fahrenheit, Celsius).	368–369

OBJECTIVE	PUPIL EDITION AND TEACHER EDITION PAGES
GEOMETRY	
Competency Goal 3: The learner will recognize and use basic geometric properties of two- and three-dimensional figures.	
3.01 Use appropriate vocabulary to compare, describe, and classify two- and three-dimensional figures.	384–387, 388–389, 390–391, 392–395, 396–399, 400–401, 408–409, 410–411, 412–413, 416–417, 424–427, 428–429, 430–431, 432–435, 436–437
3.02 Use a rectangular coordinate system to solve problems.	328–329
a) Graph and identify points with whole number and/or letter coordinates.	328–329
b) Describe the path between given points on the plane.	328–329
DATA ANALYSIS AND PROBABILITY	
Competency Goal 4: The learner will understand and use data and simple probability concepts.	
4.01 Collect, organize, analyze, and display data (including circle graphs and tables) to solve problems.	198–199, 302–303, 304–305, 306–307, 308–309, 310–313, 314–315, 322–323, 324–325, 326–327, 330–331, 375, 498–499, 500–501
4.02 Determine the number of permutations and combinations of up to three items.	498–499, 500–501
4.03 Solve probability problems using permutations and combinations.	498–499, 500–501
ALGEBRA	
Competency Goal 5: The learner will recognize, determine, and represent patterns and simple mathematical relationships.	
5.01 Describe and extend numeric and geometric patterns.	4–5, 30–31, 180–181, 212–215, 216–217, 330–331, 470–473, 474–475, 476–477, 478–479, 480–481
5.02 Extend and find missing terms of repeating and growing patterns.	470–473, 474–475, 476–477, 480–481
5.03 Use symbols to represent unknown quantities in number sentences.	4–5, 178–179, 182–184, 186–187, 212–214, 242–245
5.04 Find the value of the unknown in a whole number sentence.	4–5, 80–81, 186–187, 194–195, 196–197, 242–245, 246–249

OBJECTIVE	PUPIL EDITION AND TEACHER EDITION PAGES
CONCEPTS/SKILLS TO MAINTAIN	
Addition and subtraction of multi-digit numbers	8–9, 10–11, 12–13, 70–71, 72–73, 76–79, 90–91, 92–95, 96–97, 98–101, 120–121
Length and time	128–131, 132–133, 134–135, 136–137, 338–341, 342–343, 350–351, 358–361, 362–363
Symmetry and congruence	408–409, 410–411, 416–417
Line plots, tallies, pictographs	198–199, 302–303, 306–307, 310–313, 488–489, 490–491, 492–495, 496–497
Venn diagrams	400–401

Teaching Notes

Additional Ideas:

Good Questions to Ask:

Additional Resources:

Notes for Next Time:

Teaching Notes

Additional Ideas:

Good Questions to Ask:

Additional Resources:

Notes for Next Time: